A Note from the Publisher

The Educational Book Division of Prentice–Hall, Inc. is committed to the publication of outstanding textbooks. One important measure of a book's excellence is how well it communicates with its readers. To assure a highly readable book, the content for this text was selected, organized, and written at a level appropriate for the intended audience. The Dale–Chall readability formula was used to control readability level. An inviting and meaningful design was created to enhance the book's visual appeal as well as to facilitate the reading process. In addition, a consistent organization was used throughout so that all units, chapters, and sections will meet the reader's expectations. The authors, editors, and designers are confident that the students for whom this book is intended will read it, comprehend it, and learn from it.

The following paragraphs describe additional features that should prove useful to both students and teachers. A page reference is given to provide an example of each feature.

Clear Rules and Examples: Easy-to-read rules for *all* major concepts are presented in colored print throughout the text (page 172). These combined with numerous examples showing the many different ways in which each rule can be applied (page 172) provide the core of the learning experience.

Numerous Exercises and Applications: *Every* subsection has at least one exercise (page 106), allowing a direct and immediate evaluation of skills learned. *Every* section has at least one Application (page 108), which puts the various skills learned to some immediate use, generally through written expression.

Helpful Charts and Checklists: Colorful charts are found *throughout* the text, highlighting the elements involved in understanding basic concepts (page 585) and presenting step-by-step approaches to the mastery of various skills (page 492). Also in chart form are a number of checklists (page 650) that can be used to check mastery of skills.

Composition Steps and Models: Composition skills are taught not through rules alone but through a thorough analysis of the elements involved in *every* form examined (pages 612–634) and through the use of clear and easy-to-follow planning, writing, and revising steps, again given for *every* form examined (pages 634–665). Numerous student and professional models (page 668) are given *throughout* to increase further the reader's understanding of what is involved in each form.

Three Easy-to-Use Reference Aids: The Table of Contents (pages 5–14) lists *all* topics covered, including subsections with page references. The Key of Major Concepts at the end of the text lists *all* major concepts. The Index (pages 815–830) offers a comprehensive, thoroughly cross-referenced guide to *all* points in the text, with rules and definitions printed in bold.

Prentice-Hall

Grammar
and
Composition

Level 4

Annotated Teacher's Edition

Prepared by Gary Forlini

Pelham High School, Pelham, New York

PRENTICE-HALL, INC., Englewood Cliffs, New Jersey

Acknowledgments

Chapter 14, adapted from *The United States: A History of the Republic* by Mark Lytle and Jim Davidson. Englewood Cliffs, N.J.: Prentice-Hall, Inc. 1981. **Chapter 15,** from *Famous American Books* by Robert B. Downs. New York: McGraw-Hill, 1971. **Chapter 15,** *The Red-Headed League* by Sir Arthur Conan Doyle. Providence, R.I.: Jamestown Publishers, 1976.

ISBN 0-13-696831-7

10 9 8 7 6 5 4 3 2 1

Prentice-Hall International, Inc., London
Prentice-Hall of Australia, Pty. Ltd., Sydney
Prentice-Hall of Canada, Ltd., Toronto
Prentice-Hall of India Private Ltd., New Delhi
Prentice-Hall of Japan, Inc., Tokyo
Prentice-Hall of Southeast Asia Pte. Ltd., Singapore
Whitehall Books Limited, Wellington, New Zealand

Contents

Scope and Sequence

LEVEL FOUR (Grade 10)	LEVEL FIVE (Grade 11)	LEVEL SIX (Grade 12)
1 Nouns, Pronouns, and Verbs 2 Adjectives and Adverbs 3 Prepositions, Conjunctions, and Interjections 4 Analyzing Parts of Speech 5 Basic Parts of a Sentence 6 Phrases 7 Clauses 8 Sentence Faults	1 The Parts of Speech 2 Analyzing Parts of Speech 3 Basic Sentence Parts and Patterns 4 Phrases and Clauses 5 Avoiding Sentence Faults	1 The Parts of Speech 2 Basic Sentence Parts and Patterns 3 Phrases and Clauses 4 Correcting Sentence Faults
9 Verb Usage 10 Pronoun Usage 11 Agreement 12 Adjective and Adverb Usage 13 Special Problems in Usage	6 Verb Usage 7 Pronoun Usage 8 Agreement 9 Adjective and Adverb Usage 10 Miscellaneous Usage Problems 11 Levels of Language	5 Verb Usage 6 Pronoun Usage 7 Agreement 8 Adjective and Adverb Usage 9 Miscellaneous Usage Problems 10 Levels of Language

LEVEL FOUR (Grade 10)	LEVEL FIVE (Grade 11)	LEVEL SIX (Grade 12)
14 Capitalization and Abbreviation 15 Punctuation	12 Capitalization and Abbreviation 13 Punctuation	11 Capitalization and Abbreviation 12 Punctuation
16 Vocabulary Building 17 Spelling Improvement	14 Vocabulary Building 15 Spelling Improvement	13 Vocabulary Building 14 Spelling Improvement
18 Basic Study Skills 19 Reading and Test-Taking Skills 20 Library and Reference Skills	16 Basic Study Skills 17 Test-Taking Skills 18 Library and Reference Skills	15 Basic Study Skills 16 Test-Taking Skills 17 Library and Reference Skills
21 The Right Words and Tone 22 Sentence Variety and Logic 23 Paragraphs 24 Kinds of Paragraphs 25 Essays 26 Kinds of Essays 27 Library Papers 28 Letters 29 Essay Examinations	19 Sentence Length and Structure 20 The Use of Words 21 Clear Thinking in Writing 22 Effective Paragraphs 23 Kinds of Paragraphs 24 Essays 25 Library Papers 26 Papers About Literature 27 Letters and Précis 28 Essay Examinations	18 Word Choices 19 Sentence Style 20 Logical Thinking in Writing 21 Effective Paragraphs 22 Paragraphs with Different Purposes 23 Essays 24 Research and Writing 25 Papers Analyzing Literature 26 Letters and Applications 27 Précis and Essay Examinations

Introduction to the Student's Text

The goal of *Prentice-Hall Grammar and Composition* is one shared by teachers across the country: to help students deal more effectively with the English language. To achieve this goal, the authors and editors began by asking teachers what they wanted in such a series. The answers were not always uniform, but several points were clear. First, a good series must be comprehensive, with enough content, examples, and exercises to meet most, if not all, of the daily classroom needs. Second, a good series must be organized clearly and simply and contain enough learning aids to make it possible for students to become comfortable with the books quickly, both as texts and as reference tools. Third, a good series must present not just a series of exercises but a complete and thorough exercise program, giving students a chance to test their mastery of all skills in a variety of contexts. Finally, a good series must contain excellent coverage of composition, providing material that encourages students to expand their writing skills, not only through rules and analysis but also by following useful steps, studying numerous models, and experimenting with new ideas.

In preparing this series, the authors and editors have focused on these four points, producing a series that is (1) sufficiently comprehensive to meet your daily needs, (2) organized and presented in a fashion that will make each book readily accessible to students as a reference tool and as a text, (3) filled with exercises that offer students a number of different ways to test and use the skills they are gaining, and (4) viable as the basis for a complete course in composition. The following paragraphs will give you details about how these features have been implemented.

Content: A Comprehensive Package, Clearly Developed from Level to Level. The Scope and Sequence chart beginning on page T-4 offers a general guide to the coverage in each level. Basic topics are retaught at each higher level along with new and interesting details, giving older students a chance to review previously studied topics while gaining additional information about the way in which the English language works.

To get a clearer idea of what is covered in each unit of your text, you can check the Table of Contents. There, the titles of all subsections are given to allow you and the students quickly to find the topics you wish to cover. A glance through the text itself will show you the wealth of examples and exercises included. Notice no topics are introduced without an accompanying exercise. Notice also the valuable material contained in the study skills unit, material that can help your students succeed not only in their English courses but in other courses as well.

Organization: A Clear and Logical Format, Enhanced by Numerous Learning and Reference Aids. By choosing a simple, consistent format for each chapter, each section, and each subsection, the authors and editors have been able to present a series that will be immediately accessible both as a text and as a handbook. Whether the book is being used in class or is being consulted as a reference tool, a student's understanding will be enhanced not only by the consistency and simplicity of the format, but also by the fact that (1) all rules appear in bold, colored type, (2) all examples and models are clearly labeled, and (3) numerous charts are used to offer visual keys to important concepts. In addition, special care has been taken to provide enough examples to clarify the variations that may occur in applying each rule.

Recognizing that not all students use the same techniques for finding information in a text, the series provides three reference aids: the Table of Contents at the front of the book, the Key of Major Concepts at the back of the book, and the fully cross-referenced Index that precedes the Key.

Exercises: A Special Program with Different Levels of Skills Evaluation and Application. The series presents three types of exercises which, when taken together, give the students a chance to practice, combine, and apply skills in endless ways. First, each *subsection* ends with at least one set of basic exercises, giving students immediate feedback, allowing you to conclude a day's lesson at any point, and assuring that no concept is overlooked. Second, each *section* ends with one or more Applications, giving students a chance to begin combining the skills they have learned in a very practical way, generally through writing. Finally, the grammar, usage, and mechanics units end with sets of Review Exercises that give students a chance to monitor their skill development and restudy material they are having difficulty with.

Composition: A Complete Program That Motivates Students to Succeed. In teaching composition, rules and analysis alone are not enough; likewise, special skill building techniques can do only part of the job. Instead of relying on any of these in isolation, *Prentice-Hall Grammar and Composition* presents a solid approach for teaching writing, including a recognition of the importance of audience, purpose, and tone. For each type of writing assignment, students are also given practical steps to follow, steps which they are encouraged to expand and adapt to personal tastes in the higher levels. In addition, numerous fully labeled models are given, along with charts and checklists, to highlight the most important concepts. A special section on manuscript preparation, which includes steps for the technical polishing of a written work, follows immediately after the composition unit in Levels 3–6.

The series authors and editors believe that these four features—comprehensiveness, clarity of organization, a full exercise program, and an emphasis on writing as a vehicle of clear communication—will make *Prentice-Hall Grammar and Composition* especially valuable to both you and your students.

Introduction to the Annotated Teacher's Edition

Each Annotated Teacher's Edition has been designed to offer not only general strategies for course planning and evaluation but also specific section-by-section suggestions that can be used on a daily basis. The following paragraphs offer details about these particular features.

Strategies for Using the Text. The flexibility of the series is seen in its many possible applications both as a text and as a reference work. Beginning on page T-11, you will find suggestions for using the series in a variety of settings.

Time-Allocation Chart. On page T-16, you will find a chart giving suggested time allocations for each section of the course. Whatever sections you choose to teach, in whatever order you choose to teach them, the chart should prove helpful in gauging time, for a week, a semester, or a year.

Evaluation Procedures. The section on page T-20 starts with a description of the complete test program available with the series, moves on to specific suggestions for developing your own pretests and post-tests using text material, and then offers ideas for charting progress and developing additional exercises based on text material. The final part of the section is devoted to a discussion of various methods that can be used to evaluate student writing.

Bibliography. The bibliography of general reference works compiled by the authors and editors of the series may prove useful both in your own work and in offering suggestions to students at higher levels.

Teaching Suggestions. The bulk of the teacher's guide portion of the Annotated Teacher's Edition is devoted to a section-by-section coverage of the text. Here you will find objectives to help you plan your coverage of individual sections, suggestions for adapting each section for more and less advanced students, and specific ideas for additional exercises or activities. The objectives, which are correlated on a one-to-one basis with each subsection, should prove especially useful in planning which areas to emphasize and which exercises to assign to meet the particular needs of your own students.

Additional Answers to Text Exercises. Although most of the answers to text exercises are found directly on the text pages, a few, particularly for the diagraming exercises, are found here.

Strategies for Using the Text

Before starting a course, you will certainly want to consider how best to utilize the text to fit the needs of your students and the curriculum. For example, you may choose to teach the complete grammar and composition course in the order presented or you may choose to use the text for a course in either grammar or composition, as the basic adjunct to a literature course, as a source book for improving basic skills, or as a handbook for the correction of errors in composition. Options and possible strategies for using the text in any of these different settings are given in the following paragraphs.

As a Text for Teaching Grammar and Composition. The units in the text are presented in the traditional order of rhetoric handbooks with grammar taking the preeminent position. Although this order works well, other orders can easily be followed. You may, for example, find it more useful to begin the year with study skills (especially the first two chapters), perhaps combining the unit with vocabulary. If you do choose to begin with grammar, you may want to start with the final chapter on sentence faults, then move into a quick review of the parts of speech followed by a more leisurely progression through the chapters on sentence parts.

Still another popular and easily managed strategy is one that merges the work on grammar and usage. The usage chapters on verbs, adjectives, and adverbs can be covered with parts of speech, while the chapters on pronouns and agreement can be taught with the review of sentence parts. Certain sections of the mechanics unit can also be taught with grammar and usage, particularly those dealing with end marks, commas, colons, and semicolons.

Following any of these strategies, you still face two basic choices on the teaching of composition. You may decide to leave all of the composition unit for later in the year, when you can give it your complete attention, or you may want to enliven the study of grammar, usage, and mechanics by interspersing groups of chapters on composition throughout the year.

Regardless of the order in which you choose to teach the course, you will probably find that pretests given early in the year will be very helpful in deciding which sections need the most emphasis. Ideas for pretests can be found in the following section. Once you have basic information about a new group of students, the time chart beginning on page T-16 will help you draft your general plan for the year.

The following chart shows just three of the many possibilities for course organization.

THREE BASIC COURSES IN GRAMMAR AND COMPOSITION

Grammar (Ch. 1-8)	Study Skills (Ch. 18-20)	Grammar: Parts of Speech (Ch. 1-4)
Usage (Ch. 9-13)	Vocabulary (Ch. 16)	Usage: Verbs, Adjectives, and Adverbs (Ch. 9, 12)
Mechanics (Ch. 14-15)	Grammar (Ch. 1-8)	Grammar: Sentence Parts (Ch. 5-8)
Vocabulary and Spelling (Ch. 16-17)	Composition: Sentences (Ch. 21-22)	Usage: Pronouns and Agreement (Ch. 10-11)
Study Skills (Ch. 18-20)	Usage (Ch. 9-13)	Composition (Ch. 21-29)
Composition (Ch. 21-29)	Composition: Paragraphs (Ch. 23-24)	Mechanics (Ch. 14-15)
	Mechanics and Spelling (Ch. 14-15, 17)	Vocabulary, Spelling, and Special Usage Problems (Ch. 16-17, 13)
	Composition: Longer Works (Ch. 25-29)	Study Skills (Ch. 18-20)

As a Text for Teaching Grammar. If your curriculum calls for a grammar course alone, you can use either the first few units of the text in the given order or rearrange them in one of the ways suggested previously. Again the pretest section and the time chart should prove useful in initial planning.

THREE BASIC COURSES IN GRAMMAR

Grammar (Ch. 1-8)	Study Skills (Ch. 18-20)	Grammar: Parts of Speech (Ch. 1-4)
Usage (Ch. 9-13)	Vocabulary (Ch. 16)	Usage: Verbs, Adjectives, and Adverbs (Ch. 9, 12)
Mechanics (Ch. 14-15)	Grammar (Ch. 1-8)	Grammar: Sentence Parts (Ch. 5-8)
Vocabulary and Spelling (Ch. 16-17)	Usage (Ch. 9-13)	Usage: Pronouns and Agreement (Ch. 10-11)
Study Skills (Ch. 18-20)	Mechanics and Spelling (Ch. 14-15, 17)	Mechanics (Ch. 14-15)
		Vocabulary, Spelling, and Special Usage Problems (Ch. 16-17, 13)
		Study Skills (Ch. 18-20)

Because of the written nature of most of the Applications found at the end of every section in the text, your students will still have a chance to do some work in composition, directly related to their studies of grammar, usage, and mechanics.

Although the exercise program within the first few units is extensive, in teaching a course devoted solely to the areas of grammar, usage, and mechanics you may find the practical section-by-section suggestions for additional activities in the later portion of this guide particularly valuable.

As a Text for Teaching Composition. As already noted, the comprehensive unit on composition has been designed to present a complete course in writing with emphasis not merely on rules, analysis, and special techniques, but also on the way these can be combined with a more thorough understanding of the purposes involved and the steps and methods that can be used to achieve success.

For a course on composition, text material can be used in the given order, or it can be rearranged or divided in several other ways. Although the two chapters on sentences make a logical starting place, you may, instead, wish to start with paragraphs (or, if your students are particularly adept, with kinds of paragraphs). One especially useful way of organizing the course is around major assignments, either derived from the Applications at the end of each section or developed to fit your own classes' needs. This system works particularly well if you begin with paragraphs. The following chart shows two of the many plans that might be followed in using the text for a course in composition.

TWO BASIC COURSES IN COMPOSITION

Sentences (Ch. 21-22)	Paragraphs——Major Assignment (Ch. 23)
Paragraphs (Ch. 23)	Kinds of Paragraphs——Major Assignment (Ch. 24)
Kinds of Paragraphs (Ch. 24)	
Essays (Ch. 25-26)	Essays——Major Assignment (Ch. 25-26)
Library Papers (Ch. 27)	Sentences——Major Assignment in Paragraph or
Letters (Ch. 28)	Essay Form (Ch. 21-22)
Essay Examinations (Ch. 29)	Library Papers——Major Assignment (Ch. 27)

Again, the materials in the evaluation section that follows can help you pretest your students to determine where to place emphasis and how ambitious you may want to be with any group. The following section also offers ideas for evaluating written work that can help you find enough time to carry out ambitious plans.

The other units in the text will undoubtedly prove of value as you discover mechanical problems in written work. You may want to use the correction symbols in the manuscript preparation section that follows the composition unit or work out your own system with the students. From time to time, you may also want to check papers with particular questions in mind. Perhaps most or all of the students could benefit not only by a reference to but also by an extended lesson on a particular section of one of the earlier units. The chapter on sentence faults is especially likely to fall into this category.

Most students will also benefit from a review of outlining and library skills; both are covered in the unit on study skills.

As a Textbook to Use in Conjunction with a Literature Course. If you are using the text in a literature course, you may want to place special emphasis on the composition unit. Students can learn about literature through an analysis of what good writing should be. Conversely, they can express their opinions about literature through writing. The following chart shows some of the ways in which the studies of literature and composition can complement each other.

STUDYING LITERATURE THROUGH COMPOSITION	
Analysis of Good Writing	**Writing About Literature**
Sentences (Ch. 21-22)	Persuasive Paragraphs (Ch. 24)
Paragraphs (Ch. 23-24)	Persuasive Essays (Ch. 26)
Essays (Ch. 25-26)	Library Papers (Ch. 27)
	Essay Examinations (Ch. 29)

The composition chapters on sentences should prove especially useful in helping students recognize the importance of the way in which authors use words. As the composition chapters increase the students' awareness of literary value, the study of literary models combined with those models already found in the text should expand the students' own ideas of what they can begin to aspire to.

Paragraphs and essays can be studied, not so much in terms of wording, but in terms of logical communication. Although students may not always find topic sentences and thesis statements in literary models, they will certainly find transitions, persuasive organizations, and a general flow of ideas that can again help them in their own writing.

Persuasive paragraphs and essays can in turn be used by students to express their own opinions about the works they are studying. In an ambitious combination of the two disciplines, a library paper can offer a student the chance, even at this level, to begin analyzing literature on a higher, more critical level. The section on essay examinations, on the other hand, should prove useful in any literature course.

As a Source Book for Teaching Basic Skills. If your students have had little training in the basic skills needed to achieve success in English classes or in school in general, you will probably want to choose only a few of the topics in the text and give extra attention to each. Perhaps the best place to start is with a thorough pretesting of present skills, following the suggestions in the next section.

Once you have solid data on your students' needs, you can follow any one of a number of plans. The unit on study skills is an excellent starting place for a course of this sort. You may wish to follow this with the material on vocabulary and spelling, again to give students help with skills that can improve their ability to deal with all subject matter. You will probably want to teach most of grammar, dropping occasional topics listed in the objectives and following many of the adaptation suggestions found in the section-by-section portion of the guide that begins on page T-29. In general, you are likely to find that the first few subsections of each section contain the most basic material. This same principle carries, in a general way, throughout the units on usage and mechanics.

The time you wish to devote to composition in such a course will vary. Perhaps the most useful approach is an in-depth coverage of the first chapter on paragraphs. This coverage can, like that of the other chapters and units, be adapted and expanded by following the section-by-section suggestions that begin on page T-29.

ONE POSSIBLE COURSE IN BASIC SKILLS

Study Skills (Ch. 18-20)	The Basic Paragraph (Ch. 23)
Vocabulary and Spelling (Ch. 16-17)	Some Work on Sentences (Ch. 21-22)
Most of Grammar (Ch. 1-8)	Letters (Ch. 28)
Most of Usage (Ch. 9-13)	Essay Examinations (Ch. 29)
Most of Mechanics (Ch. 14-15)	

As a Handbook for Correcting Errors in Composition. If most of your students are above grade level and can already handle the composition process with relative ease, you will find that this text fits the reference needs of such students admirably.

In teaching such a course, you may want to conduct a short workshop session on the use of a handbook sometime early in the course. Students can be asked to brainstorm for ideas about the ways in which they might find a handbook useful—both in correcting mistakes and in developing ideas for compositions. With such a list in hand, they can then be asked to use one of the three reference aids in the text to find the areas they would consult, listing page numbers for each problem or source of ideas.

The following chart lists some of the areas that might be explored in such a session.

POSSIBILITIES FOR A WORKSHOP SESSION ON THE USE OF A HANDBOOK

For Correcting Mistakes	For Getting Ideas
1. What mistakes have students made on past compositions?	1. How can vocabulary be of help in composition?
2. What are their biggest problem areas in grammar, usage, punctuation, and spelling?	2. What should students be trying to achieve with their sentences? Their paragraphs? Their longer works?
3. What are some of the technical problems that may arise in putting their work in final form?	3. How important are audience and purpose?

Time-Allocation Chart

UNIT **II**

Usage

Estimated Class Sessions

UNIT **III**

Mechanics

Estimated Class Sessions

Chapter 15: Punctuation

UNIT **IV**

Vocabulary and Spelling

Estimated Class Sessions

Chapter 16: Vocabulary Building

Chapter 17: Spelling Improvement

UNIT **V**

Study Skills

Estimated Class Sessions

Chapter 18: Basic Study Skills

Chapter 19: Reading and Test-Taking Skills

Chapter 20: Library and Reference Skills

UNIT VI
Composition

Evaluation Procedures

Almost the only things that are certain about the evaluation procedures used in teaching a course in grammar and composition are (1) that they will probably be multifaceted and (2) that they will probably take up a considerable amount of a teacher's time. The following suggestions cover most of the different facets—general pretesting and post-testing, drill work, and the variety of special techniques that can be used in grading compositions. Many of the latter suggestions are specifically directed at reducing the work a teacher of composition can expect to face. Throughout, the focus is on using evaluation procedures to communicate with the students and help them achieve greater success.

Using the Accompanying Test Package. The *Prentice-Hall Grammar and Composition Test Program*, available separately, offers a complete pretest and a complete post-test for each unit in each text, as well as a mastery test for each chapter. Because the various sections involved are clearly marked along the left-hand side of each test, you can use any of the tests to cover any or all of the sections contained in a larger division. If, for example, students are taking a chapter test on verb usage, but you have decided to omit the section on active and passive voice, simply instruct the students to omit those labeled portions of the test.

Although the focus in the test package is mainly on objective questions, the tests covering the composition unit combine questions that call for objective identification with other questions that call for writing samples. Possible scoring systems are given for each of the samples, although you can, of course, change the weighting of parts or substitute a more holistic evaluation.

The following charts show some of the possible uses of the various components in the test package. First, they can be used in the most traditional sense of pretest and post-test evaluation.

FOR OVERALL EVALUATION		
Unit Pretests	**Chapter Tests**	**Unit Post-Tests**
Administer all or most of the pretests at the beginning of the year to identify strengths and weaknesses; then use the section numbers on the tests to plan lessons.	Administer the chapter tests at the end of each chapter in the traditional manner.	Administer all or most of the post-tests at the end of the year, or in groups at the end of each semester, to gauge overall progress during the period by comparison with pretest scores.

The tests can also serve for planning and testing each unit.

FOR UNIT-BY-UNIT PLANNING AND EVALUATION

Unit Pretests	Chapter Tests	Unit Post-Tests
Administer the pretests unit by unit as students approach each new area; encourage students to recognize their own strengths and weaknesses.	Use the chapter tests as the first stage in a recycling system that allows students to note problem areas that need extra attention.	Use the post-tests as the second stage in the recycling system, either by chapter, following the section numbers on the tests, or by unit.

Among the other uses of the tests are previewing, skills evaluation, and student self-testing.

FOR PREVIEWING, SKILLS EVALUATION, OR SELF-TESTING

Unit Pretests	Chapter Tests	Unit Post-Tests
Following the section numbers on the tests, use portions of the pretests before each chapter or section as a preview of a week's lesson.	Use the chapter tests (or the post-tests) as part of an open-book evaluation of students' ability to use the book as a reference tool.	Use the post-tests (or the chapter tests) as a vehicle that allows students to monitor their own progress in mastering basic skills.

Any of the suggestions in the charts can also, of course, be used with tests you construct yourself. The following ideas can help you construct such tests using the material in the text.

Developing Your Own Pretests and Post-Tests. The wealth of exercise material contained in the text makes it possible to pull selected material for special testing purposes without destroying the later value of the exercises themselves.

The following chart lists possibilities for constructing pretests directly from the material in the text.

CONSTRUCTING PRETESTS USING TEXT MATERIAL

1. Pull two or three exercise items from each set of exercises in the section, chapter, or unit you wish to pretest, keying them for later reference.

2. Use or adapt the Applications at the end of each section. Their cumulative nature makes them readily useful in a general pretesting of section objectives. Again, key them for later reference.

3. Use or adapt the Review Exercises at the end of the grammar, usage, and mechanics units, keying them in a more general way to the chapters covered.

Pretests can also be created by using the objectives in the section-by-section portion of this guide. The objectives can be used either to construct a series of individual questions for each objective or as a guide to decide on one or more major tasks the students might attempt in order to show the extent of their mastery of an overall concept. The following chart lists some of the major tasks that might be considered for each of the units in the text.

SAMPLE PRETESTS BASED ON OBJECTIVES FOR EACH SECTION

---

1. **Grammar:** Students can be given a series of sentences and asked first to label parts of speech, second to label sentence parts, and finally to label the sentences themselves by structure and by function. You would probably want to include a list of terms to be used in carrying out each part of this four-part assignment.

2. **Usage:** Students can be given one or more passages that contain the various errors in usage detailed in the objectives. After being told the number of errors contained in each passage, they can then be asked to locate and correct each error. Important in this kind of test is the immediate provision of corrections after students have completed the test, possibly through the use of a second sheet of error-free passages that students can study after the test.

3. **Mechanics:** Again, passages containing the major errors covered in the objectives can be distributed, with an emphasis on those that cause confusion in communication. Students should again be given the number of errors in each passage and corrected passages to study immediately after the test.

4. **Vocabulary and Spelling:** To test general strategies for developing vocabulary, you might give students a sample paragraph, ask them to identify the words they do not know, make guesses about the words telling why they made those guesses, tell how they would check the words' meanings, and how they would go about learning the words for future use. A general spelling test might ask students to choose among ten pairs of correct and incorrect spellings used in context, tell why they picked each word, and then tell how they would go about memorizing any words they have missed. As with the suggested usage and mechanics tests, correct answers should be supplied to the students immediately after the test.

5. **Study Skills:** To test the students' current knowledge of the study skills taught in this text, you might ask a series of short questions: (1) What basic study skills can help a student learn more efficiently? (2) What methods can be used to take notes and outline ideas for a paper? (3) What methods can be used to memorize material for a test? (4) How does one find a book in the library? (5) What reference books are especially useful in carrying out school assignments? (6) What can be found in a dictionary other than the meanings of words?

6. **Composition:** Your choices in designing a pretest in composition are perhaps the broadest. You can measure objective knowledge, identification skills, or writing skills. The best single method is

probably to ask for a paper of three to five paragraphs. It can then be analyzed in terms of all the different elements involved. A knowledge of the skills involved in writing library papers, letters, and answers to essay exam questions can be evaluated following a process similar to that suggested for study skills.

Post-tests for sections, chapters, and units can be constructed in similar fashion, using the text material directly or working with the guide objectives. If you are particularly interested in measuring overall attainment across a period of time, you will probably find it useful to use the same technique in constructing both the pretests and the post-tests. The following chart lists methods that might be used, including those that parallel the methods for constructing pretests.

METHODS FOR DEVELOPING POST-TESTS

1. As suggested for the pretests, pull items from the exercises in each section, use or adapt Applications, or use or adapt Review Exercises.

2. Again, as suggested for the pretests, use the guide objectives to develop individual questions for each objective or more general questions covering broader skills.

3. Use students' corrected homework papers to identify special problem areas, discuss these areas in class, and concentrate on them in preparing tests.

Whatever methods you use to evaluate student progress, you may find it useful to chart results at various stages and share these results with students.

Charting Student Progress. One of the major reasons for pretesting is so that you will be able to measure student progress, especially in those areas where the greatest problems seem to lie. Although grades can certainly be marked in grade-books, a more visual charting of scores can be more dramatic, particularly when it is shared with students at each testing stage. You may even want to ask students to construct their own charts, beginning with the results of their pretests, then moving on to other post-test stages.

To be most valuable, such charts should show individual scores for discrete portions of the work. This will give students a chance to identify those areas that are in particular need of improvement. The following chart shows three sets of scores on the usage unit: the lowest set on the unit pretest, a better set on the chapter tests, and a greatly improved set on the final unit post-test. Since one score in each set is needed for each chapter, the unit tests have been scored not in an overall fashion but chapter by chapter.

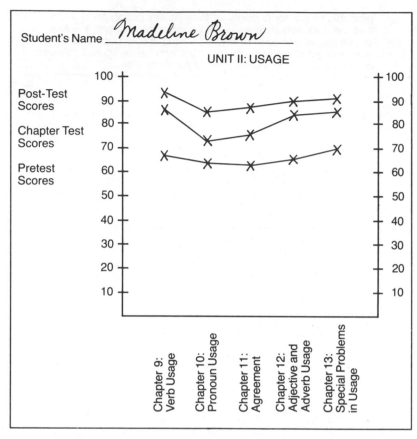

Student's Name _Madeline Brown_

UNIT II: USAGE

Post-Test Scores

Chapter Test Scores

Pretest Scores

Chapter 9: Verb Usage
Chapter 10: Pronoun Usage
Chapter 11: Agreement
Chapter 12: Adjective and Adverb Usage
Chapter 13: Special Problems in Usage

Such charts are probably most useful when teaching grammar, usage, and mechanics. With care, however, they can also be used to measure the more mechanical aspects of skills in other units.

Developing Additional Drill Material. Although you will generally find more than enough exercise material to cover the needs of most classes, individual students or groups of students may from time to time need extra work in some areas.

IDEAS FOR ADDITIONAL DRILL WORK

---

1. Use the additional activities in the section-by-section portion of the guide, along with the ideas for adapting the sections to fit the needs of different ability groups.
2. Adapt exercise sets from other areas of the book to follow the specific instructions for the exercises you are covering.
3. Have the students themselves construct new exercises, while gaining a new perspective from which to view the task at hand. After you have examined the exercises for accuracy, they can be exchanged repeatedly among the students.

As in charting student progress, you will most likely find that these ideas work best for the units presented at the beginning of the book. The last unit, composition, demands its own evaluation procedures.

Using Special Strategies for Evaluating Composition Skills. A number of different evaluation techniques can be used for grading compositions, some of which take considerable time, others of which can drastically reduce the time you spend without greatly changing the overall benefit to the student. Many experts, however, suggest that you consider using a mixture of techniques, cutting down the time you need to grade most papers while giving a thorough analysis to others.

The most traditional method of grading composition work is the most time consuming. Each error is marked for correction and an attempt is made to cover all aspects of good writing, from ideas to spelling. The result is generally a single grade covering the entire piece of writing, combined in most cases with comments that will encourage students while directing them to specific areas that can be improved.

A variation of this approach divides the general analysis into specific criteria, which can then be graded individually. The following two charts show ways in which this system can be implemented. The chart on the left gives letter grades for nine equal criteria. The chart on the right gives number grades for seven weighted criteria.

COMPOSITION EVALUATION FORM

Student's Name _Sandy Girello_

1. Sentence variety — _B_
2. Sentence style — _B-_
3. Clarity of main idea and purpose — _A_
4. Development of ideas — _A-_
5. Unity — _A_
6. Coherence — _B_
7. Ideas presented — _A_
8. Grammar and usage — _C-_
9. Mechanics and spelling — _B_

Composite Grade — _B_

COMPOSITION EVALUATION FORM

Student's Name _Greg Campbell_

1. Sentence style and variety — _8_ (10)
2. Clarity of main idea and purpose — _9_ (10)
3. Development of ideas — _8_ (10)
4. Unity and coherence — _8_ (10)
5. Spelling — _10_ (10)
6. Grammar, usage, and mechanics — _18_ (20)
7. Ideas presented — _26_ (30)

Composite Grade — _87_ (100)

The criteria used and any weighting given will depend, of course, on what you are trying to measure in each assignment. The charts, if used, should also be seen as simply one more way to communicate clearly with students. They cannot replace the notes of encouragement and individual directives that may still be included on the papers along with requests for corrections.

Another increasingly popular method of grading composition papers is the holistic method. It has two basic purposes and a number of variations. The first purpose is to save time, thus making it possible to assign more papers, giving students more chances to practice their skills. The second purpose is to keep the focus on the quality of the entire paper and not on individual, miscellaneous faults. The basic method calls for the rapid reading and ranking of a group of papers on a scale of one to five (or one to four, or one to three, depending on the variation). The papers are then rapidly read and ranked by a second teacher and the scores are compared, with perhaps a third teacher acting as mediator on papers where the two sets of scores differ greatly.

The following chart shows an adaptation of the holistic method that you can use alone.

SUGGESTIONS FOR USING A CLASSROOM ADAPTATION OF THE HOLISTIC METHOD

1. Cover the students' names to guard against expectations.
2. Spend no more than a minute reading each page of a group of papers, getting a general feel for the quality of each work.
3. After reading each paper, place it in one of four piles which range from excellent to good to fair to not good. If necessary, include a fifth pile for papers that are for some reason impossible to grade—perhaps because a student has produced a good or promising paper that does not quite fit the assignment.
4. Briefly consider the possibility of reranking some of the papers. (If you are in doubt, you will generally find it best to stick with your first opinion.)
5. Add grades and comments.

The peer-grading method has also gained favor among some teachers in recent years. Like holistic grading, it saves time and makes it possible for the students to complete more assignments. In addition, it widens the audience for which each student is writing, while giving students further models of what the members of their own peer group can accomplish. Unless it is carefully managed, however, it can cause certain problems, including the reinforcement of errors. The following suggestions may make the system more manageable in your own classroom.

SUGGESTIONS FOR USING PEER GRADING

1. Before students are asked to evaluate each other's papers, discuss what specific things they should look for and how they should go about checking and marking these things.

2. Emphasize the importance of noting the good things and offering criticism in a constructive way.
3. From time to time, consider the possibility of having more than one student evaluate each paper.
4. Also from time to time, review sets of papers and conduct a general classroom review of the criteria to be used (not specifying any particular papers).

Perhaps the most ambitious system, not so much in terms of a teacher's workload, but in terms of true student progress, is one that relies on increasing self-evaluation. The revision checklists in the text can be part of such a system, along with any or all of the suggestions in the following chart.

SUGGESTIONS FOR DEVELOPING A SYSTEM OF SELF-EVALUATION

1. As in peer grading, discuss with students the specific qualities they should look for in a written work.
2. Have students begin their self-evaluation simply by conducting two revisions, with the second revision taking place at least a day after the first.
3. In each revision, ask students to mark their original work as a teacher might with internal corrections and margin comments.
4. After they have completed the final revision, ask students to list what they believe are the strengths and weaknesses of the work. These notes should be placed in a notebook along with ideas for future works.
5. Analyze the groups of revised works from time to time to see what progress the students are making. If possible, hold individual conferences.

Few if any of the methods discussed here can be used as the sole method of evaluation in the typical classroom. However, a judicious mixture may save time while giving students greater opportunities to develop their skills.

Bibliography

Armstrong, William B. *Study Tips.* Woodbury, N.Y.: Barron's Educational Series, 1975.

Baker, Sheridan. *The Practical Stylist,* 3rd ed. New York: Crowell, 1973.

D'Angelo, Frank J. *Process and Thought in Composition,* 2nd ed. Cambridge, Mass.: Winthrop Publishers, 1980.

DeSola, Ralph. *Abbreviations Dictionary.* New York: Meredith Press, 1967.

Follett, Wilson. *Modern American Usage.* New York: Hill and Wang, 1966.

Froe, Otis D. and Froe, Otyce B. *Easy Way to Better Grades.* New York: Arco Publishing Co., 1976.

Gilbert, Doris Wilcox. *Breaking the Word Barrier.* Englewood Cliffs, N.J.: Prentice-Hall, 1972.

Gorrell, Robert and Laird, Charlton. *Modern English Handbook,* 4th ed. Englewood Cliffs, N.J.: Prentice-Hall, 1967.

Hill, Robert H. *Dictionary of Difficult Words.* New York: John Day, 1971.

Kilner, Bernard G. *Learn How to Study.* Chicago: Science Research Associates, 1975.

Koch, Carl and Brazil, James M. *Strategies for Teaching the Composition Process.* Urbana, Ill.: National Council of Teachers of English, 1978.

Leggett, Glenn, Mead, David C., and Charvat, William. *Essentials of Grammar and Composition.* Englewood Cliffs, N.J.: Prentice-Hall, 1978.

Macrorie, Ken. *Telling Writing.* New York: Hayden Book Co., 1970.

Marshak, David. *HM Study Skills Program, Part I and II.* Reston, Va.: National Assoc. of Secondary School Principals, 1979.

Memering, Dean and O'Hare, Frank. *The Writer's Work.* Englewood Cliffs, N.J.: Prentice-Hall, 1980.

Myers, L. M. *Guide to American English,* 4th ed. Englewood Cliffs, N.J.: Prentice-Hall, 1968.

Quaintance, William. *Learning to Learn.* Portland, Me.: J. Weston Walsh Publishers, 1976.

Smelt, Elsie. *Speak, Spell and Read English,* 2nd ed. Hawthorn, Victoria, Australia: Longman, 1976.

Spargo, Edward. *The New Student.* Providence, R.I.: Jamestown Publishers, 1977.

Struck, William. *Study Skills for Success in School and College.* Danbury, Conn.: Grolier Educational Corp., 1978.

Two Hundred Tips to Students on How to Study. Danville, Ill.: Interstate Printers and Publishers, 1979.

West, William W. *Developing Writing Skills,* 3rd ed. Englewood Cliffs, N.J.: Prentice-Hall, 1980.

Teaching Suggestions

Grammar

The first chapters in this unit describe the eight parts of speech: nouns, pronouns, and verbs first; then the modifiers, adjectives and adverbs; and finally prepositions, conjunctions, and interjections. The chapters that follow explore the basic parts of sentences (subjects, predicates, complements), and succeeding chapters build upon simple sentences with studies of phrases, verbals, and clauses. The last chapter, Sentence Faults, explores syntactical problems, such as sentence fragments and faulty parallelism, which students can solve using their knowledge of grammar and sentence structure. Also within this unit are sections on diagraming to help students visualize the sentence structures that they have been studying. These sections, however, are optional and can be omitted without loss of continuity, although they do provide an efficient means of review.

All of the sections in this unit are planned for students of average ability. Numerous charts and examples illustrate the concepts in the text; exercises, which follow each subtopic, test and reinforce the learning.

The pretest for the unit, available in the *Prentice-Hall Grammar and Composition Test Program*, can be used to help determine your students' need for instruction in the skills presented in the unit. Chapter tests and a unit post-test are also available in the test program.

CHAPTER 1 Nouns, Pronouns, and Verbs
(pp. 18–39)

The first section in this chapter describes compound, common, and proper nouns. The second section discusses the different kinds of pronouns. The first of two sections on verbs explains the difference between action and linking verbs. The second section on verbs describes verb phrases and helping verbs and teaches students how to locate them in sentences.

Each of the four sections in this chapter may require one or two class sessions, depending on student needs and abilities. The exercises in each section give students an opportunity to apply the principles presented.

■ 1.1 Nouns (pp. 18–22)

Objectives: After completing this section, students should be able to

- Identify nouns.
- Recognize compound nouns.
- Distinguish between common and proper nouns.

Adapting for Different Abilities. While students of varying abilities should find the material and exercises in this section accessible, you may find that some students have difficulty identifying compound nouns, particularly those formed by two separate words. You might want to do some further work with compound nouns by distributing dictionaries and asking students to find two-word compound nouns.

You might also pose the following problem to a group of advanced students: Why are the words *old age* and *old master* considered compound nouns, whereas *old car* and *old shoes* are not? After some deliberation students should figure out that the words acting as compound nouns signify more than the words themselves denote, whereas the words not acting as compound nouns do not. *Old age* does not actually mean "an age that is old," but rather "an advanced stage in a human life." Similarly, *old master* does not mean "a master who is old," but "a great European painter before the eighteenth century" or "a work by such a painter." Once this distinction is understood, students should be able to pick out the compound noun easily in such pairs as *natural history* and *natural result* or *free enterprise* and *free sample*.

Suggestions for Additional Activities. You might want to distribute a dittoed sheet with seven columns of boxes with the headings "Concrete," "Abstract," "Collective," "Compound," "Common," "Proper," and "Not a Noun." On the left side of the chart, list different kinds of nouns and a few other parts of speech such as adjectives or verbs, as shown in the following chart. Students can then check off as many boxes as apply to the words.

	Con-crete	Abstract	Collec-tive	Com-pound	Common	Proper	Not a Noun
golden retriever	X			X	X		
Great Britain	X			X		X	
sad							X
guilt		X			X		
Supreme Court	X		X	X		X	

■ 1.2 Pronouns (pp. 22-30)

Objectives: After completing this section, students should be able to

- Recognize the relationship between pronouns and their antecedents.
- Identify personal pronouns and distinguish between reflexive and intensive pronouns.
- Recognize demonstrative, relative, and interrogative pronouns.
- Identify indefinite pronouns.

Adapting for Different Abilities. What makes work with pronouns difficult for less advanced students is the nomenclature; students must not only recognize seven types of pronouns but also learn the labels for them. You might decide not to hold students accountable for all seven different labels; instead, you might require only that they be able to identify personal, relative, and indefinite pronouns. Because students must understand relative pronouns to study clauses and must know about indefinite pronouns to study subject-verb agreement, these pronouns should be mastered.

Suggestions for Additional Activities. Since the ability to recognize pronouns is important primarily as a basis for correct usage, you may at this time want to supplement this section with work in Chapter 10, Pronoun Usage, and Chapter 11, Agreement. Although material presented in these chapters requires the ability to analyze the structure of sentences, you may find that your students have had adequate preparation in earlier years to enable them to undertake this work now.

■ 1.3 Action and Linking Verbs (pp. 31-37)

Objectives: After completing this section, students should be able to

- Recognize action verbs.
- Distinguish between transitive and intransitive action verbs.
- Recognize forms of *be* and other verbs as linking verbs.
- Recognize that some verbs may be used as either linking verbs or action verbs.

Adapting for Different Abilities. You will probably expect all students to master action and linking verbs, but may find that less advanced students have trouble with transitive and intransitive action verbs. For these students you might postpone a discussion of this topic until they study direct objects in Section 5.3.

Suggestions for Additional Activities. To clarify the concept that most action verbs can be transitive or intransitive, depending on use, but some are either always transitive or always intransitive, you might want to supplement this section with dictionary work. For example, have students look up the verbs in Exercise B and check to see how they can be used. Explain that dictionaries distinguish between the transitive and intransitive definitions of verbs with the abbreviations *v.t.* and *v.i.*

You may want to carry this activity further by having your students use both the dictionary and their answers to Exercise B in writing new sentences. If a verb in the exercise is transitive, students should use it intransitively, and vice versa. For example, *swung* in Sentence 1 is intransitive. An acceptable new sentence would be *He swung the lantern to warn the train's engineer.* All of the verbs in the exercise except *shuddered* in Sentence 4 can be reused.

■ 1.4 Helping Verbs (pp. 37–39)

Objectives: After completing this section, students should be able to

- Recognize the role that helping verbs play in the formation of verb phrases.
- Locate helping verbs in sentences.

Adapting for Different Abilities. All students should find the work in this section manageable. You might want advanced students to work the five items in the Application into a single unified paragraph.

Suggestions for Additional Activities. Students can redo Exercise A in Section 1.3, this time supplying verb phrases in the blanks.

CHAPTER 2 Adjectives and Adverbs (pp. 40–51)

In two sections, one for adjectives and one for adverbs, this chapter covers all types of single-word modifiers. It explains the concept of modification as well as the situations in which adjectives and adverbs function. You may need only one class session for each section, unless your students have trouble distinguishing between adjectives and adverbs or recognizing adverbs that modify adjectives and other adverbs. In either of these cases, you may need two or three class sessions for the second section.

The concepts in this chapter are important since your students' work with phrases and clauses will require a knowledge of modification. Their work in Chapter 12, Adjective and Adverb Usage, will also rely on mastery of this chapter.

■ 2.1 Adjectives (pp. 40-47)

Objectives: After completing this section, students should be able to

- Recognize adjectives as modifiers of nouns and pronouns.
- Recognize compound and proper adjectives.
- Recognize nouns, different kinds of pronouns, and verbs used as adjectives.

Adapting for Different Abilities. While your students should have little difficulty recognizing adjectives once they understand the concept of modification, the nomenclature may prove burdensome for some students. For these students you might eliminate such terms as *demonstrative, interrogative,* and *indefinite* and choose instead to focus on recognition skills, the main point of this study.

Suggestions for Additional Activities. To reinforce the concept of modification, you might list on the board ten or more words that can be used as adjectives, such as *small, that, neither, fewer, nearsighted, autumn, California, my, which,* and so on. Ask students to think of nouns that could be modified by the adjectives and then to form phrases using as many of the adjectives as possible: *my small, nearsighted Hungarian uncle* or *that small California bear,* for example. Another activity that can both sharpen your students' use of precise words and clarify the concept of modification is modeled on the television show *Password.* To play the game, show a student a common object that the rest of the class cannot see. Using one adjective at a time, the student should then describe the object as precisely as possible until a classmate identifies it correctly. Rules governing the number of clues allowed, points to be won, and penalties for failing to use an adjective should be set at the start. Objects you might use are a scouring pad, a roll of tape, a paper clip, a bar of soap, and so on. Allowable clues for the scouring pad could be *scratchy, soapy, wet, abrasive, small, roundish, metal,* and *food-removing.*

■ 2.2 Adverbs (pp. 47-51)

Objectives: After completing this section, students should be able to

- Recognize adverbs as modifiers of verbs, adjectives, and other adverbs.
- Recognize nouns used as adverbs.
- Distinguish between adverbs and adjectives.

Adapting for Different Abilities. Most students will be able to complete Exercise A, Recognizing Adverbs, successfully. However, recognizing nouns used as adverbs and distinguishing between adverbs and adjectives may be a bit more difficult. With a group of less advanced students, you may want to work in class on the first sentences of Exercise B, Recognizing Nouns Used as Adverbs, and Exercise C, Distinguishing Between Adverbs and Adjectives. After this preparation students can complete each of the exercises independently in class or as homework. If your students have difficulty with the Application, Writing Sentences with Adverbs, you can place a list of adverbs on the board. The students can then choose appropriate words to add to the sentences.

If your advanced students keep composition folders, you can suggest that they analyze one of their compositions for use of adverbs. They should note any adverbs they used and indicate any sentences that could have been improved by the addition of adverbs.

Suggestions for Additional Activities. To give students practice in using adverbs, you might list ten adverbs, including some that can also be used as adjectives. Have students write a sentence for each word, underline the word within the sentence, draw an arrow from the word to the word it modifies, and identify the part of speech of the word modified. You might want to use the following list:

hopelessly	upstairs	too	right	mildly
extremely	in	down	very	gladly

CHAPTER 3 Prepositions, Conjunctions, and Interjections (pp. 52–62)

With this chapter students will complete their study of the eight parts of speech. The two sections of this chapter cover the last three parts of speech. Section 3.1 defines prepositions and shows students how to locate them in sentences. It also prepares students for later work with prepositional phrases and shows students how certain words can be either prepositions or adverbs, depending on their use in sentences. Section 3.2 covers conjunctions and interjections. The work with interjections is brief and simple, but students will need to concentrate on conjunctions since there are several different types of conjunctions with different functions. A maximum of three class sessions should be sufficient to cover the work in this chapter.

■ 3.1 Prepositions (pp. 52–56)

Objectives: After completing this section, students should be able to

- Recognize single-word and compound prepositions in sentences.
- Identify prepositional phrases.
- Distinguish between prepositions and adverbs in sentences.

Adapting for Different Abilities. By studying the text and carrying out the exercises, average and advanced students should find all material in the section accessible. Less advanced students may have difficulty distinguishing between prepositions and adverbs. You might create a drill for these students using the list of frequently used prepositions on page 52. Have them use each word first as a preposition and then, if possible, as an adverb.

Students should come to realize that any word in the list is a preposition when it is followed by an object, as in *aboard the ship*, but that the word is an adverb when it is used alone after a verb, as in *go aboard*.

Suggestions for Additional Activities. Once students can recognize different prepositions and prepositional phrases, you might have students choose five or ten prepositions from the chart on page 52 and use them in original sentences.

For another activity, you might have students take each adverb that they identified in Exercise C and use it in a new sentence as a preposition.

■ 3.2 Conjunctions and Interjections (pp. 56–62)

Objectives: After completing this section, students should be able to

- Identify coordinating, correlative, and subordinating conjunctions.
- Distinguish between a conjunction and a preposition or adverb.
- Recognize conjunctive adverbs and their use in sentences.
- Recognize interjections.

Adapting for Different Abilities. This section focuses primarily on conjunctions because students need little instruction in recognizing interjections. The exercises are manageable for all levels, especially if students work closely with the charts and examples provided in the text. With some students, you may want to dispense with the nomenclature, requiring only recognition of the conjunctions. If you choose this approach, you should simplify the Application by providing a list of conjunctions from which the students can choose the appropriate word.

Suggestions for Additional Activities. To give students practice writing sentences that contain different types of conjunctions, you might list five or ten short sentences that can be combined in various ways with any of the types of conjunctions:

We knew our boat had drifted perilously close to shore.
A warning buoy sounded nearby.
Waves broke over the bow.
Visibility was near zero.
Neither of us was afraid of running aground.

Since many students tend to string ideas together with *and*, you might direct students to use a coordinating conjunction only once in this practice session and rely instead on subordinating conjunctions.

CHAPTER 4 Analyzing Parts of Speech
(pp. 63–66)

This short chapter reviews the eight parts of speech by capsulizing the rules and concepts covered in Chapters 1, 2, and 3. It also provides summary exercises on all parts of speech. One class session should be sufficient for this chapter.

■ 4.1 Identifying Parts of Speech According to Use (pp. 63–66)

Objective: After completing this section, students should be able to

- Identify the part of speech of a word according to its use in a sentence.

Adapting for Different Abilities. Since this section is essentially a review of material already covered, and since the material is graphically illustrated by charts, most students should be able to achieve the objective with ease. With less advanced students, you may find it helpful to have them use the charts as you work through the first few sentences of each exercise in class. Students should then be able to complete the rest of the exercises independently.

Suggestions for Additional Activities. You might assign the following activity for homework. Ask each student to locate a short passage in a newspaper, book, or magazine. The passage should contain examples of seven or eight parts of speech (interjections can be omitted). Students should copy the selections onto their papers and follow these instructions:

1. Circle an example of each part of speech; copy the word beneath the passage and label its part of speech.
2. Underline one word in the passage that could be used as another part of speech. Write a sentence of your own, illustrating the word used as a different part of speech.

CHAPTER 5 Basic Parts of a Sentence
(pp. 57–103)

Chapters 5, 6, and 7 explore English syntax: the basic subject–verb–complement structure of simple sentences, the ways different phrases expand this basic pattern, and the way clauses expand the pattern even further to form complex as well as compound-complex sentences.

Chapter 5 contains six sections: 5.1 and 5.2 are devoted to subjects and verbs, 5.3 and 5.4 to complements, and 5.5 to the basic patterns and variations in which simple English sentences are written. Section 5.6 is the first of three sections in the unit on diagraming, which you may or may not elect to teach your students. Though suitable for review, the section may also be taught piecemeal as you introduce each concept to which the diagrams apply.

Since this chapter provides an important foundation for later work with sentence structure as well as with usage and composition, you may need as many as ten or twelve class sessions with these six sections, especially if students display need for additional explication and drill.

■ 5.1 Subjects and Predicates (pp. 67–75)

Objectives: After completing this section, students should be able to

- Recognize a sentence as a group of words consisting of a complete subject and a complete predicate.
- Distinguish between a sentence and a fragment.
- Find simple subjects and simple predicates in sentences.
- Recognize compound subjects and verbs in sentences.

Adapting for Different Abilities. Less advanced students who have problems with fragments in their writing may benefit by examining one of their own compositions, in light of the concepts presented in this section. Work with them in small groups or individually to help them find the subjects and verbs in their own sentences and to correct any fragments that they locate.

Advanced students can also benefit by examining their own sentences, especially if their sentence patterns tend to be overly involved and confusing. Have these students identify their subjects and verbs, correct any fragments, and break up overly long sentences. Stress that such reexamination is an essential part of the writing process. In this way you will help your students adjust to the tasks of proofreading and revision.

Suggestions for Additional Activities. To reinforce recognition skills, you might select a group of simple sentences from an exercise preceding this chapter and have students make two columns on their paper:

Complete Subject	Complete Predicate

Students can then spend a few minutes dividing the sentences and placing the two parts in the appropriate columns.

For another reinforcing activity, you can place on the board (or on dittoed sheets) any number of sentence fragments and ask students to fill in subjects or verbs or complete predicates—whatever is needed to make a fragment into a complete sentence.

■ 5.2 Hard-to-Find Subjects (pp. 75-80)

Objectives: After completing this section, students should be able to

- Find an understood subject in orders or directions.
- Find the subject in different kinds of inverted sentences.

Adapting for Different Abilities. Most students should find the exercises in this section easy after they have studied the text. Less advanced students may need help completing the Application. You can have these students work in groups or individually, with your guidance.

Suggestions for Additional Activities. You might place on the board some sentences such as the following and ask students to find the subject:

> Come here now.
> Where did you go yesterday?
> There is a bat in my room.
> From her shopping bag emerged a furry kitten.

Some students may choose the first word or the first noun as the subject. Have those who choose the correct word explain the reason for their choice.

■ 5.3 Direct Objects, Indirect Objects, and Objective Complements (pp. 80-86)

Objectives: After completing this section, students should be able to

- Recognize direct objects in sentences.
- Recognize indirect objects in sentences.
- Recognize objective complements in sentences.

Adapting for Different Abilities. It may be necessary to have some students review the distinction between transitive and intransitive verbs (Section 1.3). After a review, you can place on the board a sentence that needs a direct object in order to make sense. Here is an example:

> Jasper's dog bit _____.

Have a volunteer point out the action verb and then ask others to suggest nouns or pronouns that make sense in the blank. Explain that these words are called direct objects. At this point, you could return to the text, or you could continue this process by providing more sentences with blanks to be filled with indirect objects and objective complements:

Mother gave ＿＿＿＿＿＿ a ride to the station.

I named the kitten ＿＿＿＿＿＿.

After students have offered suitable answers and you have introduced the terms, explain that these two kinds of complements only appear in sentences that already have direct objects. You might challenge students to find the direct objects in the examples.

Average and advanced students should find work with direct and indirect objects manageable; however, all students may need extra time to master objective complements. With less advanced students, you might consider eliminating this topic altogether, or you might instruct students to include objective complements with direct objects as they identify and label them. Identification of an objective complement can be accomplished without the terminology by including all words as part of the direct object and simplifying study in the manner shown in the following example:

Complete		Complete
Subject	V	Direct Object

Intense heat made [my hands red and sticky.]

Suggestions for Additional Activities. Here and in the following sections, you may find that sentence combining is an enjoyable way to encourage your students' creativity and revision skills while they focus on a particular grammatical structure. For the material in this section, you can offer pairs of sentences that, when combined, will produce compound direct objects, indirect objects, and objective complements. Here are three sentence pairs suitable for combining:

1. I received a new sweater on my birthday. I also received a belt.
2. Janice bought me an ice cream. She also bought one for my little sister.
3. We painted the kitchen yellow. We painted the living room blue.

■ 5.4 Subject Complements (pp. 86–89)

Objectives: After completing this section, students should be able to

- Recognize predicate nominatives in sentences.
- Recognize predicate adjectives in sentences.

Adapting for Different Abilities. Now that students have to remember five terms for complements—direct object, indirect object, objective complement, predicate nominative, and predicate adjective—less advanced students may have trouble keeping track of the nomenclature. If you want them to remember these different terms in addition to understanding the concepts, these students will need extra practice applying the specific labels. Exercises such as the ones suggested for Section 5.3, as well as sentences that you create and place on dittoed handouts, would be suitable for this purpose.

Suggestions for Additional Activities. If you need more exercises for drill work or for homework assignments, instruct students to turn again to the exercises in Section 1.3. Exercises C and D (pp. 35–36) contain sentences with linking verbs and subject complements. As they complete these exercises this time, students can find the three sentence parts and place their answers in columns, under the following three heads. Have students specifically label each complement in the third column.

<u>Subject</u>   <u>Linking Verb</u>   <u>Subject Complement</u>

■ 5.5 Reviewing Basic Sentence Patterns
(pp. 89–94)

Objectives: After completing this section, students should be able to

- Recognize basic sentence patterns made up of subjects, verbs, and complements.
- Recognize inverted sentence patterns.

Adapting for Different Abilities. With less advanced students, you might want to approach the section this way. Before having students study the charts that present the sentence patterns, illustrate on the board what the abbreviations signify. Begin by presenting a sentence containing at least three different structural parts, and ask students first for the subject. When they tell you, write an S over it. Then ask for the verb and write an AV or LV above it, and so forth. Shortly, you will have in front of students one of the sentence patterns, as in this example:

S   AV   DO
Our bank issued new credit cards.

As these students work on the exercises, encourage them to use the charts in the section. You may want to remind them of the differences between action and linking verbs and of the different subject complements each verb takes.

Advanced students might enjoy oral drill; as they develop proficiency with the patterns, you can dictate sentences aloud. At their seats, students can write the patterns that they hear, using the abbreviations.

Suggestions for Additional Activities. To encourage students to experiment with different patterns, you might conduct a "pattern bee." List on the board all the patterns from the charts in the section and number them. Then in spelling-bee fashion, have students in turn improvise sentences to match a pattern that you assign at random. Grant a suitable award to the winner.

■ 5.6 Diagraming the Basic Parts of Sentences (pp. 94–103)

Objectives: After completing this section, students should be able to

- Diagram sentences with subjects, verbs, modifiers, and conjunctions.
- Diagram sentences with compound subjects and verbs.
- Diagram orders and sentences beginning with *there* or *here*.
- Diagram sentences with complements.

Adapting for Different Abilities. Students who have difficulty with verbal explanations of grammatical concepts often find diagraming helpful because it provides visual reinforcement. With less advanced students, however, you may want to omit some of the refinements presented in this section, specifically those under the heading "Orders and Sentences Beginning with *There* or *Here*." You may also want to provide these students with diagram skeletons for most or all of the sentences in the exercises.

If you decide not to teach your students to diagram sentences, the exercises in this section are available for additional drill, which can be more or less rigorous depending on student needs. All students should be able to complete the following identification tasks for the sentences in any designated exercise:

1. Underline the subject once.
2. Underline the verb twice and label it AV or LV.
3. Place a box around any complement, labeling it DO, IO, OC, PN, or PA.
4. Circle any modifiers.
5. Draw wavy lines under conjunctions.

Suggestions for Additional Activities. If you have opted to work with diagraming, students can use sentences from the exercises in preceding sections. Working individually or in pairs, they can diagram these sentences on the board or at their seats.

CHAPTER 6 Phrases (pp. 104–135)

In its first five sections, this chapter presents the definitions and principles needed to understand different kinds of phrases in sentences: prepositional, appositive, participial, gerundive, and infinitive. Section 6.6, at the end of the chapter, shows students how to diagram these phrases.

You will probably need at least one class session for each one of the sections. In order to gain a full understanding of the three kinds of verbal phrases that involve complements, your students may also need additional time with Sections 6.3, 6.4, and 6.5.

■ 6.1 Prepositional Phrases (pp. 104–109)

Objectives: After completing this section, students should be able to

- Identify prepositional phrases used as adjectives.
- Identify prepositional phrases used as adverbs.

Adapting for Different Abilities. If your students studied Section 3.1, they should already be familiar with prepositional phrases. For some students, a review of this earlier section might be beneficial. Once students can recognize prepositional phrases in sentences, they can more easily learn how these phrases act as adjectives and adverbs.

For less advanced students, you may also want to use the following activity. To illustrate how a prepositional phrase acts in the same way as a single-word modifier does, you might write the following sentence on the board and ask a volunteer to identify the underlined word:

Janice ran <u>away</u>.

Students should recognize that *away* is an adverb that modifies the verb *ran* by telling where.

Now erase the word *away* and write in its place *out of the house*. Ask students to explain how these words are related to *ran*. Lead the students to discover that *out of the house* also tells where Janice ran and that although the phrase contains several words it performs the same function in the sentence that *away* did only in a more detailed way. You might repeat this process to illustrate the adjectival function of prepositional phrases. Begin with a sentence such as "The *gray-haired* man was the last to speak" and show students that *with gray hair* would have the same function.

Suggestions for Additional Activities. Ask students to make up prepositional phrases for you to write on the board, leaving enough room at the right or left for sentences. When you have five phrases, discuss each one with the students, asking them to decide whether the phrase could be used as an adjective, as an adverb, or as both in a sentence.

When you are satisfied with the discussion, ask students to write a sentence for each phrase on paper. Have them underline the phrase, draw an arrow to the word the phrase modifies, and label the phrase adjective or adverb. Then you can ask volunteers to place their answers on the board next to each of the phrases you have written.

■ 6.2 Appositives and Appositive Phrases

(pp. 109–113)

Objectives: After completing this section, students should be able to

- Identify appositives in sentences.
- Identify appositive phrases in sentences.

Adapting for Different Abilities. If less advanced students have difficulty with the Application, you might help them complete the first one or two combinations by showing them how to rearrange and eliminate words.

With a group of advanced students, you might place on the board a pair of sentences such as the following:

> Czeslaw Milosz won the Nobel Prize for Literature in 1980. He is a <u>professor of Slavic languages at the University of California at Berkeley</u>.

Ask students to explain how the underlined words in the second sentence can be made part of the first. Guide the class in rearranging the words:

> Czeslaw Milosz, <u>a professor of Slavic languages at the University of California at Berkeley</u>, won the Nobel Prize for Literature in 1980.

You might take the discussion a step further by asking students to compare the two examples and explain the change in emphasis. Students should realize that the combined sentence stresses what Milosz did rather than what he is. The two separate sentences do not exhibit this stress.

Suggestions for Additional Activities. To give students practice in creating appositives of their own, have them turn to Section 3.1, Exercises A and B, and rewrite at least five of the sentences in each exercise, adding an appositive somewhere in each sentence.

For another activity, you might direct students to redo items 1, 4, and 5 in the Application by recombining the pairs of sentences in a manner different from the way they first combined them. Have them discuss the differences in stress or meaning that result.

■ 6.3 Participles and Participial Phrases

(pp. 113–119)

Objectives: After completing this section, students should be able to

- Identify present and past participles.
- Distinguish between verbs and participles.
- Recognize participial phrases.
- Recognize nominative absolutes.

Adapting for Different Abilities. You will probably want all students to recognize that participles and participial phrases act as adjectives. With less advanced students, however, you might focus on the first three subsections and skip the work under the heading "Nominative Absolutes." In addition, you might give these students more practice combining sentences such as the following, which could include participial phrases when combined.

Jack was watching the game on television. He saw his sister in the stands.

We could not take another step. We were exhausted by the hike.

That joke has been told too many times. It no longer elicits laughs.

Suggestions for Additional Activities. To give students practice in writing original participial phrases, you can start them with the following lists of simple sentences and single-word participles. Tell them to write five sentences by creating phrases out of the participles and then adding these to any of the short sentences in the first column.

Sentences	Participles
Bill worked in a restaurant.	squawking
A spacecraft hovered overhead.	spinning
Cracks appeared in the foot of the dam.	owned
Birds rested on the telephone wires.	tired
We were asleep within minutes.	frightening

■ 6.4 Gerunds and Gerund Phrases (pp. 119–123)

Objectives: After completing this section, students should be able to

- Identify gerunds used in sentences.
- Distinguish gerunds from verbs and participles.
- Identify gerund phrases.

Adapting for Different Abilities. Students who have mastered the study of participles and participial phrases should have no trouble with this section on gerunds. With less advanced students, however, you may want to reinforce learning of this and the previous section by having students do extra work with -*ing* words. You might, for example, put a list of words such as the following on the board: *unpacking, digging, splashing, floating, struggling.* Then assign a word to a student and have him or her use it in a sentence first as a verb, then as a participle, and finally as a gerund. As the students become proficient with this mental exercise, require them to create participial and gerund phrases from the words and to use the gerunds in different parts of sentences.

Suggestions for Additional Activities. To give students practice in writing original gerund phrases, you can start them with the following lists of sentence fragments and gerunds. Tell students to write five sentences by creating phrases out of the gerunds and then adding these to any of the short fragments in the first column.

Fragments	Gerunds
Sandra denied.	watching
Was how he forgot his troubles.	telling
All of his effort was given to.	taking
We learned to sky-dive by.	practicing
Is not fair to others.	playing

■ 6.5 Infinitives and Infinitive Phrases
(pp. 123–127)

Objectives: After completing this section, students should be able to

- Identify infinitives used in sentences.
- Distinguish between prepositional phrases and infinitives.
- Identify infinitive phrases.

Adapting for Different Abilities. Some students may need extra practice distinguishing between infinitives and prepositional phrases. Since infinitive phrases can serve different functions within sentences and occupy various positions, students must draw upon their knowledge of parts of speech (Chapters 1 through 4) and their understanding of syntactical relationships (Chapter 5). You might want to direct students to the specific areas where they seem to need review.

To focus students' attention on the difference between an infinitive phrase and a prepositional phrase that begins with the word *to*, place a sentence such as this on the board:

To learn singing, Lloyd went to a voice teacher.

You can ask students which of the underlined word groups is a prepositional phrase. With further questioning, you can help them realize that the first phrase begins with *to* and a verb.

Once you have established the basic distinction between an infinitive and a prepositional phrase, discuss differences in uses between the two phrases. In this case, both are adverb phrases modifying the verb *went,* but they tell different things about the verb. The first phrase tells why while the other tells where.

Suggestions for Additional Activities. To give students practice in writing original infinitive phrases, you can start them with the following two lists—one of sentences and fragments and one of infinitives. Tell them to write five sentences by creating phrases out of the infinitives and then adding these to any of the items in the first column.

Sentences and Fragments	Infinitives
Mr. Williamson decided.	to hear
She turned up the volume.	to become
Our dog was determined.	to lead
Was her goal in life.	to bring
Everyone in class was told.	to find

■ 6.6 Diagraming Phrases (pp. 127–135)

Objectives: After completing this section, students should be able to

- Diagram sentences with prepositional phrases.
- Diagram sentences with appositives and appositive phrases.
- Diagram sentences with participles and participial phrases.
- Diagram sentences with gerunds and gerund phrases.
- Diagram sentences with infinitives and infinitive phrases.

Adapting for Different Abilities. With less advanced students, you may again want to provide diagram skeletons for most or all of the sentences in the exercises.

If you decide not to teach your students to diagram sentences, the exercises in this section can be used for additional drill. You might ask all students to copy sentences from any of the exercises and do the following with each one:

1. Underline the subject once.
2. Underline the verb twice and label it AV or LV.
3. Place a box around any complement, labeling it DO, IO, OC, PN, or PA.
4. Place parentheses around every phrase and write the type of phrase above it.

With average and advanced students, you might also ask for an identification of the function of the phrases. If the phrase is prepositional, participial, or, in some cases, infinitive, have them draw an arrow to the word modified by the phrase. If the phrase is a gerund or infinitive used as a noun, have them tell how the phrase is used in the sentence.

Suggestions for Additional Activities. To give students more practice in diagraming phrases, select sentences from the exercises in Sections 6.1 through 6.5 and have students (individually or in pairs) diagram these sentences on the board, so that they can bc discussed later by the entire class.

With this chapter, students complete their study of the parts of sentences. The last three structural parts—adjective, adverb, and noun clauses—are each presented in a separate section, 7.1, 7.2, and 7.3. Then, in Section 7.4, students learn to classify sentences by the number and types of clauses they contain (simple, compound, complex, and compound-complex) as well as by their function (declarative, interrogative, imperative, or exclamatory). The chapter ends with a final section on diagraming.

The first three sections on clauses will probably need the most time since they require students to learn new terms and analyze complicated sentences. You might need at least two class sessions for each of Sections 7.1, 7.2, and 7.3, whereas the study of sentence classifications in Section 7.4 might require only one. Allow two more class sessions if you assign Section 7.5 on diagraming.

■ 7.1 Adjective Clauses (pp. 137– 143)

Objectives: After completing this section, students should be able to

- Identify adjective clauses in sentences.
- Recognize the functions of relative pronouns and relative adverbs within adjective clauses.

Adapting for Different Abilities. You may want to make sure that less advanced students understand the difference between independent and subordinate clauses before they concentrate on three types of subordinate clauses. To do this, try placing on the board a sentence like the one that follows and then asking students to find the part that can stand by itself as a complete sentence:

I need time when I can be alone.

Students should quickly see that *I need time* can be a complete sentence but that *When I can be alone* cannot. At this point explain that both sets of words are clauses because each has a subject and verb, and that the first is independent, whereas the second is subordinate because it depends upon the other part for completeness. You may want to test your students' understanding of these basic concepts by having them analyze additional sentences on the board.

For another approach with less advanced students, consider skipping the subsection headed "Different Kinds of Introductory Words." You can then use Exercise B to drill students on their ability to find adjective clauses and identify the modified words.

Suggestions for Additional Activities. One of the best methods of teaching the skills needed to write adjective clauses is sentence combining. You might do the Application as an oral activity in class and also prepare dittoed handouts containing sentence pairs for combining. Here are five possibilities to include:

1. We found an old wooden chest. It had been stored behind boxes in the attic.
2. Nobody knew the answer to the question. Mrs. Harris asked the question.
3. Quito rests on the equator. It is the capital city of Ecuador.
4. Our old house remained vacant. It needed a painting.
5. I bought a new pen. It leaked almost immediately.

As students work on combining sentences, you might instruct them to underline each adjective clause and to circle the word that it modifies.

■ 7.2 Adverb Clauses (pp. 143–147)

Objectives: After completing this section, students should be able to

- Identify adverb clauses in sentences.
- Recognize elliptical adverb clauses and supply the missing words.

Adapting for Different Abilities. To help less advanced students recognize clauses that can be used as adverbs, you might place a simple sentence on the board and ask students to make up a word group that answers such adverbial questions as *Why?* or *When?*

If you place a sentence like this on the board,

Our game was canceled.

ask students to think of a group of words that will tell *Why?* when added to the sentence. Students might offer a phrase like this:

Our game was canceled because it began to rain.

Then ask for a group of words that will tell *When?* Students might offer a phrase like this:

Our game was canceled after it began to rain.

Once you have a few examples on the board, circle the subordinating conjunctions and explain how such words connect an adverb clause to an independent clause.

An advanced group might move directly to Section 10.2 and complete the work under the subsection "Using Pronouns Correctly in Elliptical Clauses."

Suggestions for Additional Activities. To give students practice in writing adverb clauses, you can place on the board two

T–48

columns of information—the first column containing independent clauses and the second containing subordinating conjunctions. Instruct students to use each of the subordinating conjunctions in an adverb clause that can be integrated with one of the independent clauses. Following are two sample columns:

Independent Clauses	Subordinating Conjunctions
No one was allowed to water a lawn	as long as
Nelson swam for shore	as if
My group hung decorations	while
Our crops were ruined	before
She stood nervously before the camera	although

When students complete this activity, you might notice that most of their sentences begin with the independent clause and end with the adverb clause. Ask them to rewrite some of the sentences, reversing the order. At this point, you might want to remind students to use a comma after an introductory adverb clause.

■ 7.3 Noun Clauses (pp. 147–150)

Objectives: After completing this section, students should be able to

- Identify noun clauses in sentences.
- Recognize the different uses of introductory words in noun clauses.

Adapting for Different Abilities. To explain the concept of a noun clause to less advanced students, you might place on the board a simple sentence containing a single-word noun or pronoun that can be replaced by a noun clause. Using the following sentence, you can tell students that *someone* can be replaced by an entire clause:

Someone will win ten dollars.

Now, by erasing *someone* and replacing it with *Whoever writes the best composition*, you can show that the clause acts in exactly the same way as the single word did except that it provides more information:

Whoever writes the best composition will win ten dollars.

When students recognize this concept, the material in this section will become more accessible to them.

Another approach in working with less advanced students is to omit the second objective, recognizing the different uses of introductory words in noun clauses, and its related exercise.

Many students may be puzzled by the fact that when a noun clause is subtracted from a complex sentence, the remainder is not a full independent clause. They can find this hard to reconcile with what they learned in the last two sections about the independent/subordinate clause combinations. It may help to explain that the independent clause in such a sentence needs the noun clause to be grammatically complete and that a noun clause functions as does a single word.

Suggestions for Additional Activities. If your students have difficulty determining the function of the noun clauses in the sentences in Exercise A, you can suggest this activity. Have them rewrite each sentence to eliminate the noun clause. For example, the first sentence can be rewritten: *Everyone will like the book Foxfire.* It now becomes much easier to see that the noun clause in the original sentence was the subject.

■ 7.4 Sentences Classified by Structure and Function (pp. 150–155)

Objectives: After completing this section, students should be able to

- Identify the structure of sentences as simple, compound, complex, or compound-complex.
- Identify the function of sentences as declarative, interrogative, imperative, or exclamatory.

Adapting for Different Abilities. Some students may find study of the four sentence structures challenging. For this reason, you may need to supply additional explanation and activities. You might, therefore, refer students to the material on relative pronouns (Section 1.2, pp. 27–28) and on coordinating, correlative, and subordinating conjunctions (Section 3.2, pp. 57–58). You might also use Exercise A in Section 3.2 to demonstrate that the clauses in a compound sentence are joined by coordinating or correlative conjunctions, while those in a complex sentence are joined by subordinating conjunctions. After such a review, students might find Exercise A in this section easier if they look for conjunctions before determining the structure of a whole sentence.

Suggestions for Additional Activities. To reinforce the idea of classifying sentences by structure, you can try the following activity. Place on the board these patterns:

$$\underline{S}\ \underline{\underline{V}}$$

$$\underline{S}\ \underline{\underline{V}}\ \text{but}\ \underline{S}\ \underline{\underline{V}}$$

$$\underline{S}\ \underline{\underline{V}}\ \text{because}\ \underline{S}\ \underline{\underline{V}}$$

$$\underline{S}\ \underline{\underline{V}}\ \text{because}\ \underline{S}\ \underline{\underline{V}}\ \text{but}\ \underline{S}\ \underline{\underline{V}}$$

Ask students to suggest subjects and verbs and any other words needed to complete the patterns. One solution, which builds on preceding patterns, may be:

The ship sank.

The ship sank, but everyone was rescued.

The ship sank because it had hit a reef.

The ship sank because it had hit a reef, but everyone was rescued.

Next, review the four terms and definitions on pages 150–152 and ask students to label the patterns and examples accordingly. Point out in particular the differences between compound and complex sentences.

■ 7.5 Diagraming Different Sentence Structures (pp. 155–162)

Objectives: After completing this section, students should be able to

- Diagram compound sentences.
- Diagram complex sentences with adjective, adverb, and noun clauses.
- Diagram compound-complex sentences.

Adapting for Different Abilities. For many students, especially those who are less advanced, you may want to provide diagram skeletons for some or all of the sentences in the exercises.

If you decide not to teach your students to diagram sentences, the exercises in this section can be used for additional drill. Although less advanced students may need more guidance, most students should be able to complete the following instructions using the sentences in any designated exercise:

1. Underline all subjects once.
2. Underline all verbs twice and label them AV or LV.
3. Place a box around any complement, labeling it DO, IO, OC, PN, or PA.
4. Place parentheses around every phrase and write the type of phrase above it.
5. Place brackets around every clause and identify its type.
6. Next to the sentence, write S, CD, CX, or CD–CX to identify the structure of the whole sentence.

Suggestions for Additional Activities. To provide more practice in diagraming the four kinds of sentence structures, you can assign the sentences from Exercise A in Section 7.4.

CHAPTER 8 Sentence Faults (pp. 163–181)

This chapter presents the most common syntactical errors that novice writers commit—fragments, run-ons, misplaced and dangling modifiers, and faulty parallelism—and indicates how they can be corrected. You may assign this chapter now while your students' knowledge of sentence parts and the principles of modification is still fresh in their minds, or you may assign it just before Chapter 21 at the start of the composition unit.

You might plan to spend two or three class sessions each on Sections 8.1 and 8.3, and one or two sessions on Section 8.2 depending, of course, on the abilities of your students.

■ 8.1 Fragments and Run-ons (pp. 163–170)

Objectives: After completing this section, students should be able to

- Recognize and correct different kinds of fragments in writing.
- Recognize and correct run-on sentences in writing.

Adapting for Different Abilities. Many of the students will probably have only an occasional problem with fragments and run-ons in their writing. Those who have persistent problems, however, usually recognize the faults quickly if they read their work aloud. You might, therefore, want to work with such students individually when you find such problems in their compositions, having them first locate problems and then offer solutions orally. The corrected sentences can then be incorporated into their work during revision.

For students who need more help in understanding the basic concepts, you might begin by placing on the board groups of words such as the following and asking students to provide additional words to make each fragment a complete sentence:

Behind the door.

Making rattling noises.

Students should easily be able to complete each fragment:

Behind the door <u>was a skeleton</u>.

<u>It was</u> making rattling noises.

Next, you might write the two sentences as one run-on:

Behind the door was a skeleton it was making rattling noises.

Students should quickly recognize that two separate sentences have been fused, and you can explain that this fusion is wrong. At this point you can illustrate some of the methods used for correcting run-ons:

Behind the door was a skeleton; it was making rattling noises.

Behind the door was a skeleton making rattling
noises.

Suggestions for Additional Activities. After students complete
Exercise B, you might ask them to explain the fault they found
and the method of correction they used for each of the sentences.
Then, you can reassign the exercise, instructing students to recor-
rect each of the sentences using a different method from the first
one chosen.

To reinforce the concept that fragments and run-ons are sentence faults, you may have students attempt diagrams of some of
the examples from the charts in the text. The very fact that
fragments and run-ons defy diagraming should make the point
clear. You can then show how the corrected faults are easily
diagramed.

■ 8.2 Misplaced and Dangling Modifiers
(pp. 170–175)

Objectives: After completing this section, students should be
able to

- Recognize misplaced and dangling modifiers in sentences.
- Correct misplaced modifiers by moving them closer to the
  words they modify.
- Correct dangling modifiers by rewriting sentences to include
  the modified words.

Adapting for Different Abilities. Most students should complete the work in this section with little difficulty. With less
advanced students, however, you might omit the classification of
misplaced or dangling modifiers. Students can usually make the
corrections based on logic and their own sense of language.

Suggestions for Additional Activities. You might want to emphasize the fun that students seem to have discovering misplaced
and dangling modifiers. Think of some errors that sound out-
rageous, and place one or two of these on the board. Students
should readily grasp how logic can be abused through examples of
this kind of error. Two examples follow:

Speechless and still shaking, the plane landed
and passengers stumbled out.

Grinning from ear to ear, the fish was displayed
by the proud boy.

To provide additional practice in correcting misplaced and
dangling modifiers, you can have the students turn back to Exercise A and rewrite correctly the sentences that contain misplaced
or dangling modifiers.

■ 8.3 Faulty Parallelism (pp. 175–181)

Objectives: After completing this section, students should be able to

- Recognize parallel ideas and structures in sentences.
- Recognize and correct faulty parallelism in sentences.

Adapting for Different Abilities. For students who are experiencing difficulty with this section, you might place on the board an example of faulty parallelism such as the following sentence:

> Swimming, jogging, and to get enough rest are elements of successful relaxation.

Tell students to look for either a compound or a series. They should identify *swimming, jogging,* and *to get enough rest.* If you point out that the third item is not a gerund, as are the other two, they should readily grasp the meaning of parallelism when you suggest the following correction:

> Swimming, jogging, and <u>getting</u> enough rest are elements of successful relaxation.

Suggestions for Additional Activities. If you feel that students need more practice correcting faulty parallelism, ask several to attempt to create some flawed sentences at the board. Then ask the class to offer corrections.

■ Review Exercises (pp. 181–190)

These review exercises can be used to assess your students' grasp of the material covered in Chapters 1 through 8.

The time you allot to this review will depend on your students' abilities and on their needs for review and reinforcement. The review exercises can be assigned as classwork, homework, or as testing material.

UNIT II

Usage

This unit contains five chapters, Verb Usage, Pronoun Usage, Agreement, Adjective and Adverb Usage, and finally Special Problems in Usage. Since many topics of study in this unit depend on the students' understanding of grammar and sentence structure, you may want to include some time for review when you schedule the unit.

The pretest for the unit, available in the *Prentice-Hall Grammar and Composition Test Program*, can be used to help determine your students' need for instruction in the skills presented in the unit. Chapter tests and a unit post-test are also available in the test program.

CHAPTER 9 Verb Usage (pp. 192–223)

The three sections in this chapter describe the formation and use of the various tenses of both regular and irregular verbs in the active and passive voice. Section 9.1, The Tenses of Verbs, is the longest, containing lists of the principal parts of common irregular verbs. Students will need time to study these lists and to commit them to memory. You may want to plan on two or three class sessions to cover this material adequately. Section 9.2 may also require a few days, while Section 9.3 may be covered in a day.

■ 9.1 The Tenses of Verbs (pp. 193–207)

Objectives: After completing this section, students should be able to

- Recognize the six tenses in their basic, progressive, and emphatic forms.
- Form and identify the principal parts of verbs.
- Recognize the difference between regular and irregular verbs.
- Conjugate the basic, progressive, and emphatic forms of verbs.

Adapting for Different Abilities. The lists in the text group the irregular verbs according to shared characteristics of their principal parts. Such groupings should make studying them easier than it would be if they were merely listed in alphabetical order. Oral drill repeated over a period of days should help students learn the principal parts of these verbs.

With less advanced students, you may want to explain that verbs usually have a number of different spellings represented by the four principal parts: the present, the present participle, the past, and the past participle. Draw a chart on one side of the board and ask volunteers to supply the principal parts for sample verbs. In this way you can focus on troublesome verbs such as *lie* and *lay*. Next, discuss tense formations, explaining that simple recipes exist to construct each of the tense forms using the principal parts and some helpers. You can then give students a recipe for each form: "The simple present is the first principal part"; "The present perfect is the past participle plus the helper *has* or *have*"; and so on.

Suggestions for Additional Activities. Drill is the key to learning the principal parts and tenses of verbs. Oral drill can be

T–55

simple. For example, you can dictate a verb at a time, asking a volunteer to supply the principal parts. To involve all students and to reinforce auditory learning, you can ask the class to respond in unison as you supply a verb and ask for its principal parts. Written drill may be a better way for students to practice forming the different tenses. To this end, you can provide lists of sentences calling for the addition of the correct verb forms. Your sentences could look like these:

1. Evelyn (*ride*, past perfect progressive) her bicycle all afternoon.
2. School (*begin*, future) an hour later next Friday.

■ 9.2 Expressing Time Through Tense
(pp. 207–218)

Objectives: After completing this section, students should be able to

- Recognize the various uses of tense in present time.
- Recognize the various uses of tenses in past time.
- Recognize the various uses of tenses in future time.
- Avoid shifting tenses unnecessarily.
- Clarify tenses with modifiers that describe time.

Adapting for Different Abilities. To make the material in this section more accessible to less advanced students, you might begin by putting two similar sentences such as the following on the board and asking students to explain the similarities and differences in meaning:

She <u>jogs</u> in the park.

She <u>is jogging</u> in the park.

Students should be able to identify each verb as being a different form of the present tense. They should also realize that *jogs* expresses an action that happens repeatedly though not necessarily at this very moment and that *is jogging* expresses a continuous action now taking place. With examples such as these, you can make the point that even slight changes in the form of a verb can have profound effects on the meaning of a sentence and that writers are responsible for making sure that they use correct verb forms.

Suggestions for Additional Activities. Once students have read about and discussed the particulars of each tense form, you might have them make a handy reference guide in their notebooks. Next to each form, they can list the specific time relationship involved and add an illustrative sentence or two from literature or newspapers.

To aid in discussions of the uses of different forms, you might place on the board sentences with blanks where verbs would ordinarily specify a particular time relationship. If you present only the present form of the verb, you can instruct students to write the correct form and to explain why that particular form best completes each sentence. Following are three examples:

1. After we _(finish)_ eating, we heard police sirens.
2. Betty Jo _(write)_ her report by next Tuesday.
3. We knew that Bill _(sleep)_ while we worked.

■ 9.3 Active and Passive Voice (pp. 218–223)

Objectives: After completing this section, students should be able to

- Distinguish between verbs in the active and passive voice.
- Form the various tenses of verbs in the passive voice.
- Recognize the different uses of the active and passive voice.

Adapting for Different Activities. For less advanced students, you may want to place on the board the following sentence:

A bouquet was received by my sister.

and then ask students for the subject and verb. Explaining that in this sentence the verb is passive because its subject does not perform the action, you can illustrate how this construction emphasizes the receiver of the action, _bouquet_, by placing it in an unusual place in the sentence. Then you can ask students how the sentence could be rewritten to put _sister_ first:

My sister received a bouquet.

Explaining that the verb is now active because its subject performs the action, you can point out that this construction is more concise and straight-forward than the other.

Suggestions for Additional Activities. Since the most helpful application of this material is to guide students away from overuse of passive verbs in their sentences, you may want to concentrate on training students to seek the active voice wherever possible and appropriate. To this end, you can take a passage from almost anywhere—a short story, a news article—and rewrite as many verbs as you can into passive voice. Then, after duplicating the rewritten passage and distributing it to your students, you can ask them to rewrite the passage themselves—this time looking for all possible changes to active voice.

CHAPTER 10 Pronoun Usage (pp. 224–243)

Containing two sections, this chapter explains the function of the three cases in English and gives guidance for the correct use of personal pronouns as well as of *who/whom* and *whoever/whomever*. The chapter also explains how to use personal pronouns correctly in elliptical clauses.

You will probably want to spend one or two days on Section 10.1, The Case of Pronouns, and two or three class sessions on 10.2, Special Problems with Pronouns.

■ 10.1 The Case of Pronouns (pp. 224–232)

Objectives: After completing this section, students should be able to

- Identify the case of personal pronouns.
- Use pronouns in the nominative case correctly.
- Use pronouns in the objective case correctly.

Adapting for Different Abilities. For some students, a review of all positions that pronouns can occupy in sentences is a helpful prelude to this section. You might place on the board a sentence containing blanks where nouns or pronouns could go and ask students to identify each position, as in the following example:

_____ took _____ to an art exhibition.

Students should easily identify the blanks as "subject" and "direct object" positions. With nouns inserted, the sentence is complete, of course:

$$\underset{\text{S}}{\underline{\text{Anne}}} \text{ took } \underset{\text{DO}}{\underline{\text{Edna}}} \text{ to an art exhibition.}$$

Suggestions for Additional Activities. To reinforce the principle that syntax determines case, you can ask students to identify the sentence parts occupied by the pronouns in Exercises B and C. In Exercise C, for example, you might have students write their answers in this way:

1. them—used as the object of a preposition (objective)
2. her—used as an indirect object (objective)

■ 10.2 Special Problems with Pronouns
(pp. 232–243)

Objectives: After completing this section, students should be able to

- Recognize and use the various forms of *who* and *whoever*.
- Use personal pronouns correctly in elliptical clauses.

Adapting for Different Abilities. An effective device for demonstrating the problem of elliptical clauses is to place on the board an example with a blank where a pronoun can be supplied, as in this example:

Jane can run as fast as _____ (I or me?)

Asking students which pronoun they would choose, you may find wide disagreement among them because they have not completed the clause mentally. Since their attention will be focused on the point of controversy, you have a dramatic moment for introducing the correct answer as well as the meaning of the term *elliptical*.

Advanced students might enjoy creating their own sentences with elliptical clauses, leaving blanks for pronouns. They can then exchange sentences, asking partners to fill in suitable pronouns.

Suggestions for Additional Activities. To help your students increase their awareness of the problems involving *who/whom* and *whoever/whomever*, you might ask students to listen carefully for instances of these pronouns used in conversation or on radio or television. Have them record what they hear and then report their findings to the class, which can then discuss the examples and determine a percentage of correct use.

CHAPTER **11** Agreement (pp. 244–267)

This chapter groups the study of agreement into two sections: Section 11.1 covers subject/verb agreement; Section 11.2 covers pronoun/antecedent agreement.

If you assign some of the exercises for homework, you may need no more than two class sessions for each section.

■ **11.1** Subject and Verb Agreement
(pp. 244–258)

Objectives: After completing this section, students should be able to

- Identify the number of nouns, pronouns, and verbs.
- Make singular and plural subjects agree with their verbs.
- Make various confusing subjects agree with their verbs.

Adapting for Different Abilities. Less advanced students might have more success mastering the basic concepts of this section if you eliminate the material under the heading "Confusing Subjects." In addition, to clarify the concept of agreement, you might place on the board a sentence, such as the following, that sounds odd because of faulty agreement:

Will John goes with us?

Students should swiftly recognize the error of *goes*, and with some prodding they should identify *John* as the key connection in the error. From this discussion, you can identify the two sides of any agreement problem—in this case, the subject and verb—and proceed with an explanation of number, giving additional examples if necessary.

Suggestions for Additional Activities. After a point, all students should recognize simple agreement and make correct choices more or less automatically. However, compound subjects and confusing subjects may still prove difficult for many students. Students who persistently make mistakes might benefit by categorizing their errors. They may find that their problem involves only one or two of the agreement rules. By concentrating only on the problems that affect them personally, they should succeed in learning to avoid the mistakes.

■ 11.2 Pronoun and Antecedent Agreement
(pp. 259–267)

Objectives: After completing this section, students should be able to

- Make personal pronouns agree with their antecedents in number, person, and gender.
- Make personal pronouns agree with antecedents that are indefinite pronouns.
- Make sure reflexive pronouns have clearly stated antecedents.
- Avoid four special problems of pronoun agreement.

Adapting for Different Abilities. If you are working with less advanced students you might want to review Section 1.2 to make sure that your students understand both what antecedents are and what kinds of antecedents the various pronouns should and should not have.

Another device to illustrate the basic relationship between a pronoun and its antecedent is to place on the board a sentence with an error in it that students are likely to commit. A sentence such as this one may seem correct to students:

Every book on that shelf has pages torn from them.

If students are unable to find and correct the error, you may want to point out the connection between *book* and *them*, explaining the disagreement in number and demonstrating the need to examine pronouns and antecedents carefully in order to make accurate choices.

Suggestions for Additional Activities. Students may need extra drill involving agreement with indefinite pronouns. You might, therefore, prepare dittoed activities similar to Exercise B on page 263. As you spot the weaknesses in your classes, you should weight the exercises with the types of agreement problems your students have the most trouble with. You might also ask students to construct exercises for each other. If you choose to do this, you might ask students to hand in their exercises and answers for a quick check before exchanging them.

CHAPTER **12** Adjective and Adverb Usage
(pp. 268–279)

The two sections of this chapter describe the formation of the inflected forms of adjectives and adverbs and instruct students in avoiding common usage problems involving comparisons. One class session for each section should be adequate.

■ **12.1** Degrees of Comparison (pp. 268–275)

Objectives: After completing this section, students should be able to

- Recognize the positive, comparative, and superlative degrees of adjectives and adverbs.
- Form the comparative and superlative degrees of regular adjectives and adverbs.
- Form the comparative and superlative degrees of irregular adjectives and adverbs.

Adapting for Different Abilities. If some of your students need practice in recognizing degrees of comparison, you might have them volunteer some examples of adjectives, such as *simple, good, beautiful,* and *funny,* to be written on the board. To illustrate that modifiers have various forms that indicate degrees of comparison, ask students to make up sentences, leaving blank spaces for each of the listed adjectives. The sentences should involve comparisons, such as those shown in the following examples:

Our team is ⎯⎯⎯⎯⎯⎯ than yours.

Our team is the ⎯⎯⎯⎯⎯⎯ in the league.

As you place the students' sentences on the board, you can either introduce or elicit the terms *positive, comparative,* and *superlative.*

Suggestions for Additional Activities. You may want to drill students orally to help them learn the irregular forms of modifiers listed on page 273. You might begin by allowing students to keep the lists in front of them until they feel sure they can repeat the forms from memory.

■ 12.2 Clear Comparisons (pp. 275-279)

Objectives: After completing this section, students should be able to

- Use the comparative and superlative degrees correctly.
- Make balanced comparisons.
- Use *other* and *else* correctly in comparisons.

Adapting for Different Abilities. If any of your students have difficulty with the material in this section, you can place sentences such as these on the board:

This storm is the worse I've ever experienced.

Tonight's assignment is even worst than last night's.

As you ask students to pinpoint the error in each sentence, ask them to use the words *comparative* and *superlative* in their explanations.

Suggestions for Additional Activities. Working with the class, you might write on the board a list of comparative and superlative adjectives and adverbs. Then, you can ask for volunteers to offer, verbally or in writing at the board, a sentence for one of the modifiers. As the student offers the original sentence, he or she should identify the degree of comparison used.

CHAPTER 13 Special Problems in Usage
(pp. 280–301)

The first section of this chapter teaches the proper use of negative words, including contractions that include *not*. The second section, entitled Sixty Common Usage Problems, is a miscellany of words that are commonly misused. These include words sometimes confused by students—*accept* and *except*, for instance—and substandard usages that students should learn to recognize and avoid.

Section 13.1 can be covered quite easily in one class session. Allow a few more sessions if you decide to use Section 13.2 as a lesson rather than a reference tool.

■ 13.1 Negative Sentences (pp. 280-284)

Objectives: After completing this section, students should be able to

- Avoid double negatives in speech and writing.
- Recognize different ways of making sentences negative.

Adapting for Different Abilities. Once students recognize what is meant by the term *double negative*, many examples should come to their minds. To help establish the concept when working with less advanced students, you might ask students for sentences that they may have heard in conversation and put them on the board. You might explain that double negatives are acceptable in many English dialects but that they are considered unnecessary in standard English.

Suggestions for Additional Activities. To offer students an exercise that they might find fun, you could look through the work of Mark Twain for lines of dialogue in which characters use double negatives. You may find a page or two with plenty of examples. If you reproduce such passages, you can ask students to locate sentences with double negatives and to correct them.

■ 13.2 Sixty Common Usage Problems
(pp. 284–301)

Objective: After completing this section, students should be able to

- Avoid various common usage problems in their speaking and writing.

Adapting for Different Abilities. Instead of using this section as the focus of a class lesson, you might approach the material as remediation for individual students who display some of these problems in their work. Or, if you find that many of your students make the same types of errors, such as misusing *already* and *all ready*, you might make each specific usage problem a "Usage Tip for the Day" and encourage students to avoid it in their speaking and writing.

Individuals who repeatedly display certain usage problems could use the text as a model and keep an alphabetical list of their specific problems. In a looseleaf binder or on 3 × 5 cards, students could enter each problem word, write a brief rule, and then illustrate it with sentences showing the correct usage and the usage to avoid. Another approach is to encourage students to keep a personal "don't" list for use as they draft and revise their compositions. Such a list might include, for example, "Don't use the *reason is because*. See item 18 on page 287." Such study skills as these, when made routine, are effective in making students aware of those problems that directly affect the quality of their work.

Suggestions for Additional Activities. You might have students refer to this section regularly to check their compositions. With the text in front of them, students can first scan their papers looking for any of the words in the text listing, circling their words, and then checking with the text to see if their own usage is accurate.

■ Review Exercises (pp. 301–306)

At the end of this unit, you will find review exercises that offer additional practice in the usage problems presented in the preceding five chapters. You may decide to assign these exercises as students complete each of the chapters, or you might assign them as review tests at the end of the unit.

UNIT III

Mechanics

Unit III, Mechanics, is divided into two chapters: Chapter 14, Capitalization and Abbreviation, and Chapter 15, Punctuation. The first chapter has two sections containing rules and examples governing the use of capitals and abbreviations. Because this chapter is not directly dependent on material covered in other units, you may have your students review or study Chapter 14 at any time during the year. The eight sections of the second chapter, Punctuation, will probably demand more time and attention. This study also requires mastery of numerous rules and examples, but, in addition, a study of punctuation depends on a foundation of grammar and sentence structure. Therefore, you will probably want to assign students the second chapter only after they have completed or reviewed the work of Unit I, Grammar.

As you assign the sections in each chapter, keep in mind the complexity of this unit: Capitalization, abbreviation, and punctuation involve many rules, exceptions, and patterns. To prevent this study from becoming tedious for students, you may wish to interrupt it with other assignments involving literature, composition, or vocabulary. You might also vary your approach by employing devices such as the overhead projector to encourage students' interest.

The amount of time you spend on this unit depends primarily on your students' prior knowledge of the mechanics of written English. For advanced students, a review of the points covered may be all that is necessary. Less advanced students may require up to a month of intensive study to master the material. All students will benefit from using this unit as a reference tool when specific problems in mechanics confront them.

The pretest for the unit available in the *Prentice-Hall Grammar and Composition Test Program* can be used to help determine your students' need for instruction in the skills presented in the unit. Chapter tests and a unit post-test are also available in the test program.

CHAPTER **14** Capitalization and Abbreviation (pp. 307–344)

This chapter can be assigned at any time during the school year because it does not require prior knowledge of other material. You may choose to assign study of the chapter early in the year before students begin working on composition, or you may wish to teach skills presented in the chapter as the need for them becomes apparent.

Depending on the ability levels of your students, you may need to spend two to three days on the numerous rules and examples in Section 14.1, Rules for Capitalization. Because the use of abbreviations is restricted in formal writing, you may wish to spend only one or two class sessions studying or reviewing the material in Section 14.2, Rules for Abbreviation.

■ 14.1 Rules for Capitalization (pp. 307–328)

Objectives: After completing this section, students should be able to

- Place capitals correctly at the start of sentences and certain phrases.
- Recognize and capitalize all proper nouns.
- Recognize and capitalize all proper adjectives.
- Place capitals correctly in all types of titles.
- Use capitals correctly in the salutations and closings of letters.

Adapting for Different Abilities. You may want to vary your approach for less advanced students by providing additional explanation and drill. For such groups, you might use the overhead projector to present sentences from the exercises that the students must capitalize correctly. You might use odd-numbered exercise items for this purpose and assign even-numbered exercise items to be done individually. Average and advanced students might write original sentences using examples other than those in the text to illustrate each of the various rules.

Suggestions for Additional Activities. Drill work can be the key to mastering capitalization. Following study of the rules and examples and work with the exercises, you might take a page from a social studies or science textbook and reproduce it without capital letters except for those in the title and at sentence beginnings. The following excerpt from *United States: A History of the Republic* offers a sample of this kind of exercise. Students should insert capitals where needed and supply the reason each was required.

Mary McLeod Bethune

Soon after his inauguration, president franklin roosevelt called together a group of black americans to advise him on programs and policies. Among the members of this so-called black cabinet were robert c. weaver, who later served in the department of federal housing; robert l. vann, a special assistant to the attorney general; william hastie, assistant solicitor in the department of the interior; and ralph bunch, who later won a nobel peace prize. Mary mcleod bethune, a well-known educator, also served in the black cabinet.

Bethune had been an adviser to president coolidge. Impressed with her abilities, roosevelt asked bethune to serve on the committee that helped establish the national youth administration (nya) in 1934. The nya made it possible for thousands of hard-pressed high school and college students to continue their educations. In 1936, when the division of negro affairs of the nya was established, bethune was appointed to direct it. She was the first black american to head a government agency.

Bethune served as director of the nya from 1936 to 1944. In 1945 she served as a consultant on interracial understanding at the san francisco conference of the united nations. Mary mcleod bethune worked tirelessly in government service and education. She received many honors including in 1935 the spingarn medal for outstanding achievement, awarded annually by the naacp. She is pictured below in the 1950's.—Adapted from Mark Lytle and Jim Davidson

■ 14.2 Rules for Abbreviation (pp. 328–344)

Objectives: After completing this section, students should be able to

- Abbreviate titles of people correctly.
- Abbreviate time references and geographical locations appropriately.
- Recognize when to abbreviate Latin phrases, measurements, and numbers.
- Know when to abbreviate names of businesses, organizations, and government agencies.

Adapting for Different Abilities. Although no subsection of this material is more challenging than any other, you still may want to adjust the amount of material you cover or the number of exercises you assign to accord with the ability level of your students. For less advanced students, you may decide to eliminate one or more of the subsections and exercises. With average or advanced students, you may decide to use the section mainly for reference.

Suggestions for Additional Activities. An important goal of this section is for students to know not only correct forms of abbreviations but also when and where their uses are appropriate. To begin a lesson that introduces this expanded theme, you might first place on the board a number of classified ads such as the two that follow:

MECHANIC—TRUCK

Trucking co needs qual person w knowl of gas & diesel. We offer steady job w good pay & benefits to person w min of 5 yrs exp.

Office Mgr

Org & responsible indiv needed to asst sr partner of int'l corp; deal w hi level execs; mgmt exp req; flex hrs & gd benfts.

Then you might ask students to identify the meaning of each abbreviation and discuss the reasons why such abbreviations are often used in classified ads (to save space, minimize cost of ad, and so on), pointing out that most of the abbreviations would not be acceptable in formal writing.

CHAPTER 15 Punctuation (pp. 345–420)

This chapter contains eight sections and presents rules, charts, and examples to instruct students in the proper uses of punctuation marks. Because the chapter is lengthy, you may want to spend a considerable amount of time on it. As you present the rules governing punctuation, you will probably need to reinforce students' previous learning of syntax and sentence structure.

Fifteen or more class sessions may be required to cover the material in the chapter adequately. Section 15.1, End Marks, may require only one day, but Section 15.2, Commas, may require a week or more. One or two days' study may be needed for each of the other sections in the chapter: Semicolons and Colons (Section 15.3), Quotation Marks with Direct Quotations (Section 15.4), Underlining and Other Uses of Quotation Marks (Section 15.5), Dashes and Parentheses (Section 15.6), Hyphens (Section 15.7), and Apostrophes (Section 15.8).

■ 15.1 End Marks (pp. 346–353)

Objectives: After completing this section, students should be able to

- Place the appropriate end mark at the conclusion of sentences and phrases.
- Recognize the other uses of the period and the question mark.

Adapting for Different Abilities. No one subsection presents material more difficult than any other; therefore, you will probably just want to tailor the material to suit your particular students' needs. You might just review this section briefly with advanced students but have less advanced students do all the exercises to become more proficient in using the various end marks correctly.

Suggestions for Additional Activities. Perhaps one of the most useful by-products of a study of end marks is "sentence sense," which such a study reinforces. You could begin the section by placing on the board a series of two or three run-on sentences, asking students first to identify groups of words that form complete sentences and then to provide appropriate end marks. The following passage might be suitable:

> Why didn't the phone ring I just couldn't figure it out
> Angela had promised to call, but had she forgotten

To give students additional practice identifying complete sentences and appropriate end marks, you can then ask each student in turn to read a sentence he or she has prepared. The appropriate end mark might be supplied by another student.

■ 15.2 Commas (pp. 353–368)

Objectives: After completing this section, students should be able to

- Employ commas to separate the parts of compound sentences.
- Use commas appropriately to separate items in a series and, when necessary, to separate certain kinds of adjectives.
- Use commas correctly after introductory material.
- Use commas appropriately to set off parenthetical expressions and nonessential material.
- Use commas correctly in other special situations.

Adapting for Different Abilities. Less advanced students may have difficulty learning some of the rules governing commas. You might allow them more study time and give additional drill in class. Odd-numbered items in Exercises A through G may be worked on and discussed in class, while even-numbered items may be done individually outside of class. Additional review of grammar and sentence structure may also be necessary for such students.

Average and advanced students may find it challenging to choose passages from written works and determine why commas were used in each case. The following excerpt written about Frank Lloyd Wright can be used to introduce this type of activity.

> Great ideas in architecture are rare. Throughout history,
> beginning with the Greeks or even with earlier civilizations,
> there have been scarcely half a dozen structural innovations.
> The Greeks perfected the use of the lintel. The Romans

added the arch, the vault, and the dome, and Byzantine culture added the square surmounted by the dome. The great Gothic contribution was the flying buttress, designed to counter the thrust of huge vaults. From the Gothic period until Mr. Wright's time no new principle was added to our architectual vocabulary.—Edward Durrell Stone

Suggestions for Additional Activities. Students may enjoy writing sentences in which commas are necessary for clarity or to avoid unfortunate misunderstandings as in this example:

> After Alex ate the dog wanted a walk.

At first glance, a reader might think that Alex ate the dog. A comma after the introductory adverb clause would avoid any such misunderstanding:

> After Alex ate, the dog wanted a walk.

A study of commas is useful far beyond the simple knowledge of where to place these marks. If students learn the principles governing comma placement, then they will also understand how the parts of sentences function structurally. Because of the importance of this type of study, it may be wise to provide as much drill as possible. Students can be asked to make up their own sentences illustrating various situations requiring commas and present them in class for their classmates to punctuate and explain.

■ 15.3 Semicolons and Colons (pp. 368–379)

Objectives: After completing this section, students should be able to

- Use the semicolon correctly to join certain independent clauses and to avoid confusion in sentences already containing internal punctuation.
- Use the colon correctly as an introductory device and in certain conventional situations.

Adapting for Different Abilities. Depending on your time limitations, you might spend more time on some topics within the section than on others. For instance, less advanced students may need more in-class practice with semicolons (the more challenging and perhaps more vital of the two areas). Average and advanced students may find it challenging to do the Application, Using Conjunctions and Conjunctive Adverbs in Sentences, on page 62, following these instructions for the five pairs of sentences:

1. Combine the two sentences using a conjunctive adverb.
2. Combine the two sentences using a transitional expression.
3. Combine the two sentences without using a conjunction.

4. Rewrite the sentences as one, making *Goldilocks* a formal appositive.
5. Change the first sentence to a subordinate clause and combine it with the second sentence, creating one independent clause. Add another independent clause that summarizes or explains the first one and punctuate the combined independent clauses appropriately.

Suggestions for Additional Activities. To review this section, you might have students write an original example sentence of their own to illustrate each of the rules presented in the section. Students might also write sets of sentences illustrating that two methods of punctuation are possible in some situations. You can illustrate these situations by using the following pairs of sentences to introduce the activity:

Ann enjoys playing tennis. Sheila prefers playing badminton.

Ann enjoys playing tennis; Sheila prefers playing badminton.

The lecture covered two vital areas, conservation and recycling.

The lecture covered two vital areas: conservation and recycling.

■ 15.4 Quotation Marks with Direct Quotations (pp. 379–388)

Objectives: After completing this section, students should be able to

- Use quotation marks to indicate all types of direct quotations.
- Use quotation marks correctly with other punctuation marks.
- Use quotation marks in special situations involving direct quotations.

Adapting for Different Abilities. You might eliminate study or note-taking of minor points within the text for less advanced students and spend more class time with them on drill and explanation. Average and advanced students can be asked to write original dialogues of their own.

Suggestions for Additional Activities. You can use oral drill work to give students extra practice with quotation marks. Read a passage that includes dialogue and have them write down what they hear, paragraphing as best they can. Then, allow them a few minutes to rewrite the passage, checking their paragraphing and adding quotation marks and other types of punctuation. You can use an overhead projector or the board to go over the students' work in class or papers may be checked individually. The following passage from Arthur Conan Doyle's *The Red-Headed League* may be suitable for such an activity:

> . . . . With an apology for my intrusion, I was about to withdraw, when Holmes pulled me abruptly into the room and closed the door behind me.
>
> "You could not possibly have come at a better time, my dear Watson," he said, cordially.
>
> "I was afraid that you were engaged."
>
> "So I am. Very much so."
>
> "Then I can wait in the next room."
>
> "Not at all. This gentleman, Mr. Wilson, has been my partner and helper in many of my most successful cases, and I have no doubt that he will be of the utmost use to me in yours also."—Sir Arthur Conan Doyle

■ 15.5 Underlining and Other Uses of Quotation Marks (pp. 388–395)

Objectives: After completing this section, students should be able to

- Recognize titles, names, and words that require underlining.
- Determine which titles need quotation marks.
- Recognize those titles and names that require neither underlining nor quotation marks.

Adapting for Different Abilities. Less advanced students may benefit by giving more attention to those types of titles and to those situations they are likely to use in their own writing. Odd-numbered items in Exercises A and B could be done as a group in class and even-numbered items could be done individually. All students could compile additional lists of examples illustrating each rule. Advanced students may compile in their notebooks a list of foreign words and phrases and their definitions.

Suggestions for Additional Activities. You could conduct a "spelling-bee" type of contest by giving each student in turn a title to write on the board. Titles should be familiar to the students and may be those of books, films, magazines, newspapers, TV shows, record albums, poems, plays, short stories, paintings, and so forth. This activity can serve as a review of capitalization rules as well as practice in underlining and use of quotation marks. Students who have made errors and are no longer competing may suggest titles for others to write on the board, write all subsequent titles on their own paper, or be called on to find errors in titles written on the board by students who are still competing.

■ 15.6 Dashes and Parentheses (pp. 395–403)

Objectives: After completing this section, students should be able to

- Determine when to use the dash to set off parts of a sentence.
- Insert parentheses appropriately and correctly around supplementary material in a sentence.

Adapting for Different Abilities. Average and advanced students may enjoy doing the Application on page 403 in which they create sentences of their own as examples of each rule governing the use of dashes and parentheses. You might even ask them to make such an activity part of their notes. At the same time, you might work separately with any students who need extra time for explanations, practice, and exercise work in class.

Suggestions for Additional Activities. You may ask students to bring to class dashes and parentheses they find in their outside reading. Sentences can be displayed on an overhead projector or written on the board. The class can then determine the rule that governs each use of dashes or parentheses.

■ 15.7 Hyphens (pp. 403–411)

Objectives: After completing this section, students should be able to

- Use hyphens correctly in numbers, word parts, and other words that require them.
- Divide words correctly at the ends of lines using hyphens.

Adapting for Different Abilities. You may wish to concentrate on the first objective in this section with your less advanced students. These students can avoid dividing words at the ends of lines, thus eliminating the possibility of one type of error in their written work. Average and advanced students, in particular, might enjoy participating in a "spelling-bee" type of contest in which they divide words correctly. You can supply the words using a dictionary, or students can take turns supplying each other with words to be divided.

Suggestions for Additional Activities. Students can be asked to write original sentences in which hyphens are needed between words to prevent readers from falsely combining them. You can introduce the activity with the following sentence:

Six foot soldiers rested by the side of the road.

Does the writer mean "six foot-soldiers" or "six-foot soldiers"? The need to use a hyphen to clarify the meaning should be clear.

Students can then construct sentences of their own using hyphens in this way.

■ 15.8 Apostrophes (pp. 411–420)

Objectives: After completing this section, students should be able to

- Use the apostrophe correctly to form possessive nouns.
- Use the apostrophe correctly with pronouns.
- Determine where to place the apostrophe in contractions.
- Recognize the special uses of the apostrophe.

Adapting for Different Abilities. Less advanced students can work as a group on odd-numbered items in Exercises A through F. Even-numbered items in Exercises A through F can then be done individually. Average and advanced students can be asked to write a paragraph containing three different possessive personal pronouns with appropriate antecedents and two contractions of pronouns and verbs.

Suggestions for Additional Activities. Students may be given or may suggest to each other phrases to be put in the possessive using the names of classmates. They can also be asked to indicate singular or plural or individual or joint ownership. This activity can be either a written or oral one.

■ Review Exercises (pp. 421–426)

At the end of this unit, you will find review exercises that offer additional practice in the capitalization, abbreviation, and punctuation skills presented in the previous two chapters. You may decide to assign these exercises as students complete each of the chapters in the unit, or you might assign them as a review at the end of the unit study.

UNIT IV

Vocabulary and Spelling

This unit, divided into two chapters, concentrates first on vocabulary skills and then on skills necessary for spelling improvement. Since both chapters can be taught without prerequisite, you can elect to study them at any time.

The pretest for the unit, available in the *Prentice-Hall Grammar and Composition Test Program*, can be used to help determine your students' need for instruction in the skills presented in this unit. Chapter tests and a unit post-test are also available in the test program.

CHAPTER 16 Vocabulary Building
(pp. 428–445)

The first section in this chapter presents techniques students can use to enlarge their vocabularies. The second section gives students practice in determining the meaning of words through context clues. The last section provides charts of prefixes, roots, and suffixes—the tools by which students can analyze the structure of words and thereby enrich their vocabularies.

The three sections can be covered in six to seven class sessions. You will probably want to point out to your students that the charts in Section 16.3 are reference tools rather than material to be memorized.

■ 16.1 Building Your Vocabulary (pp. 428–433)

Objectives: After completing this section, students should be able to

- Use a dictionary and a special vocabulary section of a notebook to build vocabulary.
- Use one or more special review techniques to remember the meanings of new words.

Adapting for Different Abilities. Less advanced students may need your help and encouragement in the initial setting up of their vocabulary notebooks. You may wish to clarify the concept of bridge words by going over the text examples with them. To spark their thinking, have one student mention a known word and another student respond with a related word—whatever word immediately comes to mind.

Suggestions for Additional Activities. You might want to organize a competition similar to a spelling bee, using the words from the students' vocabulary lists.

To encourage dictionary use, the following activity can be tried. Place on the board a number of words with interesting origins. For example, you could group them this way:

Food	Clothing	Place Names
chocolate	parka	Philadelphia
coffee	dungarees	Lake Michigan
spaghetti	shawl	Kansas
mayonnaise	Levi's	Cheyenne
tomatoes	denim	Minnesota

You can then group the students according to the category they select, and the group that finds and learns the origins of their five words first is the winner.

■ 16.2 Using Context (pp. 433–439)

Objectives: After completing this section, students should be able to

- Determine from context the meanings of unfamiliar words in daily reading.
- Determine from context the meanings of unfamiliar words in textbooks.
- Determine from context the meanings of unfamiliar words in research work.

Adapting for Different Abilities. With less advanced students, you may want to stress the five steps for using context clues, using a sentence to illustrate the process. One of the sentences in the chart entitled Types of Context Clues on pages 433–434 can be used for this purpose.

Suggestions for Additional Activities. You may want to suggest that students bring to class sentences extracted from their outside reading or from their other textbooks. They can underline any words they consider difficult, and then exchange sentences with a partner. Using the recommended steps, students can try to determine the meanings of the words and then indicate any context clues present in the sentences.

■ 16.3 Using Structure (pp. 439–445)

Objectives: After completing this section, students should be able to

- Use prefixes as aids in determining the meanings of new words.
- Use roots as aids in determining the meanings of new words.
- Use suffixes as aids in determining the meanings of new words.

Adapting for Different Abilities. You may want to make it clear to your students that the charts in this section are to be used as reference tools. Depending on the abilities of your group, you can decide how many of the word parts are to be learned at this time and whether or not to stress origins.

You might, for less advanced students, combine the study of prefixes with some dictionary practice. You can suggest that, for every prefix listed on the chart, they supply one or two words that could replace the examples in the chart. There may be some confusion because of the different meanings for the prefix *in-* but when your students grasp this difference they will also have a clearer understanding of the function of prefixes.

Suggestions for Additional Activities. You might want to point out that knowing the meaning of a number of word parts helps in decoding the meaning of whole families of related words.

To make this point, try this activity: Turn to the chart on page 442 and elicit any words your students can think of that share the root -*ject*-. As they volunteer the words, a student can write them on the board. They may know some of the following: *eject, inject, injection, project, projection, object, objection, objective, subject, subjection, subjective, reject, rejection, interject, interjection, conjecture.*

When all the -*ject*- words they can think of have been listed, students can volunteer to underline the prefixes and circle the suffixes. Then they can define the words by using their knowledge of the component parts. Encourage them to check meanings in a dictionary.

This activity can be continued using any of the roots in the chart in this section.

CHAPTER 17 Spelling Improvement
(pp. 446–460)

This chapter consists of two sections. The first gives students techniques for spelling improvement. The second reviews basic spelling rules. Each section can be covered in two class sessions. Both the list of spelling demons in Section 17.1 and the charts that summarize rules in Section 17.2 can be used as references for the students to consult at any time.

■ 17.1 Improving Spelling Skills (pp. 446–452)

Objectives: After completing this section, students should be able to

- Use a personal spelling list to keep track of problem words.
- Use a step system to study problem words.
- Develop and use memory aids for spelling difficult words.
- Memorize spelling demons.

Adapting for Different Abilities. Less advanced students may benefit by working together as a class on the steps recommended in the chart entitled Learning to Spell Problem Words, on page 448. You can write on the board five or more difficult words, taken, if you wish, from the list of spelling demons. Have your students go through the steps one by one until they become comfortable with the system. It is possible, also, to use these same words to demonstrate the use of memory aids.

Suggestions for Additional Activities. You might want to motivate your students to keep their personal spelling lists up to date in the following way. Encourage students to enter any words they have misspelled in their written work in all subjects. They can date their entries and later note the date they check off a word as mastered. They may be interested in analyzing why some words take longer than others to learn.

For another activity, you can organize a spelling bee based on the words in their personal spelling lists. This gives more immediacy to the contest than if you were to use a textbook listing of words.

■ 17.2 Recognizing Basic Spelling Rules
(pp. 452–460)

Objectives: After completing this section, students should be able to

- Master the spelling of words that are governed by the *ie/ei* rule.
- Spell noun plurals correctly.
- Spell words correctly when adding prefixes.
- Spell words correctly when adding suffixes.
- Distinguish between confusing pairs of suffixes.

Adapting for Different Abilities. For less advanced students, you may want to use a flash card technique. Students can copy their personal spelling lists on index cards—one word to a card. An important part of this activity is to have the students check carefully the spelling of each word copied. You can have them drill in small groups or as a class. Words that are repeatedly missed should be set aside and analyzed as to which of the basic spelling rules apply. The final phase of this activity is to have students review the rules that apply to the kinds of errors made.

Suggestions for Additional Activities. One useful activity makes use of board work. You can have students take turns at the board. Seated students can then take turns calling out a word to be written on the board. If a student writes the work incorrectly, he or she should take a seat and the one who called out the word should write the word correctly on the board and then proceed with the next word called out.

You may also want to have students list on a piece of paper a certain number of words taken from their personal spelling lists. Then they can determine which of the basic spelling rules applies in each case. You might suggest that they analyze each of their problem words in this way so they can pinpoint any areas of difficulty and focus their study on the rules they need to know.

UNIT V
Study Skills

The three chapters in this unit can be most helpful in teaching or reinforcing those basic skills that students need not only in their English courses but in all their school courses.

Chapter 18, Basic Study Skills, offers guidelines and practice in setting up study routines and in organizing information. Chapter 19, Reading and Testing-Taking Skills, reinforces reading techniques and test-taking skills. Chapter 20, Library and Reference Skills, covers essential library and reference procedures. Together, the three chapters teach skills that students can use in any learning situation. If you begin the school year with this unit, you may find that returning to it for reinforcement during the year will help you attain your teaching goals.

The pretest for the unit, available in the *Prentice-Hall Grammar and Composition Test Program*, can be used to help determine your students' need for instruction in the skills presented in the unit. Chapter tests and a unit post-test are also available in the test program.

CHAPTER **18 Basic Study Skills** (pp. 462–482)

Chapter 18 encourages students to evaluate their own private study habits while they explore new ideas about the ways people think and learn. You might need two or three class sessions for the two sections.

If you present this chapter early in the school year, discuss with students the type of notebook appropriate for their work in English during the year. Since much of their work will probably involve paperwork in the form of notes, outlines, homework, and compositions, students may find it convenient to arrange papers in categories such as literature, composition, and vocabulary and spelling. You might suggest that students select either a looseleaf notebook, or a notebook with several pockets for filing classwork and homework.

■ **18.1 Practicing Basic Study Skills** (pp. 462–468)

Objectives: After completing this section, students should be able to

- Identify their present study skills and problem areas.
- Set their own goals and plan an effective schedule for studying.
- Improve their powers of concentration.

Adapting for Different Abilities. While the material in this section is suitable for all ability levels, less advanced students may need more time and attention and more concentrated practice. You might, therefore, choose to help each student individually to complete the Application (p. 468), meeting privately to monitor and guide progress.

Suggestions for Additional Activities. Since open dialogue is often an excellent means of encouragement for students who have real difficulties in studying, you might consider having the class complete some of the exercises together. With Exercise C (p. 466), for example, you might have several students volunteer to place their study schedules on the board, on a dittoed sheet, or on an acetate projection sheet for the entire class to see and comment on and improve, if necessary. Students can make revisions and additions to their own study schedules as this activity proceeds.

You can repeat this type of activity with the goal charts that students prepare, and you might have volunteers offer their responses to the Application (p. 468), which asks them to evaluate their progress as a result of their study of the section.

■ 18.2 Understanding and Organizing Information (pp. 468–482)

Objectives: After completing this section, students should be able to

- Determine which learning styles work best for them.
- Listen for directions, main ideas, and supporting details.
- Take notes using modified outlines, summaries, and free-style outlines.
- Use formal topic and sentence outlines for note-taking and organizing their thoughts.

Adapting for Different Abilities. Some students can learn summarizing and outlining skills more quickly if they work with a recording of a newscast or speech rather than with written material. You may, therefore, want to allow poor readers in your class to adapt Exercises E, F, and G to an aural format.

Suggestions for Additional Activities. As a homework assignment, you might have your students listen to a news broadcast or talk show on some controversial subject. They should take notes, writing a modified or free-form outline first and then a summary.

Since formal outlining requires knowledge of specific rules, students may need additional practice with it. You may want to distribute an interesting article (one that can be reduced to a formal outline) and have your students work on it in class. Then you can guide them as they need it, helping individuals with the placement of information and with the use of letters and numbers.

CHAPTER 19 Reading and Test-Taking Skills (pp. 483–506)

This chapter provides information about different reading techniques. It also provides guidance in preparing for and taking tests. Section 19.1, Increasing Your Reading Speed, familiarizes students with three common types of reading speeds that they can use for different activities and shows students how to gauge their own reading speed. In addition, this section offers practical methods for improving reading speed and developing skimming and scanning skills.

Section 19.2, Taking Tests, gives practical suggestions that students will find helpful in all test situations.

You can probably cover this material in two to three class sessions. Since this chapter strengthens skills useful in all subject areas, you might study or review either Section 19.1 or 19.2 at various times during the school year whenever it would be most helpful.

■ 19.1 Increasing Your Reading Speed
(pp. 483–496)

Objectives: After completing this section, students should be able to

- Recognize three types of reading speeds and their uses.
- Determine their phrase reading rate and comprehension.
- Improve their phrase reading rate through practice on their own.
- Improve their skimming skills.
- Improve their scanning skills.

Adapting for Different Abilities. If you find some students' reading speeds alarmingly low, you might set up small group sessions within class or after school during which you can provide additional time trials. You may find also that you need to work with a few of these students on an individual basis. One method that can be used is to have the student face the page as you cover it with a sheet of paper or a ruler. Beginning a time trial, you can move your paper or ruler down, revealing one line of type at a time at a regular but brisk pace. Tell the student to grasp as much information as possible per line as long as you allow the paper or ruler to stay there, but instruct him or her to move down line-by-line as you do. To check the student's comprehension, ask questions about the passage informally to see how much he or she has actually absorbed. Although this process can be somewhat time-consuming, it can often dramatically help a student who persists in reading individual words rather than phrases.

Suggestions for Additional Activities. While this section contains several activities students can practice on their own, you may feel it necessary to give your classes additional reinforcement by providing particular reading selections on dittoed handouts and by running time trials with students. (See Exercise B for a model of this kind of activity.) Each day for a week, you might begin class with a reading selection, timing your students for one, two, or three minutes. At the end of the time limit, ask students to compute and record their reading speed on a chart. Depending on your course objectives, you may or may not want to grade the students' progress. If you do assign grades, however, do not let the hope of a better grade induce students to inflate their computations.

Maintaining a good reading speed requires regular practice. You might, therefore, consider running time trials for a full week every month during the school year.

■ 19.2 Taking Tests (pp. 496–506)

Objectives: After completing this section, students should be able to

- Use various mnemonics to recall information.
- Interpret different kinds of questions on objective tests.
- Use test periods well.

Adapting for Different Abilities. Most students will find work in class with this material rewarding. It will develop students' skills at almost every level of competency or awareness.

You may find that some students have difficulty previewing tests. For them the problem is usually needless haste and anxiety. You may help such students by allowing them extra time to use the checklist, Previewing a Test, on page 505 and by helping them budget their time: For example, during your own tests you might tell them, "At this time you should be finishing Part One and starting to think about Part Two."

Suggestions for Additional Activities. Since this section is limited to test-taking techniques for objective tests, you may want to expand the coverage at this time to include the techniques for answering essay examination questions found in Chapter 29.

CHAPTER 20 Library and Reference Skills (pp. 507–548)

This chapter contains essential information that your students need for success in any academic pursuit. While students can study many library and research techniques in the classroom, you may consider having your class make special visits to the library. If possible, you should coordinate this study with the school librarian, who can guide students' work with the chapter's exercises. Moreover, during class study of the material, you might send students in groups, or individually, to use the library as they work on the exercises.

If you choose to study this chapter early in the year, you might turn to it again for review if you cover Chapter 27, Library Papers, later in the year.

You may need at least five class sessions for this chapter, or even more if you send students to the library or if you enlist help from the school librarian. Often, the librarian will offer to give a guided tour or special presentations and explanations of the library's reference materials. You might plan a day or two in your curriculum for the librarian to take over completely.

■ 20.1 Using the Library (pp. 507–522)

Objectives: After completing this section, students should be able to

- Recognize and locate the information they need to take with them when they use a library.
- Use a card catalog effectively.
- Interpret call numbers and other symbols needed to locate materials in the library.

Adapting for Different Abilities. If some students find the Dewey Decimal System difficult to follow, you might present them, instead, with a detailed map of the library to study. Then, they can try to identify the location on the map where each one of a random list of books can be found. Finally, you can take the students to the library to check these locations.

Less advanced students may also need extra practice using the skills in this section. By duplicating the exercises, as suggested under Suggestions for Additional Activities, you can give these students a chance to correct mistakes or clarify areas of confusion.

Suggestions for Additional Activities. If you find that you need to supplement the exercises to provide sufficient practice, copy a subject card on the top of a dittoed sheet and have students answer the questions in Exercise C, using the new card for information.

For additional practice with the Dewey Decimal System and the Library of Congress call numbers, you can make another list as in Exercise F. Place it at the top of a dittoed sheet and have students repeat the exercise using the new call numbers. Similarly, you can have students repeat Exercise G by assigning five additional items such as the following:

1. A recording of a classical symphony (if your library stores tapes and records)
2. An autobiography by a sports personality
3. A novel by Emily Brontë
4. A book about Russian history
5. A pamphlet about career counseling

■ 20.2 Using Reference Materials (pp. 522–535)

Objectives: After completing this section, students should be able to

- Use general reference books to check basic facts or to get an overview of a topic.
- Use specialized reference books to gather specific details about a narrow part of a broad field.
- Use periodicals to supplement research with specialized or current information.

Adapting for Different Abilities. Average and advanced students will probably find all topics in this section helpful and manageable and all exercises accessible and enjoyable. For less advanced students, you may wish to limit their study to the reference material that is appropriate to their needs, such as encyclopedias, almanacs, and atlases.

Suggestions for Additional Activities. If you can borrow reference books from the library, bring to class an assortment—encyclopedia volumes, atlases, periodicals, pamphlets, and so forth—so that each student will have one. Then write on the board a question such as this:

How many feet above sea level is Boulder, Colorado?

Tell your students to raise their hands if they can find the answer to this particular question in the reference material they have in front of them. Not all students will raise their hands, of course, but those who do should be instructed to locate the answer. In the moment that the rest of the class waits, you can check to see if any others should have raised their hands. Doing this will encourage them to think twice about whether or not the particular reference works you are consulting will answer the question you have posed.

You can repeat this activity any number of times by writing additional questions on the board. Try to vary the type of question so that every student in class locates the required information at least one time.

■ 20.3 Using the Dictionary (pp. 535-548)

Objectives: After completing this section, students should be able to

- Select a dictionary suited to their needs.
- Use the various parts of dictionary entries to their best advantage.

Adapting for Different Abilities. Students, especially those who are less advanced, should be reminded that all dictionaries are not the same. A word entered in one dictionary may not be included in another. The number and order of definitions for a word in one dictionary may be quite different for the same word in another dictionary. Thus, if the dictionaries you use in class are not all the same, some students may have difficulty finding certain information called for in the exercises. The authors and editors, however, have made every effort to ensure that the answers to the exercises can be found in most if not all current school dictionaries.

Students should have little difficulty with Exercises A through D although you may decide to complete Exercise A together in class. Less advanced students, however, may need help completing Exercises E through J. You might have these students work in small groups so that you can monitor their work and offer assistance where needed. You might also decide to omit some of these exercises if you judge that certain skills are less essential than others.

Suggestions for Additional Activities. You might decide to repeat some exercises that you find especially helpful for students. You can give students additional words for alphabetizing (Exercise B) or more words that have preferred and variant spellings (Exercise C) or other words with difficult pronunciations (Exercise D). You can even take Exercise D further by having students place the phonetic transcriptions of words on the board for volunteers to pronounce.

UNIT VI

Composition

This unit, consisting of nine chapters with 22 sections, teaches students to recognize styles and structures of different types of writing and suggests processes to follow in the planning, drafting, and revising of written material. The material within the unit can be divided into three general categories: sentence writing (Chapters 21 and 22), paragraph writing (Chapters 23 and 24), and composition writing (Chapters 25 through 29). You might elect to teach each category at a different time, or you might choose particular chapters from the unit in the order that best suits your purposes. The introduction to each chapter indicates the amount of time necessary to complete its various sections, enabling you to plan accordingly.

The pretest for the unit, available in the *Prentice-Hall Grammar and Composition Test Program*, can be used to help determine your students' need for instruction in the skills presented in the unit. Chapter tests and a unit post-test are also available in the test program.

CHAPTER **21** **The Right Words and Tone**
(pp. 550–583)

This chapter concentrates on word choices within sentences while Chapter 22 focuses on the writing of sentences that are varied and logical. The two chapters are related and may be most effective when taught together.

The first section in Chapter 21 shows students how to write concisely. The second section helps students develop precision in their statements and freshness in their language choices. The third section directs students to consider a sentence for its effect upon a reader's perceptions by examining word choices that can establish tone and mood in writing.

You can plan on approximately five class sessions to complete the chapter.

■ 21.1 Writing Concisely (pp. 550–560)

Objectives: After completing this section, students should be able to

- Eliminate deadwood and other unnecessary words from sentences.
- Reduce wordy clauses and phrases.
- Correct redundant words, phrases, and clauses in sentences.
- Change unnecessary verbs in the passive voice and remove needless verb/noun constructions.

Adapting For Different Abilities. Students who have special difficulty writing concisely may need drill using samples of their own writing. You will probably find this problem frequently among advanced students. You might have these students bring to class a number of compositions they have written in their other subjects. They can work independently or in groups to identify instances of wordiness and to rewrite such passages.

Suggestions for Additional Activities. You might have your students bring to class examples of redundancy, wordiness, and deadwood that they have found in newspapers and magazines as well as examples they have heard on radio and television. Select five to ten of these and reproduce them so that your students can revise and rewrite them.

■ 21.2 Writing Precisely (pp. 560–571)

Objectives: After completing this section, students should be able to

- Choose strong, specific words instead of weak, general words.
- Avoid worn-out expressions by creating original ways to express ideas.
- Replace overused and expected words with more varied words.

Adapting for Different Abilities. The exercises in this section are accessible for all ability levels. The only adaptations you may want to make are likely to be in subtopics that you assign for study or requirements that you set for the use of terminology. Less advanced students may not, for example, need to identify words as *clichés* to recognize imprecise language. Instead, these students can practice improving word choices just by following the guidelines in the section.

Suggestions for Additional Activities. As a homework assignment, you might ask students to listen to quiz shows, talk shows, or other regular television programs and jot down examples of clichés, passive constructions, and other examples of weak language. Instruct students to list at least five that they hear to share in class the next day.

■ 21.3 Maintaining an Appropriate Tone
(pp. 572–583)

Objectives: After completing this section, students should be able to

- Consider audience, subject, and purpose in choosing an appropriate tone for each piece of writing.
- Make the tone of their writing clear and consistent by choosing words the audience will understand.
- Avoid certain other problems in tone by considering the response of the audience to the words chosen.

Adapting for Different Abilities. Less advanced students may find the second subsection, "Avoiding Words That Might Be Misunderstood," more rewarding than the first, "The Ingredients of Tone." For these students, you may want to postpone or eliminate the first topic and its related exercise.

Advanced students will probably enjoy writing three versions of an account of an imaginary occurrence. The first could be directed to a young child, the second to a classmate, the third to a friend who is just learning the English language.

Suggestions for Additional Activities. Once students have read the text and have begun to identify slang, jargon, emotional language, and euphemisms, have them apply this skill to their own writing. They can bring to class recently written compositions, then exchange papers and do the following four things.

1. Identify the audience the composition was probably written for.
2. Use the chart on page 574 in the text to identify the tone of the composition.
3. Locate any problems involving tone.
4. On a separate paper, suggest revisions to correct the problems.

CHAPTER **22** Sentence Variety and Logic
(pp. 584–611)

In this chapter, students will examine the ways in which sentences function within passages or compositions. In the first section (22.1), students will learn how to vary the lengths and structures of sentences in series to produce a style that is neither choppy nor monotonous. In the second section (22.2), students will learn methods of joining ideas with subordinating and coordinating words as well as with transitions to promote logical connections and improve writing style.

To complete this work with students, you might plan on approximately two days per section, or four to five days for the entire chapter.

■ 22.1 Writing Varied Sentences (pp. 584–597)

Objectives: After completing this section, students should be able to

- Expand and join short sentences for variety.
- Reduce long sentences for variety.
- Begin sentences in different ways.
- Use different sentence structures for emphasis.

Adapting for Different Abilities. For less advanced students you can modify Exercise A, Adding Details to Short Sentences, by changing the parenthetical expressions. Some suggestions for making these changes follow:

Sentence 1 (to go where?)
Sentence 2 (describe the house)
Sentence 3 (identify Mrs. Hamilton)

Advanced students can reread recently written compositions to look for choppiness, rambling sentences, or static sentence openers. Discuss these items as a class or with individual students as they perform this activity. To conclude the exercise you may want to assign revision work.

Suggestions for Additional Activities. To reinforce the study of sentence openers, you can have students turn to the chart, Varying Sentence Openers, on page 592 and supply additional examples for each of the methods given in the chart.

■ 22.2 Using Logic to Connect Ideas
(pp. 597–611)

Objectives: After completing this section, students should be able to

- Use transitions to connect the ideas in different sentences logically.
- Use coordination to combine related and equal ideas.
- Use subordination to combine ideas that are related but unequal.
- Order ideas logically within and between sentences.

Adapting for Different Abilities. Less advanced students may find the textual material in this section intimidating. You may want to read it over with them and work together on one or two sentences before students work on the exercises individually. To show how simple it is to use connecting words and to order ideas logically, you can place on the board a series of ideas such as the following:

> Roger looked in every room of the house.
>
> He could not find his car keys.
>
> He even checked the street outside.

By asking students to include the three ideas in a single sentence, you force them to add connecting words and to choose a new order for the ideas. As they offer answers, discuss the types of connecting words they are using. Students will realize that order and connection are both logical processes which will improve their writing.

Suggestions for Additional Activities. You might suggest the students bring to class a copy of a recipe or a paragraph of instructions for assembling something. You can have them rewrite the recipe or instructions, scrambling the sentences. Then they can exchange papers and reorder the sentences logically.

CHAPTER 23 Paragraphs (pp. 612–665)

Divided into four sections, this chapter analyzes the key features of good paragraphs and instructs students in planning, writing, and revising paragraphs. You might teach this material immediately after students have completed Chapters 21 and 22 on sentence writing, since it puts into practice the skills taught there. Or you may find it helpful to assign this work just prior to major writing assignments.

You may want to devote a whole unit of course time to a study of paragraphs. This chapter and Chapter 24 can serve as the basis for this study, requiring approximately fourteen class sessions for the work of both chapters. You may find, however, that Section 23.3 requires the most time—you could spend as much as three or four days—as students follow the steps in planning and writing paragraphs.

■ 23.1 Recognizing Clear Topic Sentences and Strong Support (pp. 612–620)

Objectives: After completing this section, students should be able to

- Locate the topic sentence in a paragraph.
- Recognize if a paragraph has adequate support for the topic sentence.

Adapting for Different Abilities. To help less advanced students analyze a paragraph, you might point to the first paragraph of the section (p. 612) as an example of a well-written paragraph. Begin by asking students to read the paragraph and then to find the one sentence that presents the main idea. (Answer: Sentence 1, which states "Paragraphs vary in many ways, including length, organization, and purpose, but most good paragraphs have some similarities.") Have a volunteer read the sentence out loud, and then ask students what information they would expect to follow this sentence. (They should expect explanations of how paragraphs "vary" and they should expect to find information about the "similarities" of paragraphs.)

Suggestions for Additional Activities. Ask students to scan their social studies or science textbooks for paragraphs with easily identifiable topic sentences. As an assignment, students can copy or reproduce one such paragraph to bring to class. On their papers, have them indicate the topic sentence and identify the kinds of support used. Volunteers can then read their paragraphs aloud to see if the class agrees with their work.

■ 23.2 Recognizing Unity and Coherence
(pp. 620–634)

Objectives: After completing this section, students should be able to

- Recognize if a paragraph has unity.
- Recognize if a paragraph has coherence.

Adapting for Different Abilities. With less advanced students, you may want to use Paragraph 4 on page 615 in the last section to discuss the features that make the paragraph well written. Your discussion should lead to the idea that all sentences work together, creating a *unity* among all ideas. You may want to ask students to find a pattern behind the development of ideas. This discussion should help students grasp the concept of coherence and will prepare them for the second subtopic within the text.

Suggestions for Additional Activities. You may want to have students reread the following paragraphs in the text and complete the instructions given for each:

1. Read the paragraph about quarterbacks on page 614 and write down the transitions that are used.
2. Read Paragraph 2 on page 615 and the paragraph on page 617 beginning "In April, 1912, the RMS *Titanic*...." For each of these paragraphs, write the main words that have been repeated and any synonyms or pronouns used for coherence.
3. Read the paragraph on page 625 beginning "Students who wish to become doctors..." and write down any parallel sentences or parts of sentences.

■ 23.3 Planning and Drafting Your Paragraphs (pp. 634–649)

Objectives: After completing this section, students should be able to

- Write a topic sentence that expresses a single main idea.
- Gather enough unified supporting information to develop a topic sentence.
- Organize a paragraph logically for coherence.
- Draft a complete, coherent paragraph.

Adapting for Different Abilities: With some groups of students, you may need to make it clear that they can take inspiration for their writing from almost anywhere—their fantasies and dreams, their hobbies and interests, their environments, and their hopes for the future. As students offer subject ideas, no matter how fanciful, you might write these on the board or else instruct several members of the class to act as "recorders." A master list of topics can serve now and later as a source of ideas.

Suggestions for Additional Activities. To illustrate the brainstorming step, an important part of the process of paragraph writing, you might place three or four topics (or even topic sentences) on the board. Then allow fifteen or twenty minutes of class time for students to suggest support for each of the topics listed. You might then take the process a step further by asking students to choose one set of information and write a paragraph.

■ 23.4 Revising and Rewriting Paragraphs (pp. 649–665)

Objectives: After completing this section, students should be able to

- Identify and improve weak topic sentences.
- Revise weaknesses in supporting information.
- Correct paragraphs that lack unity and/or coherence.

Adapting for Different Abilities. If your students need some clarification of the concepts of unity and coherence, you might use Exercise A, Identifying Paragraphs with Unity, and Exercise B, Recognizing the Devices That Add Coherence, in Section 23.2. The exercises can be used as a review, or if your class has not covered Section 23.2, they can serve as introductory material to the present section.

Suggestions for Additional Activities. As you study the text with students, you might consider establishing a system that you can continue to use in marking and editing students' papers. Together with the class, set up a system by identifying symbols that you will use to note certain weaknesses. Here are some possibilities:

GEN TS   = Overly General Topic Sentence
NAR TS   = Overly Narrow Topic Sentence
INAD   = Inadequate Support
INAPP   = Inappropriate Support
EXTR   = Extraneous Idea(s); Broken Unity
ILLOG   = Illogical Order
TRANS   = Wrong Transition or Transition Needed
X CONN   = Poor Connections Among Ideas

Students will know that these marginal notations can be corrected by following the suggestions in the corresponding subsections of the text.

CHAPTER 24 Kinds of Paragraphs
(pp. 666–696)

Based on the assumption that students have had practice and have gained competency in the writing of paragraphs, this chapter focuses on the purposes of paragraphs. The three sections of the chapter define these purposes or approaches to a topic: expository (Section 24.1), persuasive (Section 24.2), and descriptive and narrative (Section 24.3). Each section also provides suggestions for planning, writing, and revising such paragraphs. You may choose one of the sections, depending on the type of writing you wish to teach, or you might assign all three sections.

You would probably want to plan about six days for the entire chapter, or about two class sessions for each section. Keep in mind, however, that the sections need not be taught in sequence, but that students should have practiced paragraph writing (the work of Chapter 23) before attempting this chapter.

■ 24.1 Expository Paragraphs (pp. 666–672)

Objectives: After completing this section, students should be able to

- Recognize the main features of an expository paragraph: an explanatory purpose and tone.
- Plan, draft, and revise an expository paragraph by focusing on an explanatory purpose and the goal of making the audience understand.

Adapting for Different Abilities. Less advanced students may find it easier to develop expository paragraphs if you stress that the topic sentence often gives a clue to the way the paragraph should be organized. When they have written their topic sentences for Exercise C, they can read them aloud. Then other students can suggest the order in which the paragraph should be developed.

You can then give them sample topic sentences such as the following to illustrate the idea:

(Chronological)   If I review the events of the day just as they happened, you may understand why I am not only exhausted, but confused.

(Comparison/Contrast)   While soccer could be considered a kind of football game, there are many differences in the way the two games are played.

Suggestions for Additional Activities. If you have taught Section 23.2, you might want to have your students look over the compositions they wrote for Exercise F, Writing Paragraphs, in that section. Have them pick out paragraphs that meet the criteria for expository paragraphs set forth in this section. You might want to screen their choices and select a few of the better paragraphs to be duplicated and distributed. Then the class can analyze them as to purpose, tone, topic sentence, and organization. An evaluation can follow. To protect the feelings of the students who wrote the paragraphs, remind the class of the value of constructive criticism and of the fact that the paragraphs were chosen because they were basically well-written.

■ 24.2 Persuasive Paragraphs (pp. 672–681)

Objectives: After completing this section, students should be able to

- Recognize the main features of a persuasive paragraph: a persuasive purpose and tone.
- Plan, draft, and revise a persuasive paragraph by focusing on a persuasive purpose and the goal of making the audience agree or act in some particular way.

Adapting for Different Abilities. Depending on the abilities of your group, you can use advertisements in various ways. With advanced students, you can initiate a discussion of institutional advertising. They can bring to class examples of such advertising and/or write an original paragraph in which they attempt to influence public attitudes concerning a controversial issue.

Less advanced students may enjoy bringing to class various advertisements taken from magazines and newspapers or written copies of ones heard on TV and radio. They can analyze these in terms of intended audience, emotional language, tone, and purpose.

Suggestions for Additional Activities. You can also have your students bring to class samples of persuasive paragraphs taken from the editorial page of a newspaper or from their own school paper. Working in groups, they can discuss the issue, the tone, the intended audience, the use of emotional language, and the validity of the supporting arguments. Each group can choose one member to present their conclusions to the class.

■ 24.3 Descriptive and Narrative Paragraphs (pp. 681–696)

Objectives: After completing this section, students should be able to

- Recognize the main features of a descriptive paragraph: a descriptive purpose and descriptive language that appeals to the senses and imagination.
- Plan, draft, and revise a descriptive paragraph by focusing on describing something so that a reader can see or experience it.
- Recognize the main features of a narrative paragraph: a narrative purpose and definite point of view and the use of graphic language.
- Plan, draft, and revise a narrative paragraph that tells a story.

Adapting for Different Abilities. You might want to have less advanced students make up a list of five items similar to but different from those in Exercise C, Using Sensory Impressions. Then each student can write a short descriptive paragraph based on one of the items. You can carry the activity a step further by having students choose partners. Each of the partners can write a descriptive paragraph based on the same item. Then students can exchange papers and read each other's paragraphs. In a discussion, you can make them aware of the importance of observing their surroundings and of the effect on a reader of strong descriptive language.

Suggestions for Additional Activities. You can have students choose one of the items below or one of their own. They can follow the steps for planning, brainstorming, organizing, and drafting a descriptive paragraph. Once they have drafted the paragraph, they can copy it, leaving a blank space each time they have named the object. Then they can exchange paragraphs with someone who does not know what has been described. Each student should read his or her partner's paragraph and guess what the paragraph describes. Each student might also be asked to draw a picture of the object, based on the description. The papers should then be returned to the original author with the drawings or with questions if the partner was unable to guess the object being described. Finally, the paragraph should be revised to improve, clarify, or supply any necessary details.

An unusual tool	A piece of camera equipment
An unusual holiday decoration	An unusual antique
	A kitchen utensil

An unusual piece of jewelry	A household knicknack
A piece of sports equipment	A part of a car of bicycle
A new or very old toy	A part of a clock, radio, or
An unusual musical instrument	television set

CHAPTER 25 Essays (pp. 697–733)

The work done in Chapters 23 and 24 is excellent preparation for this chapter. The first section presents the parts of an essay: thesis statement, title, introduction, body development with topic sentences and coherence, and conclusions. The second section gives students easy-to-follow steps for writing essays of their own.

You might require four to six class sessions for this chapter. Keep in mind, however, that the second section will probably take longer than the first, especially if your students do some of their writing in class.

■ 25.1 Characteristics of Good Essays
(pp. 697–715)

Objectives: After completing this section, students should be able to

- Recognize the main features of an essay: a thesis statement, a title, an introduction, a body, and a conclusion.
- Examine an essay for unity and coherence.

Adapting for Different Abilities. To give less advanced students the clearest picture possible of an essay, you might use the diagram on page 698 (or a diagram of your own that makes the same comparison) to show students schematically the parts of an essay, how they function individually, and how they work together to create a unified body.

Suggestions for Additional Activities. By the tenth grade, students have probably written essays and other types of longer compositions. If so, you might have them bring to class such works and examine them for the characteristics defined in this section. This kind of activity will reinforce recognition skills, will promote class discussion, and can even serve as motivation for students to include such features in future writing attempts.

For another activity, you can choose a sample thesis statement from the text and place it on the chalkboard or on a dittoed handout. Students can then offer topic sentences for body paragraphs and the conclusion. These you can place on the board or have students add them to their dittoes. You might even draw rectangles to represent the separate paragraphs that would form the essay.

read the essay, you can have an oral discussion based on the questions that follow the essay in Exercise A. Then, in workshop sessions, you can work with them in planning their own essays.

Suggestions for Additional Activities. You can suggest that students bring to class a persuasive essay taken from the editorial pages of the newspaper. These can be read to the class and discussed, using as guidelines the questions in Exercise A.

■ 26.3 Personal Experience Essays (pp. 750-756)

Objectives: After completing this section, students should be able to

- Recognize the main features of a personal experience essay: a narrative purpose and descriptive and lively language.
- Plan, draft, and revise a personal experience essay by focusing on recreating a personal experience for the reader.

Adapting for Different Abilities. You might want to have some of your students work in small groups. Each student can relate a personal experience. Then the group can choose the most interesting account and working together think of a title, formulate a thesis statement, order the events, and collaborate on an outline. Finally, each student can write the essay, using the common outline as a guide.

Suggestions for Additional Activities. You can use any available literature texts and have the students choose a personal experience essay to read. Then each student can analyze the essay in terms of the questions that follow the essay in Exercise A.

CHAPTER 27 Library Papers (pp. 757-783)

A study of the library paper builds upon students' work in research skills (Chapter 20) as well as their knowledge of writing essays (Chapters 25 and 26). Structurally, a library paper is an extended essay so that skills taught in the previous sections will help substantially in this chapter.

The first section of this chapter (Section 27.1) shows students the key features of library papers: the structural parts that resemble essays as well as special features such as footnotes and a bibliography, which document the research. In the second section (27.2), students will follow steps in the process of planning, drafting, and revising a library paper of their own. While you might require only two or three class sessions with the first section, your students will require more time for the work in the second. You might assign as much as a week during which students can work on their library papers in class, in the library, and at home. Or you might extend the work over a longer period of time, while pursuing other curriculum goals simultaneously. You might spend two class sessions on planning activities such as narrowing topics and collecting data and then assign the drafting steps for homework during the next week.

■ 27.1 Characteristics of the Library Paper
(pp. 757–769)

Objectives: After completing this section, students should be able to

- Acknowledge outside sources of information in a library paper in an appropriate and consistent manner.
- Recognize the structure and special features of a library paper: a title, an introduction with a thesis statement, a body, a conclusion, footnotes or internal citations, and a bibliography.

Adapting for Different Abilities. While average and advanced students should be sufficiently challenged by the work in this section, less advanced students may need extra time and attention. You might provide practice in writing footnotes, bibliography cards, and bibliographies. Group work in the library during free periods or after school is helpful. Also, if students can bring to class research papers written for other classes, you might have them work in groups to analyze these papers, comparing the features with those described and illustrated in the text. In particular, you might have them examine structure and documentation, showing them how to make improvements in these areas, if necessary.

Suggestions for Additional Activities. The students' understanding of the reasons for full citations may be enhanced by a discussion of the problems and the benefits involved, first from the perspective of the writer and then from the perspective of the reader.

■ 27.2 Steps in Writing a Library Paper
(pp. 769–783)

Objectives: After completing this section, students should be able to

- Select a topic that can be supported with available research materials and presented in a short library paper.
- Plan and carry out research on a topic.
- Draft a library paper from a thesis statement and an outline.
- Produce a finished, revised copy of a library paper that includes citations, a bibliography, and a title page.

Adapting for Different Abilities. For students who need preparation for the whole process of planning and writing, you might post an outline of all the steps they will need to follow, from choosing a topic through writing the final draft. If you think it will help to guide such students, you can include dates for the completion of each step. Here is a sample schedule that you might post in the room, or distribute on a handout:

Activity	Place	Date
1. Choose and narrow a topic.	In class	Mon., April 3
2. Select sources for your research.	Library	Tues., April 4
3. Scan sources for relevant information. Prepare bibliography cards.	At home	Tues., April 4 Weds., April 5
4. Present bibliography cards. Develop a thesis statement.	In class At home	Thurs., April 6 Thurs., April 6
5. Take notes. Develop an outline.	In class	Fri., April 7
6. Present a first draft.	In class	Mon., April 10

Suggestions for Additional Activities. A visit to the library might be very useful. The librarian can help students locate sources for their topics as you help others with this and other planning stages. As students locate and scan their sources, you can help them prepare bibliography cards and take notes. This will also give you an opportunity to help some students redefine or narrow further their topic choices.

If one of your students is working much faster than others, you might have this student prepare a preliminary outline for the paper on a dittoed handout so that you can use it next day in class as a model for the other students. You might even have the student present his or her bibliography cards and notes to explain how he or she proceeded from notes to outline.

Later in the process, when students present their first drafts, you might have them exchange papers and perform one of several activities. One such activity could be to check footnote and bibliography forms against the charts of examples on pages 760 and 764. Also, students can use the checklist on page 769 to look for and note weaknesses in each other's papers.

CHAPTER **28** Letters (pp. 784–801)

In two sections, this chapter presents models of letters written both for social and business purposes and explains their style and structure. The material can be assigned at any time and without prerequisite, but you might preface it with the chapters on paragraph writing. You will probably want to spend a total of two or three days on the chapter's work.

■ 28.1 Personal Letters (pp. 784–792)

Objectives: After completing this section, students should be able to

- Recognize the basic structure of a personal letter as well as the different styles that can be used in writing and sending such letters.
- Write a variety of different types of personal letters, including a friendly letter and a letter of invitation.

Adapting for Different Abilities. For students who need extra help, you might place on the board or on a dittoed handout a poorly structured and arranged personal letter. The errors and omissions should be obvious. Elicit from the students their reactions to such a letter. As you discuss it together, you can introduce the terminology—salutation, body, closing, and so on. You might then have the students rewrite the letter or have them construct a skeleton letter in the style they choose. They can then use this as a guide for future work.

Suggestions for Additional Activities. You might want to have the class brainstorm to think of a single situation that might require the writing of several different kinds of personal letters. For example, they can pretend they are seniors who are arranging a reunion party for students who have graduated during the last five years. They can list the kinds of letters that might be involved in planning such a party:

1. A letter announcing tentative plans for a reunion of recent graduates
2. A letter replying positively to the first letter
3. A letter responding negatively to the first letter and giving a reason for the negative response
4. A letter of invitation to be written when the date has been set
5. A letter of acceptance
6. A letter of regret
7. A letter describing the reunion to a friend who could not attend

You may then have the students collaborate on the letters or choose from the list and work independently.

■ 28.2 Business Letters (pp. 792–801)

Objectives: After completing this section, students should be able to

- Recognize the basic structure of a business letter as well as the different styles that can be used in writing and sending such letters.
- Write a variety of different types of business letters, including a letter of request and an order letter.

Adapting for Different Abilities. Among students who need extra help, you may have some who find it easier to learn by way of a strong visual presentation. You can ask volunteers to make poster-size models of the three styles for business letters. These can be posted in a prominent place. If you wish to simplify the lesson, you can decide on one style or have the students select a style and use that style throughout the section.

Suggestions for Additional Activities. For extra practice in writing business letters, you can have students assume various roles—job applicant, customer ordering a product, customer returning defective merchandise, vacationer making hotel reservations, manufacturer responding to a complaint, student writing a letter of opinion to school paper, parent writing a letter of opinion to a television station or to an advertiser. This activity can become especially interesting when the students pair off in their roles and respond to each other's letters. To add interest, you can suggest that students design letterheads for their business stationery, thus reinforcing the learning of the details of the inside address.

CHAPTER **29 Essay Examinations** (pp. 802–810)

This chapter provides some useful techniques to help students cope successfully with essay examinations. You may want to assign this chapter after completing Chapters 23 through 26. In addition, students will probably appreciate its value more if they study this chapter just before taking a major essay-type test.

You might plan on about two class sessions for this work, especially if students complete any of the exercises in class.

■ **29.1 Preparing Answers to Essay Exam Questions** (pp. 802–810)

Objectives: After completing this section, students should be able to

- Plan their timing logically at the beginning of an essay exam.
- Interpret essay exam questions quickly.
- Outline either a paragraph-length or essay-length answer.
- Write a clear answer and proofread it rapidly for errors.

Adapting for Different Abilities. Less advanced students may benefit from a class discussion of test-taking problems as a prelude to the section. As they identify problems they face in taking tests—shortage of time, blockage of ideas, and so on—elicit suggestions from the class for overcoming these problems. You may even want to outline on the board the techniques for effective, successful test-taking before turning to the text.

Suggestions for Additional Activities. To facilitate learning, you might have students take notes and construct a guide sheet for answering tests. They can place their guide sheets at the front of their notebooks for use during exams.

Another type of activity is timing your students' writing. As you give students sample questions to answer and as they complete exercises in the text, you can act as timekeeper. For instance, you might allow students twenty minutes to complete Exercise D on page 809.

Additional Answers to Test Exercises

Unit I Grammar

Section 5.6 Diagraming the Basic Parts of Sentences

Exercise A (p. 96)

1.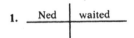

2.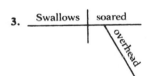

3.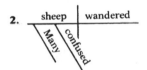

4.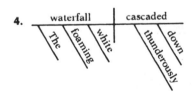

5.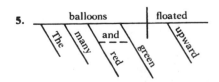

Exercise B (pp. 98-99)

1.
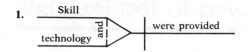

Skill
technology **and**
were provided

2.
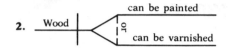

Wood
can be painted
or
can be varnished

3.
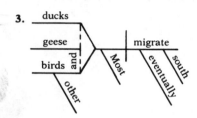

ducks
geese
birds **and**
other
Most migrate eventually south

4.
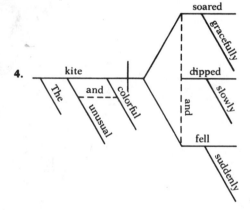

The kite **and** unusual colorful
soared gracefully
dipped slowly **and**
fell suddenly

5.
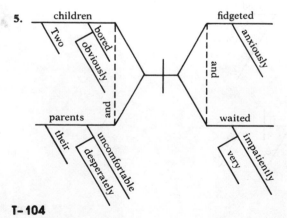

Two children obviously bored **and**
parents their uncomfortable desperately
fidgeted anxiously **and**
waited very impatiently

6.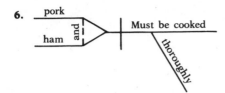

7.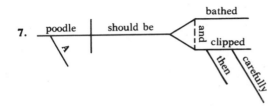

8.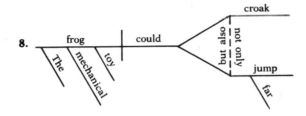

9.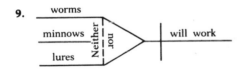

10.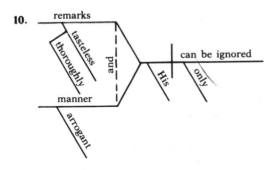

Exercise C (p. 100)

1.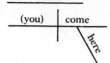
   Mr. Ricardo
   (you) | come
   here

2.
   Vera
   (you) | Go
   ahead

3.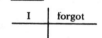
   Uh
   I | forgot

4.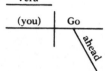
   pharmacy | is
   the   Here

5.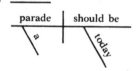
   There
   parade | should be
   a   today

Exercise D (pp. 102-103)

1.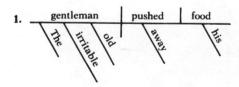
   gentleman | pushed | food
   The irritable old away   his

2.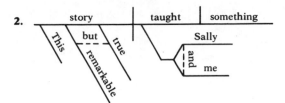

3.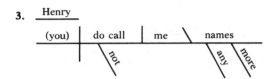

4.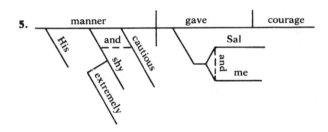

5.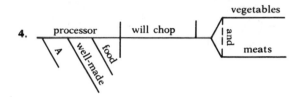

Exercise E (p. 103)

1.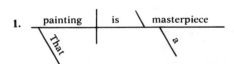

2.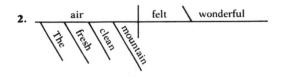

3.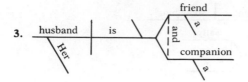

4.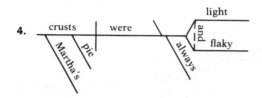

5.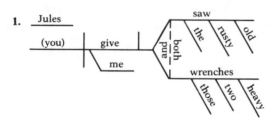

Application (p. 103)

1.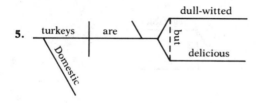

2.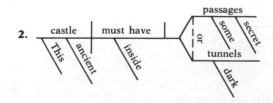

3.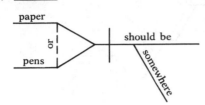

4.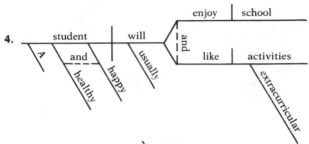

5.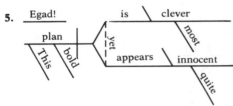

Section **6.6** **Diagraming Phrases**

Exercise A (pp. 128-129)

1.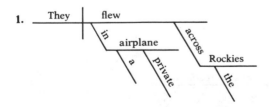

2.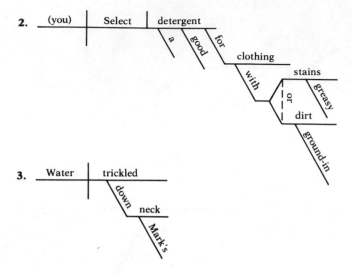

3.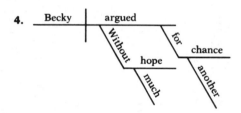

4.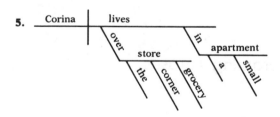

5.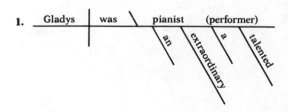

Exercise B (p. 130)

1. Gladys | was \ pianist (performer)

2.

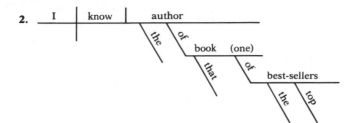

3.

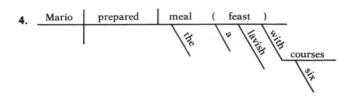

4.

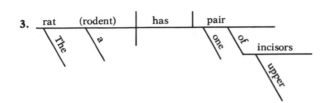

5.

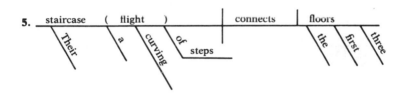

Exercise C (p. 132)

1.

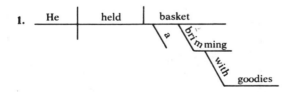

2.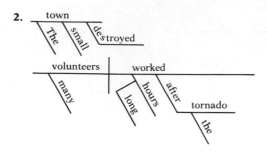

3.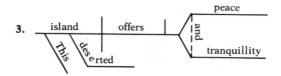

4.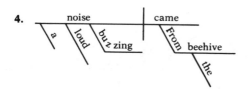

5.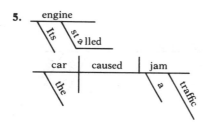

Exercise D (p. 133)

1.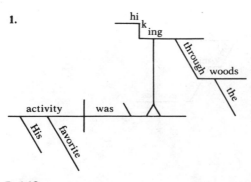

2.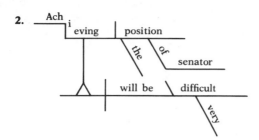

3.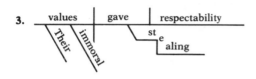

4.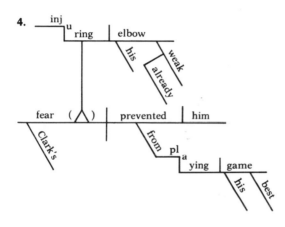

5.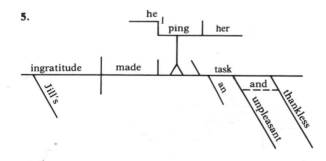

1.

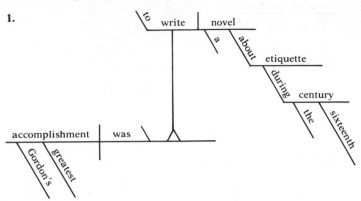

2.

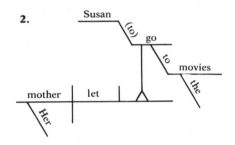

3.

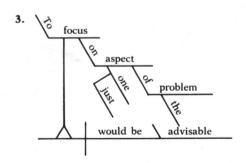

4.

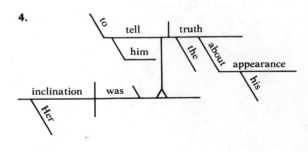

5.

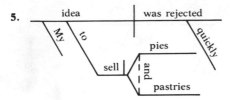

Application (p. 135)

1.

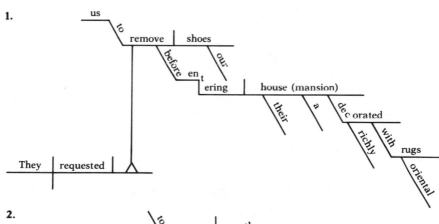

2.

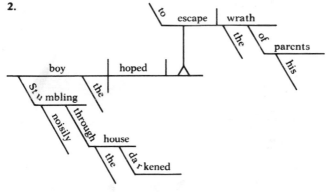

3.

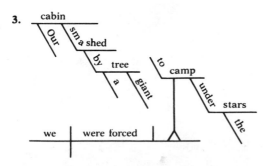

4.

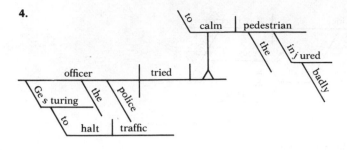

5.

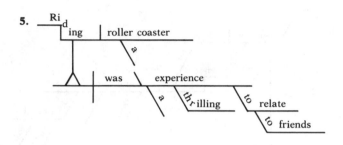

Section **7.5 Diagraming Different Sentence Structures**

Exercise A (p. 156)

1.

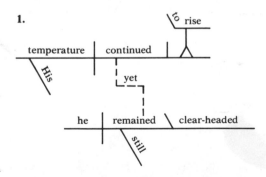

2.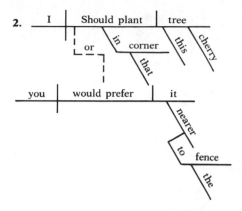

3.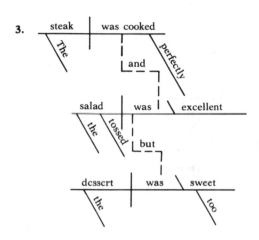

4.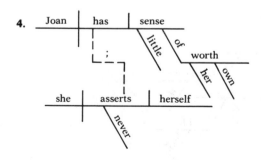

5.

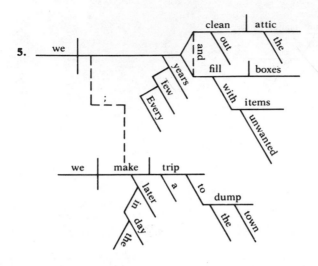

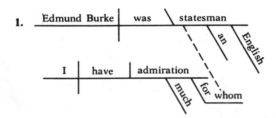

Exercise B (pp. 160-161)

1.

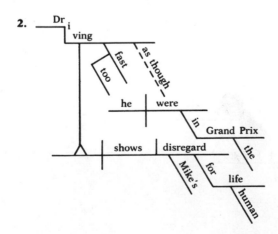

2.

3.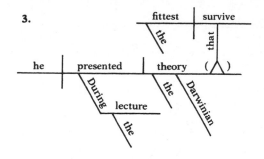

4.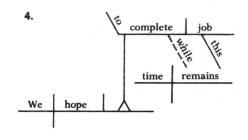

5.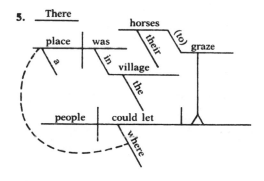

6.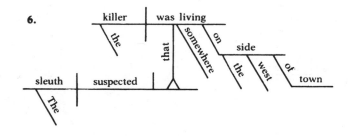

7.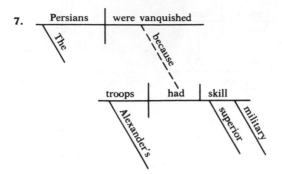

8.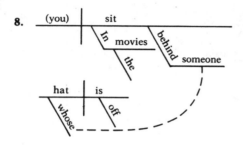

9.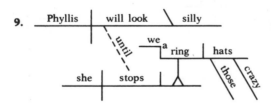

10.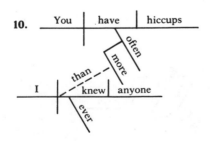

Exercise C (p. 162)

1.

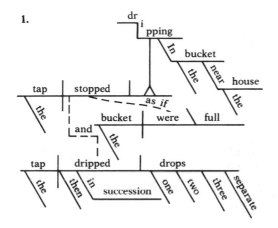

2.

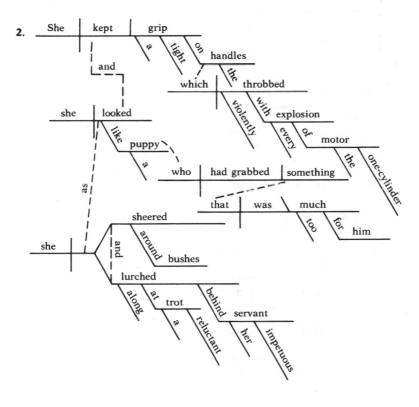

■ Review Exercises: Grammar

Review Exercise 1 (p. 181)

1. story: abstract; common
   Pompeii: concrete; proper
   people: concrete; common
2. Italy: concrete; proper
   Pompeii: concrete; proper
   city: concrete; common
   Mount Vesuvius: concrete; proper
   79: abstract; proper
3. citizens: concrete; common
   thousand: concrete; common
4. tragedy: abstract; common
   people: concrete; proper
   warnings: abstract; common
   volcano: concrete; common
5. years: abstract; common
   earthquake: concrete; common
   Pompeii: concrete; proper
   neighbors: concrete; common
   Naples: concrete; proper
   Herculaneum: concrete; proper
6. crater: concrete; common
   signs: abstract; common
   life: abstract; common
   attention: abstract; common
7. centuries: abstract; common
   Pompeii: concrete; proper
   ash: concrete; common
8. sightseers: concrete; common
   streets: concrete; common
   ruins: concrete; common

Review Exercise 2 (p. 182)

1. who — people: relative
2. themselves — fish: intensive
   their — fish: personal
3. what — methods: interrogative
   some — methods: indefinite
   their — fish: personal
4. its — archerfish: personal
   its — archerfish: personal
5. (No pronouns)
6. it — decoy fish: personal
   this — fin: demonstrative
   its — decoy fish: personal
7. its — prey: personal
8. these — ways: demonstrative
   few — ways: indefinite
   themselves — fish: reflexive

■ Review Exercises: Usage

Review Exercise 1 (pp. 301-302)

1. Verb tenses signify the time of an occurrence.
2. present, past, future, present perfect, past perfect, future perfect
3. present, present participle, past, past participle
4. The progressive is formed by the conjugation of *to be* added to the present participle.
5. The two emphatic forms add *do* and *did* as helpers to the first principal part.
6. Regular verbs form the past and past participle by adding *-d* or *-ed* to the present form. Irregular verbs may vary in several ways from that pattern.
7. A conjugation uses the personal pronouns as subjects for a verb in all the tenses and forms.
8. A verb's conjugation can aid a writer in establishing agreement between subject and verb, in avoiding tense switches, and in using the proper verb form and spelling in sentences.
9. Present, past, and future are the three major time categories. Perfect tenses express past and future time.
10. In the active voice, the subject acts. In the passive voice, the subject is acted upon. Only transitive verbs can be expressed in the passive voice.
11. Case depends upon the sentence function of nouns and pronouns, the two parts of speech using case.
12. Nominative case is used for subjects and predicate nominatives. Objective case is used for direct and indirect objects, objects of verbals, and objects of prepositions. The possessive case is used to show ownership or to precede a gerund.
13. An elliptical clause is one in which a subject or predicate is inferred. Such clauses cause problems with pronouns because important words are missing, and the writer must reconstruct them in order to use the correct case.
14. Agreement means that the subject and verb both show the same number, and that the pronoun and antecedent share the same person, number, and gender.
15. Such verbs end in *-s* or *-es*.
16. Pronouns must agree with their antecedents in person, number, and gender.
17. These modifiers, when regular, show comparison by adding *-er*, *-est*, *more*, or *most*.
18. Comparative degree is for comparing two things: *happier than she, better than he, bigger than it.* Superlative degree compares three or more things: *happiest of all, best of the lot, biggest of the three.*

19. Irregular modifiers are those that do not follow the rules cited in answer to Question 17.
20. Though once fashionable and correct, double negatives are now considered unnecessary and wrong.

Review Exercise 10 (p. 306)

1. to modify an adjective or adverb; to replace *also*
2. *accept* is a verb/*except* a preposition or verb meaning "excluding"
3. double negative
4. second mentioned/first mentioned
5. change *of* to *have*
6. in good health/conducive to good health
7. subject + verb form/possessive pronoun/adverb or expletive
8. double negative
9. change it to *since* or *because*
10. adverb/pronoun + adjective
11. eliminate *and*
12. double negative
13. change *don't* to *doesn't*
14. distance/degree, extent, addition
15. adverb *well* needed to modify verb; *good* is an adjective
16. not a conjunction or conjunctive adverb/change to *as* or *as if*
17. to move upward (intransitive verb)/to lift (transitive)
18. persons/things/*that* can be substituted for either of them
19. change it to *in school, at school,* or some other adverbial phrase
20. to overcome an opponent/to achieve victory in a contest

Unit III **Mechanics**

Section **15.4 Quotation Marks with Direct Quotations**

Exercise E (p. 387)

"Today we are lucky to have Dr. Richard Sherman to discuss the subject of dreams."

"It is a pleasure to be with you today," Dr. Sherman began. "As I talk, please feel free to interrupt and ask questions."

Someone in the audience raised a hand: "Will you cover the interpretation of dreams?"

"Yes," the doctor replied, "but first let me talk about the importance certain cultures place on dreams. For instance, the Cheyenne Indians sent their boys out to dream a vision that would reveal their destinies. In the Ibans tribe in Borneo, they believe that a secret helper comes in a dream to provide advice for the troubled dreamer."

"I have heard that people have gotten inspirations and inventions from their dreams. Can you verify this?" an individual asked.

The doctor turned to the questioner: "Mozart reported that he saw whole musical pieces composed in his dreams, and Fredrich Kekulé solved the structure of benzene based on his dream."

"And did Einstein discover the theory of relativity through a dream?" someone in the back of the room challenged.

"As a matter of fact," the lecturer explained, "he had been sick from overwork; and while experiencing a feverish dream, he worked out this now-famous theory."

"I find this fascinating," a girl in the front row whispered.

After another thirty minutes of discussion, the speaker concluded: "Thus we should welcome our dreams—not fear them. Let me leave you with these words from William Wordsworth: 'Come blessed barrier between day and day.'"

Unit IV Vocabulary and Spelling

Section 16.1 Building Your Vocabulary

Exercise B (p. 432)

1. mythological Titan who supported world on his shoulders as a punishment for defying Zeus
2. style of sweater named for the Earl of Cardigan
3. named after a 17th-century hangman
4. one who goes mad from looking too long at the moon (luna)
5. great prince (Chinese)
6. day's-eye (Old English)
7. hunters of wild oxen in Haiti who later became pirates
8. time of festivity before Lent, the season when meat was prohibited: *carne* (meat) + *vale* (good-bye)
9. originally small candies (Italian)
10. "I have found (it)!" — attributed to Archimedes
11. from the Italian word for Mosul, the city in Iraq where the fabric was made
12. mokhisson (North American Indian)
13. originally sold only on Sunday but people objected to using the same spelling as the Sabbath
14. like Don Quixote
15. named for the Muse with the beautiful voice: *Kallos* (beauty) + *ops* (voice)

Unit V Study Skills

Section 18.2 Understanding and Organizing Information

Exercise H (p. 481)

I. Musk deer
  A. Habitat
      1. Himalaya Mountains
      2. India
  B. Size
      1. Small animal
      2. Height of a man's knee
  C. Uses
      1. Scent used in perfume
      2. Gland under abdomen carries scent
II. Yak
  A. Habitat
      1. Asia
      2. Tibet, near China
  B. Size
      1. Small ox
      2. Shoulder height of tall man
  C. Uses
      1. Milk
      2. Meat
      3. Cloth woven from hair

Section 20.3 Using the Dictionary

Exercise F (p. 547)

1. from Thomas Derrick, London hangman of early 17th century
2. acronym for Radio Detecting and Ranging
3. Lit., white-robed, for Roman office-seekers, who wore white gowns
4. Latin: paene (almost) + insula ([an] island)
5. Latin: in (not) + nocuus (harmful)
6. Portuguese: doudo (stupid)
7. Old French: dent de lion (tooth of [the] lion), because of shape of leaves
8. Latin: verbosus (full of words)
9. Latin: mellifluus (honey + flow [of])
10. Greek: sophos (wise) + mōros (foolish)

PRENTICE-HALL

Grammar and Composition

Level 4

SERIES CONSULTANTS

Level 1
Ellen G. Manhire
English Consultant Coordinator
Fresno, California

Level 2
Elizabeth A. Nace
Supervisor, Language Arts
Akron, Ohio

Level 3
Jerry Reynolds
Supervisor, Language Arts
Rochester, Minnesota

Level 4
Marlene Corbett
Chairperson, Department of English
Charlotte, North Carolina

Level 5
Gilbert Hunt
Chairperson, Department of English
Manchester, Connecticut

Level 6
Margherite LaPota
Curriculum Specialist
Tulsa, Oklahoma

CRITIC READERS FOR LEVEL 4

Susan B. Baum
Lake Brantley High School
Altamonte Springs, Florida

Florence C. Bumgardner
Okaloosa District Schools
Fort Walton Beach, Florida

Burdette Connell
Southern High School
Durham, North Carolina

James E. Coomber
Concordia College
Moorhead, Minnesota

Myles D. Eley
Warren Central High School
Indianapolis, Indiana

Patricia F. Eyring
Council Rock High School
Newtown, Pennsylvania

Connie Gifford
Hazelwood School District
Florissant, Missouri

Franklin E. May
Westside High School
Omaha, Nebraska

Howard D. Peet
North Dakota State University
Fargo, North Dakota

Lois Reemer
Glastonbury High School
Glastonbury, Connecticut

James W. Reith
Scottsdale Unified School District #48
Phoenix, Arizona

Robert E. Zach
Poudre School District R-1
Fort Collins, Colorado

Prentice-Hall

Grammar
and
Composition

Level 4

SERIES AUTHORS

Mary Beth Bauer, Language Arts Consultant, Houston, Texas

Lawrence Biener, Chairperson, Department of English, Locust Valley, New York

Linda Capo, Writer and English Teacher, Ithaca, New York

Gary Forlini, Writer and English Teacher, Pelham, New York

Karen L. Moore, English and Speech Teacher, Saratoga, California

Darla Shaw, Reading Coordinator, Ridgefield, Connecticut

Zenobia Verner, Professor of Curriculum and Instruction, Houston, Texas

PRENTICE-HALL, INC., Englewood Cliffs, New Jersey

SERIES TITLES

Prentice-Hall Grammar and Composition: Level 1
Prentice-Hall Grammar and Composition: Level 2
Prentice-Hall Grammar and Composition: Level 3
Prentice-Hall Grammar and Composition: Level 4
Prentice-Hall Grammar and Composition: Level 5
Prentice-Hall Grammar and Composition: Level 6

SUPPLEMENTARY MATERIALS

Annotated Teacher's Editions—Levels 1–6
Testing Program—Levels 1–6

Acknowledgments: page 830

© 1982 by Prentice-Hall, Inc., Englewood Cliffs, New Jersey 07632. All rights reserved. No part of this book may be reproduced in any form or by any means without permission in writing from the publisher. Printed in the United States of America.

ISBN 0-13-696823-6

10 9 8 7 6 5 4 3 2 1

Prentice-Hall International, Inc., London
Prentice-Hall of Australia Pty. Ltd., Sydney
Prentice-Hall of Canada, Ltd., Toronto
Prentice-Hall of India Private Ltd., New Delhi
Prentice-Hall of Japan, Inc., Tokyo
Prentice-Hall of Southeast Asia Pte. Ltd., Singapore
Whitehall Books Limited, Wellington, New Zealand

Contents

8 *Contents*

Preface

This book has a single purpose—to help you deal more effectively with the English language. The content, organization, and special features have all been designed to help you reach this goal.

Content

Unit One, Grammar, covers parts of speech and the parts of sentences, while giving you a number of useful methods for correcting basic sentence faults. Unit Two, Usage, zeroes in on problems that may arise in using verbs, pronouns, adjectives, and adverbs and includes a special section listing sixty common usage problems along with their solutions. Unit Three, Mechanics, helps you decide when to capitalize, when to abbreviate, and when to use commas, quotation marks, and other forms of punctuation. Unit Four, Vocabulary and Spelling, provides strategies for building your knowledge of words and improving your spelling. Unit Five, Study Skills, offers numerous ideas for getting more out of the time you spend studying, listening to classroom lectures, reading, taking tests, and researching topics in the library. Unit Six, Composition, begins with ideas for making your sentences clearer and more interesting, moves on to steps for writing paragraphs, and ends with steps and other useful methods for writing essays, library papers, letters, and answers to questions on essay examinations.

Organization

While your class may study any or all of the sections in the book in depth, you will find that the book has an equally important use as a reference work, not only in your English classes but also on any other occasion when you want to write or speak with particular effectiveness.

As a Textbook. All the units are divided into chapters, each of which is divided into sections. The sections themselves are then divided into subsections. A glance at the Table of Contents, which begins on page 5, and a brief survey of a few of the text chapters should show you how this works.

The sections are short and can usually be covered in a day or two. Before beginning each section, you will find it useful to preview the subsections. Which areas do you consider yourself strong in? Which areas are you weak in? As you work through the subsections, you will find one or more exercises at the end of each subsection. You can use these to preview or test your understanding of the topics covered. At the end of each section, you will find an Application which asks you to put all the skills you have reviewed or learned in the section to work in a practical exercise. This will give you a chance to check your overall understanding and ability to use the material in the section.

As a Reference Tool. In and out of school, you are likely to find situations in which knowing correct punctuation, correct spelling, and standard usage can make a difference. If you have questions on these matters, there are three places you can go in this book to find the answers. You can check the Table of Contents at the front of the book, you can check the Key of Major Concepts at the back of the book, or you can use the Index. Note that the Index uses bold numbers to show you where to find rules and definitions.

Special Features

In addition to becoming familiar with the overall organization of the text, you may find it useful to explore some of the special features.

Clear Rules. All major rules and definitions are printed in bold type and written in easy-to-understand language. The bold numbers in the index indicate the pages where rules and definitions can be found.

Numerous Examples. For most rules you will find a number of examples, each pointing out a different aspect of the rule. Whether you are studying a section or using it for quick reference, make sure you check all of the examples to be certain you understand all aspects of the rule.

Exercises for Each Subsection. Each subsection has one or more exercises. This will make it possible for you to tell what concepts you have mastered completely and what concepts you will need to review more thoroughly.

Applications for All Sections. The practical Application at the end of each section lets you put what you have been learning to work, generally in some writing exercise. At the same time, you will be checking your mastery of the ideas in the section.

Charts Covering Important Concepts. Throughout the book you will find important concepts highlighted in charts. This will make it possible for you quickly to identify and check your understanding and knowledge of essential ideas.

Charts Offering Useful Steps. Charts are also used to illustrate step by step processes: for making subjects and verbs agree, for making summaries, for developing different materials in compositions, and for numerous other topics.

Checklists. One of the most important uses of charts is for revision checklists. What should you do when you have finished writing the first draft of a paragraph or essay? The checklists in the composition unit give some valuable suggestions.

Numerous Composition Models. One of the best ways to increase your own writing skill is to examine the works of professional writers and of other students. Throughout the composition unit you will find models by other writers with important elements clearly labeled.

A Special Unit on Study Skills. The study skills unit can help you review and develop a number of skills that will be immediately useful in a number of situations. If you are interested in increasing your reading speed, for example, see Section 19.1.

A Special Section on Manuscript Preparation. This section at the end of the book can be immensely useful any time you need to prepare a written work that you want to be well received.

Three Reference Aids. The Table of Contents, the Index, and the Key of Major Concepts at the back of the book all can help you zero in on the rules and examples you need when you are using the book for quick reference.

Chapter 1

Nouns, Pronouns, and Verbs

Each word you use in the English language can be classified as one of the eight *parts of speech:* nouns, pronouns, verbs, adjectives, adverbs, prepositions, conjunctions, and interjections.

In English, *nouns* and *pronouns* are the two parts of speech used to name people, places, and things. *Verbs* are words that tell something about nouns and pronouns, often by expressing some kind of action. The next three sections will explain these three parts of speech.

1.1 Nouns

In grammar, the names people give to themselves and others, to the places they live, and to the things that surround them are called *nouns.*

A **noun** is the name of a person, place, or thing.

■ Words That Name

Nouns name objects you can see and touch as well as things you cannot see or touch. In the following chart, notice the many different categories into which nouns fall.

CATEGORIES OF NOUNS			
Persons:	Mark	citizen	Australians	Aunt Jo
Places:	beach	hotel	Wisconsin	Europe

Living Things:	moose	daisy	tree	mosquito
Nonliving Things:	sand	hat	table	lightning
Ideas:	freedom	patriotism	religion	friendship
Actions:	decision	treatment	punishment	judgment
Conditions:	health	poverty	happiness	oppression
Qualities:	wisdom	innocence	courage	honor

Ideas, actions, conditions, and qualities are all types of things—things that cannot be seen or touched but nevertheless have names. Nouns that name things that can be seen, touched, or recognized through any of the five senses are called *concrete nouns*. Nouns that name things that cannot be seen, touched, or recognized through any of the five senses are called *abstract nouns*.

Another special type of noun is used to name groups of persons or things. Nouns of this type are called *collective nouns*.

COLLECTIVE NOUNS:	team	flock
	community	household
	jury	troupe

EXERCISE A: Identifying Nouns. Each of the following sentences contains two nouns: one concrete noun and one abstract noun. Write the two nouns from each sentence on your paper. Then identify each noun as either *concrete* or *abstract*.

1. An <u>inventor</u> must have a good <u>imagination</u>. *con/ab*
2. Their <u>excitement</u> at the <u>zoo</u> was anticipated. *ab/con*
3. The <u>election</u> was held in the <u>auditorium</u>. *ab/con*
4. Poor <u>health</u> kept the frail <u>child</u> indoors. *ab/con*
5. Wild <u>animals</u> in <u>captivity</u> often seem pathetic. *con/ab*
6. The <u>artist</u> thought about her <u>plan</u> and began to paint. *con/ab*
7. The young <u>widower</u> did not want to know what the <u>future</u> held. *con/ab*
8. The <u>average</u> of his <u>tests</u> was not satisfactory. *ab/con*
9. Amazingly, our <u>team</u> scored once more and won the <u>championship</u>. *con/ab*
10. Her <u>presentation</u> to the <u>class</u> was entertaining and informative. *ab/con*

■ Compound Nouns

Some nouns, such as *high school* and *son-in-law*, consist of two or more words acting as a unit.

A **compound noun** is a noun that is made up of more than one word.

The following chart shows three ways compound nouns are formed.

TYPES OF COMPOUND NOUNS		
Separate Words	Hyphenated Words	Combined Words
fire engine	commander-in-chief	toothbrush
soap opera	jack-of-all-trades	dishwasher

EXERCISE B: Recognizing Compound Nouns. Each of the following sentences contains two or more nouns. Write the nouns from each sentence on your paper. Then circle the noun in each sentence that is compound.
Compound nouns are shaded.

1. The maid-of-honor at the wedding cried.
2. The back of the station wagon was loaded with luggage for the trip.
3. The gardener and his son filled the trash bags with leaves from the yard.
4. Jane has a good relationship with her mother-in-law.
5. The table was covered by a fine tablecloth and set with gleaming silver.
6. In the attic the children found a lampshade which had belonged to their aunt.
7. The fisherman wore a red feather tucked in his hat.
8. Few households are without an ironing board and iron.
9. A spoonful of butter was added to the lima beans.
10. After years of hard work, she reached the position of editor-in-chief.

■ Common and Proper Nouns

All nouns may be categorized as either *common nouns* or *proper nouns*.

A **common noun** names any one of a class of people, places, or things.

A **proper noun** names a specific person, place, or thing.

Proper nouns always begin with a capital letter, as the following chart indicates.

Common Nouns	Proper Nouns
novelist	Willa Cather, Henry James
continent	North America, Africa
planets	Mercury, Venus

NOTE ABOUT COMMON AND PROPER NOUNS: Some nouns that name family members may be either common or proper, depending upon the way they are used. A family name used to indicate a person's role is a common noun. A family name used as a title before a personal name is a proper noun.

COMMON: My best friend is my *cousin.*

PROPER: My best friend is *Cousin* Barry.

A *noun of direct address*—that is, the name of a person you are directly talking to—is always proper.

DIRECT ADDRESS: Please, *Dad,* may I go out tonight?

EXERCISE C: Distinguishing Between Common and Proper Nouns. Some of the following words are common nouns; some are proper nouns. For each common noun write two proper nouns that fall into the same category. For each proper noun write one common noun that falls into the same category. *Answers will vary; samples given.*

EXAMPLES: language   French, Spanish

              Nile   river

1. town *Dover, Liverpool*
2. book *Jane Eyre, Black Beauty*
3. author *Dickens, Alcott*
4. Labor Day *holiday*
5. state *Texas, Ohio*
6. woman *Mom, Ms. Wilson*
7. *Gone with the Wind* *novel*
8. lake *Lake Huron, Great Salt Lake*
9. George III *king*
10. organization *Girl Scouts, Kiwanis*

11. boy *Louis, Paul*   16. car *Ford, Toyota*
12. statue *the Pietá, Statue of Liberty*   17. mountain
13. relative *Grandma, Uncle Al*   18. United States *country*
14. building *Sears Tower, White House*   19. animal *Bambi, Lassie*
15. Asia *continent*   20. country *Canada, Bolivia*
17. Mt. St. Helen's, Mt. Everest

APPLICATION: Using Nouns in Sentences. Complete each of the following sentences with common and proper nouns as indicated. *Answers will vary; samples given.*

EXAMPLE: (Proper) paid a (common) for the (common).

Jenny paid a dollar for the bagels.

1. The (common) cheered with (common) during the (common). *crowd/delight/game*
2. Her (compound common) asked (proper) to buy (compound proper). *mother-in-law/Jane/Reader's Digest*
3. (Proper) was so excited that he broke a (common) and some (common). *Lou/glass/pencils*
4. The (common) looked forward to the (common) to (compound proper). *family/trip/Yellowstone Park*
5. (Proper) and (proper) trembled with (common) as the (common) came closer. *Ted/Antonia/fear/sound*
6. (Compound proper) and (proper) went shopping for (compound common). *Aunt Esther/Miriam/blue jeans*
7. The (common) ate the (common) and dreamed of (common). *man/cheese/demons*
8. A (compound common) was given to the (common) for (common). *sewing machine/woman/therapy*
9. (Common) and (common) are frequently found in (common). *gold/silver/mountains*
10. The (common) presented (proper) with a (common). *child/Edgar/rose*

1.2 Pronouns

Instead of repeating the same noun many times in conversation and writing, speakers and writers use substitutes called *pronouns.*

A **pronoun** is a word used to take the place of a noun or group of words acting as a noun.

In the following examples, the arrows point from the pronouns to the nouns they stand for. In the first sentence, the pronouns *you* and *your* stand for the noun *Tom.* In the second sentence, the pronoun *it* stands for *making lasagna for dinner.*

EXAMPLES: Tom, the editor, wants *you* to submit *your* article on football.

Making lasagna for dinner was easy, and *it* will be fun to do again.

■ Antecedents

A pronoun gets its meaning from the noun it stands for. This noun is called an *antecedent.*

> An **antecedent** is the noun (or group of words acting as a noun) for which a pronoun stands.

A pronoun's antecedent usually comes before the pronoun, as in the preceding examples. Sometimes, however, this pattern is reversed.

EXAMPLES: *That* is the best book I have ever read.

When *she* fell on the ski slope, Karen fractured her hip.

As you will see, pronouns usually have specific antecedents, but there are some exceptions. The rest of this section will present the different types of pronouns and discuss their antecedents.

EXERCISE A: Recognizing Antecedents. The underlined words in the following sentences are pronouns. Write the antecedent of each underlined pronoun on your paper.

1. Betty accomplished all of this work <u>herself</u>. *Betty*
2. The rocking horse was <u>one</u> that had been made in England. <u>It</u> was painted by hand. *rocking horse/rocking horse*
3. Mr. Jenkins gave a bonus to <u>all</u> of <u>his</u> employees and to <u>himself</u> also. *employees/Mr. Jenkins/Mr. Jenkins*
4. The audience was disappointed with the play, and <u>many</u> left before <u>it</u> was over. *audience/play*
5. Magnolias are trees <u>that</u> grow in the South. <u>They</u> produce beautiful white blossoms. *trees/Magnolias*

6. The class gave their petitions to the senator <u>himself</u>, <u>who</u> was glad to receive <u>them</u>. *senator/senator/petitions*
7. Jonathan, <u>these</u> are the best coffee beans grown in Brazil. Where did <u>you</u> buy <u>them</u>. *coffee beans/Jonathan/coffee beans*
8. <u>Those</u> are the strangest tropical fish in the store. *fish*
9. The group gave <u>themselves</u> credit for <u>their</u> hard work on the project. *group/group*
10. How could Matt prove <u>he</u> wrote that paper <u>himself</u>? *Matt/Matt*

■ Personal Pronouns and Reflexive and Intensive Pronouns

The pronouns you use most often to refer to yourself, to other people, and to things are called *personal pronouns. Reflexive* and *intensive pronouns* are formed by adding *-self* or *-selves* to some of the personal pronouns.

Personal Pronouns.   Personal pronouns are used more often than any other type of pronoun.

> **Personal pronouns** are pronouns that refer to (1) the person speaking, (2) the person spoken to, or (3) the person, place, or thing spoken about.

First-person pronouns refer to the person who is speaking. *Second-person pronouns* refer to the person spoken to. *Third-person pronouns* refer to the person, place, or thing spoken about.

PERSONAL PRONOUNS		
	Singular	**Plural**
First Person:	I, me, my, mine	we, us, our, ours
Second Person:	you, your, yours	you, your, yours
Third Person:	he, him, his, she her, hers, it, its	they, them, their, theirs

In the following examples, personal pronouns and their antecedents are used in sentences. In the first example, the antecedent is the person speaking. In the second example, the antecedent is the person being spoken to. And in the last example, the antecedent is the thing spoken about.

FIRST PERSON: *My* name is not George.

SECOND PERSON: After *you* left for school, I noticed *you* forgot *your* lunch.

THIRD PERSON: Don't judge a book by *its* cover.

Reflexive and Intensive Pronouns.   Pronouns ending in *-self* or *-selves* are either reflexive or intensive.

A **reflexive pronoun** is a pronoun ending in *-self* or *-selves* that adds information to a sentence by pointing back to a noun or pronoun near the beginning of the sentence.

An **Intensive pronoun** is a pronoun ending in *-self* or *-selves* that simply adds emphasis to a noun or pronoun.

The eight reflexive and intensive pronouns are shown in the following chart.

REFLEXIVE AND INTENSIVE PRONOUNS		
	Singular	**Plural**
First Person:	myself	ourselves
Second Person:	yourself	yourselves
Third Person:	himself, herself, itself	themselves

A reflexive pronoun always gives additional information in a sentence. It cannot be left out without changing the meaning of the sentence. In the first sentence in the following examples, *himself* tells whom Michael taught. In the second sentence, *herself* tells for whom the jeans were bought.

REFLEXIVE: Michael taught *himself* to play the piano.

Gloria bought *herself* a new pair of jeans.

An intensive pronoun does not add information. Instead, it gives emphasis to its antecedent. If an intensive pronoun is removed from a sentence, the sentence will still have the same meaning.

Usually an intensive pronoun immediately follows its antecedent, as shown in the first sentence in the following examples. Sometimes, however, an intensive pronoun is located in another part of the sentence, as shown in the second sentence.

INTENSIVE: The President *himself* attended the gala opening of the opera.

We spliced the film *ourselves*.

EXERCISE B: Identifying Personal Pronouns and Reflexive and Intensive Pronouns. Write the pronoun from each of the following sentences on your paper. Then identify each pronoun as *personal, reflexive,* or *intensive.*

1. Wearing a hat in winter conserves twenty percent of your body heat.   *pers*
2. Laura made herself a white satin dress for the dance.   *refl*
3. I can't concentrate on homework while the radio is playing.   *pers*
4. If the guests are going to be late, we should stop rushing.   *pers*
5. The Queen herself is coming to launch the ship.   *intens*
6. Jack promised himself a reward for faithfully sticking to the diet.   *refl*
7. A flying squirrel uses its tail as a rudder.   *pers*
8. The family harvested the wheat themselves.   *intens*
pers 9. Louise's good judgment while driving saved their lives.
intens 10. The sun itself is the source of energy, light, and warmth.

■ Demonstrative, Relative, and Interrogative Pronouns

Three other kinds of pronouns, called *demonstrative, relative,* and *interrogative* pronouns, have very special uses.

Pronouns That Point Out.   Pronouns that direct your attention to one or more nouns are called *demonstrative pronouns.*

A **demonstrative pronoun** is a pronoun that directs attention to a specific person, place, or thing.

The following chart shows the four demonstrative pronouns.

DEMONSTRATIVE PRONOUNS	
Singular	**Plural**
this, that	these, those

Demonstrative pronouns may be located before or after their antecedents.

BEFORE: *That* is the house I would like to own.

These are the colors I selected.

AFTER: The child asked for ⌐ice cream.⌐ *This* was her favorite dessert.

The florist delivered ⌐carnations and roses,⌐ but *those* were not the flowers I had ordered.

Pronouns That Relate. One of the demonstrative pronouns, *that,* can also be used as a *relative pronoun.*

A **relative pronoun** is a pronoun that begins a subordinate clause and relates it to another idea in the sentence.

Chapter 7 offers a discussion of clauses. The following chart shows the five relative pronouns that are used to introduce many clauses.

RELATIVE PRONOUNS				
that	which	who	whom	whose

The sentences in the following chart show relative pronouns used to connect one group of words, a subordinate clause, to another group of words, an independent clause.

Independent Clause	Subordinate Clause
He found the money	*that* he had lost.
I own one horse,	*which* has never won a race.
Jim is the carpenter	*who* made that bench.

Carl is the secretary *whom* the class elected.

We applauded the contestant *whose* answer was right.

NOTE ABOUT *WHO, THAT,* AND *WHICH:*   The relative pronoun *who* is always used to refer to people. The relative pronoun *that* can refer either to people or to things. The relative pronoun *which* is always used to refer to things.

PEOPLE: My cousin, *who* has lived in Florida all his life, is planning to move to Alaska.

The woman *that* bought his house came, coincidentally, from Alaska.

THINGS: The shoes *that* I bought last week hurt my feet.

Our barn, *which* was struck by lightning during yesterday's storm, luckily did not catch fire.

Pronouns That Ask Questions.   All of the relative pronouns except *that* can also be *interrogative pronouns.*

An **interrogative pronoun** is a pronoun used to begin a question.

The following chart shows the five interrogative pronouns.

INTERROGATIVE PRONOUNS
what   which   who   whom   whose

In the following examples, notice that some of the interrogative pronouns do not have specific antecedents.

EXAMPLES: *What* did you say?

There are many possible answers. *Which* is best?

Who is the person on the telephone?

With *whom* did you wish to speak?

Mine is blue. *Whose* is red?

EXERCISE C: Recognizing Demonstrative, Relative, and Interrogative Pronouns. Write the pronoun from each of the following sentences on your paper. Then identify each pronoun as *demonstrative, relative,* or *interrogative.*

1. The suspect gave the answer <u>that</u> the police were waiting for. *rel*
2. <u>Whom</u> did the Smiths invite to the beach party? *inter*
3. <u>That</u> is the screeching noise Jane told Lee about. *demon*
4. Jack the Ripper was a notorious killer <u>whom</u> the police never caught. *rel*
5. <u>Which</u> of the tables will look best in the kitchen? *inter*
6. Is <u>this</u> the book Steve wanted Dee to read? *demon*
7. <u>Which</u> of the planets are known to have rings? *inter*
8. Do <u>these</u> seem stronger than the other chairs? *demon*
9. Sal was the foreign visitor <u>whom</u> the students entertained. *rel*
10. Uranus, <u>which</u> is the seventh planet from the sun, has a ring. *rel*

■ Indefinite Pronouns

Besides interrogative pronouns, another kind of pronoun that often lacks a specific antecedent is the *indefinite pronoun.*

Indefinite pronouns are pronouns that refer to people, places, or things, often without specifying which ones.

Some of the most frequently used indefinite pronouns are shown in the following chart.

INDEFINITE PRONOUNS			
Singular		**Plural**	**Singular or Plural**
another	much	both	all
anybody	neither	few	any
anyone	nobody	many	more
anything	no one	others	most
each	nothing	several	none
either	one		some
everybody	other		
everyone	somebody		
everything	someone		
little	something		

Although indefinite pronouns often do not have specific antecedents, sometimes they may.

NO SPECIFIC ANTECEDENT: *Each* ate *everything* offered.

Somebody had *more* than *one*.

SPECIFIC ANTECEDENT: *Several* of the hockey players were injured this season.

You may have *both* of the cupcakes that are left.

EXERCISE D: **Identifying Indefinite Pronouns.** Copy the following sentences onto your paper, filling in the blanks with indefinite pronouns that will make the sentences logical. Avoid using the same pronoun more than once.
Answers will vary; samples given.

1. Jonathan has forgotten ___*everything*___ he learned.
2. ___*Nothing*___ has been done to inform ___*anyone*___ .
3. Does ___*anybody*___ know where the supplies are?
4. You may take ___*some*___ of the packages, but do not take ___*all*___ .
5. They sent ___*most*___ of the invitations to their friends.
6. As a visitor to this country, he knew ___*something*___ of the customs but ___*little*___ of the language.
7. Are ___*any*___ of the guests here yet?
8. Rebecca has lost ___*none*___ of her charm.
9. He shares what he has with ___*everyone*___ and still Owen has ___*more*___ than he needs.
10. ___*One*___ of the boys looks a lot like his father.

APPLICATION: **Writing Sentences with Pronouns.** Copy the following paragraph onto your paper, supplying a pronoun for each blank. Write the type of pronoun—*personal, reflexive, intensive, demonstrative, relative, interrogative,* or *indefinite*—over each pronoun you supply. *Answers will vary; samples given.*

Maude's parents took (1) ___*her–pers*___ to the finest restaurant in town. The hostess led (2) ___*them–pers*___ to a table (3) ___*that–rel*___ was located in the center of the dining room. Maude's father said (4) ___*everyone–indef*___ could order (5) ___*anything–indef*___ (6) ___*that–rel*___ was on the menu. He (7) ___*himself–intens*___ preferred the veal cutlet, and (8) ___*his–pers*___ wife always had shrimp. Maude ordered lobster for (9) ___*herself–refl*___ . After dinner the waiter asked, "Would (10) ___*you–pers*___ like some dessert?" (11) ___*No one–indef*___ wanted (12) ___*anything–indef*___ . Later, (13) ___*all–indef*___ agreed the evening was (14) ___*one–indef*___ (15) ___*that–rel*___ they would remember.

Action and Linking Verbs 1.3

Nouns are an essential part of language because they name all persons, places, and things. Verbs are also essential because they give life to nouns by allowing people to make statements about them.

A **verb** is a word that expresses time while showing an action, a condition, or the fact that something exists.

Action	Condition	Existence
Sue *threw* the ball.	The puppy *is* sick.	People *were* everywhere.

This section will discuss the two main kinds of verbs: *action verbs* (verbs that express action) and *linking verbs* (verbs that express condition).

■ Verbs That Show Action

Verbs that tell what someone or something does, did, or will do are called *action verbs*.

An **action verb** is a verb that tells what action someone or something is performing.

In the first sentence in the following examples, the verb tells what action Hank performed. Similarly in the second sentence, the verb tells what the parakeet does.

ACTION VERBS: Hank *painted* the tool shed.

The parakeet *swings* back and forth in its cage.

The person or thing that performs the action is called the *subject* of the verb. In the preceding examples, the subject *Hank* did the painting, and the subject *parakeet* does the swinging.

The examples used thus far show action verbs that represent visible action. Some action verbs, however, represent mental actions, which are not visible. When people *forget,* *believe,* or *think,* they are performing mental actions.

MENTAL ACTION: Jefferson *thought* about the problem.

Other verbs, such as *sleep, hear,* or *relax,* also seem to show little action, but they are still action verbs.

EXERCISE A: Recognizing Action Verbs. Write an action verb that completes each of the following sentences on your paper. After each verb, write *visible* or *mental* to identify the kind of action the verb shows. *Answers will vary; samples given.*

1. They ___wondered___ about life on the planet Mars. *mental*
2. Someone ___said___ it was almost midnight. *visible*
3. The ping-pong ball ___bounced___ from the table to the floor. *visible*
4. A dog house ___shelters___ its inhabitant from the rain. *visible*
5. The witches ___stirred___ their terrible brew. *visible*
6. Why don't you ___relax___ for a few minutes after such a hard day? *visible*
7. No one ___expected___ the dismal weather. *mental*
8. The carpenter ___planed___ the pine boards. *visible*
9. The waitress ___stared___ at the soggy mess. *visible*
10. How did the pilot ___know___ where to land? *mental*

■ Transitive and Intransitive Action Verbs

An action verb may be *transitive* or *intransitive* depending on whether or not it transfers its action to another word in the sentence.

An action verb is **transitive** if it directs action toward someone or something named in the same sentence.

An action verb is **intransitive** if it does not direct action toward someone or something named in the same sentence.

The word that receives the action of a transitive verb is called the *object* of the verb. In the following examples, *pictures* is the object of *took,* and *something* is the object of *baked.*

TRANSITIVE VERBS: The camera *took* clear pictures.

Irene *baked* something for the bake sale.

Intransitive verbs do not have objects. The action is not directed toward any noun or pronoun in the sentence.

INTRANSITIVE VERBS: The hurricane *blew* over the mainland.

Sandy *smiled* happily.

To find out whether a verb used in a sentence is transitive or intransitive, ask *Whom?* or *What?* after the verb. If there is an answer in the sentence, the verb is transitive. If no answer can be found, the verb is intransitive.

TRANSITIVE: Robert *polished* his shoes.

(Polished *what?*)

shoes

INTRANSITIVE: Linda *waited* for the bus.

(Waited *what?*)

no answer

Most action verbs can be transitive or intransitive, depending on their use in the sentence. Some, however, can be either transitive or intransitive, but not both.

TRANSITIVE OR INTRANSITIVE: I *wrote* that letter.

The secretary *wrote* quickly.

ALWAYS TRANSITIVE: California wines now *rival* those of France.

ALWAYS INTRANSITIVE: When the dentist touched my tooth, I *winced*.

Consult a dictionary if you are uncertain about whether an action verb should have an object.

EXERCISE B: Distinguishing Between Transitive and Intransitive Action Verbs. Write the verb from each of the following sentences on your paper. After each verb, write *transitive* or *intransitive* to identify how the verb is used. If the verb is transitive, write its object as well. *Objects are shaded.*

1. The birdcage <u>swung</u> from a golden chain. *intrans*
2. Margaret angrily <u>crumpled</u> her letter in her fist. *trans*
3. Someone <u>answered</u> that question. *trans*
4. He <u>shuddered</u> with fright during the scary part of the movie. *intrans*

5. The rats <u>chewed</u> their way into the old house. *trans*
6. Acorns <u>drop</u> from the trees every fall. *intrans*
7. Charlie <u>combed</u> his hair nervously before the dance. *trans*
8. We <u>bought</u> paper napkins for the picnic. *trans*
9. Zelda <u>smiled</u> at the thought of a parade in the snow. *intrans*
10. Fish and potatoes <u>sizzled</u> in the pan. *intrans*

■ Verbs That Link

Verbs that do not show action are called *linking verbs* because they link, or join, two or more words in the sentence.

A **linking verb** is a verb that connects its subject with a word at or near the end of the sentence.

Linking verbs allow the words at or near the end of a sentence to express the condition of the subject. In the following examples, *was* connects *Queen* with the subject *Victoria*, and *is* connects *miserable* with the subject *child*.

LINKING VERBS:　Victoria *was* Queen from 1837 to 1901.

The feverish child *is* miserable.

Forms of Be.　The preceding examples both use verbs that are forms of *be*, the most common linking verb, but also the one with the most variety of forms. Take some time to study the following chart so that you will recognize this important verb in all of its different forms.

THE FORMS OF *BE*			
am	am being	can be	have been
are	are being	could be	has been
is	is being	may be	had been
was	was being	might be	could have been
were	were being	must be	may have been
		shall be	might have been
		should be	must have been
		will be	shall have been
		would be	should have been
			will have been
			would have been

NOTE ABOUT VERBS EXPRESSING EXISTENCE: The forms of *be* do not always function as linking verbs. Instead, they may express existence, usually by showing where something is located.

EXAMPLES: The guests *may be* here soon.

Your shirt *is* in the closet.

There *are* several mistakes in that article.

Other Verbs That Link.   Forms of *be* are the most commonly used linking verbs, but some other verbs may also be linking verbs.

OTHER LINKING VERBS					
appear	feel	look	seem	sound	taste
become	grow	remain	smell	stay	turn

The verbs shown here act as linking verbs in the same way the forms of *be* do. These verbs also allow words at or near the end of the sentence to name or describe the subject of the sentence.

EXAMPLES: He *remained* a hermit for many years.

The music *sounded* tuneless to her.

EXERCISE C: **Recognizing Forms of *Be* Used as Linking Verbs.** Copy each of the following sentences onto your paper. Underline the form of *be* in each. Then draw a double-headed arrow to show which words are linked by the verb.

EXAMPLE: We should have been the champions.
Words linked are shaded.

1. English setters are good field dogs.
2. Albert was being very gentle with the newborn kittens.
3. A chef should be creative in the kitchen.
4. The sharp knife is the one on the counter.
5. She should have been an Olympic gold medalist.
6. This doughnut is not very fresh.
7. They are being very prompt with their payments.
8. At sunset the sky was a soft pink.
9. We will be the first customers in the door.
10. It had been a long and difficult day.

EXERCISE D: Identifying Other Linking Verbs. Copy each of the following sentences onto your paper. Underline the linking verb in each. Then draw a double-headed arrow to show which words are linked by the verb.

EXAMPLE: Many people seemed confused.

1. She turned blue from the cold.
2. The foghorn sounded strange in the darkness.
3. Those crabapples on the ground taste bitter.
4. After years of crime, he finally became a good citizen.
5. They remained cheerful in spite of their hardships.
6. Ken and Murray stayed business partners for many successful years.
7. An expensive perfume smells different from a cheaper one.
8. They appeared older after their terrifying experience.
9. The baby's hair felt sticky from the candy.
10. This coat looks too small for you.

■ Linking or Action?

Most of the verbs in the chart on page 35 can be used as either linking or action verbs, as the following examples show.

LINKING: The warm milk *turned* sour.

ACTION: She *turned* the handle. (transitive)

LINKING: The suede *felt* soft.

ACTION: Marion *felt* for the lightswitch. (intransitive)

To decide whether a verb is being used as a linking verb or as an action verb, substitute *am, are,* or *is* for the verb. If the substituted verb makes sense while connecting two words, then the original verb is a linking verb. If the substituted verb makes an illogical sentence or fails to connect two words, then the original verb is an action verb.

EXAMPLES: The sea breeze *felt* refreshing.

The sea breeze *is* refreshing.
Linking

Henry *felt* the rough surface.

Henry *is* the rough surface.
Action

EXERCISE E: Distinguishing Between Linking Verbs and Action Verbs. Each of the verbs in the following list should be used twice to complete the following sentences—once as an action verb and once as a linking verb. Write an appropriate form of the verb for each sentence on your paper. After each verb, write *action verb* or *linking verb*.

> feel   grow   look   sound   taste

1. His voice ___*sounds*___ peculiar on the phone. *LV*
2. In their garden they ___*grow*___ tomatoes, lettuce, and carrots. *AV*
3. Marion's clam sauce always ___*tastes*___ slightly sweet. *LV*
4. If Jeff ___*feels*___ sick, he should stay home. *LV*
5. The soldier's face ___*grew*___ pale when he heard the sad news. *LV*
6. Mr. Blake ___*felt*___ a bump rising on his aching forehead. *AV*
7. Our furniture ___*looks*___ new after being reupholstered. *LV*
8. The boy on horseback ___*sounded*___ the alarm as the enemy approached. *AV*
9. Let's ___*look*___ for a birthday card after school. *AV*
10. Just ___*taste*___ this homemade fudge. *AV*

APPLICATION: Writing Sentences with Linking and Action Verbs. Use each of the following verbs in two sentences of your own. In the first sentence, use the verb as a linking verb. In the second, use the same verb as an action verb.
Answers will vary; samples given for first and last.

> appear   feel   grow   look   smell

1. The actor appeared nervous.   *5. The milk smells fresh.*
Storm clouds appeared on the horizon.   *Ferdinand smelled the flowers.*

Helping Verbs 1.4

A single verb may consist of as many as four words. Functioning as a unit, these words are called a *verb phrase*.

Helping verbs are verbs that can be added to another verb to make a single **verb phrase.**

■ Helping Verbs

All the forms of *be* listed on page 34 can be used as helping verbs. The verbs listed in the following chart can also be helping verbs.

HELPING VERBS OTHER THAN *BE*			
do	have	shall	can
does	has	should	could
did	had	will	may
		would	might
			must

Helping verbs are sometimes called *auxiliary verbs* or *auxiliaries* because they help add meaning to other verbs. Notice how helping verbs change the meaning of the following sentences.

Without Helping Verbs	With Helping Verbs
I *talk* on the telephone.	I *will talk* on the telephone.
The sparrows *repaired* their nest.	The sparrows *must have repaired* their nest.
He *returned* that book.	He *should have returned* that book.

EXERCISE A: **Supplying Helping Verbs.** Complete each of the following sentences with appropriate helping verbs. Add the number of helping verbs indicated by the numbers in the blanks. *Answers will vary; samples given.*

1. A shark ___was 1___ swimming in the shallow water.
2. Todd's car ___will be 2___ repaired at the gas station.
3. In the winter, our driveway ___should be 2___ plowed after a heavy snowfall.
4. ___Have 1___ we ___been 1___ keeping our equipment in the locker room?
5. The woodcutter ___had been 2___ sawing more carefully.
6. Carol ___should 1___ certainly not ___be 1___ going to the fair.
7. Poodles ___could 1___ be the smartest of the canines.
8. Sandals ___are 1___ not considered appropriate for a vacation in Siberia.
9. How many planets ___will 1___ we ___have 1___ discovered by the year 2000?
10. No species of insect ___has 1___ yet become extinct.

■ Locating Helping Verbs in Sentences

As you can see in Exercise A, a verb and its helping verbs are often interrupted by other words, especially in questions.

UNINTERRUPTED VERB PHRASE: The groundhog *will see* its shadow.

INTERRUPTED VERB PHRASES: The groundhog *will* probably never *see* its shadow.

Will the groundhog *see* its shadow?

EXERCISE B: **Locating Verbs with Helping Verbs.** The following paragraph contains twenty-five verb phrases. Write each of the verb phrases on your paper. Then circle the helping verbs. *Verb phrases are underlined; helping verbs are shaded.*

(1) Contact lenses are becoming increasingly popular today. (2) Many people are finding that the convenience is worth the expense. (3) If you are presently considering whether or not you should invest in contacts, which can be bought almost anywhere glasses are sold, you should definitely know these facts. (4) More contacts have been lost down the drain as they were being inserted than while the lenses were actually being worn. (5) Therefore, lenses should be inserted carefully. (6) If you do drop a lens, you must remember that if you should step on it, you will probably scratch it. (7) Then replacement of the lens would be necessary. (8) A scratch on the lens might seriously damage your eye. (9) Precautions must also be taken so that all protein deposits are removed. (10) Even a thin film of protein build-up can impair your vision. (11) Will you be happy with contact lenses? (12) Will the problems outweigh the benefits? (13) Will you be one of the successful wearers, or will you join the ranks of those who have failed?

APPLICATION: Writing Sentences with Helping Verbs. Use each of the following verb phrases in a sentence as indicated. *Answers will vary; samples given for first two.*
1. had been talking (Use the verb phrase in a question.)
2. might know (Interrupt the verb phrase with *not.*)
3. could have been laughing (Interrupt the verb phrase with *certainly.*)
4. will have left (Use the verb phrase in a question.)
5. can be used (Interrupt the verb phrase with *hardly ever.*)
1. Had you been talking on the phone? 2. I might not know my kindergarten teacher now.

Chapter 2

Adjectives and Adverbs

If the English language were limited to nouns, pronouns, and verbs, only the simplest kind of communication would be possible. These three parts of speech are used to convey essential ideas, such as "I need food," but for more descriptive and detailed communication two other parts of speech are necessary: *adjectives* and *adverbs*. Without adjectives you would not be able to describe, for example, what kind of food you need (*fresh, hot, nutritious,* and so on) or how much (*enough, little, much*). Moreover, without adverbs you would not be able to indicate, for example, when the food is needed (*now, soon, daily*).

These two parts of speech that add description and detail to your written and spoken words are called *modifiers*. How adjectives and adverbs modify other words will be shown in the next two sections.

2.1 Adjectives

Whenever you want to create a clearer picture of a person, place, or thing, you are likely to use adjectives.

An **adjective** is a word used to describe a noun or pronoun or to give a noun or pronoun a more specific meaning.

The means by which an adjective describes a word or makes it more specific is called *modification*.

■ The Process of Modification

Modification is the act of changing something slightly. An adjective modifies a noun or pronoun by adding information that answers any of the following four questions: *What kind? Which one? How many? How much?* In the following chart, the examples show adjectives that answer these questions.

What Kind?	
large couch	*lost* boy
metallic gleam	*purple* sage
Which One?	
that necklace	*those* carts
other door	*last* opportunity
How Many?	
both apples	*some* possibilities
five dollars	*frequent* interruptions
How Much?	
enough homework	*more* fun
sufficient time	*adequate* pay

As shown in the preceding examples, an adjective usually comes before the noun it modifies. Sometimes, however, an adjective follows the noun, as shown in the second example that follows.

BEFORE THE NOUN: The *silver* ornament was in the window.

AFTER THE NOUN: The ornament in the window was *silver*.

When an adjective modifies a pronoun, the most common pattern is for the adjective to follow the pronoun, usually after a linking verb, such as *are* or *become*. However, it may also precede the pronoun.

AFTER THE PRONOUN: They were *hungry* after the hike.

BEFORE THE PRONOUN: *Hungry* after the hike, they stopped to eat.

Two or more adjectives can be used to modify the same word. In the following example, all the adjectives modify *mutts*.

EXAMPLE: *Several large shaggy* mutts were in the kennel.

NOTE ABOUT *A, AN,* AND *THE*:   Three adjectives—*a, an,* and *the*—are called *articles. The* is termed a *definite article* because it refers to a specific noun. *A* and *an* are termed *indefinite articles* because they refer to any one of a class of nouns. In the following examples, *the* refers to a specific book, whereas *a* refers to any kind of *car*, and *an* refers to any kind of *answer.*

DEFINITE: Let me see *the* book.

INDEFINITE: We would like *a* new car.

Lynn wants *an* answer.

EXERCISE A: Recognizing Adjectives. The following sentences contain a total of twenty adjectives, not including articles. Write the adjective(s) in each sentence on your paper. Be prepared to identify the words modified by the adjectives. *Modified words are shaded.*

1. The dull walls and dingy carpet give the room a somber atmosphere.
2. The lonesome howl of a coyote came from the woods.
3. With gray faces and hesitant steps, they approached the haunted house.
4. After an airplane crash, there are usually few survivors.
5. On the last day of the month, you have an important medical appointment.
6. There wasn't enough money to pay the bill.
7. If you add milk to the scrambled eggs, a dozen eggs will feed everyone.
8. Bluefish give fishermen a good fight.
9. The brilliant diamonds decorated red and calloused hands.
10. The knife was silvery in the shadows.

■ Compound and Proper Adjectives

Adjectives share some of the characteristics of nouns.
Compound Adjectives.   Like nouns, adjectives can be compound.

A **compound adjective** is an adjective that is made up of more than one word.

Most compound adjectives are hyphenated, but some are written as combined words.

Hyphenated	Combined
freeze-dried coffee	*farsighted* planner
heavy-duty boots	*underpaid* staff

If you are uncertain about the spelling of a compound adjective, consult a dictionary.

Proper Adjectives. Also like nouns, some adjectives can be proper.

A **proper adjective** is an adjective formed from a proper noun.

Like proper nouns, proper adjectives begin with a capital letter.

Proper Nouns	Proper Adjectives
Shakespeare	*Shakespearean* play
Germany	*Germanic* tribes

EXERCISE B: Recognizing Compound and Proper Adjectives. Each of the following sentences contains one or two adjectives, not including articles. List them on your paper. Then label them *compound* or *proper*.

1. The red-cheeked girl on the corner was selling Turkish taffy. *cpd/prop*
2. The foolishness of the actions was self-evident. *cpd*
3. The wide-mouthed bass struggled to free itself from the hook. *cpd*
4. At the hospital open-heart surgery is performed by a well-qualified surgeon. *cpd/cpd*
5. In combat the horse remained steadfast. *cpd*
6. We bought the Victorian table for the hallway. *prop*
7. Although Phil was well-liked, he preferred to live in an out-of-the-way place. *cpd/cpd*

8. Years after Les moved to Wisconsin, he still had a <u>Bostonian</u> accent. *prop*
9. He wore a <u>waterproof</u> <u>Icelandic</u> parka. *cpd/prop*
10. The hostess served a <u>Scandinavian</u> meal to the guests. *prop*

■ Nouns, Pronouns, and Verbs Used as Adjectives

Each of the three parts of speech presented in the last chapter—nouns, pronouns, and verbs—can be used as adjectives.

Nouns Used as Adjectives.   Many common and proper nouns can be used as adjectives. They become adjectives when they modify other nouns by answering either the question *What kind?* or the question *Which one?*

Nouns	Adjectives
Common Nouns	
pineapple	*pineapple* juice (*What kind* of juice?)
summer	*summer* vacation (*Which* vacation?)
Proper Nouns	
Vermont	*Vermont* cheddar (*What kind* of cheddar?)
Brahms	the *Brahms* symphony (*Which* symphony?)

Pronouns Used as Adjectives.   Just as nouns can be used as adjectives, so can certain pronouns. Used as adjectives, pronouns become *possessive adjectives, demonstrative adjectives, interrogative adjectives,* or *indefinite adjectives.*

Seven of the personal pronouns function as *possessive adjectives.* They are still pronouns because they have antecedents, but they are also adjectives because they answer the question *Which one?*

POSSESSIVE ADJECTIVES
my   your   his   her   its   our   their

The team found *their* lost mascot.

(As a pronoun, *their* has the antecedent *team*.) │ (As an adjective, *their* modifies *mascot*.)

Whether you discuss these words as adjectives or as pronouns, remember the essential word is *possessive*.

All of the demonstrative pronouns may also be used as *demonstrative adjectives.* As adjectives, each must modify a noun that follows it within a sentence. Though other words can come between a demonstrative adjective and the word it modifies, the adjective is never immediately followed by a verb.

DEMONSTRATIVE ADJECTIVES	
this that these those	
Demonstrative Pronouns	**Demonstrative Adjectives**
Did you buy *this*?	Did you buy *this* book?
Those are old newspapers.	*Those* old newspapers have turned yellow.

Like demonstrative pronouns, three of the interrogative pronouns become *interrogative adjectives* when they modify a noun within a sentence.

INTERROGATIVE ADJECTIVES	
which what whose	
Interrogative Pronouns	**Interrogative Adjectives**
What happened?	*What* color looks best?
Whose is that?	*Whose* scarf is orange?

Many of the indefinite pronouns may, in like manner, become *indefinite adjectives* when they modify a noun within the sentence. Whether they are used to modify singular or plural nouns is shown in the following chart.

INDEFINITE ADJECTIVES		
Used with Singular Nouns	**Used with Plural Nouns**	**Used with Singular or Plural Nouns**
another	both	all
each	few	any

either	many	more
little	several	most
much		other
neither		some
one		

Indefinite Pronouns	Indefinite Adjectives
I would like *another*.	He asked for *another* piece.
Few remembered the event.	Very *few* people will come.
They needed *some* for today.	He will think of *some* excuse.
	Mary wants *some* colored pencils.

Notice that, in the third sentence on the right, *some* modifies a singular noun, *excuse*. In the last sentence, *some* modifies a plural noun, *pencils*.

Verbs Used as Adjectives.   Many verbs, especially those forms ending in *-ing* or *-ed*, can also be used as adjectives.

Verbs	Adjectives
The chipmunk *was chattering* noisily.	The *chattering* chipmunk was noisy.
The chocolate *melted* in the sun.	The *melted* chocolate had been in the sun.

More detailed information about verbs used as adjectives is found in Section 6.3.

EXERCISE C: Recognizing Nouns, Pronouns, and Verbs Used as Adjectives. Each of the following sentences contains one blank where an adjective should be added. Write each sentence on your paper, supplying the kind of adjective indicated. *Answers will vary; samples given.*

1. The ___*hockey*___ player was cheered by the crowd. (noun used as an adjective)
2. ___*Our*___ bus never came, and we were late for work. (personal pronoun used as an adjective)

3. Harvey will never wear ___*those*___ ties. (demonstrative adjective)
4. ___*What*___ human being could endure such a climate? (interrogative adjective)
5. Max told his ___*giggling*___ son to be quiet. (verb used as an adjective)
6. I misplaced ___*my*___ keys and I can't get in the house. (personal pronoun used as an adjective)
7. Inside the ___*school*___ yard children romped and played. (noun used as an adjective)
8. ___*Whose*___ mail was placed in our mailbox? (interrogative adjective)
9. Roger declared ___*neither*___ candidate was qualified for the job. (indefinite adjective)
10. She paid too much for the ___*raccoon*___ coat. (noun used as an adjective)

APPLICATION:Writing Sentences with Adjectives. Rewrite each of the following sentences to include two or more adjectives. Use at least one compound adjective, one proper adjective, and one noun, pronoun, or verb used as an adjective. *Answers will vary; samples given.*

1. He could not swallow the food. *terrible, overcooked*
2. Mickey bought a sweater and a pair of pants. *brown/matching corduroy*
3. The seagull's wing trailed on the sand. *broken/Canadian*
4. Mistletoe is a plant whose berries are poisonous. *Christmas/tiny white*
5. Snow covered the branches and ground. *Glistening/pine/surrounding*
6. Donald finally selected a toy for his sister. *wind-up/younger*
7. They made posters to announce the coming of the carnival. *colorful/traveling*
8. A stream flowed past the fence. *narrow/pasture*
9. In the evening, fireflies flashed in the darkness. *July/blinking*
10. At the zoo they saw seals begging for fish. *San Diego/many barking*

Adverbs 2.2

Like adjectives, adverbs are used to describe or add information about other words.

An adverb is a word that modifies a verb, an adjective, or another adverb.

Just as adjectives answer specific questions about nouns and pronouns, adverbs answer questions about verbs, adjectives, and other adverbs. When an adverb modifies a verb, it answers any of these four questions: *Where? When? In what manner? To what extent?* When an adverb modifies an adjective or another adverb, it answers the question *To what extent?*

■ Adverbs with Verbs, Adjectives, and Other Adverbs

The following chart shows adverbs answering each of these four questions. Notice the positions of the adverbs. When an adverb modifies a verb or verb phrase, it may come after or before the verb or verb phrase. Frequently it comes within the verb phrase. If an adverb modifies an adjective or another adverb, it generally comes immediately before the adjective or other adverb.

ADVERBS MODIFYING VERBS	
Where?	**When?**
slide *under*	*often* asks
move *near*	sails *daily*
sit *there*	should have answered *promptly*
slipped *between*	*soon* will depart
In What Manner?	**To What Extent?**
reacted *positively*	*widely* read
silently nodded	*barely* walks
rudely laughed	had *just* started
was *cheerfully* humming	must *not* have finished
ADVERBS MODIFYING ADJECTIVES	**ADVERBS MODIFYING ADVERBS**
To What Extent?	**To What Extent?**
very tall	search *very* thoroughly
somewhat satisfied	*not* exactly right
frequently absent	jumped *more* quickly
not sad	*quite* definitely decided

EXERCISE A: Recognizing Adverbs. Eight of the following sentences contain one adverb. Two sentences contain two adverbs. Divide your paper into three columns as shown. Then write the necessary words in the appropriate columns.
Modified words are shaded; answers at right give part of speech of words modified and question answered.
EXAMPLE: The otter swam very rapidly.

Adverb	Modified Word and Part of Speech	Question Answered by the Adverb
rapidly	swam, verb	in what manner
very	rapidly, adverb	to what extent

1. We will be going to the movies soon. *verb–when*
2. The starving refugees needed much more food. *adj–extent*
3. Will you definitely move to Ohio? *verb–extent*
4. Everyone thought the movie was too violent. *adj–extent*
5. He frowned rather sternly at the boy's antics. *verb–manner/adv–extent*
6. Our cat does not like cat food but prefers people food. *verb–extent*
7. They released multicolored balloons which floated away. *verb–where*
8. Some students have nearly completed their term papers. *verb–extent*
9. Todd accepted the suggestion surprisingly quickly.
10. Sharon was remarkably indifferent to her surroundings.
9. verb–manner/adv–extent   10. adj–extent

■ Nouns Used as Adverbs

A few words that are usually nouns can also be used as adverbs that answer the question *Where?* or *When?* Some of these words are *home, yesterday, today, tomorrow, mornings, afternoons, evenings,* and *nights.*

Nouns	Adverbs
Our *home* is in Lubbock.	Let's go *home*. (Go *where?*)
The summer *nights* have been humid.	My father works *nights*. (Works *when?*)

EXERCISE B: Recognizing Nouns Used as Adverbs. There are ten adverbs in the following sentences; four of them are nouns used as adverbs. List the ten adverbs on your paper and circle the ones that are nouns used as adverbs.
Nouns used as adverbs are shaded.
1. Evenings they would sit by the fire and vehemently discuss politics.

2. The nurse sent me home because I had a very high fever.
3. Tuesday was a bad day for me: Sometime during the afternoon I lost my wallet; later, I broke my glasses.
4. You must definitely see a doctor today.
5. If you decide to visit me tomorrow, please come early.

■ Adverb or Adjective?

Some words can be either adjectives or adverbs, depending upon how they are used in sentences.

ADVERB: He walked *straight* down the path.

ADJECTIVE: The path was *straight*.

ADVERB: She dived *deep* below the surface.

ADJECTIVE   The *deep* water was dark blue.

Most often, however, adjectives and adverbs do not share the same form. Many adverbs, in fact, are formed by adding *-ly* to an adjective.

Adjectives	Adverbs with *-ly* Endings
honest answer	answered *honestly*
quick movement	moved *quickly*
perfect knowledge	knows *perfectly*

All words ending in *-ly*, however, are not adverbs. Some adjectives have *-ly* endings.

ADJECTIVES: Carla's *weekly* allowance was not much.

The bread I baked was *mealy*.

EXERCISE C: Distinguishing Between Adverbs and Adjectives. In the following pairs of sentences, one sentence contains an underlined adverb, and the other contains the same word, or a different form of the word, used as an adjective. Indicate on your paper which of the underlined words is an adverb and which is an adjective. Then write the modified word and be prepared to tell its part of speech.

EXAMPLE: His room was very <u>neat</u>. adjective room

He <u>neatly</u> put his room in order. adverb put

1. The mounted moosehead looked <u>real</u>. *adj–moosehead (noun)*
   I <u>really</u> believed the weather forecast. *adv–believed (verb)*
2. Bertram walks to the office <u>daily</u>. *adv–walks (verb)*   *adj–news-*
   Our office runs advertisements in the <u>daily</u> newspaper. *paper (noun)*
3. Matilda spoke <u>darkly</u> of her husband's past. *adv–spoke (verb)*
   No light filtered into the <u>dark</u> cell. *adj–cell (noun)*
4. The immigrants who laid the railroad tracks worked
   <u>hard</u>. *adv–worked (verb)*
   Sandstone is not a <u>hard</u> rock. *adj–rock (noun)*
5. Zack is an <u>early</u> riser. *adj–riser (noun)*
   Mildred starts the day <u>early</u> and finishes late. *adv–starts (verb)*
6. I will <u>gladly</u> finish the dishes. *adv–will finish (verb)*
   We are <u>glad</u> to have you as a friend. *adj–we (pron)*
7. When he received his inheritance, he was suddenly <u>rich</u>.
   The musketeer was <u>richly</u> dressed in velvet and doeskin.
8. After scrubbing the floor, his hands were <u>rough</u>. *adj–hands (noun)*
   He <u>roughly</u> stroked the German shepherd. *adv–stroked (verb)*
9. We stared <u>dismally</u> at the destruction. *adv–stared (verb)*
   Her outlook on life is <u>dismal</u>. *adj–outlook (noun)*   *adj–cost*
10. Today's <u>high</u> cost of living causes people to be thrifty. *(noun)*
    His past employer spoke <u>highly</u> of him. *adv–spoke (verb)*

7. adj–he (pron)   adv–was dressed (verb)

APPLICATION: Writing Sentences with Adverbs. Rewrite each
of the following sentences to include two or more adverbs.
Include at least one noun used as an adverb.
Answers will vary; samples given.

1. Tony will go to the grocery store for us. *Surely/today*
2. Barn swallows are helpful because they eat insects. *often very*
3. His poor posture made him seem shorter than he was.
4. The sorcerer cast a terrible spell upon the town. *Then/truly*
5. We were sad about the end of summer. *Naturally/rather*
6. Many people think snails are delicious. *today/extremely*
7. The boat docked and lowered its sails. *smoothly/then*
8. Their enthusiasm faded. *suddenly/dramatically*
9. Night fell and the celebration began. *finally/immediately*
10. Can a helicopter rescue those men? *really/today*

3. sometimes/really

Chapter 3

Prepositions, Conjunctions, and Interjections

The next two sections will deal with the last three parts of speech. As you will see, prepositions relate words, conjunctions join words, and interjections serve as attention-getters.

3.1 Prepositions

Although there are fewer prepositions in English than there are nouns, verbs, adjectives, or adverbs, prepositions are essential for clear communication. They are needed to relate one word to another within sentences.

 A **preposition** is a word that relates the noun or pronoun following it to another word in the sentence.

■ Words Used as Prepositions

Sixty of the words most often used as prepositions are listed in the following chart.

FREQUENTLY USED PREPOSITIONS				
aboard	before	despite	off	throughout
about	behind	down	on	till
above	below	during	onto	to
across	beneath	except	opposite	toward
after	beside	for	out	under

against	besides	from	outside	underneath
along	between	in	over	until
amid	beyond	inside	past	up
among	but	into	regarding	upon
around	by	like	round	with
at	concerning	near	since	within
barring	considering	of	through	without

Some prepositions consist of more than one word and are called *compound prepositions.*

COMPOUND PREPOSITIONS			
according to	because of	in place of	next to
ahead of	by means of	in regard to	on account of
apart from	in addition to	in spite of	out of
as of	in back of	instead of	owing to
aside from	in front of	in view of	prior to

Notice in the following examples how the choice of preposition affects the relationship between the italicized words. By changing the relationship between the words, each preposition gives the sentence a completely different meaning.

EXAMPLES: We were frightened by a *snake* $\begin{cases} \text{inside} \\ \text{near} \\ \text{underneath} \\ \text{in back of} \end{cases}$ the *house.*

He *spoke* $\begin{cases} \text{about} \\ \text{with} \\ \text{without} \\ \text{in spite of} \end{cases}$ *pain.*

EXERCISE A: Recognizing Prepositions. Write each of the following sentences on your paper, filling in the blanks with appropriate prepositions of the types indicated.

Answers will vary; samples given.

1. Every store ___*except*___ this one is having a sale.
   (single preposition)
2. Water lilies floated ___*on*___ the surface of the pond.
   (single preposition)
3. Some dwarf fruit trees grew ___*next to*___ the house.
   (compound preposition)

4. _According to_ the authorities, the alleged robbers were caught. (compound preposition)
5. A lantern's gleam could be seen ____ _in_ ____ the tunnel. (single preposition)
6. Please buy construction paper _in addition to_ scissors and glue. (compound preposition)
7. Wonder Woman jumped ____ _from_ ____ the balcony. (single preposition)
8. Randy has strong feelings ____ _about_ ____ discrimination. (single preposition)
9. _Because of_ the water shortage, we will be careful. (compound preposition)
10. His ancestors left Ireland ____ _during_ ____ the potato famine. (single preposition)

■ Prepositional Phrases

Within a sentence a preposition is always followed by a noun or pronoun. The group of words beginning with a preposition and ending with a noun or pronoun is called a *prepositional phrase*. The noun or pronoun that follows a preposition is called the *object of the preposition*. One preposition can have two or more objects, as the last example in the following chart shows.

PREPOSITIONAL PHRASES	
Preposition	**Object of the Preposition**
for	*you*
throughout	the *school*
ahead of	*schedule*
between	*you* and *me*

A prepositional phrase usually consists of only two or three words; it can, however, be much longer. Length depends on the number of modifiers before the object of the preposition, the number of objects, and the length of the preposition itself.

EXAMPLES: *in* a *community*

in a small agricultural *community*

because of her *temper* and *irritability*

because of her terribly vicious, unpredictable *temper* and general *irritability*

EXERCISE B: Identifying Prepositional Phrases. Write the prepositional phrase or phrases from each of the following sentences on your paper. Then underline the prepositions and circle their objects. *Phrases are underlined; prepositions are underlined twice; objects are shaded.*

1. In back of the shop the owner and his son baked bread.
2. Step outside the door and see the sunset.
3. We ran out of money during our shopping spree.
4. According to the President's speech, we need a greater awareness of pollution problems.
5. Chinese lanterns were hung from the ceiling.
6. He carefully placed the glass figurine next to the vase.
7. The terrified rabbit slipped between the fence posts and ran to safety.
8. Billy the Kid stayed ahead of his pursuers by means of a stolen horse.
9. Don't walk in the rain without an umbrella and galoshes.
10. The long-distance runner fell behind the others.

■ Preposition or Adverb?

Many of the words listed as prepositions can also be adverbs, depending on how they are used in sentences. Notice in the following chart that prepositions are always part of a phrase.

Prepositions	Adverbs
The smoke drifted *up* the chimney.	The smoke drifted *up*
Flowers grew *along* the path.	Won't you come *along* with us?
The park is *near* our house.	We knew help was *near*.

EXERCISE C: Distinguishing Between Prepositions and Adverbs. Identify each underlined word as either a preposition or an adverb. If the word is a preposition, write the entire prepositional phrase on your paper. If the word is an adverb, simply write *adverb*. *Prepositional phrases are shaded.*

1. Hang <u>on</u> and don't let go! *adv*
2. The snoring told him someone slept <u>within</u>. *adv*
3. No one can make that horse go <u>over a bridge</u> but him. *prep*
4. The snail crept <u>along the bottom</u> of the sandy fishtank. *prep*
5. On account of your continual lateness, you have fallen <u>behind</u>. *adv*
6. Walk right <u>in</u> if you don't find us at home. *adv*
7. She put her work <u>aside</u> and talked with me. *adv*
8. The balloon floated <u>up</u> higher and higher. *adv*
9. <u>Beneath our house</u> are the remains of a colonial cabin. *prep*
10. We searched <u>around</u> all day for the lost money. *adv*

APPLICATION: **Completing Sentences with Prepositions.**
Copy the following paragraph onto your paper, filling in the blanks with appropriate prepositions. *Answers will vary; samples given.*

Jackie wished she had learned to sew (1) ___*in*___ the past. Now she had just two minutes left and the dress (2) ___*for*___ the dance wasn't finished. (3) ___*Because of*___ her carelessness, she would need to undo most (4) ___*of*___ the seams and begin once more. She looked (5) ___*at*___ her mistakes. The collar was sewn (6) ___*inside*___ the neck and the zipper had come away (7) ___*from*___ the material. None (8) ___*of*___ the buttonholes were (9) ___*next to*___ the buttons. One sleeve had been stitched (10) ___*to*___ the side (11) ___*of*___ the dress, and the other sleeve dangled (12) ___*from*___ one thread. The dress was one (13) ___*of*___ a kind. Certainly she had never seen anything (14) ___*like*___ it. Since there was nothing suitable (15) ___*in*___ her closet to wear, Jackie made a brave decision. (16) ___*With*___ great difficulty, she struggled (17) ___*into*___ the dress. When she heard the doorbell ring, she slipped (18) ___*into*___ her coat and walked (19) ___*to*___ the door. She hoped her date would have a sense (20) ___*of*___ humor.

3.2 **Conjunctions and Interjections**

Unlike prepositions, which show the relationship between words, *conjunctions* draw a direct connection between words.

> A **conjunction** is a word used to connect other words or groups of words.

■ Three Kinds of Conjunctions

Three main kinds of conjunctions are used in English to connect words: *coordinating conjunctions, correlative conjunctions,* and *subordinating conjunctions.*

Coordinating Conjunctions. Coordinating conjunctions connect words that are the same part of speech, or they connect groups of words that are grammatically alike. There are seven of these conjunctions.

COORDINATING CONJUNCTIONS			
and	for	or	yet
but	nor	so	

In the following examples, coordinating conjunctions connect similar parts of speech.

WITH NOUNS AND PRONOUNS: Joaquín *and* I are good friends.

WITH VERBS: Amos trembled *yet* continued on his way.

WITH ADVERBS: Marjorie churned the butter slowly *but* skillfully.

Coordinating conjunctions can also connect groups of words that are grammatically alike, as in the following examples.

WITH PREPOSITIONAL PHRASES: The dog ran out the door *and* across the field.

WITH DEPENDENT IDEAS: Veronica wrote that she was enjoying London *but* that she had been ill a few days.

WITH COMPLETE IDEAS: The bear slept soundly, *for* winter had come.

Correlative Conjunctions. Correlative conjunctions are similar to coordinating conjunctions. They differ only in that they are always used in pairs.

CORRELATIVE CONJUNCTIONS		
both . . . and	neither . . . nor	whether . . . or
either . . . or	not only . . . but also	

The following examples show some of the many ways to use these pairs of conjunctions.

WITH NOUNS: He owned *neither* a coat *nor* a hat.

WITH NOUNS AND PRONOUNS: They asked *whether* Edith *or* we had seen the movie.

WITH ADJECTIVES: *Both* gold *and* beige are warm colors.

WITH PREPOSITIONAL PHRASES: The guilt was shared *not only* by him *but also* by us.

WITH COMPLETE IDEAS: *Either* Brenda forgot about the meeting, *or* she is sick.

Subordinating Conjunctions.   Subordinating conjunctions connect two complete ideas by making one of the ideas subordinate, or dependent, upon the other.

FREQUENTLY USED SUBORDINATING CONJUNCTIONS			
after	because	now that	until
although	before	since	when
as	even if	so that	whenever
as if	even though	than	where
as long as	if	though	wherever
as soon as	in order that	till	while
as though	lest	unless	

The following examples show how subordinating conjunctions are used to begin dependent ideas.

| Dependent Idea | Main Idea |

EXAMPLES: *Because* Carolyn practices, she is a good musician.

| Main Idea | Dependent Idea |

He ran *as though* a pack of wolves were after him.

EXERCISE A: Identifying Conjunctions. Write the conjunction from each of the following sentences on your paper and label it *coordinating, correlative,* or *subordinating.*

1. During his fast he <u>neither</u> ate any food <u>nor</u> drank any liquids. *correl*

2. They promised to return, <u>for</u> a good time was had by everyone. *coord*
3. Gordon bit his nails <u>whenever</u> he was nervous. *subord*
4. The judge listened to the explanation <u>in order that</u> he might decide fairly. *subord*
5. The joke Evan told was <u>not only</u> impolite <u>but also</u> senseless. *correl*
6. Already ten inches of rain had fallen, <u>yet</u> the downpour continued. *coord*
7. <u>Since</u> Ben refuses to vote, he shouldn't complain about our country's leadership. *subord*
8. Was the opossum actually dead <u>or</u> just pretending? *coord*
9. Belinda had never succeeded in the past <u>nor</u> would she now. *coord*
10. Buffalo are scarce today <u>because</u> people in the last century indiscriminately slaughtered them. *subord*

■ Subordinating Conjunction, Preposition, or Adverb?

After, before, since, till, and *until* can be subordinating conjunctions or prepositions. *After, before, when,* and *where* can also be adverbs. Whether these words are conjunctions, prepositions, or adverbs is determined by their use within a sentence.

SUBORDINATING CONJUNCTION: He started to run *before* the signal was given.

PREPOSITION: David never speaks *before* breakfast.

ADVERB: Haven't you ever been here *before?*

EXERCISE B: Identifying Words as Conjunctions, Prepositions, or Adverbs. In the following sentences, the underlined words may be either subordinating conjunctions, prepositions, or adverbs. Write the part of speech of each underlined word on your paper.

1. Their house will be vacant <u>till</u> next summer. *prep*
2. The child had never ridden a merry-go-round <u>before</u>. *adv*
3. Never stand under a tree <u>when</u> there is lightning. *conj*
4. Tin is rarely used for foil <u>since</u> aluminum is available. *conj*
5. <u>Where</u> are you going at this late hour? *adv*

6. The band did not begin to play <u>until</u> it reached the town. *conj*
7. Don't stop working <u>before</u> noon. *prep*
8. Dolores always brushes her teeth <u>after</u> meals. *prep*
9. Crops were grown <u>where</u> once there had been only desert. *conj*
10. They never rise <u>till</u> the rooster crows. *conj*

■ Conjunctive Adverbs

While some words can be used either as a conjunction or as an adverb, other words act as both a conjunction and an adverb at the same time. Words that combine the qualities of both adverbs and conjunctions are called *conjunctive adverbs*. Since their primary function is to connect words, they are classified as conjunctions.

> A **conjunctive adverb** is an adverb that acts as a conjunction to connect complete ideas.

Conjunctive adverbs are also called *transitions* because they serve as links between different ideas. They help, for example, to contrast or compare ideas, or to show a result.

FREQUENTLY USED CONJUNCTIVE ADVERBS		
accordingly	for example	nevertheless
again	furthermore	on the other hand
also	however	otherwise
besides	in addition	then
consequently	indeed	therefore
finally	moreover	thus

The following examples show how conjunctive adverbs work to make different kinds of transitions between related ideas.

EXAMPLES: It rained until the field was soggy; *consequently*, the game was canceled.

Ann certainly doesn't have a green thumb; *nevertheless*, she considers gardening an enjoyable activity.

They had never been in a large city before. *Indeed*, they had never been away from home.

Notice the punctuation in the preceding sentences. In the first and second sentences, a semicolon is used along with a conjunctive adverb to tie two closely related ideas together. In the last sentence, a period is used so that the conjunctive adverb, *indeed*, will add extra emphasis to the second idea. Notice also in all of the examples that when a semicolon or period precedes a conjunctive adverb, the conjunctive adverb is followed by a comma.

EXERCISE C: Recognizing Conjunctive Adverbs. Rewrite each of the following pairs of sentences to contain a suitable conjunctive adverb. Use either a semicolon or a period to divide the two ideas. *Answers will vary; samples given.*

1. His plane was delayed in Chicago. It arrived two hours behind schedule. *; consequently,*
2. I have listened long enough to your excuses. I am tired of your lack of originality. *; moreover,*
3. Some materials are more expensive than others. Wool and linen are often costly. *; indeed,*
4. Fewer people bought new cars this year. There was less profit for the automotive industry. *; therefore,*
5. First Frank smiled. He laughed heartily. *; then,*
6. Raymond can be demanding and impatient. He is sometimes very helpful and understanding. *; however,*
7. Please bring paper cups and napkins. Bring something to drink. *; also,*
8. The general instructed the soldiers to move ahead. They advanced several paces. *; accordingly,*
9. Blanche has a beautiful voice. She is often asked to sing at weddings. *; indeed,*
10. Rosemary has many trophies over the fireplace. I assumed she had won them. *; therefore,*

■ Interjections

The only part of speech that exists independently from other words in a sentence is the *interjection*.

An **interjection** is a word that expresses feeling or emotion and functions independently of a sentence.

Some of the many feelings or emotions expressed by interjections are shown in the following examples.

JOY: *Hurray!* We won!

SURPRISE: *Aha!* I found the missing cuff link.

EXHAUSTION: *Whew!* That was hard work.

SORROW: She said that, *alas*, she had lost her way.

Notice the punctuation in the preceding examples. Since interjections are independent from all other words in the sentences, they are set off either by exclamation marks or by commas.

EXERCISE D: Recognizing Interjections. The following words express general emotions or feelings. Write ten sentences on your paper, each using an interjection that shows the indicated emotion. Underline the interjection in each sentence.
Answers will vary; samples given for first two.

1. anger	6. annoyance
2. joy	7. hesitation
3. dislike	8. concern
4. humor	9. surprise
5. pain	10. fear

1. Scat! Get away from that bird!   *2. Wow! We won!*

APPLICATION: Using Conjunctions and Conjunctive Adverbs in Sentences. Connect each of the following pairs of sentences, using the type of conjunction or conjunctive adverb indicated. Then underline the words you have added.
Answers will vary; samples given.

1. Rhoda had rescued a small boy from a blazing building. She was afraid of heights.   (subordinating conjunction)
2. The puppy might be hiding in the closet. He might be hiding under the bed.   (coordinating conjunction)   *, or*
3. Paula works days as a cashier. She takes classes in the evenings.   (correlative conjunction)   *not only/but also*
4. Goldilocks slept soundly. The three bears came home. (subordinating conjunction)   *until*
5. We had warned him not to swim in that river. He was devoured by crocodiles.   (conjunctive adverb)   *; indeed,*

1. although

Chapter 4

Analyzing Parts of Speech

At this point you should be familiar with the eight parts of speech. Perhaps you did not realize that every word you read or speak can be assigned to one of these categories. The following section offers a summary of the parts of speech and gives you a chance to practice categorizing words.

Identifying Parts of Speech According to Use **4.1**

Never assume you know a word's part of speech until you examine how it is used in its sentence.

The way a word is used in a sentence determines what part of speech it is.

Notice in the following examples that the part of speech of the word *left* changes according to the way it is used.

AS A NOUN: Our house is the one on the *left*.

AS A VERB: We *left* shortly after midnight.

AS AN ADJECTIVE: Susan's *left* shoe is untied.

AS AN ADVERB: Turn *left* when you reach the center of town.

■ Parts of Speech in Sentences

The following charts should help you review the parts of speech. The column labeled *Questions to Ask Yourself* is particularly important.

Nouns, Pronouns, and Verbs. A noun names a person, place, or thing. A pronoun stands for a noun. A verb shows action, condition, or existence.

Part of Speech	Questions to Ask Yourself	Examples
Noun	Does the word name a person, place, or thing?	*Cliff* rode a *camel* in *Egypt.*
Pronoun	Does the word stand for a noun?	*We* bought *several* of *them.*
Verb	Does the word tell what someone or something did?	They *raised* the flag.
	Does the word link the noun or pronoun before it with an adjective or noun that follows?	Pat *is* angry. She *will be* vice-president.
	Does the word merely indicate that something exists?	Here I *am.*

Modifiers. There are two kinds of modifiers: adjectives and adverbs. An adjective modifies a noun or pronoun. An adverb modifies a verb, adjective, or another adverb.

Part of Speech	Questions to Ask Yourself	Examples
Adjective	Does the word tell what kind, which one, how many, or how much?	A game like *this* one is *difficult.*
Adverb	Does the word tell where, when, in what manner, or to what extent?	Papers blew *everywhere.* Leave *now.* She smiled *sadly.* Jim has *just* finished.

Prepositions, Conjunctions, and Interjections. A preposition relates a noun or pronoun following it to another word. A conjunction connects words or groups of words. An interjection expresses feelings or emotions.

Part of Speech	Questions to Ask Yourself	Examples
Preposition	Is the word part of a phrase that ends with a noun or pronoun?	The pony ran *beside* the train. Buy envelopes *in addition to* stamps.
Conjunction	Does the word connect other words in the sentence?	He wants to sleep, *yet* he can't. Kurt will *either* get lost *or* show up late.
Interjection	Does the word express feelings or emotions and function independently of the sentence?	*Wow!* That's amazing.

EXERCISE A: Identifying Nouns, Verbs, and Adjectives. Identify the underlined word in each of the following sentences as a *noun, verb,* or *adjective.*

1. This restaurant serves delicious <u>green</u> salad. *adj*
2. Put some <u>greens</u> in the vase with the flowers. *noun*
3. Spring sunshine will quickly <u>green</u> the lawns. *verb*
4. The grammar <u>test</u> will be easy. *noun*
5. The lawyers say the trial will be a <u>test</u> case. *adj*
6. This machine <u>tests</u> blood for anemia. *verb*
7. A firm mattress is needed to give good <u>back</u> support. *adj*
8. They painted a colorful mural on the <u>back</u> of the barn. *noun*
9. The volunteers promised they would <u>look</u> everywhere for the child lost in the wilderness. *verb*
10. A wistful <u>look</u> appeared on his face as he gazed at the playground. *noun*

EXERCISE B: Identifying Pronouns and Adjectives. Identify the underlined word in each of the following sentences as a *pronoun* or an *adjective.*

1. If Charlotte makes her apple pie, you should have <u>some</u>. *pron*
2. <u>Some</u> fragments of the Indian arrowheads were found. *adj ind-*
3. <u>Which</u> is harder, a diamond or an emerald? *pron interrog*
4. Please decide <u>which</u> hat is the most flattering. *adj interrog*
5. The museum uses <u>these</u> soft overhead lights to illuminate the paintings. *adj demons,*

6. Throw <u>these</u> out with the rest of the trash. *pron*
7. An unsupervised dog will eat <u>more</u> than is good for it. *pron*
8. Year by year, she added <u>more</u> clocks to her collection. *adj*
9. Never again will I try to entertain <u>this</u> little monster. *adj*
10. She sang a lullaby, and <u>this</u> put the baby to sleep. *pron*

EXERCISE C: Identifying Nouns, Prepositions, and Adverbs.
Identify the underlined word in each of the following sentences as a *noun, preposition,* or *adverb.*

1. Our cat is deaf and cannot go <u>outside</u>. *adv*
2. On the <u>outside</u> the house was drab. *noun*
3. Arnold's parrot greets visitors and sometimes flies <u>outside</u> the house. *prep*
4. There was a terrible, dark secret about the family's <u>past</u>. *noun*
5. Larry cannot see <u>past</u> his actions to the consequences. *prep*
6. Their cabin is so far in the woods that you can drive <u>past</u> without seeing it. *adv*
7. These comforters are very warm because they are filled with <u>down</u>. *noun*
8. Don't look <u>down</u> before you jump into the safety net. *adv*
9. In most cultures there is a belief in life <u>beyond</u> death. *prep*
10. She gazed in horror at what lay <u>beyond</u>. *adv*

EXERCISE D: Identifying Conjunctions, Prepositions, and Adverbs.
Identify the underlined word in each of the following sentences as a *conjunction, preposition,* or *adverb.*

1. He ran <u>about</u> wildly, shouting for help. *adv*
2. As your parents, we are concerned <u>about</u> your health. *prep*
3. The wheat must be harvested <u>before</u> the rainy season. *prep*
4. Judd stepped into the road <u>before</u> the light changed. *conj*
5. I never saw that man <u>before</u>. *adv*
6. Many people prefer to sleep with a pillow <u>underneath</u> their heads. *prep*
7. The door will be locked, so just slip my mail <u>underneath</u>. *adv*
8. <u>After</u> the factories closed, the town was strangely silent. *conj*
9. Wendy usually goes straight home <u>after</u> school. *prep*
10. The boys remained <u>after</u> and picked up the papers. *adv*

APPLICATION: Using Words as Different Parts of Speech.
Use each of the following words in two sentences of your own. Use the word as a different part of speech in each sentence. Then underline the word and identify its part of speech. *Answers will vary; samples given for first two.*

past   turn   blue   look   beyond

1. We regretted our <u>past</u> mistakes. (adj)   Turn right just <u>past</u> the library. (prep)
2. Whose <u>turn</u> is it? (noun)   That tree <u>turns</u> red in autumn. (verb)

Chapter 5

Basic Parts of a Sentence

You will begin in this chapter to take a closer look at a familiar means of communication. You use sentences every time you speak or write, yet you may not be aware of their essential parts. Knowing how the parts of speech work to form sentences will give you a better understanding of how words communicate ideas.

Subjects and Predicates 5.1

Language is a tool with which people communicate their ideas to others, either through speaking or through writing. Many things can go wrong with this process and prevent a listener or reader from understanding the intended idea. A writer, for example, may use words that the reader cannot understand. A dictionary solves this problem easily enough. A more serious problem, however, occurs when a writer tries—usually unintentionally—to communicate with words that do not form sentences. The result is a short circuit, and communication comes to a dead stop. Recognizing that every sentence must have two key parts will help you avoid this problem in your own writing.

■ The Complete Subject and Complete Predicate

Every sentence that is grammatically correct consists of two parts: a *complete subject* and a *complete predicate*.

67

A **sentence** is a group of words with two main parts: a complete subject and a complete predicate. Together these parts express a complete thought.

The complete subject includes a noun or pronoun that names the person, place, or thing that the sentence is about. The complete predicate includes a verb or verb phrase that tells something about the complete subject. In the following examples, you can see that a complete subject or complete predicate may consist of only a single essential word (a noun or pronoun for the complete subject, a verb for the complete predicate). Or a complete subject or complete predicate may consist of many words that modify and expand upon the essential words.

EXAMPLES: *They* | *were stumbling* through briars and branches.

Complete Subject | Complete Predicate ⟶

The captured *spy*, in fear for his life, | *spoke.*

⟵ Complete Subject | Complete Predicate

EXERCISE A: Recognizing Complete Subjects and Complete Predicates. Divide your paper into two columns. Label the left column *Complete Subject* and the right column *Complete Predicate*. Copy each of the following sentences onto your paper, placing the sentence parts under the appropriate headings. *The complete subject includes all the words to the left of the vertical line; the complete verb, the words to the right.*

1. The new puppy|won't leave the older dog alone.
2. An old-fashioned spinning wheel|sat in the corner.
3. Seasonal wind changes in India|are called monsoons.
4. New skin|was grafted onto his burned leg.
5. We|should have been on the road before now.
6. Anyone|could have made a mistake like that.
7. My umbrella handle|is carved from ivory.
8. The Sons of Liberty|was a secret society.
9. Mink oil|is excellent for conditioning leather.
10. Her stationery|is always simple but elegant.

■ Sentence or Fragment?

A group of words lacking a complete subject or a complete predicate, or both, is called a *fragment*.

A **fragment** is a group of words that does not express a complete thought.

The following chart contrasts fragments with the sentences they become after the italicized words are added. Notice how the fragments pose problems for a reader because they leave out essential ideas.

Fragments	Complete Sentences
Wild Bill Hickok, a famous frontiersman.	Wild Bill Hickok, a famous frontiersman, *was an honest marshal.*
Shot several men in the line of duty.	*He* shot several men in the line of duty.
In a saloon in Dakota.	*Hickok was shot to death* in a saloon in Dakota.

In the first sentence, the italicized words make up the complete predicate. In the second sentence, one word is added to make up the complete subject. In the last sentence, a complete subject, *Hickok,* and the essential part of a complete predicate, *was shot to death,* are added to form a complete sentence.

Though fragments, like those in the preceding chart, are confusing to a reader, they sometimes can express complete thoughts to a listener in a conversation.

Conversational Fragments. In conversation, you are often able to express clear ideas in fragments. When you speak, repetition, the tone of your voice, your gestures, and your facial expressions all help add meaning to your words.

The following conversation, consisting of both sentences and fragments, is easily understood.

SENTENCE: When did you last see Jane?

FRAGMENT: Yesterday.

SENTENCE: I thought she already left for her vacation.

FRAGMENT: No, not yet.

SENTENCE: Will she leave next weekend?

FRAGMENT: Probably sooner than that.

Written Fragments. As you have just seen, fragments can sometimes be an acceptable means of communication in conversation. However, with few exceptions, you should avoid fragments in your writing. One permissible use of fragments in writing is to represent speech. Another use is the *elliptical sentence*, in which the missing word or words are obvious and can easily be understood. Even these elliptical sentences should be used sparingly, especially in formal writing.

ELLIPTICAL SENTENCES: (I) Thank you.

Why (are you) so sad?

EXERCISE B: **Distinguishing Between Sentences and Fragments.** Identify each of the following items as either a *sentence* or a *fragment*. If the group of words is a fragment, rewrite it to make it a sentence. Then indicate whether you have added words to form a complete subject, a complete predicate, or both.
Answers will vary for all except 3 and 8; samples given for first two.

EXAMPLE: Without thinking about it.

fragment   I answered without thinking about it.   both

1. A sewing machine with all the frills.∧ *is expensive. (pred)*
2. ∧Some wonderful stories about creatures in the ocean's depths. *I read (both)*
3. Jan did not finish her breakfast.
4. Jumped higher and higher on the trampoline.
5. Few, if any.
6. Basketball, the most popular spectator sport.
7. Wearing a white, heavy knit sweater.
8. A stitch in times saves nine.
9. Trembled and shook with fear.
10. Beside the pool, soaking up the sunshine.

■ The Simple Subject and Simple Predicate

Every complete subject and complete predicate contains a word or group of words that is essential to the sentence.

The **simple subject** is the essential noun, pronoun, or group of words acting as a noun that cannot be left out of the complete subject.

The **simple predicate** is the essential verb or verb phrase that cannot be left out of the complete predicate.

In the following examples, notice that all the other words in the complete subject modify or add information to the simple subject. In the same manner, all the other words in the complete predicate either modify the simple predicate or help it complete the meaning of the sentence.

EXAMPLES:

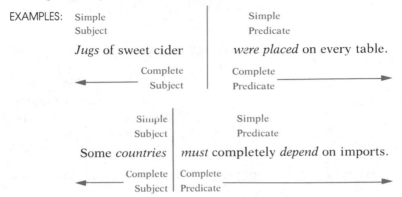

Notice in the first example that the simple subject of the sentence is *jugs*, not *cider*. The object of a preposition can never be a simple subject. Notice also that in the last example, the verb phrase *must depend* is split by an adverb, *completely*.

NOTE ABOUT THE TERMS *SUBJECT* AND *VERB*: From this point on in this book, the word *subject* will refer to the simple subject, and the word *verb* will refer to the simple predicate.

Knowing how to find the subject and verb in your written sentences will help you to write more clearly and effectively. The same skill will also help you to improve your understanding of more difficult sentence patterns.

If you prefer to find the subject of a sentence before you find the verb, first ask yourself, "What word is the sentence about?" Then, once you have found the subject, ask yourself, "What did the subject *do?*" The answer will be an action verb. If there is no answer to the last question, look for a linking verb.

EXAMPLE: The stream trickled slowly down the ravine.

Subject: stream

Question: What did the stream *do?*

Answer: trickled

On the other hand, you may find it easier to locate the verb before the subject. In that case, first look for an action verb or a linking verb. Having found the verb, ask *Who or what?* before the verb. The answer will be the subject.

EXAMPLE: A wasp's nest was hanging above the porch.

  Verb: was hanging

  Question: Who or what was hanging?

  Answer: nest

EXERCISE C: Recognizing Subjects and Verbs. Write the subject and verb from each of the following sentences on your paper. Then underline each subject once and each verb twice.

1. Greek literature contains many stories about Amazons.
2. Supposedly living near the Black Sea, they were a nation of women warriors.
3. Not enjoying the presence of men, the Amazons lived apart in their own cities.
4. Ares, the god of war, was worshipped in their temples.
5. They fought against the Greeks during the Trojan War, according to Pausanias.
6. They were also fearless hunters.
7. Their bravery made them famous.
8. Many Greek statues of Amazons with bows and arrows can be seen today in museums.
9. These women never really existed, however, according to some scholars.
10. They are merely the product of the Greeks' imagination.

■ Compound Subjects and Verbs

The word *compound* is used to describe a noun, adjective, or preposition with more than one part. *Station wagon*, for example, is a compound noun. The word *compound* is also used to describe subjects or verbs connected by conjunctions such as *and* or *or*.

Compound Subjects.   The complete subject of a sentence may contain two or more subjects.

A **compound subject** is two or more subjects that have the same verb and are joined by a conjunction such as *and* or *or*.

In the following examples, the parts of the compound subject are underlined once and the verbs twice.

EXAMPLES: His constant threats and warnings frightened the children away from his yard.

Parsley, sage, dill, and rosemary were growing in the dry soil.

Compound Verbs.   Sentences may also contain two or more verbs in the complete predicate.

A **compound verb** is two or more verbs that have the same subject and are joined by a conjunction such as *and* or *or*.

EXAMPLES: You either apologize or accept the punishment.

The star signed autograph books, smiled at her fans, and then departed in a limousine.

Sentences may also have both compound subjects and compound verbs.

EXAMPLE: Mr. Willis and his neighbor argued and shouted at each other over the fence.

NOTE ABOUT COMPOUND VERBS: When a compound verb consists of two or more verb phrases, the helping verb is not repeated if doing so makes the sentence sound awkward.

AWKWARD REPETITION: The banjo player was strumming his banjo, was stomping his feet, and was singing enthusiastically.

HELPING VERB NOT REPEATED: The banjo player was strumming his banjo, stomping his feet, and singing enthusiastically.

EXERCISE D: Recognizing Compound Subjects and Compound Verbs. Each of the following sentences has either a compound subject, a compound verb, or both. Copy the sentences onto your paper. Underline the subjects once and the verbs twice.

1. A hat, mittens, scarf, and warm coat should be worn in this weather.
2. Our grandmother and grandfather visit us every year and bring many beautiful gifts.
3. Both salt and pepper are good seasonings.
4. In the summer my friends and I swim and ride our bicycles on country roads.
5. Moles have very poor eyesight and therefore burrow in dark tunnels underground.
6. Thor Heyerdahl not only navigated the Pacific in a raft but also wrote a book about it.
7. Hair dyes and lipsticks come in almost every shade.
8. The mother cat and her kittens mewed pitifully and rubbed against our legs.
9. High above the ground, a Piper Cub was gliding and spiraling for the people below.
10. At twilight large moths clustered on the screen and beat their wings.

EXERCISE E: **Finding Simple and Compound Subjects and Verbs.** Divide your paper into two columns. Label the left column *Subject* and the right column *Verb*. Then list the subjects and verbs in the following sentences under the appropriate headings. Some of the sentences contain compound subjects and verbs.

1. The nozzle of the garden hose was clogged with dirt.
2. Many people have trouble with the high note of "The Star-Spangled Banner."
3. Rats and mice eat huge quantities of valuable grains.
4. On Sunday Aunt Jennie and Uncle Nick will have been married for fifty years and will celebrate their golden anniversary.
5. Miners and their families do not lead easy lives free from worry.
6. Emanuel can hear a tune once and afterwards whistle it perfectly.
7. Any remedy for a cold usually does not do much good.
8. During the dry season campfires and carelessly-tossed matches can cause raging forest fires.
9. Hilary, Miranda, and their cousin could dance, sing, and play musical instruments with great enjoyment but little talent.
10. Phoebe's ignorance of the law and her trusting nature led her to commit a felony.

APPLICATION: **Developing Sentences from Subjects and Verbs.** The following two lists consist of subjects and verbs.

In both lists, the last five groups of words are compound parts. Write ten sentences of your own, using all of the subjects in the given order and the verbs in any order you choose. Underline the subjects once and the verbs twice.
Answers will vary; two samples given.

1. child	grew
2. people	poured
3. painting	were lying
4. water	are required
5. colt	go
6. Alma, Gilbert	cried, laughed
7. iron, copper	played, entertained
8. ketchup, mustard	was torn, was ripped
9. sand, gravel	can be used, may provide
10. knife, fork	was running, was jumping

1. The <u>child</u> <u>grew</u> larger and wiser.

2. The <u>painting</u> <u>was torn</u> by one child and <u>was ripped</u> by another.

Hard-to-Find Subjects 5.2

The sentences in the last section all followed the usual pattern of English sentences: subject followed by verb. Many sentences, however, do not follow this pattern. In this section, you will examine sentences with subjects that are less obvious.

■ Understood Subjects in Orders and Directions

In sentences that give orders or directions, the subject is usually not expressed.

In sentences that give orders or directions, the subject is understood to be *you*.

The following chart contrasts sentences with and without the understood *you*. The subjects are underlined once; verbs, twice. Notice in the last sentence that even when a person is addressed, the subject is still understood to be *you*.

Order or Direction	With Understood *You* Added
<u>Dust</u> the furniture and then <u>wax</u> the floor.	(<u>You</u>) <u>dust</u> the furniture and then <u>wax</u> the floor.

Before the clay hardens, <u>mold</u> it with your hands.	Before the clay hardens, (<u>you</u>) <u>mold</u> it with your hands.
Kim, <u>let</u> me see your drawing.	Kim, (<u>you</u>) <u>let</u> me see your drawing.

EXERCISE A: Finding Subjects in Orders or Directions. Use the following list of verbs to create ten sentences of your own. Let your first five sentences give orders and your last five give directions. Include at least three sentences in which a person is addressed. Underline each verb twice and place a caret (∧) to indicate *you* as the understood subject.
Answers will vary; samples given for first two.

EXAMPLE: lend

Joe, ∧ <u>lend</u> me your pen.

1. give
2. wipe
3. speak
4. wash
5. step

6. drive
7. clean
8. brush
9. rake
10. mix

1. ∧ <u>Give</u> the pen back to Greta, Louis.   *2. ∧ <u>Wipe</u> your feet before coming in.*

■ Subjects in Inverted Sentences

In some sentences the usual subject-verb order is inverted—that is, reversed. Sentences that may be inverted in English include questions and sentences beginning with *there* or *here*. In addition, some sentences are inverted for emphasis.

Subjects in Questions. One of the ways to form questions in English is to invert the usual subject-verb order.

In questions, the subject often follows the verb.

An inverted question can begin with a verb, a helping verb, or one of the following words: *what, which, whose, who, when, why, where,* or *how.*

A good way to find the subject in an inverted question is to rephrase the question mentally as a statement. Then the subject and verb will fall into the most common pattern of subject followed by verb.

Question	Question Rephrased as a Statement
<u>Was</u> the <u>meal</u> satisfactory, sir?	The <u>meal</u> <u>was</u> satisfactory, sir.
<u>Do</u> <u>you</u> <u>like</u> raisins in your cereal?	<u>You</u> <u>do like</u> raisins in your cereal.
Where <u>was</u> the <u>car</u> <u>parked</u>?	The <u>car</u> <u>was parked</u> where.

NOTE ABOUT QUESTIONS: Some questions are not inverted. Those beginning with an interrogative adjective or pronoun may be in the usual subject-verb order.

EXAMPLES: Which <u>poet</u> <u>won</u> the Pulitzer Prize this year?

Who <u>cares</u> about such nonsense?

Sentences Beginning with *There* or *Here*. Two words that are often found at the beginning of inverted sentences are *there* and *here*.

There or *here* is never the subject of a sentence.

The only exception to this rule occurs when *there* or *here* is referred to as a word, as in the rule itself.

When *there* or *here* begins a sentence, the subject usually follows the verb. As with inverted questions, a mental rephrasing of the sentence will help you find the subject. Simply rearrange the sentence logically so that it does not begin with *there* or *here*.

Sentence Beginning with *There* or *Here*	Sentence Rephrased with Subject Before Verb
Here <u>is</u> a <u>patch</u> for your sleeve.	A <u>patch</u> for your sleeve <u>is</u> here.
There <u>is</u> my battered <u>suitcase</u>.	My battered <u>suitcase</u> <u>is</u> there.
There <u>are</u> the <u>tools</u> for the garden.	The <u>tools</u> for the garden <u>are</u> there.

In the sentences in the chart, *there* and *here* are adverbs; they modify the verbs and tell where. Occasionally *there* is merely used to help the sentence get started and does *not* modify the verb. When *there* is used in this manner, it is not an adverb but an *expletive*.

EXAMPLES: There is no bridge across this river.

     There will be a drastic change in the weather.

In sentences where *there* is used as an expletive, rephrasing to find the subject may not work. To find the subject in this situation, mentally drop *there* and ask *Who or what?* before the verb.

Sentence with Expletive *There*	Question for Finding the Subject
There are some crumbs on your chin.	*Question: Who or what* are? *Answer*: crumbs
There may not be any logical answer to that question.	*Question: Who or what* may be? *Answer*: answer

NOTE ABOUT SENTENCES BEGINNING WITH *THERE* OR *HERE:* Some sentences beginning with *there* or *here* are not in inverted order.

EXAMPLE: There you are!

Inverted Order for Emphasis. Sometimes the usual subject-verb order is deliberately inverted to emphasize the last words in the sentence.

In some sentences the subject is placed after the verb in order to receive greater emphasis.

On the left in the following chart, notice how the inverted subject-verb order directs attention to the subjects at the ends of the sentences. Rephrased in normal subject-verb order, the sentences are less dramatic.

Sentences with Inversion for Emphasis	Sentences Rephrased with Subject Before Verb
Near the entrance to a dark cave <u>lurked</u> the wounded <u>bear</u> and her <u>cubs</u>.	The wounded <u>bear</u> and her <u>cubs</u> <u>lurked</u> near the entrance to a dark cave.
Beneath the ruined temple <u>waited</u> the deadly <u>cobra</u>.	The deadly <u>cobra</u> <u>waited</u> beneath the ruined temple.

EXERCISE B: Finding the Subject in Questions. Copy the following sentences onto your paper. Underline the subjects once and the verbs twice.

1. <u>Is</u> a <u>tomato</u> a fruit or a vegetable?
2. Where <u>did</u> <u>you</u> <u>put</u> the buttered rolls?
3. Which <u>shade</u> of blue <u>looks</u> best?
4. <u>Should</u> a <u>murderer</u> <u>be released</u> from prison so quickly?
5. <u>Who</u> <u>won</u> the prize for the silliest costume?
6. <u>May</u> <u>we</u> <u>have</u> a little peace and quiet?
7. <u>Was</u> the <u>key</u> under the mat?
8. How long <u>will</u> <u>you</u> <u>take</u> to decide?
9. Whose <u>honor</u> <u>was</u> at stake?
10. <u>Can</u> <u>Marge</u> and her <u>friend</u> <u>climb</u> mountains safely?

EXERCISE C: Finding the Subject in Sentences Beginning with *There* **or** *Here.* Write the subject or subjects from each of the following sentences on your paper.

1. Here are your <u>gloves</u> and fur <u>hat</u>.
2. There was the leaky <u>pipe</u>.
3. There <u>he</u> was, with no bus fare.
4. Here are some <u>suggestions</u> for your composition.
5. There are several possible <u>locations</u> for the new shopping center.
6. There were the lost <u>documents</u>.
7. Here is a new <u>slant</u> on that topic.
8. Here come <u>Megan</u> and <u>Suzanne</u>.
9. Here is your <u>change</u> from the dollar bill.
10. There are no <u>mistakes</u> in this needlepoint sampler.

EXERCISE D: Finding the Subject in Sentences Inverted for Emphasis. Copy the following inverted sentences onto your paper. Underline the subjects once and the verbs twice.

1. Into the valley of death <u>rode</u> the <u>six hundred</u>.
2. Far from town on the top of a mountain <u>lived</u> the bitter <u>recluse</u>.
3. Near a clearing in the woods <u>lay</u> the <u>musket</u> and the dying <u>soldier</u>.
4. With respect and understanding <u>comes</u> <u>compassion</u> for others.
5. From the kitchen <u>was drifting</u> the <u>smell</u> of baking bread.

APPLICATION: Writing Sentences with Hard-to-Find Subjects.
Write a sentence for each of the following directions. Underline your subjects once and your verbs twice.
Answers will vary; samples given for first two.
1. Write a sentence that gives an order. Place a caret where *you* is understood.
2. Write a question that begins with a helping verb.
3. Write a question that begins with *where*.
4. Write an inverted sentence with *there* used as an expletive.
5. Write an inverted sentence that emphasizes the subject at the end.

1. ʌ <u>*Clean*</u> *your room.*   *2.* <u>*Do*</u> *<u>you</u> <u>know</u> the answer?*

5.3 Direct Objects, Indirect Objects, and Objective Complements

In addition to the main verb, a complete predicate may also have a *complement*.

> A **complement** is a word or group of words that completes the meaning of the predicate of a sentence.

The following examples show the five basic patterns for sentences containing complements. As you can see, the complements are nouns, pronouns, or adjectives. Notice also that the subjects are underlined once; the verbs, twice.

EXAMPLES: The <u>invaders</u> <u>plundered</u> the town.
                                                         Complement

                    Complements
             <u>Allison</u> <u>told</u> her a secret.

                              Complements
             The <u>President</u> <u>appointed</u> her Attorney General.

Complement

That <u>tree</u> <u>is</u> an oak.   Complement

The frozen <u>lake</u> <u>looked</u> smooth.

Since a complete predicate may consist of only one word, a verb, sentences do not have to contain complements. Most, however, do. The following examples show sentences that obviously need complements.

COMPLEMENTS NEEDED: Grace <u>sent</u>.

The <u>people</u> <u>elected</u>.

Wild <u>animals</u> <u>are</u>.

This section and the next deal with the five different kinds of complements used in sentences: direct objects, indirect objects, objective complements, predicate nominatives, and predicate adjectives. These last two are often grouped together as subject complements.

■ Direct Objects

Sentences with action verbs often contain complements called *direct objects*.

A **direct object** is a noun, pronoun, or group of words acting as a noun that receives the action of a transitive verb.

To find a direct object, ask *What?* or *Whom?* after an action verb.

What?
DO
EXAMPLES: The <u>carpenter</u> <u>is sanding</u> the bookcase.

Whom?
DO
The army <u>blanket</u> <u>covered</u> the old soldier.

In the first sentence, the question is *Is sanding what?* and the answer is *bookcase*. In the second sentence, the question is *Covered whom?* and the answer is *soldier*. *Bookcase* and *soldier* are both direct objects.

NOTE ABOUT ACTION VERBS: Only transitive action verbs are followed by direct objects; these verbs direct their action toward something or someone—the direct object. Intransitive verbs do not have direct objects.

TRANSITIVE: The tidal <u>wave</u> <u>sank</u> the ship.

INTRANSITIVE: The <u>wheels</u> <u>sank</u> into the mud.

Compound Direct Objects.   When an action verb directs action toward more than one direct object, the result is a *compound direct object*. If there is a compound direct object in a sentence, asking *What?* or *Whom?* after the verb will give you two or more answers.

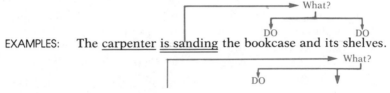

EXAMPLES: The <u>carpenter</u> <u>is sanding</u> the bookcase and its shelves.

The <u>blanket</u> <u>covered</u> the old soldier and his rifle.

Direct Object or Object of a Preposition?   A direct object is never the noun or pronoun at the end of a prepositional phrase. Do not confuse these two sentence parts.

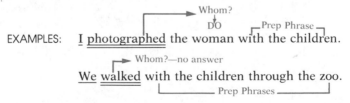

EXAMPLES: I <u>photographed</u> the woman with the children.

We <u>walked</u> with the children through the zoo.

EXERCISE A: Recognizing Direct Objects. Write the direct object from each of the following sentences on your paper. If a direct object is compound, write all of the parts and label them *compound*.

1. No one heard the <u>announcement</u> on the radio.
2. His nephew searched <u>closets</u>, <u>drawers</u>, and <u>cupboards</u> for the will. *cpd*
3. Torches lit the <u>tunnels</u> in the gloomy mine shaft.

4. Amy's mother invited <u>most</u> of her friends and relatives to the shower.
5. The dog guarded his sleeping <u>mistress</u> and her sick <u>child</u>. *cpd*
6. The mob threw rotten <u>fruits</u> and <u>vegetables</u> at the well-dressed noble. *cpd*
7. Janet jogs two <u>miles</u> through Central Park every day.
8. Jackals gnaw <u>bones</u> with their powerful jaws.
9. His furious look frightened not only the <u>company</u> but also his <u>wife</u>. *cpd*
10. The lumbering elephant crashed his <u>way</u> through the thicket.

■ Indirect Objects

Sentences with direct objects sometimes have *indirect objects* too.

An **indirect object** is a noun or pronoun that comes after an action verb and before a direct object. Its purpose is to name the person or thing that something is given to or done for.

To find an indirect object, first be certain that the sentence has a direct object. Then, having found the direct object, ask *To or for whom?* or *To or for what?* after the action verb.

EXAMPLES: Camille <u>promised</u> her sister a reward for good behavior.

We <u>should give</u> Fred's idea a fair chance.

Compound Indirect Objects. Like direct objects, indirect objects may be compound. When there is a compound indirect object in a sentence, asking *To or for whom?* or *To or for what?* after the verb will lead to two or more answers.

EXAMPLES: Camille <u>promised</u> her sister and brother a reward for good behavior.

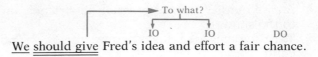

We <u>should give</u> Fred's idea and effort a fair chance.

Indirect Object or Direct Object?   To avoid confusing an indirect object with a direct object, remember that an indirect object always comes between the verb and the direct object. The pattern is always verb-indirect object-direct object. Notice this pattern in the following example.

EXAMPLE: <u>Uncle Charlie</u> <u>handed</u> the bellhop a tip.

Asking yourself the questions for direct and indirect objects will help you distinguish between the two kinds of complements. In the preceding example, the question for direct objects—*Handed what?*—gives the answer *tip*. The question for indirect objects—*Handed to whom?*—leads to the indirect object *bellhop*.

Indirect Object or Object of a Preposition?   You should also be careful not to confuse an indirect object with an object of a preposition. An indirect object is never preceded by the word *to* or *for* in the sentence. Moreover, it never follows the direct object. In the first sentence in the following examples, *friends* is the object of a preposition and is located *after* the direct object. In the second sentence, there is no preposition and *friends* comes before the direct object.

EXAMPLES:
                     DO   Obj of Prep
     <u>Angela</u> <u>told</u> the news to her friends.

                  IO   DO
     <u>Angela</u> <u>told</u> her friends the news.

EXERCISE B: Recognizing Indirect Objects. Each of the following sentences contains a direct object. Some of the sentences contain one or more indirect objects. Others contain a prepositional phrase instead. Divide your paper into three columns and label them *Direct Object, Indirect Object,* and *Object of a Preposition.* List the parts from each sentence under the appropriate headings. If the indirect object is compound, write *compound*.

1. Trading vessels brought <u>people</u> exotic <u>spices</u>. *IO/DO*
2. Our committee distributed <u>fliers</u> to our <u>neighbors</u>. *DO/obj of prep*
3. Mr. Hinkle taught <u>Harriet</u> and <u>Alberta</u> a good <u>lesson</u>. *cpd IO/DO*
4. Please bring the <u>children</u> and <u>me</u> some <u>ice cream</u>. *cpd IO/DO*
5. The Constitution guarantees <u>freedom</u> to <u>all</u>. *DO/obj of prep*
6. She sold her <u>home</u> for very little <u>profit</u>. *DO/obj of prep*
7. When will Lena tell <u>him</u> the <u>truth</u>? *IO/DO*
8. Higher education gives <u>men</u> and <u>women</u> better <u>opportunities</u>. *cpd IO/DO*
9. Lucille made <u>herself</u> some hot <u>chocolate</u>. *IO/DO*
10. The article had a <u>message</u> for cigarette <u>smokers</u>. *DO/obj of prep*

■ Objective Complements

A third kind of complement, one that comes after the direct object, is called an *objective complement*. Its purpose is to give additional information about the direct object.

> An **objective complement** is an adjective, noun, or group of words acting as a noun that follows a direct object and describes or renames it.

Objective complements occur infrequently because they follow only such verbs as *appoint, name, make, think,* or *call.*

An objective complement can be found only in a sentence that has a direct object. To determine whether a word is an objective complement, say the verb and the direct object, and then ask *What?*

EXAMPLES: <u>Ben</u> <u>called</u> his dog Rover.

The <u>beautician</u> <u>made</u> Marlene's hair short and curly.

Notice that the objective complement in the last example is compound.

EXERCISE C: Recognizing Objective Complements. Eight of the following sentences contain an objective complement. The other two sentences have compound objective complements. Write the objective complements on your paper.

1. The neighborhood bully considered Martin a <u>sissy</u>.
2. A card for Father's Day makes my dad very <u>happy</u>.
3. That unpleasant gentleman called me a <u>fool</u> and a <u>liar</u>.
4. The most stubborn of men, Mr. Fenston thinks other people <u>obstinate</u>.
5. John's uncle makes everyone <u>welcome</u>.
6. His close friends nominated him <u>master of ceremonies</u>.
7. The ointment made the wound less <u>red</u> and <u>sore</u>.
8. Tired of the same decor, she painted the doors to the dining room <u>pink</u>.
9. The boss appointed Ms. Brady <u>chairwoman</u> of the committee.
10. Such experiences make life <u>worthwhile</u>.

APPLICATION: Writing Sentences with Direct Objects, Indirect Objects, and Objective Complements. Write a sentence on your paper for each of the following directions. Label all the direct objects *DO*, all the indirect objects *IO*, and all the objective complements *OC*. Answers will vary; samples given for first two.

1. Write a sentence with a direct object. Use *Alice* as the subject and *described* as the verb.
2. Write a sentence with a compound direct object. Use *electrician* and *plumber* as the subject and *checked* as the verb.
3. Write a sentence with a direct object and an indirect object. Use *catcher* as the subject and *tossed* as the verb.
4. Write a sentence with a direct object and a compound indirect object. Use *Sid* as the subject and *owes* as the verb.
5. Write a sentence with an objective complement. Be sure to include a direct object. Use *I* as the subject and *called* as the verb.

1. *Alice described the suspect accurately.*   DO
2. *An electrician and a plumber checked the wiring and pipes.*   DO   DO

5.4 Subject Complements

The previous section showed how transitive action verbs are followed by a complement, a direct object that helps complete the meaning of the sentence. Many of these sentences also contain indirect objects or objective complements. In this section you will see that sentences with linking verbs have a different kind of complement, called a *subject complement*.

A **subject complement** is a noun, pronoun, or adjective that follows a linking verb and tells something about the subject of the sentence.

A subject complement may be either a *predicate nominative* or a *predicate adjective.*

■ Predicate Nominatives

The word *nominative* comes from the Latin word *nomen* meaning "name." The words *noun* and *pronoun* are also derived from *nomen.*

A **predicate nominative** is a noun or pronoun that follows a linking verb and renames, identifies, or explains the subject of the sentence.

A subject and a predicate nominative are two different words for the same person, place, or thing. Acting like an equal sign, the linking verb joins these two parts and equates them.

Notice in each of the following examples that the subject and the predicate nominative are both representing the same noun or pronoun.

EXAMPLES: Emily Brontë became a famous author.

The best person for the job is you.

Like other sentence parts, predicate nominatives may be *compound.*

EXAMPLES: Two of spring's flowers are crocuses and tulips.

A good nominee might be either Dean or Richard.

EXERCISE A: **Recognizing Predicate Nominatives in Sentences.** Write the noun or pronoun used as the predicate nominative in each of the following sentences on your paper. Some of the predicate nominatives are compound.

1. The girl in the green sweater is <u>she</u>.
2. Bill's favorite sports were <u>hockey</u> and <u>football</u>.
3. Possible sources of protein might be <u>eggs</u>, <u>meat</u>, or certain <u>kinds</u> of beans.
4. Agatha remained an <u>athlete</u> in spite of her illness.
5. The winning composition will be the <u>one</u> with the most originality.
6. John Audubon was an American <u>naturalist</u> and <u>artist</u>.
7. Two valuable metals have always been <u>gold</u> and <u>silver</u>.
8. Peace of mind and a clear conscience are <u>everything</u>.
9. Bob's idea for the assembly seems the <u>best</u>.
10. My best friends are <u>you</u> and <u>he</u>.

■ Predicate Adjectives

The second kind of subject complement is the *predicate adjective*.

A **predicate adjective** is an adjective that follows a linking verb and describes the subject of the sentence.

In sentences with predicate adjectives, the linking verb joins the subject with the predicate adjective. Notice in the following examples how the predicate adjectives refer to the subjects.

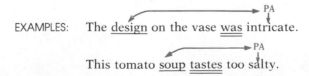

EXAMPLES: The <u>design</u> on the vase <u>was</u> intricate.

This tomato <u>soup</u> <u>tastes</u> too salty.

Like predicate nominatives, predicate adjectives may be compound.

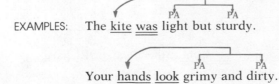

EXAMPLES: The <u>kite</u> <u>was</u> light but sturdy.

Your <u>hands</u> <u>look</u> grimy and dirty.

EXERCISE B: Recognizing Predicate Adjectives in Sentences. Write the predicate adjective in each of the following sentences on your paper. Some of the predicate adjectives are compound.

1. Her voice on the telephone sounded muffled.
2. After hours of hard work, Eugene's muscles felt stiff and sore.
3. The mayor's policy is important to our city's welfare.
4. Our sandwiches at the beach were gritty and inedible.
5. Joan grew kinder and more understanding with time.
6. A crossword puzzle should be fairly difficult.
7. This item on the list appears unnecessary.
8. The lieutenant's criticism was harsh yet impersonal.
9. Because of his frightening experience, Steve's face looked drawn and colorless.
10. Janice became successful overnight.

APPLICATION: Writing Sentences with Subject Complements. Write a sentence for each of the following sets of directions on your paper. Label all of the predicate nominatives *PN* and all of the predicate adjectives *PA*.

Answer will vary; samples given for first two.

1. Write a sentence with a noun as a predicate nominative. Use *Adam* as the subject and *became* as the verb.
2. Write a sentence with a noun as a predicate nominative. Use *Bill* as the subject and *remained* as the verb.
3. Write a sentence with two or more nouns as a compound predicate nominative. Use *insects* as the subject and *are* as the verb.
4. Write a sentence with two pronouns as a compound predicate nominative. Use *friends* as the subject and *were* as the verb.
5. Write a sentence with a compound predicate adjective. Use *plants* as the subject and *looked* as the verb.

            PN   PN
1. Adam became class president.   *2. Bill remained treasurer for another year.*

Reviewing Basic Sentence Patterns   5.5

English sentences fall into certain patterns. This section will help to increase your awareness of some of the basic patterns available to you for your speaking and writing.

■ Basic Sentence Patterns

Sentences with complements follow predictable patterns.

In the English language, subject, verbs, and complements follow five **basic sentence patterns.**

The following charts should clarify the way the different kinds of complements are used in sentences. In addition to the basic *Subject-Verb* pattern, the charts point out the five basic sentence patterns for sentences with complements. With transitive verbs the patterns are *Subject-Verb-Direct Object*, *Subject-Verb-Indirect Object-Direct Object*, and *Subject-Verb-Direct Object-Objective Complement*. With linking verbs the patterns are *Subject-Verb-Predicate Nominative* and *Subject-Verb-Predicate Adjective*. In the examples, subjects have been underlined once; verbs, twice. Complements are boxed and labeled. The unmarked words act as modifiers.

The Basic Subject-Verb Pattern.   The most basic sentence pattern is a *subject* followed by a *verb*.

Pattern	Examples
S-V	The <u>fire</u> <u><u>crackled</u></u>. <u>It</u> <u><u>is</u></u> over there.

Patterns with Transitive Verbs.   Transitive action verbs are always followed by direct objects. They may also be followed by indirect objects or objective complements.

Pattern	Examples
S-AV-DO	<u>Bill</u> <u><u>presented</u></u> a formal $\boxed{\text{speech}}^{\text{DO}}$. <u>They</u> <u><u>chose</u></u> $\boxed{\text{me}}^{\text{DO}}$.
S-AV-IO-DO	His <u>teacher</u> <u><u>wrote</u></u> $\boxed{\text{him}}^{\text{IO}}$ a $\boxed{\text{recommendation}}^{\text{DO}}$.
S-AV-DO-OC	My <u>parents</u> <u><u>named</u></u> the $\boxed{\text{baby}}^{\text{DO}}$ $\boxed{\text{Jenny}}^{\text{OC}}$. The team's <u>victory</u> <u><u>made</u></u> $\boxed{\text{him}}^{\text{DO}}$ $\boxed{\text{happy}}^{\text{OC}}$.

Patterns with Linking Verbs.   Linking verbs are always followed by either a predicate nominative or a predicate adjective.

Pattern	Examples
S-LV-PN	A <u>pit viper</u> <u>is</u> a poisonous $\overset{\text{PN}}{\boxed{\text{snake}}}$.
	The <u>winner</u> <u>is</u> $\overset{\text{PN}}{\boxed{\text{she}}}$.
S-LV-PA	<u>She</u> <u>is</u> $\overset{\text{PA}}{\boxed{\text{ill}}}$ today.

Compound Patterns. Any of these basic patterns can be expanded by making any of the sentence parts compound.

EXAMPLE: S-S-AV-DO-DO-DO

Both <u>Herman Melville</u> and <u>James Joyce</u> <u>wrote</u> $\overset{\text{DO}}{\boxed{\text{poetry}}}$, $\overset{\text{DO}}{\boxed{\text{short stories}}}$, and $\overset{\text{DO}}{\boxed{\text{novels}}}$.

Experimenting with these patterns will give your writing variety and style.

EXERCISE A: Recognizing Basic Sentence Patterns. Copy the following sentences onto your paper. Underline the subjects once, the verbs twice, and draw a box around the complements. Then, identify the sentence patterns using the abbreviations found in the preceding charts. Some sentences contain compounds.

Complements are shaded.

1. <u>Warren</u> <u>ran</u> around the block. *S/V*
2. <u>Dennis</u> <u>nicknamed</u> me Buzzy. *S/AV/DO/OC*
3. This Irish <u>stew</u> <u>is</u> hearty and delicious. *S/LV/PA/PA*
4. <u>Phyllis</u> <u>sent</u> Mike and me a wonderful surprise. *S/AV/IO/IO/DO*
5. The most helpful <u>suggestions</u> <u>were</u> yours and mine. *S/LV/PN/PN*
6. <u>Jill</u> <u>dyed</u> her hair bright orange. *S/AV/DO/OC*
7. After years of exile, <u>Philip Nolan</u> <u>felt</u> desperate for news. *S/LV/PA*
8. A powerful <u>telescope</u> <u>gives</u> astronomers a better look at the universe. *S/AV/IO/DO*
9. Pileated <u>woodpeckers</u> <u>are</u> large, red-crested birds. *S/LV/PN*
10. <u>Hubert</u> <u>covered</u> the walls with peanut butter. *S/AV/DO*

■ Inverted Sentence Patterns

The patterns shown in the preceding charts are not the only sentence pattern possibilities.

In an inverted sentence pattern, the subject is never first.

Variations of the basic patterns occur in most questions, in sentences beginning with *there* or *here*, and in sentences inverted for emphasis.

Patterns in Inverted Questions.   Although some questions beginning with interrogative adjectives or pronouns are not inverted, most questions rely on inversion. In a question containing a single form of the verb *be*, for example, the subject often follows the verb.

Pattern	Examples
V-S	Are the peaches from California?
	Why are they here?

Another inverted pattern may occur in questions containing verb phrases. Then the order will generally be *Helping Verb-Subject-Verb*.

Pattern	Examples
HV-S-V	Will Joe arrive today?
	Where is he going?

Complements usually follow the subject and verb in inverted questions. Sometimes, however, the direct object may begin the sentence.

Pattern	Examples
V-S-COMP	Was Robert delirious? (PA)
HV-S-V-COMP	Are you reading that novel? (DO)
COMP-HV-S-V	Which necklace did the jeweler sell? (DO)

Patterns in Sentences Beginning with *There* or *Here*. Sentences beginning with *there* or *here* are almost always inverted: The subject follows the verb.

Pattern	Example
V-S	There <u>is</u> an <u>owl</u> in the barn.

Patterns in Sentences Inverted for Emphasis. In sentences in which inversion is used to emphasize the subject, the subject follows the verb.

Pattern	Example
V-S	Above the dying animal <u>soared</u> a dozen <u>vultures</u>.

Sometimes a sentence is inverted not to emphasize the subject at the end but to stress the complement at the beginning.

Pattern	Examples
COMP-S-V	What a DO [victory] <u>we</u> <u>had</u>!
COMP-V-S	How PA [fragile] <u>was</u> that <u>peace</u>!

EXERCISE B: Recognizing Inverted Sentence Patterns. Copy the following sentences onto your paper. Underline the subjects once, the verbs twice, and draw a box around the complements. Then, identify the sentence patterns using the abbreviations found in the preceding charts.
Complements are shaded.

1. Why <u>does</u> <u>everyone</u> always <u>suspect</u> the butler? *HV/S/V/COMP*
2. Back and forth, through the hospital corridors, <u>paced</u> the anxious <u>father</u>. *V/S*
3. "What a piece of work <u>is</u> <u>man</u>!" *COMP/V/S*
4. How many trees <u>will</u> <u>they</u> <u>plant</u>? *COMP/HV/S/V*
5. Deep under the sea <u>lay</u> the ancient Spanish <u>galleon</u>. *V/S*
6. <u>Was</u> <u>Marlene</u> <u>trapped</u> in the broken elevator? *HV/S/V*
7. When <u>was</u> <u>De Gaulle</u> President of France? *V/S/COMP*
8. <u>Is</u> this frayed <u>wire</u> dangerous? *V/S/COMP*
9. What beautiful weather <u>we</u> <u>have been enjoying</u>! *COMP/S/HV/HV/V*
10. <u>Could</u> <u>you</u> <u>imagine</u> such a spectacular sight? *HV/S/V/COMP*

APPLICATION: Writing Sentences in a Variety of Patterns. Write sentences of your own, using the following patterns.

Then underline your subjects once, underline your verbs twice, and draw a box around the complements.

Answers will vary; samples given for first two.

1. S-V
2. S-AV-IO-DO
3. S-AV-DO-OC
4. S-LV-PN
5. HV-S-V

6. V-S-COMP
7. HV-S-V-COMP
8. COMP-HV-S-V
9. COMP-V-S
10. S-S-AV-IO-IO-DO

1. The <u>boy</u> <u>cried</u> out for help.   *2. The <u>teacher</u> <u>gave</u> you a cynical look.*

5.6 Diagraming the Basic Parts of Sentences

Diagraming is a visual way of reinforcing your understanding of sentences and of each of their parts. Like a blueprint, a diagram can make a fuzzy mental picture of a sentence clear and logical.

■ Subjects, Verbs, Modifiers, and Conjunctions

The simplest sentence pattern to diagram contains just a subject and a verb. When modifiers and conjunctions are added, the process becomes a little more complicated.

Subjects and Verbs. To diagram a sentence with just a subject and a verb, draw a horizontal line, place the subject on the left, the verb on the right, and then draw a vertical line to separate the subject from the verb.

EXAMPLE: Adriana laughed.

Adriana	laughed

Names, compound nouns, and verb phrases are diagramed in the same way.

EXAMPLE: George Fredericks must have arrived.

George Fredericks	must have arrived

When a sentence is inverted, as in a question or for emphasis, the diagram remains the same as it would for a sentence in the usual subject-verb order.

EXAMPLE: Did Norman finish?

Adjectives. Adjectives are placed on slanted lines directly below the nouns or pronouns they modify. The possessive forms of personal pronouns (*my, your, his, hers,* and so on) are always diagramed as adjectives.

EXAMPLE: My fragile antique glass shattered.

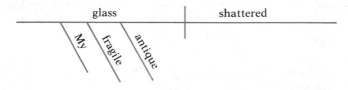

Adverbs. Adverbs are placed on slanted lines directly beneath the verbs, adjectives, or adverbs they modify. Notice the extra line that connects an adverb to an adjective or another adverb.

EXAMPLE: Quite confident, Jane soon answered very wisely.

When an adverb splits a verb phrase, it is diagramed in the same way that any adverb modifying a verb would be.

EXAMPLE: Freda could not decide.

Conjunctions. Conjunctions are diagramed on dotted lines drawn between the words they connect. In the following examples, coordinating conjunctions join both adjectives and adverbs.

EXAMPLE: A beautiful but dangerous stallion galloped smoothly and swiftly.

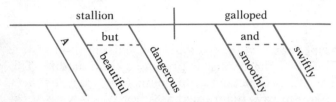

EXERCISE A: Diagraming Subjects, Verbs, Modifiers, and Conjunctions. Each of the following sentences contains a subject and a verb. Some contain adjectives and adverbs. Diagram each sentence on your paper. *Answers on page T-103.*

1. Ned waited.
2. Many confused sheep wandered.
3. Swallows soared overhead.
4. The foaming white waterfall cascaded thunderously down.
5. The many red and green balloons floated upward.

■ Compound Subjects and Verbs

When compound subjects and verbs are diagramed, each of the separate compound parts is placed on a line of its own.

Compound Subjects. The following example shows how compound subjects are placed on a diagram. Notice the position of the conjunction.

EXAMPLE: Wool and cotton can shrink.

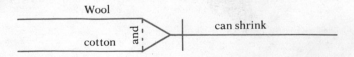

It is important to be careful with the placement of adjectives when compound subjects are diagramed. Notice the position of the adjectives in the following example. Since *several* modifies both parts of the compound subject it is positioned under the stem of the diagram.

EXAMPLE: Several piercing shrieks and desperate yells were heard.

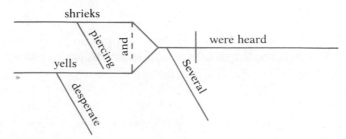

Compound Verbs.   The diagram for compound verbs is similar to that for compound subjects. If an adverb modifies both parts of the compound verb, it is placed on the stem. However, if it modifies just one of the verbs, it is placed directly below it.

EXAMPLE: Marcus usually slept fitfully and tossed restlessly.

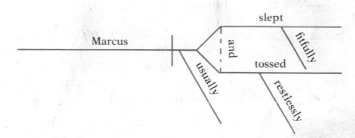

When a helping verb is shared by both parts of a compound verb, the helping verb is positioned on the stem of the diagram. However, if each part of the compound verb has its own helping verb, each helping verb is positioned on the line with its verb.

EXAMPLE: The cattle would bellow and stampede.

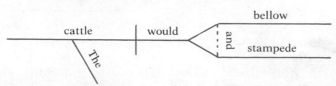

EXAMPLE: This proposal might be accepted or might be rejected.

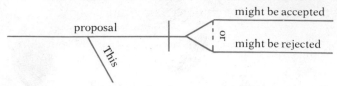

If a sentence contains both a compound subject and a compound verb, the diagram will look similar to the following example. Notice the position of the correlative conjunction in the subject.

EXAMPLE: Neither Tracy nor Silvia will lie, steal, or cheat.

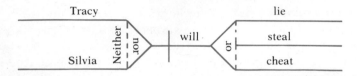

EXERCISE B: Diagraming Compound Subjects and Compound Verbs.

The following sentences contain a compound subject, a compound verb, or both. Some of the sentences contain adjectives and adverbs. Copy the skeletons for the first two onto your paper and diagram each sentence. Then diagram the remaining sentences. *Answers on page T-104.*

1. Skill and technology were provided.

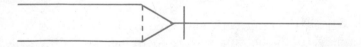

2. Wood can be painted or can be varnished.

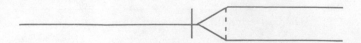

3. Most ducks, geese, and other birds eventually migrate south.
4. The unusual and colorful kite soared gracefully, slowly dipped, and suddenly fell.

5. Two obviously bored children and their desperately uncomfortable parents fidgeted anxiously and waited very impatiently.
6. Must pork and bacon be cooked thoroughly?
7. A poodle should be bathed and then carefully clipped.
8. The mechanical toy frog could not only croak but also jump far.
9. Neither worms, minnows, nor lures will work.
10. His thoroughly tasteless remarks and arrogant manner can only be ignored.

■ Orders and Sentences Beginning with *There* or *Here*

Sentences that give orders and sentences that begin with *there* or *here* are easily diagramed once you know the method.

Orders. The understood *you*, the implied subject in orders and directions, is written in parentheses.

EXAMPLE: Stand up.

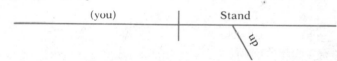

Sentences Beginning with *There* or *Here*. Usually when *there* or *here* begins a sentence, it will function as an adverb modifying the verb.

EXAMPLE: Here comes Bob.

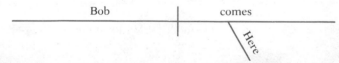

If *there* is used as an expletive to get the sentence started, it is positioned on a short line over the subject.

EXAMPLE: There were a few possibilities.

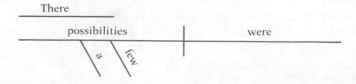

NOTE ABOUT EXPLETIVE STYLE: The expletive style is also used for interjections and nouns of direct address.

EXAMPLE: Alas, my friend, you lost.

EXERCISE C: Diagraming Orders and Sentences Beginning with *There* or *Here*.

Diagram each of the following sentences on your paper. Make sure that the understood subjects, adverbs, expletives, interjections, and nouns of direct address are positioned correctly in your diagrams. *Answers on page T-106.*

1. Mr. Ricardo, come here.
2. Go ahead, Vera.
3. Uh, I forgot.
4. Here is the pharmacy.
5. There should be a parade today.

■ Complements

The five kinds of sentence complements are diagramed in four different ways.

Direct Objects.   A direct object is positioned on the main horizontal line after the verb. A short vertical line separates the direct object from the verb.

EXAMPLE: Carol selected a small golden locket.

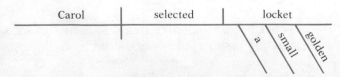

Compound direct objects are diagramed like compound subjects and verbs. If an adjective modifies both parts of the compound direct object, it is placed under the stem of the diagram. If it modifies only one of the direct objects, it is placed directly under the direct object.

EXAMPLE: Evan wrote several articles and book reviews.

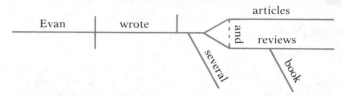

Indirect Objects.   An indirect object is positioned on a short horizontal line extending from a slanted line directly below the verb.

EXAMPLE: Louis always gives his brother lectures.

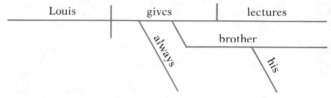

The following example shows how a compound indirect object is diagramed.

EXAMPLE: Mr. Willowby promised Ellie and Tom a reward.

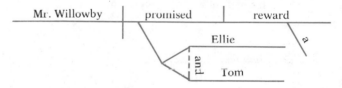

Objective Complements.   Since an objective complement helps complete the meaning of a direct object, they are positioned next to each other. A short slanted line separates them.

EXAMPLE: The President named him Chief-of-Staff.

President | named | him \ Chief-of-Staff

The

Subject Complements.   Both predicate nominatives and predicate adjectives are positioned in the same way on the main horizontal line after linking verbs. A short, slanted line is used to separate them from the verb.

PREDICATE NOMINATIVE: A spaniel is a gentle, intelligent pet.

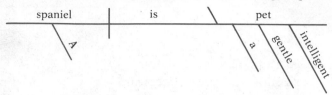

PREDICATE ADJECTIVE: Cashmere sweaters should be luxuriously soft.

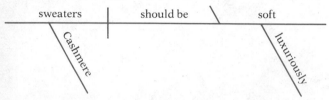

A compound subject complement is diagramed just like a compound direct object, but the line separating the complement from the verb is slanted.

EXAMPLE: We felt very tired and somewhat grouchy.

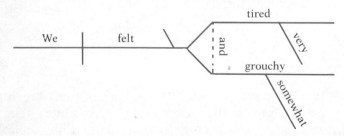

EXERCISE D: Diagraming Direct Objects, Indirect Objects, and Objective Complements. The following sentences contain direct objects, indirect objects, and objective complements. Some of the direct objects and indirect objects may be compound. Diagram each sentence on your paper.
Answers on page T-106.

1. The irritable old gentleman pushed his food away.
2. This remarkable but true story taught Sally and me something.
3. Henry, do not call me any more names!

4. A well-made food processor will chop vegetables and meats.
5. His extremely shy and cautious manner gave Sal and me courage.

EXERCISE E: Diagraming Subject Complements. The following sentences contain predicate nominatives and predicate adjectives. Some are compound. Diagram each sentence on your paper. *Answers on page T-107.*

1. That painting is a masterpiece.
2. The fresh, clean mountain air felt wonderful.
3. Her husband is a friend and a companion.
4. Martha's pie crusts were always light and flaky.
5. Domestic turkeys are dull-witted but delicious.

APPLICATION: Diagraming Different Sentence Parts. The following sentences contain all of the sentence parts covered in this section: subjects, verbs, modifiers, conjunctions, and complements. Diagram each sentence on your paper. *Answers on page T-108.*

1. Jules, give me both the rusty old saw and those two heavy wrenches.
2. This ancient castle must have some secret passages or dark tunnels inside.
3. There should be paper or pens somewhere.
4. A healthy and happy student will usually enjoy school and like extracurricular activities.
5. Egad! This bold plan is most clever yet appears quite innocent.

Chapter 6

Phrases

A verb phrase, consisting of two or more words, functions just as a single verb would. Prepositional phrases and other kinds of phrases, as you will see in this chapter, function similarly.

A **phrase** is a group of words, without a subject and verb, that functions in a sentence as one part of speech.

There are several kinds of phrases: prepositional phrases, appositive phrases, participial phrases, gerund phrases, and infinitive phrases. The last three types of phrases may be grouped together as verbal phrases. In this chapter you will learn how phrases can be used to add meaning and variety to your sentences.

6.1 Prepositional Phrases

A prepositional phrase is a group of words that begins with a preposition and ends with a noun or pronoun called the object of the preposition. A single prepositional phrase may have two or more objects joined by a conjunction.

EXAMPLES:
Prep   Obj
over their heads

Prep   Obj   Obj
between the window and the wall

In this section you will learn how prepositional phrases function either as adjectives or as adverbs within sentences.

■ Adjectival Phrases

A prepositional phrase that acts as an adjective is called an *adjectival phrase*.

An **adjectival phrase** is a prepositional phrase that modifies a noun or pronoun by telling what kind or which one.

The following chart contrasts adjectives with adjectival phrases.

Adjectives	Adjectival Phrases
He admired a *beautiful* painting.	He admired a painting *of great beauty.*
The woman sang a *sentimental* song.	The woman sang a song *with sentiment.*
Mary took a *boxed* lunch.	Mary took lunch *in a box.*

A prepositional phrase that answers the adjectival questions *What kind?* or *Which one?* will be an adjectival phrase. In the first sentence on the right in the chart, for example, the question *What kind of painting?* is answered by *of great beauty*.

Adjectival phrases usually modify nouns functioning as subjects, direct objects, indirect objects, or predicate nominatives.

MODIFYING A SUBJECT:

The mansion *across the road* has been abandoned.

MODIFYING A DIRECT OBJECT:

Marilyn erased the poem *on the blackboard.*

MODIFYING AN INDIRECT OBJECT:

A realtor sold our neighbors *above us* a beautiful country home.

MODIFYING A PREDICATE NOMINATIVE:

A unicorn is a mythical horselike animal *with a single horn.*

A sentence may often have a series of two or more adjectival phrases. When this happens, each succeeding phrase may modify the object of the preceding phrase.

EXAMPLE:　The wind blew down the tree *on the corner of the block.*

The adjectival phrase *on the corner* describes *tree*. The adjectival phrase *of the block* modifies *corner*.

In other situations, more than one adjectival phrase may describe the same noun.

EXAMPLE:　New England women brought patches *with bright colors for a quilting bee.*

Both *with bright colors* and *for a quilting bee* are adjectival phrases that tell what kind of *patches*.

EXERCISE A: Identifying Adjectival Phrases.

Each of the following sentences contains one or more adjectival phrases. Write the adjectival phrase or phrases in each sentence on your paper. Then write the modified word and indicate its function in the sentence as a *subject, direct object, object of a preposition,* and so on.
Modified words are shaded.

EXAMPLE:　Tom's mother wrote a note for her son's absence.

　　　　　for her son's absence　note　direct object

1. Agatha Christie was a widely read writer of mysteries. *PN*
2. The article about Indian folklore is fascinating. *S*
3. My uncle designed the props for the play by Ibsen. *DO/obj*
4. Her masterpiece is a book with three parts. *PN*　　　*of prep*
5. A trellis near the cottage door supported the climbing vines. *S*
6. We painted the ceilings throughout the house and shampooed the carpeting on the stairs and floors. *DO/DO*
7. Bring me the wagon beside the door of the barn. *DO/obj*
8. A rendezvous at the outdoor café was canceled. *S*　*of prep*

9. Some of the boys and girls in the class showed interest in mechanical drawing. *S/obj of prep*
10. The Danish ballet dancers made a favorable impression upon the audience. *DO*

■ Adverbial Phrases

A prepositional phrase that acts as an adverb is called an *adverbial phrase*.

An **adverbial phrase** is a prepositional phrase that modifies a verb, adjective, or adverb by pointing out where, when, in what manner, or to what extent.

The following chart shows that adverbial phrases function in a manner similar to single-word adverbs.

Adverbs	Adverbial Phrases
She ran *swiftly*.	She ran *with speed*.
They were happy *there*.	They were happy *at the picnic*.
Alex was *never* afraid.	Alex was afraid *of nothing*.

If a prepositional phrase is adverbial, it will answer one of the adverbial questions: *Where? When? In what manner?* or *To what extent?* In the first example on the right in the chart, the question *Ran in what manner?* is answered by *with speed*, an adverbial phrase.

Unlike an adjectival phrase, which almost always follows the word it modifies, an adverbial phrase may either follow the word it modifies or be located elsewhere in the sentence.

EXAMPLES: The slumbering village vanished *during the avalanche.*

During the avalanche the slumbering village vanished.

Like single-word adverbs, adverbial phrases can modify either verbs, adjectives, or adverbs.

MODIFYING A VERB: The marathon runner dashed *past the spectators.*

MODIFYING AN ADJECTIVE: The forest became quiet *before daybreak.*

MODIFYING AN ADVERB: He arrived late *for class.*

Like adjectival phrases, two or more adverbial phrases may modify the same word.

EXAMPLE: *In the evening, after dinner,* my friends and I walked *to the movies.*

EXERCISE B: Identifying Adverbial Phrases. Each of the following sentences contains one or more adverbial phrases. Write the adverbial phrase or phrases in each sentence on your paper. Then write the modified word and indicate its part of speech as *verb, adjective,* or *adverb.*

EXAMPLE: He rapped loudly upon the door.

upon the door   rapped   verb

1. The Pied Piper lured the children from the village. *verb*
2. Calcium is essential for strong bones and teeth. *adj*
3. A crab is fairly safe inside its skeleton. *adj*
4. After the wedding ceremony, the bride left in the groom's car. *verb/verb*
5. The whale died in silent agony on the beach. *verb/verb*
6. After the lecture, she was enthusiastic about military service. *adj/adj*
7. In a flash, the mischievous child plucked all the flowers from the neighbor's garden. *verb/verb*
8. During the afternoon, the crowds drifted to the ice-cream stands. *verb/verb*
9. The editorial is rich in sarcasm. *adj*
10. When children worked in factories, their lives were often worth little. *verb*

APPLICATION: Adding Adjectival and Adverbial Phrases. Copy the following paragraph onto your paper, filling in each blank with an adjectival or adverbial phrase. Be prepared to tell whether the phrase is adjectival or adverbial. *Answers will vary; samples given.*

The snow (1) __on the ground__ had been falling (2) __since midnight__ . (3) __On the morning__ (4) __after the storm__ Mike sat (5) __at the window__ and watched as the drifts grew higher. Soon they would reach the top (6) __of the dog house__ . One huge drift (7) __from the east__ was moving (8) __toward it__ . Mike stared (9) __in disbelief__ as he watched the drift slowly spread (10) __over everything__ .

1. adj   2. adv   3. adv   4. adj   5. adv   6. adj   7. adj   8. adv   9. adv   10. adv

(11) ___except the roof___ . He jumped (12) ___from his bed___ and ran (13) ___out the door___ . There was no time to lose, and (14) ___without hesitation___ , he grabbed (15) ___for the snow shovel___ . (16) ___After a moment___ (17) ___of strenuous effort___ Mike knew there was nothing to fear. He had succeeded (18) ___in his rescue___ . His story (19) ___of his dog's escape___ could be told (20) ___to everyone___ .

11. adj   12. adv   13. adv   14. adv   15. adv   16. adv   17. adj   18. adv   19. adj   20. adv

Appositives and Appositive Phrases 6.2

The term *appositive* comes from a Latin verb meaning "to put near or next to." Using appositives in your speaking and writing is an easy way to give additional meaning to nouns and some pronouns.

An appositive is a noun or pronoun placed after another noun or pronoun to identify, rename, or explain it.

■ Appositives

A word *in apposition* is "placed next to" another word. In the following chart, each appositive is placed next to the word it identifies, renames, or explains.

APPOSITIVES
Her greatest attribute, *charm*, was not enough.
Some villagers, the *old-timers*, prefer the dirt roads.
Wapiti (*elk*) are the largest kind of deer in North America.

Notice that all the examples in the chart are set off by commas or other punctuation. The punctuation is used because these appositives are *nonessential*. In other words, they could be omitted from the sentences without altering the sentences' basic meaning.

Some appositives, however, are not set off by any punctuation because they are *essential* to the meaning of the sentence. As you read the following examples, notice how much of the sentences' meaning would be lost if the appositives were removed.

EXAMPLES: The artist *Van Gogh* cut off his ear.

A successful play was made out of the story found

in the book *Look Homeward, Angel.*

For more about punctuating appositives, see Section 15.2.

NOTE ABOUT TERMS: Sometimes the terms *nonrestrictive* and *restrictive* are used in place of *nonessential* and *essential*.

EXERCISE A: **Identifying Appositives.** Each of the following sentences contains an appositive. Write the appositive from each sentence on your paper. Then write the words that the appositives rename. *Words renamed are shaded.*

1. Edna discussed her favorite topic, <u>food</u>.
2. My cousin <u>Phyllis</u> will spend this summer with us.
3. We thought he would give Cara, <u>a girlfriend</u>, something for Valentine's Day.
4. Herman Melville wrote the novel <u>*Moby Dick*</u>.
5. Our cat, <u>a Manx</u>, has free run of the house.
6. The movie <u>*Gone with the Wind*</u> was a great success on TV.
7. Douglas looks good in his favorite color, <u>blue</u>.
8. We remembered one important item, <u>a can opener</u>, as we set up camp on the mountainside.
9. She played a woodwind instrument, <u>the clarinet</u>, in addition to the harp.
10. The inventor <u>Frankenstein</u> created a monster that eventually destroyed him.

■ Appositive Phrases

When an appositive is accompanied by its own modifiers, it forms an *appositive phrase*.

An **appositive phrase** is a noun or pronoun with modifiers, placed next to a noun or pronoun to add information and details.

The modifiers within an appositive phrase can be adjectives, adjectival phrases, or other groups of words functioning as adjectives.

Appositives	Appositive Phrases
Amethyst, a *birthstone*, is for people born in February.	Amethyst, *a purple birthstone,* is for people born in February.
The sailor had scurvy, a *disease.*	The sailor had scurvy, *a disease caused by a lack of vitamin C.*
Fred explained numismatics, a *hobby.*	Fred explained numismatics, *the interesting hobby of coin collecting.*

Appositives and appositive phrases may follow nouns or pronouns used in almost any role within a sentence. The following examples show a few of the positions in which appositives may be found.

WITH A SUBJECT:

Ernest Hemingway, *a famous author,* wrote in a terse style.

WITH A DIRECT OBJECT:

Eve wore a sequined shirt, *the latest fad.*

WITH AN INDIRECT OBJECT:

I bought my brother, *a boy of six,* a pet turtle.

WITH AN OBJECTIVE COMPLEMENT:

They painted the house purple, *an unusual color for a house.*

WITH A PREDICATE NOMINATIVE:

A porcupine's best defense is its quills—*sharp, barbed spines.*

WITH AN OBJECT OF A PREPOSITION:

The bins in the root cellar, *a cool, dry room,* stored potatoes and apples.

Appositives and appositive phrases may also be compound. In the following examples, notice that the compound parts of the appositives are joined by the conjunctions *and* and *both . . . and.*

EXAMPLES:

We visited several Hawaiian islands: *Oahu, Maui,* and *Molokai*.

Armand, *both his schoolmate and his confidant*, was always a welcome presence in the house.

When appositives or appositive phrases are used to combine sentences, they help to eliminate unnecessary words. The following examples show how two sentences may be smoothly joined as one.

TWO SENTENCES: Jules Verne wrote about a submarine before it had even been invented. He was a remarkable man.

SENTENCE WITH APPOSITIVE PHRASE: Jules Verne, *a remarkable man*, wrote about a submarine before it had ever been invented.

TWO SENTENCES: Vermont is a state with breathtaking scenery. It has brilliant foliage in the fall and snowy mountain peaks in the winter.

SENTENCE WITH APPOSITIVE PHRASE: Vermont, *a state with breathtaking scenery*, has brilliant foliage in the fall and snowy mountain peaks in the winter.

NOTE ABOUT APPOSITIVE PHRASES WITH *NOT:* Sometimes an appositive phrase may begin with the word *not*. Its effect is to set up a sharp contrast.

EXAMPLE: The good old days, *not the bad old days*, were remembered.

EXERCISE B: Identifying Appositive Phrases. Each of the following sentences contains an appositive phrase. Some are compound. Write the appositive phrase from each sentence on your paper. Then write the words the appositive phrases rename.

1. Tammy learned the Heimlich maneuver, a technique for saving people from choking.
2. The bobcat, an endangered species, has been hunted as a pest in the East.

3. At the circus the clown rode a dromedary, a one-humped camel, rapidly around the ring.
4. He was proud of owning his first car, an old jalopy.
5. The office workers named Don Jones chairman, a well-deserved title.
6. I will tell you, my good friend, an intriguing story.
7. Herb will read anything—matchbooks, junk mail, or the backs of cereal boxes—whenever a book isn't handy.
8. Marsha gave the baby some stuffed animals: a white, woolly lamb, a huggable teddy bear, and a huge, floppy elephant.
9. My family took our guests to a French restaurant, one of the best places in the city.
10. Bill excelled in two outdoor sports, archery and canoeing.

APPLICATION: **Writing Sentences with Appositives and Appositive Phrases.** Combine each of the following pairs of sentences to make one sentence containing an appositive or appositive phrase. *Answers will vary; samples given for first two.*

1. An ostrich is a native of Africa and parts of Asia.
   The ostrich is the largest of all birds.
2. Mrs. Gordon always kept a melodeon in her parlor.
   Her parlor was a room for special guests.
3. The restaurant serves lobster in a delicious Newburg sauce.
   Newburg sauce is a creamy sauce with butter and wine.
4. Marjorie is one of the most interesting people I know.
   She is a gourmet, an expert ventriloquist, and a very good photographer.
5. Donny's father is a neurologist.
   He is a specialist on the nervous system.
   1. An ostrich, the largest of all birds, is a native of Africa and parts of Asia.
   2. Mrs. Gordon always kept a melodeon in her parlor, a room for special guests.

Participles and Participial Phrases 6.3

When a verb is used as a noun, adjective, or adverb, it is called a *verbal*. Although a verbal does not function as a verb, it still retains two characteristics of verbs: (1) It can be modified by adverbs and adverbial phrases, and (2) it can have a complement. If a verbal has modifiers or a complement, it is called a *verbal phrase*. This section will explain the kind of verbal that functions as an adjective.

■ Present Participles and Past Participles

Many of the adjectives you use are actually verbals known as *participles*.

A participle is a form of a verb that acts as an adjective.

There are two kinds of participles: *present participles* and *past participles*. These two kinds of participles can be distinguished from each other by their endings. Present participles end in *-ing (frightening, entertaining)*. Past participles usually end in *-ed (frightened, entertained)*, but many have irregular endings such as *-t* or *-en (burst, written)*. (See Section 9.1 for more information on irregular verb endings.)

The following charts show participles modifying nouns within sentences.

PRESENT PARTICIPLE

Limping, a *returning* hiker favored his *aching* ankle.

PAST PARTICIPLE

Confused, Nan returned to her *interrupted* work.

Notice that participles answer the adjectival questions *What kind?* or *Which one?*

EXAMPLES: Irma's *shining* eyes betrayed her excitement.

What kind of eyes?   *shining* eyes

The *shattered* window needs replacement.

Which window?   the *shattered* window

NOTE ABOUT *BEING* AND *HAVING*:   The present participles *being* and *having* may be followed by a past participle.

EXAMPLES: *Being informed*, I knew what to expect.

Having decided, Adele acted quickly.

EXERCISE A: Identifying Present and Past Participles. Each of the following sentences contains a present or past participle. Write the participle from each sentence on your paper. Then identify it as *present* or *past*.

1. Grandmother Jefferson's <u>fractured</u> hip is very painful. *past*
2. A <u>fluttering</u> white flag was held over the soldiers' heads. *pres*
3. Water surged over the banks of the <u>swollen</u> river. *past*
4. This arsonist has an <u>established</u> pattern for fires. *past*
5. <u>Drizzling</u> rain kept us all housebound. *pres*
6. We sat and listened to the <u>pounding</u> waves and the cry of seagulls. *pres*
7. The handyman left <u>splattered</u> paint all over the floor. *past*
8. <u>Lisping</u>, the child told us about the Tooth Fairy. *pres*
9. During the storm, a <u>broken</u> branch fell onto our roof. *past*
10. <u>Disgusted</u>, his mother glowered at the horrible mess. *past*

■ Verb or Participle?

It is easy to confuse a participle with a verb since they share the endings *-ing* and *-ed*. The following chart shows words used first as verbs and then as participles. Notice that as verbs the words tell what someone or something does or did. As participles, however, the same words describe someone or something.

Verbs	Participles
The dog is *snarling* at the plumber. (What is the dog doing?)	The *snarling* dog attacked the plumber. (Which dog?)
The singers *delighted* their audience. (What did the singers do?)	*Delighted*, the audience applauded. (What kind of audience?)

EXERCISE B: Distinguishing Between Verbs and Participles. Identify each of the underlined words in the following sentences as a *verb* or a *participle*. If the word is a participle, indicate the word it modifies on your paper.
Modified words are shaded.
1. At the birthday party, the loud bang of a <u>punctured</u> balloon startled everyone. *part*
2. The front tire could have been <u>punctured</u> when it ran over a nail. *verb*

part 3. My flashlight illuminated the <u>towering</u> walls of the cave.
4. Myriad stars were <u>glittering</u> in the night sky. *verb*
5. The cracked eggs should be <u>removed</u> from the carton. *verb*
6. <u>Separated</u>, the twins were inconsolable. *part*
verb 7. In the alley, a forlorn puppy was <u>whimpering</u> with fear.
8. An angry mother hushed her <u>sobbing</u> child. *part*
9. A <u>torn</u> parachute must be either thoroughly mended or discarded. *part*
10. The old parchment has been <u>ripped</u> in half. *verb*

■ Participial Phrases

Participles become *participial phrases* when they have their own modifiers or complements.

A **participial phrase** is a present or past participle that is modified by an adverb or adverbial phrase or that has a complement. The entire phrase acts as an adjective in a sentence.

The following examples show different ways that participles may be expanded into phrases.

EXAMPLES: *Jumping high*, Brad hit his head on the ceiling.

The chemist, *blinded by smoky fumes*, stumbled out of the laboratory.

Scanning the textbook, Craig spotted an important passage.

In the first sentence, an adverb modifies the participle *jumping*. In the second sentence, an adverbial phrase modifies *blinded*. In the last sentence, *scanning* has a direct object.

Participial phrases are punctuated according to their use within a sentence. The following chart contrasts nonessential and essential participial phrases. In the sentences on the left, the participial phrases could be removed without altering the sentences' basic meaning. However, if you remove the participial phrases from the sentences on the right, the sentences' meaning will not be the same.

Nonessential Phrases	Essential Phrases
There is my brother, *standing by the bus stop.*	The boy *standing by the bus stop* is my brother.
Painted by Leonardo in 1497, the mural of *The Last Supper* is almost beyond repair.	The famous mural *painted by Leonardo in 1497* is almost beyond repair.

In the first sentence on the left in the chart, *standing by the bus stop* merely adds information about *brother,* who has already been identified. In a similar sentence on the right, however, the same phrase is essential for the identification of *boy* since there could be many different boys in view. In the second sentence on the left, *painted by Leonardo in 1497* is an additional description of *mural,* which is adequately identified by the prepositional phrase that follows it. In the sentence on the right, the phrase is essential. It identifies the mural that is being discussed. For more about punctuating participial phrases, see Section 15.2.

EXERCISE C: Recognizing Participial Phrases. Write the participial phrase from each of the following sentences on your paper. Then indicate the word it modifies. Finally, indicate whether the phrase is *nonessential* or *essential.*

1. Andrea, waking from a terrifying dream about monsters, cried fearfully. *noness*
2. Slumped over a chair, I could only think of sleep. *noness*
3. The speedboat, making large waves, threatened to overturn the sailboats. *noness*
4. Near the road, Mrs. Foley picked up debris thrown by a careless motorist. *ess*
5. Feeling jaunty in his borrowed tuxedo, Barney sauntered into the room. *noness*
6. We stared at the horizon, broken only occasionally by small dwellings. *noness*
7. As Zack fell, he grabbed onto a branch jutting out from the cliff. *ess*
8. Shivering in anticipation, I could hardly wait for the conclusion to Poe's *The Pit and the Pendulum. noness*

9. Her husband, a man with a hearty appetite, always orders a plate piled high with flapjacks. *ess*
10. She saw in the mirror a face streaked with tears. *ess*

■ Nominative Absolutes

Sometimes the noun or pronoun modified by a participle or participial phrase belongs neither to the complete subject nor to the complete predicate of the sentence. Such constructions are called *nominative absolutes*.

> A **nominative absolute** is a noun or pronoun followed by a participle or participial phrase that functions independently of the rest of the sentence.

Although a nominative absolute is grammatically separate from the rest of the sentence, it is still closely related because it indicates time, reason, or circumstance for the rest of the sentence. In the following examples, the subjects are underlined once; the verbs, twice.

TIME: *Three hours having passed,* we could wait no longer.

REASON: *His task completed,* Andy asked for payment.

CIRCUMSTANCE: The car came to a halt, *its tires sinking into the mud.*

NOTE ABOUT *BEING*:   Sometimes the participle *being* is left out of the nominative absolute. In the following examples, parentheses indicate where the word *being* is omitted.

EXAMPLES: Lenny was caught in the act, *his hand (being) in the cookie jar.*
My mind (being) vacant, I could think of nothing.

EXERCISE D: Recognizing Nominative Absolutes. Each of the following sentences contains a nominative absolute. Write the nominative absolute from each sentence on your paper.

1. Her smile vanishing from her face, Julia listened in stunned silence.

2. Six huskies pulled the sled, <u>its runners skimming over the ice.</u>
3. <u>His glasses at home,</u> Mr. Owens squinted with bleary eyes.
4. <u>Several minutes having gone by,</u> the bank teller finally pushed the alarm button.
5. Roger whittled a stick, <u>his dog Briar lying at his feet.</u>
6. <u>A bonnet tied around her head,</u> Lisa resembled a Puritan woman.
7. <u>Candles on every table,</u> the room had a soft, inviting look.
8. <u>Several delays being unavoidable,</u> our guests finally departed.
9. <u>Midnight striking,</u> she hurried down the steps toward her carriage.
10. <u>The furnace broken,</u> we huddled under blankets and waited for dawn.

APPLICATION: **Writing Your Own Sentences with Participial Phrases.** Follow the directions to write sentences of your own containing participial phrases.
Answers will vary; samples given for first two.

EXAMPLE: Use *walk* as a present participle.

A man *walking down the road* asked for directions.
Telling no one, Janet slipped out the
1. Use *tell* as a present participle. *back door.*
2. Use *burn* as a past participle. *The badly burned cookies tasted awful.*
3. Use *hurl* as a past participle.
4. Use *work* as a present participle.
5. Use *having left* in a nominative absolute.

Gerunds and Gerund Phrases 6.4

Many nouns ending in *-ing* are actually verbals known as *gerunds*.

A **gerund** is a form of a verb that acts as a noun.

■ Verbs That Act as Nouns

Gerunds are not difficult to recognize once you realize that they always end in *-ing* and always function as nouns.

The following examples show some of the ways gerunds may be used just as nouns would be.

GERUNDS
As a subject: *Sailing* is my favorite sport.
As a direct object: Your hospitality makes *visiting* a pleasure.
As an indirect object: Mr. Mendoza's lecture gave *traveling* a new dimension.
As an object of a preposition: Their well-behaved dog showed signs of *training*.
As a predicate nominative: Walter's most annoying habit is *interrupting*.
As an appositive: Brady's profession, *advertising*, is very competitive.

D.C.   She gave the walls a painting. (IO)

EXERCISE A: Identifying Gerunds. Each of the following sentences contains at least one gerund. Write the gerunds from each sentence on your paper. Then identify each gerund's function in the sentence as *subject, direct object*, and so on.

1. <u>Gardening</u> can be enjoyable and profitable. *S*
2. The school offered classes in <u>weaving</u> and <u>sculpting</u>. *obj of prep/ obj of prep*
3. Denise's hobby, <u>sky-diving</u>, is a thrilling one. *appos*
4. The man's crimes were <u>counterfeiting</u> and <u>stealing</u>. *PN/PN*
5. <u>Milking</u> was one of Wilbur's chores. *S*
6. To avoid his dentist appointment, Fred started <u>pro-crastinating</u>. *DO*
7. Esther's favorite occupation, <u>eavesdropping</u>, can be most unpleasant. *appos*
8. My father enjoys the art of <u>fencing</u>. *obj of prep*
9. <u>Owning</u> and <u>maintaining</u> a home can be very satisfying. *S/S*
10. With this machine, <u>vacuuming</u> seems easy. *S*

■ Verb, Participle, or Gerund?

Words ending in *-ing* may be either verbs, participles, or gerunds. A verb ending in *-ing* will always be part of a verb phrase. A participle ending in *-ing* will always function as an adjective. And a gerund, which must end in *-ing*, will always function as a noun. If you keep these ideas in mind, it will not be difficult to tell them apart.

Verb	Participle	Gerund
Kevin is *yawning*.	The *yawning* boy was very tired.	*Yawning* is contagious.

EXERCISE B: **Distinguishing Between Verbs, Participles, and Gerunds.** Identify the underlined word in each of the following sentences as either a *verb*, a *participle*, or a *gerund*.

1. Do we have any <u>wrapping</u> paper left? *part*
2. The detective was <u>wrapping</u> up the case. *verb*
3. <u>Wrapping</u> the gifts for Joanna's party took longer than expected. *ger*
4. Emma must have been <u>dreaming</u> about a handsome prince. *verb*
5. The <u>dreaming</u> boy stared absently out the window. *part*
6. Rarely do I remember <u>dreaming</u>. *ger*
7. Many athletes use <u>running</u> as a means of exercise. *ger*
8. Our summer cabin has <u>running</u> water in the kitchen. *part*
9. <u>Shopping</u> can become tiresome after a few hours. *ger*
10. Lou is <u>shopping</u> for a new trenchcoat. *verb*

■ Gerund Phrases

Like participles, gerunds may be joined by other words to make *gerund phrases*.

A **gerund phrase** is a gerund with modifiers or a complement, all acting together as a noun.

The following examples show just a few of the ways that gerunds may be expanded into gerund phrases.

GERUND PHRASES
Gerund with adjectives: *His constant, angry frowning* made wrinkles in his face.
Gerund with adjectival phrase: *Arguing about grades* will get you nowhere.
Gerund with adverb: *Walking briskly* is good exercise.

Gerund with adverbial phrase:	The park prohibits *walking on the grass.* #10
Gerund with direct object:	Russell was incapable of *recovering the ball.* #1, 2, 3, 4 ..
Gerund with indirect and direct objects:	Mrs. Jeffries tries *giving her students praise.*

PN - #7 , DO-OC Mrs. Jeffries tried painting her walls blue

NOTE ABOUT GERUNDS AND POSSESSIVE PRONOUNS: Always use the possessive form of a personal pronoun before a gerund.

INCORRECT: We never listen to *him boasting.*

CORRECT: We never listen to *his boasting.*

EXERCISE C: Identifying Gerund Phrases. Each of the following sentences contains at least one gerund phrase. Write each gerund phrase on your paper. Be prepared to identify the modifiers and complements that help make up the phrases.

1. She is good at <u>remembering trivia and unimportant details.</u>
2. The most amusing event, <u>catching a greased pig,</u> was the highlight of the fair.
3. As a child, his household tasks were <u>setting the table before dinner</u> and <u>washing the dishes afterwards.</u>
4. <u>Caring for pets</u> is a good way of <u>learning responsibility.</u>
5. During the summer Hal taught <u>canoeing to the youngsters</u> and <u>riding to the adults.</u>
6. <u>Drying fruits and vegetables for winter use</u> is good for <u>cutting down expenses.</u>
7. Morris's worst habits are <u>complaining about everyone's faults</u> and <u>worrying unceasingly.</u>
8. At the Olympics we enjoyed <u>trading stories with the other spectators.</u>
9. To me, summer, fall, and winter mean <u>mowing grass,</u> <u>raking leaves,</u> and <u>shoveling snow.</u>
10. <u>Hoarding money under the mattress</u> is not the best way to beat inflation.

APPLICATION: Writing Your Own Sentences with Gerund Phrases. Follow the directions to write sentences of your own containing gerund phrases. Underline the gerund phrase in each sentence. *Answers will vary; samples given for first two.*

1. Use *cooking* as a direct object.
2. Use *preparing* as a predicate nominative.
3. Use *explaining* as the object of a preposition.
4. Use *huddling* as a subject.
5. Use *directing* as a predicate nominative.

1. I enjoy <u>cooking for company</u>.
2. The worst part of the job is <u>preparing the surface</u>.

Infinitives and Infinitive Phrases 6.5

The third and last kind of verbal is the *infinitive*.

An **infinitive** is a form of a verb that comes after the word *to* and acts as a noun, adjective, or adverb.

■ The Different Uses of Infinitives

As nouns, infinitives can be used in almost as many ways as gerunds.

INFINITIVES USED AS NOUNS
As a subject: To *understand* required maturity and acceptance.
As a direct object: Working hard at her new job, Brenda hoped *to succeed*.
As a predicate nominative: The hunter's only defense against the bear was *to run*.
As an object of a preposition: With his muscles tensed, the inexperienced parachuter was about *to jump*.
As an appositive: You have only one choice, *to go*.

Unlike gerunds, infinitives can also act as adjectives and adverbs.

INFINITIVES USED AS MODIFIERS
As an adjective: The eager villagers showed a willingness *to cooperate*.
As an adverb: Some people are unable *to adjust*.

EXERCISE A: Identifying Infinitives. Each of the following sentences contains an infinitive. Write the infinitive from each sentence on your paper. Then identify it as a *noun, adjective,* or *adverb*. If the infinitive is a noun, further identify it as a *subject, direct object, predicate nominative, object of a preposition,* or *appositive*.

1. To fantasize was his only way out of a dreary life. *noun–S*
2. We were reluctant to leave. *adv*
3. Worried by my decision, I decided to reconsider. *noun–DO*
4. Seth had only one alternative, to flee. *noun–appos*
5. The teacher assigned us too many pages to read. *adj*
6. Our best tactic is to watch. *noun–PN*
7. To build was the architect's fondest dream. *noun–S*
noun–obj 8. To escape, the cat clawed at the top of the box. *adv*
of prep 9. Hated by the people, the king was about to abdicate.
10. The Wright brothers produced one of the first airplanes to fly. *adj*

■ Prepositional Phrase or Infinitive?

The difference between a preposition and an infinitive is easy to recognize once you are aware of it. A prepositional phrase always ends with a noun or pronoun, whereas an infinitive always ends with a verb.

Prepositional Phrase	Infinitive
The soldier listened *to the command.*	A general's purpose in the army is *to command.*

EXERCISE B: Distinguishing Between Prepositional Phrases and Infinitives. Each of the following sentences contains either a prepositional phrase or an infinitive beginning with *to*. Write the phrase or infinitive on your paper and identify it as a *prepositional phrase* or an *infinitive*.

EXAMPLE: When I am in New York, I like to shop.

   to shop   infinitive

infin 1. At the outdoor market, my grandmother likes to bargain.
2. Would you try to explain? *infin*
3. Give an explanation to Glenn. *prep phr*

4. To believe took considerable faith. *infin*
5. Lindsey wrote letters to friends. *prep phr*
6. After working so hard, he wanted to rest. *infin*
7. Our trip to China was filled with surprises. *prep phr*
8. Baxter's gift to me was too extravagant. *prep phr*
9. When do you plan to graduate? *infin*
10. On Bill's way to town he had a flat tire. *prep phr*

■ Infinitive Phrases

Like other verbals, infinitives can be joined with other words to form phrases.

An **infinitive phrase** is an infinitive with modifiers, a complement, or a subject, all acting together as a single part of speech.

The following examples show just a few of the ways infinitives can be expanded into phrases.

INFINITIVE PHRASES
Infinitive with adverb: Jeffrey's entire family likes *to rise early.*
Infinitive with adverbial phrases: *To skate on the ice without falling* was not easy for Dennis.
Infinitive with direct object: Oliver was not able *to discuss emotions.*
Infinitive with indirect and direct objects: They promised *to show everyone their slides.*
Infinitive with subject and complement: I would like *her to determine her own goals.*

NOTE ABOUT INFINITIVES WITHOUT *TO*:   Sometimes infinitives do not include the word *to*. When an infinitive follows one of the eight verbs listed here, the *to* is generally omitted.

dare	help	make	see
hear	let	please	watch

EXAMPLES: She doesn't dare *go* without permission.

They heard the canary *sing* its song.

Dale helps me *clean* the house.

Let's *be* on our way.

EXERCISE C: Identifying Infinitive Phrases. Each of the following sentences contains at least one infinitive phrase. Write the infinitive phrase from each sentence on your paper. If it is used as a noun, identify it as a *subject, direct object, predicate nominative, object of a preposition,* or *appositive.* If it is used as an adjective or adverb, label it *adjective* or *adverb.*

EXAMPLE: I have an assignment to finish before tomorrow.

to finish before tomorrow   adjective

1. To <u>describe the hockey game in an understandable manner</u> required gestures. *noun–S*
2. The birdwatcher's ambition was <u>to see one hundred different species during one weekend</u>. *noun–PN*
3. My friends and I went <u>to see the exhibit on Indian art</u> and <u>to gather material for our reports</u>. *adv/adv*
noun–DO 4. Huck and Tom swore <u>to keep the secret about Injun Joe</u>.
5. <u>To inhale these fumes</u> is <u>to die instantly</u>. *noun–S/noun–PN*
6. With no money <u>to pay our bill</u>, we had no choice but <u>to wash dishes</u>. *adj/noun–obj of prep*
7. <u>To heed his somber warning</u> was <u>to be prepared for every eventuality</u>. *noun–S/noun–PN*
8. Ray hopes <u>to become a veterinarian</u>. *noun–DO*
adv 9. Children must have vitamins <u>to grow strong and healthy</u>.
10. Since we were about <u>to sink in the leaky boat</u>, there was nothing <u>to do</u> except <u>to bail it out</u>. *noun–obj of prep/ adj/noun–obj of prep*

APPLICATION: Writing Your Own Sentences with Infinitive Phrases. Write sentences of your own using each of the following infinitives according to the directions. Underline the infinitive phrase in each sentence.
Answers will vary; samples given for first two.
1. Use *to swing* as a subject.
2. Use *to draw* as a predicate nominative.
3. Use *to examine* as an adjective.
4. Use *to show* as a direct object.
5. Use *to begin* as the object of a preposition.
6. Use *to seem* as an adverb.
7. Use *to wander* as a subject.
8. Use *to mail* as a direct object.

1. <u>To swing on a trapeze</u> was Gretchen's unrealized dream.

2. My hope is <u>to draw him into the conversation</u>.

9. Use *to fly* as an appositive.
10. Use *to assist* as a direct object.

Diagraming Phrases 6.6

Each kind of phrase is diagramed in a slightly different way. As you study the following models, keep in mind that any phrase functioning as an adjective or adverb will be diagramed beneath the word it modifies. In addition, keep in mind that phrases are never diagramed on a single straight horizontal or vertical line.

■ Prepositional Phrases

The diagram for a prepositional phrase begins with a slanted line, for the preposition, and ends with a horizontal line, for the object of the preposition. Any words that modify the object of the preposition are placed on slanted lines below the horizontal line. Adjectival phrases are placed directly below the noun or pronoun they modify. Adverbial phrases are placed directly below the verb, adjective, or adverb they modify.

In the following example, an adjectival phrase modifies the subject *child*, and an adverbial phrase modifies the verb *skipped*.

EXAMPLE: The child with the orange ball skipped through the park.

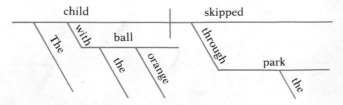

A prepositional phrase with a compound object is diagramed in the same way as the other compound parts of a sentence. The following example shows an adjectival phrase that modifies a direct object.

EXAMPLE: We need a house with three bedrooms, a den, and adequate storage space.

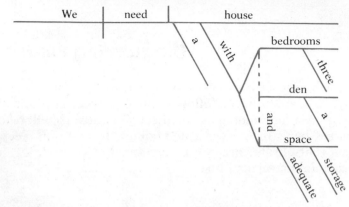

An adjectival phrase that modifies the object of the preposition of another prepositional phrase goes below the other phrase.

EXAMPLE: Take the ceramic cup on the counter near the stove.

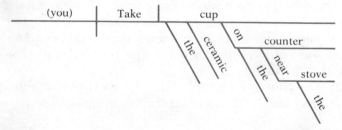

When an adverbial phrase modifies an adverb or an adjective, the diagram for the phrase changes slightly. Notice the extra line in the following example.

EXAMPLE: The confusion began yesterday before daybreak.

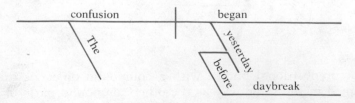

EXERCISE A: Diagraming Prepositional Phrases. Each of the following sentences contains one or more adjectival phrases, one or more adverbial phrases, or both. Copy the skeletons for 1 and 2 onto your paper and diagram each sentence. Then diagram the remaining sentences. *Answers on page T-109.*

1. They flew in a private airplane across the Rockies.

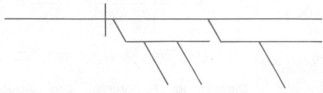

2. Select a good detergent for clothing with greasy stains or ground-in dirt.

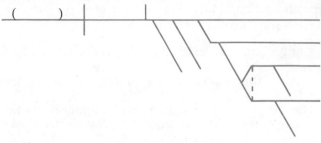

3. Water trickled down Mark's neck.
4. Without much hope, Becky argued for another chance.
5. Corina lives over the corner grocery store in a small apartment.

◼ Appositives and Appositive Phrases

An appositive is placed in parentheses beside the noun or pronoun it identifies, renames, or explains.

EXAMPLE: Her old friend Harriet Danby is a lawyer.

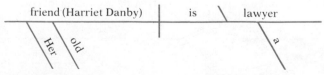

An appositive in an appositive phrase is diagramed in the same manner. Any adjectival or adverbial phrases included in the appositive phrase are placed directly beneath the appositive.

EXAMPLE: We took him to the Lincoln Memorial, a place of great beauty.

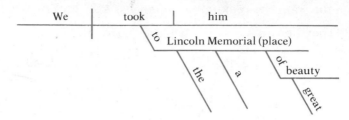

EXERCISE B: Diagraming Appositives and Appositive Phrases.

Each of the following sentences has an appositive or appositive phrase that renames either a subject, direct object, predicate nominative, or object of a preposition. Diagram each sentence. *Answers on page T-110*

1. Gladys was an extraordinary pianist, a talented performer.
2. I know the author of that book, one of the top best-sellers.
3. The rat, a rodent, has one pair of upper incisors.
4. Mario prepared the meal, a lavish feast with six courses.
5. Their staircase, a curving flight of steps, connects the first three floors.

■ Participles and Participial Phrases

Since participles always act as adjectives, they are always placed directly beneath the noun or pronoun they modify. Unlike adjectives, however, participles are positioned partly on a slanted line and partly on a horizontal line that extends from the slanted line.

EXAMPLE: I have a tingling sensation in my left arm.

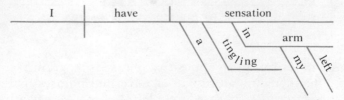

A participial phrase with one or more adverb modifiers is diagramed in the following way.

EXAMPLE: Suddenly quite embarrassed, Megan turned bright red.

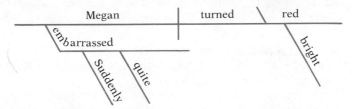

When a participle is modified by an adverbial phrase, the phrase is placed in the usual position, directly below the horizontal line.

EXAMPLE: Striving for some recognition, the man raved about his accomplishments.

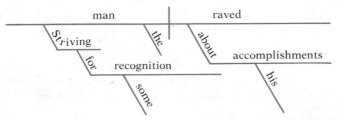

When a participle has a complement, the complement is also placed in its normal position, on the horizontal line with the participle, separated by a short vertical line.

EXAMPLE: Reviewing books for children, Russell stays busy.

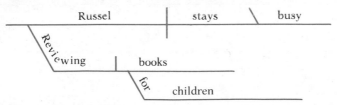

A nominative absolute is diagramed in the same way an expletive is. Grammatically independent, a nominative absolute is positioned over the rest of the sentence.

EXAMPLE: His speech finished, everyone applauded.

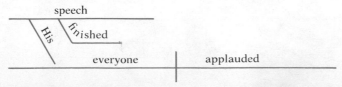

EXERCISE C: Diagraming Participles and Participial Phrases. Each of the following sentences contains a participle or a participial phrase. Diagram each sentence.
Answers on page T-111.

1. He held a basket brimming with goodies.
2. The small town destroyed, many volunteers worked long hours after the tornado.
3. This deserted island offers peace and tranquillity.
4. From the beehive came a loud buzzing noise.
5. Its engine stalled, the car caused a traffic jam.

■ Gerunds and Gerund Phrases

Since all gerunds function as nouns, they can be subjects, complements, objects of prepositions, or appositives.

A gerund that acts as a subject, direct object, or predicate nominative is diagramed on a pedestal above the main horizontal line of the diagram. Notice the shape of the line on which the gerund rests.

EXAMPLE: Slouching is bad posture.

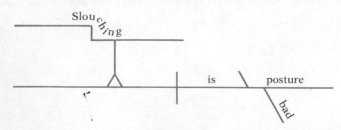

A gerund that acts as an indirect object or an object of a preposition is placed on a line slanting down from the main horizontal line.

EXAMPLE: His lecture gave traveling new dimensions.

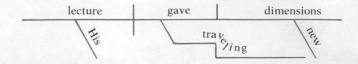

A gerund that acts as an appositive is placed on a pedestal, in parentheses, next to the noun or pronoun it accompanies.

EXAMPLE: We enjoy a summer sport, surfing.

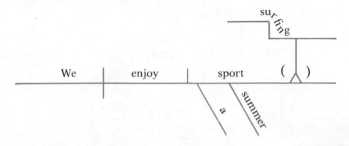

Gerund phrases with modifiers or one or more complements also act as nouns. The position of the gerund in the sentence diagram remains the same even when it is part of a gerund phrase. The modifiers and complements are just added to the diagram in the usual way.

EXAMPLE: Our lease forbids keeping pets on the premises.

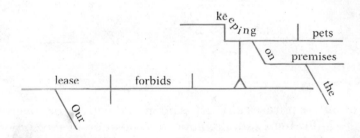

EXERCISE D: Diagraming Gerunds and Gerund Phrases.

Each of the following sentences contains a gerund or a gerund phrase. Diagram each sentence.
Answers on page T-112.

1. His favorite activity was hiking through the woods.
2. Achieving the position of senator will be very difficult.
3. Their immoral values gave stealing respectability.
4. Clark's fear, injuring his already weak elbow, prevented him from playing his best game.
5. Jill's ingratitude made helping her an unpleasant and thankless task.

■ Infinitives and Infinitive Phrases

Infinitives can act as nouns, adjectives, or adverbs. An infinitive acting as a noun is diagramed on a pedestal just as a gerund is, but the line on which the infinitive rests is simpler. The following example shows infinitives acting as a subject and a predicate nominative.

EXAMPLE: To think is to exist.

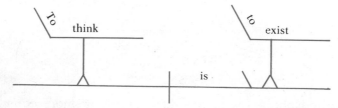

An infinitive acting as an adjective or adverb is diagramed much as a prepositional phrase is. In the following example, an infinitive is used as an adverb to modify the predicate adjective *proud*.

EXAMPLE: Beth is too proud to beg.

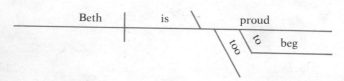

Infinitive phrases also act as nouns, adjectives, or adverbs. In the following example, notice the position of the subject of the infinitive and of the indirect and direct objects of the infinitive. The entire infinitive phrase is the direct object of the sentence.

EXAMPLE: We want Blanche to show us her stamp collection.

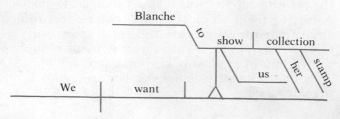

When an infinitive in a sentence does not include the word *to*, add it to the sentence diagram anyway, but in parentheses.

EXAMPLE: Clancy dared me climb the water tower behind the school.

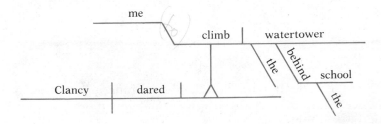

EXERCISE E: **Diagraming Infinitives and Infinitive Phrases.** Each of the following sentences contains an infinitive or an infinitive phrase. Diagram each sentence.
Answers on page T-114.

1. Gordon's greatest accomplishment was to write a novel about etiquette during the sixteenth century.
2. Her mother let Susan go to the movies.
3. To focus on just one aspect of the problem would be advisable.
4. Her inclination was to tell him the truth about his appearance.
5. My idea to sell pies and pastries was quickly rejected.

APPLICATION: **Diagraming Various Kinds of Phrases.** The following sentences contain all of the different kinds of phrases covered in this section. Diagram each sentence on your paper. *Answers on page T-115.*

1. They requested us to remove our shoes before entering their house, a mansion richly decorated with oriental rugs.
2. Stumbling noisily through the darkened house, the boy hoped to escape the wrath of his parents.
3. Our cabin smashed by a giant tree, we were forced to camp under the stars.
4. Gesturing to halt traffic, the police officer tried to calm the badly injured pedestrian.
5. Riding a roller coaster was a thrilling experience to relate to friends.

Chapter 7

Clauses

Chapter 6 dealt with how a phrase functions within a sentence. Chapter 7 deals with a similar but more complex structure called a *clause*.

A **clause** is a group of words with its own subject and verb.

The two basic kinds of clauses are the *independent clause* and the *subordinate clause*.

An **independent clause** can stand by itself as a complete sentence.

A **subordinate clause,** although it has a subject and verb, cannot stand by itself as a complete sentence; it can only be part of a sentence.

The following examples illustrate the three ways in which independent clauses can function. In the first example, an independent clause stands alone. In the second example, a single sentence is made up of two independent clauses joined by a coordinating conjunction. In the third example, an independent clause is joined to a subordinate clause. Notice that each independent clause could stand by itself as a complete sentence, just as the first example does. The subjects are underlined once; the verbs, twice.

ONE INDEPENDENT CLAUSE:

That <u>girl</u> <u>teaches</u> sign language to the deaf.

TWO INDEPENDENT CLAUSES:

Great <u>mud slides</u> <u>will engulf</u> these hillside homes, and <u>some</u> <u>will be ruined</u>.

136

INDEPENDENT CLAUSE AND SUBORDINATE CLAUSE:

Brian asked to be excused from class because *he was* ill.

The basic difference between a subordinate clause and an independent clause is that a subordinate clause, even though it also has a subject and a verb, does not express a complete thought and cannot stand alone as a sentence. It must be part of a sentence that contains at least one independent clause if it is to express its meaning.

SUBORDINATE CLAUSES: That *girl* whom *I introduced* to you *teaches* sign language to the deaf.

Unless the rain stops, great *mud slides will engulf* these hillside homes, and *some will be ruined.*

Brian asked that he be excused from class.

Like phrases, subordinate clauses can function as adjectives, adverbs, and nouns in sentences. The next three sections will discuss each of these three functions in turn. A fourth section will explain how sentences can be classified by structure and by function. Using clauses in your writing will allow you to express ideas of greater complexity.

Adjective Clauses 7.1

One way to add description and detail to a sentence is by using an *adjective clause*.

An **adjective clause** is a subordinate clause that modifies a noun or pronoun by telling what kind or which one.

■ Clauses That Modify Nouns and Pronouns

Most often adjective clauses begin with one of the relative pronouns: *who, whom, whose, which,* or *that.* (See Section 1.2 for a review of relative pronouns.) Sometimes, however, they may begin with a *relative adverb*, such as *when*, *where*, *why*, *before*, or *since*. All of these words relate the clause to the word it modifies.

In the following chart, the adjective clauses are italicized. Arrows indicate the noun or pronoun modified by each clause. You can tell that these are adjective clauses because they answer the adjectival questions *What kind?* and *Which one?* Notice also that the first three clauses begin with relative pronouns, the last two with relative adverbs.

ADJECTIVE CLAUSES

Anyone *who is calm* will be good in an emergency.

The American hockey team won the medal *that the Soviets coveted*.

We gave the stray mutt, *which we found*, a hearty meal.

Spring is the time *when peepers make their shrill evening sound*.

Our trip to Holland ended with a visit to the town *where my parents were born*.

Like single-word adjectives or adjectival phrases, adjective clauses may modify any noun or pronoun in a sentence. In the first sentence in the chart, the subject is modified. In the second and third sentences, a direct object and then an indirect object are modified. In the fourth sentence, a predicate nominative is modified. And in the last sentence, the object of a preposition is modified.

Adjective clauses, like appositive and participial phrases, are set off by punctuation only when they are not essential to a sentence's meaning. The following chart contrasts nonessential and essential adjective clauses. In the sentences on the left, the adjective clauses could be omitted without changing the sentences' basic message. However, if you were to take away the adjective clauses from the sentences on the right, the sentences' message would not be complete. For more about punctuating adjective clauses, see Section 15.2.

Nonessential Adjective Clauses	Essential Adjective Clauses
One of Dickens' best novels is *Great Expectations, which first appeared in serial form in 1860–61.*	The novel *that everyone must read by Monday* is not too long.
John McCurdy, *who studied three hours each evening for a month,* won the statewide competition.	A student *who studies regularly* usually finds test-taking easy.

In the sentences on the left, the commas indicate that the clauses give additional information, whereas in the sentences on the right the lack of commas shows that the clauses are needed to define the words they modify. By reading the contrasting sentences aloud, you will hear that you naturally pause before and after the nonessential clauses and that your voice drops as you say the words in the clauses. Realizing this should help you recognize the clauses in your own writing that need to be set off with commas.

EXERCISE A: Identifying Adjective Clauses and the Words They Modify. Each of the following sentences contains an adjective clause. Write the adjective clause from each sentence on your paper. Then, write the word modified by the adjective clause. Finally, indicate whether the clause is *nonessential* or *essential.* Words modified are shaded.

1. The student whom Mr. Stendal recommended was first in her class. *ess*
2. Is this the year when the planets will align? *ess*
3. Henry VIII was the king whose many wives fared badly. *ess*
4. It has been three years since I visited my aunt in Miami. *ess*
5. Our school play, which lasted two hours, bored everyone in the audience. *noness*
6. Books that deal with current events in an exciting way often become bestsellers. *ess*
7. My father works in an office where everyone helps each other. *ess*
8. George Washington's false teeth, which were probably made of ivory or animal bones, must have been uncomfortable. *noness*
9. The position that Jackie wanted was already filled. *ess*

10. The man whose playing you were ridiculing is an internationally recognized chess champion. *ess*

■ Different Kinds of Introductory Words

The words that introduce adjective clauses—relative pronouns or relative adverbs—have two functions in sentences.

A relative pronoun or relative adverb (1) connects the adjective clause to the modified word and (2) acts within the clause as a subject, direct object, or other sentence part.

Learning to recognize the function of these words within the clause can also help you recognize when you should use *who* and *whom*. (See Section 10.2 for a discussion of the use of these pronouns.)

Relative Pronouns A relative pronoun acts within the clause as either a subject, a direct object, an object of a preposition, or an adjective.

To tell how a relative pronoun is being used within a clause, separate the clause from the rest of the sentence and then find the subject and verb in the clause. Quite often you may need to turn the words in the clause around as you would with an inverted sentence.

THE USES OF RELATIVE PRONOUNS IN CLAUSES
As a Subject
A house *that is built on a good foundation* is built to endure. *Clause*: that is built on a good foundation *Subject*: that · *Verb*: is built *Use of relative pronoun*: subject
As a Direct Object
My brother-in-law, *whom my sister met at college*, is a poet. *Clause*: whom my sister met at college *Reworded clause*: my sister met whom at college · *Subject*: sister *Verb*: met *Use of relative pronoun*: direct object

As an Object of a Preposition
This is the restaurant *about which I read enthusiastic reviews*.   *Clause*: about which I read enthusiastic reviews   *Reworded clause*: I read enthusiastic reviews about which   *Subject*: I   *Verb*: read   *Use of relative pronoun*: object of a preposition
As an Adjective
The senator *whose honesty was in question* refused to speak to the press.   *Clause*: whose honesty was in question   *Subject*: honesty   *Verb*: was   *Use of relative pronoun*: adjective

NOTE ABOUT UNDERSTOOD WORDS: Sometimes in writing and in speech, a relative pronoun is left out of an adjective clause. The omitted word, though simply understood, still functions in the sentence.

EXAMPLES: The suggestions *(that) they made* were ignored.

The legendary heroes *(whom) we studied* were great men and women.

Relative Adverbs. Unlike a relative pronoun, a relative adverb has only one use within a clause. It always acts as an adverb.

THE USE OF RELATIVE ADVERBS WITHIN CLAUSES
Pat looked forward to the day *when she could walk without crutches*.   *Clause*: when she could walk without crutches   *Reworded clause*: she could walk when without crutches   *Subject*: she   *Verb*: could walk   *Use of relative adverb*: adverb

EXERCISE B: Recognizing the Uses of Relative Pronouns and Relative Adverbs. Each of the following sentences contains an adjective clause beginning with either a relative pronoun or a relative adverb. Write the adjective clause from each sentence on your paper and circle the relative pronoun or relative adverb. If the clause begins with a relative pronoun, identify its function within the clause as *subject, direct object, object of a preposition,* or *adjective.* If the clause begins with a relative adverb, draw an arrow from the adverb to the word it modifies within the clause. *Relative pronouns and adverbs are shaded; words modified by adverbs are in parentheses.*

1. We look forward to a weekend when we (can have) some rest.
2. A sales representative whose approach is too insistent may anger potential customers. *adj*
3. The person with whom you spoke is my father. *obj of prep*
4. In the time since Maria (returned) she has talked only about her trip.
5. My friend whom you admired liked you also. *DO*
6. Dolphins are mammals that communicate with high-pitched sounds. *subj*
7. In the centuries before the car (was invented) people relied on horses for transportation.
8. An historian who knows the facts can compare the past with the probable future. *subj*
9. Physics is a subject about which I know nothing. *obj of prep*
10. The first man on the moon walked on land where no man (walked) before.

APPLICATION: Combining Sentences Using Adjective Clauses. Combine the following pairs of sentences into single sentences by using one of the sentences in each pair as an adjective clause. Then underline the adjective clause in each sentence and draw an arrow from it to the word it modifies. *Answers will vary; samples given for first two.*

EXAMPLE: Dr. Perone is a good veterinarian. I always take our dog to Dr. Perone.

I always take our dog to Dr. Perone, who is a good veterinarian.

1. This store sells crafts. These crafts were made by Navajo artists.
2. Fall is the season before winter. Life slows down in the fall.
3. Their apartment is in the city. Their apartment has all the modern conveniences.
4. Mr. Hart spoke kindly of his worst enemy. Mr. Hart always saw good instead of evil.

1. *The store sells crafts that were made by Navajo artists.*

2. *Life slows down in the fall, which is the season before winter.*

5. These old photographs recall happy moments. My father took the photographs.
6. We walked silently through the forest. In the forest great pines gave us a sense of peace.
7. Our dog is like a member of the family. Our dog's tail never stops wagging.
8. The summer house borders on a lake. As children, we swam and paddled our canoe in the lake.
9. The highway went straight through the desert. We saw no signs of life in the desert.
10. Colleen has a terrific record collection. Sometimes Colleen lets me borrow records.

Adverb Clauses 7.2

In addition to acting as adjectives, subordinate clauses can also act as adverbs.

An **adverb clause** is a subordinate clause that modifies a verb, adjective, adverb, or verbal by pointing out where, when, in what manner, to what extent, under what condition, or why.

■ Clauses That Act as Adverbs

Every adverb clause begins with a subordinating conjunction. The following chart shows some of the most frequently used subordinating conjunctions. For a more complete list, see Section 3.2.

SUBORDINATING CONJUNCTIONS			
after	before	so that	when
although	even though	than	whenever
as	if	though	where
as if	in order that	unless	wherever
as long as	since	until	while
because			

Being familiar with these words will help you identify adverb clauses. In the following examples, the adverb clauses are italicized. Arrows indicate the words modified by the clauses. You can tell that these clauses are adverbial because they answer adverbial questions. The first adverbial clause answers *When?*, the second *Where?*, and so on. The last two clauses are different because they provide information that a single adverb cannot. The first of these two clauses answers *Under what condition?* and the second answers *Why?*

ADVERB CLAUSES

Modifying a Verb

When the fog is dense, you should use low beams.

Modifying an Adjective

Wherever Tricia was, she seemed happy.

Modifying an Adverb

Faster *than the eye could follow*, the race car sped down the track.

Modifying a Participle

Laughing uncontrollably *until he gasped for breath*, the boy could not finish his oral report.

Modifying a Gerund

Driving a car *if you do not have a license* is illegal.

Modifying an Infinitive

We decided to remain in our seats *so that we could watch the movie again*.

As you can see in the preceding examples, adverb clauses may be placed at the beginning, in the middle, or at the end of sentences. Sometimes, however, the placement of an adverb clause can affect the meaning of the entire sentence.

EXAMPLE: *Before the day was over*, we planned to visit Mr. Barnes.

We planned to visit Mr. Barnes *before the day was over*.

EXERCISE A: Identifying Adverb Clauses and the Words They Modify. Each of the following sentences contains an adverb clause. Copy the sentences onto your paper, underline the adverb clauses, and circle the subordinating conjunctions. Then draw an arrow from the adverb clause to the modified word in each sentence and label the modified word *verb, adjective, adverb, participle, gerund,* or *infinitive*. Subordinating conjunctions are shaded; modified words are identified at the end of each sentence.

1. Before he gave the assignment, Mr. Martin explained the method for reviewing. *explained–verb*
2. Mark looks gloomy whenever that topic is brought up. *gloomy–adj*
3. After the sun goes down, the temperature drops several degrees. *drops–verb*
4. We wanted to drive slowly so that we could enjoy the scenery. *slowly–adv*
5. Germany has been divided since World War II ended in 1945. *has been divided–verb*
6. Miserable unless there is work, my father aimlessly putters in his workshop. *miserable–adj*
7. Picked when they are ripe, fresh strawberries have a luscious taste. *picked–part*
8. More delicately than a mouse would eat, Mary nibbled her sandwich. *more–adv*
9. Winking as if he knew a secret, old Mr. Bumble gave the child a peppermint. *winking–part*
10. Susan planned to remain in the country until her visa expired. *to remain–infin*

▨ Elliptical Clauses

Sometimes words are omitted in adverb clauses, especially in those clauses that begin with *as* or *than* and are used to express comparisons. Such clauses are said to be *elliptical*.

An **elliptical clause** is a clause in which the verb or subject and verb are understood but not actually stated.

Even though the subject or the subject and the verb have been left out of an elliptical clause, they still function to make the clause express a complete thought. In the following examples, the understood words have been added in parentheses. The sentences are alike except for the words *he* and *him*. In the first sentence, *he* is a subject. In the second sentence, *him* functions as a direct object. The use of each word is easy to see when the omitted words are added.

VERB UNDERSTOOD: She resembles their father more *than he (does).*

SUBJECT AND VERB UNDERSTOOD: She resembles their father more *than (she resembles) him.*

When you read or write elliptical clauses, mentally include the omitted words. Doing this should help clarify the meaning you intend.

EXERCISE B: Recognizing Elliptical Adverb Clauses. Each of the following sentences contains an adverb clause. If the clause is complete, write *complete* on your paper. If the clause is elliptical, copy it onto your paper, adding the understood word or words.

1. We think our cheerleaders are better <u>than theirs</u>. *are*
2. Blake is happier working with people <u>than he is working by himself</u>. *complete*
3. My younger brother is as tall <u>as I</u>. *am*
4. Small children sometimes appreciate classical music <u>more than nursery jingles</u>. *they appreciate*
5. In Riley's backyard you can find junk heaped <u>wherever there is an inch of space</u>. *complete*
6. Joe pitches better <u>than he</u>. *pitches*
7. Professor Horton is more interested in ancient history <u>than in the day's events</u>. *he is*
8. I like green beans better <u>than he</u>. *likes them*
9. Everyone was as discontented with the situation <u>as I was</u>. *complete*
10. Look to find assistance <u>wherever likely</u>. *it is*

APPLICATION: Combining Sentences Using Adverb Clauses. Combine the following pairs of sentences into single sentences by using one of the sentences in each pair as an adverb clause. Then underline the adverb clause in each of your sentences. *Answers will vary; samples given for first two.*

1. Her mother called the doctor in the middle of the night <u>because her child's temperature was abnormally high</u>.

EXAMPLE: Livia is unhappy. Her parakeet died.

Livia is unhappy <u>because her parakeet died</u>.

1. Her mother called the doctor in the middle of the night. Her child's temperature was abnormally high.
2. The beach house was swept away. Enormous waves were carried inland by the storm.
3. We toasted marshmallows over the dying embers. We silently shared a feeling of closeness.
4. Randolph will never learn to study. He learns to concentrate.
5. Give me some more ideas. I can think of a topic for the paper.
6. Everyone reported to class late. The bell had rung.
7. The settlers chose that wooded area for their homestead. A clear stream provided fresh water.
8. Our trip to Washington D.C. will be canceled. We are not able to raise sufficient funds.
9. She had a bad cough. She still insisted upon going to work.
10. You find the time. Write your uncle a get-well note.

2. The beach house was swept away <u>when enormous waves were carried inland by the storm</u>.

Noun Clauses 7.3

In addition to acting as adjectives and adverbs, subordnate clauses can also act as nouns.

A **noun clause** is a subordinate clause that acts as a noun.

■ Clauses That Act as Nouns

A noun clause acts in almost the same way as a single-word noun does in a sentence. It can function in any of the roles shown in the following chart.

NOUN CLAUSES
As a subject: *Who wins the contest* is determined by a panel of judges.
As a direct object: Please invite *whomever you want* to the festivities.

As an indirect object: His blunt manner gave *whoever approached him* a shock.

As an object of a preposition: Use the money for *whatever purpose you choose.*

As a predicate nominative: Our problem is *whether we should stay here or leave.*

As an appositive: The occupied country rejected our plea, *that orphans be cared for by the Red Cross.*

EXERCISE A: Identifying Noun Clauses. Each of the following sentences contains one noun clause. Write the noun clause from each sentence on your paper and then identify the function of the noun clause as *subject, direct object, indirect object, object of a preposition, predicate nominative*, or *appositive*. Answers follow sentences; answers for Exercise B given below.

1. Whoever is interested in past generations will like the book *Foxfire*. S
2. The governor's dilemma, how it would be possible to please both factions, required hard thinking. *appos*
3. No one cares about what you wear to the party. *obj of prep*
4. Whether the play is a financial success depends much upon the critics' reviews. S
5. Leon discusses politics with whoever is unfortunate enough to sit next to him. *obj of prep*
6. The planning committee needed more suggestions, whatever ideas people thought would be workable. *appos*
7. The brochure describes what a tourist can expect to see in Kenya. DO
8. Tell Ms. Pleanty when she should expect you to arrive. DO
9. Carmella's selection of fabrics will be whichever ones she orders from the retailer. PN
10. Mr. Randolph gave whoever came into his store a warm greeting. IO

1. S   2. adv   3. DO   4. no function   5. S   6. adj   7. DO   8. adv
9. adj   10. S

■ Words That Begin Noun Clauses

Noun clauses frequently begin with the words *who, whom, whose, which,* or *that,* the same words that are used to begin adjective clauses. Variants of these words, *whoever, whomever,* or *whichever,* may also be used as introductory words. Other noun clauses begin with the words *what, whatever, where, how, when, if, whether,* or *why.*

In addition to beginning the clause, these introductory words usually function within the clause as subjects, direct objects, or some other sentence part. The examples in the following chart show a few of the possible uses. Notice that the introductory word *that* in the last example has no function except to introduce the clause.

THE USE OF INTRODUCTORY WORDS IN NOUN CLAUSES

Adjective: The little girl could not decide *which flavor of ice cream she would like.*

Direct object: *Whatever Robbie could accomplish* would be good enough.

No function in clause: The officials determined *that the voting polls had been rigged.*

Most of the words that begin a noun clause may also introduce an adjective clause or adverb clause. Therefore, to decide whether a clause acts as a noun, you must look at the clause's role in the sentence. In the following examples, all three of the subordinating clauses begin with *where*, but only the first one is a noun clause because it functions in the sentence as a direct object.

NOUN CLAUSE: The advertisement told people *where they should call for suicide prevention.*

ADJECTIVE CLAUSE: They took him to the emergency ward *where a doctor examined his cut.*

ADVERB CLAUSE: Tammy lives *where the weather is warm all year.*

NOTE ABOUT INTRODUCTORY WORDS: Frequently in both writing and speech, the introductory word *that* is omitted from a noun clause. In the following example, the understood *that* is in parentheses.

EXAMPLE: The secretary suggested *(that) you leave your name and number.*

EXERCISE B: Recognizing the Different Uses of Introductory Words. Reread the items in Exercise A. Write the function of each introductory word within the clause on your paper. If the introductory word has no function within the clause, write *no function*. *Answers appear below Exercise A.*

APPLICATION: Writing Sentences with Noun Clauses.
Following the directions, write ten sentences of your own
containing noun clauses. *Answers will vary; samples given for first two.*

1. Use *who* as an introductory word; the clause should
   function as the subject of the sentence.
2. Use *how* as an introductory word; the clause should
   function as the subject of the sentence.
3. Use *whatever* as an introductory word; the clause should
   function as a direct object in the sentence.
4. Use *that* as an understood introductory word; the clause
   should function as a direct object in the sentence.
5. Use *whoever* as an introductory word; the clause should
   function as an indirect object in the sentence.
6. Use *whomever* as an introductory word; the clause
   should function as an object of a preposition in the
   sentence.
7. Use *whom* as an introductory word; the clause should
   function as an object of a preposition in the sentence.
8. Use *whether* as an introductory word; the clause should
   function as a predicate nominative in the sentence.
9. Use *wherever* as an introductory word; the clause should
   function as a predicate nominative in the sentence.
10. Use *that* as an introductory word; the clause should
    function as an appositive in the sentence.

1. *Who made the statement is not known.*
2. *How we proceed depends on weather conditions.*

7.4 Sentences Classified by Structure and Function

Every sentence you read, speak, or write can be classified
both by its structure and by its function.

■ The Four Structures of Sentences

The two main kinds of clauses, independent and subordinate, may be joined in different ways to form the four
basic sentence structures: *simple, compound, complex,* and
compound-complex.

A **simple sentence** consists of a single independent clause.

A **compound sentence** consists of two or more independent clauses joined by a comma and a coordinating conjunction *(and, but, for, nor, or, so, yet)* or by a semicolon.

A **complex sentence** consists of one independent clause and one or more subordinate clauses.

A **compound-complex sentence** consists of two or more independent clauses and one or more subordinate clauses.

In the following charts, notice that even a simple sentence, a single independent clause, may have a compound subject, compound verb, or both. The subjects in the examples are underlined once; the verbs, twice.

FOUR STRUCTURES OF SENTENCES

Simple Sentences

The big day arrived early.

Both Mom and Dad saw the holdup and reported it to the police.

Struck by the novelty of the idea, Pat grinned with appreciation.

Compound Sentences

We went to three auctions yesterday, but we did not bid for anything.

Sue is a nightowl; therefore, she sleeps until late in the afternoon. *(See p. 60 and note punctuation)*

Complex Sentences

Main Clause   Subordinate Clause

My brother's pet boa constrictor was the culprit that ate my white mice.

Main Clause — Subordinate Clause

The Red Cross, which gives invaluable assistance, was flown in to help people who were made homeless by the flood.

Subordinate Clause

> ```
>                ──────── Main Clause ────────
>   ┌─────────────────────────────────────┐
>   │  Subordinate Clause                  │
>   Whoever wants this job can have it.
> ```

Compound-Complex Sentences

```
                    Main Clause
  The truck dropped its load of gravel onto the driveway

    Subordinate Clause              Main Clause
  where the car was parked, and then it drove off.

     Subordinate Clause      Main Clause        Main Clause
  When the lights went out, we felt uneasy, but we knew
                Subordinate Clause
  that morning would eventually come.
```

Notice that in complex and compound-complex sentences the independent clauses are called *main clauses* to distinguish them from subordinate clauses. The subject and verb of a main clause, in turn, are usually called the *subject of the sentence* and the *main verb* to distinguish them from the other subjects and verbs. You should also note that sometimes in a complex or compound-complex sentence an entire noun clause may be the subject of the sentence, as it is in the first sentence in the chart at the top of the page.

EXERCISE A: Identifying the Structure of Sentences. Identify each of the following sentences as *simple, compound, complex,* or *compound-complex*.

1. People often spend money foolishly during times of prosperity but forget the lean years. *smp*
2. The movie is about three men who try to dig under Fort Knox. *cpx*
3. The author's prose is stuffy; he uses too many archaic words. *cpd*
4. The artist whom you admire painted her most famous portraits, which hang in the gallery, when she was almost blind; her style, as you can see, is abstract. *cpd–cpx*
5. She seethed with anger over the well-deserved reprimand. *smp*
6. After the war, John could not sleep without having nightmares. *smp*

7. How many jellybeans are in the jar) is the question that must be answered correctly to win the contest) *cpx*
8. Their standard of living is much higher than ours.) *cpx*
9. Since Ted is a forest ranger) he knows a lot about fire prevention, and he often talks about the damage that fire can do *cpd–cpx*
10. The dusty caravan filed through the tortuous streets and finally reached the marketplace. *smp*

■ The Four Functions of Sentences

Sentences may be classified not only by structure but also by *function*. A sentence may be *declarative, interrogative, imperative,* or *exclamatory.*

A **declarative sentence** states an idea and ends with a period.

An **interrogative sentence** asks a question and ends with a question mark.

An **imperative sentence** gives an order or a direction and ends with a period or an exclamation mark.

An **exclamatory sentence** conveys strong emotion and ends with an exclamation mark.

The type of sentence most often used in both writing and speaking is the declarative sentence. All questions that actually demand answers, either spoken or unspoken, are interrogative. Whether a sentence is imperative or exclamatory is determined by the intent of the sentence. If its primary purpose is to give an order or direction, it is an imperative sentence; if its purpose is to show emotion, it is exclamatory.

In the following chart, the third example of an imperative sentence is actually a question intended as an order. The first three examples of exclamatory sentences show a declarative, an interrogative, and an imperative sentence, all intended to show strong feeling. Note also that there is really very little difference between an imperative sentence with an exclamation mark and an exclamatory sentence that expresses an order.

FOUR FUNCTIONS OF SENTENCES
Declarative Sentences
She is an expert in karate. Icarus fell into the ocean because the sun melted his wax wings.
Interrogative Sentences
When did Hannibal cross the Alps? Did you renew your magazine subscription?
Imperative Sentences
Brush the crumbs off the table. Run! Will someone please take these packages before I drop them.
Exclamatory Sentences
The roof is collapsing! Would you look at that! Leave me alone! An avalanche! Late again!

The subject of most imperative sentences is understood to be *you*, as it is in the first two examples of imperative sentences. Sometimes, however, an imperative sentence does contain a subject, as in the third example, an imperative sentence phrased as a question without the question mark. The important thing here is not whether the sentence contains an understood *you*, but rather whether it gives an order or direction.

Notice also that exclamatory sentences may have an understood subject, understood verb, or both, as shown in the last three examples.

EXERCISE B: Identifying the Function of Sentences. Identify each of the following sentences by its function: *declarative, interrogative, imperative,* or *exclamatory.* After each function write the appropriate punctuation mark for that sentence.

1. Look in both directions before crossing the street . *imper*
2. When the alarm sounds, it summons firefighters . *declar*
3. Your dress is ruined . *declar* or*!* *exclam*
4. All four of my tires are flat . *declar* or*!* *exclam*
5. Is there any way to tell when the corn is ripe *?* *interrog*
6. Will you please turn off the light before you leave . *imper*
7. Should we whitewash this wall or just leave it as it is *?* *interrog*
8. The toast *!* *exclam*
9. Oil the hinges and this door will no longer squeak . *imper*
10. If you look next to that tall tree, you will see the boundary marker . *declar*

Did you lose a thousand dollars!

APPLICATION: **Writing Sentences with Different Structures and Functions.** Following the directions in the two columns, write sentences of your own with different structures and functions. Underline each independent clause.
Answers will vary; samples given for first two.

EXAMPLE: Structure   Function

complex   interrogative

<u>Did you request an interview with Mr. Wharton,</u> who manages personnel?

Structure	Function
1. compound	exclamatory
2. simple	imperative
3. complex	declarative
4. simple	interrogative
5. complex	imperative
6. simple	exclamatory
7. compound	declarative
8. compound-complex	interrogative
9. compound-complex	declarative
10. complex	interrogative

1. *<u>I won't stand for it</u> and <u>you shouldn't either!</u>*   2. *<u>Take off your shoes.</u>*

Diagraming Different Sentence Structures   **7.5**

Diagrams of simple sentences are placed on one main horizontal line. Diagrams of more complicated sentence patterns require more than one main horizontal line.

■ Compound Sentences

If you know how to diagram simple sentences, diagraming compound sentences, which are combinations of two or more simple sentences, should be relatively easy. To diagram a compound sentence, just diagram each simple sentence, or independent clause, separately. Then join them at the verbs with a dotted line on which the conjunction or semicolon is placed.

EXAMPLE: A gentle breeze blew across the lake, and the raft floated inland.

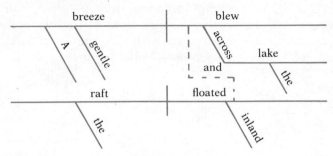

EXERCISE A: Diagraming Compound Sentences. Diagram
each of the following compound sentences on your paper.
Answers on page T-116.

1. His temperature continued to rise, yet he still remained clear-headed.
2. Should I plant this cherry tree in that corner, or would you prefer it nearer to the fence?
3. The steak was cooked perfectly and the tossed salad was excellent, but the dessert was too sweet.
4. Joan has little sense of her own worth; she never asserts herself.
5. Every few years we clean out the attic and fill boxes with unwanted items; later in the day, we make a trip to the town dump.

■ Complex Sentences

Complex sentences consist of a main clause and one or more subordinate clauses which may be adjective clauses, adverb clauses, noun clauses, or any combination of these. Each clause is placed on a separate horizontal line.

Adjective Clauses. To diagram an adjective clause, first diagram the main clause. Then diagram the adjective clause beneath it, connecting the two clauses with a dotted line. This line should extend from the modified noun or pronoun in the main clause to the relative pronoun or relative adverb in the adjective clause.

The first of the following examples shows a relative pronoun acting as the direct object of the adjective clause. In the other examples, notice how the position of the relative pronoun changes depending on its function in the adjective clause. *S, Do., O.P.*

EXAMPLE: Our mutual friend whom you always mention has just completed his autobiography.

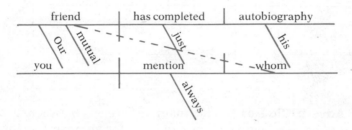

EXAMPLE: Our team cheered for the boy who made the touchdown.

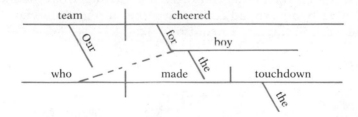

EXAMPLE: This vacation is the reward for which I worked so hard.

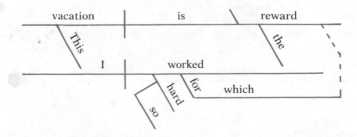

EXAMPLE: We know the Fensons whose cottage you rented.

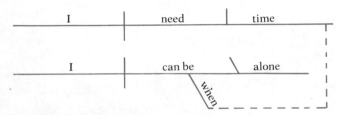

A relative adverb that introduces an adjective clause is placed just as any other adverb would be.

EXAMPLE: I need time when I can be alone.

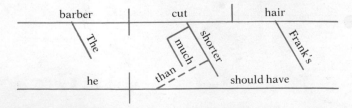

Adverb Clauses.   The main difference between a diagram for an adjective clause and one for an adverb clause is that the subordinating conjunction for an adverb clause is written on the dotted line. This line extends from the modified verb, adverb, adjective, or verbal in the main clause to the verb in the adverb clause.

EXAMPLE: Look for happiness wherever you can find it.

EXAMPLE: The barber cut Frank's hair much shorter than he should have.

EXAMPLE: To look before you leap is good advice.

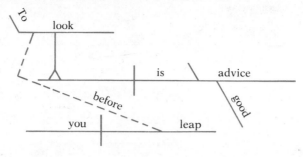

If the adverb clause is elliptical, the understood words are placed in the diagram in parentheses, as shown in the following example.

EXAMPLE: Barbara seems more tense than before the accident.

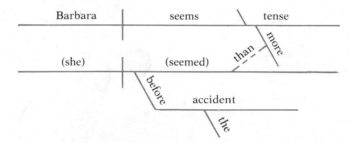

Noun Clauses.   When diagraming a sentence with a noun clause, first diagram the main clause. Then place the entire noun clause on a pedestal extending upwards from the position the noun clause fills in the main clause. In the first of the following examples, the noun clause acts as the subject of the main clause. Notice that the pedestal meets the noun clause at the verb.

EXAMPLE: Whatever you decide is fine with me.

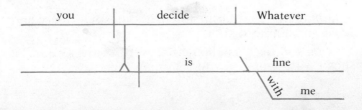

EXAMPLE: The sponsors will give whoever loses a small consolation prize.

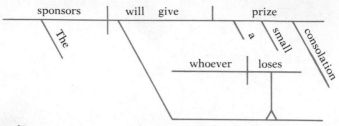

EXAMPLE: You may write an essay on whatever topic interests you.

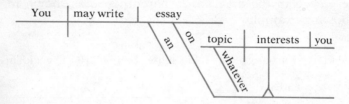

When an introductory word in a noun clause has no function in the clause, it is written alongside the pedestal.

EXAMPLE: The question, whether Jonas is truly sorry, will be revealed in the next episode.

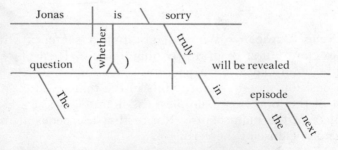

EXERCISE B: Diagraming Complex Sentences.

Each of the following sentences contains an adjective clause, an adverb clause, or a noun clause. Diagram each sentence.
Answers on page T-118.

1. Edmund Burke was an English statesman for whom I have much admiration.

2. Driving too fast, as though he were in the Grand Prix, shows Mike's disregard for human life.

3. During the lecture he presented the Darwinian theory that the fittest survive.
4. We hope to complete this job while time remains.
5. There was a place in the village where people could let their horses graze.
6. The sleuth suspected the killer was living somewhere on the west side of town.
7. The Persians were vanquished because Alexander's troops had superior military skill.
8. In the movies, sit behind someone whose hat is off.
9. Phyllis will look silly until she stops wearing those crazy hats.
10. You have hiccups more often than anyone I ever knew.

■ Compound-Complex Sentences

Once you know how to diagram compound and complex sentences, you will have no difficulty in diagraming compound-complex sentences.

To diagram a compound-complex sentence, begin by diagraming and connecting each of the independent clauses just as you would if you were diagraming a compound sentence. Then diagram and connect each subordinate clause as you would if you were diagraming a complex sentence.

EXAMPLE: We just bought a microwave oven, which should make life simpler, and we can hardly wait until we get home to use it.

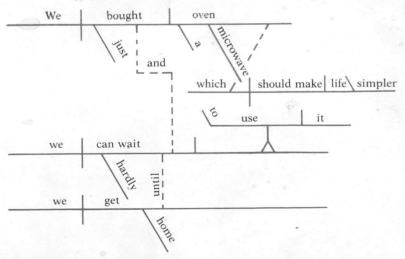

EXERCISE C: Diagraming Compound-Complex Sentences.
Diagram each of the following quotations correctly on your
paper.   *Answers on page T-121.*

1. In the bucket near the house the tap stopped dripping, as
   if the bucket were full, and then the tap dripped one, two,
   three separate drops in succession.—Virginia Woolf
2. She kept a tight grip on the handles, which throbbed violently with every explosion of the one-cylinder motor,
   and as she sheered around bushes and lurched along at a
   reluctant trot behind her impetuous servant, she looked
   like a puppy who had grabbed something that was too
   much for him.—E.B. White

APPLICATION: Diagraming Various Sentence Structures.
In a novel or textbook, find four sentences: one simple, one
compound, one complex, and one compound-complex. Then
diagram each sentence.

*Answers will vary; if students find some sentences too difficult you may want to
encourage them to continue searching until they find sentences they can diagram.*

Chapter 8

Sentence Faults

Once you understand the structure and function of sentences, you can begin to recognize and correct different kinds of errors in your writing. The sections in this chapter will help you recognize and correct such common sentence faults as fragments and run-ons, incorrectly placed modifiers, and nonparallel constructions.

Fragments and Run-ons 8.1

Fragments and run-on sentences are two errors commonly found in writing. Section 5.1 dealt briefly with fragments—groups of words masquerading as complete sentences. This section will give you more practice with fragments by showing you several ways to correct them. You will also practice correcting run-on sentences. These are two or more sentences that are mistakenly joined as if they were one sentence.

■ Different Kinds of Fragments

A fragment, a group of words that does not express a complete thought, is generally considered an error in writing. Sometimes a phrase, a subordinate clause, or words in a series are misused as fragments in writing.

Do not capitalize and punctuate phrases, subordinate clauses, or words in a series as if they were complete sentences.

163

Fragments in writing are usually the result of carelessness and haste. If you find you are having a problem with fragments, take the time to check your work. Read it aloud, listening to the natural pauses and stops. You should hear where your sentences actually begin and end.

Most often you will find that a fragment can be corrected simply by linking it up with the words that come before or after it. Sometimes, however, you will need to add words to the fragment in order to make it into a complete sentence, one that has both a subject and a verb.

Phrase Fragments. Phrase fragments may consist of modified nouns without verbs (sometimes called *noun phrases*), predicates without subjects, or prepositional, appositive, or verbal phrases. Avoid treating any of these phrases as sentences.

The following examples show different ways a noun phrase may be used as part of a sentence containing a subject and verb. Notice that the fragment consists of a noun, *rose*, which is modified by adjectives and an adjective clause.

NOUN FRAGMENT: A single long-stemmed rose that smelled like rare perfume.

AS A SUBJECT: *A single long-stemmed rose that smelled like rare perfume* stood in a crystal bud vase.

AS A DIRECT OBJECT: Pierre selected *a single long-stemmed rose that smelled like rare perfume.*

AS AN OBJECT OF A PREPOSITION: Dew drops glistened on *a single long-stemmed rose that smelled like rare perfume.*

AS AN APPOSITIVE: He gave her a love token, *a single long-stemmed rose that smelled like rare perfume.*

Just as a noun and its modifiers cannot stand alone as a sentence, a verb with its modifiers and complements cannot stand alone. Always make sure all of your verbs have subjects.

VERB FRAGMENT: Soon will be ready for restoration.

AS A PREDICATE: The turn-of-the-century house *soon will be ready for restoration.*

Prepositional, appositive, and verbal phrases must also be written as parts of larger sentences. The following chart shows a few of the ways such phrase fragments can be corrected.

CORRECTING PREPOSITIONAL, APPOSITIVE, AND VERBAL PHRASE FRAGMENTS	
Sentence and Prepositional Phrase	**Corrected Sentence**
Wild blackberries grew there. *By the roadside.*	Wild blackberries grew *by the roadside.*
Sentence and Appositive Phrase	**Corrected Sentence**
Bill handed Sue her gift. *A box of chocolates.*	Bill handed Sue her gift, *a box of chocolates.*
Sentence and Participial Phrase	**Corrected Sentence**
The car looked immaculate. *Washed clean by the rain.*	*Washed clean by the rain*, the car looked immaculate.
Sentence and Gerund Phrase	**Corrected Sentence**
It is a daily habit. *Winding my watch.*	*Winding my watch* is a daily habit.
Infinitive Phrase and Sentence	**Corrected Sentence**
To walk to school in good weather. I prefer that.	I prefer *to walk to school in good weather.*

Clause Fragments. Subordinate clauses are another construction that should not be capitalized and punctuated as sentences. Instead, they should be joined to one or more independent clauses.

CORRECTING CLAUSE FRAGMENTS	
Sentence and Adjective Clause	**Corrected Sentence**
I read a book about mountain climbing. *Which I enjoyed.*	I read a book, *which I enjoyed*, about mountain climbing.

Sentence and Adverb Clause	Corrected Sentence
Don't skate there. *Where the ice is thin.*	Don't skate there *where the ice is thin.*

Noun Clause and Sentence	Corrected Sentence
Whoever needs a ride. They may come with us.	*Whoever needs a ride* may come with us.

Series Fragments.   Once in a while, a series of words or phrases may be so long that it fools you into thinking it is a complete sentence. To avoid writing series fragments, be sure that each of your sentences has a subject and verb. Notice how the following series fragment can easily be made into a complete sentence.

CORRECTING SERIES FRAGMENTS	
Sentence and Series Fragment	Corrected Sentence
Every spring his garden is alive with color. *A flowering pink cherry tree near the fence, red and yellow primroses along the border, and neat rectangular beds of orange and yellow tulips.*	Every spring his garden is alive with color. *A flowering pink cherry tree* blooms *near the fence, red and yellow primroses* dot *the borders, and neat rectangular beds* blaze *with orange and yellow tulips.*

EXERCISE A: **Correcting Phrase Fragments, Clause Fragments, and Series Fragments.** Identify each of the following fragments as a *phrase fragment*, a *clause fragment*, or a *series fragment*. Then rewrite the fragments as sentences.
Revisions will vary; samples given for first two.
 1. Laughed, shouted, and romped. *ser frag*
 2. While she was running after the bus. *cl frag*
 3. Frequent loud interruptions. *phr frag*
 4. Petrified dinosaur bones. *phr frag*
 5. Where cattails and reeds grew high. *cl frag*
 6. Sometimes downcast, frequently deeply depressed, never really happy. *ser frag*
 7. Watching, stalking, pouncing on its victim. *ser frag*
 8. Which recalled a time of carefree days. *cl frag*
 9. Must have been abandoned by an indifferent person. *phr frag*
10. Whomever he invites. *cl frag*

1. The children laughed, shouted, and romped.

2. While she was running after the bus, Cindy fell and broke her ankle.

■ Different Kinds of Run-ons

Another kind of sentence error is the *run-on sentence,* often called simply a *run-on.* A run-on sentence is two or more complete sentences that are capitalized and punctuated as if they were one. Unlike fragments, which have too little information, run-ons are to be avoided because they have too much information.

Use punctuation, conjunctions, or other means to join or separate the parts of a run-on sentence.

There are two common types of run-on sentences. One kind consists of two or more sentences that arc not scparated or joined by any punctuation at all. The other kind of run-on is made up of two sentences with only a comma to separate them.

WITH NO PUNCTUATION: ⌐He rushed down the subway steps⌐ ⌐an

angry woman followed in close pursuit⌐.

WITH ONLY A COMMA: ⌐This is a very belated birthday card, ⌐my

birthday was three months ago⌐.

Like fragments, run-ons arc usually the result of carelessness and haste. Avoid them by rereading your work, aloud if necessary. Listen for the natural stops that indicate where your sentences end. If you find run-ons in your writing, you can correct them easily by adding punctuation and conjunctions or by rewriting.

Correcting Run-ons with Punctuation and Conjunctions. The following chart shows three ways that run-ons may be corrected with punctuation and conjunctions.

USING PUNCTUATION AND CONJUNCTIONS	
Run-ons	**Sentences with End Marks**
Will summer ever come we doubt it very much.	Will summer ever come? We doubt it very much.
Edith slumped into a chair, her worst fear was realized.	Edith slumped into a chair. Her worst fear was realized.

Run-ons	Sentences with Commas
A storm was predicted soon lightning lit up the sky.	A storm was predicted, and soon lightning lit up the sky.
They may have stopped to eat, they may be lost.	They may have stopped to eat, or they may be lost.

Run-ons	Sentences with Semicolons
He doesn't merely like fishing, he is addicted to it.	He doesn't merely like fishing; he is addicted to it.
Charlene is a disaster in the kitchen, she never invites anyone for dinner.	Charlene is a disaster in the kitchen; therefore, she never invites anyone for dinner.

In the last example, notice that even though the conjunctive adverb *therefore* is added between the independent clauses, a semicolon is still necessary.

Correcting Run-ons by Rewriting.   Sometimes the best way to correct a run-on sentence is by rewriting. The following examples show run-ons rewritten to form parts of simple sentences.

RUN-ON: Julie sometimes comes over to visit us, her little brother comes too.

SENTENCE WITH COMPOUND SUBJECT: *Julie and her little brother* sometimes come over to visit us.

RUN-ON: Leaping from behind the chair, the kitten batted the yarn with her paw, then she dashed across the rug.

SENTENCE WITH COMPOUND VERB: Leaping from behind the chair, the kitten *batted the yarn with her paw and then dashed across the rug.*

RUN-ON: William Shakespeare wrote tragedies, comedies, and histories, he was the finest of playwrights.

SENTENCE WITH APPOSITIVE PHRASE: William Shakespeare, *the finest of playwrights*, wrote tragedies, comedies, and histories.

Run-ons can also be rewritten to form complex sentences. Notice in the following example that the second clause in the run-on is already subordinate to the other clause—it implies a condition.

RUN-ON: The picnic may be canceled, it may rain.

SENTENCE WITH SUBORDINATE CLAUSE: The picnic may be canceled *if it rains.*

Sometimes a run-on may be corrected by rewriting it as a complex sentence even though neither clause seems subordinate to the other.

RUN-ON: I like to watch a good movie twice, I do this every time I can.

SENTENCE WITH SUBORDINATE CLAUSE: I like to watch a good movie twice *whenever I can.*

EXERCISE B: **Correcting Run-on Sentences.** Rewrite the first five run-ons by adding either appropriate end marks, commas and conjunctions, or semicolons. Rewrite the last five as simple or complex sentences.

Answers will vary; samples given for first two at bottom of page.

1. They bought an old mill, eventually they were able to make it into a unique and beautiful home.
2. Every year at this time the snow melts and the creek flows, six months from now, however, it will be dry.
3. Jason dropped out of school in his junior year, he received a diploma years later from a correspondence school.
4. Days turned into years, the years seemed an eternity.
5. Will he leave his job and its security to try his luck at farming it seems unlikely.
6. Sir Winston Churchill was a brilliant man he was a famous English Prime Minister during World War I.
7. Stalin was a ruthless dictator, he slaughtered millions of innocent people.
8. Marty was afraid of bees, he had a severe allergic reaction to their stings.
9. In the spring cardinals come to our birdfeeder, an occasional bluejay also makes an appearance.
10. Rapunzel let her long hair fall to the ground, her name means "lettuce."

APPLICATION: **Correcting Sentence Errors in Compositions.** Some of the sentences in the following paragraphs are

1. They bought an old mill, and eventually they were able to make it into a unique and beautiful home.   2. Every year at this time, the snow melts and the creek flows; six months from now, however, it will be dry.

faulty. Rewrite the composition correcting each fragment and run-on, using any method of correction you wish.
Faulty sentences are underlined. Revisions will vary; sample given for first paragraph.

(1) The storm had come upon them suddenly. (2) <u>Taking the two boys by surprise.</u> (3) Their lightweight jackets offered no protection from the drenching rain. (4) <u>Jack, who led the way, pointed to the cabin, it was almost hidden by the trees.</u> (5) Within minutes they stood on the porch. (6) <u>The door opened effortlessly they entered, throwing their backpacks onto the floor.</u>

(7) <u>Phil let his eyes grow accustomed to the darkness, Jack felt for the lantern.</u> (8) <u>Which he knew was on the table.</u> (9) If they had started out even half an hour later, they would have been caught in the downpour. (10) <u>Unable to reach the cabin before nightfall.</u>

(11) <u>When the lantern was lit, Jack gasped in astonishment, the doors to the cupboard which had been so carefully stocked by his father were opened, revealing empty shelves.</u> (12) <u>Walking numbly back onto the porch.</u> (13) He stared at the place where they had stacked nearly half a cord of wood. (14) Obviously someone had been warm and well-fed at their expense. (15) <u>Phil, he knew, would accept his apology, that was a small consolation for the uncomfortable night they would pass before tomorrow came.</u> (16) <u>At least a lesson had been learned, in the future he would be prepared for all eventualities.</u>

1. . . . them suddenly. 2. taking the two boys by surprise. 4. . . . to the cabin, which was almost hidden by the trees. 6. When the door opened effortlessly, they entered. . . .

8.2 Misplaced and Dangling Modifiers

The correct placement of phrase or clause modifiers within a sentence is one essential ingredient of clear speaking and writing.

A modifier should be placed as close as possible to the word it modifies.

■ Problems with Modifiers

Two common sentence errors occur (1) when modifiers are placed too far from the modified word or (2) when the modified word appears to be missing from the sentence.

Misplaced Modifiers. A *misplaced modifier* seems to modify the wrong word in a sentence. In the following example, notice how the italicized modifier confuses the reader.

MISPLACED MODIFIER: *Slithering through the wet grass,* we watched the garden snake.

Although *slithering through the wet grass* logically should modify *snake,* the modifier is positioned as though it modified *we.* The sentence should be rewritten so that the modifier is closer to the modified word.

CORRECTED SENTENCE: We watched the garden snake *slithering through the grass.*

Dangling Modifiers. A *dangling modifier* seems to modify either the wrong word or no word at all because the word it should modify is missing from the sentence. To understand the sentence, the reader must pause and guess what the missing word should be, as in the following example.

DANGLING MODIFIER: *Pausing briefly to congratulate Barbara,* the conversation continued.

The italicized dangling modifier appears to describe *conversation,* which, according to the sentence, "paused to congratulate Barbara." The sentence can be rewritten logically to include the missing word.

CORRECTED SENTENCE: *Pausing briefly to congratulate Barbara,* we continued the conversation.

EXERCISE A: Recognizing Misplaced and Dangling Modifiers. Each of the following sentences contains an underlined phrase or clause. Indicate on your paper whether the modifier is *misplaced, dangling,* or *correct.*

1. Carefully trained for months, the dog owner hoped to win a blue ribbon. *dang*
2. Don't try to board the bus until it comes to a complete stop. *C*
3. They planned to win before the game started. *misp*
4. To succeed in a job interview, the employer must be impressed by your desire to do the work. *dang*
5. She flew in a small aircraft trembling with fear. *misp*
6. Jumping out of his seat, Milton shouted with surprise. *C*

7. <u>Carefully reading the directions</u>, the test could be taken with confidence. *dang*
8. This letter, <u>which I found behind a drawer</u>, was written over a century ago. *C*
9. She fearfully pointed to the spider over her head <u>that hung from a transparent web</u>. *misp*
10. We joined the crowd in applauding the winner <u>with enthusiasm</u>. *misp*

■ Correcting Misplaced Modifiers

A misplaced modifier is usually a prepositional phrase, verbal phrase, or adjective clause.

Correct a sentence containing a misplaced modifier by moving the phrase or clause closer to the word it should logically modify.

Notice how the following misplaced modifiers can be corrected.

MISPLACED PREPOSITIONAL PHRASE: The lake attracted many birds *with gentle waves.*

CORRECTED SENTENCE: The lake *with gentle waves* attracted many birds.

MISPLACED PARTICIPIAL PHRASE: *Balanced on one leg,* the boys stared at the flamingo.

CORRECTED SENTENCE: The boys stared at the flamingo *balanced on one leg.*

MISPLACED ADJECTIVE CLAUSE: Gazing upwards at the bats, the spelunkers shone their flashlights *that hung by the thousands from the roof of the cave.*

CORRECTED SENTENCE: Gazing upwards, the spelunkers shone their flashlights at the bats *that hung by the thousands from the roof of the cave.*

EXERCISE B: Correcting Misplaced Modifiers. Rewrite the following sentences to correct the misplaced modifiers. Then underline the corrected modifier in each sentence and draw an arrow from it to the word it modifies.

Misplaced modifiers are underlined. Revisions will vary; samples given for first two.

1. They gave him a watch for a gift <u>that was self-winding</u>.
2. Lionel sold his bicycle to his brother <u>with four speeds</u>.
3. The zookeeper captured the escaped iguana <u>brandishing a net in his upraised hand</u>.
4. The boys ran from the haunted house <u>noticeably trembling</u>.
5. Brenda put oranges into the punch <u>that came from California</u>.
6. We saw a deer bound across the road and into the woods <u>in alarm</u>.
7. Jed ordered a steak and a salad <u>cooked medium rare</u>.
8. She had a gold tooth in her mouth <u>that gleamed whenever she smiled</u>.
9. Perched on top of the counter <u>with a lollipop</u>, the child sat contentedly.
10. <u>Leaving the party after midnight</u>, we waved farewell to the happy guests.

1. For a gift they gave him a watch that was self-winding.

2. Lionel sold his bicycle with four speeds to his brother.

■ Correcting Dangling Modifiers

A dangling modifier is usually a verbal phrase or an adverb clause.

Correct a sentence containing a dangling modifier by rewriting the sentence to include the missing modified word.

If the dangling modifier is a verbal phrase, the missing word or words can be added after the phrase, or the verbal phrase can be rewritten as a clause containing the missing word or words. In the following set of examples, the first corrected sentence shows the addition of missing words. The second corrected sentence shows a verbal phrase expanded into a clause.

DANGLING PARTICIPIAL PHRASE: *Looking at the stars through a telescope, a meteor suddenly flashed across the sky.*

CORRECTED SENTENCE: *Looking at the stars through a telescope, we saw a meteor suddenly flash across the sky.*

CORRECTED SENTENCE: *As we were looking at the stars through a telescope, a meteor suddenly flashed across the sky.*

If the dangling modifier is a clause, the problem will often involve the use of pronouns. In the following set of examples, the adverb clause dangles because of a confusion between *Sarah* and *Sarah's mother*. The sentence is corrected by making clear exactly who "was just a baby."

DANGLING ADVERB CLAUSE: *When she was just a baby,* Sarah's mother read her colorfully illustrated stories.

CORRECTED SENTENCE: *When Sarah was just a baby,* her mother read her colorfully illustrated stories.

EXERCISE C: Correcting Dangling Modifiers. Rewrite the following sentences to eliminate the dangling modifiers. In your rewritten sentence, underline the modifier that was dangling in the original. Then draw an arrow from it to the word it modifies. *Dangling modifiers are underlined. Revisions will vary; samples given for first two at bottom of page.*

1. To understand his philosophy, certain books must be read.
2. Picketing for improved working conditions, the strike continued.
3. In searching for the missing diamond ring, every possible nook and cranny was explored.
4. To swallow the bitter medicine, sugar was needed.
5. Lost in a daydream, my teacher's words went unheard.
6. When he was barely nine months old, Jeremy's father taught him to swing by himself.
7. Flying from Los Angeles to Santa Fe, the desert looked like the moon.
8. To achieve maximum efficiency, incentive must be provided.
9. Waving the baton at the musicians, the orchestra began to play.
10. A reward was received by returning the wallet.

APPLICATION: Correcting Misplaced and Dangling Modifiers in Compositions. Rewrite the following paragraph to correct any misplaced or dangling modifiers. *Misplaced and dangling modifiers are underlined. Revisions will vary; samples given for 2 and 4.*

(1) Stan is a successful architect and interior designer whose custom-built homes stagger the imagination. (2) Priced beyond what the average person can afford, his unique inspiration can be seen in the house on the corner. (3) The front of the house is made entirely of glass. (4) Ex-

1. *To understand his philosophy, you must read certain books.*   2. *Picketing for improved working conditions, the workers continued the strike.*

tended outward from the second floor, eight vertical steel pillars support a balcony. (5) Within the center of the house, a huge tropical aquarium rests on a marble floor five feet in diameter. (6) A wrought iron staircase winds its way around the aquarium connecting the first and second stories. (7) Recessed in the ceilings, each room is softly lit by fluorescent lights. (8) To enjoy music in any location, there is a dial on the wall next to the thermostat. (9) In the winter, fireplaces provide warmth; in the summer, cool air is circulated by fans. (10) By closing your eyes and dreaming, the house can become yours.

2. Priced beyond what the average person can afford, his houses have a unique inspiration that can be seen in the house on the corner.   4. Extending outward from the second floor, the balcony is supported by eight vertical pillars.

Faulty Parallelism   8.3

Besides fragments, run-ons, and misplaced or dangling modifiers, another sentence fault that can confuse a listener or reader is faulty parallelism.

■ Parallelism in Sentences

Parallelism is a big word for a simple, logical idea.

Parallelism is the placement of equal ideas in words, phrases, or clauses of similar types.

Checking your sentences for the correct use of parallelism is one way to ensure that your ideas are expressed clearly and logically.

Correct Use of Parallelism.   Whenever you present a comparison or a series of ideas that are equal in importance, you should express them in equal—that is, parallel—grammatical structures. Parallel structures can be two or more words of the same part of speech, two or more phrases of the same type, or two or more clauses of the same type. A coordinating conjunction such as *and* or *or* usually helps link parallel structures.

PARALLEL WORDS: The school board reviewed several aspects of redistricting: *social*, *educational*, and *financial*.

PARALLEL PHRASES: She loves *to swim in the ocean* and *to water ski at the lake*.

PARALLEL CLAUSES: We wondered *what was in the box, where it came from, who had sent it,* and *why it had not been unwrapped.*

Parallel structures may also be written with an understood word that is omitted after the first item in a series. In the following example, notice that the word *by* begins the first phrase but has been omitted in the second and third phrases. The understood word is shown in brackets.

PARALLEL PHRASES: I am planning to improve my health *by eating properly,* [by] *sleeping regularly,* and [by] *exercising daily.*

Sometimes the conjunction may also be omitted between parallel structures.

PARALLEL CLAUSES: *If you do no homework,* [and] *if you show no interest in class,* you will undoubtedly fail the course.

Faulty Use of Parallelism.   Faulty parallelism results when ideas of equal importance are not expressed in equal grammatical structures. The last idea in the following sentence, for example, is not parallel to the others.

FAULTY PARALLELISM: The waiter suggested *lamb chops, green beans,* and *that we try the scalloped potatoes.*

The direct objects in this sentence are not parallel: The first two are nouns; the third is a noun clause. The easiest solution is to make them all nouns.

CORRECTED SENTENCE: The waiter suggested *lamb chops, green beans,* and *scalloped potatoes.*

EXERCISE A: Recognizing Parallel Ideas.   Each of the following sentences contains two or more parallel ideas. Some are expressed correctly in parallel structures; others are not. Write the parallel ideas on your paper. Then identify each as *correct parallelism* or *faulty parallelism.*
Parallel ideas are in parentheses.

EXAMPLE: In her lecture the professor discussed migration, courtship, and how birds establish nesting territories.

migration, courtship, how birds establish nesting territories   faulty parallelism

1. Good speech must (be audible) and (have clarity.) *faulty*
2. My paper received a high grade for (originality) and for (thorough research.) *correct*
3. Claire dislikes (hiking for great distances) but prefers (to stroll leisurely.) *faulty*
4. You can adjust the swing either (by lengthening the one rope) or (you can shorten the other rope.) *faulty*
5. The insurance agent sold my parents (a homeowners' policy) and also (a life insurance policy for me.) *correct*
6. The clock is (compact), (silent,) and (runs accurately.) *faulty*
7. (To err is human;) (forgiving is divine.) *faulty*
8. We interviewed (the mayor,) (a council member,) and (with the sheriff.) *faulty*
9. The football sailed (across the yard,) (over the fence,) and (into our neighbor's bed of prize dahlias.) *correct*
10. We saw neither (the Ganges) nor (went to the Taj Mahal) when we were in India. *faulty*

■ Correcting Faulty Parallelism

To correct a sentence containing faulty parallelism usually takes only a few moments of thinking and a quick rewriting.

Correct a sentence containing faulty parallelism by rewriting it so that each parallel idea is expressed in the same grammatical structure.

As you will see, faulty parallelism can involve not only words, phrases, or clauses in a series but also words, phrases, or clauses in a comparison.

Nonparallel Words. When ideas are presented in a series of words, each word should be the same part of speech. You should also be careful not to match a series of words with a phrase or a clause.

CORRECTING NONPARALLEL WORDS	
Nouns and a Phrase	**Nouns**
The qualities of a good scout are *loyalty, honesty,* and *being brave.*	The qualities of a good scout are *loyalty, honesty,* and *bravery.*

Adverbs and a Phrase	Adverbs
A well-trained dog obeys *willingly*, *completely*, and *with speed*.	A well-trained dog obeys *willingly*, *completely*, and *quickly*.
Verbs and a Clause	**Verbs**
The class *analyzed*, *discussed*, and *we raised questions about the new rules*.	The class *analyzed*, *discussed*, and *questioned* the new rules.

Nonparallel Phrases.　When ideas are presented in a series of phrases, make sure each phrase is the same type: prepositional, participial, gerundive, or infinitive. In addition, make sure the series contains nothing but phrases.

CORRECTING NONPARALLEL PHRASES	
Prepositional and Predicate Phrases	**Prepositional Phrases**
They traveled *to Oregon*, *to California*, and *visited Mexico*.	They traveled *to Oregon*, *to California*, and *to Mexico*.
Participial Phrase and Clause	**Participial Phrases**
The accused faced his trial, *believing in his own innocence* and *he desired the truth*.	The accused faced the trial, *believing in his own innocence* and *desiring the truth*.
Gerund and Infinitive Phrases	**Gerund Phrases**
You should always find time for *doing your daily chores*, *enjoying leisure time*, and *to think of others*.	You should always find time for *doing your daily chores*, *enjoying leisure time*, and *thinking of others*.

Nonparallel Clauses.　When ideas are presented in a series of subordinate clauses, each clause should be of the same type: adjective, adverb, or noun.

CORRECTING NONPARALLEL SUBORDINATE CLAUSES	
Adjective and Adverb Clauses	**Adjective Clauses**
Our lawyer accepts cases *that deserve representation* and *if she feels she will win.*	Our lawyer accepts cases *that deserve representation* and *that she feels she will win.*
Noun Clause and Independent Clause	**Noun Clauses**
The examination showed *that my height had increased,* but *I weighed less.*	The examination showed *that my height had increased* but *that my weight had dropped.*

Ideas presented in two or more independent clauses placed together in a single sentence should also be parallel in structure.

CORRECTING NONPARALLEL INDEPENDENT CLAUSES	
Gerund and Infinitive Openers	**Gerund Openers**
Knowing how to swim is important; *to know* where to swim is even more important.	*Knowing* how to swim is important; *knowing* where to swim is even more important.

Nonparallel Comparisons. A common saying warns, "Don't compare apples with oranges." This saying can easily be applied to sentences that compare two things: A comparison should not be worded so that one grammatical structure is compared to another.

CORRECTING NONPARALLEL COMPARISONS	
Phrase and Clause	**Prepositional Phrases**
My report received a low grade more *for its grammatical mistakes* than *what was said in it.*	My report received a low grade more *for its grammatical mistakes* than *for its content.*

Gerund and Infinitive Phrases	Gerund Phrases
Giving an oral presentation can require more preparation than *to write a term paper.*	*Giving an oral presentation* can require more preparation than *writing a term paper.*
Noun and Gerund Phrase	**Gerund Phrases**
I like *television* as much as *going to see new movies.*	I like *watching television* as much as *going to see new movies.*

EXERCISE B: Correcting Faulty Parallelism of Words, Phrases, and Clauses in a Series. Each of the following sentences is awkward because of words, phrases, or clauses that are not parallel. Rewrite each sentence so that it contains parallel constructions.
Revisions may vary; samples given.

1. We were happy to hear the good news and <u>for being</u> the first to congratulate them. *to be*
2. The florist arranged the flowers, placing a few ferns here and there and then <u>added</u> a ribbon. *adding*
3. Searching for buried treasure was fun, but <u>to find</u> real pirate booty was astounding. *finding*
4. In my family we talk to one another, not ~~talking~~ about one another.
5. By thinking clearly and ~~with~~ being patient, you can unscramble an anagram.
6. The man and his wife were served soup that offended them, a main course that sickened them, and <u>the dessert</u> made them nauseated. *a dessert that*
7. My desires were to visit the museum and <u>seeing</u> everything in the displays. *to see*
8. These plants need <u>water</u> and looking after. *watering*
9. In the pond small beetles darted to and fro, pollywogs <u>wriggling</u>, and snails <u>clinging</u> to stems. *wriggled/clung*
10. He agreed to participate in the talent show but refused <u>singing</u> without a microphone. *to sing*

EXERCISE C: Correcting Faulty Parallelism in Comparisons. Each of the following sentences is awkward because the ideas being compared are not expressed in parallel structures. Rewrite each sentence so that it contains parallel constructions. Revisions may vary; samples given.

EXAMPLE: Joel likes imitating people and to tell jokes.

Joel likes imitating people and telling jokes.

1. Swimming in the lake during the summer is more fun than to skate on it in the winter. *skating*
2. Some people learn more from careful observation of the world around them than by diligently reading books. *carefully observing*
3. I like listening to music less than a good game of chess with a friend. *playing*
4. Sailing the boat well is more important to them than to win the regatta. *winning*
5. She prefers staying at home to parties. *going to parties*

APPLICATION: Writing Sentences with Parallel Structures.
Follow the directions to write sentences of your own. Underline the parallel ideas in each of your sentences.
Answers will vary; samples given for first two at bottom of page.
1. Use *or* to join three parallel gerund phrases.
2. Use *and* to join two parallel subordinate clauses.
3. Use *either* and *or* to join parallel infinitive phrases.
4. Write a comparison beginning "Listening to the radio is often more interesting than. . ."
5. Use *and* to join three parallel prepositional phrases.

Review Exercises: Grammar

REVIEW EXERCISE 1: Nouns

The following paragraph contains thirty nouns. First, list the nouns in each sentence. Next, indicate whether the nouns are *concrete* or *abstract*. Then, label the nouns *common* or *proper*. *Labels on page T-122.*

(1) The story of Pompeii fascinates most people. (2) Located in Italy, Pompeii was a prosperous city that vanished after Mount Vesuvius erupted in 79 A.D. (3) Although many of its citizens escaped, over a thousand died. (4) This tragedy could have been avoided if the people had heeded the warnings of the volcano. (5) Sixteen years earlier, an earthquake had damaged Pompeii and her neighbors, Naples and Herculaneum. (6) Afterwards, the crater began to show signs of life, but no one paid any attention. (7) For centuries, Pompeii lay buried under hardened volcanic ash. (8) Now, sightseers walk through the excavated streets and marvel at the ancient ruins.

1. *Getting up in the morning, eating during the day,* and *going to bed at night* are what nearly everyone does 365 days a year.   2. *Although he hated violence* and *he loathed muscular bodies,* he married a woman wrestler.

REVIEW EXERCISE 2: Pronouns

The following paragraph contains fifteen pronouns. First, list the pronouns in each sentence. Next, indicate the antecedent for each pronoun. (Some of the antecedents may be located in preceding sentences.) Then, identify the type of pronoun as *personal, reflexive, intensive, demonstrative, relative, interrogative,* or *indefinite. Identifications on page T-122.*

(1) People who fish often need to be tricky. (2) The fish themselves, however, also need to be tricky in order to catch their prey. (3) What are some of their trickier methods? (4) The archerfish shoots its insect victims with drops of water from its tongue. (5) The decoy fish has a fin resembling a tiny fish. (6) It uses this to lure its victims close enough to be caught. (7) The frogfish fools unsuspecting prey into thinking there is a bit of food floating over its head. (8) These are just a few of the unusual ways fish provide nourishment for themselves.

REVIEW EXERCISE 3: Verbs

Write the verb or verb phrase contained in each of the following sentences on your paper. Identify each verb or verb phrase as *action* or *linking.* If the verb is an action verb, label it *transitive* or *intransitive.*

1. Small legs appear on the tadpole's body in this stage of growth. *AV intrans*
2. In their family, red hair and blue eyes have always been hereditary. *LV*
3. I am usually full of self-pity during an illness. *LV*
4. An oboe may sound either harsh or sad. *LV*
5. The sign on the gate warns visitors of the watchdog inside. *AV trans*
6. My mouth feels strange because of the novocaine. *LV*
7. Irma stunned the audience with her performance. *AV trans*
8. We saw her cousins at the barbecue. *AV trans*
AV trans 9. Bank tellers count money very rapidly and accurately.
10. These after-dinner mints are especially good with Turkish coffee. *LV*
AV trans 11. With fury, Gwen tore the picture into tiny fragments.
12. The oak tree's leaves turn dark brown at this time of year. *LV*
AV trans 13. The startled fawn leaped from its cover in the bushes.
14. He did not want any of the things offered. *AV trans*
15. Because of his cold, Jack could not smell the coffee's aroma. *AV trans*

16. His hands <u>had become</u> raw in the cold. *LV*
17. This royal palace <u>was</u> several centuries old. *LV*
18. Sherlock Holmes always <u>found</u> unusual clues. *AV trans*
19. A lion tamer <u>must be</u> very patient and careful. *LV*
20. Tina <u>can stay</u> underwater nearly three minutes. *AV intrans*

REVIEW EXERCISE 4: Adjectives

The following words are nouns. Write two adjectives on your paper that can be used in the blanks before each noun. For numbers 1 to 10, include two of each of the following four kinds of adjectives: *proper, compound, definite articles, indefinite articles.* For numbers 11 to 20, include two of each of these four kinds of adjectives: *possessive, demonstrative, interrogative, indefinite.* Answers will vary; samples given.

1.	*the*	*red*	grapefruit	11.	*his*	*chapped* hands
2.	*a*	*pretty*	hat	12.	*three*	*American* tourists
3.	*two*	*Greek*	shepherds	13.	*that*	*dirty* spoon
4.	*the*	*Swiss*	watch	14.	*their*	*neighbor's* dirt
5.	*one*	*hard*	knock	15.	*these*	*pine* trees
6.	*hot*	*homemade*	pastries	16.	*many*	*a* mousetrap
7.	*soft*	*eiderdown*	blanket	17.	*some*	*African* reptiles
8.	*an*	*ancient*	coin	18.	*British*	*Crown* jewels
9.	*new*	*designer*	jacket	19.	*which*	*bright* color
10.	*tiny*	*lovely*	camera	20.	*whose*	*past* experience

REVIEW EXERCISE 5: Adverbs

Each of the following sentences contains at least one adverb. Write the adverbs on your paper. After each, write the verb, adjective, or other adverb that the adverb modifies. Then write the information given by the adverb: *where, when, in what manner,* or *to what extent.* Modified words are shaded.

1. He <u>courageously</u> dived into the river and <u>quickly</u> rescued the unconscious woman. *verb–manner/verb–manner*
2. Gail is <u>certainly</u> <u>very</u> reliable. *adj–extent/adj–extent*
3. After the party she was <u>still</u> depressed and <u>somewhat</u> sad. *adj–when/adj–extent*
4. The yellow butterfly <u>lightly</u> floated on a current of air. *verb–manner*
5. <u>Yesterday</u> my brother's elementary school class visited a paint factory. *verb–when*
6. An enraged rhino runs <u>much</u> <u>more</u> rapidly than you think it could. *adv—extent/adv—extent/verb—manner*
7. Make your move <u>soon</u> but think <u>carefully</u> first.
8. A rabbit <u>hungrily</u> nibbled the lettuce leaves that grew there. *verb–manner/verb–where*

7. verb—when/verb—manner/verb—when

9. She was <u>too</u> thin and <u>not</u> tall <u>enough</u> to be a model.
10. The mouse <u>hardly</u> had a chance to run. *verb–extent*

9. adj—extent/adj—extent/adj—extent

REVIEW EXERCISE 6: Prepositions

Each of the following sentences contains a preposition or an adverb that can be used as a preposition. If the sentence contains a preposition, write the preposition and its object on your paper. If the sentence contains an adverb that can be used as a preposition, write the adverb and label it *adverb*. *Preposition and adverbs are underlined, objects of prepositions are not.*

1. Please lean <u>across the</u> table and hand me the salt. *prep*
2. We had few supplies <u>after the</u> long winter months. *prep*
3. Anthony spent his money and then had to go <u>without</u>. *adv*
4. Look <u>around</u> and see what you want. *adv*
5. I put the cat <u>inside</u> and locked the door. *adv*
6. They glanced <u>behind them</u> to see if they were being followed. *prep*
7. Rachel Carson wrote books <u>about the</u> environment. *prep*
8. An eagle swooped <u>down</u> and struck its victim. *adv*
prep 9. The vastness of the universe is <u>beyond our</u> imagination.
10. You will find the toolshed <u>beside the</u> garage. *prep*

REVIEW EXERCISE 7: Conjunctions

Complete each of the following sentences with an appropriate coordinating conjunction, correlative conjunction, subordinating conjunction, or conjunctive adverb. Write the conjunction on your paper and identify what kind it is.
Answers will vary: samples given.
1. Sometimes it helps to take a break from studying; ___*otherwise*___ , your eyes become too tired. *conj adv*
2. Curry is a good seasoning, ___*but*___ too much can be overwhelming. *coord*
correl 3. Bill ___*not only*___ won the race ___*but also*___ set a record.
4. Snowshoe rabbits have white fur ___*until*___ summer comes. *subord*
5. The traveler spoke ___*as if*___ he were weary of his journey. *subord*
6. Ponce de Leon searched for the Fountain of Youth, ___*but*___ he did not find it. *coord*
7. Some old houses cannot be insulated; ___*therefore*___ , they are often drafty and cold. *conj adv*
8. Gerry would rather stay here and read ___*than*___ go for a walk. *subord*

9. Watch for quail hidden in the tall grass ___*or*___ near those rocks. *coord*
10. Marie Antoinette said the French people should eat cake ___*if*___ they couldn't afford bread. *subord*

REVIEW EXERCISE 8: Interjections

Complete each sentence by filling in the blank with an appropriate interjection. *Answers will vary; samples given.*

1. ___*Oh*___, I forgot to turn off the water faucets!
2. ___*Ah*___! Isn't that a cute little kitten?
3. This butter tastes rancid! ___*Yech*___!
4. He knew, ___*alas*___, that no one cared.
5. ___*Phew*___, this trunk is too heavy for one person.
6. ___*Phooey*___! Who could believe a word of that?
7. The exam has been cancelled. ___*Hallelujah*___!
8. I'm afraid, ___*darn*___, that I've lost the address.
9. ___*Oops*___! The carton of eggs fell on the floor.
10. ___*Rats*___, the umpire made another mistake.

REVIEW EXERCISE 9: All Eight Parts of Speech

Write ten sentences of your own containing each of the following words as directed. *Answers will vary; samples given for first three at bottom of page.*

1. *master* as a noun
2. *master* as a verb
3. *master* as an adjective
4. *inside* as an adverb
5. *inside* as an adjective
6. *inside* as a preposition
7. *inside* as a noun
8. *after* as a conjunction
9. *after* as an adverb
10. *after* as a preposition

REVIEW EXERCISE 10: Using Basic Sentence Parts

For each of the following items, write a sentence containing the designated sentence parts in the order given. Underline and label the sentence parts as follow: *S* for a subject; *V* for a verb; *HV* for a helping verb; *DO* for a direct object; *IO* for an indirect object; *OC* for an objective complement; *PN* for a predicate nominative; *PA* for a predicate adjective. Try to include at least ten words in each of your sentences. *Answers will vary; samples given for first two.*

EXAMPLE: subject, verb, direct object, objective complement

                S   V   DO   OC
    The <u>students</u> <u>elected</u> <u>CharlesLee</u> <u>president</u> of the junior class.

1. The dog followed his master.   2. Will he ever master factoring?
3. Later he became a master plumber.

1. subject, verb, predicate nominative
2. subject, subject, verb, indirect object, direct object, direct object
3. subject, verb, direct object, objective complement
4. helping verb, subject, verb, direct object
5. subject, verb, verb, predicate nominative
6. subject, verb, indirect object, indirect object, direct object
7. helping verb, subject, verb, predicate nominative
8. subject, subject, verb, verb, indirect object, direct object
9. subject, subject, verb, predicate nominative
10. helping verb, subject, subject, verb, predicate nominative

  S V   PN   S   S V IO DO   DO
1. She was a movie star. 2. Poseidon and Athena gave the Greeks water and the olive tree.

REVIEW EXERCISE 11: Expanding Sentences with Prepositional Phrases and Appositives

Combine each of the following pairs of sentences into one sentence containing either an appositive or a prepositional phrase. Indicate the kind of phrase you included after each sentence. *Answers will vary; samples given for first two.*

EXAMPLE: You can write your answers with pen. You can also use a pencil.

     You can write your answers with a pen or with a pencil. prepositional phrase

1. We sent my grandmother a gift. The gift was a new tennis racket.
2. A kangaroo rat gets its name because of the way it jumps. This rodent has a long tail and strong back legs.
3. Kyle bought a silk scarf. The scarf had a designer's signature.
4. The teacher told us some interesting facts. The topic was astronomy.
5. Tom wrote his girlfriend a long letter. Tom's girlfriend's name is Patricia.
6. Our neighbors just bought a new house. A lake is nearby.
7. Mr. Armstrong travels from campus to campus, giving lectures. He is an environmentalist.
8. The girl caught everyone's attention. She had stilts.
9. This type of toadstool grows on trees. It is a poisonous one.
10. The dachshund puppy growled ferociously at me. It had a giant bone in its mouth.

1. We sent my grandmother a gift, a new tennis racket. (appos)
2. The kangaroo rat, a rodent with a long tail and strong back legs, gets its name because of the way it jumps. (appos)

REVIEW EXERCISE 12: Expanding Sentences with Verbals and Verbal Phrases

Each of the following sentences contains at least one verbal. Expand each verbal into a verbal phrase by adding one or more modifiers or complements to it. Write the expanded sentences on your paper and label each verbal phrase as *participle* (for a participial phrase), *gerund* (for a gerund phrase), or *infinitive* (for an infinitive phrase).
Sentences will vary; samples given for first two.

1. I tried to remember.
2. Fascinated, we watched the film about sky-diving.
3. A good book to read is this one.
4. Jogging and bicycling are good exercise.
5. He noticed his supervisor frowning.
6. Relaxing, Hal tried to unwind.
7. She found it difficult to breathe.
8. After swimming, they unpacked a picnic lunch.
9. Abe, hesitating, was afraid to speak.
10. Spying is an unpopular vocation.

1. I tried to remember the plot of the novel. (inf)

2. Totally fascinated, we watched the film about sky-diving. (part)

REVIEW EXERCISE 13: Identifying Subordinate Clauses

Each of the following sentences contains a subordinate clause. Write the subordinate clause from each sentence on your paper. Then label it as an *adjective clause*, an *adverb clause*, or a *noun clause*.

1. <u>Since Ed grew a beard</u>, his friends are hardly able to recognize him. *adv*
2. You are <u>what you eat</u>. *noun*
3. Pastels, <u>which are considered cold colors</u>, are not my choice for classroom walls. *adj*
4. <u>As levels of carbon dioxide in the earth's atmosphere rise</u>, our planet's average temperature also rises. *adv*
5. <u>How much you weigh</u> will be a vital factor in your becoming a successful jockey. *noun*
6. Charlie attends a school <u>where a strict dress code is observed</u>. *adj*
7. He died <u>before he could atone for his mistakes</u>. *adv*
8. A travel agency of questionable merit arranged for them to stay at a hotel <u>where cockroaches scuttled across the floor</u>. *adj*
9. We give <u>whatever we can</u> to the Community Chest. *noun*
10. A person <u>whose attitude is condescending</u> will not succeed as a social worker. *adj*

REVIEW EXERCISE 14: Writing Simple, Compound, Complex, and Compound-Complex Sentences

Follow the directions to combine each of the following groups of sentences into one sentence. Place brackets around your independent or main clauses; underline your subordinate clauses. *Answers will vary; samples given for first two.*

EXAMPLE: Write a complex sentence with one main clause and two subordinate clauses.

The musicians tuned their instruments. The concert had not begun. They were waiting for the conductor to make her entrance.

Before the concert began, [the musicians tuned their instruments] while they waited for the conductor to make her entrance.

1. Write a simple sentence.
   The guard dog attacked the dummy. The dog sank its teeth into the dummy's leg.
2. Write a simple sentence.
   A woman stepped out of the taxi. She was dressed entirely in black.
3. Write a compound sentence with two independent clauses.
   Orson Welles frightened thousands with his story of alien invaders. Many people panicked.
4. Write a compound sentence with three independent clauses.
   She ignored him. She laughed at him. She apologized for her rude behavior.
5. Write a complex sentence with one main clause and one subordinate clause.
   We didn't dare remove our snow tires yet. More snow was predicted.
6. Write a complex sentence with one main clause and two subordinate clauses.
   The telephone rings. A recorded voice will give you brief instructions. You can leave a message.
7. Write a complex sentence with one main clause and one subordinate clause.
   The manager expected us to arrive early. The manager expected us to work late. The manager expected us to work without complaining. The manager was soon forced to resign.

1. [The guard dog attacked the dummy and sank its teeth into the dummy's leg.]

2. [A woman dressed entirely in black stepped out of the taxi.]

8. Write a compound-complex sentence with two main clauses and one subordinate clause.
   Beat a pint of heavy cream. It will form stiff peaks. Put it on warm gingerbread.
9. Write a compound-complex sentence with two main clauses and two subordinate clauses.
   The detective looked for clues. There were no clues. Finally he accused a person. The person was obviously innocent.
10. Write a compound-complex sentence with two main clauses and two subordinate clauses.
    There is a thunderstorm. You should lie flat on the ground. The ground should be in a depressed area. You should not touch anything made of metal. Metal attracts lightning.

REVIEW EXERCISE 15: Correcting Sentence Faults

Each of the following sentences contains a structural error. Identify the error in each sentence as a *fragment*, a *run-on*, a *misplaced modifier*, a *dangling modifier*, or *faulty parallelism*. Then rewrite the sentence to correct the error. *Errors are underlined. Sample revisions are given along with labels. Answers for 2. 4. 9 at bottom of page.*

1. On weekends we like to see a good movie and <u>going</u> to a nice restaurant afterward. *go (faulty parallelism)*
2. <u>Without a chance of coming out of the desert alive.</u>
3. <u>~~Teetering high above the net~~</u>, the crowd watched the amateur acrobat. *. . . teetering high above the net. (misp mod)*
4. <u>Neatly arranged in rows as she had left them.</u>
5. <u>Waiting patiently at the door</u>, the friend I searched for never arrived. *While I waited . . . (misp mod)*
6. He could hardly wait to taste the fudge <u>it</u> smelled so good. *which (RO)*
7. We were convinced that we should have a legal contract and <u>having</u> a lawyer represent us too. *have (faulty parallelism)*
8. <u>Fighting to stay afloat</u>, the raft rose and fell with the waves. *Even as we were fighting to stay afloat . . . (dang mod)*
9. Lucy wore perfume behind her ears <u>~~with a strong scent~~</u>.
10. The children made a snowman, <u>it</u> melted later in the day. *that (RO)*

REVIEW EXERCISE 16: Summary of Sentence Parts

Follow the directions to write ten sentences of your own. Underline the indicated sentence part in each sentence. *Answers will vary; samples given for first two on the following page.*
1. Write a simple sentence containing an appositive phrase.
2. Write a simple sentence containing an infinitive phrase.
2. . . . , we felt hopeless. (frag) 4. . . . were the toy soldiers. (frag) 9. with a strong scent (misp mod)

3. Write a simple sentence containing parallel verbs.
4. Write a compound sentence containing two gerund phrases.
5. Write a compound sentence containing a participle.
6. Write a complex sentence containing a gerund.
7. Write a complex sentence containing parallel subordinate clauses.
8. Write a complex sentence containing an appositive and a prepositional phrase.
9. Write a compound-complex sentence containing parallel main clauses.
10. Write a compound-complex sentence containing a participial phrase and an infinitive.

1. Julius Caesar, *a play by Shakespeare*, is often required reading for ninth graders.
2. The fastest way *to get to Atlanta* is by plane.

Chapter 9

Verb Usage

Grammar explains the form of a language—how all the parts work together to express meaning. Usage, on the other hand, explains how that language is actually used by speakers and writers. Though English grammar has remained much the same for the last several centuries, English usage is constantly changing.

Because usage varies, a word or expression is never right or wrong in itself. Correct usage is language that suits the time, the place, and the occasion.

In this and following chapters, you will find rules for what is called *standard English usage*. This is the usage considered appropriate most of the time, on most occasions, by most educated Americans today.

The unit begins with one of the more difficult aspects of usage: verbs. Even the best speakers and writers sometimes have trouble choosing the correct form of a verb from the variety of forms and uses that verbs have in the English language. It is easy to misuse the forms of certain verbs. For example, how often have you heard "I sung the song" instead of "I sang the song"?

Although a good memory is helpful to good verb usage, you will find that correctness is often more a matter of making sensible choices. For example, neither "I wrote that essay" nor "That essay was written by me" is wrong, but there are times when one is more appropriate than the other.

In this chapter you will employ both your powers of recall and your ability to discriminate between choices to develop a better command of verbs. You will look first at the tenses of verbs and then at the way tense forms are used within sentences. Finally, you will look at the passive forms of verbs and learn when to use the passive voice.

The Tenses of Verbs 9.1

One of the most important uses of verbs is to indicate when something happens. A verb will tell you if an event occurred two months ago, yesterday, or an hour ago. It will tell you if something is happening right now. It will tell you if an event will happen later in the day, next week, or some time in the distant future. The *tense* of a verb tells the time period in which an event takes place.

A **tense** is a form of a verb that shows time of action or state of being.

Examine the following sentences, noting the changes in time. Although the same verb, *work*, is used in each example, notice how the verb changes with each change in time.

EXAMPLES: She *works* hard all the time.

Last week, she *worked* many hours on her report.

She *will work* on her science project tomorrow.

She *has worked* on her speech all morning.

She *had worked* on the poster from seven until ten.

By the end of this week, she *will have worked* at her new job for three months.

In each sentence the tense of the verb indicates the time something happens.

■ The Six Tenses of English Verbs

As the preceding examples show, time can generally be expressed by using one of six tenses. There are three *simple tenses*: *present*, *past*, and *future*. There are also three *perfect tenses*: *present perfect*, *past perfect*, and *future perfect*.

Each of the six tenses has two forms: *basic* and *progressive*. A third form, the *emphatic*, occurs only in the present and past tenses. The following chart shows all fourteen forms of the verb *use*.

THE BASIC, PROGRESSIVE, AND EMPHATIC FORMS OF THE SIX TENSES

Tense	Basic Form	Progressive Form	Emphatic Form
Present	use	am using	do use
Past	used	was using	did use
Future	will use	will be using	
Present Perfect	have used	have been using	
Past Perfect	had used	had been using	
Future Perfect	will have used	will have been using	

EXERCISE A: Recognizing Tenses. Study the preceding chart. Then copy the following verbs onto your paper. After each, name the tense and the form if the form is not basic.

EXAMPLES: will appear   future

had been writing   past perfect progressive

do jump   present emphatic

1. noted *past*
2. had swum *past perf*
3. was taking *past prog*
4. have been *pres perf*
5. lie *pres*
6. am going *pres prog*
7. went *past*
8. had striven *past perf*
9. will have chosen *fut perf*
10. did eat *past emph*
11. spring *pres*
12. am being *pres prog*
13. will grow *fut*
14. do write *pres emph*
15. will be teaching *fut prog*
16. will have been seeing *fut perf prog*
17. am bursting *pres prog*
18. have shown *pres perf*
19. had been hurting *past perf*
20. will hit *fut prog*
21. do let *pres emph*
22. am speaking *pres prog*
23. have been learning *pres perf prog*
24. had slain *past perf*
25. will be *fut*

■ The Principal Parts of Verbs

To use the English language most effectively, it is necessary to know how to form all the different verb tenses. Luckily it is not necessary to memorize all the forms for the thousands of verbs in the English language. A shortcut is to learn the *principal* parts of verbs.

Each tense of a verb is formed from one of the verb's four principal parts. Except in the basic forms of the present and the past tense, a helping verb is used with the principal part.

A verb has four principal parts: the **present** (base form), the **present participle**, the **past**, and the **past participle**.

Here, for example, are the principal parts of the verb *use*.

PRINCIPAL PARTS			
Present	Present Participle	Past	Past Participle
use	using	used	used

The basic, progressive, and emphatic forms in the chart on page 194 are all formed from these four principal parts. You will want to refer to the chart as you read the explanation of how each of these tenses is formed.

The first principal part, the *present*, is used for the basic forms of the present *(I use)* and the future *(I will use)*. This principal part is also used for the two emphatic forms: present emphatic *(I do use)* and past emphatic *(I did use)*.

The second principal part, the *present participle*, is used along with a number of different helping verbs to form all six of the progressive forms *(I am using, I was using, and so on)*.

The third principal part, the *past*, is used for just one basic form: the past *(I used)*. As in the present, the principal part stands alone.

The fourth principal part, the *past participle*, is used with various helping verbs for the basic forms of the three perfect tenses: the present perfect *(I have used)*, the past perfect *(I had used)*, and the future perfect *(I will have used)*.

EXERCISE B: Identifying Principal Parts in Sentences. Find the verb in each of the following sentences and write it on your paper. Then underline the main verb and identify it as one of the four principal parts.

EXAMPLES: By tomorrow, we will have chosen our captain.
will have <u>chosen</u>   past participle

I do believe his explanation.
do <u>believe</u>   present
Verbs are shaded; main verbs are underlined.

1. My father will <u>arrive</u> home from his trip in two days. *pres*
2. Our class is <u>going</u> to the science museum. *pres part*
3. Barry had <u>begun</u> his research paper a month ago. *past*
4. I did <u>expect</u> a much easier test. *pres part*
5. His country home <u>lies</u> in a beautiful valley. *pres*
6. By next year the mining company will have <u>taken</u> all the ore from the silver mine. *past part*
7. The dancers were <u>performing</u> a tango. *pres part*
8. In "The Fifty-First Dragon" Gawaine <u>slew</u> the first fifty monsters without much difficulty. *past*
9. I do <u>spend</u> too much money. *pres*
10. My family will be <u>going</u> to Florida for the holidays. *pres part*

■ Regular and Irregular Verbs

Depending on their principal parts, verbs are classified into two types: *regular* and *irregular*. The principal parts of regular verbs follow a set pattern. The third and fourth principal parts of irregular verbs, however, differ from verb to verb and have to be learned individually.

Regular Verbs.   Most verbs in English are regular.

The past and past participle of a **regular verb** are formed by adding *-ed* or *-d* to the present form.

Verbs such as *ask* and *open* form the past and the past participle by adding *-ed*. Verbs that already end in an *e*, such as *move* and *love*, simply add *-d* to form the same two principal parts. Compare the principal parts of the regular verbs in the following chart.

PRINCIPAL PARTS OF REGULAR VERBS			
Present	**Present Participle**	**Past**	**Past Participle**
ask	asking	asked	(have) asked
open	opening	opened	(have) opened
move	moving	moved	(have) moved
love	loving	loved	(have) loved

Though the past and past participle of regular verbs are identical, the past is a tense while the past participle is not.

A helping verb such as *has* or *have* is always needed with a past participle to form the perfect tenses.

Irregular Verbs. Some of the most common verbs in English are irregular.

The past and past participle of an **irregular verb** are not formed by adding *-ed* or *-d*.

The origin of irregular verbs can be traced back to Old English, the form of English used over 800 years ago. Verbs such as *begin* (OE. *beginnan*), *freeze* (OE. *frēosan*), and *hide* (OE. *hȳdan*) appear in the earliest written English. Over the years, the forms changed and different principal parts developed. Most of our regular verbs, on the other hand, come from Latin and other foreign languages. As they became a part of the English language, they did not form their past and past participles according to the irregular patterns of the native English verbs.

Since irregular verbs form their past and past participles in different ways, there is no simple method that can be used to learn them all. They must be memorized. To help you, they have been arranged in convenient groups in the following charts.

In the final column of each chart, note that the helping verb *have* appears in parentheses in front of the past participle. It is there to remind you that the past participle cannot stand alone as a tense.

IRREGULAR VERBS WITH THE SAME PAST AND PAST PARTICIPLE			
Present	Present Participle	Past	Past Participle
bind	binding	bound	(have) bound
bring ✔	bringing	brought	(have) brought
build	building	built	(have) built
buy	buying	bought	(have) bought
catch	catching	caught	(have) caught
fight	fighting	fought	(have) fought
find	finding	found	(have) found
get	getting	got	(have) got *or* gotten
grind	grinding	ground	(have) ground
hang	hanging	hung	(have) hung

hold	holding	held	(have) held
keep	keeping	kept	(have) kept
lay✓	laying	laid	(have) laid
lead	leading	led	(have) led
leave	leaving	left	(have) left
lose	losing	lost	(have) lost
pay	paying	paid	(have) paid
say	saying	said	(have) said
sell	selling	sold	(have) sold
send	sending	sent	(have) sent
show	showing	showed	(have) showed *or* shown
sit ✓	sitting	sat	(have) sat
sleep	sleeping	slept	(have) slept
spend	spending	spent	(have) spent
spin	spinning	spun	(have) spun
stand	standing	stood	(have) stood
stick	sticking	stuck	(have) stuck
strike	striking	struck	(have) struck
swing	swinging	swung	(have) swung
teach✓	teaching	taught	(have) taught
win	winning	won	(have) won
wind	winding	wound	(have) wound
wring✓	wringing	wrung	(have) wrung

IRREGULAR VERBS WITH THE SAME PRESENT, PAST, AND PAST PARTICIPLE

Present	Present Participle	Past	Past Participle
bid	bidding	bid	(have) bid
burst✓	bursting	burst	(have) burst
cost	costing	cost	(have) cost
cut	cutting	cut	(have) cut
hit	hitting	hit	(have) hit
hurt	hurting	hurt	(have) hurt
let	letting	let	(have) let
put	putting	put	(have) put

set ✓	setting	set	(have) set
shut	shutting	shut	(have) shut
split	splitting	split	(have) split
spread	spreading	spread	(have) spread
thrust	thrusting	thrust	(have) thrust

IRREGULAR VERBS THAT CHANGE IN OTHER WAYS

Present	Present Participle	Past	Past Participle
arise	arising	arose	(have) arisen
begin	beginning	began	(have) begun
blow	blowing	blew	(have) blown
break	breaking	broke	(have) broken
choose ✓	choosing	chose	(have) chosen
come	coming	came	(have) come
do	doing	did	(have) done
draw	drawing	drew	(have) drawn
drink ✓	drinking	drank	(have) drunk
drive	driving	drove	(have) driven
eat	eating	ate	(have) eaten
fall	falling	fell	(have) fallen
fly	flying	flew	(have) flown
freeze	freezing	froze	(have) frozen
give	giving	gave	(have) given
go	going	went	(have) gone
grow	growing	grew	(have) grown
know	knowing	knew	(have) known
lie ✓	lying	lay	(have) lain
ride	riding	rode	(have) ridden
ring ✓	ringing	rang	(have) rung
rise ✓	rising	rose	(have) risen
run	running	ran	(have) run
see	seeing	saw	(have) seen
shake	shaking	shook	(have) shaken
shrink ✓	shrinking	shrank	(have) shrunk
sing	singing	sang	(have) sung

sink	sinking	sank	(have) sunk
slay	slaying	slew	(have) slain
speak	speaking	spoke	(have) spoken
spring	springing	sprang	(have) sprung
steal	stealing	stole	(have) stolen
stride	striding	strode	(have) stridden
strive	striving	strove	(have) striven
swear	swearing	swore	(have) sworn
swim	swimming	swam	(have) swum
take	taking	took	(have) taken
tear	tearing	tore	(have) torn
throw	throwing	threw	(have) thrown
wear	wearing	wore	(have) worn
weave	weaving	wove	(have) woven or wove
write	writing	wrote	(have) written

The easiest way to learn these irregular verbs is to read the charts several times. Pay close attention to spelling as you study. A number of present participles in both regular and irregular verbs double a consonant (beginning, bidding, cutting, swimming, winning). There are similar changes in some past participles as well (gotten, ridden, stridden, written).

Dictionaries usually list the principal parts of irregular verbs right after the part-of-speech label. If you are in doubt about the principal parts or spelling of an irregular verb, check your dictionary.

EXERCISE C: Completing the Principal Parts of Regular and Irregular Verbs. Copy the following headings onto your paper and write the given words in the appropriate columns, as shown. Without referring to the charts in your book, complete each line by filling in the three missing principal parts.

Present	Present Participle	Past	Past Participle
1. slay	slaying	slew	slain
2. grind	grinding	ground	ground
3. lie	lying	lay	lain
4. drive	driving	drove	driven

	Present	Present Participle	Past	Past Participle
5.	thrust	*thrusting*	*thrust*	*thrust*
6.	*weave*	weaving	*wove*	*woven* ()
7.	*write*	*writing*	wrote	*written*
8.	*cut*	*cutting*	*cut*	cut
9.	pay	*paying*	*paid*	*paid*
10.	*open*	*opening*	*opened*	opened
11.	*leave*	leaving	*left*	*left*
12.	*stride*	*striding*	strode	*stridden*
13.	ask	*asking*	*asked*	*asked*
14.	*bring*	*bringing*	*brought*	brought
15.	*fly*	flying	*flew*	*flown*
16.	*say*	*saying*	said	*said*
17.	offer	*offering*	*offered*	*offered*
18.	*strike*	*striking*	*struck*	struck
19.	*shut*	shutting	*shut*	*shut*
20.	choose	*choosing*	*chose*	*chosen*
21.	*teach*	*teaching*	taught	*taught*
22.	*begin*	*beginning*	*began*	begun
23.	*sleep*	sleeping	*slept*	*slept*
24.	wear	*wearing*	*wore*	*worn*
25.	*wring*	*wringing*	*wrung*	wrung

■ Conjugating the Tenses

Conjugating a verb is one way to learn all of its forms.

A **conjugation** is a list of the singular and plural forms of a verb in a particular tense.

In the conjugation of any tense, there will be three singular forms and three plural forms. The first person, second person, and third person of each of the personal pronouns will each have a singular and a plural form.

In the following charts the irregular verb *take* is conjugated in the basic, progressive, and emphatic forms. Before examining the conjugation, review the principal parts of *take*.

PRINCIPAL PARTS OF *TAKE*			
Present	**Present Participle**	**Past**	**Past Participle**
take	taking	took	(have) taken

As you study the conjugation of *take*, note that only three of the principal parts—the present, the past, and the past participle—are used to form the six basic tenses.

CONJUGATION OF THE BASIC FORMS OF *TAKE*		
Present	Singular	Plural
First Person	I take	we take
Second Person	you take	you take
Third Person	he, she, it takes	they take
Past		
First Person	I took	we took
Second Person	you took	you took
Third Person	he, she, it took	they took
Future		
First Person	I will take	we will take
Second Person	you will take	you will take
Third Person	he, she, it will take	they will take
Present Perfect		
First Person	I have taken	we have taken
Second Person	you have taken	you have taken
Third Person	he, she, it has taken	they have taken
Past Perfect		
First Person	I had taken	we had taken
Second Person	you had taken	you had taken
Third Person	he, she, it had taken	they had taken
Future Perfect		
First Person	I will have taken	we will have taken
Second Person	you will have taken	you will have taken
Third Person	he, she, it will have taken	they will have taken

Only one principal part, the present participle, is used for the six progressive forms.

CONJUGATION OF THE PROGRESSIVE FORMS OF *TAKE*		
Present Progressive	Singular	Plural
First Person	I am taking	we are taking
Second Person	you are taking	you are taking
Third Person	he, she, it is taking	they are taking
Past Progressive		
First Person	I was taking	we were taking
Second Person	you were taking	you were taking
Third Person	he, she, it was taking	they were taking
Future Progressive		
First Person	I will be taking	we will be taking
Second Person	you will be taking	you will be taking
Third Person	he, she, it will be taking	they will be taking
Present Perfect Progressive		
First Person	I have been taking	we have been taking
Second Person	you have been taking	you have been taking
Third Person	he, she, it has been taking	they have been taking
Past Perfect Progressive		
First Person	I had been taking	we had been taking

Second Person	you had been taking	you had been taking
Third Person	he, she, it had been taking	they had been taking

Future Perfect Progressive		
First Person	I will have been taking	we will have been taking
Second Person	you will have been taking	you will have been taking
Third Person	he, she, it will have been taking	they will have been taking

To conjugate the emphatic forms, two forms of the helping verb *do* are placed in front of the first principal part of the verb—the present.

CONJUGATION OF THE EMPHATIC FORMS OF *TAKE*		
Present Emphatic	Singular	Plural
First Person	I do take	we do take
Second Person	you do take	you do take
Third Person	he, she, it does take	they do take
Past Emphatic		
First Person	I did take	we did take
Second Person	you did take	you did take
Third Person	he, she, it did take	they did take

NOTE ABOUT THE CONJUGATION OF *BE:*　Perhaps the most frequently used verb in English is *be*. It is also one of the most irregular. Note its principal parts.

PRINCIPAL PARTS OF *BE*			
Present	**Present Participle**	**Past**	**Past Participle**
am	being	was	(have) been

Notice also the forms of *be* used in conjugating the basic and progressive forms of the six tenses.

PRESENT: I *am;* he, she, it *is;* we, you, they *are*

PAST: I, he, she, it *was;* we, you, they *were*

FUTURE: I, he, she, it, we, you, they *will be*

PRESENT PERFECT: I, we, you, they *have been;* he, she, it *has been*

PAST PERFECT: I, he, she, it, we, you, they *had been*

FUTURE PERFECT: I, he, she, it, we, you, they *will have been*

PRESENT PROGRESSIVE: I *am being;* he, she, it is *being;* we, you, they *are being*

PAST PROGRESSIVE: I, he, she, it *was being;* we, you, they *were being*

The verb *be* does not have the other four progressive forms. It also does not have emphatic forms.

EXERCISE D: Conjugating Verbs. Along the left side of your paper list in order the six basic forms, the six progressive forms, and the two emphatic forms. (Make your list from the conjugation of *take* that begins on page 202.) Next to this list, make three columns. Title the first *I*, the second *she*, and the third *they*.

EXAMPLE:

Tense	I	She	They
Present			
Past			
Future			

Then choose three verbs from the following list and conjugate them according to the "person" listed at the top of each column. Follow patterns on pages 202–205. Note that all but open are irregular.

1. sell
2. drive
3. swim
4. write
5. see

6. open
7. hold
8. teach
9. grow
10. be

EXERCISE E: Identifying the Tenses of Verbs in Sentences.
Find the verb in each of the following sentences and write it
on your paper. Then identify the tense of each verb and its
form if the form is not basic.

1. I almost <u>froze</u> after two hours in the storm. *past*
2. Surprisingly, Betty <u>has written</u> an unusually beautiful
   poem. *pres perf*
3. This year my parents <u>are spending</u> a lot of money to ren-
   ovate the house. *pres prog*
4. Bill <u>rises</u> at dawn to do his exercises. *pres*
past 5. My mother <u>had shut</u> all the windows before leaving.
perf 6. In an hour we <u>will have arrived</u> at the airport. *fut perf*
7. Hopefully, we <u>will be going</u> to Mexico City this summer. *fut*
past 8. Much to our amazement, my brother <u>ate</u> the entire cake. *prog*
9. The documents <u>were lying</u> under the desk all the time. *past*
10. Mr. Williams <u>did try</u> to explain the importance of the *prog*
    test. *past emph*
11. Who <u>is driving</u> to town for the supplies? *pres prog*
fut 12. By the end of the term, we <u>will have moved</u> to California.
perf 13. Several people <u>have</u> already <u>swum</u> across this lake. *pres perf*
14. Last year our hockey team <u>strove</u> to improve its record. *past*
15. Almost in tears, my grandmother <u>was standing</u> alone in
    the rain. *past prog*
16. For the last time, I <u>will explain</u> the rules of the game. *fut*
17. As part of my job, I <u>fly</u> to London twice a year. *pres*
18. Disappointed, our fullback <u>burst</u> into the locker room. *past*
19. The criminal <u>has paid</u> his debt to society. *pres perf*
20. Charles <u>does expect</u> to be accepted to law school. *pres emph*
21. <u>Will</u> you <u>be speaking</u> to your mother this evening? *fut prog*
22. The villagers <u>were wringing</u> their hands in dismay. *past prog*
23. The committee <u>has been</u> in session all morning. *pres perf*
24. What <u>did</u> the volunteers <u>hope</u> to achieve with their
    campaign? *past emph*
25. In spite of the warning, she <u>thrust</u> herself in front of the
    line. *past*

APPLICATION: Writing Sentences Using Different Tenses.
Write an original sentence using the form given for each of
the following verbs. *Answers will vary; samples given for first two.*

1. Present progressive of *go*   Mr. Weatherbee <u>is going</u> to art class.
2. Past of *wring*   Barbara <u>wrung</u> her hands in dismay.
3. Future perfect of *show*
4. Past emphatic of *wait*
5. Present of *slay*
6. Present perfect of *be*
7. Past progressive of *take*

8. Present emphatic of *eat*
9. Future progressive of *spend*
10. Present of *lie*
11. Past of *fly*
12. Present progressive of *play*
13. Past perfect of *put*
14. Future of *be*
15. Past of *shrink*
16. Past emphatic of *belong*
17. Present perfect of *bring*
18. Future progressive of *open*
19. Past perfect of *win*
20. Present emphatic of *know*
21. Future perfect of *do*
22. Past progressive of *begin*
23. Present progressive of *write*
24. Future perfect progressive of *raise*
25. Future of *lay*

Expressing Time Through Tense 9.2

In speaking and writing, there are three main categories of time: present, past, and future. Both the basic and the progressive forms of the six tenses of verbs express time in all three categories. The two emphatic forms deal with time only in the present and past.

All fourteen forms are shown in the following chart. Notice that the term *simple* is used to describe the basic forms of the present, past, and future tenses.

THREE CATEGORIES OF TIME		
Past	**Present (now)**	**Future**
simple past	simple present	simple future
past progressive	present progressive	future progressive
past emphatic	present emphatic	future perfect
present perfect		future perfect progressive
present perfect progressive		
past perfect		
past perfect progressive		

The different tenses, when used correctly in sentences, show the relationship in time of one event to another. This section will explain some of the many ways the tenses work to express these relationships in time.

■ Uses of Tense in Present Time

The simple present, the present progressive, and the present emphatic are all used in slightly different ways to express present time.

The three forms of the present tense can be used to show present actions or conditions as well as various continuous actions or conditions.

The simple present has three main uses: (1) to show present actions or conditions, (2) to show regularly occurring actions or conditions, and (3) to show actions or conditions that are constantly true.

USES OF THE SIMPLE PRESENT
Present action: Here they *come.*
Present condition: The air in the room *is* stale.
Regularly occurring action: Grandfather *sings* in the shower.
Regularly occurring condition: The park *is* most beautiful in spring.
Constant action: The sun *sets* in the west.
Constant condition: The heart *is* a pump.

The present progressive form is used to express continuous actions or conditions now taking place. The continuous action or condition of the present progressive can be of long or short duration. Building a model ship, for example, may take many months, while whistling a tune takes only a few minutes.

USES OF THE PRESENT PROGRESSIVE
Long continuing action: My uncle *is building* a three-masted coastal schooner.
Short continuing action: I *am whistling* a tune from *Oklahoma.*
Continuing condition: Gloria *is being* extra helpful around the house.

The present emphatic form is used to emphasize a statement or to deny a contrary assertion.

USES OF THE PRESENT EMPHATIC
Emphasizing a statement: I *do believe* you dropped this.
Denying a contrary assertion: Despite the claim in the review, that restaurant *does bake* all its own pies daily.

EXERCISE A: Using the Present Tense. All of the verbs in the following sentences are in the present tense. Read each sentence carefully and decide which use of the present tense is intended. For each sentence write the letter of the choice that best indicates the use of the verb.

A. Present action or condition
B. Regularly occurring action or condition
C. Constant action or condition
D. Continuing action or condition
E. Emphasized statement or denial of contrary assertion

1. My brother *is waiting* for Father at the station. *D* (*p. 208 box*)
2. Cereals *increase* bulk in the diet. *C*
3. Now the president *approaches* the podium. *A*
4. I *jog* three miles every morning before going to school. *B*
5. In spite of warnings, my little sister still *chews* her nails. *B*
6. The weather *is* bad along the entire East Coast. *A*
7. The members *are growing* impatient with his actions. *D*
8. Mumps and measles *are* widespread this year. *A*
9. My old aunt *walks* to town almost every morning. *B*
10. I *do see* a ship approaching the bridge. *E*

Uses of Tenses in Past Time

As the chart at the beginning of the section shows, there are seven ways to express past time. The seven forms are the simple past, the past progressive, the past emphatic, the present perfect, the present perfect progressive, the past perfect, and the past perfect progressive.

The seven forms of the three tenses that express past time can be used to show a variety of actions and conditions that began in the past.

The simple past is the most frequently used of the seven forms. It is used to show that an action is completed or that a condition no longer exists.

USES OF THE SIMPLE PAST
Completed action: Judy *finished* her science project.
Condition no longer existing: Father *was* terribly depressed.

Notice that these verbs show completed actions or conditions that took place at some *indefinite* time. The time expressed by the simple past can be made definite by adding such words as *last year, yesterday,* or *this morning.*

The past progressive is used to show that a continuous action or condition took place in the past. As with the present progressive, an action or condition expressed by this tense can be of long or short duration.

USES OF THE PAST PROGRESSIVE	
Long continuing action in the past:	Last year my uncle *was building* a three-masted coastal schooner.
Short continuing action in the past:	I *was whistling* a tune from *Oklahoma* when the telephone rang.
Continuing condition in the past:	Frank *was* not *being* careful with the pesticide.

The past emphatic is used to emphasize a statement or deny a contrary assertion that occurred in the past.

USES OF THE PAST EMPHATIC	
Emphasizing a statement:	I *did favor* his candidacy until a short while ago.
Denying a contrary assertion:	But I *did do* my homework!

In spite of its name, the present perfect expresses past time. It is used to show that an action was completed at some indefinite time in the recent past or that an action or condition has continued to the present.

There are two ways this form differs from the simple past. Unlike the simple past, the present perfect *cannot* be made definite by adding such words as *last year, yesterday,* or *this morning.* Again unlike the simple past, the present perfect *can* be used to show actions or conditions continuing to the present.

USES OF THE PRESENT PERFECT

Completed action (indefinite time): Bob *has completed* his job.
Completed condition (indefinite time): She *has been* there, too.
Action continuing to present: We *have worked* in the city for three years.
Condition continuing to present: She *has been* here ever since.

The present perfect progressive has a single use: to show that an action began at some indefinite time in the past and has continued to the present.

USE OF THE PRESENT PERFECT PROGRESSIVE

Past action continuing to the present: Bob *has been studying* the catalogs of many colleges.

The past perfect shows a connection between two events in the past. It is used to show that an action or condition was completed before some other action or condition began.

USES OF THE PAST PERFECT

Action completed before another past action: Bob *had studied* all the college catalogs before he filled out his first application.
Condition completed before another past condition: I *had been* a member of the club long before you were.

Avoid using the past perfect unless you are showing a relationship to another action or condition in the past.

The past perfect progressive form is used to show that an action was continuous from some indefinite time in the past until some definite time in the past.

USE OF THE PAST PERFECT PROGRESSIVE

Past action continuing from indefinite to definite time: The wheat crop *had been thriving* until it was attacked by locusts.

---

212 *Verb Usage*

EXERCISE B: Using Tenses in Past Time. In each of the following sentences, one of the verbs in parentheses is better than the other. Write the verb you should use in each sentence on your paper.

1. Joshua (has been reading, <u>had read</u>) all of the book before the quiz yesterday.
2. The train (<u>pulled</u>, has pulled) into the station at seven.
3. Katherine (had been working, <u>has been working</u>) on that poem for a month, and it's still not finished.
4. Every day last week the mail carrier (<u>brought</u>, has brought) me at least one letter.
5. When we drank the soda, we noticed it (has lost, <u>had lost</u>) its fizz.
6. Before he spoke, the demonstrators (<u>rushed</u>, have rushed) down the aisle.
7. We (have, <u>had</u>) never seen a bald eagle before yesterday.
8. I (<u>developed</u>, have developed) this new process a week ago.
9. The lawyer's request for leniency (has been, <u>was</u>) granted yesterday.
10. Richard (<u>was working</u>, worked) when a thunderstorm suddenly began.

■ Uses of Tenses in Future Time

Four forms are used to express the future: the simple future, the future progressive, the future perfect, and the future perfect progressive.

The four forms of the two tenses in future time can be used to express various actions or conditions that will occur in the future.

The simple future is used to show that an action or condition will occur in the future.

USES OF THE SIMPLE FUTURE
Action in the future: Sally *will race* in the main event.
Condition in the future: The room *will be* warm in a few minutes.

The future progressive is used to show an action will be continuous at a future time.

USE OF THE FUTURE PROGRESSIVE
Continuous action in the future: Our football team *will be practicing* during July and August.

The future perfect is used to predict that a future action or condition will be completed before another time in the future.

USES OF THE FUTURE PERFECT
Future action completed before another: By the end of the month *I will have completed* my term paper.
Future condition completed before another: My sister *will have been* out of college for five years by the time I graduate.

Like the future progressive, the future perfect progressive describes a certain kind of continuous action in the future. This form, however, particularly shows that a continuous action in the future will be in the past by the time some other future action occurs.

USE OF THE FUTURE PERFECT PROGRESSIVE
Continuous action completed before another future action begins: By the time we play our first game in September, I *will have been practicing* for more than two months.

NOTE ABOUT THE SIMPLE FUTURE AND THE FUTURE PROGRESSIVE: The simple present and the present progressive often are used with other words to convey future time. In this use, they take the place of the simple future and the future progressive.

SIMPLE PRESENT SUGGESTING FUTURE: Ted finally *gets* to play Romeo tomorrow night.

PRESENT PROGRESSIVE SUGGESTING FUTURE: My aunt and uncle *are flying* to Spain next month.

EXERCISE C: Using Tenses in Future Time. Copy each of the following sentences onto your paper, adding the form of the verb indicated. Be prepared to explain what kind of action each tense indicates.

1. The plane from Boston (arrive—*simple future*) in about two hours. *will arrive*
2. By the time I return home in September, I (travel—*future perfect progressive*) for six months. *will have been traveling*
3. Before school ends, Steven (make—*future perfect*) his career decision. *will have made*
4. We (visit—*future progressive*) parts of Canada in June.
5. In another fifteen years they (open—*simple future*) the time capsule. *will open*
6. The orchestra (perform—*future perfect progressive*) for three months by the time they reach Sweden.
7. On September 1, she (be—*future perfect*) vice-president for a year. *will have been*
8. The teachers (go—*future progressive*) to the Chicago convention in April. *will be going*
9. Before college, Terry (work—*simple future*) for a year.
10. At the end of this month, I (be—*future perfect*) in South America for three years. *will have been*

4. will be visiting   6. will have been performing   9. will work

■ Shifts in Tense

In sentences with more than one verb, it is important to keep the time sequence consistent.

When showing a sequence of events, do not shift tenses unnecessarily.

A sentence with a compound verb should have both verbs in the same time frame.

INCORRECT: Father *turned* the key and *starts* the car.
                    Past   Present

CORRECT: Father *turned* the key and *started* the car.
                Past   Past

The same principle applies when two or more sentences deal with the same period of time. Keep the tenses logical throughout: If you are describing past events, do not shift from past time to present time.

INCORRECT: We *thought* the actor *had collapsed* on the stage.
           Past   Past Perf

Suddenly, however, he *is sitting* up and *is* all right.
                 Present Prog   Present

Then we *realized* it *is* all part of the show.
             Past   Present

Past   Past Perf
CORRECT: We *thought* the actor *had collapsed* on the stage.
               Past   Past
              Suddenly, however, he *sat* up and *was* all right. Then
              Past   Past
              we *realized* it *was* all part of the show.

After you write a paragraph or a composition, check your sentences for consistency of tense. It is an important proof-reading skill to develop.

EXERCISE D: Avoiding Unnecessary Shifts in Tense. One tense in each of the following sentences is incorrect. Rewrite each sentence, correcting the tense. Then underline the verb you have changed.

1. My father growled at the salesman and <u>tells</u> him to leave. *told*
2. I <u>reach</u> Stockholm, found a taxi, and arrived an hour later at my hotel. *reached*
3. Beethoven conducted the first performance of his Ninth Symphony when he <u>is</u> already deaf. *was*
4. It <u>is</u> several years since I <u>had seen</u> my grandfather.
5. Although I <u>offered</u> to buy his collection, he <u>refuses</u> to sell. *have offered* or *refused*
6. As soon as the operation was over, I <u>visit</u> him at the hospital. *visited*
7. He <u>exercises</u> in the health spa before he <u>left</u> for work.
8. The visitor <u>had told</u> two stories that <u>are</u> hard to believe.
9. The first story Hemingway wrote was "Up in Michigan," and the last <u>is</u> "Old Man at the Bridge." *was*
10. The referee approached the fighter, <u>asks</u> a question or two, and stopped the fight. *asked*
11. The car <u>has</u> front-wheel drive and <u>was equipped</u> with power brakes. *had* or *is equipped*
12. If Susan wins first prize, she <u>will have been getting</u> many offers to perform. *will be getting*
13. They <u>were sailing</u> to Bermuda when you <u>are</u> on your trip. *will be sailing* or *were*
14. My family had dinner at a Japanese restaurant, and then they <u>go</u> to the movies. *went*
15. When she completed the assignment, she <u>achieves</u> a first for an American architect. *achieved*
16. When I <u>have been driving</u> for five or six hours, I <u>got</u> very tired. *had been driving* or *get*
17. This museum <u>is</u> open seven days a week, but the art gallery <u>was</u> not. *was* or *is*
18. Father <u>walks</u> into the factory and saw an unbelievable sight. *walked*

4. had been or *have seen*   *7. exercised* or *leaves*   *8. told* or *were*

19. By the time I <u>reached</u> him, he will have contacted his sister. *reach* or *had contacted*
20. The receptionist <u>sits</u> at his desk and ignored my request for an interview. *sat*

EXERCISE E: Proofreading to Catch Unnecessary Shifts in Tense. The following paragraph contains many errors in tense. Rewrite the paragraph, making the necessary corrections. Then circle the verbs that you have corrected.
Verbs likely to be changed are shaded; samples given.

is (1) Bucharest, the capital of Romania, has a charm that *was* unique in Eastern Europe. (2) There *have been* still *are* *survived* many old, elaborately decorated Baroque buildings that *survive* the bombings of World War II. (3) The National Gallery *features* of Art, open daily except Mondays, *featured* the work of Constantin Brancusi. (4) It is a short distance to the Presidential *are* Palace from the museum. (5) Both *were* close to the colorful *is* Cismigiu Gardens. (6) If your legs hold out, it *will be* only a short walk to the National Opera House or even to famous Stavropoleos Church. (7) Most of the time you will probably *use* *used* the excellent public transportation to get around the *is* city. (8) Fare on the trolleys and trams *was* only seven cents. (9) Most of the time, you will want to walk since the down- *is* town area *was* only two miles across. (10) For a side excursion, you may want to visit the Black Sea coast, only two *may* hundred miles to the East. (11) Or you *may have wished* to *wish* travel south to see the beautiful Danube River which separates Romania from Bulgaria.

■ Modifiers That Help Clarify Tense

Often it is possible to make an idea clearer by adding a modifier. Useful modifiers include adverbs such as *always*, *frequently*, *occasionally*, and *often*. Phrases such as *at times*, *now and then*, and *at some earlier period* can also be used to improve the clarity of the tenses you use.

Use modifiers to help clarify the time expressed by a verb.

EXAMPLES: Prehistoric mammals lived *at some earlier time* in this western desert.

Grandmother walks *occasionally* in the park.

Now and then, I try to bake fresh bread.

In the evening she wandered into the French Quarter.

EXERCISE F: Using Modifiers to Improve Meaning. Copy each of the following sentences onto your paper. In the space indicated, supply a modifier. Use words such as *at times, now and then, later, once in a while, occasionally, next week, in three hours,* or other appropriate words of your own choice.
Answers will vary; samples given.

1. *Usually,* Sandy walks to the bus terminal.
2. Mom and Dad expect to visit me *next week* at college.
3. Our principal *recently* has been going to conventions in other states.
4. *Tomorrow* I will speak to the manager about a raise.
5. She developed *gradually* into a fine artist.
6. The agent said the flight will arrive *in an hour*.
7. *Sometimes* I enjoy driving alone into the country.
8. I wrote to the hotel for directions *last week*.
9. The missing child appeared *eventually*, terribly confused.
10. *For ten years* my father had worked as a leather craftsman.

APPLICATION: Using the Correct Tense in Your Writing. Begin or complete each of the following sentences with words of your own choice. Underline all verbs. Make sure that the tense you use in your part of the sentence is consistent with the tense already given in the other part.
Answers will vary; samples given.

1. We are going to the movies after *we eat supper*.
2. The committee has reached a decision and *will publish it tomorrow*.
3. *Dora will come* as soon as she can.
4. If he is disappointed with our choice, *he will have to bear his chagrin*.
5. By the time the basketball game ends, *the papers will have gone to press*.
6. *We worked hard* and finished before the last deadline.
7. When I phoned the office later, *the secretary was quite nasty*.
8. I really do intend to attend the exhibition if *I can still get a ticket*.
9. He had been working on his stamp collection when *the news was broadcast*.
10. The jury agreed that *the defendant was innocent*.
11. *Ann is taking driver ed* since she really wants to drive.
12. Jasper answered the bell, opened the door, and *accepted the package*.
13. I had hoped that *someone else had done the dishes*.
14. *She lost her way* and then she saw the bridge.
15. The driver who had reached the crossroads *didn't know which way to turn*.

16. *Paul entered the room*____ and with great joy hugged his father.
17. My sister did expect an offer *but it was never made*____.
18. Our old roof often leaks when *it rains*____.
19. He will have earned half a million dollars before *he is thirty*____.
20. Before we leave California, *we want to visit Big Sur*____.

9.3 Active and Passive Voice

In addition to showing time by their tense, verbs also show whether the subject is performing an action or having an action performed on it. This quality of a verb is called *voice*.

Voice is the form of a verb that shows whether or not the subject is performing the action.

There are two voices in English: *active* and *passive*. Only action verbs show voice; linking verbs do not.

■ Differences Between Active and Passive Verbs

Most action verbs can be used in either the active or the passive voice.

A verb is **active** when its subject performs the action.

In both of the following examples, the subjects perform the action. This is true whether or not the sentence has a direct object.

ACTIVE VOICE:
$$\overset{S}{Allan} \overset{V}{bought} \text{ a new } \overset{DO}{typewriter}.$$

$$\overset{S}{\text{My sister }} \overset{V}{drives} \text{ carefully}.$$

In the first sentence *Allan*, the subject, performs the action. *Typewriter*, the direct object, receives the action. *Sister* performs the action in the second sentence; there is no receiver of the action.

A verb is **passive** when its action is performed upon the subject.

In a sentence with a passive verb, the verb is often followed by a prepositional phrase beginning with *by* that identifies the performer of the action. Notice how the words change in the following examples. In the first sentence, *Allan*, the original subject, still buys a typewriter, but *Allan*, the performer of the action, is now the object of the preposition *by*. What was the direct object is now the subject: *typewriter* has the action of the verb performed on it. In the second sentence, *sister* is still the subject but no longer the performer of the action; the person who did the driving is not identified.

| | S | V | Obj of Prep |
PASSIVE VOICE: A new typewriter *was bought* by Allan.

My sister *was driven* to school.

EXERCISE A: **Distinguishing Between Active and Passive Voice.** Find each verb or verb phrase in the following sentences and write it on your paper. Then label each one *active* or *passive*.

1. The letter was obviously written by a stranger. *pass*
2. The gates in front of the embassy were closed permanently. *pass*
3. Several business people raced through the airport to catch their flights. *act*
4. I try to watch as little television as possible. *act*
5. Most of the books have been chosen by the librarians. *pass*
6. All four of these magnificent symphonies were composed by Brahms. *pass*
7. The next morning we began our long trek through the jungle. *act*
8. The air conditioner was delivered later in the day. *pass*
9. The mayor asked for volunteers to serve on the committee. *act*
10. A decaying tooth was extracted by my dentist. *pass*
11. The patient was being taken by ambulance to the plane. *pass*
12. With wild abandon the players charged across the field. *act*
13. My mother saves manufacturers' discount coupons. *act*
14. On a trip across country, the car will have been driven by several people. *pass*
15. He explained his theory to a rather uninterested audience. *act*
16. The lawyers were suddenly called to the judge's chamber. *pass*
17. A strange creature has been spotted for some time now in the mountains. *pass*

18. Gordon Grant <u>painted</u> magnificent sailing ships on stormy seas. *act*
19. The crates <u>were received</u> months late on the wharf. *pass*
20. Safes <u>should be made</u> of reinforced steel. *pass*

■ The Forms of Passive Verbs

In changing from the active to the passive voice, the form of the verb is altered. Passive verbs always have two parts.

A **passive verb** is always a verb phrase made from a form of *be* plus the past participle of a transitive verb.

A transitive verb, as you may recall, is one that can have a direct object. (For a review of transitive and intransitive verbs, see Section 1.3.)

The helping verb *be* determines the tense of a passive verb. In the passive verb *was bought*, for example, the helping verb *was* makes the verb phrase past tense. Even if the helping verb changes (*is* bought, *has been* bought), the past participle remains the same.

The following chart gives a short conjugation in the passive voice of the verb *drive* with the pronoun *he*. Notice that there are only two progressive forms in the passive voice instead of six. Moreover, there are no passive emphatic forms.

THE VERB *DRIVE* IN THE PASSIVE VOICE	
Tense	**Passive Voice**
Simple Present	he is driven
Simple Past	he was driven
Simple Future	he will be driven
Present Perfect	he has been driven
Past Perfect	he had been driven
Future Perfect	he will have been driven
Present Progressive	he is being driven
Past Progressive	he was being driven

EXERCISE B: Forming the Tenses of Passive Verbs. Using the preceding chart as your model, conjugate the following five verbs in the passive voice with the indicated pronouns.
Follow the pattern of the preceding chart. Note that give, tell, *and* send *are irregular verbs.*

1. give (with *we*)
2. call (with *you*)
3. tell (with *they*)
4. send (with *she*)
5. open (with *it*)

■ Using Voice Correctly

Having studied examples of verbs in the active and passive voice and having learned how to form verbs in the passive voice, you may wonder when to use which voice. Good writers follow certain conventions with regard to voice.

Use the active voice whenever possible.

Good writing is as concise as possible. A short, direct sentence is better than one with unnecessary words. Sentences with active verbs have fewer words since there is no need for the helping verb *be* or for a prepositional phrase beginning with *by* at the end of the sentence. Moreover, unless you have a good reason, the performer of an action should be the subject. Compare these examples.

ACTIVE VOICE: Billy *delivered* the clarinet.

PASSIVE VOICE: The clarinet *was delivered* by Billy.

There are, of course, proper uses for the passive voice.

Use the passive voice to emphasize the receiver of an action rather than the performer of the action.

Placing a word in an unexpected position at or near the beginning of a sentence helps emphasize its importance in the sentence. When you want to stress the importance of the receiver of the action rather than the importance of the performer then it is proper to use the passive voice.

PASSIVE VOICE: The $10,000 reward *was given* to Mr. Stevens by the bank manager.

PASSIVE VOICE: The signal to ride *was* finally *seen* by Paul Revere.

The passive voice is also used effectively when there is no performer of the action.

Use the passive voice to point out the receiver of an action when the performer is unknown or unimportant and not named in the sentence.

PERFORMER UNKNOWN: A warning *was received* the next morning.

PERFORMER UNIMPORTANT: With great care the nuclear material *was removed* to a safer location.

EXERCISE C: **Using the Active Voice.** Twelve sentences in Exercise A have verbs in the passive voice. Rewrite each of the sentences, placing the verb in the active voice. Change or add words as necessary. When you are finished, proofread your sentences carefully. Be prepared to explain why the active voice is better in your rewritten sentences.
Answers will vary; sample given for first one. 1. A stranger obviously wrote the letter.

EXERCISE D: **Correcting Overuse of the Passive Voice.** Most of the italicized verbs in the following paragraph are in the passive voice. Rewrite the paragraph, changing the passive verbs into active verbs when you think you should. It is not necessary to change every passive verb.
Answers will vary; sample changes given on page 223.

(1) After eighty years of use, aspirin today *is* still *regarded* as a "wonder drug." (2) Aspirin, acetylsalicylic acid, *was* first *developed* as a painkiller by Felix Hoffman, a German chemist, in 1893. (3) He *had been asked* by his father, who *was suffering* from rheumatism, to develop a pain-reliever that *would* not *irritate* the stomach. (4) Though the formula worked, how it worked *could* not *be told* by scientists. (5) Since its introduction, aspirin *has been used* successfully to reduce fever, pain, and inflammation. (6) Not long ago, a new use for aspirin *was uncovered* by researchers. (7) The one major drawback of aspirin *has* always *been* its tendency to cause intestinal bleeding. (8) This drawback now *has been turned* into an advantage. (9) It *has been discovered* that this quality of aspirin *may prevent* blood clots that often *lead* to heart attacks and strokes. (10) This *is* welcome news to the aspirin industry. (11) About 12,000 tons of aspirin *are produced* by the American pharmaceutical industry every year. (12) The equivalent of 150 aspirins *is taken* by every adult and child each year in our country.

APPLICATION: Using the Active and Passive Voice in Writing. Write a short description of something exciting that happened to you recently. Include two appropriate sentences using the passive voice correctly: one with a prepositional phrase beginning with *by*, the other without. Make sure all the other sentences in your description use the active voice.

Answers will vary; make certain that students use active and passive voice appropriately.

Answers for Exercise D:

2. *Felix Hoffman, a German chemist, first developed aspirin, acetylsalicylic acid, as a painkiller, in 1893.*
3. *His father, who was suffering from rheumatism, asked him to develop . . .*
4. *Though the formula worked, scientists could not tell how it worked.*
6. *. . . researchers uncovered a new use . . .*
9. *Researchers have discovered that this quality may prevent . . .*
11. *The American pharmaceutical industry produces about 12,000 tons of aspirin every year.*
12. *Every adult and child in our country takes the equivalent of 150 aspirins each year.*

10

Pronoun Usage

Not only does a pronoun take the place of a noun, it also occupies the same positions in a sentence as a noun. A pronoun used as a subject will usually come before a verb. A pronoun used as a direct object comes after the verb, and so on.

Pronouns and nouns share another characteristic. At one time, both nouns and pronouns always changed their forms to indicate how they were being used in a sentence. Now, nouns change form only to show possession: A noun is made possessive by adding an apostrophe and an *s* (a *girl's* gloves) or just an apostrophe (three *boys'* hockey sticks).

With the exception of possession, nouns no longer change form to indicate their use in a sentence. The noun *apple*, for example, looks the same whether it is used as a subject (*Apples* are delicious) or as a direct object (I like *apples*). Pronouns, however, do change form depending upon their use in the sentence. *They*, for example, is used for subjects (*They* are delicious) and *them* for direct objects (I like *them*). This chapter will explain the various forms of pronouns and their uses in sentences.

10.1 The Case of Pronouns

Case is a term used in grammar to describe a characteristic of nouns and pronouns.

Case is the form of a noun or pronoun that indicates how it is used in a sentence.

There are three cases in English: *nominative, objective,* and *possessive.* The following chart shows the various uses of the three cases.

Case	Use in Sentence
Nominative	subject of verb predicate nominative
Objective	direct object indirect object object of verbal object of a preposition
Possessive	to show ownership

■ The Cases of Personal Pronouns

Depending upon their use in a sentence, personal pronouns change form to show case. In the following chart, the personal pronouns are grouped by case.

THE CASES OF PERSONAL PRONOUNS			
	Nominative	**Objective**	**Possessive**
Singular	I	me	my, mine
	you	you	your, yours
	he, she, it	him, her, it	his, her, hers, its
Plural	we	us	our, ours
	you	you	your, yours
	they	them	their, theirs

Study and learn the pronouns in the chart. You will need them as you learn more about the uses of these pronouns in the different cases.

EXERCISE A: Identifying Case. Divide your paper into two columns. Title the first column *Case*, the second, *Use*. For each of the following sentences, write the case of the underlined pronoun (*nominative, objective,* or *possessive*) and its use in the appropriate columns.

EXAMPLE: The witness finally told the truth about <u>them</u>.

Case   Use
objective   object of a preposition

For answers to 4 and 13 see below.

1. Father and <u>he</u> will meet Mother at the station. *nom–S*
2. Please give <u>him</u> the letter now. *obj–IO*
3. <u>Our</u> reasons are not really important. *poss–own*
4. The doctor agreed to discuss the symptoms with <u>them</u>.
5. Between you and <u>me</u>, I don't think Bill is telling the truth. *obj–obj of prep*
6. The team captain is <u>she</u>. *nom–PN*
7. <u>Our</u> poster is the best so far. *poss–own*
8. In the morning <u>they</u> began to cross the lake. *nom–S*
9. Are you sure that's <u>her</u> work? *poss–own*
10. The principle spoke to <u>us</u>. *obj–obj of prep*
11. My friends and <u>I</u> intend to collect funds for cancer research. *nom–S*
12. <u>Your</u> congressional representative just phoned. *poss–own*
13. This unpleasant matter is between <u>him</u> and <u>them</u>.
14. I gave <u>her</u> a number of ideas about the campaign. *obj–IO*
15. Bring the reports to <u>us</u> at once. *obj–obj of prep*
16. Won't <u>you</u> tell the reporters what really happened? *nom–S*
17. Undoubtedly, those keys belong to <u>them</u>. *obj–obj of prep*
18. <u>We</u> want to pay <u>our</u> fair share. *nom–S/poss–own*
19. A special effort was made by <u>her</u>. *obj–obj of prep*
20. I know <u>my</u> records are there. *poss–own*

4. obj–obj of prep   13. obj–obj of prep/obj–obj of prep

■ The Nominative Case

There are two important uses of pronouns in the nominative case.

Use the nominative case for the subject of a verb and for a predicate nominative.

The following chart shows both of these uses.

NOMINATIVE PRONOUNS	
Use	**Example**
Subject	*She* is the president of our club.
	I will wait only a few minutes.
	They are planning a dance.
Predicate Nominative	The president is *she*.
	It is *I*.
	Our delegates have always been *they*.

As the last three sentences in the chart show, it is grammatically correct to use the nominative case after a linking verb. To some people, however, this usage sounds unnatural. Because they are uncomfortable with these forms, they tend to say instead, "The president is *her*," "It is *me*," or "Our delegates have always been *them*." This use of the objective pronoun after a linking verb has long been common in conversation and informal writing. It is still considered proper, however, to use the nominative pronouns in formal writing such as essays and term papers.

Use of Nominative Pronouns in Compounds. Problems sometimes occur with the use of a pronoun when it is part of either a compound subject or a compound predicate nominative. In both situations, it is important to check that the pronoun is correctly in the nominative case.

AS A COMPOUND SUBJECT:

Marie and *I* often study together. (*Not* "Marie and me . . .")

He and Beth will take care of the arrangements. (*Not* "Him and Beth . . .")

Dr. Smith said that *they* and *we* were exposed to the infection. (*Not* ". . . them and us . . .")

AS A COMPOUND PREDICATE NOMINATIVE:

The winners were Hank and *I*. (*Not* ". . . Hank and me.")

The most popular candidates have always been Leslie and *she*. (*Not* ". . . Leslie and her.")

The musicians who performed were Gordy and *they*. (*Not* ". . . Gordy and them.")

To check whether the pronoun is correct in a compound subject, skip the noun and use the pronoun separately. In the sentence "*He* and Beth will take care of the arrangements," for example, try the pronoun without *Beth*. "*He* . . . will take care . . ." is correct since a nominative pronoun is needed for a subject. Pronouns in compound predicate nominatives can be checked the same way. In the sentence "The winners were Hank and *I*," skip *Hank* and use the pronoun separately. "The winner was . . . *I*." *I* is correct since a predicate nominative should be in the nominative case.

Use of Nominative Pronouns with Appositives. Appositives follow immediately after a noun or pronoun and rename or identify it. Do not let an appositive mislead you into putting a pronoun into the wrong case. Check whether the pronoun is correct by skipping the appositive and using the pronoun by itself.

In the following examples both the pronoun and the noun are in the nominative case.

EXAMPLES:

        S   Appos

We cheerleaders attend every home game. (*Not* "Us . . . attend . . .")

                  PN   Appos

The ones who suffer are *we* the students. (*Not* ". . . are us . . .")

EXERCISE B: Using Pronouns in the Nominative Case.

Complete each of the following sentences by writing a nominative pronoun. Then tell how each pronoun is used in the sentence. *Answers will vary; samples given.*

1. Fred and __she__ will finish all the chores. *S*
2. __We__ volunteer fire fighters will respond to the call. *S*
3. The leaders of the combat team are __they__ . *PN*
4. Have __they__ seriously considered his offer? *S*
5. __It__ is snowing more than an inch an hour. *S*
6. __She__ has been elected captain of the Boosters.
7. The lieutenant is __she__ . *PN*
8. __He__ himself agreed to speak to the captain. *S*
9. Yes, __she__ is my favorite grandmother. *S*
10. The bakers are Betty and __he__ . *PN*
11. The real culprits are __we__ second-year players. *PN*
12. __I__ can't be expected to do it all. *S*
13. Mr. Bogan and __she__ decided to speak to the principal. *S*
14. Honestly, __we__ men will prepare the entire picnic. *S*
15. I believe the winner is __he__ . *PN*
16. My brother and __she__ are best friends. *S*
17. The last leader of the Brownies was __she__ . *PN*
18. __They__ won't believe my astonishment. *S*
19. Jerry and __he__ are being sent to the American Legion Model Congress. *S*
20. It is __he__ who revealed the secret. *PN*

■ The Objective Case

The objective case is used with the objects of both verbs and verbals as well as with the objects of prepositions.

Use the **objective case** for the object of any verb, verbal, or preposition.

The following chart shows the use of the objective case with direct objects, indirect objects, participles, gerunds, infinitives, and prepositions.

USES OF PRONOUNS AS OBJECTS	
Use	**Example**
Direct Object	I baked *them* yesterday. Our teacher praised *her*.
Indirect Object	Give *him* the news. Alice gave *us* our tickets.
Object of Participle	Racing *her*, he crashed into a fence. The girl chasing *them* was her sister.
Object of Gerund	My parents like helping *me* with my problems. Warning *them* was my primary concern.
Object of Infinitive	To tell *him* clearly, he had to shout. He wants to ask *me* about the party.
Object of Preposition	Between *us*, there are no secrets. Walk beside *them*.

Use of Objective Pronouns in Compounds. Like compound subjects and predicate nominatives, compound objects may make it more difficult to choose the correct pronoun.

EXAMPLES: Max conferred with Judy and *me*. (*Not* ". . . with Judy and I.*")

Stand beside Mary and *him*. (*Not* ". . . beside Mary and he.*")

If you skip the noun in a compound and try the pronoun by itself, you will find it easier to see whether you have made the correct choice. In the sentence "Stand beside Mary and *him*," after eliminating *Mary*, the sentence reads, "Stand beside . . . *him*." The pronoun *him* used as the object of the preposition is correct.

A common error often occurs with the use of *between* in a compound construction. *I*, the nominative pronoun, should never be used after this preposition.

INCORRECT: This matter is between you and *I*.

CORRECT: This matter is between you and *me*.

Use of Objective Pronouns with Appositives.   Sometimes an appositive appears after a pronoun used as a direct object, indirect object, or object of a preposition. The pronoun for all of these forms should be in the objective case. The appositive should not affect your choice of the correct case of the pronoun.

EXAMPLES: The dean reprimanded *us* girls. (*Not* ". . . we girls.")

They awarded *us* leaders a service letter. (*Not* ". . . we leaders . . .*")

All of *us* troublemakers were punished. (*Not* ". . . we troublemakers . . .*")

NOTE ABOUT PRONOUNS IN THE POSSESSIVE CASE: The possessive case of pronouns does not generally cause the same problems as the other two cases do. Nevertheless, you should be aware of three rules involving these forms.

First, use the possessive case for a pronoun before a gerund.

EXAMPLES: *Your* complaining bothers us all. (*Not* "You complaining . . .*")

We were upset by *his* going. (*Not* ". . . him going.")

Second, remember that certain possessive pronouns are used by themselves. Do not add an apostrophe to them.

EXAMPLES: The camera and the manual are *ours*. (*Not* "our's")

Were these presents *yours*? (*Not* "your's")

The coats are *theirs*. (*Not* "their's")

Third, do not confuse a possessive pronoun with a contraction.

INCORRECT: The dog looked for *it's* master.

CORRECT: The dog wagged *its* tail furiously.

EXERCISE C: Using Pronouns in the Objective Case. Complete each of the following sentences by writing an objective pronoun on your paper. Then tell how each pronoun is used in the sentence. *Answers will vary; samples given.*

1. Of all of _____*them*_____ , I like Mary the best. *obj of prep*
2. Bruce told _____*me*_____ his side of the story. *IO*
3. The clerk can't imagine how he found _____*it*_____ . *DO*
4. I expect it will have to be settled between Bob and _____*her*_____ . *obj of prep*
5. Your plan pleased Sue and _____*him*_____ . *DO*
6. The coach scolded _____*us*_____ girls. *DO*
7. You must give Arthur and _____*me*_____ the entire report. *IO*
8. To you and _____*him*_____ , I must apologize for my rashness. *obj of prep*
9. Grandfather always gave _____*us*_____ good advice. *IO*
10. I bought new sweaters for Charles and _____*him*_____ . *obj of prep*
11. The teacher handed Mary, Louise, and _____*me*_____ our consent slips. *IO*
12. Between you and _____*me*_____ , I know that I am right. *obj of prep*
13. I gave _____*her*_____ a chance to try out. *IO*
14. From _____*him*_____ , we got much useful information. *obj of prep*
15. They lent _____*us*_____ boys a trailer. *IO*
16. I warned Bess about Michael and _____*her*_____ . *obj of prep*
17. Give _____*me*_____ another week to reach a decision. *IO*
18. I refused to speak about _____*it*_____ . *obj of prep*
19. Monet's work gave _____*him*_____ new ideas about style. *IO*
20. Without Steven and _____*him*_____ , we would have failed. *obj of prep*

EXERCISE D: Using Case Correctly. Complete each sentence by choosing one of the words in each set of parentheses. Write the correct word or words for each sentence on your paper. Be prepared to explain your choices.

1. The doctor told both Mary and (she, <u>her</u>) his reason for leaving. *IO*
2. (<u>He</u>, Him) and (<u>she</u>, her) make a fine team. *S/S*
3. (<u>Their</u>, They're) contributions cannot be over-estimated. *own*
4. These sketches are definitely (her's, <u>hers</u>). *own*
5. Mozart and the young Beethoven were similar in (<u>their</u>, they're) musical styles. *own*
6. Why can't we reach David and (they, <u>them</u>)? *DO*
7. The reporters said the outstanding speaker was (<u>she</u>, her). *PN*
8. Between (we, <u>us</u>), nobody expected such a victory. *obj of prep*
9. Those skates surely are (their's, <u>theirs</u>). *own*
10. The team waited for (<u>him</u>, he) until (<u>he</u>, him) arrived. *obj of prep/S*

own/obj

11. The company broke (its, it's) promise to (us, we) all. *of prep*
12. Next to (he, him), our section leader is a saint. *obj of prep*
13. No question about it, the two best runners are (they, them). *PN*
14. Disraeli and (he, him) were the two best English prime ministers. *S*
15. (They're, Their) by far our best musicians. *they are*
16. With (your's, your) experience, we should succeed. *own*
17. The Student Council president told (we, us) girls the bad news. *IO*
18. Is (her, she) really serious about going to Europe? *S*
19. I told my boss that it was (he, him) who left early. *PN*
20. Won't you join (us, we) players for a game of bridge? *DO*

APPLICATION: Using Case Correctly in Sentences. Identify each of the pronouns in the following items as *nominative, objective,* or *possessive.* Then write complete sentences of your own using each item.

Cases identified for all. Sentences will vary; samples given for first two.

EXAMPLE: my mother and her

possessive   objective   I told the news to my mother and her.

1. my staff and he   *poss nom*
2. them and Pedro   *obj*
3. his friends and I   *poss nom*
4. our team and they   *poss nom*
5. you and me   *obj*
6. Rickey and him   *obj*
7. we and the Smiths   *nom*
8. he and my father   *nom poss*
9. Veronica and her   *obj*
10. Bill, Ellen, and she   *nom*
11. the coach and I   *I nom*
12. she and they   *nom*
13. us and you   *obj*
14. your dog and me   *poss obj*
15. you and him   *obj*
16. her and Ms. Wallenberg   *obj*
17. us football players   *obj*
18. the rest of the players and I   *nom*
19. we sophomores   *nom*
20. us cheerleaders   *obj*
21. she and I   *nom*
22. their cat and me   *poss obj*
23. her request and his   *poss*
24. the team and I   *nom*
25. you and me   *obj*

1. *My staff and he are cooperating.*

2. *Seeing them and Pedro together, the teacher realized what had happened.*

10.2   Special Problems with Pronouns

Because the pronouns *who* and *whoever* change form to indicate case, many people find them particularly troublesome. Moreover, pronouns in elliptical clauses often confuse the most careful speakers and writers. For example, did you know that *"Who* are you looking for?" and "Gloria is a better musician than *me"* are considered incorrect in formal speaking and writing? This section will explain the use of *who* and *whoever* in their various forms and will clarify the use of pronouns in elliptical clauses so that you can make informed choices in your use of pronouns.

■ The Cases of *Who* and *Whoever*

Choices involving *who* and *whoever* are less confusing when the specific uses of the words are understood. *Who* can be used in questions or to begin subordinate clauses in complex sentences. Most often, *whoever* is used to begin subordinate clauses. Examine the forms of both pronouns in the following chart.

THE CASES OF *WHO* AND *WHOEVER*			
	Nominative	**Objective**	**Possessive**
Singular	who	whom	whose
	whoever	whomever	whosever
Plural	who	whom	whose
	whoever	whomever	whosever

Notice that both the singular and plural forms are the same. It also helps to understand that the uses of *who* and *whom* correspond to most of the uses of the personal pronouns. Review these uses now in the following chart.

THE USES OF *WHO, WHOM, WHOSE, WHOEVER, WHOMEVER,* AND *WHOSEVER*		
Case	**Pronoun**	**Use**
Nominative	who, whoever	subject of verb predicate nominative
Objective	whom, whomever	direct object object of verbal object of a preposition
Possessive	whose, whosever	to show ownership

The possessive is easier to use correctly than the other two cases. Just one potential problem deserves a quick review. Do not confuse the contraction *who's*, which means *who is*, with the possessive pronoun *whose*.

CONTRACTION: *Who's* our first singer tonight?

PRONOUN: *Whose* short story won the writing contest?

The rest of this section deals with pronouns in the nominative and objective cases.

The Nominative Case: *Who* and *Whoever*.   The nominative case has two uses: for subjects and for predicate nominatives.

Use *who* or *whoever* when the pronoun is the subject of the verb.

EXAMPLE: *Who* is the only president to serve more than two terms?

In addition to acting as the subject in main clauses, *who* and *whoever* are often used as the subject of subordinate clauses.

EXAMPLES: I know *who* was the most valuable player last year.

He chose *whoever* volunteered to serve.

Both of these examples are complex sentences. Each has a main clause and a subordinate clause. In these sentences *who* and *whoever* are used to begin the subordinate clauses. The correct case of the pronoun is determined by the pronoun's use in the subordinate clause.

Consider the use of the pronoun in the following sentence. Is it in the correct case?

EXAMPLE: I will accept help from *whoever* will offer it.

The first step in checking whether the case of the pronoun is correct is to isolate the subordinate clause. In this example the subordinate clause is *whoever will offer it*, a noun clause acting as the object of the preposition *from*. The next step is to see how the words in the subordinate clause are used. In this one, *will offer* is the verb; it is followed by a direct object, *it. Whoever* is the subject. Since a subject must be in the nominative case, *whoever* is correct.

A second use of the nominative case is as a predicate nominative.

Use *who* or *whoever* when the pronoun is a predicate nominative.

EXAMPLE: The victim is *who?*

A problem may arise when the pronoun is the predicate nominative in a subordinate clause.

EXAMPLE: The police do not know *who* the victim is.

Again follow the same steps. First, isolate the subordinate clause (*who the victim is*). Next, determine each word's use within the clause. Since this clause is inverted, put it into normal word order: *the victim is who*. Examining the clause now, you can see that its subject is *victim*, that the verb is *is*, and that *who* is the predicate nominative of the linking verb. Since the nominative case is needed for predicate nominatives, *who*, a nominative pronoun, is correct.

The Objective Case: *Whom* and *Whomever*.   The objective case of these pronouns is used for direct objects of both verbs and verbals and for objects of prepositions.

Use *whom* or *whomever* when the pronoun is the direct object of a verb or verbal.

In the following example, *whom* is the object of the infinitive *to find*.

EXAMPLE: *Whom* did you expect to find? (You did expect to find *whom?*)

Pronouns in the objective case also occur in the subordinate clauses of complex sentences. In the following examples, *whom* is the direct object of *chose. Whomever* is the direct object of *want*.

EXAMPLES: She invited *whom* he chose.

You can select *whomever* you want.

The process of analysis is the same as before. Isolate the subordinate clause (*whom he chose, whomever you want*). Rearrange the clauses in normal word order: *he chose whom, you want whomever*. It now becomes clear that the subjects are *he* and *you* and that the direct objects are correctly *whom* and *whomever*.

The second use of the objective case is for objects of prepositions.

Use *whom* or *whomever* when the pronoun is the object of a preposition.

Whom is the object of the preposition in both of the following examples even though it is separated from the preposition in the second example.

EXAMPLES: From *whom* did you receive the message?

Whom did you receive the message from?

Again, it is necessary to check more carefully when the pronoun is used to connect the clauses of a complex sentence. The pronoun *whom* follows right after its preposition in the first sentence in the following examples. In the second, however, it is separated by many words from its preposition *with*.

EXAMPLES: I spoke again to the artist with *whom* we had lunch.

I spoke again to the artist *whom* we had lunch with.

To check whether the case of the pronoun is correct, once more isolate the subordinate clause: *whom we had lunch with*. In normal word order the clause changes to *we had lunch with whom*. The clause has a subject (*we*), a verb (*had*), and a direct object (*lunch*). It also has a prepositional phrase (*with whom*). The object of a preposition is always in the objective case. *Whom*, of course, is correct.

Checking Case in Subordinate Clauses with Parenthetical Expressions.   Occasionally, parenthetical expressions such as *I think*, *we all suppose*, or *critics believe* are included in subordinate clauses. These expressions do not affect the rest of the clause and should be ignored in checking the case of *who* and *whom*. The parenthetical expressions are set off by commas in the following examples.

EXAMPLES: John Steinbeck was the writer *who*, critics believed, deserved the Nobel Prize.

John Steinbeck was the writer to *whom*, the critic correctly predicted, the judges would award the Nobel Prize.

NOTE ABOUT *WHOM* AND *WHOMEVER* IN SPOKEN ENGLISH: *Whom* and *whomever* are used less frequently in speaking than in writing. *Who* and *whoever* are satisfactory except at those times when *whom* and *whomever* obviously sound better. *Who* sounds correct in the first example that follows since it is separated from its preposition, *from*. In the second example, however, *whom* is preferred because it stands right after its preposition.

INFORMAL: *Who* did you receive a letter from?

FORMAL AND INFORMAL: From *whom* did you receive a letter?

EXERCISE A: Using *Who* Correctly in Questions. Choose the correct form of the pronoun in each of the following sentences and write it on your paper. Be prepared to explain your choices.

1. (Who, Whom) will you choose to represent us? *DO*
2. (Who, Whom) is our new foreign language teacher? *S*
3. About (who, whom) are you speaking? *obj of prep*
4. The principal chose (who, whom)? *DO*
5. (Whose, Who's) pen did you borrow? *own*
6. (Who, Whom) has been elected to the council? *S*
7. From (who, whom) did you hear that rumor? *obj of prep*
8. (Who, Whom) on our staff can read Spanish? *S*
9. (Whose, Who's) the Speaker of the House? *who is*
10. (Who, Whom) did you ask about the football tickets? *DO*

EXERCISE B: Determining the Use of *Who* and *Whoever* in Clauses. Each of the following sentences is correct. Write the subordinate clause in each sentence on your paper. Indicate whether the introductory word is *nominative* or *objective* and explain how it is used in the subordinate clause.

EXAMPLE: He will select whoever is available.
whoever is available   nominative   subject

1. He is the legislator <u>who always researches both sides of an issue</u>. *nom–S*

2. The generals knew <u>whom they needed for the special mission</u>. *obj–DO*
3. We spoke to <u>whoever answered the phone</u>. *nom–S*
4. <u>Whoever is chosen</u> will have complete authority. *nom–S*
5. I approached the clerk <u>from whom I received the information</u>. *obj–obj of prep*
6. Finally, he told us <u>who was in charge</u>. *nom–S*
7. Allison wondered <u>whom you agreed to sponsor</u>. *obj–obj of infin*
8. <u>Whomever she wants</u> can have the position. *obj–DO*
9. The penalty will be given to <u>whoever is responsible</u>. *nom–S*
10. Tell <u>whomever you wish</u> the good news. *obj–DO*
11. The singer <u>whom they picked</u> was unattractive. *obj–DO*
12. They always agree with <u>whoever speaks the loudest</u>. *nom–S*
13. Would you tell us <u>whom he picked</u>? *obj–DO*
14. This is the writer <u>whom I like the best</u>. *obj–DO*
15. Only those <u>who are on line</u> will be admitted. *nom–S*
16. I bought my camera from a dealer <u>who has a shop in the neighborhood</u>. *nom–S*
17. I cannot understand <u>who would attempt something like that</u>. *nom–S*
18. The committee will accept <u>whomever they nominate into the legislative council</u>. *obj–DO*
19. A person <u>who is honest</u> should have nothing to fear from the authorities. *nom–S*
20. She is a member of the debate team <u>whom we vanquished</u>. *obj–DO*

EXERCISE C: Using *Who* and *Whoever* in Questions and Clauses. Choose the correct form of the pronoun in each of the following sentences and write it on your paper. Be prepared to explain your choices.

1. (Who, <u>Whom</u>) were you arguing with? *obj of prep*
2. I wonder (<u>who</u>, whom) he thinks will win. *S*
3. (Whose, <u>Who's</u>) the spokesperson for the company? *who is*
4. The director (<u>who</u>, whom) was fired left the city. *S*
5. The shortstop is the player (<u>who</u>, whom) experts feel will achieve stardom. *S*
6. (Whoever, <u>Whomever</u>) they select will represent us in Vienna. *DO*
7. Dr. Goodman is the only professor (who, <u>whom</u>) I still respect. *DO*
8. Give (<u>whoever</u>, whomever) appears the package for the post office. *S*
9. (<u>Who</u>, Whom) has been your delegate to the convention? *S*

10. About (who, <u>whom</u>) were they talking? *obj of prep*
11. The lady (who, <u>whom</u>) I usually see is ill. *DO*
12. I telephoned the person (<u>who</u>, whom) makes most of the decisions. *S*
13. (<u>Whose</u>, Who's) car will we take this time? *own*
14. (<u>Who</u>, Whom) is Gustav Mahler? *S*
15. About (who, <u>whom</u>) did Thomas Mann write "Death in Venice"? *obj of prep*
16. Margery Smolins is the only jeweler (who, <u>whom</u>) I trust. *DO*
17. She is the woman (<u>who</u>, whom) I believe is the leading candidate. *S*
18. Is it he (<u>who</u>, whom) was rejected? *S*
19. It is Vince Lombardi (who, <u>whom</u>) I think he named one of the greatest of all football coaches. *DO*
20. (Who, <u>Whom</u>) can we refer them to? *obj of prep*

EXERCISE D: Supplying the Correct Word. Choose an appropriate pronoun for each of the following sentences and write it on your paper. Choose from among *who, whom, whoever, whomever, whose, whosever,* and *who's.*

1. She is a teacher ___*whom*___ we all admire.
2. ___*Who*___ is your favorite recording star?
3. The policeman asked ___*whom*___?
4. Tell ___*whomever*___ you want about the discovery.
5. He wonders ___*who*___ cheated on the exam.
6. She is the artist ___*who*___ I feel has the least talent.
7. ___*Who's*___ the trainer of the hockey team?
8. A person ___*who*___ is persistent has a good chance of success.
9. ___*Whomever*___ they choose will be a disappointment to some.
10. ___*Whom*___ do you intend to visit in Chicago?
11. With ___*whom*___ were you planning to go?
12. ___*Whoever*___ he is can expect my support.
13. Bring the package to ___*whomever*___ you were told.
14. ___*Whom*___ have you raced with?
15. I cannot support ___*whoever*___ he feels will be selected.
16. Is it she to ___*whom*___ I should report?
17. Those ___*who*___ train diligently usually finish the event.
18. ___*Whose*___ dictionary is this?
19. They are actors ___*who*___ can play a variety of roles.
20. Under ___*whose*___ authority was this order issued?

■ Using Pronouns Correctly in Elliptical Clauses

Another problem with pronouns involves choosing the correct case for a pronoun in an elliptical clause. In an elliptical clause, some words are omitted because they are understood. Sentences with elliptical clauses usually draw a comparison and are generally divided into two parts connected by *than* or *as*: *I am smarter than he* or *She is as happy as I*. It is in the second part of the comparison that some words are understood rather than fully stated. Sometimes only a pronoun is stated. In selecting the case of the pronoun in the elliptical clause, it is necessary to know what the unstated words are.

> In elliptical clauses beginning with *than* or *as*, use the form of the pronoun that you would use if the clause were fully stated.

In the following models, each box represents a clause. The boxes are connected by the conjunction *than* or *as*. Study the boxes on the right carefully. They explain why a nominative pronoun is used in one elliptical clause and an objective pronoun in another. The case of the pronoun depends upon whether the omitted words belong before or after the pronoun.

Words Left Out After Pronoun

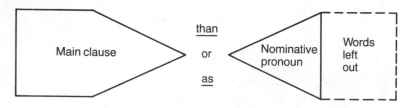

Words Left Out Before Pronoun

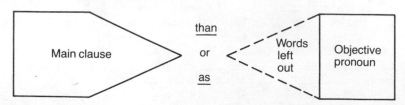

Compare these models with the two examples that follow. Notice both the pronoun used in each elliptical clause and the position of the omitted words in relation to the pronoun. The words understood are in parentheses.

WORDS LEFT OUT AFTER PRONOUN: She is as talented as *he* (is talented).

WORDS LEFT OUT BEFORE PRONOUN: The principal gave her the same choices as (the principal gave) *him.*

Often the entire meaning of the sentence can depend on the case of the pronoun. Compare, for example, the meanings of the following sentences.

WITH A NOMINATIVE PRONOUN: Stan inspired us more than *she* (inspired us).

WITH AN OBJECTIVE PRONOUN: Stan inspired us more than (he inspired) *her.*

Always follow these steps in making your decision.

STEPS FOR CHOOSING A PRONOUN IN ELLIPTICAL CLAUSES

1. Consider the choices of pronouns: nominative or objective.
2. Mentally complete the elliptical clause.
3. Base your choice on what you find.

EXERCISE E: Choosing the Correct Pronoun in Elliptical Clauses. Each of the following sentences contains an elliptical clause. Copy each sentence onto your paper and complete the elliptical clause. Then cross out the incorrect pronoun from the choices in the parentheses.
Choices may vary in many items; sample answers given.

EXAMPLE: She is more beautiful than (I, me).

She is more beautiful than (I, ~~me~~) am beautiful.

1. He is happier with the choice than (I, ~~me~~). *am.*
2. Steven is as dedicated as (she, ~~her~~). *is.*
3. This assignment is more important to me than to (~~he~~, him). *it is*
4. Sam is as disappointed with him as (they, ~~them~~). *are.*

5. This novel affected me more deeply than (she, ~~her~~). *did.*
6. Under the circumstances Lucy is as pleased as (he, ~~him~~). *is.*
7. The coin collection means more to me than (she, ~~her~~). *does.*
8. I love life in the country as much as (they, ~~them~~). *do.*
9. I think he is more aggressive than (I, ~~me~~). *am.*
10. Shostakovich was at least as successful as (they, ~~them~~). *are.*
11. My mother loved her more than (I, ~~me~~). *did.*
12. Some critics believe Bruckner was a greater composer than (he, ~~him~~). *was.*
13. The storekeeper gave them more than (we, ~~us~~). *did.*
14. I admire Picasso as much as (she, ~~her~~). *does.*
15. Without a doubt you are as misguided as (he, ~~him~~). *is.*
16. My brother helped him less than (I, ~~me~~). *did.*
17. Are they as pleased with their new plants as (we, ~~us~~)? *are.*
18. You can tell her as easily as (I, ~~me~~). *can.*
19. The investment was more costly to them than (we, ~~us~~). *were.*
20. Judy can dance better than (she, ~~her~~). *can.*

APPLICATION 1: Writing Sentences with *Who* and *Whoever*.
For each of the following pronouns, write a sentence using the form of the pronoun indicated.
Answers will vary; samples given for first two.
EXAMPLE: *Whom* (as a direct object)

Darius is the Persian king whom Alexander defeated.

1. *Who* (as a subject) *Who won the race?*
2. *Whom* (as an object of a preposition) *To whom should I give this?*
3. *Whomever* (as a direct object)
4. *Whomever* (in a question)
5. *Whoever* (as a subject)
6. *Whom* (at the beginning of a question)
7. *Who* (as the subject of a subordinate clause)
8. *Whom* (as a direct object)
9. *Who* (as a predicate nominative)
10. *Whom* (as an object of a preposition in a subordinate clause)

APPLICATION 2: Writing Sentences with Elliptical Clauses.
Write sentences of your own containing the following elliptical clauses. Check to see that the pronouns are used correctly by mentally completing the elliptical clauses.
Answers will vary; samples given for first two.
EXAMPLE: as strong as *I*

My brother is as strong as I.

1. taller than *she*
2. as capable as *they*
3. less than *him*
4. much more cooperative than *we*
5. more than *her*
6. as well as *they*
7. as much as *them*
8. as poorly as *he*
9. much happier than *them*
10. better than *us*

1. My sister is taller than she.
2. In home economics, we boys are as capable as they.

Chapter 11

Agreement

A car is a masterpiece of machinery. A battery feeds energy to the starter, which cranks the engine. A carburetor supplies fuel to the cylinders where it is burned, turning the drive shaft. A transmission shifts the gears smoothly. Everything works together to make the car go—in short, all of the parts *agree*.

A sentence is not quite as complicated. Nevertheless, the many parts of a sentence must work together to communicate your ideas clearly and effectively. Your words must be arranged in an understandable pattern, and the sentence must express a complete thought. Moreover, within the sentence itself, the words must have certain relationships to one another; that is, they must have agreement.

Getting subjects and verbs to agree is one task the writer faces. Another is making certain that pronouns agree with their antecedents. This chapter will deal with these tasks. After you understand a number of important rules, you will be able to make the various parts of your sentences fit together perfectly.

11.1 Subject and Verb Agreement

There is one general rule of subject and verb agreement.

A subject must agree with its verb in number.

Although you seldom consciously think of them, there are three steps in making a subject and verb agree.

STEPS FOR MAKING A SUBJECT AND VERB AGREE
1. Find the subject of the sentence.
2. Determine whether that subject is singular or plural.
3. Distinguish between the singular and plural forms of a verb, and match your choice to the subject.

Usually you perform these steps automatically as you form a sentence in your mind. Your experience in writing and speaking helps you make the correct choice, but sometimes you can make a mistake. If problems arise, you should consciously slow down the process and carefully check the steps.

You should be able to identify the subject of a sentence without much difficulty. If you cannot, review Sections 5.1 and 5.2. Otherwise, begin your study of agreement at the second and third steps and learn about the *number* of nouns, pronouns, and verbs.

■ Number: Singular and Plural

Understanding the grammatical concept of number is no problem at all.

Number refers to the two forms of a word: **singular** and **plural**. Singular words indicate *one;* plural words indicate *more than one.*

The word *car,* for example, refers to one object and is singular. *Cars* refers to more than one and is, of course, plural. Only nouns, pronouns, and verbs have number; the other parts of speech do not.

The Number of Nouns and Pronouns.   You should have no trouble recognizing the difference between singular and plural nouns and pronouns. Compare these forms of nouns in the following chart.

NOUNS			
Singular	Plural	Singular	Plural
record	records	child	children
tax	taxes	goose	geese

As you know, most nouns form their plurals by adding -*s* or -*es* to the singular (record*s*, tax*es*). Some, however, form plurals in other ways (child*ren*, g*ee*se). Whenever you have a problem with the number of a noun, check a dictionary.

The singular and plural forms of pronouns are presented in Section 1.2. *I, he, she,* and *it* are singular; *we* and *they* are plural. *You* can be either singular or plural.

The Number of Verbs. Verbs also have number. Two problem areas are number in the simple present tense and in tenses using a form of *be* as a helping verb. The following chart shows two verbs in the simple present tense.

SINGULAR AND PLURAL VERBS IN THE PRESENT TENSE		
Singular		**Plural**
First and Second Person	**Third Person**	**First, Second, and Third Person**
(I, you) write	(he, she, it) write*s*	(we, you, they) write
(I, you) go	(he, she, it) go*es*	(we, you, they) go

Verbs in the present tense change form only in the third-person singular. An -*s* or -*es* is added to create this form (write*s*, go*es*). People sometimes forget that, unlike nouns, verbs ending in -*s* or -*es* are always singular.

Forms of *be* are used as helping verbs and often indicate whether a verb phrase is singular or plural. Study the forms of the verb *be* in the following chart.

THE HELPING VERB *BE*	
Singular	**Plural**
(I) am	(we) are
(he, she, it) is	(they) are
(I, he, she, it) was	(we, they) were
(he, she, it) has been	(they) have been

The forms in the chart are in the present, past, and present perfect tenses. These are the only forms of *be* that change form from singular to plural and thus are the only ones that may cause agreement problems.

EXERCISE A: Determining the Number of Nouns, Pronouns, and Verbs. Determine whether each of the following nouns, pronouns, and verbs is singular or plural. A few may be both. Write the answer on your paper.

1. animals *pl*	6. try	11. delivers	16. it *sing*
2. we *pl*	7. agree	12. river *sing*	17. tulips *pl*
3. child *sing*	8. they *pl*	13. have	18. collapses
4. is *sing*	9. elephant	14. apples *pl*	19. shatter *sing* or *pl*
5. candle *sing*	10. grasps	15. were	20. geese *pl*

6. sing noun/sing or pl verb   7. sing or pl   9. sing   10. pl noun/sing verb   11. sing
13. sing or pl verb   15. sing or pl   18. pl noun/sing verb

■ Singular and Plural Subjects

The general rule that a subject and verb must agree has two simple extensions depending upon whether the subject is singular or plural.

A singular subject must have a singular verb.

A plural subject must have a plural verb.

Subjects are underlined once and verbs twice in the following examples.

SINGULAR SUBJECT AND VERB: Father always drives to work.

She is about to leave for school.

Charlie was reading the paper.

PLURAL SUBJECT AND VERB: The Smiths drive to work.

They are about to leave for school.

My brothers were reading the paper.

In each of these examples, the verb is close to the subject. Such sentences seldom pose an agreement problem. Sometimes, however, a phrase or clause comes between the subject and verb. Do not let it mislead you when you are checking for agreement.

A phrase or clause that comes between a subject and its verb does not affect subject-verb agreement.

In the first sentence in the following examples, the participial phrase *most admired by the students* ends with a plural noun. The subject of the sentence, however, is *actor*, which is singular; therefore the verb, *is*, is singular. In the second sentence, the adjective clause *that were being chased by our dog* ends with a singular noun but the verb that follows, *were seen*, is plural since the subject *raccoons* is plural.

EXAMPLES: The <u>actor</u> most admired by the students <u>is</u> often on TV.

The two <u>raccoons</u> that were being chased by our dog <u>were</u> last <u>seen</u> climbing a tree.

EXERCISE B: Making Singular and Plural Subjects Agree with Their Verbs. Write the subject from each of the following sentences on your paper. Then write the verb that agrees with the subject. *Subjects are shaded; verbs are underlined.*

1. The yellow and brown boxes (was, <u>were</u>) destroyed in the fire.
2. The concert (<u>begins</u>, begin) at eight.
3. Of all my subjects, woodworking (<u>was</u>, were) my favorite.
4. Old clocks (has, <u>have</u>) interesting histories.
5. My grandfather often (<u>goes</u>, go) to the adult center.
6. In desperation the heroine (<u>clutches</u>, clutch) for air.
7. John Cheever (<u>has</u>, have) finally received proper literary recognition.
8. Yesterday, both dictionaries (was, <u>were</u>) on that desk.
9. I guess this (<u>is</u>, are) the only possible explanation.
10. Lately, our evergreen plants (has, <u>have</u>) been yellowing.

EXERCISE C: Making Separated Subjects and Verbs Agree. Write the subject from each of the following sentences on your paper. Then write the verb that agrees with the subject. *Subjects are shaded; verbs are underlined.*

1. The old books in the attic (was, <u>were</u>) thrown away.
2. A representative of several student clubs (<u>is</u>, are) asking to speak.
3. A carton of grapefruits from Florida (<u>was</u>, were) delivered.
4. The vegetables in the stew (is, <u>are</u>) unusually tasty.
5. The trucks approaching the bridge often (races, <u>race</u>) their engines.
6. Flights from this airport to cities in Central America (leaves, <u>leave</u>) infrequently.
7. Our neighbor who has been traveling in Africa for several years (<u>appears</u>, appear) to have returned.

8. Four columns of infantry (was, <u>were</u>) advancing across the marsh.
9. A bouquet of flowers (<u>has</u>, have) a special magic for some people.
10. The speakers in my stereo (is, <u>are</u>) poorly balanced.

■ Compound Subjects

A compound subject has two or more subjects usually connected by *or* or *and*. Depending upon the combinations, several rules apply.

Two or more singular subjects joined by *or* or *nor* must have a singular verb. Two or more plural subjects joined by *or* or *nor* must have a plural verb.

In the first of the following examples, two singular subjects are connected by *or*. Together they form a singular compound subject: Either a bus or a car is recommended, not both. In the second example, once again a choice is offered: fathers *or* mothers. But since both subjects are plural, the compound subject requires a plural verb.

SINGULAR SUBJECTS CONNECTED BY *OR*: A <u>car</u> or <u>bus</u> <u>is</u> the only means of travel upstate.

PLURAL SUBJECTS CONNECTED BY *OR*: Only the <u>fathers</u> or the <u>mothers</u> <u>are</u> to be invited.

Sometimes, however, one subject in a compound is singular and the other is plural.

If one or more subjects are singular and the others are plural and they are joined by *or* or *nor*, the subject closest to the verb determines the agreement.

In the first sentence in the following examples, *parents*, a plural subject, stands closest to the verb, requiring a plural form. In the second sentence, *David*, a singular subject, is closer; the verb, therefore, is singular.

EXAMPLES: Neither <u>David</u>, <u>Judy</u>, nor my <u>parents</u> <u>are going</u> to the wedding.

Either my <u>parents</u> or <u>David</u> <u>is going</u> to the wedding.

Another rule applies to compound subjects connected by *and*.

A compound subject joined by *and* is generally plural and must have a plural verb.

The conjunction *and* usually acts as a plus sign. It does not matter whether there are two or more singular subjects, two or more plural subjects, or any combination of singular and plural subjects. Subjects joined by *and* add up to a plural compound subject.

EXAMPLES: One <u>boy</u> and one <u>girl</u> <u>are willing</u> to speak at the assembly.

Two <u>boys</u> and three <u>girls</u> <u>were chosen</u>.

Only two <u>boys</u> and one <u>girl</u> <u>were chosen</u>.

This rule has two exceptions. If the parts of a compound subject add up to one thing, the compound subject is singular and requires a singular verb. The second exception involves the words *every* and *each*. Either of these words in front of a compound subject indicates the need for a singular verb.

SINGULAR COMPOUND SUBJECT: <u>Corned beef and cabbage</u> <u>is</u> a holiday treat in our house. (Corned beef and cabbage = one dish)

EVERY WITH A SINGULAR VERB: Every (or Each) <u>dog</u> and <u>cat</u> in the kennel <u>was</u> inoculated. (Every dog and cat = each one)

EXERCISE D: Making Compound Subjects Agree with Their Verbs.

Write the compound subject from each of the following sentences on your paper. Then write the verb that agrees with the subject. *Subjects are shaded; verbs are underlined.*

1. My boss and her partner both (collects, <u>collect</u>) coins.
2. Trish or Kathy (<u>plans</u>, plan) to represent us.
3. Either my grandparents or I (shops, <u>shop</u>) for milk each morning.
4. Snow, hail, and sleet (has been, <u>have been</u>) forecast for the weekend.

5. Fruits and vegetables (provides, provide) many minerals.
6. Spaghetti and meatballs with mushrooms (is, are) her favorite dish.
7. A train or several buses (is, are) available on Sundays.
8. Either my uncle or my aunt (phones, phone) each week.
9. Several photographs or a large mural (seems, seem) just right for that large wall.
10. Books and magazines always (is, are) well received by patients in a hospital.
11. Neither the sedan nor the station wagon (has, have) a spare tire.
12. Three men and a woman (was, were) approaching the door.
13. The three daughters and their father (has, have) a special relationship.
14. The lamps or the end tables (is, are) on sale tomorrow.
15. In the morning a robin or two bluejays (perches, perch) on our windowsill.
16. Every apple and pear (was, were) eaten by the guests.
17. Franks and beans or corned beef and cabbage (is, are) my choice.
18. Phil or Mary usually (opens, open) the office each morning.
19. Certain drugs and alcohol seriously (impairs, impair) the body's reflexes.
20. Three candles or a strong flashlight (is, are) necessary for emergencies.

■ Confusing Subjects

Many subjects can be confusing and lead to faulty agreement. Among them are subjects in unusual positions, subjects of linking verbs, collective nouns, plural-looking nouns, indefinite pronouns, titles, and amounts or measurements.

Subjects in Unusual Positions. Subjects that follow their verbs often cause problems in agreement.

A verb that comes before its subject must still agree with it in number.

Sentences in which the subject comes after the verb are in inverted word order. In the following example, the subject is *silos*, not *hill*. This plural subject agrees with the plural verb *are*. Agreement is not affected by the two prepositional phrases at the beginning of the sentence.

EXAMPLE: At the crossroads in front of the hill <u>are</u> two picturesque <u>silos</u>.

Some inverted sentences begin with *there* or *here*. In the first sentence in the following examples, the plural subject *photos* agrees with the plural verb *are*. In the second sentence, *edition*, a singular subject, agrees with *is*, a singular verb.

EXAMPLES: There <u>are</u> the <u>photos</u> of the castle.

Here <u>is</u> the revised <u>edition</u> of that book.

NOTE ABOUT *THERE'S* AND *HERE'S*:   Both of these words are contractions containing the singular verb *is: there is* and *here is*. They should not be used with plural subjects.

CORRECT: There<u>'s</u> only one <u>concert</u> planned for this semester.

There <u>are</u> two <u>concerts</u> planned for this semester. (*Not* "There's two concerts . . .")

Subjects of Linking Verbs.   Sometimes a sentence with a linking verb and a predicate nominative presents a problem in agreement.

A linking verb must always agree with its subject, regardless of the number of its predicate nominative.

In some sentences the subject and the predicate nominative may not be the same in number. One may be singular while the other is plural. In the first sentence in the following examples, the plural subject *stereos* agrees with the plural verb *are* although the predicate nominative *reason* is singular. In the second sentence, the opposite is true. *Reason*, the singular subject, agrees with *is*, a singular verb. They are not affected by the plural predicate nominative *stereos*.

EXAMPLES: Loud <u>stereos</u> <u>are</u> one reason for increased hearing problems among teen-agers.

One <u>reason</u> for increased hearing problems among teen-agers <u>is</u> loud stereos.

Collective Nouns. Collective nouns pose yet another agreement problem. Words such as *audience, class, couple, crowd, family, faculty, group, orchestra, team,* and *United States* can be either singular or plural depending upon use.

A collective noun is singular and agrees with a singular verb when the group it names is considered to be a **single unit.** It is plural and agrees with a plural verb when the group it names is considered to be **individuals** with different feelings or points of view.

SINGULAR: The <u>orchestra</u> <u>is playing</u> at Symphony Hall tonight.

The football <u>team</u> <u>has been invited</u> to a bowl game.

PLURAL: The <u>jury</u> <u>have been</u> unable to agree on a verdict.

The <u>faculty</u> <u>have been discussing</u> the new testing policy.

Plural-Looking Nouns. Other confusing subjects are plural-looking nouns, such as those ending in *s,* that are actually singular in meaning.

Nouns that are plural in form but singular in meaning agree with singular verbs.

A number of these special nouns name branches of knowledge: *economics, ethics, physics, politics, acoustics, mathematics, social studies,* and so on. Others, like collective nouns, have singular meaning because they name single units or ideas: *spaghetti, measles, news.*

SINGULAR: For me, <u>mathematics</u> <u>is</u> always difficult.

The <u>news</u> from the Middle East today <u>is</u> good.

Some of these words can be tricky. When words such as *ethics* and *acoustics* do not name branches of knowledge but rather indicate characteristics or qualities, their meanings are plural. Similarly, words such as *eyeglasses, pliers,* and *scissors,* although they name single items, generally take plural verbs. Whenever you have a question about these special nouns, check a dictionary.

PLURAL: The <u>acoustics</u> in the school auditorium <u>are</u> bad.

The senator's <u>ethics</u> <u>have been questioned</u>.

The <u>scissors</u> <u>are</u> in the top drawer.

Indefinite Pronouns. Indefinite pronouns used as subjects often cause problems in agreement.

Depending on its form and meaning, an indefinite pronoun can agree with either a singular or a plural verb.

The following chart shows three groups of indefinite pronouns: those always singular, those always plural, and those which can be either.

INDEFINITE PRONOUNS			
Singular		**Plural**	**Singular or Plural**
another	much	both	all
anybody	neither	few	any
anyone	nobody	many	more
anything	no one	others	most
each	nothing	several	none
either	one		some
everybody	other		
everyone	somebody		
everything	someone		
little	something		

The following examples illustrate each of these groups.

ALWAYS SINGULAR: <u>Each</u> of the players <u>was cited</u> for excellence.

<u>Either</u> of the dancers <u>has</u> the potential to become a star.

ALWAYS PLURAL: <u>Few</u> <u>were</u> at the concert.

<u>Several</u> of the students <u>are changing</u> their plans now.

EITHER SINGULAR OR PLURAL: <u>Some</u> of the stew <u>is</u> spoiled. <u>Some</u> of of the cars <u>are</u> expensive.

In the last set of examples, the objects of the prepositions determine whether the verb should be singular or plural. *Stew*, considered one unit, makes *some* singular. *Cars*, obviously plural, makes *some* plural.

NOTE ABOUT *MANY A, NONE,* AND *ANY:*   *Many a* is used in front of a singular subject and always takes a singular verb.

EXAMPLE: Many a <u>writer</u> <u>has contributed</u> to this project.

None and *any* can sometimes take a singular verb even when the nouns they stand for are plural. In this sense, *none* means "not one," and *any* means "any one."

EXAMPLES: <u>None</u> of the vegetables <u>was spoiled</u>.

<u>Has</u> <u>any</u> of the crates <u>been opened</u> yet?

Titles.   The title of a book or other work of art, regardless of whether or not it sounds plural, always takes a singular verb.

A title is singular and must have a singular verb.

In the following examples, the plural words *Lives* and *Tales* do not make the titles plural.

EXAMPLES: <u>*Atlantic Brief Lives*</u> <u>is</u> a useful reference.

Offenbach's <u>*The Tales of Hoffmann*</u> <u>has been performed</u> often at the Metropolitan Opera.

Amounts and Measurements.   Although they sometimes appear to be plural, many amounts and measurements express single units or ideas.

A noun expressing an amount or measurement is usually singular and must usually have a singular verb.

In the first three sentences in the following examples, the subjects require singular verbs. *Seventy-nine cents* is one sum of money; *four feet*, a single measurement; and *three quarters*, one part of a container. The last sentence is different: *Half* refers to a number of individual chickens and is, as a result, plural.

EXAMPLES: Seventy-nine cents is the price for two.

Four feet was the height of the recommended chain link fence.

Three quarters of the bushel of fruit was thrown away.

Half of the chickens were diseased and ordered destroyed.

EXERCISE E: Making Confusing Subjects Agree with Their Verbs.
Divide your paper into three columns. Title the first *Subject*, the second *Singular or Plural*, and the third *Verb*. For each of the following sentences, write the subject in the first column. Then decide whether the subject is singular or plural and write your answer in the second column. Finally, choose the correct verb and write it in the third column. *Subjects are shaded; verbs are underlined.*

sing 1. Physics (is, are) my brother's favorite subject.
2. (There's, There are) an old raincoat and umbrella in the
pl garage.
pl 3. In the back of the closet (is, are) two 60-watt bulbs.
sing 4. The United States (is, are) one nation indivisible.
pl 5. Here (is, are) three examples of the Romantic Period.
sing 6. The news (hasn't, haven't) changed for days.
sing 7. Smallpox (was, were) once a serious disease.
pl 8. Storms at sea (is, are) a reason for extreme caution.
sing 9. Many a criminal (pleads, plead) for a second chance.
sing 10. Another cause of accidents (was, were) poor, unlit roads.
sing 11. Someone among them (has, have) to assume leadership.
pl 12. There (has been, have been) three attempts on his life.
sing 13. A group of pilgrims (arrives, arrive) at the shrine daily.
sing 14. Finally, the jury (has, have) rendered a verdict.
sing 15. Local politics (has, have) always shown favoritism.
pl 16. After the long, impressive corridor (is, are) three elevators.
sing 17. All of the soup (was, were) spilled on the new floor.
sing 18. (Here's, Here are) one last question from the director.
pl 19. The acoustics in the studio (was, were) excellent.
pl 20. The committee (has, have) regrouped themselves into three factions.
pl 21. A candidate's ethics (is, are) an important consideration.
sing 22. Near the fence between two trees (lies, lie) the treasure.
sing 23. Fifty cents (is, are) not much of a tip these days.
sing 24. None of the tomatoes (has, have) ripened.
sing 25. *The Adventures of Sherlock Holmes* still (retains, retain) much of its popularity.

EXERCISE F: More Practice with Confusing Subjects.
Follow the directions in Exercise E. *Subjects are shaded; verbs are underlined.*

1. Ten feet of cement (<u>is</u>, are) what we want for the patio. *sing*
2. Most of the reports (was, <u>were</u>) of poor quality. *pl*
3. Civics (<u>has</u>, have) not been taught as a subject in many schools for some time now. *sing*
4. At the top of the hill (stands, <u>stand</u>) two majestic oaks. *pl*
5. *The Brothers Karamazov* (<u>ranks</u>, rank) as an outstanding Russian novel. *sing*
6. There (was, <u>were</u>) several weaknesses in that survey. *pl*
7. Now the audience (<u>rises</u>, rise) as one in appreciation. *sing*
8. Each of the turntables (<u>has</u>, have) a drawback. *sing*
9. Dirty streets (is, <u>are</u>) just one of our complaints. *pl*
10. The couple (disagrees, <u>disagree</u>) with each other about where they should spend their vacation. *pl*
11. Where (is, <u>are</u>) my new pliers? *pl*
12. Others in the council (joins, <u>join</u>) in criticism. *pl*
13. The jury (is, <u>are</u>) arguing over the details of the case. *pl*
14. One fifth of our income (<u>goes</u>, go) for taxes. *sing*
15. Bartlett's *Familiar Quotations* (<u>has</u>, have) always been a fine resource for speakers. *sing*
16. In back of the house (is, <u>are</u>) planted beans and cucumbers. *pl*
17. Half of the new cars (has, <u>have</u>) significant defects. *pl*
18. *The Best of the Beatles* (<u>was</u>, were) bound to be a classic from the beginning. *sing*
19. (<u>There's</u>, There are) only one person I can recommend. *sing*
20. Four inches of growth in a year (<u>is</u>, are) outstanding. *sing*

EXERCISE G: Using All of the Rules of Subject and Verb Agreement. Write the subject from each of the following sentences on your paper. Then write the verb that agrees with the subject. *Subjects are shaded; verbs are underlined.*

1. My brother or my mother (<u>wants</u>, want) to meet the train.
2. Both sailors (was, <u>were</u>) attempting to grasp the lifeline.
3. Most of the roast (<u>seems</u>, seem) too dry.
4. Fine artists often (collaborates, <u>collaborate</u>) in a performance.
5. Everyone (<u>knows</u>, know) what to expect from her.
6. Fruits or assorted nuts (is, <u>are</u>) excellent to serve.
7. Many a political cause (<u>dies</u>, die) soon after birth.
8. Trips to Europe (has, <u>have</u>) become more expensive.
9. The new series of recitals (<u>appears</u>, appear) to be successful.
10. That couple (has, have) been living there for years.
11. *The Sense of the 60's* (<u>depicts</u>, depict) a particularly turbulent era.

258   *Agreement*

12. Examples of his poor judgment (has, <u>have</u>) been documented.
13. At the other end of town (<u>is</u>, are) a fine French restaurant.
14. More of our teammates now (agrees, <u>agree</u>) with me.
15. The Marx Brothers' films still (delights, <u>delight</u>) audiences.
16. Either two friends or my teacher (<u>is</u>, are) planning to visit Bill in the hospital.
17. Hockey and football (has, <u>have</u>) always been particularly aggressive sports.
18. The strings in the orchestra (is, <u>are</u>) outstanding.
19. Either (<u>has</u>, have) been acceptable to us for some time.
20. Three fifths of the population (<u>supports</u>, support) it.

APPLICATION: Applying the Rules of Subject and Verb Agreement. Complete each of the following sentences with an appropriate verb in the present tense.
Answers will vary; samples given.

1. *Great Expectations* ___is___ one of my favorite novels.
2. Everybody always ___attends___ the annual picnic.
3. Our class ___has___ voted unanimously to put on a play.
4. An umbrella or a raincoat ___is___ a good choice today.
5. One of our radios ___has___ not been working well lately.
6. Two thirds of the cake ___is___ covered with whipped cream.
7. Several copies of *Page One* ___are___ in the library.
8. Many an animal ___needs___ regular vaccinations and proper care.
9. There ___is___ only one possible excuse for their lateness.
10. Economics ___is___ a subject I can't understand.
11. Sixty-five cents ___is___ too much for a pencil.
12. Every flower and plant ___has___ been fed properly.
13. In front of the magazine ___are___ two unusual photographs.
14. The jury ___have___ returned to their seats.
15. Here ___are___ two reasons to support her campaign for senator.
16. A reason for possible breakdowns ___is___ poor original designs.
17. A trip to Europe or Asia ___is___ out of the question.
18. Tennis and golf now ___are___ at their height of popularity.
19. Most of the plants ___are___ in good health.
20. Outdoor lights or a strong reflector ___is___ an absolute must to prevent accidents.

Pronoun and Antecedent Agreement 11.2

In Section 1.2 an antecedent is defined as the noun (or group of words acting as a noun) for which a pronoun stands. Although the word *antecedent* comes from a Latin word that means "to go before," an antecedent often follows its pronoun.

■ Agreement Between Personal Pronouns and Antecedents

One general rule of pronoun and antecedent agreement governs all the others.

A personal pronoun must agree with its antecedent in number, person, and gender.

Understanding number, person, and gender is not as difficult as it might sound. Number, as noted in Section 11.1, is either sigular or plural. Person, as noted in Section 1.2, is divided into three groups: A first-person pronoun indicates the person speaking; a second-person pronoun, the person spoken to; and a third-person pronoun, the person, place, or thing spoken about.

You may also be familiar with gender from studying a foreign language. In English, nouns and pronouns have gender, which may be *masculine, feminine,* or *neuter.* As the following chart indicates, masculine words refer to males and feminine words to females. Neuter words refer to neither males nor females. Notice that the pronouns in the chart are all third-person singular. The other personal pronouns are not listed because they can apply to any of the three genders.

GENDER OF NOUNS AND PRONOUNS					
Masculine		Feminine		Neuter	
Noun	Pronoun	Noun	Pronoun	Noun	Pronoun
father	he	mother	she	book	it
nephew	him	niece	her	truth	its
boy	his	girl	hers	London	

In the following example, note how the pronoun agrees with its antecedent in number, person, and gender.

EXAMPLE: *Byron* received *his* M.A. degree from Cambridge in 1808.

Byron is the antecedent. It is singular in number, third-person, and masculine in gender. *His*, the pronoun referring to *Byron*, is also singular, third-person, and masculine.

Making Personal Pronouns Agree with Antecedents in Number.   As you write, pay special attention to personal pronouns and their antecedents so that they will agree in number. Be particularly careful when you use compound antecedents. A compound antecedent consists of two or more nouns joined by the conjunction *and*.

Use a plural personal pronoun with two or more antecedents joined by *and*.

EXAMPLE: As *Byron*, *Hunt*, and *Trelawny* prepared Shelley's body for cremation, *they* found a copy of Keats' poems in the drowned poet's pocket.

Use a singular personal pronoun with two or more singular antecedents joined by *or* or *nor*.

EXAMPLE: Neither *Byron* nor *Hunt* could believe *his* (not *their*) eyes: Shelley's heart was not consumed by the flames.

Avoiding Shifts in Person and Gender.   A personal pronoun and its antecedent will not agree if there is a shift in either person or gender in the second part of the sentence.

Do not shift person or gender between a pronoun and its antecedent.

SHIFT IN PERSON: *Michele* is doing volunteer work in a home for the aged, the kind of service *you* need if *you* want to qualify for a service award.

CORRECT: *Michele* is doing volunteer work in a home for the aged, the kind of service *she* needs if *she* wants to qualify for a service award.

SHIFT IN GENDER: *Vienna* is noted for *its* musical and artistic activities as well as *her* other cultural highlights.

CORRECT: Vienna is noted for *its* musical and artistic activities as well as *its* other cultural highlights.

It is easy to correct errors caused by shifts in person and gender. Simply find the antecedent and determine its person and gender. Then make sure each pronoun referring to it matches.

Dealing with Generic Masculine Pronouns.   With an antecedent whose gender is not specified as either masculine or feminine, a masculine personal pronoun has traditionally been used. The term *generic* means "general." Thus, a generic masculine pronoun covers both genders in general statements.

Use a masculine pronoun *(he, him,* and *his)* with a singular antecedent whose gender may be either masculine or feminine.

The gender of *guest* in the following example is not indicated.

EXAMPLE: An overnight *guest* normally thanks *his* host by means of a small gift.

Many modern writers attempt to avoid using generic pronouns altogether. What they do instead is rephrase the sentence.

EXAMPLES: An overnight *guest* usually thanks the host by means of a small gift.

Overnight *guests* usually thank *their* host by means of a small gift.

EXERCISE A: Making Personal Pronouns Agree with Their Antecedents. Complete each of the following sentences by writing an appropriate personal pronoun on your paper. Be sure your pronoun agrees with the antecedent in each sentence.

1. Uncle Stan sent us _____*his*_____ best wishes.
2. My brother and sister later explained _____*their*_____ objections.
3. Each student designed _____*his*_____ own poster.
4. Lisa briefly described the city and then related in detail _____*her*_____ experiences there.

5. Neither Bob nor Jerry wanted to drive ___*his*___ car to the station.
6. I expected two crates of fruit from Florida, but ___*they*___ apparently got lost somewhere.
7. The waiter asked us for ___*our*___ preference in salad dressings.
8. The delegates rose as one and thundered ___*their*___ approval.
9. My grandmother and grandfather urged us to use ___*their*___ cottage.
10. The car has trouble with ___*its*___ transmission.

■ Agreement Between Personal Pronouns and Indefinite Pronouns

Indefinite pronouns, such as *each, either, somebody, both, few,* and *all,* occasionally cause agreement problems with personal pronouns. (See page 254 for a complete list of indefinite pronouns.)

Use a singular personal pronoun when the antecedent is a singular indefinite pronoun.

An interrupting phrase does not affect the agreement of a pronoun with its antecedent. *Recordings,* the object of a preposition in the first sentence in the following examples, does not affect the agreement of the pronoun *its* with its antecedent *each.* In the next two sentences, notice that the *number* of the personal pronouns (*her, his*) is determined by the singular antecedents (*each, neither*) but that the *gender* in both sentences is determined by the objects of the preposition (*girls, firemen*).

EXAMPLES: *Each* of the borrowed recordings must be returned to *its* (not *their*) original owner.

Each of the girls handed in *her* (not *their*) assignment.

Neither of the two firemen has yet recovered from *his* (not *their*) injuries.

NOTE ABOUT *EVERYONE* AND *EVERYBODY*:   The singular indefinite pronouns *everyone* and *everybody* require singular pronouns, particularly in formal writing. In speaking and in informal writing, the plural pronoun *their* is frequently used instead. Another choice, in formal and informal writing, is to rewrite the sentence. Your teacher will tell you which style to use in your classroom work.

FORMAL: *Everyone* wants to express *his* opinion.

INFORMAL: *Everybody* wants to express *their* opinions.

FORMAL AND INFORMAL: *All* of them want to express *their* opinions.

EXERCISE B: Making Personal Pronouns Agree with Indefinite Pronouns. Write the correct pronoun for each of the following sentences on your paper. Be prepared to explain your choices. *Pronouns are underlined; antecedents are shaded.*

1. Both of the delivery vans had received (its, <u>their</u>) state inspection.
2. Everyone on the committee gave (<u>her</u>, their) approval to the plan.
3. Each of the soldiers completed (<u>his</u>, their) assignment.
4. Several of the dancers promised (her, <u>their</u>) autographs.
5. Tomorrow everyone should bring (<u>his</u>, their) recommendations to the meeting.
6. Nobody on the team could express (<u>his</u>, their) feelings about the loss.
7. Neither of the girls offered to lend me (<u>her</u>, their) notes.
8. Finally, one of the victims volunteered to tell (<u>his</u>, their) story.
9. All of the members agreed to double (his, <u>their</u>) contributions to the club.
10. Many of the witnesses offered (his, <u>their</u>) opinions about the incident.
11. The next morning everybody apologized for (<u>his</u>, their) poor behavior.
12. Few of the reporters have (her, <u>their</u>) credentials with them.
13. Neither the men nor the women wanted (his, her, <u>their</u>) names in the paper.
14. Only one of the speakers gave logical reasons for (<u>her</u>, their) objections to the proposed law.
15. Each of the musicians had (<u>his</u>, their) music ready.
16. Somebody shouted (<u>his</u>, their) criticism into the microphone.
17. Which one of the women wanted (<u>her</u>, their) coat?
18. Some of the townspeople have always supported (its, <u>their</u>) volunteer firefighters.

19. Neither of them will bring (his, their) garden tools.
20. Someone on the council gave (his, their) consent to the scheme.

■ Agreement with Reflexive Pronouns

Reflexive pronouns end in *-self* or *-selves* and refer to an antecedent occurring earlier in the sentence, as in "Marie told herself to stay calm."

A reflexive pronoun must agree with an antecedent that is clearly stated.

Do not use a reflexive pronoun when a personal pronoun can do the job. Notice that the antecedent of *myself* in the following example does not appear in the sentence. The personal pronoun *me* should be used instead.

POOR: The messenger brought Peter and *myself* good news.

CORRECT: The messenger brought Peter and *me* good news.

EXERCISE C: Checking Reflexive Pronouns for Agreement. Two of the following sentences are correct; the others have errors involving reflexive pronouns. For each correct sentence, write the reflexive pronoun and its antecedent. Rewrite each of the other sentences to correct the error.
Antecedents for reflexive pronouns are shaded.

- 1. My grandmother knitted the scarves, a white one for me and a red one for herself. *c*
  2. Either Myra or myself will speak with the counselor. *I*
  3. We gave ourselves three hours to reach the boat. *c*
  4. The president wants the secretary, the treasurer, and yourself to make the presentation. *you*
  5. The person with the best chance for success is herself. *she*

■ Four Special Problems in Pronoun Agreement

One special kind of error in agreement occurs when writers or speakers use personal pronouns without clearly identifying their antecedents. Such sentences should be rephrased to include a personal pronoun with a clear antecedent or to eliminate the personal pronoun altogether.

A personal pronoun should always have an antecedent that is either stated or clearly understood.

In the first sentence in the following examples, the pronoun *they* does not have an antecedent. To whom does *they* refer? In the second sentence, *they* is replaced with *it,* which clearly refers to *movie.* In the third sentence, a noun is used in place of *they.*

POOR: The movie was disappointing because *they* never made the relationships between the characters clear.

CORRECT: The movie was disappointing because *it* never made the relationships between the characters clear.

CORRECT: The movie was disappointing because *the director* never made the relationships between the characters clear.

The second special agreement rule involves *ambiguous* pronouns—that is, pronouns that refer to two or more possible antecedents.

A personal pronoun should always refer to a single, obvious antecedent.

A sentence containing a pronoun with two or more possible antecedents should be rephrased. In the following sentence, for example, it is difficult to tell whether Mary has lost the *letter* or the *book.*

POOR: Mary put the letter between the pages of a book, but now she cannot locate *it.*

CORRECT: Mary cannot find the letter that she put between the pages of a book.

CORRECT: Mary cannot find the book in which she put the letter.

The third special agreement rule concerns personal pronouns that are not close enough to their antecedents.

A personal pronoun should always be close enough to its antecedent to prevent confusion.

If a personal pronoun is too far from its antecedent, the reference is no longer clear. In the following example, the pronoun *he* is too far from its antecedent, *Macbeth*. The best solution is to rewrite the sentence or sentences to move the pronoun closer.

POOR: At the banquet Macbeth was stunned by the appearance of Banquo's ghost. Lady Macbeth and the guests showed their concern but, shaken at the sight of the apparition, *he* paid them no heed.

MOVED CLOSER: The appearance of Banquo's ghost at the banquet stunned Macbeth. Although Lady Macbeth and the guests showed their concern, *he* was too shaken by the apparition to heed them.

The fourth rule deals with the use of *you* in general statements.

The personal pronoun *you* should be used only when the reference is truly to the reader or the listener.

In the following example, the pronouns are imprecise because a reader or listener could not possibly have been in ancient Rome.

POOR: In ancient Rome, the emperors often made *you* offer sacrifices to the gods as a sign of *your* loyalty to the state.

CORRECT: In ancient Rome, the emperors often made *citizens* offer sacrifices to the gods as a sign of *their* loyalty to the state.

EXERCISE D: Correcting Special Problems in Pronoun Agreement. Each of the following sentences contains at least one problem in pronoun agreement. Rewrite the sentences to correct the errors, changing individual words or rephrasing the sentences as necessary. *Answers will vary; samples given.*

1. Take the papers from the pile of folders and then file ~~them.~~ *the papers.*
2. ~~At school they expect you to~~ report to the attendance office. *At school, students must*
3. Marge told Gloria about the bazaar and they decided not to go today. ~~She~~ said that perhaps they could go later in the week. *Marge*
4. The quarterback faded to pass. The receiver and the defender converged on the ball, and ~~he~~ dropped it. *the receiver*
5. ~~When~~ Mother spoke to Alice, ~~she~~ nodded. *who*

6. Take the breadbox off the table and clean ~~it.~~ the breadbox.
7. My sister read her story to Fran. When Fran criticized the opening, ~~she~~ wanted another opinion. *my sister*
8. ~~It~~ says that ~~you~~ should be able to type and take shorthand. *The ad/an applicant*
9. My brothers chased the intruders ~~until they~~ fell. *who finally*
10. If you decide to go to college out of town, ~~it sometimes makes you~~ terribly lonely. *you will sometimes be*
11. When I visited Athens in 1968, ~~you~~ were still permitted to walk inside the Parthenon. *tourists*
12. A person's integrity should be very important to ~~them.~~ *him*
13. Even if a college application does not call for letters of recommendation, ~~they expect you~~ to submit them nevertheless. *applicants are expected*
14. ~~Bob told Billy he is the new monitor.~~
15. My teacher assigned Mary to rewind the film, Sue to pull up the screen, and Beth to unpack the other reel. ~~But she didn't do it.~~ *Beth, however, did not perform her task.*
16. If ~~they want~~ the term paper to have a certain format, you should not change it. *your teacher wants*
17. Bring the bushel of apples into the kitchen and sort ~~it.~~ *them.*
18. When my father was in college ~~they expected you~~ to wear academic gowns to class. *students were expected*
19. When Sally makes lunch for my mother, ~~she~~ is always sorry. *Mother*
20. Father put the phone number in his wallet, but he can't find ~~it.~~ *his wallet.*

14. Bob said, "Billy, I'm the new monitor."

APPLICATION: Writing Paragraphs in Which the Pronouns Agree with Their Antecedents. For each of the following items, write an original paragraph of four or five sentences. Follow the directions carefully. Make sure you proofread each paragraph carefully to see that all the pronouns agree with their antecedents. *Answers will vary; students might read paragraphs to class to check clarity and agreement among pronouns.*

1. Write a paragraph about your father or another male relative. Begin with the word *Father* or the person's name. In the following sentences use the pronouns *he*, *him*, and *his* to refer to him.
2. Write a paragraph about your family. Begin the first sentence with the words "The members of my family have always been . . ." In the rest of the paragraph refer to them with the pronouns *they, them, their, theirs*.
3. Write a paragraph about your sister or a girl you know. Begin the first sentence with the person's name. Then use the pronouns *she, her,* and *hers* to refer to her in the rest of the paragraph.

Chapter 12

Adjective and Adverb Usage

Adjectives and adverbs play an important role in sentences. They describe, they add color, they clarify, and they make distinctions. A carefully chosen adjective or adverb often turns an ordinary phrase or sentence into a superior one.

Adjectives and adverbs perform still another function. They make comparisons. In daily conversation or in writing, people constantly make comparisons, comparing one television program with another, one nation with another, or one political candidate with several others. The speaker or writer of each sentence usually wants to show a specific difference between two or more people, objects, or ideas.

In the first section of this chapter, you will learn how to form the various adjectives and adverbs used in comparisons. The second section, which puts this information to use, will help you avoid a number of common usage problems involving comparisons.

12.1 Degrees of Comparison

In English most adjectives and adverbs have three forms, called *degrees*, that are used to modify and make comparisons.

Adjectives and adverbs have different forms to show degrees of comparison.

The three degrees are called *positive*, *comparative*, and *superlative*.

THE THREE DEGREES OF COMPARISON

1. The *positive* degree is the base form of the word, the one under which definitions are listed in a dictionary. It is the form used when a comparison is *not* being made.
2. The *comparative* degree is the form used to compare two persons, places, things, or ideas.
3. The *superlative* degree is the form used to compare three or more persons, places, things, or ideas.

■ Recognizing Degrees of Comparison

Adjectives and adverbs have different ways of forming the comparative and superlative degrees. Notice, for example, how the forms of the adjectives and adverbs in the following chart change to show the three degrees.

DEGREES OF ADJECTIVES		
Positive	**Comparative**	**Superlative**
simple	simpler	simplest
impressive	more impressive	most impressive
good	better	best

DEGREES OF ADVERBS		
Positive	**Comparative**	**Superlative**
simply	more simply	most simply
impressively	more impressively	most impressively
well	better	best

EXERCISE A: Recognizing Positive, Comparative, and Superlative Degrees. Each of the following sentences contains an adjective or adverb in the positive, comparative, or superlative degree. Write each modifier on your paper and identify its degree.

EXAMPLE: He is the tallest player on the team.

             tallest   superlative

1. My father is far <u>more industrious</u> than I. *compar*
2. Sometimes it is <u>best</u> not to argue. *sup*
3. I think she is <u>hungry</u> now. *pos*
4. *Giants in the Earth* is one of the <u>most impressive</u> American novels I've read. *sup*
5. You will be <u>more rested</u> after a nap. *compar*
6. I like the Mozart's *Jupiter Symphony* <u>better</u> than the *Prague*. *compar*
7. Her <u>swollen</u> arm requires treatment. *pos*
8. The banker is the <u>richest</u> person in town. *sup*
9. This is the <u>most informative</u> article I've read regarding Yeats' symbolism. *sup*
10. My brother has <u>more</u> money now than when he returned to school. *compar*
11. For those who want to work, this course is the <u>most challenging</u>. *sup*
12. Who do you think is <u>prettier</u>? *compar*
13. Of all my uncle's careers, working as a potter, he always said, was the <u>most satisfying</u>. *sup*
14. The <u>happiest</u> day of my vacation was Friday. *sup*
15. You are <u>better</u> at statistics than he. *compar*
16. She is the <u>choosiest</u> person I know. *sup*
17. Unfortunately, he is <u>more talkative</u> than he used to be. *compar*
18. Judy apparently is <u>sleepy</u> this morning. *pos*
19. In your opinion, which photo is <u>more attractive</u>? *compar*
20. Clark was the <u>most qualified</u> candidate in the group. *sup*

■ Regular Forms

Adjectives and adverbs, like verbs, can be either regular or irregular. Most modifiers, fortunately, form their comparative and superlative degrees regularly. The rules depend on the number of syllables in the modifier. There is one rule for modifiers of one or two syllables, another for modifiers of three or more syllables.

Use *-er* or *more* to form the comparative degree and *-est* or *most* to form the superlative degree of most one- and two-syllable modifiers.

In general, one- and two-syllable words form their comparative and superlative degrees with *-er* and *-est* rather than with *more* and *most*. Although either method can be used in most situations, avoid using *more* and *most* when they sound awkward, particularly with modifiers of one syllable. It is better, for example, to say *shorter* than *more short*, *later* than *more late*.

The following examples show the degrees of one- and two-syllable modifiers formed by the usual method of adding *-er* and *-est*.

EXAMPLES:

tall	taller	tallest
nice	nicer	nicest
simple	simpler	simplest
shiny	shinier	shiniest

Sometimes, *-er* and *-est* sound awkward with certain one- and two-syllable modifiers. In such instances, use *more* and *most*. Your ear will tell you which method sounds better. Try, for example, using *-er* and *-est* to form the comparative and superlative degrees of the following modifiers. Notice how awkward they would sound.

EXAMPLES:

lost	more lost	most lost
famous	more famous	most famous
obese	more obese	most obese
pungent	more pungent	most pungent

Regardless of the number of syllables, adverbs ending in *-ly* always form their comparative and superlative degrees with *more* and *most*.

EXAMPLES:

justly	more justly	most justly
evenly	more evenly	most evenly

With modifiers of three or more syllables, there is no choice in forming the comparative and superlative degrees. You must use *more* and *most*.

Use *more* and *most* to form the comparative and superlative degrees of all modifiers of three or more syllables.

EXAMPLES:

regular	more regular	most regular
problematic	more problematic	most problematic
independently	more independently	most independently

NOTE ABOUT COMPARISONS WITH *LESS* AND *LEAST*:   *Less* and *least*, the opposite of *more* and *most*, are also used to form the comparative and superlative degrees of most modifiers.

EXAMPLES: tall   less tall   least tall
            hopeless   less hopeless   least hopeless

EXERCISE B: Forming Regular Comparative and Superlative Degrees. In each of the following groups are three sentences. The first sentence, which is complete, has a modifier in the positive degree. The two sentences that follow need to be completed with comparative and superlative forms of the same modifier. Copy all three sentences in each group onto your paper, filling in the correct forms.

EXAMPLE: My mother is beautiful.
           My older sister is even more beautiful.
           My youngest sister is the most beautiful of all.

1. Baseball is exciting to watch.
   Football is _more exciting_ than baseball.
   Hockey, however, is the _most exciting_ of all.
2. Television is an informative news medium.
   Newspapers, in my opinion, are _more informative_.
   Many think, however, that weekly journals are the _most informative_.
3. Rice is not as fattening as bread.
   Chicken is even _less fattening_.
   Green vegetables, of course, are the _least fattening_.
4. Yesterday, the weather was cold.
   Today, the temperature is five degrees _colder_.
   Tomorrow may be the _coldest_ day of the month.
5. This fabric is unusually light.
   My new blouse is even _lighter_.
   My favorite scarf is the _lightest_.
6. Chicago is a popular exhibition center.
   New York is even _more popular_.
   Miami may be the _most popular_ of all.
7. Bread is a nutritious food.
   Enriched cereal may be even _more nutritious_.
   Wheat germ is perhaps the _most nutritious_.
8. Allison is an impressive speaker.
   Kathy is _more impressive_ most of the time.
   Mary Elizabeth is by far the _most impressive_.

9. My sister is <u>hungry</u>.
   Mother seems even __*hungrier*__ .
   Father is always the __*hungriest*__ .
10. Bus transportation is <u>fast</u>.
   Train transportation is even __*faster*__ .
   Flying, of course, is the __*fastest*__ by far.

■ Irregular Forms

A few commonly used adjectives and adverbs form their comparative and superlative degrees in unpredictable ways.

The irregular comparative and superlative forms of certain adjectives and adverbs must be memorized.

It is important to memorize the irregular forms in the following chart since these modifiers are frequently used in everyday speech and writing.

IRREGULAR MODIFIERS		
Positive	**Comparative**	**Superlative**
bad	worse	worst
badly	worse	worst
far	farther	farthest
far	further	furthest
good	better	best
ill	worse	worst
late	later	last *or* latest
little (amount)	less	least
many	more	most
much	more	most
well	better	best

NOTE ABOUT DOUBLE COMPARISONS: Do not add both *-er* and *more (less)* or *-est* and *most (least)* to the same modifier. One or the other is sufficient. Moreover, never add any of these endings or words to the *irregular* forms. They are not needed.

INCORRECT: That race care is *more faster* than the others.

CORRECT: That race car is *faster* than the others.

INCORRECT: This pudding is the *least smoothest* I've ever tasted.

CORRECT: This pudding is the *least smooth* I've ever tasted.

INCORRECT: John's stereo is *more better* than mine.

CORRECT: John's stereo is *better* than mine.

INCORRECT: The outpost is at the *most farthest* point on the map.

CORRECT: The outpost is at the *farthest* point on the map.

EXERCISE C: Forming Irregular Comparative and Superlative Degrees.
This exercise is similar to Exercise B. In this exercise, however, all the modifiers are irregular. Follow the same directions.

1. Verdi's *Macbeth* is a good opera.
   His *Rigoletto* is considered even _____better_____ .
   Of course, *Otello* is accepted as one of his _____best_____ .
2. Grandmother was ill months ago.
   She was _____worse_____ last week.
   This is the _____worst_____ I've seen her.
3. I did badly on the PSAT's.
   My neighbor did even _____worse_____ .
   My best friend did the _____worst_____ of all.
4. We have many books at home.
   Our school library has _____more_____ books.
   The public library has the _____most_____ in town.
5. The caffeine in soda is bad for many people.
   The caffeine in tea is even _____worse_____ .
   The caffeine in coffee is the _____worst_____ .
6. In my opinion Glenn will go far.
   Janet will go even _____farther_____ .
   José, however, will go the _____farthest_____ of all.
7. Richard Tucker was a good tenor.
   Jan Peerce was even _____better_____ .
   Caruso was the _____best_____ tenor of all.
8. This is a late version of the recording.
   I know that this is a _____later_____ version.
   Here right out of the carton is the _____latest_____ .
9. I have little interest in pop music.
   I have _____less_____ interest, however, in jazz.
   I find opera the _____least_____ interesting of all.
10. The lawn needs much care.
    The flower garden needs _____more_____ attention than the lawn does.
    The vegetable garden, however, takes the _____most_____ time.

Application: Correcting Faulty Degrees. Twenty of the following sentences contain double or awkward comparisons. Five are correct. If the sentence is correct, write *correct* on your paper. If not, write a correct version of the sentence.

1. My sister is ~~more~~ happier than she has ever been.
2. He is undoubtedly the least impressive doctor I know. *C*
3. My friend described the ~~most~~ weirdest adventure.
4. She is ~~more~~ worse today than she has ever been.
5. A ~~more~~ handsomer actor she had never seen. *or more handsome*
6. One of the finest performers of all is Laurence Olivier. *C*
7. My sister is the ~~talentedest~~ person I know. *most talented*
8. He is the ~~least luckiest~~ of all the businessmen. *least lucky*
9. Is this television ~~more~~ costlier? *or more costly*
10. The quarterback is the ~~frightenedest~~ of all. *most frightened*
11. I've never heard ~~an excitinger~~ story. *a more exciting*
12. His wrist is more swollen now than it was yesterday. *C*
13. She is the most ~~willingest~~ worker in the campaign.
14. Big Bill Russell may have been the ~~bestest~~ center of all time.
15. She is the ~~most shortest~~ of the two girls. *shorter*
16. Who in your opinion was the ~~more~~ better center fielder, Mantle or Mays?
17. This is a ~~more~~ later edition than the other.
18. Grandmother is ~~less happier~~ than a week ago. *less happy*
19. This is the ~~bestest~~ time I've ever had.
20. My uncle is friendlier than my aunt. *C*
21. The Rolling Stones are ~~talenteder~~ than The Who. *more talented*
22. Of the two brothers, he is the ~~childisher~~. *more childish*
23. *Die Fledermaus* has the most delightful music of all Strauss's operas. *C*
24. Is San Francisco or Los Angeles the ~~more~~ warmer in January?
25. Willa Cather was a ~~more~~ better writer than Edith Wharton.

Clear Comparisons 12.2

Speakers and writers sometimes have problems with comparisons. These problems usually are of three types: using the comparative or superlative degree incorrectly, comparing unrelated things or ideas, and comparing items illogically. This section will illustrate some poor comparisons and show you how to make them clear and exact.

■ Using Comparative and Superlative Forms in Comparisons

The basic rule of comparison has two parts.

Use the comparative degree to compare *two* persons, places, things, or ideas. Use the superlative degree to compare *three or more* persons, places, things, or ideas.

Specific numbers need not be mentioned in making comparisons. Instead, the entire sentence should be phrased in a way that indicates whether you are comparing two items or three or more items.

COMPARATIVE: In humid weather an air conditioner is *more effective* than an electric fan.

My report is *more detailed* than his.

The hotel is considerably *nearer* than the cottages.

SUPERLATIVE: He wants to take you to the *most expensive* restaurant in the city.

I like Denmark the *best* of all the European nations.

This hospital has the *largest* clinic in the state.

In the first set of examples, notice the *two* items being compared: an air conditioner and an electric fan; one report and another; a hotel and a group of cottages. In the second set, the superlative form indicates more than two items are being compared: one restaurant to all others in a city; one nation to all other European nations; one clinic to all others in a state.

EXERCISE A: **Using Comparative and Superlative Forms Correctly.** Write the correct comparative or superlative form for each of the following sentences on your paper.

1. Boston is perhaps the (more, <u>most</u>) historic of all cities in the United States.
2. His condition is (<u>poorer</u>, poorest) this week than last.
3. Which of the triplets is the (prettier, <u>prettiest</u>)?
4. Mrs. Willis gave him a (<u>better</u>, best) introduction than her.
5. This is the (less, <u>least</u>) I can do for you.

6. Which of the three cars is the (cheaper, cheapest)?
7. She is (more, most) willing to help than I.
8. Is this the (worse, worst) case you have seen?
9. Of the two brothers, which is the (faster, fastest)?
10. She is the (more, most) able legislator in the House of Representatives.
11. In some features this camera is (best, better) than that one.
12. The museum is the (better, best) tourist attraction in the city.
13. Marianne is the (older, oldest) of the two sisters.
14. I feel that *My Ántonia* is the (better, best) book Willa Cather ever wrote.
15. This scenery is the (more, most) dramatic in the North.
16. He is the (more, most) capable hair stylist I know.
17. Who was the (greater, greatest) of all Presidents?
18. Of Macbeth and Lady Macbeth, who is the (stronger, strongest) character?
19. In many ways she is the (warmer, warmest) person on the staff.
20. Who is the (more, most) talented musician in that string quartet?

■ Balanced Comparisons

Generally, you should have little difficulty in developing sentences with proper comparative and superlative forms. At times, however, especially when you are in a hurry, you may inadvertently compare two or more unrelated items. It is necessary then to rephrase the sentence so that the comparison is properly balanced.

Make sure that your sentences compare only items of a similar kind.

Because an unbalanced comparison is illogical, it may be unintentionally humorous. For instance, in the first sentence in the following examples, the size of one animal's brain is being compared to another entire animal. In the second unbalanced sentence the meaning is cloudy because the sentence's structure matches *speed* with *air*.

UNBALANCED: A dolphin's *brain* is bigger than a *shark*.

BALANCED: A dolphin's *brain* is bigger than a *shark's*.

UNBALANCED: The *speed* of sound through dry air is greater than humid *air.*

BALANCED: The *speed* of sound through dry air is greater than the *speed* of sound through humid air.

Always check your comparisons for balance so that your writing will clearly express the relationships you intend.

EXERCISE B: Making Balanced Comparisons. Rewrite each of the following sentences to correct the poorly balanced comparison. *Errors underlined. Revisions will vary; samples given.*

1. Aren't my new pants more attractive than Jacqueline?
2. The four-cylinder engine in the sedan is more powerful than the station wagon. *the engine in the station wagon*
3. Trish's debating record is better than Mary. *Mary's*
4. The motor in my electric typewriter is quieter than your typewriter. *the one in your typewriter.*
5. Are the vitamins in a lemon better than an orange?
6. My grandfather's stamp collection is in better condition than my uncle. *that of my uncle*
7. At the meeting Bruce's presentation was better than Charles. *Charles's*
8. The sails of a clipper ship were stronger than a schooner.
9. A larger orchestra is needed to perform a Bruckner symphony than Haydn. *one by Haydn*
10. An infection of the liver is as dangerous as the kidneys. *an infection of the kidneys*

1. Jacqueline's   5. those in an orange   8. those of a schooner

■ The Use of *Other* and *Else* in Comparisons

A common error is to compare something with itself.

When comparing one of a group with the rest of the group, make sure that your sentence contains the word *other* or the word *else.*

Unless you add *other* or *else* in this type of comparison, you create an illogical situation. In the first set of examples, the *Beatles* as a group must be compared with *other* groups, not *all* groups, a category that includes the Beatles themselves. In the second set, *Rosa* as one employee in a company must be compared with everyone *else* in that company, not with *everyone,* which includes herself.

ILLOGICAL: The Beatles were *greater than any* group.

LOGICAL: The Beatles were *greater than any other* group.

ILLOGICAL: Rosa has served *more years than anyone* in the company.

LOGICAL: Rosa has served *more years than anyone else* in the company.

EXERCISE C: Using *Other* and *Else* in Comparisons. Rewrite each of the following sentences to correct the illogical comparisons.

1. Marguerite Young's *Miss MacIntosh, My Darling* is longer than any˄American novel. *other*
2. My friend Pepe plays soccer better than anyone˄I know. *else*
3. Our apartment is longer than any˄in the building. *other*
4. Mrs. Thalenburg said my term paper was more carefully researched than every˄student's in the class. *other*
5. Your contribution to the fund was more than any˄we received. *other*
6. My room is colder than any˄in the house. *other*
7. Eric skated faster than everyone˄in the competition. *else*
8. Robert Frost's poetry is probably more widely read than any˄American poet's. *other*
9. Mount Everest is higher than any mountain. *other*
10. This brand of writing paper contains at least as much cotton fiber as any˄on the market. *other*

APPLICATION: Writing Clear Comparisons. Write an original sentence for each of the following comparisons. Check to make sure that the comparison is balanced and logical.
Answers will vary; sample given for first one.

EXAMPLE   Compare the weather in two states.

I like California's dry summers more than the humid summers we had in Georgia.

1. Compare the leading characters of two television comedies.
2. Compare the writing styles of two authors whom you have read recently.
3. Compare the personalities of two pet dogs (or cats, birds).
4. Compare the service at three restaurants.
5. Compare one area of your city or town to all the others.

1. I like Ann Romano's humor better than Archie Bunker's.

Chapter 13

Special Problems in Usage

In this unit so far, the usage of verbs, pronouns, adjectives, and adverbs has been presented. One chapter has also dealt with agreement. There are still, however, other aspects of usage with which you should be familiar. In this chapter you will learn about negative words and certain differences between standard and nonstandard usage as well as between preferred and less acceptable usage. Additional problems involve words that are confused and misused because they have similar meanings or spellings.

By this time you may have mastered the skills needed to use most of these words correctly. If you have not, you will have an opportunity here to learn how to avoid a number of important usage errors. You will want to refer to this chapter periodically for help, particularly to Section 13.2, which offers an alphabetical list of problem words.

13.1 Negative Sentences

There are many negative words in English: *no, not, never, nothing,* and *nobody,* among others. At one time, it was correct to use as many negative words as possible in a sentence. It was correct, for example, to say, "Father *didn't* tell *nobody nothing.*" As time passed, this usage changed. Now, one negative is considered sufficient to deny something. Today, the sentence above would be phrased in one of two ways: "Father *didn't* tell anybody anything" or "Father told *nobody* anything."

■ Double Negatives

Some people still use too many negatives. A sentence with a *double negative* contains two negative words when only one is needed.

Do not write sentences with **double negatives**.

The first sentence in each of the following examples has a double negative. Each has a negative contraction as well as another negative word or expression. Notice also that each faulty sentence can be corrected in two ways.

DOUBLE NEGATIVE: Bill *hasn't* invited *no one.*

CORRECT: Bill has invited *no one.*

Bill *hasn't* invited anyone.

DOUBLE NEGATIVE: As guests, the girls *shouldn't* bring *nothing.*

CORRECT: As guests, the girls should bring *nothing.*

As guests, the girls *shouldn't* bring anything.

EXERCISE A: Avoiding Double Negatives. Rewrite each of the following sentences to eliminate the double negative.
Answers may vary; samples given.
1. Our new car isn't no gas guzzler. *is*
2. He hasn't eaten none of his food. *any*
3. That lady hasn't never purchased anything in our store. *has*
4. She couldn't have told them nothing important. *anything*
5. No one in the office reviewed none of the reports. *any*
6. You shouldn't ask nobody for directions. *anybody*
7. Nobody said nothing to me about a quiz today. *anything*
8. I don't need no money from you. *any*
9. She hadn't never told us what she did in those two years. *had*
10. Chinese vegetables shouldn't never be cooked too long. *should*

■ Three Methods of Using Negative Words Correctly

Negative sentences are formed correctly in one of three ways. Learn these and avoid using double negatives with each type.

The Use of a Single Negative Word. The simplest and most common way to make a statement negative is with a single negative word, such as *no, not, none, nothing, never, nobody,* or *nowhere,* or with the contraction *-n't* added to a helping verb. Avoid using any two of these together in one clause.

DOUBLE NEGATIVE: He *hasn't never* told us the truth.

CORRECT: He has *never* told us the truth.

He *hasn't* ever told us the truth.

DOUBLE NEGATIVE: She *wouldn't* give them *no* contribution.

CORRECT: She *wouldn't* give them any contribution.

She would give them *no* contribution.

The Use of *But* as a Negative Word. *But* sometimes has a negative meaning. In this sense it should not be used with another negative word.

DOUBLE NEGATIVE: He *didn't* offer *but* one reasonable excuse.

CORRECT: He offered *but* one reasonable excuse.

He offered only one reasonable excuse.

The Use of *Barely, Hardly,* and *Scarcely.* These three words also have a negative sense. They should not be used with other negative words.

DOUBLE NEGATIVE: She *wasn't barely* able to recognize him.

CORRECT: She was *barely* able to recognize him.

She almost *wasn't* able to recognize him.

DOUBLE NEGATIVE: The driver *couldn't hardly* see the sign on the bridge.

CORRECT: The driver could *hardly* see the sign on the bridge.

The driver almost *couldn't* see the sign on the bridge.

DOUBLE NEGATIVE: He *hadn't scarcely* uttered a word when she began to cry.

CORRECT: He had *scarcely* uttered a word when she began to cry.

He *hadn't* uttered more than a word when she began to cry.

NOTE ABOUT NEGATIVE WORDS AND NEGATIVE PREFIXES: A negative word *can* be used correctly with a word that has a negative prefix, such as *in-* (*in*adequate), *un-* (*un*willing), or *non-* (*non*existent). The effect is usually one of understatement.

EXAMPLE: The pianist is *not un*willing to perform her new work.

This sentence implies that the pianist is not only "not unwilling" to perform but is probably very eager to play.

EXERCISE B: Choosing the Correct Form. Write the word that completes each sentence without creating a double negative.

1. You (<u>can</u>, can't) hardly mean what you say.
2. I don't owe my parents (nothing, <u>anything</u>).
3. My sister (<u>has</u>, hasn't) reported nobody.
4. There (<u>is</u>, isn't) but one possible explanation.
5. He shouldn't have told (<u>anyone</u>, no one) about the trip.
6. Don't you want (<u>anything</u>, nothing) from the bazaar?
7. Ann (had, <u>hadn't</u>) revealed the strategy to anybody.
8. The counselors did not have (<u>any</u>, no) better suggestions.
9. I (would, <u>wouldn't</u>) ever agree to such a plan.
10. We haven't traveled (<u>anywhere</u>, nowhere) in South America.
11. Can't you (<u>ever</u>, never) do anything right?
12. There (hadn't, <u>had</u>) been but two possibilities.
13. This old jalopy (<u>is</u>, isn't) never going to run properly.
14. I (do, <u>don't</u>) take the bus to school anymore.
15. Of course, she doesn't expect (<u>anything</u>, nothing).
16. On weeknights we never go (nowhere, <u>anywhere</u>).
17. The doctor (isn't, <u>is</u>) suggesting but one new treatment.
18. Weren't you (<u>ever</u>, never) able to contact him?
19. We (do, <u>don't</u>) have any plans for this evening.
20. They (<u>have</u>, haven't) never attended a concert in the city.

APPLICATION: Writing Negative Sentences. Write sentences of your own using each of the following phrases. Avoid using double negatives.
Answers will vary; samples given for first two.

1. was hardly ever
2. hasn't been anywhere
3. shouldn't ever give
4. want never
5. has but one
6. couldn't travel anywhere
7. isn't any
8. had scarcely arrived
9. is not common
10. offered nothing
11. are not inaccurate
12. can't ever make anything

1. Karen was hardly ever late for school.
2. Luigi hasn't been anywhere outside of New Jersey.

13. would barely come to
14. has not explained
15. never agreed to
16. had brought none of

17. would give no
18. has nothing to do with
19. has visited nowhere
20. will not be unopposed

13.2 Sixty Common Usage Problems

Even if you have mastered most of the usage skills in this unit, you will still encounter miscellaneous problems in usage. People commonly confuse many of the words in the following listing because of their similar spellings or similar meanings. Other terms or expressions in this section should never be used in standard English.

One way to use this miscellany of common problems is to go through it systematically, studying all the entries. Your teacher may want to assign portions of the section for you to study and later discuss in class. A second way to use this miscellany is as a reference tool. Once you are familiar with its contents, you will want to check individual words or word groups as you need them in your work.

Information that does not appear here may be found in other parts of this book. Therefore, if the miscellany does not help you with the problem you are trying to solve, check the index at the back of the book.

(1) *A* **and** *An.* The article *a* is used before consonant sounds; *an,* before vowel sounds. When using *a* and *an* before words beginning with *h, o,* or *u,* check to make sure you have chosen the correct article. Sometimes these three letters have consonant sounds; at other times they have vowel sounds.

CONSONANT SOUNDS: a *h*istory book (*h*-sound)

a *o*ne-time opportunity (*w*-sound)

a *u*nanimous decision (*y*-sound)

VOWEL SOUNDS: an *h*onor society (no *h*-sound)

an *o*nly child (*o*-sound)

an *u*gly wound (*u*-sound)

(2) *Accept* **and** *Except.* The spellings of these words are often confused. *Accept,* a verb, means "to receive." *Except,* a preposition, means "other than" or "leaving out."

VERB: We *accept* your offer to mediate the dispute.

PREPOSITION: All the singers attended *except* the tenor.

(3) Accuse and Allege. Learn to distinguish the meanings of these words. *Accuse* means "to blame" or "to bring a charge against." *Allege* means "to claim something that has not yet been proved."

EXAMPLES: The state has *accused* them of murder.

The defense will try to prove that the *alleged* crime never actually occurred.

(4) Adapt and Adopt. The meanings of these verbs are often confused. *Adapt* means "to change." *Adopt* meants "to take as one's own."

EXAMPLES: John Lanchbery *adapts* and arranges the music of others.

In the play he *adopted* an Irish accent.

(5) Advice and Advise. Check the spellings of the two forms of this word. *Advice*, a noun, means "an opinion." *Advise*, a verb, means "to give an opinion to."

NOUN: I will accept your *advice*.

VERB: His doctor *advised* him to lose weight.

(6) Affect and Effect. These words are often confused. *Affect*, almost always a verb, means "to influence" or "to bring about a change in." *Effect* may be used as a noun or as a verb. As a noun, it means "result." As a verb, it means "to bring about" or "to cause." The noun use is more common.

VERB: I was deeply *affected* by her tribute.

NOUN: Students are warned about the *effects* of alcohol.

VERB: The new managers *effected* important changes in the operation of the business.

(7) Ain't. Avoid the use of *ain't*. Originally a contraction of *am not*, it is not considered acceptable standard English.

NONSTANDARD: Your friend *ain't* prepared to speak.

CORRECT: Your friend *isn't* prepared to speak.

(8) *Allot, A Lot, and Alot.* *Allot,* a verb, means "to divide in parts" or "to give out in shares." *A lot* is an informal expression meaning "a great many." It should never be spelled as one word.

VERB: Each of us has been *allotted* ten dollars to spend at the fair.

INCORRECT: We visited *alot* of state parks last summer.

CORRECT: We visited *a lot* of state parks last summer.

(9) *All Ready and Already.* *All ready,* two separate words used as an adjective, is an expression meaning "ready." *Already,* an adverb, means "even now" or "by or before this time."

ADJECTIVE: They have been *all ready* to leave for an hour.

ADVERB: He has *already* reached Washington.

(10) *All Right and Alright.* You will occasionally see this expression spelled *alright.* The preferred spelling is still the two-word form.

PREFERRED: Grandfather's allergies are *all right* today.

LESS ACCEPTABLE: The movie was *alright.*

(11) *All Together and Altogether.* Both adverbs, these words have different meanings. *All together,* two words, means "together as a single group." *Altogether* means "completely" or "in all."

EXAMPLES: Let's sing the school song *all together.*

We were *altogether* disappointed with the play.

(12) *Among and Between.* Notice the difference in the use of these prepositions. *Among* always implies three or more. *Between* is usually used with two things only.

EXAMPLES: *Among* my five friends, I prefer Louise.

The argument is *between* Mary and me.

(13) *Anxious.* This adjective implies uneasiness, worry, or fear. Do not use it as a substitute for *eager.*

AMBIGUOUS: I am *anxious* to go to the concert tonight.

CLEAR: I am *eager* to go to the concert tonight.

CLEAR: I am *anxious* about the crowds that will be at the concert.

(14) Anywhere, Everywhere, Nowhere, and Somewhere. Never end these adverbs with an -*s*.

INCORRECT: The baby is *nowheres* in sight.

CORRECT: The baby is *nowhere* in sight.

(15) As To. This combination is considered awkward. Either eliminate it or use *about* or *of* instead.

AWKWARD: I cannot guess *as to* where he went.

CORRECT: I cannot guess where he went.

CORRECT: I have no idea *of* where he went.

(16) At. Do not use *at* after *where*. Simply eliminate it.

NONSTANDARD: We're lost and don't know *where* we are *at*.

CORRECT: We're lost and don't know *where* we are.

(17) A While and Awhile. *A while* is an article and a noun. The expression is usually used after the preposition *for*. *Awhile*, an adverb, in itself means "for a while."

NOUN: Come talk with me for *a while*.

ADVERB: Let's sit *awhile* and talk.

(18) Because. *Because* should not be used after *the reason*. Use one or the other.

NONSTANDARD: *The reason* for his happiness is *because* he was accepted at Julliard.

CORRECT: He is happy *because* he was accepted at Julliard.

   The reason for his happiness is that he was accepted at Julliard.

(19) Being That and Being As. Do not use either expression. Use *because* or *since* instead.

NONSTANDARD: *Being that* (or *as*) I hoped for a better score, I took the SAT's again.

CORRECT: *Because* (or *since*) I hoped for a better score, I took the SAT's again.

(20) *Beside* and *Besides*. These are *not* forms of the same word. *Beside* means "close to" or "at the side of." *Besides* means "in addition to."

EXAMPLES: The pool is *beside* the house.

Besides my parents, my aunt will attend the ceremony.

(21) *Bring* and *Take*. These words have distinct meanings. *Bring* means "to carry from a distant place to a nearer one." *Take* means the opposite: "to carry something from a near place to a more distant one."

EXAMPLES: *Bring* those papers to me.

Take these reports with you to the president's office.

(22) *Burst*, *Bust*, and *Busted*. Despite frequent use, *bust* and *busted* are nonstandard verb forms. The present, past, and past participle of the verb *burst* are all *burst*.

NONSTANDARD: Don't *bust* the blister.

She *busted* the cellophane wrapper.

CORRECT: The doctor *will burst* the blister.

Why *did* you *burst* the cellophane wrapper?

(23) *Can't Help But*. This is another nonstandard expression. Use *can't help* plus a gerund instead.

NONSTANDARD: He *can't help but* want another chance.

CORRECT: He *can't help wanting* another chance.

(24) *Different From* and *Different Than*. *Different from* is preferred to *different than*.

PREFERRED: His camera is much *different from* Arlene's.

LESS ACCEPTABLE: His camera is much *different than* Arlene's.

(25) Doesn't and Don't. *Doesn't* is the correct form for the third person singular (he, she, it *doesn't*). *Don't* is used with all other forms.

NONSTANDARD:　He *don't* intend to go.

It *don't* seem right.

The air conditioner *don't* work.

CORRECT:　He *doesn't* intend to go.

It *doesn't* seem right.

The air conditioner *doesn't* work.

(26) Done. Done, the past participle of *do*, should always follow a helping verb.

NONSTANDARD:　She *done* what was expected of her.

CORRECT:　She *has done* what was expected of her.

(27) Due To. *Due to* means "caused by." Use it only to begin a phrase that clearly and logically modifies a noun. If you are not sure you are correct, try using another expression, such as *because of.*

NONSTANDARD:　*Due to* a computer error, he received two checks.

CORRECT:　His receiving two checks was *due to* a computer error.

CORRECT:　*Because of* a computer error, he received two checks.

(28) Due To The Fact That. This is an awkward, wordy expression. Use *because* or *since* instead.

PREFERRED:　*Since* he had a camera, he was designated official photographer.

LESS ACCEPTABLE:　*Due to the fact that* he had a camera, he was designated official photographer.

(29) Emigrate and Immigrate. These words have opposite meanings. *Emigrate* means "to move *out of* a country." *Immigrate* means "to move *into* a country."

EXAMPLE:　Heidi *emigrated* from Austria in 1934. After many years she finally *immigrated* to Israel.

(30) *Enthusiastic* and *Enthused*. Avoid using *enthused;* it is nonstandard. Simply replace it with *enthusiastic*.

NONSTANDARD: I am *enthused* about going to Nantucket.

CORRECT: I am *enthusiastic* about going to Nantucket.

(31) *Etc.* Since *etc.* is an abbreviation for the Latin expression *et cetera*, meaning "and so forth," it is repetitive to write "and etc." In most formal writing, *etc.* should not be used at all.

INCORRECT: He told us about his stamps, his coins, his clocks, *and etc.*

CORRECT: He told us about his stamps, his coins, his clocks, *etc.*

FORMAL: He told us about his stamps, his coins, his clocks, and his other collections.

(32) *Farther* and *Further*. *Farther* is used to refer to distance. *Further* means "to a greater degree or extent" or "additional."

EXAMPLES: The college is *farther* away than I would like.

I want to develop your ideas *further*.

She expects a *further* explanation.

(33) *Fewer* and *Less*. *Fewer* is used with objects that can be counted. *Less* is used with qualities or quantities that cannot be counted.

EXAMPLES: *fewer* ships, *fewer* newspapers, *fewer* calories

less excitement, *less* water, *less* supervision

(34) *Former* and *Latter*. *Former* is used to refer to the first of two previously mentioned items. *Latter* refers to the second of the two.

EXAMPLE: We visited Mexico City and Acapulco. The *former* is a bustling city; the *latter* is a modern seaside resort.

(35) *Good* and *Well*. *Good*, an adjective, should not be used after an action verb. Use *well*, an adverb, instead.

NONSTANDARD: Charles drove *good* on his driver's test.

CORRECT: Charles drove *well* on his driver's test.

(36) *Healthy* **and** *Healthful.* People are *healthy;* things are *healthful.*

PREFERRED: Limiting your intake of bread and cake is *healthful.*

LESS ACCEPTABLE: Too much bread and cake is not *healthy* for you.

(37) *In* **and** *Into.* *In* refers to position, whereas *into* suggests motion.

POSITION: The children stood ankle deep *in* the water.

MOTION: Sean ran down the beach and dived *into* (not *in*) the surf.

(38) *Irregardless.* Avoid this word. Use *regardless* instead.

NONSTANDARD: I cannot agree, *irregardless* of her plea.

CORRECT: I cannot agree, *regardless* of her plea.

(39) *Kind Of* **and** *Sort Of.* These expressions should not be used to mean "rather" or "somewhat."

NONSTANDARD: I am *kind of* disappointed.

CORRECT: I am *rather* disappointed.

(40) *Learn* **and** *Teach.* Do not confuse the meanings of these words. *Learn* means "to acquire knowledge." *Teach* means "to give knowledge to."

EXAMPLES: I *learn* many things by myself.

Will you *teach* (not *learn*) me how to drive?

(41) *Leave* **and** *Let.* Do not reverse the meanings of these words. *Leave* means "to allow to remain." *Let* means "to permit."

NONSTANDARD: *Let* him alone in the room.

CORRECT: *Leave* him alone in the room.

NONSTANDARD: *Leave* us try once more.

CORRECT: *Let* us try once more.

(42) Lie and Lay. *Lie* means "to recline." Its principal parts are *lie, lying, lay,* and *lain.* It is never followed by a direct object. *Lay* means "to put or set down." Its principal parts are *lay, laying, laid,* and *laid,* and it is usually followed by a direct object.

LIE: I will *lie* down after I finish the work.

I *lay* down yesterday for a short nap.

I have *lain* here thinking about the party for hours.

LAY: *Lay* the tools on the bench.

He *laid* everything we needed in the car this morning.

Where have you *laid* the keys?

(43) Like, As, and As If. *Like* is a preposition. *As* and *as if* are conjunctions that begin subordinate clauses.

PREPOSITION: She drives *like* a race-car driver.

CONJUNCTION: She drives *as* (not *like*) a race-car driver would.

CONJUNCTION: She drives *as if* (not *like*) she were a race-car driver.

(44) Of. Do not use *of* after *should, would,* or *could.* Use *have* instead. *Of* after *outside, inside, off,* or *atop* is also undesirable in formal writing. Simply eliminate it.

NONSTANDARD: She would *of* wanted that role.

CORRECT: She would *have* wanted that role.

PREFERRED: The jewels were hidden *inside* a toy doll.

LESS ACCEPTABLE: The jewels were hidden *inside of* a toy doll.

(45) Plenty. *Plenty,* a noun, does not mean "very." It should be followed by *of,* as in "plenty of time."

NONSTANDARD: She was *plenty* disgusted.

CORRECT: She was very digusted.

CORRECT: She had *plenty of* time.

(46) Rise and Raise. *Rise* means "to move upward" or "to be increased." It is never followed by a direct object. *Raise* means "to lift," "to increase," or "to grow." It is usually followed by a direct object.

RISE: The sun *rises* in the east every day.

RAISE: The Cotters *raise* corn in their back field.

(47) Shall and Will. In most instances these helping verbs are interchangeable. *Shall* is preferred in questions asking for permission or agreement.

EXAMPLES: *Shall* I ask him for his autograph?

He *will* open the package later.

(48) Sit and Set. *Sit* means "to be seated." Its principal parts are *sit, sitting, sat,* and *sat.* It is never followed by a direct object. *Set* means "to put (something) in a certain place." Its principal parts are *set, setting, set,* and *set,* and it is usually followed by a direct object.

SIT: He *sits* in the front row.

He *sat* in the third row last year.

He has never *sat* in the last row.

SET: *Set* the forks on the table.

They *set* off for the Far West.

We have *set* a date for the rally.

(49) So. Do not use *so* to begin a sentence. It can be used, of course, as a conjunction.

STANDARD: Be quiet *so* I can study.

NONSTANDARD: On the first day Gawain failed. *So* the next day he tried again.

CORRECT: On the first day Gawain failed. The next day he tried once again.

(50) Than and Then. Use *than* in comparisons. *Then,* an adverb, usually refers to time.

EXAMPLES: Billy is more dependable *than* Glenn.

Having finished her speech, Ellen *then* presented the award.

(51) That, Which, and Who. Learn to use these relative pronouns properly. *That* can refer to either people or things. *Who* refers only to people. *Which* should be used to refer only to things.

PEOPLE: She is the only council member *who* (or *that*) was re-elected.

THINGS: The document *that* (or *which*) was lost was finally recovered.

(52) Their, There, and They're. These three words are sometimes confused. *Their,* a possessive pronoun, always modifies a noun (*their* hats, *their* ideas). *There* can be used either as an expletive at the beginning of a sentence or as an adverb. *They're* is a contraction for *they are.*

PRONOUN: We lost *their* immigration papers.

EXPLETIVE: *There* are three chickens in the basket.

ADVERB: The monument will be erected *there.*

CONTRACTION: *They're* ready to leave now.

(53) Them. Do not use *them* as a substitute for *those.*

NONSTANDARD: Give me *them* pliers.

CORRECT: Give me *those* pliers.

(54) This Here and That There. These are nonstandard expressions and should not be used. Simply leave out *here* and *there.*

NONSTANDARD: *This here* car is too expensive.

CORRECT: *This* car is too expensive.

(55) To, Too, and Two. Do not confuse the spellings of these words. *To,* a preposition, begins a phrase or an infinitive. *Too,* an adverb, modifies adjectives and other adverbs. *Two* is a number.

PREPOSITION: *to* the house, *to* them

INFINITIVE: *to* eat, *to* speak

ADVERB: *too* rich, *too* rapidly

NUMBER: *two* apples, *two* ships

(56) Unique. *Unique* means "one of a kind." Therefore, it is illogical to say *very unique, most unique,* or *extremely unique. Unique* by itself is enough.

NONSTANDARD: This is a *most unique* ring.

CORRECT: This is a *unique* ring.

(57) Ways. *Ways,* a plural noun, should not be used after the article *a.* Instead, use the singular noun *way.*

NONSTANDARD: The hikers have a great *ways* yet to go.

CORRECT: The hikers have a great *way* yet to go.

(58) When and Where. Do not use *when* or *where* directly after a linking verb.

NONSTANDARD: A new opportunity is *when* you can begin another career.

The discount store is *where* you can get a good buy.

CORRECT: A new opportunity will allow you to begin another career.

You can get a good buy at that discount store.

In addition, do not use *where* in place of *that.*

NONSTANDARD: Amy heard on TV *where* people are smoking less.

CORRECT: Amy heard on TV *that* people are smoking less.

(59) Win and **Beat.** *Win* means "to achieve victory in." *Beat* means "to overcome (an opponent)." Do not use *win* in place of *beat*.

INCORRECT: I *won* him again at table tennis.

CORRECT: I *beat* him again at table tennis.

(60) -wise. Do not create new words with this suffix.

PREFERRED: I did well *in school* last semester.

LESS ACCEPTABLE: *Schoolwise*, I did well last semester.

EXERCISE A: Avoiding Usage Problems (1–10).

Complete each of the following sentences with the correct expression. Try to complete the exercise without looking back in the book.

1. Unfortunately, I cannot (accept, except) your offer.
2. They were (already, all ready) to go when I arrived.
3. I am searching for (a, an) honorable solution to the problem.
4. We had (alot, a lot, allot) to eat at the picnic.
5. I hope that your mother will be (all right, alright).
6. The puppy has (already, all ready) ripped her new toy to shreds.
7. Who among them can (adopt, adapt) the play?
8. The stereo components are sold as (a, an) unit.
9. What is the (effect, affect) of the new medicine?
10. Such (advice, advise) is hardly ever helpful.
11. All of us (accept, except) Jon had a good time at the show.
12. There (ain't, isn't) a single reason for us to change our minds.
13. The Secretary of State had difficulty in (affecting, effecting) changes in the State Department.
14. An eyewitness (accused, alleged) him of the crime.
15. She (adapted, adopted) a peculiar accent after her stay in England.
16. Would you (advice, advise) him to see another doctor?
17. Coffee (affects, effects) my nerves.
18. We (accuse, allege) that they stole the typewriter.
19. She is (a, an) outstanding citizen.
20. How should we (a lot, allot, alot) the profits from the tag sale?

EXERCISE B: Avoiding Usage Problems (11–20). Complete each of the following sentences with the correct expression.

1. (Nowheres, <u>Nowhere</u>) will you get a better bargain.
2. I am (anxious, <u>eager</u>) to taste the pie you baked.
3. (Being as, <u>Since</u>) I agreed to serve, I have received several complaints.
4. (Between, <u>Among</u>) the three girls, I find Lisa the most sympathetic.
5. Do you really know where we (are at, <u>are</u>)?
6. During one ride at the amusement park, it seemed a ghost was sitting (<u>beside</u>, besides) us.
7. My teacher was (all together, <u>altogether</u>) satisfied with the paper.
8. We haven't heard (as to, <u>about</u>) her last adventure.
9. My wallet must be here (<u>somewhere</u>, somewheres).
10. His reason for failing is (because, <u>that</u>) he did not prepare for the test.
11. We swam (a while, <u>awhile</u>) and then cooked a barbecue.
12. There is a parking lot (besides, <u>beside</u>) the restaurant.
13. Working (altogether, <u>all together</u>), we should finish the job in an hour.
14. I found the rare stamp (<u>between</u>, among) the pages of an old book.
15. She invited no one from our class (beside, <u>besides</u>) you and me.
16. We were (<u>anxious</u>, eager) about how the strike would affect our vacation plans.
17. Rest for (<u>a while</u>, awhile) before you shovel any more snow.
18. I had to stay home (being that, <u>because</u>) I had no money.
19. Put the packages (<u>beside</u>, besides) the table.
20. Do you know anything (as to, <u>about</u>) his strange behavior?

EXERCISE C: Avoiding Usage Problems (21–30). Complete each of the following sentences with the correct expression.

1. Your stereo is much different (<u>from</u>, than) mine.
2. My sister just (don't, <u>doesn't</u>) agree with your decision.
3. (Bring, <u>Take</u>) these cards to the closet on the second floor.
4. (Due to the fact that, <u>Because</u>) he is ill, we had to postpone the meeting.
5. My mother (<u>burst</u>, busted) into the room and smiled.
6. I am (enthused, <u>enthusiastic</u>) about visiting Brazil next month.

7. Johnson's administration was considerably different (from, than) Eisenhower's.
8. When you come to my house this evening, (bring, take) your new record album.
9. My grandfather (immigrated, emigrated) from Poland more than fifty years ago.
10. I had to control myself so that I wouldn't (bust, burst) out laughing.
11. He (done, has done) as he was told.
12. (Due to, Because of) his absence, he was not paid this week.
13. I am late (due to the fact that, because) the train broke down.
14. I (doesn't, don't) know where she hid the presents.
15. The doctor (has done, done) everything possible.
16. I couldn't help (but cry, crying).
17. Your headaches may be (due to, because of) failing eyesight.
18. My father (immigrated, emigrated) to the United States in 1928.
19. I become (enthused, enthusiastic) whenever we start to rehearse a play.
20. It (don't, doesn't) seem possible that I could be wrong.

EXERCISE D: Avoiding Usage Problems (31–40). Complete each of the following sentences with the correct expression.

1. Mary Grace works (good, well) with the others in the class.
2. How much (farther, further) is the state park?
3. (Irregardless, Regardless) of your excuse, I am still angry.
4. Does he have (fewer, less) horses now than last year?
5. For my report I compared the agricultural methods of the United States and China. The (former, latter) I found has been making great advances since Mao Zedong's death.
6. Please purchase paper napkins, plastic spoons and forks, paper cups, (and etc., etc.)
7. The bus crashed (in, into) a telephone pole.
8. Will you (teach, learn) me how to play the guitar?
9. Wheat germ is considered (healthful, healthy) for you.
10. This milk is (sort of, somewhat) sour.
11. This cereal has (fewer, less) vitamins than the other.
12. Barbara was (kind of, rather) upset by the phone call.
13. I always do (good, well) in home economics.
14. I have decided to (learn, teach) myself to type.

15. Leave the ice cream (<u>in</u>, into) the freezer.
16. We went to the Bronx Zoo and the Botanical Gardens. At the (<u>former</u>, latter) we saw the new building in which special lighting allows the birds to be displayed without cages.
17. Because she exercises and watches her diet my grandmother is as (<u>healthy</u>, healthful) as a person half her age.
18. I feel (<u>good</u>, well) when I get high grades.
19. She has (fewer, <u>less</u>) free time now that she works after school.
20. Since I wasn't looking, I walked (in, <u>into</u>) the wall.

EXERCISE E: Avoiding Usage Problems (41–50). Complete each of the following sentences with the correct expression.

1. You should (of, <u>have</u>) reported the accident to the police.
2. We have been (<u>sitting</u>, setting) here since the office opened.
3. When he sneezes he sounds (like, <u>as if</u>) he is going to explode.
4. She plans to (<u>rise</u>, raise) at seven.
5. They are (lying, <u>laying</u>) a new sidewalk on our street.
6. (<u>Shall</u>, Will) we go on a picnic tomorrow if the weather is good?
7. (So when, <u>When</u>) he finally arrived all the food was gone.
8. You have been told twice to (<u>leave</u>, let) the dog alone.
9. I did (like, <u>as</u>) I was told to.
10. You should (<u>lie</u>, lay) down and rest.
11. Only (than, <u>then</u>) did Pharaoh give in to Moses' demands.
12. They (sat, <u>set</u>) the flowers in the vase.
13. A crow perched (<u>atop</u>, atop of) the tree.
14. The customer was (<u>very</u>, plenty) unhappy about the delay.
15. Why won't you (leave, <u>let</u>) me sit here in peace?
16. (So, <u>Then</u>) he made one more effort to see the parade.
17. The old traveler's face looked (<u>like</u>, as) a map of all his journeys.
18. Your impersonation could (of, <u>have</u>) fooled me.
19. The fox had (<u>lain</u>, laid) in the leaves for hours watching the hunters.
20. My brother is always hungrier (then, <u>than</u>) I.

EXERCISE F: Avoiding Usage Problems (51–60). Complete each of the following sentences with the correct expression.

1. The groundhog is (<u>there</u>, their, they're), in the vegetable garden.

2. I like (them, <u>those</u>) new shoes you are wearing.
3. The dean found (there, <u>their</u>) explanation hard to believe.
4. There are (to, too, <u>two</u>) ways to get to Copake from here.
5. Students (<u>who</u>, which) buy tickets now are eligible for a bonus.
6. A new job is (<u>the time when</u>, when) you can make a fresh start.
7. I am doing well this year (classwise, <u>in class</u>).
8. Flying on the Concorde is a (<u>unique</u>, most unique) experience.
9. The agent traveled a great (ways, <u>way</u>) to see you.
10. I think we can (win, <u>beat</u>) them in the second half of the game.
11. I read in this book (where, <u>that</u>) most sharks drown if they stop moving through the water.
12. (<u>That</u>, That there) restaurant serves the best steaks in town.
13. The ducks (<u>that</u>, who) were nesting near the pond didn't fly south last winter.
14. (<u>They're</u>, There) waiting for the bus on that road.
15. That custom sports car is (<u>unique</u>, more unique than any other).
16. (This here, <u>This</u>) book really is frightening.
17. Would you believe I have (won, <u>beaten</u>) him six times at chess?
18. She thinks she ate (to, <u>too</u>) much for lunch.
19. (Workwise, <u>At work</u>) I have been unusually successful.
20. We walked a long (<u>way</u>, ways) into the woods.

APPLICATION 1: Correcting Usage Problems. Fifteen of the following twenty sentences contain one error in usage. If a sentence is correct, write *correct* on your paper. Rewrite all of the other sentences, correcting all mistakes.
Revisions may vary; samples given.

1. Yesterday, I wanted ~~too~~ tell him the truth. *to*
2. ~~Due to the fact that~~ my father works for a dress manufacturing company, we asked him to buy the material wholesale. *Because*
3. My grandparents have been healthy for many years. *c*
4. She can't help ~~but want~~ another chance to make the cheering squad. *wanting*
5. Next, the villain ~~busted~~ into the room in a rage. *burst*
6. The matter was quickly settled ~~among~~ my brother and me. *between*
7. The inauguration of a President is ~~an~~ historical event. *a*
8. The ~~affect~~ of his loss destroyed his self-confidence. *effect*
9. ~~Sit~~ the glass to the right of the plate. *Set*

10. ~~Being that~~ you asked, I'll tell you my feelings about him. *Since*
11. Besides my brother and sister, only my mother wants to attend. *C*
12. ~~Their~~ are three boxes in the attic. *There*
13. ~~Partywise,~~ I have had my fill if you really want to know. *As for parties*
14. ~~So~~ she decided to apply for a job in another city.
15. Anywhere you go, you will find similar problems. *C*
16. If she were smart, she wouldn't ~~of~~ made up an excuse. *have*
17. I like rich chocolate cake ~~like~~ I've often told you. *as*
18. They're apparently lost in the wilderness. *C*
19. Everyone except them passed the exams. *C*
20. I opened canned fish, kidney beans, two types of soups, ~~and etc.~~ *and other items*

APPLICATION 2: Using Expressions Correctly. Write an original sentence for each of the following expressions. Proofread your sentences carefully after you finish writing.
Answers will vary; samples given for first two.

1. all together
2. due to
3. different from
4. can't help wanting
5. everywhere
6. etc.
7. healthful
8. between
9. alleged
10. former/latter
11. unique
12. their
13. all right
14. accept
15. the reason is
16. plenty
17. lie
18. further
19. immigrate
20. affect
21. except
22. sat
23. allot
24. all ready
25. adapt

1. We had worked all together for several hours before the dissension began.
2. My cold was due to the fall I took while skating on the Chippewa River.

Review Exercises: Usage

REVIEW EXERCISE 1: A Review of Terms

Answer each of the following questions as clearly as possible.
Answers may vary somewhat; samples given on page T-123.

1. What do the tenses of a verb tell you?
2. What are the six basic tenses?
3. What are the four principal parts of a verb?
4. How are the progressive forms of the six tenses created?
5. How are the two emphatic forms made?
6. What is the difference between a regular and an irregular verb?

7. What is a conjugation?
8. How does knowing the conjugation of a verb help you?
9. What are the three main categories of time? In which categories are the perfect tenses?
10. What is the active voice? The passive voice? What are the only verbs that can be used in the passive voice?
11. What is case? Which two parts of speech have case?
12. When is the nominative case used? The objective case? The possessive case?
13. What is an elliptical clause? What problem arises is using pronouns with elliptical clauses?
14. What is meant by the term *agreement*? How must a subject and verb agree?
15. What is the ending of verbs in the third-person singular of the present tense?
16. How must a pronoun agree with its antecedent?
17. How do adjectives and adverbs show comparison?
18. What is the comparative degree? The superlative degree? Give three examples of each.
19. What are "irregular" adjectives and adverbs?
20. Why should double negatives be avoided?

REVIEW EXERCISE 2: The Principal Parts of Verbs

Divide your paper into four columns. Title the first *Present,* the second *Present Participle,* the third *Past,* and the fourth *Past Participle.* Write the principal parts of each of the following verbs in the appropriate columns.
Follow pattern in Section 9.1. Note that only 7 and 14 are regular.

1. sell	6. lay	11. freeze	16. speak	21. shut
2. be	7. open	12. throw	17. burst	22. ring
3. sit	8. go	13. do	18. drive	23. begin
4. cost	9. sing	14. drop	19. wind	24. win
5. take	10. fly	15. spring	20. eat	25. hold

REVIEW EXERCISE 3: Conjugations

Conjugate each of the following verbs as indicated. Note that the first column calls for the basic forms, the second for the progressive forms, and the third for the emphatic forms.
Follow the pattern beginning on page 202. Note that 1–3. 7–9. and 12 are irregular.

Basic Forms	Progressive Forms	Emphatic Forms
1. say (with *he*)	6. open (with *they*)	11. stay (with *we*)
2. grow (with *we*)	7. swim (with *I*)	12. see (with *she*)
3. bring (with *she*)	8. drive (with *she*)	
4. work (with *it*)	9. go (with *it*)	
5. laugh (with *they*)	10. search (with *you*)	

REVIEW EXERCISE 4: Verb Tenses in Sentences

Copy each of the following verbs onto your paper. Identify the tense of the verb and its form if the form is not basic. Then use each verb in an original sentence.

Sentences will vary; sample given.

1. will be seeing *fut prog*
2. did remember *past emph*
3. has raised *pres perf*
4. is sleeping *pres prog*
5. will find *fut*
6. does ask *pres emph*
7. was taking *past prog*
8. had spoken *past perf*
9. will have been working
10. seeks *pres*

11. will have left *fut perf*
12. do go *pres emph*
13. has been wearing *pres perf prog*
14. will be lying *fut prog*
15. tried *past*
16. were planning *past prog*
17. did attempt *past emph*
18. had been flying *past perf prog*
19. does appreciate *pres emph*
20. are laughing *pres prog*

1. I will be seeing you tomorrow. 9. fut perf prog

REVIEW EXERCISE 5: Active and Passive Voice

Identify the voice in each of the following sentences as *active* or *passive*. Then rewrite each sentence that has a verb in the passive voice, changing it to the active voice.

Revisions will vary; sample given.

1. The packages were taken by the delivery person to the wrong department. *pass*
2. Notices for our next meeting will be sent to you by the secretary. *pass*
3. The heavy, snorting truck rumbled across the bridge. *act*
4. All of the flowers were provided by local florists. *pass*
5. Traffic is being slowed by huge snowdrifts on the highways. *pass*
6. The next week a new group of applicants will replace those already in training. *act*
7. A new route to Florida was introduced last month by the airline. *pass*
8. The theater was filled with attractive couples on opening night. *pass*
9. Many people I know jog several miles a day in good weather. *act*
10. The cassette recorder was hidden by the speaker in the lectern. *pass*

1. The delivery person took the packages to the wrong department.

REVIEW EXERCISE 6: Pronoun Usage

Complete each of the following sentences with the correct pronoun.

1. It is (he, him) who developed the master plan.

2. We can accept (whoever, <u>whomever</u>) you choose.
3. Let's keep this secret between you and (I, <u>me</u>).
4. (<u>Their</u>, Them) laughing is particularly distracting to us.
5. Do you think this report is really (<u>hers</u>, her's)?
6. The adviser told (we, <u>us</u>) boys to pack for the trip.
7. My best friend and (<u>he</u>, him) plan to attend the same college.
8. From (who, <u>whom</u>) did you receive that message?
9. I think Gail is much more talented than (<u>he</u>, him).
10. His opinion is that (its, <u>it's</u>) not possible to rebuild the engine.
11. (<u>We</u>, Us) leaders will have to provide direction to the others.
12. (<u>Whoever</u>, Whomever) speaks first will make the other introductions.
13. I will give the extra ticket to (<u>whoever</u>, whomever) wants it.
14. (<u>Who</u>, Whom) do you feel deserves the award?
15. Does he really object to (<u>my</u>, me) telling them the news?
16. Ask the woman and (he, <u>him</u>) for directions.
17. (Whose, <u>Who's</u>) the girl who volunteered to act as a master of ceremonies?
18. Mark, Michael, Judy, and (<u>I</u>, me) will prepare the burgers and steaks.
19. The committee decided not to choose between you and (she, <u>her</u>).
20. The best reporter on the staff is (<u>he</u>, him).

REVIEW EXERCISE 7: Agreement

In fifteen of the following sentences, the subject and verb or a pronoun and antecedent do *not* agree. Rewrite each of these to correct the error in agreement. Explain why the five remaining sentences are correct.

1. One of the fenders ~~were~~ damaged in the accident. *was*
2. Many a college freshman wishes ~~they~~ had studied more in high school. *he*
3. Neither Mary Grace nor Carmelina ~~are~~ prepared this morning. *is*
4. At that private school ~~you are~~ expected to wear a uniform. *one is*
5. At the end of the road ~~is~~ an old, deserted gas station and a barn. *are*
6. His grandmother ~~don't~~ care if she stays or goes. *doesn't*
7. There ~~is~~ at best three possible explanations. *are*

8. Both Faulkner and Steinbeck have won Nobel Prizes for Literature. *C—compound subject joined by* and *uses plural*
9. Each of the boys~have~ developed separate projects. *has*
10. Fifty dollars ~are~ too much to spend for a sleeveless blouse. *is*
11. The album of Britten's violin concertos was lost in the fire. *C—album is singular*
12. An apple or two pears ~is~ used in this punch recipe. *are*
13. Swimsuits or very informal outfits are not permitted in the dining room. *C—outfits takes plural*
14. The oldest village in the mountains ~were~ chosen as an historic site. *was*   *C—civics is*
15. Civics is no longer taught in some school districts. *singular*
16. ~There's~ the two girls whom he wants most to date. *There are*
17. Neither my mother nor my aunt ~expect~ to visit Mexico this summer. *expects*
18. Three quarters of the report ~are~ now completed. *is*
19. Each of the girls is required to bring her own equipment to the tournament. *C—each is singular*
20. Near several distant beaches ~are~ a fine restaurant. *is*

REVIEW EXERCISE 8: Degrees of Comparison

Each of the following sentences contains a comparative or superlative form used correctly. Indicate which type of comparison is used in each sentence. Then rewrite the sentence using the other form. *Sentences will vary; sample given.*

EXAMPLE: My dog is larger than yours.

comparative

My dog is the largest on the block.

1. Newspapers are more informative than many magazines. *compar*
2. Mike is the tallest basketball center in the league. *sup*
3. Pants are often more practical than skirts. *compar*
4. The winding mountain road is the most dangerous in the state. *sup*
5. *David Copperfield* has the most interesting characters of any novel I've read. *sup*
6. This beach is much cleaner than the other we used to visit. *compar*
7. Bob has the best stereo of all my friends. *sup*
8. Japan's population is considerably smaller than China's. *compar*
9. Flying is the most convenient way to cover large distances. *sup*
10. President Kennedy was the youngest elected President. *sup*

1. Newspapers are usually the most informative of the media.

REVIEW EXERCISE 9: Making Clear Comparisons

Each of the following sentences is incorrect. Rewrite each sentence to correct the comparison.
Answers may vary; samples given.
1. Of all the girls, Beth is the ~~better~~ artist. *best*
2. My bar graph on population growth is more accurate than ~~the books~~. *the book's*
3. His behavior at the meeting was the ~~worse~~ I've seen. *worst*
4. Of potatoes and celery, celery has ~~the fewest~~ calories. *fewer*
5. My new gloves are smaller than ~~Betty~~. *Betty's*
6. Bay scallops are usually more costly than any seafood.
7. Frank is the ~~heaviest of both~~ tackles. *heavier of the two*
8. Our ideas for the fair are much better than ~~the~~ seniors.
9. If you compare both brothers, Peter is the ~~most~~ handsome.
10. His electronic camera is more automatic than any.

6. *other*   8. *those of the*   9. *more*   10. *other on the market*

REVIEW EXERCISE 10: Special Problems of Usage
Answers may vary somewhat; samples given on page T-124.
Answer each of the following questions as clearly as possible.

1. How would you use *too* in a sentence?
2. What is the difference between *accept* and *except?*
3. Why shouldn't *barely* be used with *didn't?*
4. What is the difference between *latter* and *former?*
5. How would you improve a sentence that contained the words *should of?*
6. What is the difference between *healthy* and *healthful?*
7. How are *they're, their,* and *there* used properly?
8. What is wrong with the expression *can't help but?*
9. How would you change a sentence beginning with *being that?*
10. What is the difference between *already* and *all ready?*
11. How would you change a list that ends with *and etc.?*
12. What is wrong with the expression *hadn't done nothing?*
13. How would you change a sentence beginning with *she don't?*
14. What is the difference between *farther* and *further?*
15. Why shouldn't you say, "I did *good*"?
16. Why shouldn't *like* be used to begin a clause? What should you use instead?
17. What is the difference between *rise* and *raise?*
18. What is the difference between *who* and *which?* Which pronoun can take the place of either of these words?
19. How would you improve a sentence containing the word *schoolwise?*
20. What is the difference between *beat* and *won?*

UNIT III

Mechanics

Chapter 14

Capitalization and Abbreviation

The engravings of many ancient civilizations were originally done using all capital letters. Since this form of writing took up so much space, smaller or lower-case letters and a system of abbreviations evolved to conserve room. Capital letters continued to be used only in certain situations. Thus, a working relationship developed between capitalization and abbreviation. Though the alphabet has altered over the years, capitalization and abbreviation continue to share a working partnership. Today, they complement one another— the capital signaling important words and the abbreviation shortening others that might become repetitive. Together they help the writer to communicate efficiently and effectively.

To **capitalize** means to begin a word with a capital letter.

To **abbreviate** means to shorten an existing word or phrase.

Many rules, or conventions, currently govern the use of capitalization and abbreviation. Writers must know these to maintain clarity in their work. This chapter will introduce you to the most widely accepted conventions, showing you when and where to capitalize and abbreviate correctly.

14.1 Rules for Capitalization

Capital letters serve to make certain words stand out more prominently on a printed page; they work as a significant visual clue to the reader. Learning the conventions of capitalization is an important responsibility for writers. This section will focus on the rules used in capitalization.

■ Capitalizing First Words

Since first words in writing usually signal the beginning of a new idea, writers capitalize them. First words requiring the use of an initial capital letter occur in sentences, in quotations, and in some phrases.

In Sentences. Capital letters function most commonly at the beginning of sentences. You will always see a capital letter used in the first word of complete sentences.

Capitalize the first word in declarative, interrogative, imperative, and exclamatory sentences.

Note that each of the following sentences is complete. Each contains both a subject and a verb and makes sense by itself.

DECLARATIVE: Raoul sent the letter yesterday.

INTERROGATIVE: Did you mail the monthly bills?

IMPERATIVE: Get a stamp out of the drawer.

EXCLAMATORY: This letter says I've won the contest!

In Quotations. There is also a general rule regarding capitalization of quotations.

Capitalize the first word in a quotation if the quotation is a complete sentence.

EXAMPLE: "Man is not made for defeat."—Ernest Hemingway

Even when the quotation is preceded or followed by a "he said/she said" phrase, a capital still begins the quotation.

EXAMPLES: Maya answered, "We bought some stationery."

"Packages are difficult to wrap," the man grumbled.

If a "he said/she said" phrase comes in the middle of quoted material that is *one continuous* sentence, only the first word of the quotation gets a capital letter.

EXAMPLE: "If you go by the post office," Loren said, "please drop this letter off.

If a "he said/she said" phrase sits between *two complete* sentences, both sentences receive capital letters.

EXAMPLE: "Mail order catalogs provide hours of fun," Arleen exclaimed. "My family loves to browse through them."

When a portion of a quotation that is *not* a complete sentence is contained within a longer sentence, do not capitalize the first word of the quoted part of the sentence.

EXAMPLE: The early Pony Express riders maintained that "neither snow nor rain nor heat" would stop their deliveries.

In the preceding example, no capital is inserted at the start of the quoted fragment since it is found in the middle of a longer sentence. If, however, the quoted fragment shifts to the beginning of the sentence, the first word should then, of course, be capitalized.

EXAMPLE: "Neither snow nor rain nor heat" kept the early Pony Express riders from completing their mail deliveries.

After a Colon.   Sometimes, a complete sentence will follow a colon.

Capitalize the first word after a colon if the word begins a complete sentence.

If a list follows the colon, it is not a complete sentence and, therefore, no capital letter is used. Always check carefully before using a capital after a colon.

SENTENCE FOLLOWING COLON: We could not believe the contents of the package: It contained my lost wallet.

LIST FOLLOWING COLON: The mail carrier delivered our mail: three letters, one advertisement, and a small package.

In Interjections and Question Fragments.   Capitals are also used at the beginning of interjections and question fragments.

Capitalize the first word in interjections and question fragments.

Exclamatory interjections fall under this rule.

EXAMPLES: Fantastic!   Ouch!   Darn it!

First words of incomplete questions (or question fragments) often require a capital letter. If ending punctuation follows a fragment (as in the following examples), the fragment usually begins with a capital letter.

EXAMPLES: When?   For Maria?   How much?

In Poetry.   Generally, the first word in *each* line of poetry also needs capitalization.

Capitalize the first word in each line of most poetry.

If you examine the following poem, you will notice that a capital letter begins the second line even though the line does not begin a new sentence. Follow this policy for most poems.

EXAMPLE: Were it not better to forget
Than to remember and regret?—Letitia Elizabeth
Landon

For *I* and *O*.   Some words such as *I* and *O* require capitalization all the time, regardless of their location in the sentence.

Capitalize *I* and *O* throughout a sentence.

EXAMPLES: "I am in earnest. I will not equivocate—I will not excuse—I will not retreat an inch—and I will be heard."—William Lloyd Garrison

"But O for the touch of a vanish'd hand,
And the sound of a voice that is still!"—Alfred, Lord
Tennyson

Do not confuse *O* with the word *oh*. *Oh* only receives a capital when it serves as a first word in a sentence.

EXERCISE A: **Using Capitalization with First Words.** Copy the following sentences onto your paper, adding the missing capitals. Some sentences may require more than one capital. For those that require no capitals, write *correct*.
Underlined letters are to be capitalized.
1. good grief, Charlie Brown! you can't do anything right!
2. look at the work of Marie Curie if you want to know more about early research studies of radioactivity.
3. "In some ways," wrote Henry Wallace, "certain books are more powerful by far than any battle." c
4. is the Great Wall of China really the longest wall? where does it start? and end?
5. "your dreams o years, how they penetrate through me!" —Walt Whitman
6. in studying Latin America, you should not overlook these interesting aspects: the dress, the culture, and the food.
7. "stand with anybody that stands right," Abraham Lincoln declared. "stand with him while he is right and part with him when he goes wrong."
8. the soccer team had a successful season: it won the league championship.
9. some Japanese farmers have grown forty-pound radishes!
10. Mary, Mary, quite contrary,
    how does your garden grow?
    With silver bells and cockleshells
    and pretty maids all in a row. —Mother Goose

■ Capitalizing Proper Nouns

A proper noun is a noun that names a *specific* person, place, or thing.

Capitalize all proper nouns.

Names. Whenever a person's specific name is given, it is called a proper name, and capital letters should be used.

Capitalize each part of a person's full name.

As the following examples show, the given or first name, the initials standing for a name, and the surname or last name receive capital letters.

EXAMPLES: Chester Worth, Maria A. Lopez, S. D. Schneider

In some cases, surnames may consist of several parts. If a surname begins with *Mc*, or *O'*, or *St.*, the letter immediately following it also gets capitalized.

EXAMPLES: McGregor, O'Callahan, St. John

However, surnames beginning with *de, D', la, le, Mac, van,* or *von* are not so consistent, and the capitalization will vary.

EXAMPLES: De Mello or de Mello

La Coe or Lacoe

von Hofen or Von Hofen

In these cases, ask for a spelling of the name to insure accuracy.

Capitalize the proper names of animals.

EXAMPLES Silver, the horse; Miss Piggy, the pig; Benjie, the dog

Geographical and Place Names. When writing you will sometimes have to refer to specific places. One group of proper nouns that should be capitalized is made up of geographical names.

Capitalize geographical names.

The following chart provides examples of some of the many geographical names that require capitalization.

GEOGRAPHICAL NAMES	
Streets:	Stokes Avenue, Fallen Leaf Lane
Towns and Cities:	Elk Grove, Salinas, Miami
Counties:	Cheyenne County
States and Provinces:	Idaho, Utah, Ontario
Nations:	China, Nigeria
Continents:	Australia, North America
Mountains:	the Appalachian Mountains
Valleys and Deserts:	Imperial Valley, Mojave Desert
Islands:	the Galapagos Islands
Sections of a Country:	the Northwest

Scenic Spots:	Badlands of South Dakota, the Grand Canyon
Rivers and Falls:	Amazon River, Bridalveil Falls
Lakes and Bays:	Lake Ontario, Hudson Bay
Oceans and Seas:	Indian Ocean, the Red Sea
Celestial Bodies:	Pluto, the Milky Way

Two celestial bodies that are *not* capitalized are the moon and the sun. When you use the word *earth* as one of the planets, you should capitalize it. However, when the word *earth* is preceded by the article *the*, do not capitalize it.

EXAMPLES: The astronauts left Earth and landed on the moon.

               The astronauts left the earth and landed on the moon.

When a compass point is used merely to show direction, it is not capitalized. However, when a specific location is involved, a capital is needed.

EXAMPLES: We headed northwest.

               My cousin lives in the Southwest.

Another group of proper nouns that must be capitalized are place names such as the names of monuments, buildings, and meeting rooms.

Capitalize the names of monuments, buildings, and meeting rooms.

The following chart shows examples of monuments, buildings, and meeting rooms.

SPECIFIC PLACES	
Monuments and Memorials:	the Lincoln Memorial, the Washington Monument, the Pearl Harbor Memorial
Buildings:	the Smithsonian Institution, the Superdome, the Actor's Conservatory Theater
School and Meeting Rooms:	Room 20B, Laboratory C, the Gold Room, the Oval Office

Do not capitalize *theater, hotel,* or *university* unless it is part of a proper name.

EXAMPLES: The theater was one of the first buildings erected in Columbia.

The Fallon House Theater stands in the old ghost town of Columbia.

The word *room* is capitalized only if it refers to a specific room and is combined with a name, letter, or number.

EXAMPLES: The room was decorated in white and gold.

The exam will be given in Room 46.

Other Proper Nouns.   References to time and history also follow certain capitalization conventions.

Capitalize the names of specific events and periods of time.

The following chart illustrates several categories of specific events and periods of time covered by this rule.

SPECIFIC EVENTS AND TIMES	
Historical Periods:	the Stone Age
Historical Events:	the War of 1812
Documents and Laws:	the Gettysburg Address, the Homestead Act
Days:	Monday
Months:	April 14
Holidays:	Labor Day
Religious Days:	Good Friday, Rosh Hashana
Special Events:	the Kentucky Derby, the Senior Prom

Do not capitalize the seasons.

EXAMPLE: We felt a winter chill in the air.

The names of various groups are also capitalized.

Capitalize the names of various organizations, government bodies, political parties, races, and nationalities, as well as the languages spoken by different groups.

Study the following chart to see how each of these names is capitalized.

SPECIFIC GROUPS AND LANGUAGES	
Clubs:	Rotary Club, Lynbrook Speech Club, Lions Club
Organizations:	League of Women Voters, American Cancer Society, United Farm Workers
Institutions:	University of Miami, Marymount General Hospital, Ford Foundation
Businesses:	International Business Machines, Ford Motor Company
Government Bodies:	the Senate of the United States, the Houses of Parliament, Department of Defense
Political Parties:	the Republicans, the Communist Party
Races:	Negro, Caucasian, Mongoloid
Nationalities:	American, French, Russian, Mexican
Languages:	English, Spanish, French, Yiddish

When using words such as *black* or *white* to refer to race, however, do not use capitals.

Religious references make up another group of proper nouns that requires capitalization.

Capitalize references to religions, deities, and religious scriptures.

Each religion has a set of words referring to the important and sacred beliefs it holds. Although you may not be a believer in that faith, courtesy demands that references to each religion be capitalized. The major religious groups you are likely to refer to in your writing include Christianity, Judaism, Buddhism, Islam, and Hinduism. A partial list of words from these faiths is given below.

CHRISTIANITY: God, the Lord, the Father, the Son, the Holy Spirit, the Bible, the books of the Bible (Exodus, Mark, Romans)

JUDAISM: God, the Lord, the Prophets (Moses, Abraham), the Torah, the Talmud

EASTERN RELIGIONS: Buddhism (Buddha, the Tripitaka); Islam (Allah, the Koran); Hinduism (Brahma, the Vedas)

This list is not complete. Other references you encounter must also be capitalized. These include any pronoun references made to the Deity in Christian or Jewish writings.

EXAMPLE: Praise be to the Lord, for He made all things in heaven and on earth.

The only instance in which capitalization of religious references is not required occurs when writing about mythological gods and goddesses. Although the proper names of the gods and goddesses are capitalized, the words *god* and *goddess* are not.

EXAMPLES: the god Pluto, the goddess Athena

Special awards and presentations are often named after people. Even when they are not, awards and presentations should be capitalized.

Capitalize the names of awards.

Notice in the following examples that the word *the* is not capitalized.

EXAMPLES: the Kevin E. Morris Scholarship; the Nobel Peace Prize; the Academy Awards; the Oscar; Eagle Scout

Another group of names requiring capitalization includes the names of air, sea, land, and space craft.

Capitalize the names of specific types of air, sea, land, and space craft.

When capitalizing the names of air, sea, land, and space craft, do not capitalize the word *the* preceding a name unless the word is part of the official name.

AIR: Boeing 747   LAND: the Model T

SEA: *Lusitania*   SPACE: *Sputnik I*

As a writer, you will also need to write the names of products.

Capitalize brand names.

This rule applies both to brand names used as adjectives and to full trademark names. If the full trademark name is used, all the words in the name are considered a proper noun and should be capitalized.

EXAMPLES: a Volkswagen import

the Volkswagen Rabbit

EXERCISE B: Using Capitals in Sentences with Proper Nouns. Copy the following sentences onto your paper, adding the missing capitals. *Underlined letters are to be capitalized.*

1. tonight we will hear robert mc clanahan speak on ireland.
2. the book *Roots*, written by alex haley, helps readers understand the cultural heritage of black americans.
3. anyone who loves animal stories should read about the horse known as flicka.
4. the starring role in the movie was played by sally fields.
5. my favorite poet is edna st. vincent millay.
6. they enjoyed reading the book by e.b. white.
7. have you ever watched the television program starring a dog named boomer?
8. janet d. o'connor was the name on the door.
9. my friend nancy and i went to the concert.
10. awards were presented to three of the students: jenny lincoln, richard logan, and rose mc clure.

EXERCISE C: Adding Capitals for Geographical Places, Specific Events, Periods of Time, and Other Proper Nouns. Copy the proper nouns from the following paragraph onto your paper, adding the missing capitals. Some sentences do not need additional capitalization. *Underlined letters are to be capitalized.*

(1) The early years of this century brought with them a variety of new names, exciting events, and far-reaching ideas. (2) This century got off to a flying start when the Wright brothers took to the air in december 1903. (3) Excitement continued into the next year when the st. louis world's fair began, bringing over 20,000 visitors flocking to the city.

(4) Sports lovers also enjoyed the olympic games that were held in conjunction with the fair that year. (5) Formation of the american baseball league in 1901 had also brought the sports fans joy since it introduced a new level of competition to this popular sport. (6) Many people enjoyed activities in their own communities during the early 1900's: parades and picnics held as part of the july celebration of independence day brought pleasure to people of all ages. (7) Of course, all was not fun and games; many important laws were passed during these years. (8) One of the most influential pieces of legislation in the early 1900's was the pure food and drug act passed in the summer of 1906. (9) Advertisements of many "quack" medical cures came to a quick halt. (10) All this began in those first few years of 1900 as america boldly entered a new century—the time period labeled by some as the progressive era.

EXERCISE D: Using Capitalization with Other Proper Nouns. Copy the following sentences onto your paper, adding the missing capitals. Some sentences may require more than one capital or no additional capitals.
Underlined letters are to be capitalized.
1. After hearing the news, the united nations called a meeting of the security council.
2. The store called stamp house, inc., makes rubber stamps in one day or less.
3. Most of the people in India are hindus and worship brahma.
4. My timex is now ten years old but still works.
5. The russian spoke english very well.
6. We inducted sixty new members into the national honor society at our school last week.
7. One goddess in mythology that you will read about often is the goddess Hera. *c*
8. Illustrators of children's books all hope to win the coveted caldecott award.
9. Charles lindbergh flew the airplane named the *spirit of st. louis* across the atlantic ocean.
10. If you want passport information, contact the passport office of the state department in washington, d.c.

■ Capitalizing Proper Adjectives

A proper noun used as an adjective or an adjective formed from a proper noun is called a proper adjective.

Capitalize most proper adjectives.

EXAMPLES: Swiss government; American people; Renaissance art

Some proper adjectives are no longer capitalized, however, because they have been used for so long.

EXAMPLES: french fries; teddy bear; venetian blinds

In some cases, a brand name is used as a proper adjective and is followed by a common noun. In these situations, the brand name serves as a proper adjective describing the common noun and, thus, the brand name deserves a capital. The common noun following the brand name remains uncapitalized.

Capitalize brand names used as adjectives.

EXAMPLES: Timex watches; Samsonite luggage

Sometimes prefixes precede proper adjectives.

Do not capitalize prefixes attached to proper adjectives unless the prefix refers to a nationality.

EXAMPLES: pre-Mayan architecture; pro-American sentiment

However, if the prefix itself is a nationality, it should be capitalized.

EXAMPLES: Indo-European; Afro-American

Sometimes, proper adjectives are hyphenated in other ways.

In a hyphenated adjective, capitalize only the proper adjective.

EXAMPLE: Spanish-speaking Americans

EXERCISE E: Using Capitalization with Proper Adjectives. Copy the following sentences onto your paper, adding the missing capitals. If no capitals are needed, write *correct*.
Underlined letters are to be capitalized.

1. Charles Drew, who developed the use of plasma rather than whole blood in emergency transfusions, was an afro-american.
2. The babysitter hunted all over the house for the child's teddy bear. *C*
3. That store sells many bottles of chanel no. 5. perfume.
4. The pro-american speaker at the rally was cheered.
5. Did you use your kodak instamatic to take this photograph?
6. India's population is 77 percent indo-aryan.
7. I asked for brazilian coffee.
8. Please close the venetian blinds because the sun is in my eyes. *C*
9. The story of st. joan is one well loved by the french people.
10. My parents are italian-speaking americans.

■ Capitalizing Titles

Capitals are used to indicate titles of people and works.

Capitalize titles of people and titles of works.

Titles of People. Titles used before names and in direct address require capitalization.

Capitalize a person's title when it is followed by the person's name or when it is used in direct address.

The following chart provides examples of some of these titles and shows when they should and should not be capitalized.

SOCIAL, BUSINESS, RELIGIOUS, AND MILITARY TITLES		
With Proper Names	In Direct Address	In General References
Social:		
Sir Henry Bellamy, Dame Mary Cottrell, Lord and Lady Ansley, the Duke and Duchess of Windsor, Madame Lallemand	May I help you into the car, Sir? Could you tell me, Madame, if this is the main post office?	The duke attended the coronation. A woman who has received an order of knighthood is a dame.

Business:		
Professor Scott Casentini, Dr. Pauline Greer, Superintendent B.K. Wallaker, B. Lawley, Ph.D.	Professor, your lecture was very interesting. I feel fine, Doctor.	The doctor set the broken leg. The superintendent spoke at the meeting.
Religious:		
Reverend James, Bishop Potter, St. Bernadette, Rabbi Frankel	I received your letter, Rabbi. Are you going to deliver the sermon, Father?	The father plays the trombone. She is a saint.
Military:		
Sergeant Ford, Major D. Moyer, Lieutenant Lowe, Ensign Garcia, General Fratini	Ensign, raise the flag. I'm glad you could be here, Major.	The captain flew helicopters. Tell the sergeant what happened.

The titles of government officials also require capitalization in certain cases.

Capitalize titles of government officials when they are followed by a proper name or when used in direct address.

In the United States, titles such as supervisor, mayor, governor, congressman, congresswoman, senator, judge, and ambassador are used for different government officials. Each foreign country also has titles peculiar to that country. All of these titles receive capital letters when used in front of a proper name or in direct address. If, however, the reference is general, the capital is usually omitted.

PRECEDING A PROPER NAME: Mayor Martin Holbrook will address us.

IN DIRECT ADDRESS: Will you speak tonight, Mayor?

IN A GENERAL REFERENCE: The mayor expressed concern for the rights of city employees.

If the title is for an extremely high-ranking official (President, Vice President, Chief Justice, Queen of England), the title will always be capitalized.

Capitalize the titles of certain high government officials even when the titles are not followed by a proper name or used in direct address.

EXAMPLES: The President cut short his stay at Camp David.

He will meet with the Queen of England in a private session today.

The Supreme Court of the United States has eight justices and a Chief Justice.

Although the references to the government officials in the preceding examples are classified as general references, they still are capitalized to show the respect due the high office.

Other titles are sometimes capitalized to show special respect when referring to a specific person holding the office.

EXAMPLES: The Senator spoke in favor of the legislation.

A senator is elected for a six-year term.

Confusion often results when a title is longer than one word.

Capitalize all important words in compound titles, but do not capitalize prefixes and suffixes added to titles.

EXAMPLES: Lieutenant Governor

Assistant Secretary of the Interior

Commander in Chief

ex-Senator Jorgenson

Governor-elect Richter

Notice, in the preceding examples, that when the prefix *ex-* or the suffix *-elect* is used in connection with a title, the prefix and suffix remain uncapitalized.

In families, the titles used to refer to relatives are often capitalized.

Capitalize titles showing family relationships when the title is used with the person's name or in direct address. The title may also be capitalized when it refers to a specific person, except when the title comes after a possessive noun or pronoun.

EXAMPLES: Did Uncle John bring the package?

When did this package arrive, Dad?

This package is for Grandmother.

Watch for instances in which these names are used as common nouns, for then the capitals are dropped. It may also help to realize that when these names are preceded by a possessive pronoun such as *my*, *their*, or *our* they do not require capitalization.

EXAMPLES: Mrs. Jackson is a grandmother.

I wonder if my dad saw the package arrive.

My uncle John brought the package.

People have all kinds of titles attached to their names that identify their degrees, professions, marital status, and so forth. These kinds of titles will need capitalization.

Capitalize abbreviations of titles before and after names.

The most common abbreviations found before and after names include *Mr.*, *Mrs.*, *Jr.*, and *Sr.*

EXAMPLES: Mr. Kevin Peterson, Jr.; Mrs. Ann Sikorski

The title *Ms.* is not an abbreviation for another word. It starts with a capital and ends with a period, however, as if it were an abbreviation. You can use *Ms.* before a proper name to refer to either a single or a married woman.

Note that *Miss* should also be capitalized. It is not an abbreviation so no period is put at the end.

Titles of Things.   Since writers often make references to the titles of works, they must understand the proper way to capitalize them.

Capitalize the first word and all other important words in the titles of books, periodicals, poems, stories, plays, paintings, and other works of art.

BOOK: *Heart of Darkness*

PERIODICAL: *Better Homes and Gardens*

POEM: "Flower in the Crannied Wall"

STORY: "Bernice Bobs Her Hair"

PLAY: *How to Succeed in Business Without Really Trying*

PAINTING: *The Artist's Daughter with a Cat*

MUSIC: *The Triumph of Time and Truth*

As you look at the preceding examples, notice the following: (1) The words *a, an,* and *the* are only capitalized when they are the first word of the title. (2) Conjunctions and prepositions shorter than five letters are capitalized only when they are the first word in the title. (3) Adjectives, nouns, pronouns, verbs, and adverbs are considered important words and are always capitalized.

When capitalizing a subtitle, use the same rule that you do for capitalizing a title.

EXAMPLE: *Language: A Reflection of the People and Their Cultures*

In addition to titles of works of art, titles of courses of study sometimes require capitalization.

Capitalize titles of courses when the courses are language courses or when the courses are followed by a number.

Any references to language classes will always receive capital letters since languages are always capitalized. However, other subjects will only be capitalized when the reference is made to a *specific* course, which will generally be followed by a number or letter identifying the course.

WITH CAPITALS: Latin II, English, California History 1A

WITHOUT CAPITALS: mathematics, history, home economics

EXERCISE F: Using Capitalization with Titles of People. Copy the following sentences onto your paper, adding the missing capitals. If a sentence is correct, write *correct.*
Underlined letters are to be capitalized; capitals optional in 3 and 9.
1. Do you remember your first day of school, grandma?
2. The well-known <u>r</u>everend John Hall, <u>jr</u>., spoke at the service.
3. With no hesitation, the mayor approached the speaker's platform. *C*
4. The <u>p</u>resident of the <u>u</u>nited <u>s</u>tates held a press conference.
5. Very few officers in the service ever attain the rank of general. *C*

6. May I introduce <u>m</u>iss Anna Schmidt and <u>m</u>r. Louis Ward, <u>s</u>r.?
7. My aunt Louise is a professor at the college. *c*
8. Please give me advice, <u>r</u>abbi.
9. The commander in chief will review the troops. *c*
10. Do you know <u>s</u>enator-elect Garcia personally?

EXERCISE G: **Capitalizing Titles of Things.** Copy the following titles onto your paper, adding the missing capitals. *Underlined letters are to be capitalized.*
1. Painting: <u>at the c</u>ircus
2. Poem: "<u>l</u>ines <u>c</u>omposed a <u>f</u>ew <u>m</u>iles <u>a</u>bove <u>t</u>intern <u>a</u>bbey"
3. Short story: "<u>b</u>efore the <u>w</u>olves <u>c</u>ome"
4. School courses: <u>g</u>erman   geometry   <u>b</u>usiness 312
5. Sculpture: <u>v</u>ariation <u>w</u>ithin a <u>s</u>phere
6. Opera: <u>the s</u>iege of <u>r</u>hodes
7. Book: <u>w</u>ellington: <u>the y</u>ears of the <u>s</u>word
8. Periodical: <u>l</u>adies <u>h</u>ome <u>j</u>ournal
9. One-act play: "<u>the w</u>onderful <u>i</u>ce <u>c</u>ream <u>s</u>uit"
10. Song: "<u>b</u>y the <u>l</u>ight of the <u>s</u>ilvery <u>m</u>oon"

■ Capitalizing in Letter Salutations and Closings

Certain words in letters always require capitalization.

Capitalize the first word and all nouns in letter salutations and the first word in letter closings.

SALUTATIONS: Dear Brian,   My dear Friend,   Ladies:

CLOSINGS: With deepest regards,   Sincerely,
            In sympathy,

EXERCISE H: **Using Capitalization in a Letter.** Read the following excerpt from a letter and decide if each underlined word requires a capital. If it does, write *yes* after the corresponding number on your paper; if it does not, write *no*.

(1) <u>my</u> (2) <u>dear</u> Friends,

Recently I have discovered a brand new hobby—hot air ballooning! (3) <u>what</u> a thrill it is to drift slowly above the farms and house tops! Last week I saw the most spectacular sight: (4) <u>a</u> slender steeple rose majestically above the fog.

Of course, this new hobby is not cheap. (5) <u>do</u> you have any idea how much a hot air balloon costs? Over $5,000! Just taking a ride costs about $50. I think I will investigate building one. So far, I've learned that the baskets you ride in are usually constructed from one of four materials: (6) <u>rattan</u>, fiberglass, aluminum, or wood. (7) "<u>it's</u> possible to build the basket," a salesman told me, (8) "<u>but</u> you'll need to purchase the balloon."

Since my pocketbook is empty, I'll have to settle for an occasional flight. I guess I should try to remember the words of Dorothy in *The Wizard of Oz* when she said, (9) "<u>there's</u> no place like home."

With fondest (10) <u>regards</u>,

Archie

1. yes   2. no   3. yes   4. yes   5. yes   6. no   7. yes   8. no   9. yes   10. no

EXERCISE I: Using Capitals Throughout Writing. Copy the following sentences onto your paper, adding the missing capitals. *Underlined letters are to be capitalized.*

1. <u>a</u> mighty statue, representative of <u>a</u>merica's love of freedom, sits on <u>l</u>iberty <u>i</u>sland as a welcome to visitors from <u>e</u>urope, <u>a</u>sia, <u>l</u>atin <u>a</u>merica, and other parts of the world.
2. <u>k</u>nown as the <u>s</u>tatue of <u>l</u>iberty, it stands 151 feet, 1 inch tall.
3. <u>t</u>he statue was designed by <u>f</u>rederic <u>b</u>artholdi, a <u>f</u>renchman.
4. <u>t</u>he <u>f</u>rench government liked the designs and thus formed the <u>f</u>ranco-<u>a</u>merican <u>u</u>nion to raise funds for it.
5. <u>w</u>hen the statue was finished, it was presented formally to <u>u</u>.<u>s</u>. minister <u>m</u>orton.
6. <u>t</u>o prepare the foundation for the arriving statue, <u>j</u>oseph <u>p</u>ulitzer, for whom the <u>p</u>ulitzer <u>p</u>rize is named, helped solicit donations.
7. <u>m</u>r. <u>p</u>ulitzer was the owner of the <u>n</u>ew <u>y</u>ork <u>w</u>orld, a newspaper in the city.
8. <u>p</u>resident <u>g</u>rover <u>c</u>leveland dedicated the statue on <u>o</u>ctober 28, 1886.
9. <u>d</u>id you know that a poem by <u>e</u>mma <u>l</u>azarus entitled "<u>t</u>he <u>n</u>ew <u>c</u>olossus" was added to the pedestal in 1903?
10. <u>r</u>ecently, the <u>a</u>merican <u>m</u>useum of <u>i</u>mmigration was opened here.

APPLICATION: Using Capitals Correctly in Your Own Writing. Here is a list of some imaginary titles for the bestsellers of this decade.

1. *Deadly Danger in the Ocean Depths*
2. *A Step Through Space and Time*
3. *Why I Flunked "Physical Education 1A"*
4. *Twelve Hours to D-Day*
5. *Me and More Me—My Years as a Hollywood Star*

Choose one of these imaginary titles and write a paragraph summarizing what the plot of such a book might be. Include in your paragraph the following information, correctly capitalized. *Answers will vary; students might exchange papers to check mechanics.*

Name of the main character
Hometown and state
His/her title
His/her nationality
Business he/she works for
Organization or club he/she belongs to
A special event he/she attended
The title of a book, poem, or play that influenced the main
    character
The most famous line the main character speaks
A trade name for some object associated with the main
    character

14.2 Rules for Abbreviation

Abbreviations were first developed to enable writers to save time and space. Some abbreviated forms of words have become so popular that people no longer think of them as abbreviations; for example, *gym, auto, memo,* and *exams* fall into this category. So many abbreviated forms now exist that entire books are needed to catalog them. In order to insure some consistency in these abbreviations, certain conventions are followed. This section will focus on these abbreviation rules, showing you how and when to abbreviate correctly.

■ Titles of People

References to people are governed by a number of abbreviation rules. One of the most important rules concerns given names.

Use a person's full given name in formal writing, unless the person uses initials as part of his or her formal name.

If you consider a person important enough to mention in formal writing, that person deserves to have his or her full name included. In addresses or lists, using initials in place of the given name is considered acceptable.

IN FORMAL WRITING: My friend Steven Pratt (not S. Pratt) had knee surgery recently.

IN AN ADDRESS OR LIST: Steven Pratt *or* S. Pratt

Unlike names, the titles that precede a person's name are often abbreviated in formal writing.

Abbreviations of social titles before a proper name begin with a capital letter and end with a period. They can be used in any type of writing.

Consider first the common abbreviated titles in the following examples.

EXAMPLES: Mr., Mrs., Mme. (Madam or Madame)

Messrs. (plural of Mr.), Mmes. (plural of Mrs. or Mme.)

The title *Ms.* is not an abbreviation of another word. It begins with a capital and ends with a period as if it were an abbreviation, however. It may be used before a proper name to refer to either a single or married woman.

You may use these abbreviated titles in formal writing whenever they are followed directly by a proper name. Never use them without a proper name.

INCORRECT: The Mrs. is not at home.

CORRECT: Mrs. Birdsall is not at home.

You should also remember that the social title *Miss* is not an abbreviation. Thus, no period is placed at the end of it.

Formal titles indicating professional, religious, political, and military rank may also be abbreviated before proper names in some cases.

Abbreviations of other titles used before proper names also begin with a capital letter and end with a period. They are used less often in formal writing.

The following chart provides some of the more common abbreviations of rank and position. Study the examples closely so that you understand how the abbreviated form is constructed.

ABBREVIATIONS OF COMMON TITLES OF POSITION AND RANK			
Professional		**Religious**	
Dr.	Doctor	Rev.	Reverend
Atty.	Attorney	Fr.	Father
Prof.	Professor	Sr.	Sister
Hon.	Honorable	Br.	Brother
Political		**Military**	
Pres.	President	Sgt.	Sergeant
Supt.	Superintendent	Lt.	Lieutenant
Rep.	Representative	Capt.	Captain
Sen.	Senator	Lt. Col.	Lieutenant Colonel
Gov.	Governor	Col.	Colonel
Treas.	Treasurer	Gen.	General
Sec.	Secretary	Ens.	Ensign
Amb.	Ambassador	Adm.	Admiral

Several guidelines will help you use these abbreviations appropriately. First, when only the surname is given, write out the title: Do not use the abbreviated form. .

INCORRECT: Amb. Leonard conducted the negotiations.

CORRECT: Ambassador Leonard conducted the negotiations.

The abbreviation *Dr.* is an exception to this guideline. *Dr.* is abbreviated before a proper noun just as *Mr.* and *Mrs.* are.

EXAMPLE: Dr. Tyson gave her patient a tetanus shot.

Second, when the first name or initials are provided, you may use the abbreviated form of the title.

EXAMPLE: Our guest lecturer, Prof. Milton R. Douglas, talked about the energy shortage.

Finally, you must remember that certain religious titles (*Reverend, Father, Sister,* and *Brother*) and the professional title *Honorable* are customarily not abbreviated even when a first name or initials are used.

A number of abbreviations also exist for titles that follow immediately after a name.

Abbreviations of titles after a name start with a capital letter and end with a period. They can be used in any type of writing.

The abbreviations *Jr.* and *Sr.* appear quite regularly after names.

EXAMPLE: Roberto Garcia, Jr., looks like his father.

Academic degrees following a name adhere to this rule as well. The following chart lists common academic abbreviations.

COMMON ACADEMIC ABBREVIATIONS

B.A. (or A.B.)	Bachelor of Arts	Ph.D.	Doctor of Philosophy
B.S. (or S.B.)	Bachelor of Science	D.D.	Doctor of Divinity
M.A. (or A.M.)	Master of Arts	D.D.S.	Doctor of Dental Surgery
M.S. (or S.M.)	Master of Science		
M.B.A.	Master of Business Administration	M.D.	Doctor of Medicine
		R.N.	Registered Nurse
M.F.A.	Master of Fine Arts	Esq.	Esquire (lawyer)

Do not use the abbreviations for Junior and Senior or for academic degrees unless they follow a proper name.

INCORRECT: The M.D. checked the child's pulse.

CORRECT: Craig Fredericks, M.D., checked the child's pulse.

EXERCISE A: Abbreviating Titles of People.
A title has been written out in full in each of the following sentences. Decide how the title should be abbreviated and write the abbreviated form on your paper.

1. The will stated that Henry Larson, <u>Junior</u>, should receive half the estate. *Jr.*
2. We will attend the play with <u>Madame</u> Cousteau. *Mme.*
3. The bestseller was written by Ingrid Rowley, <u>Doctor of Philosophy</u>. *Ph.D.*
4. At graduation, <u>Admiral</u> Rupert Hawkes gave the invocation. *Adm.*
5. He wrote on the application Delmar David Benson, <u>Bachelor of Science.</u> *B.S.*
6. The judge assigned <u>Attorney</u> Howard Manthos to the case. *Atty.*
7. The news reported that <u>Captain</u> Barry Zimmer had landed safely. *Capt.*
8. The keynote speaker, <u>Representative</u> Martha Schatz, will fly in tonight. *Rep.*
9. Can you tell me, <u>Mister</u> Parks, when the homes will go on the market? *Mr.*
10. When he finished at the seminary, he had a plaque put on his office door that read, Carl Shelby, <u>Doctor of Divinity.</u> *D.D.*

■ Time References and Geographical Locations

In your writing, you will frequently need to include references to time and to geographical locations. The use of abbreviations in these situations is governed by a number of conventions.

Time References.   Time references fall into three major categories: time spans, A.M. and P.M., and B.C. and A.D. First, consider the rule governing the abbreviation of time spans.

Abbreviations for clocked time begin with a small letter and end with a period. Abbreviations for days of the week or months of the year begin with a capital letter and end with a period. These abbreviations are not used in formal writing.

TIME ABBREVIATIONS					
Clocked Time					
sec.	second(s)	min.	minute(s)	hr.	hour(s)

Days of the Week					
Mon.	Monday	Thurs.	Thursday	Sat.	Saturday
Tues.	Tuesday	Fri.	Friday	Sun.	Sunday
Wed.	Wednesday				

Months of the Year					
Jan.	January	May	May	Sept.	September
Feb.	February	June	June	Oct.	October
Mar.	March	July	July	Nov.	November
Apr.	April	Aug.	August	Dec.	December

Although the preceding abbreviations are allowed only in informal writing, the abbreviations A.M. and P.M. are permitted in both formal and informal writing.

For abbreviations of time before noon and after noon, either capital letters followed by periods or small letters followed by periods are acceptable. They can be used in any type of writing.

EXAMPLES: A.M. or a.m. (ante meridiem, before noon)

P.M. or p.m. (post meridiem, after noon)

Use these abbreviations only when referring to the time of day in numerals; otherwise, write the words out.

EXAMPLES: We had a fire drill at 11:05 a.m. today.

I have to get my haircut sometime before noon tomorrow.

The abbreviations B.C. and A.D. may be used in historical dates in both formal and informal writing.

Abbreviations for historical dates before and after the birth of Christ require capital letters followed by periods. They can be used in any type of writing.

EXAMPLES: B.C. (before Christ)

A.D. (*anno Domini*, in the year of the Lord)

334 Capitalization and Abbreviation

These two time references are usually used in conjunction with numerals. Place the B.C. after the number it refers to.

EXAMPLE: Beginning with the Eastern Cho dynasty in 770 B.C., Chinese culture started to spread to the rest of the world.

The A.D. may come before or after the number *unless* the word *century* is spelled out. In that case, the A.D. is placed after the word *century*.

EXAMPLE: The Reformation began about A.D. 1500.

The Reformation began about 1500 A.D.

The sixteenth century A.D. has been labeled the beginning of the Reformation.

Geographical Locations. Knowing when to abbreviate geographical locations is sometime confusing. Most often, abbreviations for map locations are generally used only in addresses, lists, charts, and informal writing.

Abbreviations for geographical terms before or after a proper noun begin with a capital letter and end with a period. They are seldom used in formal writing.

The following chart provides a look at some of the more common geographical abbreviations.

COMMON GEOGRAPHICAL ABBREVIATIONS					
Ave.	Avenue	Dr.	Drive	Prov.	Province
Bldg.	Building	Ft.	Fort	Pt.	Point
Apt.	Apartment	Is.	Island	Rd.	Road
Blk.	Block	Mt.	Mountain	Rte.	Route
Blvd.	Boulevard	Natl.	National	Sq.	Square
Co.	County	Pen.	Peninsula	St.	Street
Dist.	District	Pk.	Park; Peak	Terr.	Territory

Two sets of abbreviations for states exist: one traditional set and one put out more recently by the U.S. Postal Service.

Traditional abbreviations for states begin with a capital letter and end with a period. The official Postal Service abbreviations for states require capital letters with no periods. Both are seldom used in formal writing.

Study the abbreviations for the states given in the following chart, noticing how the two sets of abbreviations differ from one another.

		STATE ABBREVIATIONS			
State	**Traditional**	**Postal Service**	**State**	**Traditional**	**Postal Service**
Alabama	Ala.	AL	Montana	Mont.	MT
Alaska	Alaska	AK	Nebraska	Nebr.	NB
Arizona	Ariz.	AZ	Nevada	Nev.	NV
Arkansas	Ark.	AR	New Hampshire	N.H.	NH
California	Calif.	CA	New Jersey	N.J.	NJ
Colorado	Colo.	CO	New Mexico	N. Mex.	NM
Connecticut	Conn.	CT	New York	N.Y.	NY
Delaware	Del.	DE	North Carolina	N.C.	NC
Florida	Fla.	FL	North Dakota	N. Dak.	ND
Georgia	Ga.	GA	Ohio	O.	OH
Hawaii	Hawaii	HI	Oklahoma	Okla.	OK
Idaho	Ida.	ID	Oregon	Ore.	OR
Illinois	Ill.	IL	Pennsylvania	Pa.	PA
Indiana	Ind.	IN	Rhode Island	R.I.	RI
Iowa	Iowa	IA	South Carolina	S.C.	SC
Kansas	Kans.	KS	South Dakota	S. Dak.	SD
Kentucky	Ky.	KY	Tennessee	Tenn.	TN
Louisiana	La.	LA	Texas	Tex.	TX
Maine	Me.	ME	Utah	Utah	UT
Maryland	Md.	MD	Vermont	Vt.	VT
Massachusetts	Mass.	MA	Virginia	Va.	VA
Michigan	Mich.	MI	Washington	Wash.	WA
Minnesota	Minn.	MN	West Virginia	W. Va.	WV
Mississippi	Miss.	MS	Wisconsin	Wis.	WI
Missouri	Mo.	MO	Wyoming	Wyo.	WY

NOTE ABOUT D.C.: The traditional abbreviation for the District of Columbia is D.C.; the Postal Service abbreviation is

DC. Use the traditional abbreviation in formal writing whenever it follows the word Washington.

EXAMPLE: The meeting was held in Washington, D.C.

You should generally use the abbreviations for states only in lists, addresses, and informal writing. The Postal Service prefers that you use its method of abbreviating the states on envelopes or packages to be mailed.

In formal writing, you should also avoid abbreviations for streets, cities, counties, states, and countries. One exception to this rule does exist, however. When you refer to the U.S.S.R. or the U.S. (especially when they are used as adjectives,), abbreviations are acceptable *even* in formal writing.

EXAMPLE: The U.S.S.R. (or Union of Soviet Socialist Republics) has bought some of the U. S. (or United States) grain surpluses over the years.

EXERCISE B: Abbreviating Time References. In each of the following sentences, an abbreviated time reference is in parentheses. If the abbreviation is used correctly, write *correct* on your paper. If it is not, write *incorrect* and then write the correct form.

C 1. At 2:00 (a.m.) our cat delivered her first litter of kittens.
 2. In (A.D.) 1215, the Magna Carta was signed. *C*
 3. This (<u>Feb.</u>) I plan to watch the Winter Olympics. *February*
 4. A recent book discusses the Bronze Age, which began around 2500 (<u>b.c.</u>) *B.C.*
minutes/ 5. My brother can run the mile in (five <u>min.</u> and ten <u>sec.</u>)
seconds 6. Should the drawing be held (<u>a.m.</u> or <u>p.m</u>)? *before/after noon*
 7. My birthday falls on (<u>Dec.</u>) 13. *December*
 8. Many interesting events happened (<u>B.C.</u>).
 9. The Muslim religion started in the (<u>A.D. seventh century</u>) when Muhammad began preaching. *seventh century A.D.*
 10. As we waited for the doctor to arrive, the (<u>hr.</u>) ticked slowly by. *hour or hours*

8. in the years before the birth of Christ

EXERCISE C: Abbreviating Locations. In the following letter, most abbreviations are underlined. If the abbreviation can be used correctly, write *correct* on your paper. If it cannot, write *incorrect* and then write the correct form.

1721 Lafayette (1) <u>Dr</u>.
Buffalo, (2) <u>WY</u> 82834
July 10, 1985

Mr. Ray Byrne
326 Payne (3) <u>Ave</u>.
San Carlos, (4) <u>NM</u> 43180

Dear Mr. Byrne:

I wanted to thank you personally for that intriguing article on travel; your suggestions for unique vacations have my family extremely excited. Right now, we are considering a backpack trip to the Yukon (5) <u>Terr</u>., a trip to the Flower Festival in British Columbia, or an excursion to see our web-footed friends of the Galapagos (6) <u>Is</u>. We were at least able to eliminate the bus tour of (7) <u>Mt</u>. Rushmore and Yellowstone (8) <u>Natl</u>. Park since we've already taken that fantastic tour. One suggestion: If you decide to take that bicycle trip through Milpitas, (9) <u>CA</u>, don't forget to see the Court House (10) <u>Bldg</u>. No visitor should miss it!

Sincerely,

Arden DeMoss

1. C   2. C   3. C   4. C   5. Territory   6. Islands   7. Mount
8. National   9. California   10. Building

■ Abbreviating Latin Phrases, Measurements, and Numbers

You may also need to use abbreviations for Latin phrases, measurements, and numbers.

Latin Phrases. Take a moment to look at the way common Latin abbreviations are formed.

Use small letters and periods for most abbreviations of Latin expressions. These abbreviations are not used in formal writing.

The following common Latin abbreviations have become a part of the English language. They usually are used only in bibliographies, footnotes, and lists. In formal writing, you should use the English equivalent instead of the Latin abbreviation. An exception is *i.e.*, which is often found in formal writing.

EXAMPLES: c., ca., circ. about (used to show approximate dates)

f.   and the following (page or line)

ff. and the following (pages or lines)

e.g. for example   et al. and others

etc. and so forth   i.e. that is

Measurements.   Generally, abbreviations for traditional and metric measurements are formed according to the following rule.

With traditional measurements use small letters and periods to form the abbreviations. With metric measurements use small letters and no periods to form the abbreviations. These abbreviations are not used in formal writing except with numerals.

The typical abbreviations for these measurements are shown in the following chart.

ABBREVIATIONS OF MEASUREMENT			
Type of Measurement	Traditional		Metric	
Linear:	inch (es)	in.	centimeter(s)	cm
	foot (feet)	ft.	decimeter(s)	dm
	yard (s)	yd.	meter(s)	m
	mile(s)	mi.	kilometer(s)	km
Volume:	teaspoon(s)	tsp.	centiliter(s)	cL
	tablespoon(s)	tbsp.	deciliter(s)	dL
	pint(s)	pt.	liter(s)	L
	quart(s)	qt.	kiloliter(s)	kL
	gallon(s)	gal.		
Weight:	ounce(s)	oz.	centigram(s)	cg
	pound(s)	lb.	decigram(s)	dg
			gram(s)	g
			kilogram(s)	kg
Temperature:	Fahrenheit	F.	Celsius	C

Notice that in the volume measurement for the metric abbreviations there is an exception: A capital letter is used to designate *liter*. Capital letters are also used for both Fahrenheit and Celsius abbreviations.

For a more complete listing of all the measurements and their abbreviated forms, you can refer to a dictionary or almanac. There you are also likely to find a conversion chart that will help you change traditional measurements to metric ones.

Although abbreviations with numerals will occasionally be used in formal writing, they are generally more appropriate in informal writing. Above all, remember never to abbreviate these units when they follow a spelled-out number.

IN INFORMAL WRITING: The piano weighed 750 lb. so I decided not to move it.

IN FORMAL WRITING: The piano weighed 750 pounds, so I decided not to move it.

IN ALL TYPES OF WRITING: The child weighed seven pounds, six ounces at birth.

Numbers.   Several rules govern the abbreviation of numbers (the use of numerals rather than words).

In formal writing, spell out numbers or amounts of less than one hundred and any other numbers that can be written in two words or less.

EXAMPLES: At least seven children broke out with the measles.

The senator took in ten thousand dollars at the fund raiser.

The senior class has 623 members.

Sometimes, numbers will occur at the beginning of the sentence. If possible, relocate the number to another place in the sentence. If this cannot be done, use this rule.

Spell out all numbers found at the beginning of sentences.

EXAMPLES: Four hundred and seventy-three homing pigeons were released during the half-time show.

During the half-time show, 473 homing pigeons were released.

Certain special types of numbers are almost always abbreviated.

Use numerals when referring to fractions, decimals, and percentages.

Remember to place the numerals within, not at the beginning of, the sentence.

EXAMPLES: The boy stood 49½ inches tall.

The class tallies revealed that he captured 57 percent of the vote.

The correct answer was 61.9.

Numbers in dates should also be abbreviated.

Use numerals when referring to a date.

EXAMPLE: The man predicted the world would end January 27, 1979, but he was mistaken.

A final frequent use of numerals is in addresses. These references should always be abbreviated.

Use numerals when writing addresses.

EXAMPLE: Donald Dersh
882 Teneda Dr.
Englewood Cliffs, NJ 07631

When you write these abbreviations or others, situations will occur when you will not be completely sure whether you may use an abbreviation or not. In these cases, follow this advice: "When in doubt, spell it out."

EXERCISE D: Abbreviating Latin Phrases, Measurements, and Numbers. In each of the following items, certain words and abbreviations are in parentheses. Decide which one of the two choices is appropriate for the sentence and write it on your paper. *Correct answers are underlined.*

1. (435, Four hundred and thirty-five) citizens attended the ecology rally.

2. The antique dealer told us the chair was made (c. 1820, about 1820).
3. Porky Pig
   (21, Twenty-one) Trough Dr.
   Gorge, PA 52154
4. The man wanted to borrow ($1,000,000.00, one million dollars).
5. Figures showed that company profits had increased (28, twenty-eight) percent last year.
6. He had that surgery on June (27, twenty-seven) of this year.
7. The recipe calls for six (tbsp. tablespoons) flour and three (tbsp., tablespoons) sugar.
8. We purchased two (lb., pounds) of food for my guinea pig.
9. I put six (L, liters) of gas in the car.
10. The table stood (18½, eighteen and one-half) inches tall.

■ Other Names

A variety of methods exist for abbreviating names of businesses, organizations, government agencies, and other groups, but some of these abbreviations are not considered appropriate in formal writing.

The first type of abbreviation occurs when one word in the name (usually the last) is shortened. The names of business firms often contain this type of abbreviation.

An abbreviated word in a business name begins with a capital letter and ends with a period. Most of these abbreviations are not used in formal writing.

Some of the more frequently seen business abbreviations are included in the following examples.

EXAMPLES: Bros. (Brothers)   Ltd. (Limited)

Co. (Company)   Mfg. (Manufacturing)

Corp. (Corporation)   &   (And) This symbol for the
word *and* is called an
Inc. (Incorporated)   *ampersand.*

In formal writing, write out the full name of most businesses. Limit your use of abbreviations to *Inc.* and *Ltd.*

EXAMPLES: The Ford Motor Company produces the Mustang.

Better Homes and Gardens devoted its last issue to family finances.

The magazine *Field and Stream* provides good fishing tips.

In the last example, using the ampersand would be correct in a list or address since it serves as part of the magazine's official name.

Occasionally, names are shortened so that only the first letter of each word in the name is used. The word, when pronounced letter by letter, is called an *initial abbreviation*.

Use all capital letters and no periods to abbreviate the names of familiar organizations, large business firms, government agencies, and other things whose abbreviated names are pronounced letter by letter as if they were words. These abbreviations are often used in formal writing.

The following chart demonstrates this method.

INITIAL ABBREVIATIONS	
Organizations:	NHS National Honor Society NFL National Football League NEA National Educational Association
Business Firms:	TWA Trans-World Airlines CBS Columbia Broadcasting System RCA Radio Corporation of America
Government Agencies:	FCC Federal Communications Commission IRS Internal Revenue Service FDA Food and Drug Administration
Objects/Persons/Places:	GNP Gross National Product TV Television VP Vice President

If you study the examples in the chart, you will notice that in these abbreviations, each letter is individually pronounced. In other cases, the initials are blended together and pronounced as a single word called an *acronym.*

Use all capital letters and no periods for acronyms that form the names of organizations. These acronyms are often used in formal writing.

EXAMPLES: WIG Women's Investment Group

NASA National Aeronautics and Space Administration

FERA Federal Emergency Relief Administration

SUNFED Special United Nations Fund for Economic Development

NATO North Atlantic Treaty Organization

Both initial abbreviations and acronyms may be used in formal writing as a technique for avoiding repetition. However, before using an unfamiliar abbreviation, use the complete title first. Commonly, the title is given and the abbreviation is enclosed in parentheses immediately afterward.

EXAMPLE: The National Boxing Association (NBA) will consider some new regulations. The NBA has indicated that these regulations are necessary to improve the sport.

EXERCISE E: Abbreviating Other Names. For each of the following abbreviations write the full name. Then identify the abbreviation as one of the following.
3. Manufacturing–A   9. National Aeronautics and Space Administration–B
  A. An abbreviation that cannot be used in formal writing.
  B. An abbreviation that can be used in formal writing, in some cases, after it has been written out in full.

1. Market-All <u>Corp</u>. *Corporation–A*
2. NFL *National Football League–B*
3. Homac <u>Mfg</u>. Company
4. NEA *National Education Association–B*
5. GNP *Gross National Product–B*
6. Romaggi <u>Bros</u>. *Brothers–A*
7. CBS *Columbia Broadcasting System–B*
8. Center Paint <u>Co</u>. *Company–A*
9. NASA
10. TV *Television–B*

11. IRS *Internal Revenue Service–B*
12. Racquet Sports <u>Ltd</u>. *Limited–B*
13. FBI *Federal Bureau of Investigation–B*
14. TWA *Trans-World Airlines–B*
15. Old World Iron, <u>Inc</u>.
16. RCA *Radio Corporation of America–B*
17. FCC
18. NHS *National Honor Society–B*
19. WIG *Women's Investment Group–B*
20. *Field <u>&</u> Stream* *and–A*

15. Incorporated–B   17. Federal Communications Commission–B

APPLICATION: Using All the Abbreviation Rules. Decide if the underlined words, phrases, or abbreviations included in the following passage are used correctly. If they are correct, write *correct*; if they are not, write the correct form on your paper.

Answers for 16 and 17 may vary, depending on students' familiarity with the terms.

The oldest known written tablets date back to (1) 2,000 (2) before Christ. Even in those times, people were recording ideas, facts, procedures, (3) etc. for future generations. One leader, Ptolemy I, saw the need to centralize this kind of information, and around (4) B.C. 300, he began to collect what would become a library of over (5) 500,000 scrolls. More and more libraries grew as the (6) yrs. passed. In the (7) U.S., the first library began as a gift from (8) Rev. John Harvard in 1638. Later, (9) B. Franklin founded the library (10) Co. of Philadelphia, the first subscription library. Today, the (11) N.Y. Public Library alone is the repository of over (12) 7 million volumes. With this proliferation of material, libraries have discovered microfilm—a method of condensing huge amounts of writing into a space smaller than a (13) sq. inch. In the Library of Congress, written and microfilm records are maintained on all events of importance ((14) e.g., the election of (15) Pres. Carter, the rulings of the (16) FDA, the documents for (17) NATO). A student studying for a (18) Ph.D. and a state (19) Sen. needing updated information can come to (20) Washington, D.C. to use the archives in this library.

1. C	11. New York Public Library
2. B.C.	12. seven
3. and so forth	13. square inch
4. 300 B.C.	14. for example
5. C	15. President
6. years	16. Food and Drug Administration
7. C	17. C
8. Reverend	18. doctorate
9. Benjamin Franklin	19. senator
10. Company	20. C

Chapter 15

Punctuation

When Beethoven wrote the *Moonlight Sonata* more than 150 years ago, he included in his music not only the notes he wanted played but also *how* he wanted them played. Through the use of accepted music notation, he left precise instructions on the tempo he wished, the mood he wanted to convey in the passages, the volume, and the stops. By following Beethoven's instructions, today's musicians are able to play that piece almost exactly as Beethoven played it himself.

Just as a composer must do more than set down notes on paper, a writer must do more than set down words on paper. A writer must also provide notation telling the reader *how* the words are to be read. To facilitate this process, a set of standard marks called *punctuation* has evolved over the years.

Punctuation is a commonly accepted set of symbols used in writing to convey specific directions to the reader.

The most frequently used punctuation marks include those in the following chart.

FREQUENTLY USED PUNCTUATION MARKS	
period (.)	colon (:)
question mark (?)	quotation marks (" ")
exclamation mark (!)	dash (—)
comma (,)	parentheses (( ))
semicolon (;)	hyphen (-)

By using these marks carefully, writers tell readers to pause for clarity, to read with a particular emotion, or to stop completely. The key word here is *carefully*; you cannot insert punctuation according to your own whims but must carefully follow certain rules or conventions. Even when you follow the rules, there will be times when you have to use your own discretion. Knowing the rules, however, will enable you to make intelligent punctuation decisions at these times. This chapter will focus on the generally accepted conventions of punctuation so that you, the writer, can punctuate your own writing more effectively.

15.1 End Marks

Just as every sentence must begin with a capital letter, so every sentence must end with a carefully chosen end mark. The three most common end marks are the period (.), the question mark (?), and the exclamation mark (!). These "full stop" marks clearly indicate to a reader that you have arrived at the end of a thought. Using end marks carefully will help you avoid fragments and run-on sentences. End marks also indicate the emotion or tone of a sentence so that the reader knows with what kind of expression it should be read. End marks can serve other important functions, as well. In this section, you will have the opportunity to review the more common uses of end marks and to study some of their other functions.

■ End Marks at the End of Sentences and Phrases

The basic purpose of end marks is to end *all* sentences and *some* phrases.

Use a period (.) to end a declarative sentence, a mild imperative, and an indirect question.

Declarative sentences are defined as statements of fact or opinion. Both types of statements require a period.

STATEMENT OF FACT: Clothing styles have changed.

STATEMENT OF OPINION: The movie was boring.

You will also place a period at the end of a mildly worded order called a *mild imperative*. You will recognize these sentences easily since they often begin with a verb and have an "understood you" as their subject.

MILD IMPERATIVE: Change your shoes quickly.

If the order is delivered with more force or emotion, a writer should insert an exclamation mark instead. More information on this ending mark is provided later in this section.

Indirect questions also require a period. An indirect question needs no answer; instead, it is a statement that refers to a question that might be asked or has been asked previously.

DIRECT QUESTION: Are the pants on sale?

INDIRECT QUESTION: I asked whether the pants were on sale.

As you may recall, a sentence that asks a direct question to which an answer is desired is an interrogative sentence. Another end mark is necessary for interrogative sentences— the question mark.

Use a question mark (?) to end a direct question, an incomplete question, or a statement intended as a question.

A direct question demands an answer; it stands as a direct request for additional information. All direct questions must conclude with a question mark.

DIRECT QUESTIONS: Did you go to the discount clothing store?

What color looks best with these pants?

A helping verb or the words *who, what, where, when, why, how,* or *to what degree* at the beginning of a sentence often signal direct questions. Noticing these clues will help you put the proper punctuation at the end of the sentence.

In some cases, only a portion of the question is written out and the rest is simply understood. When this occurs, place a question mark at the end of the incomplete question.

INCOMPLETE QUESTIONS: Where? What color? How much?

In formal writing, you should avoid writing incomplete questions. Use them most often when writing conversations. Sometimes, a question is phrased as if it were a declarative sentence.

Use a question mark to show that the sentence is a question.

STATEMENTS INTENDED AS QUESTIONS: You called me?

They have four dogs?

Since some sentences express a great amount of emotion, another ending mark was developed—the exclamation mark.

Use an exclamation mark (!) to end an exclamatory sentence, a forceful imperative sentence, or an interjection expressing strong emotion.

An exclamatory sentence shows strong emphasis or emotion. It expresses more feeling than other sentences. An exclamation mark is used at the end of an exclamatory sentence to indicate the emphasis or emotion it expresses.

EXCLAMATORY SENTENCES: That evening gown looks stunning!

This dress costs $250!

A strongly worded imperative will also take an exclamation mark. Remember, the imperative must demonstrate a forcefulness or strong emotion in order to use this punctuation.

STRONG IMPERATIVE: Give me back those pearls, thief!

Occasionally (especially in conversations), one or two words are delivered emphatically. These strong interjections should be followed by an exclamation mark.

STRONG INTERJECTIONS: Breathtaking!   Ouch!   Oh dear!

Sometimes a strong interjection may precede a short exclamatory sentence. If this happens, you may choose whether you want to use a comma or exclamation mark after the interjection; both are appropriate.

WITH COMMA: My goodness, that thunder was loud!

WITH EXCLAMATION MARKS: My goodness! That thunder was loud!

According to the conventions of punctuation, both sentences are correctly punctuated.

NOTE ABOUT EXCLAMATION MARKS: Remember, overdoing the exclamation mark undoes its effectiveness. Use this mark sparingly to achieve the most effective writing.

EXERCISE A: Using the Period and Question Mark. The end marks have been left out of the following items. Copy the sentences and phrases onto your paper, adding the necessary periods or question marks.

1. Who has more bones—a baby or an adult?
2. I have often asked in what country a person can expect to live the longest.
3. What was the name of Roy Roger's horse?
4. Which state has produced the most Presidents?
5. How many?   Who?
6. The scientist questioned how long a queen termite can live.
7. Who knows what Lawrence Welk's personal license plate says?
8. Of all the animal personalities, who was first named to the Animal Hall of Fame?
9. Where can you find the tallest living thing in the world?
10. I wondered where the name Typhoid Mary came from.

EXERCISE B: Using the Period and Exclamation Mark. The end marks have been left out of the following sentences. Copy the sentences onto your paper, adding the necessary periods or exclamation marks. Answers will vary according to the way a sentence is spoken, so be prepared to defend your choices. *Answers will vary; samples given.*

1. Please bring me that pin cushion.
2. His operatic voice simply mesmerized me.
3. Don't touch that spider—it's poisonous!
4. Darn it!
5. A child is caught in that burning building!
6. Do as I say this minute, young man!
7. The house looked fresh after its new paint job.
8. Well, I have never been so insulted in my entire life!
9. Finish those essays for tomorrow, class.
10. I just won the Boston Marathon!

EXERCISE C: Using All of the End Marks. All of the end marks have been left out of the following paragraph. Copy the paragraph onto your paper, adding periods, question marks, or exclamation marks as needed.

(1) Popcorn! Get your fresh, hot, buttered popcorn right here! (2) The cry of the vendor selling popcorn has been heard for years at circuses, ball games, and county fairs. (3) But some may wonder who first learned about this delicacy. (4) Even before Columbus sailed to this continent, the Indians of Central and South America were popping little kernels of corn. (5) They ate them, made popcorn soup from them, and wore them during religious ceremonies. (6) Today popcorn is one of America's favorite snack foods. (7) Just how much popcorn do Americans eat in a year? (8) If you can believe it, they consume 450 million pounds of popcorn in twelve short months. (9) That keeps the popcorn industry happy but busy. (10) That is a lot of popcorn!

■ End Marks in Other Situations

End marks are not used exclusively to conclude sentences. Both the period and question mark serve other functions as well.

The Period. A major use of the period is found in abbreviations.

Use a period to end most abbreviations.

Some common abbreviations requiring periods include initials, titles of people, geographical locations, time references, numbers, and business terms. Study the following chart; if you want a more complete list, see Section 14.2.

SOME COMMON ABBREVIATIONS REQUIRING PERIODS				
Initials	**Titles of People**		**Geographical Locations**	
S. K. Biren	Mr.	Jr.	47 Mountain Rd.	
Matthew J. Kinney	Mrs.	Sr.	14 Peach Blossom St.	
	Dr.	M.D.	Savannah, Ga.	
	Rev.	Ph.D.	Laramie, Wyo..	
	Lt.	R.N.	U.S.A.	
			U.S.S.R.	

Time References	Numbers	Business Terms
A.M.	$7.21	Prentice-Hall, Inc.
B.C.	4.2	Smith Bros.
Mon.		U.P.S. (United Postal
Jan.		Service)

Remember that Miss is not an abbreviation, so do not use a period after it. You should also recognize that some businesses and organizations use letters but have dropped the periods after letters. FBI and NBC are two examples of these. Check a reliable source when you are in doubt.

When an abbreviation requiring a period comes at the end of the sentence, do not add an additional period as an end mark.

INCORRECT: The letter was addressed to K. Hillman, Ph.D..

CORRECT: The letter was addressed to K. Hillman, Ph.D.

If, however, the sentence requires any other punctuation mark besides the period, that punctuation mark must be inserted after the period.

EXAMPLES: Did you say that the letter was addressed to K. Hillman, Ph.D.?

The letter was addressed to K. Hillman, Ph.D., but Bob opened it anyway.

The period has yet another function you will want to know about when you write an outline.

Use a period after numbers and letters in outlines.

EXAMPLE: I. Addressing an envelope
  A. The mailing address
    1. Location on the envelope
    2. Necessary information to include
    3. Appropriate abbreviations

The Question Mark.   The question mark has another function as well as that of ending interrogative sentences.

Use a question mark in parentheses (?) after a fact or statistic to show its uncertainty.

EXAMPLE: The letter arrived on June 14(?).

Use caution when employing the question mark to show uncertainty. Its use should be limited to a fact that for some reason you simply cannot verify; do not insert it just because you do not wish to check the accuracy of a fact.

Furthermore, do not use the question mark in parentheses to indicate humor or irony.

INCORRECT: The intelligent (?) mail carrier couldn't read the address.

CORRECT: The supposedly intelligent mail carrier couldn't read the address.

In good writing, the words themselves should convey the humorous or ironic tone you are seeking. You should not have to provide visual clues for your reader.

EXERCISE D: Using End Marks in Other Situations. The periods and question marks have been left out of the following groups of words. Copy the word groups onto your paper, adding the necessary punctuation marks. Many items will require more than one mark.

1. 600 A.D.
2. Kim Partridge, Ph D
3. Lisa Holmes was born in 1905. (Show doubt about the year.) *in 1905 (?)*
4. Dr and Mrs Iseri
5. Tues, Oct 17
6. Rodriguez Enterprises, Inc

7. II The shark's teeth
   A They are in many rows
   B They never wear down
8. 7:24 a m
$6.15 9. Six dollars and fifteen cents (Use numerals.)
10. Austin, Tex

APPLICATION: Using End Marks in Your Own Writing. Follow the directions to write ten sentences of your own.
Answers will vary; samples given for first two.
1. Write a direct question about trucks.
2. Write an exclamatory sentence about barbecues.
3. Write a sentence that contains an abbreviation of a person's title.
4. Write an indirect question about baseball.
5. Write a mild imperative about stereos.
6. Write a declarative statement of fact on the topic of roller skates.
1. What mileage do these trucks get?
2. Yuk! Another rare hamburger!

7. Write a sentence with a geographical abbreviation.
8. Write a sentence about food using a question mark in parentheses to show uncertainty.
9. Write a mild imperative about a flower.
10. Write a declarative statement of opinion about a rock group.

Commas 15.2

The shape of the comma (,) resembles a fish hook, and just as a fish is caught on a hook, so a reader's voice is caught slightly on the comma. The comma tells the reader to take a short pause before continuing the sentence, and thus it brings greater clarity to the meaning of the sentence.

Writers probably use the comma more than any other internal punctuation mark. As a result more errors are made in the use of commas than in the use of any other punctuation mark. This section will focus on the comma, providing you with rules that will help you to use the comma correctly to separate basic elements and to set off added elements in sentences.

■ Commas in Compound Sentences

A compound sentence is two or more independent clauses joined by one of the following coordinating conjunctions: *and, or, nor, for, but, yet,* and *so.* A comma is needed to separate the independent clauses.

Use a comma before the conjunction to separate two independent clauses in a compound sentence.

Always check to make sure that you have written two *complete* sentences joined by a coordinating conjunction before you insert a comma.

EXAMPLES: We polished the silver, and the boys then used it to set the table.

Neither did the monkeys eat our peanuts, nor did the seals devour our gift of fish.

The most common error that writers make with this rule is not checking to make sure that complete sentences sit on *both* sides of the coordinating conjunction. They see the conjunction and automatically insert a comma. Remember, coordinating conjunctions can also join compound subjects, verbs, prepositional phrases, and clauses. When they are used in one of these ways, no comma is required.

COMPOUND VERB: The old friends chatted and laughed as they ate lunch.

COMPOUND PREPOSITIONAL PHRASE: I hit the golf ball into the water and then into a sand trap.

Sometimes, even with complete independent clauses, when both the clauses are quite short and easily understood, you may leave out the comma.

EXAMPLE: She loved long books but he preferred short ones.

EXERCISE A: **Using Commas in Compound Sentences.** Commas have been left out of some of the following sentences. Read each sentence and decide if a comma is needed. Write the word before the comma, the comma, and the conjunction following the comma on your paper. Write *not needed* for any sentences that do not need any commas.

1. The drummers beat out the rhythm, and the band marched proudly along the parade route.
2. The photograph clearly showed your feet, but somehow your head was cut off.
3. Neither did we visit the aquarium, nor did we watch the show at the planetarium.
4. You may have either hot chocolate or coffee to drink. *not needed*
5. Jack and Wendy will lead the songfest. *not needed*
6. The hateful mosquito bit me, and now I have a huge welt.
7. My mother lost her favorite earrings, so I will get her another pair for her birthday.
8. The airplane circled once and then came in for the landing. *not needed*
9. The student saved time for the last essay question, yet he found the time was not sufficient.
10. The TV blared but the child slept on. *not needed*

■ Commas in a Series and with Certain Kinds of Adjectives

Commas often are positioned internally in a sentence to set off basic elements such as the items in a series and certain kinds of adjectives.

Series.   Whenever a series of words, phrases, or clauses occurs in a sentence, you will need to insert commas.

Use commas to separate three or more words, phrases, or clauses in a series.

WORDS: I gathered the socks, shirts, and pants for the wash.

PREPOSITIONAL PHRASES: The cat carried her kittens into cupboards, under beds, and into the broom closet.

CLAUSES: The bank filled quickly with people who transferred their accounts, who cashed checks, and who opened their safe deposit boxes.

It may help you to know when you use this rule that the number of commas is one fewer than the number of items in the series. In the preceding examples, each series consists of three items; therefore, two commas are used in each of the series.

Some writers omit the last comma in a series. This is permissible as long as the writer follows a consistent pattern. The full use of commas, however, generally works better, especially in those cases where the last comma is needed to prevent confusion.

CORRECT: I gathered socks, shirts and pants for the wash.

CONFUSION: Endless streams of people, honking geese and police officers could all be seen leaving the fair.

ALWAYS CLEAR: Endless streams of people, honking geese, and police officers could all be seen leaving the fair.

Commas are not needed when all the items in a series have already been separated by conjunctions (usually *and* or *or*).

EXAMPLE: We cut *and* chopped *and* diced onions until we were all crying.

Commas should also be avoided between pairs of items that are used together so frequently that they are thought of as a single item. Notice in the following example that commas separate the pairs but not the items in the pairs.

EXAMPLE: I asked for *ham and eggs, coffee and cream,* and *bread and butter.*

Adjectives.   You should also use commas to divide adjectives of equal rank. Such adjectives are called *coordinate adjectives.*

Use commas to separate adjectives of equal rank.

To determine if adjectives in sentences are of equal rank ask yourself two questions: (1) Can you put an *and* between the adjectives and still have the sentence retain its exact meaning? (2) Can you switch the adjectives and still have a sentence that sounds grammatically correct? If the answer to the two test questions is *yes,* you have adjectives of equal rank, and a comma must be placed between them for clarity.

EXAMPLE: The dog's matted, filthy coat needed immediate washing.

In this example, *matted* and *filthy* qualify as coordinate adjectives.

If you have adjectives that must remain in a specific sequence, do not use a comma to separate them. Such adjectives are called *cumulative adjectives.*

Do not use commas to separate adjectives that must stay in a specific order.

EXAMPLE: I watched several lanky boys play basketball.

For the sentence in this example to retain its original meaning the adjectives must stay in the sequence in which they are written. Therefore, no comma is used to separate them.

EXERCISE B: Separating Items in a Series. Copy the following sentences onto your paper, adding the necessary commas. If no commas are needed, write *correct*.

1. We plan to sing and dance and act in our summer theater troupe. *C*
2. I carefully watered the philodendrons, the ivy, and the African violet.
3. The crowd sat on the edge of their seats, listened with awe, and absorbed the speaker's powerful words.
4. With great patience, diplomacy, and knowledge, the politician answered the questions from the crowd.
5. I looked under the bed, in the closet, and through my desk to find my homework.
6. Cloris Leachman, Henry Fonda, and other well-known stars performed in the play *The Oldest Living Graduate*.
7. I described the symptoms to the doctor: a temperature, aching bones, nausea, and a rash on my legs.
8. Send that letter to the President, the Secretary of State, and the Ambassador of France.
9. We went first to pick up Beth and then to find Barry and finally to get Peter. *C*
10. The sun shone brightly, the clouds drifted lazily overhead, and we waded in the warm water.

EXERCISE C: Using Commas with Adjectives. The following phrases contain either coordinate or cumulative adjectives. For each phrase, write *cumulative* if the adjectives are cumulative and require no comma. If the adjectives are coordinate, write them down, inserting the comma.

1. many delicious jams and jellies *cumulative*
2. moist, large mushrooms
3. dark, angry funnel clouds
4. several sharp pencils *cumulative*
5. the dusty, yellowed documents
6. bright red dress *cumulative*
7. disorganized, crowded cabinet
8. a clear plastic covering *cumulative*
9. hot, greasy french fries *lative*
10. a friendly, good-natured grin

■ **Commas After Introductory Material**

Commas are also used after introductory material consisting of either words, phrases, or clauses.

Use a comma after an introductory word, phrase, or clause.

Check the following chart for examples of this rule used with all types of introductory material.

KINDS OF INTRODUCTORY MATERIAL		
Words	Introductory Words:	No, I will not drive you to the bowling alley.
	Nouns of Direct Address:	Cindy, could you hold this painting?
	Common Expressions:	Of course, we can get that printed for you.
	Introductory Adverbs:	Obviously, the student had copied. Hurriedly, she hid the present she had been wrapping.
Phrases	Prepositional Phrases: (usually only if they consist of four words or more)	In the deep recesses of the couch, I found the watch I had lost.
	Participial Phrases:	Jumping over the fence, the horse caught its back hoof.
	Infinitive Phrases:	To get to the appointment on time, the man needed to leave earlier.
Clauses	Adverbial Clauses:	When the steaks were medium rare, we took them off the grill.

EXERCISE D: Using Commas After Introductory Material. Many of the following sentences contain introductory material that is not set off by commas. For each sentence, write the introductory material and the comma, if one is needed, on your paper.

1. Though we probably do not think about it often, we use soap every day.
2. In fact, a person uses an average of twenty-eight pounds of soap and detergent a year.
3. According to old legends, soap was invented over three thousand years ago.
4. On top of Sapo Hill in Rome, fat from sacrificed animals soaked through the ashes on the altar and into the soil.

5. Soon after, the women discovered that the soil produced a soapy clay that helped wash their clothes.
6. Working with caustic soda in the 1700's, Nicolas Leblanc discovered that an inexpensive soap could be produced from salt.
7. To have soap in the early days of American history, frontier women had to make lye soap themselves.
8. When the 1800's arrived, the soap industry began.
9. However, it was not until 1916 that Fritz Gunther developed the first synthetic detergent for industrial use.
10. In 1933, Proctor and Gamble began to produce household detergents for the marketplace.

■ Commas with Parenthetical Expressions and Nonessential Material

Commas are often used within a sentence to set off parenthetical expressions and nonessential material. First, consider parenthetical expressions.

Parenthetical Expressions. A parenthetical expression is a word or phrase that is unrelated to the rest of the sentence and interrupts the sentence's general flow. Study the following list of common parenthetical expressions.

NOUNS OF DIRECT ADDRESS: Denise, Mrs. Burke, my son, beloved wife

CERTAIN ADVERBS: also, besides, furthermore, however, indeed, instead, moreover, nevertheless, otherwise, therefore, thus

COMMMON EXPRESSIONS: by the way, I feel, in my opinion, in the first place, of course, on the other hand, you know

CONTRASTING EXPRESSIONS: not that one, not there, not mine

When you see any of these parenthetical expressions, use the following rule.

Use commas to set off parenthetical expressions.

Two commas are used to enclose the entire parenthetical expression when the expression occurs in the middle of the sentence.

NOUN OF DIRECT ADDRESS: We will go, Margaret, as soon as your father arrives home.

INTERRUPTING ADVERB: The boys, therefore, decided to call a tow truck.

COMMON EXPRESSION: The flowers, in my opinion, have never looked healthier.

CONTRASTING EXPRESSION: It was here, not there, that we found the answer.

If one of these expressions is used at the end of the sentence, however, only one comma is necessary.

EXAMPLE: We will go as soon as your father arrives home, Margaret.

Essential and Nonessential Expressions. Since commas are only used with nonessential expressions, writers need to learn to distinguish between essential and nonessential material. (The terms *restrictive* and *nonrestrictive* are sometimes used to refer to the same type of expressions.)

An *essential expression* is a word, phrase, or clause that provides essential information in the sentence: information that cannot be removed without changing the meaning of the sentence. In the following example, the clause following *boy* tells *which* boy the writer means, and thus, provides essential information in the sentence.

EXAMPLE: The boy who is holding the book won the contest.

Because the clause in this sentence is an essential expression, it is not set off with commas.

Nonessential expressions provide additional, but not essential, information in a sentence. You can remove nonessential material from a sentence, and the remaining sentence will still contain all the necessary information required by the reader.

EXAMPLE: Michael Weightman, who is holding the book, won the contest.

Here the boy is specifically named, and the information contained in the clause only provides an additional fact; the clause is not essential. Thus, this clause qualifies as a nonessential expression.

Once you have decided whether or not an expression is essential, you can apply this rule.

Use commas to set off nonessential expressions.

When applying the preceding rule, be alert for three types of word groups: appositives, participial phrases, and adjective clauses. They often serve as either essential or non-essential expressions. Check them carefully to avoid committing comma errors. Study the following chart until you feel confident that you can tell the difference between essential and nonessential expressions.

ESSENTIAL AND NONESSENTIAL EXPRESSIONS		
Appositives	Essential:	My sister Joanne went to the University of California at Davis.
	Nonessential:	Joanne, my sister, went to the University of California at Davis.
Participial Phrases	Essential:	The teacher wearing a blue dress took the students on the field trip.
	Nonessential:	Mrs. Goff, wearing the blue dress, took the students on the field trip.
Adjective Clauses	Essential:	The hotel that we enjoyed the most had three swimming pools and lighted tennis courts.
	Nonessential:	The Royal Tahitian Hotel, which rated as our favorite, had three swimming pools and lighted tennis courts.

The examples in the chart show only expressions that are located in the middle of the sentence; each nonessential expression is set off with two commas. If the expression shifts to the beginning or to the end of the sentence, use only one comma. *Essential: if nonsense results about it*

EXAMPLE: That evening he met Joanne, my sister.

EXERCISE E: Setting Off Parenthetical Expressions. Copy each of the following sentences onto your paper, inserting the necessary commas to set off the parenthetical expressions.

1. We have enough paper plates left over,I think.
2. The suit,nevertheless,needed drastic alterations before I could wear it.
3. When does your ship sail,Mr. Harville?
4. I will type up the letter,Kim,if you get it written by tomorrow.
5. I,therefore,went out shopping for a bathing suit.
6. My performance was absolutely perfect,of course!
7. We went,instead,to see *Romeo and Juliet*.
8. You may ask your question,Ed,as soon as I finish.
9. The candidate,furthermore,expresses support for Proposition A.
10. The newspaper,on the other hand,carries more business news than its competitor.

EXERCISE F: Distinguishing Between Essential and Nonessential Expressions. All of the following sentences contain internal expressions, some of which require commas. If the sentence contains an essential expression needing no additional commas, write *essential* on your paper. If the sentence contains a nonessential expression, copy the sentence onto your paper, adding the necessary commas.

1. Pirates,those colorful, legendary plunderers of the ocean, made many spectacular heists on the high seas.
2. Bartholomew Roberts,who allowed no drinking or gambling on board his vessel,caught and pirated over four hundred ships.
3. Long Ben Avery, beginning his pirating career at age twenty,captured $2,000,000—the largest amount of loot ever stolen.
4. The pirates,who broke almost every law in the book,still possessed a very strong code of honor within their own ranks.
5. Pirates stealing from their mates had their ears and noses cut off as punishment. *essential*
6. Ships that were attacked by pirates often sank with all the men and treasures still aboard. *essential*
7. Experts studying cases of buccaneering believe as much as forty million dollars in gold may rest in watery graves. *essential*
8. In 1962 excavators who were digging off the coast of Florida discovered three million dollars in sunken treasure. *essential*

9. Excavation for sunken treasure has recently started at the pirate city Port Royal. *essential*
10. An earthquake that hit in 1692 killed over 2,000 pirates and buried much of their wealth under water. *essential*

■ Other Uses of the Comma

Commas are used in several additional situations.

With Dates. Dates containing numbers require commas.

When a date is made up of two or more parts, use a comma after each item except in the case of a month followed by a day.

EXAMPLES: On Friday, April 17, we have a special schedule at school.

The city's new mass transit system ran its first train on June 11, 1974, after a dedication ceremony.

You may use or omit the commas if the date contains only the month and the year.

EXAMPLES: February, 1980, was one of the wettest months on record.

February 1980 was one of the wettest months on record.

If the parts of a date have already been joined by prepositions, no comma is needed.

EXAMPLE: The city's new mass transit system ran its first train on June 11 in 1974.

With Locations. Whenever you are citing a specific place, check to see if a comma is required.

When a geographical name is made up of two or more parts, use a comma after each item.

EXAMPLES: I traveled from Taos, New Mexico, to Oklahoma City, Oklahoma.

With Titles. To indicate titles following a name, you should use a comma.

When a name is followed by one or more titles, use a comma after the name and after each title.

EXAMPLE: I noticed that Jeremy McGuire, Sr., works for the law firm of Heller, Ramirez, and Donaldson, Incorporated.

In this example, notice how the comma is dropped after the word *Incorporated* because it occurs at the end of the sentence.

With Addresses.   When writing addresses consisting of two or more parts, you will need to use commas to separate the parts.

Use a comma after each item in an address made up of two or more parts.

EXAMPLE: My new address is K. Wedel, 243 Park Street, St. Louis, Missouri   63131.

If you placed this address on an envelope, most of the commas would then be omitted. Notice in both cases that extra space, instead of a comma, is left between the state and the ZIP code.

EXAMPLE: K. Wedel
243 Park Street
St. Louis, Missouri   63131

You should also avoid using commas if prepositions join the parts of the address.

EXAMPLE: K. Wedel lives on Park Street in St. Louis.

With Salutations and Closings.   You will need to use commas in the openings and closings of many letters.

Use a comma after the salutation in a personal letter and after the closing in all letters.

SALUTATIONS: Dear Rupert,   Dear Aunt Lucy,
CLOSINGS: Sincerely,   In appreciation,

With Numbers.   Certain numerical references require commas.

With numbers of more than three digits, use a comma after every third digit counting from the right.

EXAMPLES: The projected complex would house 1,245 people.

498,362,719

There are several exceptions to this rule: ZIP codes, phone numbers, and page and serial numbers do not have commas.

EXAMPLES: ZIP code   26413

Telephone number   (612) 555–3702

Page number   1047

With Omissions.   Sometimes, you will purposely omit a word or phrase from a sentence; this is then known as an elliptical sentence. For clarity, you will often need to insert a comma where words have been left out.

Use a comma to indicate the words left out of an elliptical sentence.

In the following example, the omitted word does not interfere with the meaning of the sentence, for the missing word is understood. However, the comma serves as a visual clue to the reader that an omission exists.

EXAMPLE: The man walked quickly; the woman, slowly.

With Quotations.   Commas are also used with quotations containing a "he said/she said" phrase.

Use a comma to set off the quoted words in a "he said/she said" quotation.

As the following examples demonstrate, the placement of the comma varies with the placement of the "he said/she said" phrase.

EXAMPLES: The guest asked, "Do you know of any nearby drug stores that are open all night?"

"If you don't mind a little drive," the host said, "you will find one about three miles down the road."

"Oh, that will be perfect," the guest replied.

For a more detailed study of punctuating quotations with commas, see Section 15.4.

For Clarity. You will occasionally run across a sentence structure that may be confusing without a comma. By inserting a comma, you can reduce the confusion and prevent misreading.

Use a comma to prevent a sentence from being misunderstood.

UNCLEAR: She studied French and English literature.

BETTER: She studied French, and English literature.

These sentences could easily be misread, but the addition of the comma prevents this.

NOTE ABOUT CARELESS USE OF THE COMMA: Too many commas in a paper leads to choppiness and confusion. Generally, you should not use a comma unless you have a rule clearly in mind. Study the following examples of careless overuse of commas, and try to avoid such use in your own writing.

MISUSE WITH ADJECTIVE AND NOUN: The furry, kitten padded across the floor.

CORRECT: The furry kitten padded across the floor.

MISUSE WITH COMPOUND SUBJECTS: We watched as the man, and woman executed some fancy dance steps.

CORRECT: We watched as the man and woman executed some fancy dance steps.

MISUSE WITH COMPOUND VERBS: The dancers leaped, and twirled around the stage.

CORRECT: The dancers leaped and twirled around the stage.

MISUSE WITH PREPOSITIONAL PHRASES: The dancers bowed to the audience, and to the conductor.

CORRECT: The dancers bowed to the audience and to the conductor.

MISUSE WITH SUBORDINATE CLAUSES: I won't forget that you gave me the ticket, or how much I enjoyed the performance.

CORRECT: I won't forget that you gave me the ticket or how much I enjoyed the performance.

EXERCISE G: Using Commas in Other Situations. The commas have been left out of each of the following sentences. Copy the sentences onto your paper, adding the necessary commas.

1. The drive from Seattle, Washington, to Portland, Oregon, is a pretty one.
2. He was elected on Tuesday, November 5, and inaugurated in January of the next year.
3. There were 50000 people watching the parade.
4. "Move into the left lane please," the officer patiently instructed.
5. My brother asked, "Have you eaten dinner yet?"
6. Our class will have Martin Deardorf, Ph.D., as our guest lecturer.
7. I read the address on the business card: R.P. Mendosa, 615 Taggert Lane, Cupertino, California 95014.
8. The irate customer spoke belligerently; the public relations officer, gently.
9. "When I reached the age of eight," the woman recalled, "I decided to become a dental hygienist."
10. During the afternoon, tea and pastries were always served.

EXERCISE H: Correcting Careless Use of Commas. Some of the commas have been used incorrectly in the following sentences. Rewrite each sentence, removing any incorrect commas. *Circled commas are to be omitted.*

1. During the initial training period, the falcon, sits on a gloved hand with a hood covering its head.
2. Bees have existed for about fifty million years, and live everywhere but the North and South Poles.
3. An interesting fact about the buffalo is, that it is found on the ten dollar bill.
4. Bill, don't forget to rake the leaves, and clean the garage.
5. The cost of World War II, in deaths and suffering, was enormous.
6. Hospitals use morphine for sedatives, and hypnotic analgesics.
7. If eaten, the beautiful, Christmas poinsettia is poisonous.
8. The crayfish is the freshwater counterpart of the lobster, and is found in freshwater springs and lakes.
9. The queen bee, really does not rule the colony but only serves to reproduce the bees.

10. When new seedlings begin to grow, they need water○ and sunshine.

APPLICATION: **Using Commas in Your Own Sentences.** Write ten sentences of your own, using the following sentence parts. *Answers will vary; samples given for first two.*

1. An introductory phrase
2. Two complete sentences joined by a conjunction
3. An essential clause
4. A quotation containing a "he said/she said" phrase
5. A series of items

6. A nonessential modifier
7. A parenthetical expression
8. Coordinate adjectives
9. Cumulative adjectives
10. An elliptical construction

1. Having seen one cave, Mrs. Molnar had no desire to see another.

2. Cara came late to the party, but she had more fun than anyone else.

15.3 Semicolons and Colons

The semicolon (;) is a punctuation mark that serves as the happy medium between the comma and the period. It signals to the reader to pause longer than for a comma but to pause without the finality of a period. The semicolon is used to join independent sentences or to clarify a possibly confusing sentence structure.

The colon (:) is used primarily to point ahead to additional information. It directs the reader to look on for further explanation or amplification.

The first part of this section will cover the rules that govern the use of semicolons. The last part will present the ways in which you can use colons.

■ Uses of the Semicolon

The semicolon is used to separate independent clauses that have a close relationship to each other. A semicolon is also used to separate independent clauses or items in a series that already contain commas within them.

With Independent Clauses. Semicolons are most often used between independent clauses.

Use a semicolon to join independent clauses that are not already joined by the conjunction *and, or, nor, for, but, so,* or *yet.*

Two sentences joined by a conjunction need a comma before the conjunction.

EXAMPLE: The child rode the merry-go-round, but she soon grew dizzy going in constant circles.

Since the semicolon carries more strength than the comma, it replaces *both* the comma and the conjunction. Notice in the following example that the second independent clause of two joined by a semicolon starts with a small letter. Do not use a capital following a semicolon unless the word following the semicolon is a proper noun or a proper adjective.

EXAMPLE: The child rode the merry-go-round; she soon grew dizzy going in constant circles.

You should not use the semicolon to join unrelated sentences. The semicolon should be used only when the independent clauses have a close relationship. Most often this will be a close relationship in meaning. Notice, for instance, the relationship of the clauses in the second example that follows.

INCORRECT: Alice is a good chess player; rain is expected tomorrow.

CORRECT: The dog patiently sat as near the table as permitted; he hoped some table scraps might come his way.

Sometimes, the independent clauses share a similar structure as well as a similar meaning.

EXAMPLE: With enthusiasm, he cast his line out into the lake; with pleasure, he later cooked his fish.

Notice that in this example, both sentences center around a shared subject—fishing. The sentences are also similar to one another in structure. This is a perfect situation in which to use the semicolon.

Occasionally, independent clauses may set up a contrast between one another.

EXAMPLE: My sister excels at art; I can barely draw a straight line.

As you can see in this example, the sentences center around a central subject by looking at the two extremes of that subject.

Up to this point, the discussion has concentrated on the semicolon as it applies to *two* independent clauses; however, if the independent clauses increase in number, the semicolon can still be used.

EXAMPLE: The horse nibbled at the grass; the cowboy picked despondently at his food; the prairie dog watched the scene from a safe distance.

Independent clauses also need a semicolon when they are joined by either a conjunctive adverb or a transitional expression.

Use a semicolon to join independent clauses separated by either a conjunctive adverb or a transitional expression.

Before looking at examples of this use of the semicolon, take a moment to review the following list containing common conjunctive adverbs and transitional phrases.

CONJUNCTIVE ADVERBS: also, besides, furthermore, however, indeed, instead, moreover, nevertheless, otherwise, therefore, consequently, thus

TRANSITIONAL EXPRESSIONS: as a result, at this time, first, for instance, in fact, on the other hand, second, that is

Notice in the following examples that the semicolon is placed before the conjunctive adverb or the transitional expression. A comma follows the conjunctive adverb or the transitional expression since it serves as an introductory expression in the second independent clause.

CONJUNCTIVE ADVERB: A cloudless blue sky dawned that morning; nevertheless, rain was forecast for later in the day.

TRANSITIONAL EXPRESSION: We needed to get to the spare tire in the trunk; as a result, we had to unload all the trunk's contents onto the roadside.

Since words used as conjuctive adverbs and transitions can also interrupt one continuous sentence, always check to be sure that there is an independent clause on *each* side of the conjunctive adverb or transitional expression.

INCORRECT: The team was; consequently, disqualified for cheating.

CORRECT: The team was, consequently, disqualified for cheating.

In these examples, the word *consequently* interrupts one continuous sentence; therefore, a semicolon would not be appropriate.

Using the Semicolon to Avoid Confusion.   The semicolon helps avoid confusion in sentences where other internal punctuation already exists. First, the semicolon helps avoid confusion when two independent clauses contain their own internal punctuation.

Consider the use of semicolons to avoid confusion when independent clauses already contain commas.

When a sentence consists of two independent clauses joined by a coordinating conjunction, the tendency is to place a comma before the conjunction. However, when one or both of the sentences also contain commas, a semicolon may be used before the conjunction to prevent confusion.

EXAMPLE: The thieves stole my favorite painting, a scene of a small fishing village; but they did not locate my valuable jewelry.

The semicolon also helps avoid confusion in a series of items containing their own internal punctuation.

Use a semicolon between items in a series if the items themselves contain commas.

A series generally consists of several items separated by commas.

EXAMPLE: We visited the Averills, the Wilsons, and the Garcias.

Sometimes, the items in the series may contain their own commas; in that case, a semicolon is used to prevent a whole string of commas from confusing the reader. The semicolon helps make clear to the reader where each complete item of the series ends.

EXAMPLE: We visited the Averills, who live in Wisconsin; the Wilsons, friends in Michigan; and the Garcias, former neighbors now living in North Dakota.

You will use the semicolon in a series most commonly when the items contain either nonessential appositives, participial phrases, or adjective clauses.

APPOSITIVES: I sent notes to Mr. Nielson, my science teacher; Mrs. Jensen, my history instructor; and Mrs. Seltz, my coach.

PARTICIPIAL PHRASES: My cat, meowing at the door; my dog, howling at the neighbors; and my sister, babbling on the phone, gave me a terrible headache.

ADJECTIVE CLAUSES: The tires, which were brand new; the stereo, which I had just installed; and the engine, which was newly tuned-up, helped make the trip enjoyable.

Notice in the last two examples that the last item of nonessential material is set off by a comma rather than by a semicolon.

EXERCISE A: Using the Semicolon with Independent Clauses. The semicolons have been left out of the following sentences. Read each sentence and decide where a semicolon is required. Write the word that goes before the semicolon, the semicolon, and the word that goes after it.

1. Yo-yos have been enjoyed for <u>years;in</u> fact, people in ancient Greece played with yo-yo-like toys for entertainment.
2. In France, the popularity of the yo-yo grew <u>quickly;for</u> instance, the nobles in seventeenth-century France played with yo-yos in the royal courts.
3. Napoleon's soldiers played with them while waiting to <u>fight;France's</u> prisoners supposedly played with them while waiting for the guillotine.
4. Even King George IV is pictured with a <u>yo-yo;a</u> cartoonist satirically drew him spinning his top.
5. In Europe they *played* with <u>yo-yos;in</u> the Philippines they used them for more serious purposes.

6. In the sixteenth century, the people of the Philippines hunted with yo-yo-like <u>weapons</u>;<u>they</u> sat in trees and sent the yo-yos hurtling down to stun the animals below them.
7. History reports that Donald Duncan first promoted the yo-yo in America in <u>1926</u>;<u>however</u>, recent evidence shows Lothrop Llewellyn selling a metal yo-yo as early as 1906.
8. He sold his yo-yos in <u>Gloucester</u>;<u>Llewellyn</u> even took out patent rights on his invention.
9. The latest yo-yo craze occurred in the early <u>1960's</u>;<u>indeed</u>, Duncan reportedly sold 15 million yo-yos in 1961 alone.
10. Today, the most difficult yo-yo trick is the <u>whirlwind</u>;<u>it</u> requires performing inside and outside loop-the-loops.

EXERCISE B: Using Semicolons with Internal Punctuation. The semicolons have been left out of the following sentences. Read each sentence and decide where semicolons are required. Write the word that goes before the semicolon, the semicolon, and the word that goes after it.

1. When the milk carton fell, it <u>split</u>;<u>but</u> I managed to get it up before all the milk flowed out onto the floor.
2. Joe, Maria, and I drove into the city last <u>night</u>;<u>and</u> we watched one of the most touching musicals, *Runaways*.
3. As I watched, the tall, thin man reached into the pedestrian's pocket, removing the <u>wallet</u>;<u>but</u> before I could even protest, he was lost in the crowd.
4. As she tried to lay out the pattern on the material, she finally concluded that she was short of <u>fabric</u>;<u>and</u> so she switched to another pattern, one requiring less material.
5. My grandmother knew more about people, places, and life in general than many world <u>travelers</u>;<u>yet</u> she never left the state of Nebraska.
6. When the cast was posted, you should have seen the look of joy on Martin's <u>face</u>;<u>for</u> to get a lead in the play was his dream.
7. Walking home from the store, I found an injured, frightened <u>cat</u>;<u>and</u> at that moment, I knew he was meant to be mine.
8. I peeked out of my sleeping bag and saw a squirrel, who was busily gathering his winter <u>store</u>;<u>a</u> bird, who was welcoming the morning in <u>song</u>;<u>and</u> a doe, who was surveying her peaceful domain.
9. During this morning's practice, we have to master the <u>routine</u>;<u>or</u> the coach says we work, work, work all afternoon until it looks perfect.

10. Neither did that young gymnast waver on the balance
beam, which is only four inches <u>wide;nor</u> did she make
one error on her floor exercises.

■ Uses of the Colon

The colon acts mainly as an introductory device. It is
also used in several special situations.

Colons as Introductory Devices.   To use the colon correctly as an introductory device, you must be familiar with
the different things it can introduce. Perhaps most important, the colon can introduce a list.

Use a colon before a list of items following an independent
clause.

EXAMPLE: We must bring the following items: a flashlight, a
thermos, and a blanket.

As shown in this example, the independent clause before
a list often ends in a phrase such as *the following* or *the following items*. You should familiarize yourself with these
phrases since they often indicate the need for a colon. Of
course, you should not depend on these phrases alone to signal the need for a colon. The most important point to consider is whether or not an independent clause precedes the
list. If it does, use a colon.

EXAMPLE: I bought several pieces of clothing on sale: a blouse, a
skirt, and two pairs of pants.

Colons can also be used to introduce certain quotations.

Use a colon to introduce a quotation that is formal or lengthy
or a quotation that does not contain a "he said/she said"
phrase.

Often, a formal quotation requiring a colon will consist
of more than one sentence. However, your best guideline for
inserting a colon should be the formality of the quotation.
The more formal the quotation, the more likely you will
need a colon. Do not use a colon to introduce a casual
quoted remark or dialogue, even if more than one sentence
is used.

FORMAL: Formally approaching the bench, the lawyer said: "My client pleads, 'Not guilty.' "

CASUAL: As Ann left the room, she called, "I really must hurry. I don't want to be late."

Remember, also, to notice whether or not the quotation contains a "he said/she said" phrase. You will want to use a colon to introduce even a casual quotation that does not contain a "he said/she said" phrase.

FORMAL: He walked stiffly to the door and then turned: "Your accusations are false. You have gone too far this time."

CASUAL: Teresa stood up slowly: "I think I'll go home. It's been a long day."

The colon can also serve as an introductory device for a sentence that either amplifies or summarizes what has preceded it.

Use a colon to introduce a sentence that summarizes or explains the sentence before it.

When using a complete sentence following a colon, you will need to employ the capitalization rule that appears on page 310. Capitalize the first word after a colon if the word begins a complete sentence.

EXAMPLES: The garage attendant provided me with one piece of advice: He said to check my water level often until I could get my car in for the needed repairs.

The tuna casserole lacked a rather vital ingredient: I forgot the tuna!

In both of these sentences, the colon points to the explanation contained in the next sentence. These sentences, in turn, amplify or summarize the information presented in the preceding independent clause.

Another basic use of the colon is to point to a formal appositive following an independent clause.

Use a colon to introduce a formal appositive that follows an independent clause.

Using a colon, instead of a comma, to introduce an appositive that follows an independent clause gives additional emphasis to the appositive. Thus, using a colon makes the appositive more important than using a comma would.

EXAMPLE: I missed one important paragraph lesson: writing the topic sentence.

In this example, notice that the first clause could stand alone. It contains both a subject and a verb, and it makes sense by itself. Always check to insure that the words *preceding* the colon constitute an independent clause. Do not put a colon after a verb or a preposition since that will result in a fragment.

INCORRECT: We decided: to see a movie.

CORRECT: We decided to see a movie: *The Wizard of Oz*.

INCORRECT: Our tour took us by: the rose gardens, the Japanese park, and the hanging gardens.

CORRECT: Our tour took us by some beautiful spots: the rose gardens, the Japanese park, and the hanging gardens.

Although an independent clause must *precede* a colon, it is not necessary that the words *following* the colon be an independent clause. An appositive composed of a word or short phrase may follow a colon.

EXAMPLES: From the jeep, I looked out over the dry grass and saw the king of beasts: a lion.

She asked that we play her favorite game: Boggle.

As you can see, the word *lion* is an appositive for *the king of beasts*, and the word *Boggle* is an appositive for *game*.

You could successfully argue that a comma would also be appropriate where the colon is inserted. However, the colon provides a slightly more dramatic, profound effect than that achieved by the comma. As a writer, you will have the responsibility of deciding whether the comma or the colon more precisely fits the tone you are establishing.

Special Uses of the Colon.   The colon has several specialized functions.

Use a colon in a number of special writing situations.

The special situations requiring the use of a colon include the following: time, volume and page numbers, Biblical chapter and verse references, book subtitles, business letter salutations, and labels used to introduce important ideas. Study the following chart; it provides examples of the colon's use in each of these conventional cases.

SPECIAL SITUATIONS REQUIRING COLONS	
Numerals Giving the Time:	5:22 A.M. 7:49 P.M.
References to Periodicals (Volume Number: Page Number):	*Forbes* 4:8
Biblical References (Chapter Number: Verse Number):	Genesis 1:5
Subtitles for Books and Magazines:	*Fixing Hamburger: One Hundred Ways to Prepare Delicious Meals*
Salutations in Business Letters:	Dear Mr. Biggs: Ladies: Dear Sir:
Labels Used to Signal Important Ideas:	Warning: Cigarette smoking can be hazardous to your health. Note: This letter must be postmarked no later than the tenth of this month.

EXERCISE C: **Using Colons as Introductory Devices.** Colons and some capital letters have been left out of the following sentences. Read the sentences and decide where the colons and capital letters are required. Then copy the sentences onto your paper, adding the necessary punctuation and capitalization. Underlined letters are to be capitalized.

1. This man was born December 5, 1901, and until his death in 1966, he was one of the most well-known gentlemen in the world: Walt Disney.
2. Of course, he is best remembered as the creator of some of our most beloved cartoon characters: Mickey Mouse, Pluto, and Donald Duck.
3. Walt Disney studied one subject with diligence: he concentrated on art.

4. Walt Disney felt he had to go to the one city where he could possibly become successful he headed to Hollywood.
5. In Hollywood, he made money from his drawings, but he finally hit success with a now-classic cartoon short featuring Mickey Mouse "Steamboat Willie."
6. Disney went on to create many of the following famous films Snow White and the Seven Dwarfs, Fantasia, and Mary Poppins.
7. In 1955 he started something that was to change family entertainment he opened Disneyland.
8. Parents appreciated Walt Disney "Our children can explore the worlds of Frontierland, Fantasyland, Tomorrowland, and Adventureland in a clean environment."
9. Several years later Disney directed his efforts in a new direction television.
10. Yes, Disney has left us the kind of lasting memorials that will continue to be enjoyed by millions around the globe Mickey Mouse, Snow White, Bambi, and the rest of the gang in Disney's world.

EXERCISE D: Using Colons for Special Writing Situations. The colons have been left out of the following sentences. Copy the sentences onto your paper, adding the necessary colons.

1. Warning Pull the plug after you have finished using the iron.
2. School ended at 2 35 p.m., and we were expected to be ready for the presentation at 3 00 p.m.
3. *The Readers' Guide* listed *Time* 16 23, but I could not find that issue.
4. "Dear Mr. Nielson " is the way I started my business letter.
5. The Old Testament reading came from Psalms 130:5.
6. I have been reading *Caring for Livestock A Guide for Beginners.*
7. I should be finished with my homework at 10 00 p.m.
8. Danger This water is polluted. No swimming is allowed.
9. Note The assembly will begin thirty minutes later than indicated in the bulletin.
10. The movie starts at 7 30 p.m.

APPLICATION: Writing Sentences Using the Semicolon and Colon. Using your imagination, fill in the blanks in the following sentences on your paper. Then follow the instructions given after each sentence, using the word or words you put in the blank. *Answers will vary; sample sentences given for first one.*

1. My favorite sport is _____archery_____ .
   a. Write a sentence about this, using a semicolon to join two independent clauses with a close relationship.
   b. Write a sentence using semicolons to separate a series of items that contain internal punctuation.
2. I have the hardest time doing homework when _____a movie_____ is on TV.
   a. Write a sentence with a colon pointing to a summary or explanation.
   b. Write a sentence containing a semicolon and conjunctive adverb.
3. My favorite dinner has _____meat_____ as its main course.
   a. Write a sentence with a colon pointing to a list.
   b. Write a sentence with a semicolon preceding a transitional expression.
4. If I had the money to go see a concert, I would spend it on _____records_____ .
   a. Write a sentence using time or volume and page numbers.
   b. Write a sentence with a semicolon joining two contrasting clauses.
5. The most annoying habit I can think of is _____thumb-sucking_____.
   a. Write a sentence joining two independent clauses—each with its own internal punctuation.
   b. Write a sentence with a colon pointing to a formal appositive.

a. My parents gave me an archery set for my fifth birthday; my mother showed me how to use it. b. Encouraged by my parents, I learned quickly; within a few months, I became quite proficient; and by Christmas I was demanding a better archery set.

Quotation Marks with Direct Quotations

15.4

Writers usually attempt to provide concrete support for the ideas or arguments that they put forth. Directly quoting an expert or well-known person can provide support for your statements while making your writing more colorful.

A **direct quotation** represents a person's exact speech or thoughts and is enclosed in quotation marks (" ").

EXAMPLE: "No barrier of the senses shuts me out from the sweet, gracious discourse of my book friends."—Helen Keller

Do not confuse direct quotations with those that are indirect.

An **indirect quotation** reports the general meaning of what a person said or thought and does not require quotation marks.

INDIRECT QUOTATION: Helen Keller wrote that being blind and deaf did not prevent her from enjoying reading.

Paraphrasing, like that in this example of the indirect quotation, does not lend itself to dynamic, strong writing the way a direct quote does. Therefore, you should avoid indirect quotations when possible.

This section will take a close look at direct quotations to help clarify any uncertainties you may have regarding their use.

■ Indicating Direct Quotations

All direct quotations in your writing must be indicated by quotation marks. There are various ways a writer may present a direct quotation. One way is to quote an uninterrupted sentence. Another way is to use an introductory, concluding, or interrupting expression with a quotation. Writers may also present a quoted phrase within an otherwise complete sentence.

To enclose a sentence that is an uninterrupted direct quotation, double quotation marks (" ") are placed around the quoted material. Of course, each complete sentence of any quotation begins with a capital letter.

Use quotation marks before and after an uninterrupted direct quotation.

DIRECT QUOTATION: "Suspicion always haunts the guilty mind."
—William Shakespeare

Sometimes you may wish to add a "he said/she said" expression to a quotation to show who is speaking. A "he said/she said" phrase may introduce a quoted sentence.

When an introductory expression precedes a direct quotation, place a comma or colon after the introductory expression and write the quotation as a full sentence.

INTRODUCTORY EXPRESSION: Shakespeare wrote, "Suspicion always haunts the guilty mind."

If you do not use a "he said/she said" expression to introduce a quotation or if the introductory phrase takes a more formal tone, use a colon instead of a comma.

EXAMPLES: The President turned to face the cameras: "We are pleased to announce that agreement has been reached."

Solemnly, she stated: "I will resign as treasurer of this firm, effective the first of next month."

In the second example, you could argue that a comma would also be appropriate. However, the formal tone of the phrase makes the colon a more effective method of punctuation.

On some occasions, a "he said/she said" phrase may conclude a quoted sentence.

When a concluding expression follows a direct quotation, write the quotation as a full sentence ending with a comma, question mark, or exclamation mark inside the quotation mark, and then write the concluding expression.

CONCLUDING EXPRESSION: "Suspicion always haunts the guilty mind," wrote Shakespeare.

When a direct quotation is interrupted by a "he said/she said" expression, quotation marks enclose *both* parts of the quotation.

When a direct quotation of one sentence is interrupted, end the first part of the direct quotation with a comma and a quotation mark, place a comma after the interrupting expression, and then proceed with a new quotation mark and the rest of the quotation.

INTERRUPTING EXPRESSION: "Suspicion," wrote Shakespeare, "always haunts the guilty mind."

So far, you have focused only on an interrupting expression in a single quoted sentence; however, such expressions may also be used with two sentences of directly quoted material. If so, follow the next rule.

> When two sentences in a direct quotation are separated by an interrupting expression, end the first quoted sentence with a comma, question mark, or exclamation mark and a quotation mark; place a period after the interrupter; and then write the second quoted sentence as a full quotation.

EXAMPLE: "Should we expect rain through the weekend?" the weather forecaster asked. "Looking ahead, you can plan on a pleasant, warm weekend."

Sometimes, you will insert only a quoted phrase into a sentence. Set this fragment off with quotation marks.

> When a quoted fragment is included in a sentence, enclose the quoted fragment in quotation marks, but do not use commas to set the fragment off from the rest of the sentence. Capitalize the first word of the fragment only when it falls at the beginning of the sentence or when it is a proper noun or a proper adjective.

EXAMPLES: In defining bureaucracy, Honoré de Balzac called it a "giant mechanism operated by pygmies."

"A giant mechanism operated by pygmies" is the way Honoré de Balzac referred to bureaucracy.

EXERCISE A: Indicating Quotations. Some of the following sentences contain direct quotations. Copy the sentences onto your paper, adding the necessary quotation marks. Quoted phrases are underlined so that you will know where they begin and end. If no quotation marks are needed, write *correct*.

1. Hain't we got all the fools in town on our side? And ain't that a big enough majority in any town?—Mark Twain
2. Ginny told me she did very well on her science test. *c*
3. Among mortals, Euripides commented, second thoughts are wisest.
4. Her favorite saying was to each his own.
5. James Martineau once said, Religion is no more possible without prayer than poetry without language or music without atmosphere.

6. "Wit has truth in it; wisecracking is simply calisthenics with words." —Dorothy Parker
7. My aunt told me I was the only one who remembered her birthday. *C*
8. Longfellow often expressed the philosophy that people should "act in the living present."
9. "I rode this bicycle," Felipe gasped, "at least two miles up the hill."
10. "Maybe I can go with you," Carolyn said.

EXERCISE B: Indicating and Capitalizing Quotations. The following sentences have not been correctly punctuated or capitalized. Quoted phrases are underlined. Copy the sentences onto your paper, making the necessary corrections.
Underlined letters are to be capitalized.
1. "it is better to wear out than rust out." —Bishop Cumberland
2. Marya Mannes says that in judging a work of art, you must apply standards "timeless as the universe itself."
3. "tell the truth," Sir Henry Wotton advised, "and so puzzle and confound your adversaries."
4. "honest differences of views and honest debate are not disunity. they are the vital process of policy-making among free men," wrote Herbert Hoover.
5. In one of her poems, Mary Lamb referred to a child as a "young climber-up of knees."
6. sympathy was once described by Charles Parkhurst as "two hearts tugging at one load."
7. "if you pick up a starving dog and make him prosperous, he will not bite you," Mark Twain remarked. "this is the principal difference between a dog and a man."
8. "The greatest powers of the mind are displayed in novels," Jane Austen believed.
9. "better late than never" has become a favorite proverb for those who never get anything done on time.
10. in 1957, Theodore Reid wrote these words: "work and love—these are the basics. without them there is neurosis."

■ Using Other Punctuation Marks with Quotation Marks

Whether to place the punctuation inside or outside the quotation marks presents a problem for some writers. Four basic rules, once learned, will alleviate most of the confusion.

Always place a comma or a period inside the final quotation mark.

EXAMPLES: "You exhibited greater skill in today's lesson," the driving instructor announced.

"As I passed the coffee house," Margaret explained, "the aroma of freshly brewed coffee lured me inside."

Note in the second example that the quotation is split but that this makes no difference in the placement of the comma. It still goes inside the quotation marks.

The semicolon and colon always go outside the quotation marks.

Always place a semicolon or colon outside the final quotation mark.

EXAMPLES: One repair person said, "I can't do it for less than eighty dollars"; another indicated he could fix it for half that price!

She listed the ingredients for "an absolutely heavenly salad": spinach, mushrooms, hard-boiled eggs, and bacon.

Question marks and exclamation marks are slightly more difficult to punctuate.

Place a question mark or exclamation mark inside the final quotation mark if the end mark is part of the quotation.

EXAMPLES: The patient asked, "Is my blood pressure normal?"

The TV announcer exclaimed, "You just won the $10,000 jackpot!"

On the other hand, if the exclamation mark or question mark refers to the entire sentence, the mark goes *outside* the quotation marks.

Place a question mark or exclamation mark outside the final quotation mark if the end mark is not part of the quotation.

EXAMPLES: Did you hear that speaker when he said, "Rolling blackouts will begin soon if we don't reduce energy consumption"?

I was thrilled when they said, "And for president, Debbie Schmidt"!

Occasionally, a quoted sentence may require a question mark or exclamation mark while the rest of the sentence requires a period. When this happens, drop the period.

EXAMPLE: My mother asked, "Did you feed the animals?"

EXERCISE C: Adding Other Punctuation Marks. Some commas, colons, semicolons, and end marks have been left out of the following direct quotations. Read the sentences and decide if the punctuation goes inside or outside the quotation marks. Add the missing punctuation marks and label them *inside* if they go inside the quotation marks and *outside* if they go outside the marks.

1. The woman asked the officer, "How much will this ticket cost" *? inside*
2. My mother remarked, "Today, I want you to clean your room before going out" *. inside*
3. "The next stop will be Fresno" the bus driver announced. *, inside*
4. The girl shrieked, "There is a spider on my desk" *! inside*
5. "But I have already seen that movie" I patiently explained. *, inside*
6. "What time is your orthodontist appointment" my mother inquired. *? inside*
7. She had the nerve to call it "a piece of junk not worth paying to tow away" my beloved Chevy! *: outside or , inside*
8. I let loose a blood-curdling scream when the doctor said, "This won't hurt a bit" *. inside*
9. My mother usually says, "Harry, you're getting fat around the middle" my father then tells her that she is looking at muscle, not fat. *; outside*
10. Did you hear the coach say, "Run the track *three* times" *? outside*

EXERCISE D: Adding Quotation Marks and Other Punctuation Marks. All of the punctuation and quotation marks have been left out of the following sentences. Copy the sentences onto your paper, adding the necessary quotation marks and punctuation.

1. The car keeps overheating, she explained to the mechanic.
2. We enjoyed perfect skiing weather, my friends told me. The sun came out and the wind died down completely.
3. We watched the principal on the closed circuit TV. I am pleased to announce that one of our own teachers, Mrs. Ramos, has been named Teacher of the Year.
4. Watch that child! He almost ran in front of my car, a driver called out.

5. "Will you go to the Senior Ball with me?"asked the young man shyly.
6. "Ouch!"Archie yelped."That pan is still hot!"
7. "Doesn't that kite look beautiful floating in the air up there?"the father asked his young child.
8. She explained,"I got the job at Mervyn's. I start working there tomorrow morning."
9. "I sent the package first class,"the secretary reported to the boss.
10. "Since the milk has turned sour,"the clerk apologized,"let me get you a new quart right away."

■ Using Quotation Marks in Special Situations

Several special situations may occur when you write direct quotations. These special situations include writing dialogues, quotations of more than one paragraph, and quotations that appear within other directly quoted material. First, consider the use of quotation marks when writing dialogues.

Writers may, on occasion, write a dialogue—a direct conversation between two or more people. Use quotation marks to enclose the directly quoted conversation and a new paragraph for each change of speaker.

When writing dialogue, begin a new paragraph with each change of speaker.

EXAMPLE: The station attendant shouted from behind the hood, "You're a quart low on oil, Mrs. Lowell. Would you like me to put some in for you?"
"Yes, thank you," she replied.
"What kind of oil do you use in the car?"
She hesitated and then replied, "I believe the car takes multi-grade."

In cases where one quotation consists of several paragraphs of quoted material, remember the following rule.

For quotations longer than a paragraph, put quotation marks at the beginning of each paragraph and at the end of the final paragraph.

EXAMPLE: "Experts are noticing a change in the types of food Americans are buying. More fast foods, such as TV dinners and canned meals, are being purchased by food shoppers.
"Many people who used to spend a great deal of time preparing meals now work outside their homes. Researchers conclude that this is the reason more fast foods are being purchased.
"People need well-balanced meals. They now buy meals that can be prepared quickly. Thus, people today have more time to spend at work and not in the kitchen."

Occasionally, you may need to indicate a quotation contained within another quotation.

Use single quotation marks for a quotation within a quotation.

EXAMPLE: The fund raiser concluded, saying, "As we try to raise money for this worthy cause, let us not forget that old English proverb that says, 'Where there's a will there's a way.'"

EXERCISE E: Punctuating and Capitalizing in Longer Selections. The following dialogue has no paragraphing, quotation marks, capitalization, or punctuation. Each number indicates a new speaker. Copy the dialogue onto your paper, indenting paragraphs and adding the necessary quotation marks, capitalization, and punctuation. *Answers on page T-125.*

(1) today we are lucky to have dr. richard sherman to discuss the subject of dreams (2) it is a pleasure to be with you today dr. sherman began as i talk please feel free to interrupt and ask questions (3) someone in the audience raised a hand will you cover the interpretation of dreams (4) yes the doctor replied but first let me talk about the importance certain cultures place on dreams for instance the cheyenne indians sent their boys out to dream a vision that would reveal their destinies in the ibans tribe in borneo they believe that a secret helper comes in a dream to provide advice for the troubled dreamer (5) i have heard that people have gotten inspirations and inventions from their dreams can you verify this an individual asked (6) the doctor turned to the questioner mozart reported that he saw whole musical pieces composed in his dreams and friedrich kekulé solved the structure of benzene based on his dream (7) and did ein-

stein discover the theory of relativity through a dream someone in the back of the room challenged (8) as a matter of fact the lecturer explained he had been sick from overwork and while experiencing a feverish dream he worked out this now-famous theory (9) i find this fascinating a girl in the front row whispered (10) after another thirty minutes of discussion the speaker concluded thus we should welcome our dreams—not fear them let me leave you with these words from william wordsworth come blessed barrier between day and day

APPLICATION: Punctuating Quotations in Your Own Writing. Choose one famous figure from List A and one from List B. Write a dialogue between the two in keeping with their personalities. Make the dialogue at least ten sentences long and use paragraphing, quotation marks, capitalization, and punctuation correctly. Vary the location of the "he said/she said" expressions in your sentences.
Answers will vary; dialogue could be presented in class.

List A: Reggie Jackson   *List B:* Mary Tyler Moore
Dracula   Abraham Lincoln
Susan B. Anthony   Charlie Brown
Nancy Drew   Wonder Woman

15.5 Underlining and Other Uses of Quotation Marks

In books and other printed material, italics and quotation marks are used to set some titles, names, and words apart from the rest of the text. In handwritten or typed material, the italics must be replaced by underlining.

UNDERLINING: <u>Seven Days in May</u>

ITALICS: *Seven Days in May*

Most writers know what items need to be highlighted in their writing, but some feel unsure about which method—underlining or quotation marks—is appropriate in each situation. This section will cover the rules for using both underlining and quotation marks as well as the rules for those titles and names that require neither.

■ When to Underline

You should use underlining in your writing or typing to highlight titles of long written and artistic works. You will also need to indicate certain names and foreign expressions by underlining them. Finally, you can use underlining to indicate words you want to exphasize.

The most common use of underlining is with titles of long or complete written works.

Underline the titles of long written works and the titles of publications that are published as a single work.

The following chart will show you titles of various types of works you should underline as well as examples of each.

TITLES OF WRITTEN WORKS THAT ARE UNDERLINED	
Titles of Books:	<u>Jane Eyre</u> by Charlotte Brontë
Titles of Plays:	<u>A Raisin in the Sun</u> by Lorraine Hansberry <u>The Man Who Came to Dinner</u> by Moss Hart
Titles of Periodicals: (magazines, journals, pamphlets)	<u>Skiing Magazine</u> <u>Time</u> <u>Journal of American History</u> <u>Five Ways to Keep Heating Costs Down</u>
Titles of Newspapers:	<u>The New York Times</u> the Palm Beach <u>Post</u> the Chicago <u>Sun-Times</u>
Titles of Long Poems:	<u>Idylls of the King</u> by Alfred, Lord Tennyson <u>Beowulf</u>

NOTE ABOUT NEWSPAPER TITLES: The portion of the title that should be underlined will vary from newspaper to newspaper. <u>The New York Times</u> should always be fully capitalized and underlined. Other papers, however, can usually be treated in one of two ways: the <u>Los Angeles Times</u> or the Los Angeles <u>Times</u>. Unless you know the true name of a paper, choose one of these two forms and use it consistently.

Many media presentations and pieces of artwork also require underlining.

Underline the titles of movies, TV and radio series, and works of music and art.

This rule covers a spectrum of categories. The following chart provides a closer look at each category.

TITLES OF ARTISTIC WORKS THAT ARE UNDERLINED	
Titles of Movies:	The Caine Mutiny
Titles of Radio and TV Series:	The Shadow Comedy Hour Family Feud Happy Days
Titles of Long Musical Compositions and Record Albums: (any musical work made up of several parts, such as operas, musical comedies, symphonies, and ballets)	Bach's Christmas Oratorio Puccini's Tosca Tchaikovsky's Swan Lake the Beatles' Abbey Road
Titles of Paintings and Sculpture:	Dancers at the Bar (Degas) Indian on Horseback (Mestrovic)

Not only titles but also some names need underlining.

Underline the names of individual air, sea, space, and land craft.

AIR: the Spirit of St. Louis

SEA: the S.S. Seagallant

SPACE: Explorer I

LAND: the Best Friend of Charleston

If a *the* precedes the name, do not underline or capitalize it since it is not considered part of the official name. Note also that a specific name given to a *group* of vehicles (for example, the Explorer spaceships) is capitalized but not underlined.

Occasionally, you will use a foreign phrase in your writing. If a foreign phrase still retains its foreign spelling and pronunciation, you should underline it.

Underline foreign words not yet accepted into English.

EXAMPLES: It is <u>verboten</u> to leave the building without permission. (German: forbidden)

Everyone said the <u>coq au vin</u> was delicious. (French: chicken cooked in wine)

Since the process of accepting words and phrases into the English language is a continuous one, you cannot always be certain whether a phrase is still considered foreign. Check those doubtful phrases in the dictionary. If the foreign word or phrase is not in the dictionary, you can generally consider it foreign. If it is in the dictionary, it will either be labeled with the name of the foreign language, in which case you should underline it, or it will be given standard treatment as an English word, in which case you should not underline it.

Some words, letters, and numbers also require underlining.

Underline words, letters, or numbers used as names for themselves.

WORDS: The student wrote the word <u>fluid</u>, but he meant <u>fluent</u>.

LETTERS: Is that first letter a <u>G</u> or an <u>S</u>?

NUMBER: When I say the number <u>three</u>, you start running.

Finally, underline words that you want to stress more emphatically than other words.

Underline words that you wish to stress.

EXAMPLE: We will need a <u>minimum</u> of six dollars for the field trip.

Although the underlining of the word in this example clarifies the meaning of the sentence, do not overdo underlining for emphasis. In most cases, you should rely on precise word selection to convey your meaning and emphasis.

EXERCISE A: Underlining Titles, Names, and Words. Some of the following sentences contain titles, names, or words that require underlining; others do not. Write the items that require underlining on your paper and underline them. If a sentence needs no correction, write *correct*.

1. When the producers made the movie <u>Star Wars</u>, they probably had no idea what a hit they would have.
2. Many books such as <u>Gone with the Wind</u> have been made into movies.
3. Margot Fonteyn, a famous ballerina, appeared in the production <u>Marguerite and Armand</u>.
4. My favorite record album is Linda Ronstadt's <u>Simple Dreams</u>.
5. Renoir depicts a summer outing in his painting <u>Luncheon of the Boating Party</u>.
6. The Secretary of Defense met with several Congressional subcommittees last week. *C*
7. The Washington <u>Post</u> has won several Pulitzer prizes for its fine reporting. or <u>Washington Post</u>
8. Many important historical events occurred in and around Boston's Faneuil Hall. *C*
9. In 1830, the people held a race between a horse and a train, the <u>Tom Thumb</u>; the horse won.
10. I thought I heard the clerk say the number <u>fifteen</u>, but she apparently called out the number <u>fifty</u>.

▣ When to Use Quotation Marks

In Section 15.4 the use of quotation marks (" ") to enclose spoken words or phrases was discussed. Quotation marks also set off certain titles. Quotation marks first serve to enclose titles of short literary works.

Use quotation marks around the titles of short written works.

Conventionally, *short works* include short stories, chapters from books, one-act plays, short poems, and essays and articles.

SHORT STORY: "The Jockey" by Carson McCullers

CHAPTER FROM A BOOK: "Mental Development"

ONE-ACT PLAY: "Trifles" by Susan Glaspell

SHORT POEM: "Boy Breaking Glass" by Gwendolyn Brooks

ESSAY TITLE: "Self-Reliance" by Ralph Waldo Emerson

ARTICLE TITLE: "How to Organize Your Life"

Certain titles from TV, music, and art also need quotation marks.

Use quotation marks around the titles of episodes in a series, songs, and parts of a long musical composition.

EPISODE: "The Iran File" from <u>60 Minutes</u>

SONG TITLE: "Swing Low, Sweet Chariot"

PART OF A LONG MUSICAL COMPOSITION: "Spring" from <u>The Four Seasons</u>

Occasionally, you may refer to a title of one long work contained in a larger work. Singly, each title would require underlining; when used together, another rule applies.

Use quotation marks around the title of a work that is mentioned as part of a collection.

EXAMPLE: "Plato" from <u>Great Books of the Western World</u>

EXERCISE B: Using Quotation Marks with Titles. Each of the following sentences contains a title requiring quotation marks. Copy the titles onto your paper, enclosing them in quotation marks.

1. Our teacher assigned a chapter to be read for Thursday's class: Building the Affirmative Case.
2. The only song our foreign exchange student knew from our country was The Star-Spangled Banner.
3. The short poem Ozymandias by Shelley conveys the theme that no one can achieve immortality.
4. Stevie Wonder reached new heights of success with his hit song You Are the Sunshine of My Life.
5. I tried out for a part in the one-act play called The Veldt.
6. Road to the Isles is my favorite Jessamyn West story.
7. A Modest Proposal is a satirical essay written by Jonathan Swift in 1729.

8. This month's issue had an interesting article about elephants called "What Do You Do with a 300-Pound Nose?"
9. Henry David Thoreau's famous essay "Civil Disobedience"
was first published in 1849.
10. "The Open Window," a short story by H.H. Munro, has a
surprise ending.

■ Titles Without Underlining or Quotation Marks

Some titles may at first glance appear to need underlining or quotation marks, but in reality, neither is appropriate. The first such classification consists of various religious
works.

Do not underline or place in quotation marks mentions of the
Bible, its books, divisions, or versions, or other holy scriptures,
such as the Koran.

EXAMPLE: He received a Bible on the day of his confirmation.

Similarly, you should not underline or enclose in quotation marks certain government documents.

Do not underline or place in quotation marks the titles of
government charters, alliances, treaties, acts, statutes, or
reports.

EXAMPLES: Declaration of Independence

Civil Rights Act

EXERCISE C: Punctuating Different Types of Titles. Each of
the following sentences contains one or more titles. Some require quotation marks or underlining; others do not. Copy
the titles onto your paper, either enclosing them in quotation marks or underlining them. If neither quotation marks
nor underlining are needed, write *correct*.

1. I just finished the chapter called "Life with Max" in the
book <u>Agatha Christie: An Autobiography</u>.
2. The magazine <u>Short Story International</u> published "Before the Wolves Come" by Hugh Munro.

3. I would much rather read short poems like Poe's Dream Within a Dream than long ones like Lord Byron's The Prisoner of Chillon.
4. "Waltz of the Flowers" is often a featured excerpt from The Nutcracker Suite.
5. The Treaty of Versailles officially ended World War I in 1919. *C*
6. The episode "Still Waters" from the weekly show Nova looked at the constantly changing life of a pond.
7. Genesis is the first book in the Bible. *c*
8. I love the song "Climb Every Mountain" from the musical The Sound of Music.
9. Just reading the poem The Eve of St. Agnes took me a long time.
10. In the symphony Indian by Edward MacDowell, one piece called "In War Time" consists of an arrangement of a popular song of the Atlantic coast Indians.

APPLICATION: **Writing Titles Correctly.** Number your paper from 1 to 10. Write sentences containing titles that require underlining next to numbers 1 to 4. Write sentences containing titles that require quotation marks next to numbers 5 to 8. Write sentences containing titles that do not need underlining or quotation marks next to numbers 9 and 10.
Answers will vary; samples given for 1, 5, and 9.   1. My father reads Time every week   5. Shirley Jackson's "The Lottery" first appeared in The New Yorker   9. The Book of Job is found in the Old Testament.

Dashes and Parentheses 15.6

Commas, dashes, and parentheses all perform a similar function—that of separating certain words, phrases, and clauses from the rest of the sentence. To use these marks effectively, a writer must become thoroughly acquainted with the different qualities of the three marks. The comma is the most common mark and, therefore, draws the least attention to itself. The dash sets off material more dramatically. This flamboyant mark often encloses editorial remarks from the writer. Parentheses on the other hand, are a more reserved, intellectual mark, setting off technical or explanatory material quietly, but clearly, from the rest of the sentence.

Which marks you, as a writer, choose will largely depend on your purpose in writing. This section will focus on the uses of the dash and the parentheses, providing rules to show you how to use them.

■ Use of the Dash

The dash, a long horizontal mark made above the writing line (—), functions first to set off dramatic or sudden changes in a sentence.

Use dashes to indicate an abrupt change of thought.

In the following example, notice how the writer changes direction midstream; both the idea and the structure of the sentence are shifted. Dashes effectively convey this sense of suddenly breaking off a thought.

EXAMPLE: I cannot believe what the barber did to my beautiful— oh, I don't even want to think about it!

Dashes can also set off certain words or phrases that *interrupt* the main sentence.

Use dashes to set off interrupting ideas in a dramatic fashion.

Notice in the following example that the dashes set off additional information that interrupts the main idea of the sentence.

EXAMPLE: Oatmeal—which tastes delicious with honey and raisins—makes a nutritious breakfast when served with milk.

If the interrupting idea is an exclamation or a question, place the appropriate punctuation mark before the last dash.

EXAMPLE: Next Saturday—do you have to work that day?—we want you to go fishing with us.

A dash also precedes a dramatic summary statement.

Use a dash to set off a summary statement.

When used in this manner, the dash points back to what has already been written, explaining or summarizing it in more detail.

EXAMPLES: Vanilla, rocky road, strawberry, blackberry, and butter brickle—deciding which of these flavors to get took me a full five minutes.

To see my name in lights—this was my greatest dream.

It may help to know that words such as *all*, *these*, *this*, and *that* frequently begin a summary sentence preceded by a dash.

In certain circumstances, nonessential appositives are also set off with dashes. Although nonessential appositives—those not necessary to the meaning of a sentence—are usually set off with commas, dashes are often used in the cases mentioned in the following rule.

Use dashes to set off a nonessential appositive in the middle of a sentence (1) when the appositive is long; (2) when it is already punctuated; (3) when it is introduced by words such as *for example* or *that is*; and (4) when you want to be especially dramatic.

In order for an appositive to need a dash, it must meet any *one* of the four criteria set forth in the following chart.

CONDITIONS FOR USING DASHES WITH APPOSITIVES	
Condition	**Example**
Length:	The chairperson—a socialite more concerned with her stomach than the empty stomachs of the world's hungry millions—will hold a fund-raising dinner.
Internal Punctuation:	My friends—Martha, Ray, and of course, Dennis—have agreed to paint posters.
Words such as *for instance*, *for example*, **or** *that is*:	Some of the stores in the mall—for example, The Bathing Beauties Bath Shop—never have any customers.
Strong Emphasis:	The movies—three box-office blockbusters—were not among our favorites.

A nonessential modifier, another sentence interrupter, can also benefit at times from the effective use of dashes.

Use dashes to set off nonessential modifiers (1) when the modifier is already punctuated and (2) when you want to be especially dramatic.

You should limit the use of the dash to those modifiers that contain their own internal punctuation or that you want to emphasize strongly.

INTERNAL PUNCTUATION: The mongrel—who, for some reason known only to himself, decided to follow me home—has no identifying tags.

STRONG EMPHASIS: His hopeful expression—which he has mastered so well that even Lassie could take lessons from him—is slowly winning me over.

And now, take a moment to consider the last kind of sentence interrupter—a parenthetical expression. You may recall that a parenthetical expression consists of words or phrases that are inserted into a sentence but have no essential grammatical relationship to it. Parenthetical expressions are often enclosed by dashes.

Use dashes to set off a parenthetical expression (1) when the expression is long; (2) when it is already punctuated; and (3) when you want to be especially dramatic.

Of course, not every parenthetical expression will take a dash. Short expressions such as the following would hardly need a dash.

EXAMPLES: I will, I think, go.

Give it to me, Susan.

However, as with nonessential appositives, if the parenthetical expression is long or contains its own punctuation, you will often want to set it off with dashes.

EXAMPLE: This continual downpour—we had two inches Monday, one inch yesterday, and already have had an inch today—will certainly replenish our low water supplies.

Even without internal punctuation, a parenthetical expression may sometimes require a question mark or exclamation mark at the end. In these situations, you may again choose to use dashes, placing the end mark inside the final dash.

EXAMPLE: Mr. Mathers, who was caught stealing—did you have any idea he had run so short of money?—was booked at the local police station just yesterday.

You can also enclose the parenthetical expression in dashes if you want the expression to stand out dramatically from the rest of the sentence.

EXAMPLE: At her birthday party—she actually tried to tell me that she was celebrating her twenty-ninth—she had assembled more than forty guests.

Although the dash has many valid uses, be careful not to overuse it. *Sprinkling* your writing with an occasional dash serves to add sentence variety and interest; putting dashes in too often will *drown* your paper in a series of confusing, disjointed thoughts. Therefore, look for the few opportunities (as outlined in the preceding rules) where a dash is specifically required. In all other situations, insert commas or in some cases parentheses for maximum effectiveness.

EXERCISE A: Using the Dash. The dashes have been left out of the following sentences. Copy the sentences onto your paper, adding the necessary dashes.

1. The marching band—which has been, I might point out, practicing for weeks—won a blue ribbon at the competition.
2. Our new gardener—she is a genius with all plants!—pruned the roses recently.
3. The scenery—long, sandy beaches, desolate lava beds, and fiery sunsets—brings many tourists to Hawaii.
4. Cats are so lovable and—hey, stop eating that plant, you dumb cat!
5. To be able to see exotic fish in their natural habitat—that provides one of the greatest joys of snorkeling.
6. That runner—what was his name?—didn't even look tired after his race.
7. We ordered Valentine's arrangements carnations, daisies, and roses—to be sent to our relatives.

8. The family bookkeeping system–which just looks like a jumble of numbers to me–is designed to keep me on a tight budget.
9. Some ski resorts–for example, Lake Placid in New York–provide for a variety of skiing activities.
10. Baseball, soccer, football, and tennis–these probably represent America's favorite sports.

■ Use of the Parentheses

Parentheses set off supplementary material not essential to the understanding of the sentence. Though not as dramatic as the dash, parentheses are the strongest separator a writer can use.

Rules for Using Parentheses. Several rules help you determine when using parentheses is appropriate.

Use parentheses to set off asides and explanations only when the material is not essential to the meaning of the sentence.

Note that all the material contained in the parentheses in the following examples can be lifted out without altering the meaning of the sentence.

EXAMPLES: The committee looks at each student's entire entrance file (transcript, application, recommendations, SAT scores) when deciding which students to admit.

The bill passed (only after two days of heated debate) and will now be sent to the Senate for approval.

Sometimes, this kind of parenthetical aside or explanation can consist not of just a phrase but of one or more complete sentences.

Use parentheses to set off asides and explanations that consist of one or more complete sentences.

EXAMPLE: We will pick up the stereo tomorrow afternoon. (The manager promised that she would have it ready this time.) By 5 p.m., I should be listening to my favorite records.

Supplementary numbers may also be enclosed in parentheses.

Use parentheses to set off the dates of a person's birth and death or other explanations involving numerals.

EXAMPLES: We established a memorial fund at school for Mary Tsai (1965–1981), which will be used to buy some needed books.

One half of the club's members (37) attended the pot-luck dinner.

You should also clarify in parentheses any numbers you fear may be misread.

EXAMPLE: You need to put a minimum of twenty thousand dollars ($20,000) down on the house.

Parentheses also assist in the writing of series or lists.

Use parentheses around numbers and letters marking items in a series.

EXAMPLES: Pick these items up at the market: (1) milk; (2) eggs; (3) margarine; and (4) unsweetened chocolate.

Who signed the Declaration of Independence first? (a) B. Franklin (b) P. Revere (c) J. Hancock

In following these four rules, be careful not to overuse parentheses. As with the dash, overuse can lead to choppy, unclear prose—something every good writer wants to avoid.

Capitalizing and Punctuating with Parentheses. Several guidelines will help you punctuate and capitalize the material in parentheses.

Sometimes, parenthetical sentences interrupt one continuous sentence.

When a parenthetical phrase or declarative sentence interrupts another sentence, do not capitalize the initial word or use any end mark inside the parentheses.

EXAMPLE: Lentil soup (my family tasted it for the first time in Germany) provides a delicious, filling meal.

However, if the sentence is exclamatory or interrogative, the rule changes.

When a parenthetical question or exclamatory sentence interrupts another sentence, use both an initial capital and an end mark inside the parentheses.

EXAMPLE: *Sixty Minutes* (That show has done some outstanding investigative reporting!) reaches millions of viewers.

When a parenthetical sentence falls between two complete sentences, use both an initial capital and an end mark inside the parentheses.

EXAMPLE: We drove to the Ashland Shakespeare Festival. (It took over fifteen hours.) The quality of the performances there surpassed even our high expectations.

You must also be aware of punctuation that falls *after* a parenthetical phrase.

In a sentence with a parenthetical phrase, place any punctuation belonging to the main sentence after the second parenthesis.

This rule applies to commas, semicolons, colons, and end marks.

EXAMPLES: The ocean water felt icy cold (about 45°)!

I purchased a Honda (a Prelude, to be exact), and it took four months to receive this popular car.

EXERCISE B: Using Parentheses. The parentheses have been left out of the following sentences. Copy the sentences onto your paper, adding the necessary parentheses.

1. We watched the second one-act play ("The Devil and Daniel Webster"), but then we had to leave.
2. The skater looked confident (perhaps more confident than the judges liked)as he left the ice.
3. Our new foreign exchange student (German)speaks English fluently.
4. Mopeds (motorized bicycles) first became popular in Europe.
5. Check the boat for the following safety supplies: (a)extra gas; (b)life preservers; (c)flares.
6. My sister(b. February 29, 1980)will have a birthday only once every four years.
7. I must remember to do my homework in these classes: (1)algebra; (2)speech; and (3)history.
8. This painting by Picasso (see picture on page 75)is considered one of his best.
9. My report card arrived today. (I've been meeting the

mail carrier every day for the last week.)The grades will please my parents.
10. While the lion was completely out(the effects of the tranquilizer), the vet entered the cage confidently.

EXERCISE C: Using Capitals and Punctuation with Parentheses. Each of the following sentences contains a phrase or clause enclosed in parentheses, but the punctuation and capitalization have been left out. Copy the sentences onto your paper, making the necessary corrections. If no corrections are needed, write *correct*.
Underlined letters are to be capitalized.
1. Helmers Electronic firm (did they open up in 1974)? showed a 25 percent increase in profits.
2. The sale went well (over one thousand dollars profit), and we now have room for the new merchandise.
3. After the fashion show (held at 11:00 a.m.) a lunch was served.
4. My antique music box (it was constructed in 1880 in Dusseldorf) operates with a hand wheel. C
5. The cowboy hat (i planned to wear it skiing) fit perfectly.
6. The coral reefs (what a beautiful underwater sight they make) have meant destruction for many unknowing ships.
7. I watered the plant. (it has a water indicator that shows when it needs moisture) Then, I added some fertilizer to the soil. or . . . plant (it . . . moisture). Then . . .
8. My new tires (guaranteed for a minimum of 40,000 miles) already show signs of wear. C
9. My alarm watch stopped (could the battery be dead already?) and made me late for school.
10. I purchased a new umbrella (the kind that folds up); it worked well in this heavy rainfall. or . . . that folds up). It worked well . . .

APPLICATION: Using Dashes and Parentheses in Sentences. Write one sentence to illustrate each of the six rules governing dashes. Then write four sentences to illustrate the four rules governing parentheses.
Answers will vary but should follow models beginning on pages 396 and 400.

Hyphens 15.7

As a writer, you should appreciate the versatility of the hyphen, for this punctuation mark makes it possible not only to join but also to divide certain words. Unfortunately, the hyphen is often mistaken for its cousin, the dash, since the two share a similar appearance. However, you should note that the hyphen is distinctly shorter than the dash; in fact, in typing the hyphen consists of one mark (-) while the dash is composed of two (--).

The primary uses of the hyphen are to divide certain numbers and parts of words, to join some compound words, and to divide words at the ends of lines. This section will focus on the rules governing the appropriate use of the hyphen in these cases.

■ Using the Hyphen

Hyphens are used with certain numbers, word parts, and words. First, look at the use of hyphens with numbers.

With Numbers.   When you write out numbers in words, some of them require hyphens.

> Use a hyphen when writing out the numbers *twenty-one* through *ninety-nine.*

EXAMPLE: Someone stole from her wallet a sum of twenty-seven dollars!

Some fractions also require a hyphen.

> Use a hyphen when writing fractions that are used as adjectives.

EXAMPLES: A three-fourths majority passed the controversial bill.

The gas tank registered two-thirds full.

In the preceding examples, the fractions function as adjectives. If they were used as nouns, the hyphen would then be omitted.

EXAMPLE: Three fourths of the junior class came to the meeting.

With Word Parts.   Some word parts require the use of a hyphen.

> Use a hyphen after a prefix that is followed by a proper noun or adjective.

EXAMPLES: The family vacation started in mid-August.

The country grew quickly during the pre-Revolutionary period.

Certain prefixes and suffixes also demand the use of hyphens even when no proper noun or adjective is involved.

Use a hyphen in words with the prefixes *all-, ex-, self-* and words with the suffix *-elect.*

EXAMPLES: all-powerful   ex-teacher   self-addressed

senator-elect

Always check to make sure that a complete word joins the prefix or suffix. Sometimes, prefixes and suffixes combine with only part of a word, and the resulting word does not require a hyphen.

INCORRECT: ex-ecutive

CORRECT: executive

With Compound Words.   You will also use hyphens with some compound words.

Use a hyphen to connect two or more words that are used as one word, unless the dictionary gives a contrary spelling.

The use of hyphens in compound words is a matter of changing style. The dictionary should always be your authority on this matter. Three examples, hyphenated in most dictionaries, follow.

EXAMPLES: hit-and-run   crow's-feet   life-size

You will also need to use a hyphen with certain modifiers.

Use a hyphen to connect a compound modifier that comes before a noun.

EXAMPLES: The dark clouds cast a grayish-blue tint on the water.

The well-groomed lawn added to the value of the house.

With great reluctance, the child took the cod-liver oil.

This rule has several corollaries that need closer study.

If a compound modifier comes after the noun, the hyphen is dropped.

BEFORE: We got the prescription from an all-night druggist.

AFTER: A druggist open all night filled the prescription.

The only exception to this rule is when the dictionary shows the compound modifier with a hyphen. In this case, the word remains hyphenated regardless of its sentence position.

EXAMPLES: We water skiied behind a jet-propelled boat.

Our ski boat was jet-propelled.

Hyphens should also be avoided with adverbs ending in *-ly*, in compound proper adjectives, and in compound proper nouns acting as adjectives.

Do not use a hyphen with a compound modifier that includes a word ending in *-ly* or in a compound proper adjective or a compound proper noun acting as an adjective.

INCORRECT: The badly-damaged car sat in the body shop.

CORRECT: The badly damaged car sat in the body shop.

INCORRECT: The North-American continent has some large oil supplies.

CORRECT: The North American continent has some large oil supplies.

For Clarity. Certain letter combinations may cause a reader to misread a passage. By inserting a hyphen, you can avoid this.

Use a hyphen within a word when a combination of letters might otherwise be confusing.

EXAMPLES: *co-op* versus *coop*

re-lay versus *relay*

Unusual combinations of words can also be made clearer with hyphens.

Use a hyphen between words to keep the reader from combining them erroneously.

EXAMPLES: *a new home-owner* versus *a new-home owner*

three-point makers versus *three point-makers*

EXERCISE A: Using Hyphens in Numbers, Word Parts, and Words. Read the following sentences and decide if any words or phrases require hyphenation. Write those words, correctly hyphenated, on your paper. Use a dictionary when in doubt. If no hyphen is needed, write *correct*.

1. My mother's yoga class is part of her <u>self- improvement</u> plan.
2. We had <u>forty- three</u> senior citizens on the bus trip to Boston.
3. When I was three fourths of the way to Dan's house, I realized I had left behind the folder he wanted. *c*
4. The <u>happy- go- lucky</u> child played contentedly on the swings.
5. When my cup was only <u>one-third</u> empty, the waitress refilled it.
6. Each year many <u>Chinese</u> people celebrate the Chinese New Year. *c*
7. A United Nations committee will take the proposals into consideration. *c*
8. The <u>all- important</u> decision will be handed down in the next few weeks.
9. With my last arrow, I made a <u>bull's eye.</u>
10. During the <u>post- World War II</u> days, the United States experienced a baby boom.

EXERCISE B: Using Hyphens to Avoid Ambiguity. Copy the following sentences onto your paper, adding hyphens to make each sentence clear.

1. The clay head that I had modelled was out of proportion and needed to be <u>reformed</u>. *re-formed*
2. During <u>kick- off</u>, the crowd stood to watch the football player kick off.
3. The walk up to the <u>walk- up</u> I had seen advertised in the paper turned out to be farther than I had anticipated.
4. The six <u>foot- soldiers</u> walked across the bridge; one fell off and then there were five.
5. The dress my mother made was a <u>recreation</u> of one I had seen in a store window. *re-creation*

■ Using Hyphens at the Ends of Lines

"To divide or not to divide?" This question comes up again and again when a writer reaches the end of a line of writing. In such a situation, you must decide whether to put one last word on the line, drop the word down to the next line, or divide it. The decision need not be based on the flip of a coin; certain rules govern this problem. The most important rule is the one regarding syllables.

> If a word must be divided, always divide it between syllables.

If you are in doubt about how to divide a word into syllables, check a dictionary. It will show, for example, that the word *intricately* has four syllables *in tri cate ly* and can be divided as in the following example.

EXAMPLE: The museum tapestry was a masterpiece of intri-cately woven threads.

You will notice in this example that the hyphen is placed at the point where the division occurs. Always place the hyphen at the end of the first line—never at the start of the next line.

INCORRECT: We cannot continue to sup
-port this candidate.

CORRECT: We cannot continue to support this candidate.

Prefixes and suffixes provide a natural place to divide words.

> If a word contains word parts, it can almost always be divided between the prefix and the root *or* the root and the suffix.

PREFIX: ex-tend   out-side   mis-fortune

SUFFIX: mon-arch   four-some   fif-teen

If the suffix is composed of only two letters, however, do *not* divide the word between the root and suffix.

INCORRECT: walk-ed

CORRECT: walked

In addition to avoiding a two-letter suffix, there are a number of other rules that should be followed in dividing words.

Do not divide one-syllable words.

Be on the lookout for one-syllable words that sound like two-syllable words or look as if they are long enough to be two syllables. Do not divide them.

INCORRECT: lod-ge   clo-thes   thro-ugh

CORRECT: lodge   clothes   through

Each of these examples consists of only one syllable; therefore, dividing them is inappropriate.

You will also need to watch divisions that result in a single letter standing along.

Do not divide a word so that a single letter stands alone.

INCORRECT: stead-y   a-ble   e-vict

CORRECT: steady   able   evict

Another problem occurs if you divide proper nouns or adjectives.

Do not divide proper nouns and adjectives.

The following divisions have traditionally been considered undesirable or even incorrect.

INCORRECT: We recently hired Sylvia Rodri-
                    guez.

INCORRECT: I just finished eating a Chiqui-
                    ta banana.

You may occasionally need to divide a word that already contains a hyphen.

Divide a hyphenated word only after the hyphen.

If you use the word *apple-pie* as an adjective, you would hyphenate it. When dividing the word at the end of a line, divide it only at the hyphen.

INCORRECT: Everything appeared to be in ap-
             ple-pie order.

CORRECT: Everything appeared to be in apple-
            pie order.

When you get to the end of a page, you should remember one more rule.

Do not divide a word so that part of the word is on one page and the remainder of the word is on the next page.

Often chopping up a word in this manner will confuse your readers or cause them to lose their train of thought.

EXERCISE C: **Using Hyphens to Divide Words.** In each of the following sentences, a word has been divided and hyphenated. Read each sentence and decide if the hyphenated word has been divided correctly. If it has, write *correct* on your paper. If it has not, write the correct form.

1. My father is self-em-
   ployed. *self-employed*
2. Beth injured the liga-
   ments in her knee. *C*
3. Jane pruned the hed-
   ge for us. *hedge*
4. The instructor can-
   celed the music lesson. *C*
5. At dinner, I had Roquefort dressing. *Roquefort*
6. The new house has e-
   lectric appliances. *elec-tric*
7. I measured both the length and width of the box. *length*
8. The weary campers head-
   ed back to their trailer. *headed*
9. Be sure to clip that cou
   -pon for a free dinner. *cou-pon*
10. The mannequin looked life-
    like to me. *C*

APPLICATION: **Examining the Use of Hyphens.** Choose a short magazine or newspaper article and circle all the hyphens. Write the rule that applies to each hyphen used. Note for classroom discussion any hyphens that do not follow the rules.
Answers will vary; a tally could be compiled of "most common," "next most common," and "least common" usages.

Apostrophes 15.8

Though the apostrophe (') is classified as a punctuation mark and not as a letter, its misuse can result in the misspelling of many words. The apostrophe serves two purposes: to show possession and to indicate missing letters. In most cases, you must place the apostrophe between the letters of the word, not before or after it. Thus, misplacement of the apostrophe leads to spelling errors. This section will provide you with rules so that you can use the apostrophe correctly in your writing.

■ Apostrophes with Possessive Nouns

An apostrophe must be used to indicate possession or ownership with nouns.
With Singular Nouns. First, consider possessives formed from singular nouns.

Add an apostrophe and *-s* to show the possessive case of most singular nouns.

As shown in the following examples, this rule applies to most singular nouns.

EXAMPLES: the toy of the *child* becomes the *child's* toy

the desires of the *customer* becomes the *customer's* desires

the frosting of the *cake* becomes the *cake's* frosting

the success of *Roy* becomes *Roy's* success

the sleeve of the *dress* becomes the *dress's* sleeve

Notice that even when a singular noun ends in *-s*, as in the last example, you can still follow this style in most cases. The only exception is when the additional -*s* makes the word difficult to pronounce.

AWKWARD: I like Burns's poetry.

BETTER: I like Burns' poetry.

With Plural Nouns. Showing possession with plural nouns ending in -*s* or -*es* calls for a special rule.

Add an apostrophe to show the possessive case of plural nouns ending in -*s* or -*es*.

EXAMPLES: the dishes of the *dogs* becomes the *dogs'* dishes

the words of the *speakers* becomes the *speakers'* words

the problems of the *cities* becomes the *cities'* problems

Not all plural nouns end in -*s* or -*es*, however. Another rule will help you form the possessive case of these nouns.

Add an apostrophe and -*s* to show the possessive case of plural nouns that do not end in -*s* or -*es*.

EXAMPLES: the paintings of the *women* becomes the *women's* paintings

the game of the *children* becomes the *children's* game

the songs of the *people* becomes the *people's* songs

With Compound Nouns. Sometimes, you will find that a noun showing ownership consists of several words. One primary rule governs these compound nouns.

Add an apostrophe and -*s* (or just an apostrophe if the word is a plural ending in -*s*) to the last word of a compound noun to form the possessive.

This rule refers to names of businesses and organizations, names with titles, and hyphenated compound nouns.

APOSTROPHES WITH COMPOUND NOUNS	
Businesses and Organizations:	the Good Earth's menu
	Black and Decker's tool warranty
	the Lions Clubs' motto

Names with Titles:	the Secretary of Defense's visit Edward VIII's abdication
Hyphenated Compound Nouns Used to Describe People:	my father-in-law's glasses the secretary-treasurer's notebook

With Expressions Involving Time, Amounts, and the Word Sake. If you use possessive expressions involving time, amounts, or the word *sake*, you will need to use an apostrophe.

To form possessives involving time, amounts, or the word *sake*, use an apostrophe and -*s* or just an apostrophe, depending on whether the possessive is singular or plural.

TIME: a day's journey   six years' time

AMOUNT: one quarter's worth   fifty cents' worth

SAKE: for Heaven's sake   for goodness' sake

Notice in the last example on the right that the final -*s* is often dropped in expressions involving sake.

To Show Joint and Individual Ownership. When two nouns precede a possession, you must show ownership accurately.

To show **joint ownership,** add an apostrophe and -*s* to the last noun in a series.

EXAMPLES: Roger and Jeremy's science project
            (They share the same project.)

            the husband and wife's car
            (They share one car.)

With individual ownership, the use of the apostrophe changes.

To show **individual ownership**, add an apostrophe and -*s* at the end of each noun in a series.

EXAMPLES: Roger's and Jeremy's science projects
            (They each have their own projects.)

            the husband's and wife's cars
            (Each owns a separate car.)

Checking Your Use of the Rules. Often confusion results over the application of the various rules because writers forget to ask themselves if they are writing about a singular noun or a plural noun. First, you should determine whether the owner is singular or plural. Then you should consider the word before the apostrophe you are going to add. If you place the apostrophe correctly, the letters to the *left* of the apostrophe should spell out the *owner's* complete name. Look at the checking technique in the following chart.

CHECKING THE USE OF APOSTROPHES		
Incorrect	Explanation	Correction
Jame's car	The owner is not Jame, but James.	James's
one boys' book	The owner is not *boys* but *boy*.	boy's
two girl's lunches	The owner is not *girl* but *girls*.	girls'

EXERCISE A: Using the Apostrophe with Single-Word Possessive Nouns. A noun has been underlined in each of the following sentences. The noun may be singular or plural. Copy the nouns onto your paper, putting them into the possessive form when necessary. Some nouns may not need to be put into the possessive so read the sentences carefully. For sentences that do not require possessive forms, write *correct*.

1. The <u>kittens</u> string lay in a tangled mess after they finished playing with it. *kittens'*
2. The <u>lass</u> blond curls framed her cherubic face. *lass's*
3. The <u>skater</u> sloppy leaps cost him the competition. *skater's*
4. The bright canary yellow of the <u>taxis</u> provided a splash of color against the gray of the city buildings. *c*
5. The <u>town</u> main offices were located off First Street. *town's*
6. <u>Mavis</u> eyes certainly were her nicest feature. *Mavis's*
7. We listened to the <u>waves</u> crashing against the rocks. *c*
8. The <u>babies</u> cries filled the tiny nursery. *babies'*
9. The <u>cactus</u> spines made it impossible to touch the plant. *cactus's*
10. The <u>people</u> reactions to the presidential announcement varied. *people's*

EXERCISE B: **Using the Apostrophe with Compound Nouns.** A compound noun has been underlined in each of the following sentences. Copy the nouns onto your paper, putting them into the possessive form.

1. The <u>Sierra Club's</u> actions often prevent environmental destruction.
2. My <u>great-uncle's</u> turkey farm produces many fat Thanksgiving birds.
3. The <u>National Honor Society's</u> colors consist of blue and gold.
4. <u>Jack-in-the-Box's</u> drive-up windows makes it different from many fast food chains.
5. The <u>Director of Transportation's</u> recommendations would mean an increase in mass transit fares.
6. The <u>secretary-elect's</u> first responsibility was to go over the minutes with the current officer.
7. <u>Hershey Food Corporation's</u> headquarters is located in Hershey, Pennsylvania.
8. This <u>home-owner's</u> policy gives needed protection against fire and theft.
9. <u>Queen Elizabeth II's</u> reign of twenty-five years was celebrated in 1977 with a Silver Jubilee celebration.
10. The <u>*Working Woman's*</u> fashions are designed with the career woman in mind.

EXERCISE C: **Using the Apostrophe to Show Joint and Individual Ownership.** Two nouns have been underlined and need to be put into the possessive form in each of the following sentences. Copy the nouns onto your paper, changing them to show joint or individual ownership as the instructions indicate.

1. The formal style of <u>Rhonda's and Emily's</u> dresses did not blend with the informal attire of the rest of the guests. (individual)
2. The <u>sororities and fraternities'</u> Greek heritage sets them apart from other clubs. (joint)
3. <u>Fred and Marilyn's</u> joint tax return is being audited by the IRS. (joint)
4. Since <u>Laura's and Marcello's</u> papers were identical, the teacher accused them of cheating. (individual)
5. <u>Doug's and Hy's</u> desks were covered with grafitti. (individual)
6. The <u>faculty's and administrators'</u> complaints have been formally lodged with the mediator. (individual)

7. We celebrated <u>Mike and Kristin's</u> tenth anniversary with a party. (joint)
8. <u>Richard and Karen's</u> oldest boys have graduated from college already. (joint)
9. The <u>boys' and girls'</u> teams from our school all won ribbons at the track meet. (individual)
10. <u>Phil and Ruth's</u> property taxes increased last year. (joint)

■ Apostrophes with Pronouns

Not only nouns but also some pronouns showing ownership require an apostrophe.

Use an apostrophe and -s with indefinite pronouns to show possession.

EXAMPLES: another's   nobody's   one's

anyone's   someone's   everybody's

If you form a two-word indefinite pronoun, add the apostrophe and the -s to the last word only.

EXAMPLES: nobody else's   one another's

On the other hand if you use a possessive personal pronoun, you will not need an apostrophe.

Do not use an apostrophe with the possessive forms of personal pronouns.

With the words *yours, his, hers, theirs, its, ours,* and *whose,* no apostrophe is necessary. These particular pronouns *already* show ownership.

EXAMPLES: Looking at the competition, I decided *yours* far outdistanced the other entries.

Its delicious aroma drew everyone inside for dinner.

Pay special attention to the possessive forms *whose* and *its* since they are easily confused with the contractions *who's* and *it's*. Just remember, *whose* and *its* show possession.

PRONOUNS: *Whose* wallet is this?

Its chimes rang out clearly.

Who's and *it's*, on the other hand, make up contractions from the words *who is* and *it is*. They both require apostrophes to indicate the missing letters.

CONTRACTIONS: *Who's* doing telephoning for the meeting?

It's the responsibility of the Telephone Chairman.

EXERCISE D: Using Apostrophes with Pronouns. Pronouns are used as possessives and contractions in the following sentences. Write any pronouns that are used incorrectly, making the necessary corrections. If a pronoun is used correctly, write *correct* on your paper.

1. I suppose you will say that clearing the table is nobody's job? *C*
2. Someone's else's letter came to our address. *Someone else's*
3. She gave the minutes to the one who's in charge. *C*
4. The child gave his' address to the police officer, who, in turn, called his' parents. *his/his*
5. We must not be jealous of one anothers' good fortune. *another's*
6. Your's was the most beautiful quilt on display at the fair. *Yours*
7. As I looked at the rose, I was awed by it's simple beauty. *its*
8. Is this anybody's necklace—its' clasp is broken. *its*
9. I asked whose pen it was. *C*
10. People have told me that it's a fantastic play. *C*

■ Apostrophes with Contractions

The meaning of a *contraction* is implied by its name—it is a word contracted in size by the removal of some letter or letters and the insertion of an apostrophe to indicate the missing letters. This leads to the following basic rule for contractions.

Use an apostrophe in a contraction to indicate the position of the missing letter or letters.

Contractions with Verbs. Verbs often come in contracted form. Look at the following chart, taking a moment to notice how often these verb contractions are used in common speech patterns.

COMMON CONTRACTIONS WITH VERBS		
Verb + *not*:	cannot = can't do not = don't	was not = wasn't were not = weren't
Pronoun + *will*:	he will = he'll	you will = you'll
Pronoun or noun + *to be* verb:	you are = you're Mark is = Mark's	I am = I'm where is = where's
Pronoun or noun + *would*:	we would = we'd	they would = they'd

One special contraction changes letters as well as drops them: *Will not* becomes *won't* in contracted form.

As a writer, you should try to avoid most verb contractions in formal writing. They tend to make your style more informal than you may wish.

INFORMAL: He's promised that he'll postpone the test if we're still confused about the procedure.

FORMAL: He has promised that he will postpone the test if we are still confused about the procedure.

Contractions with Years.   In writing about years, you will often need to insert an apostrophe in places where a number is left out.

EXAMPLE: Decathlon Champion of '75

Contractions with *o', d',* and *l'*.   These letters followed by the apostrophe make up the abbreviated form of the words *of the* or *the* as spelled in several different languages.

EXAMPLES: o'clock   O'Sullivan

d'Carlo   l'Abbe

As you can see, these letters and apostrophes are combined most often with surnames.

Contractions with Dialogues.   When writing dialogue, you will usually want to keep the flavor of the speaker's individual speaking style. Therefore, you should use any contractions the speaker might use. You may also want to include a regional dialect or a foreign accent; since this often includes unusual pronunciations or omitted letters, you should insert apostrophes to show those changes.

EXAMPLES: C'mon—aren't you comin' fishin'?

'Tis a fine spring morn we're havin'.

That li'l horse is afeelin' his oats!

As with most punctuation, overuse reduces the effectiveness and impact, so watch the overuse of the apostrophe with contractions—even in dialogues.

EXERCISE E: Using Apostrophes with Contractions. Various words are underlined in the following paragraph. If a contraction is underlined, write the two words that make it up. If two words are underlined, write the contraction they would form.

Graphology, the study of handwriting, (1) is not a new science. Though we (2) don't know with complete certainty, (3) it is believed that it began as far back as 1000 B.C. in China and Japan. Many historical figures (4) did not discount graphology as a "false science." In fact, Shakespeare wrote, "Give me the handwriting of a woman, and I will tell you her character." Other figures who (5) did not regard graphology as silly included Sir Walter Scott, Edgar Allan Poe, Goethe, and both of the Brownings. To prove it (6) was not false, a scientist by the name of Binet tested seven graphologists in the 1800's. He showed them the handwriting of different people and asked, "Who would you pick as intelligent, average, or dull based on their handwriting?" All the graphologists did better than mere chance would have allowed. Today, there are still people (7) who will call it a false science, but (8) that's becoming less frequent. Even the American Medical Association (9) will not call it that. (10) They have written, "There are definite organic diseases that grapho-diagnostics can help diagnose. . . ." In the business world, many people consult graphologists before they hire new employees. And so graphology, once nothing more than a silly parlor game, has grown in respectability, and it shows every sign of continuing to do this in the future.

1. isn't   2. do not   3. it's   4. didn't   5. didn't   6. wasn't   7. who'll   8. that is   9. won't   10. They've

■ Special Uses of the Apostrophe

One final method for employing the apostrophe exists—using it to show the plural of numbers, letters, symbols, and certain words.

Use an apostrophe and *-s* to write the plurals of numbers, symbols, letters, and words used to name themselves.

EXAMPLES: *64*'s (If written out in words, no apostrophe is required.)

three *!*'s

distinguishing between *b*'s and *d*'s

A's and *an*'s cause confusion.

EXERCISE F: Using the Apostrophe in Special Cases. Certain numbers, symbols, letters, and words need an apostrophe and an *-s* added in the following sentences. Copy each sentence onto your paper, adding an apostrophe and an *-s* wherever necessary.

1. Hearing all those *Merry Christmas* from people has put me into a holiday mood. *Christmas's*
2. I think you are leaving the *s* and the *ed* off the ends of your words. *s's/ed's*
3. We sing eight *do-da* in a row before we get to any lyrics in the song. *do-da's*
4. Ten , in one sentence make the sentence too choppy and confusing. *,'s*
5. Europeans put an extra line in their *7* to show they are different from their *1*. *7's/1's*
6. We both had *h* for our first and last initials. *h's*
7. The girl said twenty *however* during the course of her short speech. *however's*
8. I always get carried away writing *!* in my letters. *!'s*
9. In the *1800*, the U.S. fought several significant wars. *1800's*
10. The Emporium stores use *E* in various sizes as a symbol of their name. *E's*

APPLICATION: Using Apostrophes in Your Own Writing. Write a short passage of your own including at least one of each of the following uses of an apostrophe.

Answers will vary; students could exchange papers for evaluation.
1. An apostrophe with a possessive noun.
2. An apostrophe with a possessive pronoun.
3. An apostrophe in a contraction.
4. A special use of an apostrophe with a number, letter, symbol, or word used to name itself.
5. An apostrophe used to show ownership of something by at least two people.

Review Exercises: Mechanics

REVIEW EXERCISE 1: Capitalization

Capitals have been left out of the following sentences. Copy the sentences onto your paper, adding the necessary capitals.
Underlined letters are to be capitalized.
  1. yesterday, i went to a performance of the musical comedy *the music man.*
  2. my aunt rose lives in houston, texas, and is a member of the league of women voters.
  3. did you vote for senator smith last november?
  4. we won the game!
  5. professor elena martinez gave an interesting talk about her trip to the grand canyon.
  6. the president of the united states during world war I was woodrow wilson.
  7. ex-mayor callahan speaks french well.
  8. people of the christian religion believe in god and study the bible.
  9. in english class, we read the book *crime and punishment* by feodor dostoevski, a russian author.
 10. the ford motor company first introduced the model t in 1908.

REVIEW EXERCISE 2: Abbreviations

If the underlined word or words in each of the following sentences may be abbreviated in formal writing, write the abbreviation on your paper. If not, write *no.*

  1. Mister Arthur Holtzman has arrived. *Mr.*
  2. Ambassador Mansfield enjoyed the trip. *no*
  3. When I had the flu, I made an appointment with Doctor Fields. *Dr.*
  4. The class was taught by Alice Murphy, Doctor of Philosophy. *Ph.D.*
  5. General Motors Corporation manufactures automobiles. *no*
  6. Would you like to buy a ticket, Madame? *no*
  7. They lived on Oak Avenue in a white house. *no*
  8. When gold was discovered in the Yukon Territory, many people rushed there. *no*
  9. Socrates died in the year 399 before Christ. *B.C.*
 10. The twins were born on February second, 1981. *2*

REVIEW EXERCISE 3: End Marks

The end marks are missing from the following sentences. Copy each item onto your paper, adding the necessary end mark. Then write the name of the end mark you used.

1. Look out for that speeding car !
2. Will you be marching at the rally tonight ?
3. Dr. and Mrs. Harold Graves will attend the wedding .
4. She asked how many cars we had washed on Saturday .
5. Ouch! That grease is hot !
6. I just received a perfect score on my math test . or !
7. The *Examiner* reported on the scandal in Friday's paper .
8. What freeway turn-off should we take? How far is it ?
9. The police questioned the young woman about her activities on Thursday night .
10. Archie Schroeder, Sr., won back his city council seat this year .

REVIEW EXERCISE 4: Commas

The following paragraph contains no commas. Copy the paragraph onto your paper, adding the commas.

(1) The elephant , the largest land animal in existence , possesses some unique characteristics. (2) Though these creatures weigh only 190 pounds at birth , they may eventually reach four tons or more in weight. (3) Surprisingly , with this massive bulk , they can still swim , but they usually prefer to walk along a river-bed bottom. (4) Master bulls often stand eleven feet high and grow impressive ivory tusks. (5) Currently , the record length for the largest tusks stands at approximately 11½ feet , a great length , indeed. (6) These animals also possess one of the longer life spans in the animal kingdom , with some elephants surpassing the half-century mark. (7) In Sydney , Australia , the oldest known elephant , a senile crotchety old girl named Jessie , lived to the age of sixty-nine years. (8) Elephant courtship also has acquired a uniqueness. (9) Not one to rush into commitments , the bull may court his lady for ten full months. (10) During this time he brings her the choicest tufts of grass. (11) But with the arrival of the calf , the father disappears and leaves the mother and her female companions to care for the infant. (12) Although the bull's action may seem to fit the stereotype we have of the elephant as a dull , callow brute , these animals show a gentleness towards the young , frightened , and injured in their herd. (13) Walt Disney made the well-loved Dumbo a kind , humble little elephant , and Dr. Seuss capital-

ized on this attribute in his book *Horton Hatches an Egg.* (14) Indeed, these mammoth creatures with their gentle attitudes have always been admired by people.

REVIEW EXERCISE 5: The Semicolon and Colon

Semicolons and colons have been left out of the following sentences. Write the word that goes before the punctuation mark, the punctuation mark, and the word that comes after it. Some sentences may contain more than one mark.

1. My throat hurt;my ears throbbed;my bones ached.
2. Our eyes focused on the tiny figure on the stage:a twelve-year-old Little Orphan Annie belting out her song.
3. Our chapter of the National Honor Society gave their money to a very worthy cause;They contributed to the American Cancer Society.
4. The tenant brought in her check;the manager wrote out a receipt.
5. She had been assigned several items to bring to the car wash:soap, towels, sponges, and a hose.
6. I concentrated—or at least, I tried to concentrate—on the checkbook statement before me;but my mind kept wandering back to thoughts of that warm, relaxing day at the beach.
7. He gulped down his coffee and raced for the door;she sipped her tea and stretched back in the chair.
8. We shared one common characteristic;We both suffered from an identical eye problem.
9. I decided to increase my reading skills by reading *Faster Reading:Six Techniques to Increased Speed.*
10. The group headed off for opening night;however, the line for the show already stretched several blocks by the time they got there.

REVIEW EXERCISE 6: Quotation Marks

Quotation marks have been left out of the following sentences. The one quoted phrase is underlined. Copy each sentence onto your paper, adding the necessary quotation marks.

1. "The voice of dissent must be heard."—Henry Ford
2. The guard asked, "Do you want me to lock this gate after you leave?"
3. Adlai E. Stevenson believed in a patriotism that was not wild but instead was the "tranquil and steady dedication of a lifetime."

4. The voice over the loudspeaker announced, "A special manager's sale on toasters will begin in the Kitchenware Department in five minutes."
5. The politician remarked, "We must investigate and find out the truth of these charges of fraud, for as the Latin proverb so aptly put it, 'Truth conquers all things.'"
6. The young child shouted gleefully, "Someone just found my lost dog!"
7. "When this report is finally done," the boss stated, "we are going out to celebrate."
8. The sign said, "Two for the price of one," the manager, however, indicated that the sign was out-of-date.
9. "In my dream, I was running from a huge army," the child described.
10. Did you say, "Meet at 4:00 o'clock"?

REVIEW EXERCISE 7: Underlining and Other Uses of Quotation Marks

Copy the following items onto your paper. Underline the items that should be underlined in formal writing, and put quotation marks around the others. Some items are already correct.

1. S.S. Providence (boat)
2. "Soldier's Home" by Hemingway (short story)
3. "This Land Is Your Land" (song)
4. nouveau riche (foreign phrase)
5. Journal of Education (journal)
6. the Koran (religious book)
7. Treaty of Versailles (treaty)
8. World Press Review (magazine)
9. "What Investment Means to You" (book chapter)
10. To Sir, With Love (book)

REVIEW EXERCISE 8: Parentheses and the Dash

Boxes have been placed in the following sentences. Indicate which of the following marks should be placed in each box by writing the letter of the correct mark on your paper.

A. a parenthesis
B. a dash
C. either mark

1. The campers brought plenty to eat ⬚[C] beef jerky, crackers, and homemade trail mix ⬚[C] so they wouldn't starve.

2. We are almost ⬚ *B* oh no, I forgot my purse!
3. James Buchanan ⬚ *A* 1791–1868 ⬚ *A* believed that force was unnecessary and always desired to keep peace.
4. The cutbacks ⬚ *B* for instance, reducing the number of elective classes ⬚ *B* are bound to affect the quality of education.
5. We bought a huge roll of white ⬚ *A* paper ⬚ *A* so now we can paint our posters.
6. Meat, salad, rolls, vegetable, and dessert ⬚ *B* our guests should have enough to eat with that.
7. The teacher taught us the concept of parallellism. ⬚ *A* *Parallel* has the word *all* hidden in it which helps to spell it correctly. ⬚ *A* We are to watch our parallel structure in our thesis statements.
8. His outbursts ⬚ *C* we never know what will set off his tantrums ⬚ *C* cause me great concern.
9. The speaker made three points: ⬚ *A* 1 ⬚ *A* inflation is spiraling; ⬚ *A* 2 ⬚ *A* wage-and-price controls will not control the problem; and ⬚ *A* 3 ⬚ *A* cutting energy imports provides the best solution.
10. My brother's hand ⬚ *A* Did you know he had to get seven stitches in it last week? ⬚ *A* is healing nicely.

REVIEW EXERCISE 9: The Hyphen

A hyphen is used in each of the following sentences. If the hyphen is correctly placed, write *correct* on your paper. If the hyphen is incorrectly placed or if it is not needed, write *incorrect*.

1. The well-lighted tennis courts drew large crowds in the warm evenings. *C*
2. The bus held thirty-nine passengers. *C*
3. For ten long and cold days, the man sat stubbornly a-top the flag pole. *I*
4. The dog had a continual down-in-the-dumps expression on his face. *C*
5. The ball rolled out of bounds before Gregory Vander-bush, could get to it. *I*
6. I went out to watch the ten pigs eat from the tro-ughs. *I*
7. As the self-appointed leader, she took charge. *C*
8. Since she had just gotten her license, she classified as a new-bus driver. *I*
9. We bought the king-size box of cereal since we eat lots of it. *C*
10. We dove off the pier into the warm salt-water. *I*

REVIEW EXERCISE 10: The Apostrophe

An apostrophe has been used in each of the following phrases. If it is used correctly, write *correct* on your paper. If it is not, write *incorrect*.

1. the man and wife's charge card (joint) *c*
2. I cannot say ss' without hissing. *I*
3. one childs' toy *I*
4. It's his umbrella. *c*
5. the children's clothes *c*
6. Nobody's home. *c*
7. my only dogs' leash *I*
8. the single flower's fragrance *c*
9. Donny's and Marie's voices (individual) *c*
10. Ain't you leavin'? *c*
11. Douglas' paper *I*
12. She'll arrive soon. *c*
13. the Rotary Club's annual dinner *c*
14. It could be anyone's dollar bill. *c*
15. the gentlemen's coats *c*
16. the two swimmer's exhaustion *I*
17. Daniel's and Allison's moped (joint) *I*
18. the crowds' in the stores *I*
19. a month's trip to Canada *c*
20. seven 3's equal *21* *c*

REVIEW EXERCISE 11: Using Punctuation in Your Own Writing

Choose one of the following topics to write about. As you write, try to use all of the different punctuation marks you have learned. Do not over-punctuate.

Answers will vary; students could exchange papers to check.

1. your favorite relative
2. the closest scrape with death that you have ever had
3. your all-time favorite book
4. a community problem
5. the country you would most like to visit

Vocabulary and Spelling

Chapter 16

Vocabulary Building

One of the most useful skills you can acquire is that of learning different ways in which you can expand your vocabulary. If you can find ways to learn the new words you read and hear, if you can make reasonable guesses about the meanings of unfamiliar words, and if you can add new words to your existing vocabulary by using common prefixes, roots, and suffixes, you are well on your way to mastering a skill that will help you in all subject areas now and in later life as well.

No matter how large your vocabulary is, you can always increase your knowledge of the meaning of words. You can work on developing your vocabulary every day by recording new words as you encounter them and by looking up their meanings in a dictionary. If you do not have a dictionary handy, you can often figure out the meanings of new words from the meaning of the words around them or from the meaning of their parts. This chapter will show you how to confront unfamiliar words and how to incorporate them into your vocabulary.

16.1 Building Your Vocabulary

Developing your vocabulary is so important that you should work on it almost every day. Every subject you will study has a particular vocabulary. Knowing the meanings of the words related to each subject will enable you to understand the subject better. In order to master each subject's vocabulary, you should use the dictionary and write definitions of new words in your notebook. You can also make use of a variety of study and review techniques.

■ Using the Dictionary and Your Notebook

The best place to begin is with a dictionary and your notebook.

Use the dictionary and special vocabulary sections of your notebook regularly to build your vocabulary.

A dictionary should always be your final authority on the meaning of words. It will usually give you a number of definitions as well as examples of how to use a word correctly. You should cultivate the habit of looking up unfamiliar words by having a dictionary in your study area at home and by using the dictionaries in your classrooms. You might also want to carry a pocket dictionary. When you check a word in the dictionary, read the definitions carefully, study the definitions, and write the new word and its meaning in your notebook.

You should have a vocabulary section for each subject in your notebook. One possible way to set up vocabulary sections is explained in the following chart.

SETTING UP VOCABULARY SECTIONS IN A NOTEBOOK

Step 1: For each subject division in your notebook, designate a few pages at the beginning or end for a vocabulary section.

Step 2: Divide each page into three columns.

Step 3: Label Column 1 "Words," and use this column to write new words. Include pronunciations when necessary.

Step 4: Label Column 2 "Bridge Words," and use this column to write words or clues that will help you remember the meaning of each new word. For *oscillate*, for example, you might write the word *pendulum* as a reminder that *oscillate* means "to swing back and forth."

Step 5: Label Column 3 "Definitions," and use this column to write one or more definitions for each new word.

Once you have established vocabulary sections in your notebook, use the sections regularly by looking up unfamiliar words in a dictionary for each of your subjects and entering the words, bridge words, and definitions in the three columns.

Your vocabulary notebook might resemble the following example from a science notebook.

Vocabulary Words	Notebook Bridge Words	Science Definitions
ornithology	oriole	the study of birds
carnivorous	cannibal	flesh eating
oscillate	pendulum	swing back and forth
effervescent	champagne	bubbling
forceps	the dentist	small tongs for grasping

EXERCISE A: **Starting Vocabulary Sections of Your Notebook.** Select several pages in each of the subject areas of your notebook. Make these pages into vocabulary notebook sections by dividing them into three columns labeled *Words*, *Bridge Words*, and *Definitions*. Then write five important terms you have already encountered in each class and add bridge words and definitions. As new words come up, add them to your notebook. *Students might be encouraged to add words that come up in class, from reading assignments, and from personal reading.*

■ Reviewing and Remembering Vocabulary Words

To make a word part of your vocabulary, you should study its definition, use it in your writing and speaking, and review it from time to time until you are completely sure of it. There are a number of methods for studying and remembering words.

Use one or more special review techniques to remember the meaning of new words.

You can use your vocabulary notebook, flashcards, a tape recorder, or books on the history of words to learn new words.

Studying with Your Vocabulary Notebook. When you have free time at school or at home or when you are preparing for a test, you can use the organization of your vocabulary notebook to help you study. The following chart describes a method of studying with your vocabulary notebook.

USING YOUR VOCABULARY NOTEBOOK

Step 1: Study the word by looking across the three columns that give you the word, a bridge word or clue, and the definition.

Step 2: Take a piece of paper and cover the definition column. Using the bridge word, say or write the definition of each word.

Step 3: Then cover both the bridge word and the definition columns and try to define each word orally or in writing.

Step 4: Put a check by each word that you miss and study the three columns again.

Step 5: Finally, cover the word and the bridge word columns and try to say or write the word to match each definition.

Studying with Mini-Flashcards. One way to study vocabulary words frequently is to keep a small pack of vocabulary cards with you at all times. On one- by three-inch (2.5 by 7.5 cm) cards, you can list your vocabulary words on one side and the definitions on the other. When you have spare time—waiting for the bus, sitting in the doctor's office or in study hall—flip through the cards to see how many words you can define. As you begin to remember certain definitions, remove these cards from the pack and include new words from your classes and your reading.

Studying with a Tape Recorder. If hearing something helps you learn and remember, you might try using a tape recorder to study your vocabulary words. Speaking, repeating, and hearing new words and their definitions will reinforce your learning. The following chart explains how to use a tape recorder to study new words.

USING A TAPE RECORDER

Step 1: Read the vocabulary word into the tape recorder.

Step 2: Leave a ten-second blank space on the tape. Then state the definition and give a short sentence using the word in context.

Step 3: Continue with the remainder of the vocabulary words.

Step 4: Replay the tape, and try to give a definition and a sentence during each ten-second pause. As the tape continues, you will see if you are correct. When you have gone through your list once, start over, giving definitions and sentences for only those words you missed. Continue until you have learned all of the words.

Listening to your tape several times a week will help you make new words a permanent part of your vocabulary.

Studying Etymologies. The study of the history of a word from its earliest recorded use to its current use is called the word's *etymology*. Knowing the origin and development of a word's meaning can help you remember that word. Also, some words have unusual and fascinating histories. A word may have passed from language to language until it became part of English. The name of a character in a myth or story may have become a common word, or a famous person may have given his or her name to a thing or quality. For example, the word *sandwich* comes from the title of a man, the Earl of Sandwich, who ate meat between slices of bread so that he would not have to stop gambling to dine.

The average dictionary will give you short etymologies, but for more detail you can consult books on etymologies in the 420 section of the library. Unusual histories, such as the following, will help you remember the meaning of words.

EXAMPLE: *bonanza* = a source of wealth or profits

Spanish sailors used the word *bonanza*, related to *bonus* (good) in Latin, to describe fair weather or good fortune. Miners in the nineteenth century used *bonanza* to describe a fortunate discovery of ore. Eventually the word came to mean a source of wealth or profits in general.

EXERCISE B: Working with Etymologies. Check the origins and histories of five of the following fifteen words by using library books with numbers around 420. The library card catalog under the heading "English language" will direct you to these books. Write down the titles of the books you use. Then find the histories of your five words and write a summary for each. *Answers on page T-126.*

1. atlas	6. daisy	11. muslin
2. cardigan	7. buccaneers	12. moccasin
3. derrick	8. carnival	13. sundae
4. lunatic	9. confetti	14. quixotic
5. tycoon	10. eureka	15. calliope

EXERCISE C: Deciding on a Study Method. Decide which of the four study methods explained here will work best for you. Then choose a second method you can use occasionally to add variety to your study. Explain the reasons for both choices. *Students could be polled to determine most common method and could discuss the reasons for their choices.*

APPLICATION: Evaluating and Improving Your Vocabulary Skills. After two or more weeks of working on your vocabulary using the methods presented in this section, evaluate your skills by answering the following questions.
In addition, notebooks could be checked and class lists of new words compiled.
1. Have you used a dictionary at least five times this week?
2. Have you entered new words in your notebook this week?
3. Have you used at least two new words in your writing and speaking this week?

Using Context 16.2

The other words in the sentence or passage in which a word is found make up the word's *context.* You can use these surrounding words, or context clues, to make an educated guess about a word's meaning. By learning to interpret context clues you can figure out the meaning of many unfamiliar words when you are reading rapidly and before you can consult a dictionary for an exact definition.

Use context clues to determine the meaning of unfamiliar words.

Context clues can be of several types. A knowledge of the types of clues can help you use context most effectively. The following chart shows three common types. Notice how the italicized clues help you figure out the meaning of the underlined words.

TYPES OF CONTEXT CLUES	
Clue	Example
Key words in the sentence that point to the word's meaning	Climbing *mountains*, being in *tall* buildings, and crossing *high* bridges *frighten* me because I have <u>acrophobia</u>.
	(Italicized words suggest height and fear. <u>Acrophobia</u> means fear of high places.)

Sentences that set up comparisons or contrasts between several words and suggest that a word means the same as or the opposite of another word	One of our cats is very *courageous* and *loves adventure;* the other is very timorous. (The sentence leads you to think that timorous is the opposite of *courageous.* Timorous means fearful.)
Words or phrases that follow another word closely and seem to rename or define it	Bonsai, *the art of growing trees in small flower pots,* is well-known in Japan. (The phrase after bonsai renames and defines it. Bonsai means the art of growing trees in small flower pots.)

To use these types of context clues, you should follow a few simple steps. You can quickly perform all of the steps mentally, except for the last one.

USING CONTEXT CLUES

Step 1: Read the sentence through carefully, first with, then without, the unfamiliar word.

Step 2: Identify surrounding words that give clues and note which type of clue the sentence provides.

Step 3: Try to guess the meaning of the unfamiliar word, using the context clues.

Step 4: Read the sentence substituting your guess for the unfamiliar word.

Step 5: Check your guess in the dictionary and record the word and its definition in your vocabulary notebook.

■ Using Context in Daily Reading

After you have mastered the steps for using context clues, try your context skills on the following paragraph. It is similar to the kind of humorous article you might find in a newspaper or popular magazine. Read it and try to determine the meaning of each underlined word by its context in the sentence. On a piece of paper, jot down what you think each word means.

EXAMPLE: If a want ad for a rock star existed, it might look like this. Wanted: Young man or woman willing to <u>forgo</u> a <u>serene</u> life for the prospect of <u>incessant</u> rehearsals, months of <u>grueling</u> one-night concerts, and the probability that this lifestyle is <u>transient</u>. Applicants for the position must <u>bedeck</u> themselves in <u>flamboyant</u> outfits guaranteed to <u>bedazzle</u> fans. A repertoire of songs that will totally wreck the composure of an audience is also a requirement. A group of loyal followers who will support the singer at all times is the final <u>prerequisite</u>. Anyone who <u>aspires</u> to such a position must possess all these qualifications.

EXERCISE A: **Defining Words.** Use your list of guesses from the preceding paragraph to complete the following multiple choice questions. For each word choose the definition that most closely matches the meaning of the word as it was used in the paragraph. Write the letter next to the appropriate number on your paper. Then check your answers in a dictionary and record any words you missed in the English section of your notebook.

1. forgo: (a) <u>do without</u>; (b) precede; (c) agree; (d) assert
2. serene: (a) dead; (b) <u>peaceful</u>; (c) excited; (d) bored
3. aspire: (a) breathe; (b) <u>earnestly desire</u>; (c) influence; (d) die
4. transient: (a) random; (b) terminated; (c) legendary; (d) <u>temporary</u>
5. bedeck: (a) bend; (b) lure; (c) wear; (d) <u>adorn</u>
6. flamboyant: (a) trivial; (b) <u>overly showy</u>; (c) informal; (d) rare
7. bedazzle: (a) <u>blind, figuratively</u>; (b) adapt; (c) change for the worse; (d) affect
8. grueling: (a) <u>exhausting</u>; (b) soupy; (c) fighting; (d) racing
9. incessant: (a) tiresome; (b) uncomfortable; (c) <u>constant</u>; (d) secretive
10. prerequisite: (a) list; (b) trifle; (c) basis; (d) <u>precondition</u>

■ Using Context in Reading Textbooks

The content of the next passage is similar to material you might find in a health or science textbook. Notice, however, that some of the underlined words are words that you might meet in your general reading as well as in your school assignments. A good general vocabulary can improve your reading comprehension in all areas. As you read the passage, try to determine the meaning of each underlined word by its context in the sentence. Use the steps in the chart on page 434 to guess the meaning of the words. Then jot down on a piece of paper what you think each word means.

EXAMPLE: The field of medicine has greatly advanced from primitive attempts to help the injured and sick. The lifesaving techniques that were used then were based on <u>rudimentary</u> knowledge of the body. Much of this basic knowledge was derived from observation of animals. From various herbs and plants came salves to soothe and <u>anodynes</u> to alleviate pain. Interestingly enough, the popularity of many folk remedies is enjoying a <u>resurgence</u> today.

As knowledge about cures of diseases has increased, so too has the <u>range</u> of knowledge about the diseases themselves. Sophisticated procedures and equipment have enabled scientists to determine that there are many different viruses as well as many kinds of <u>virulent</u> bacteria. Success with curing bodily illnesses has made the search for more <u>efficacious</u> methods of treating mental illnesses even more <u>intensive</u>. <u>Prodigious</u> amounts, however, remain to be learned about the human body and brain. No one would make the <u>assertion</u> that <u>pathologists</u> have all the answers.

EXERCISE B: Defining Words. Use your list of guesses to complete the following questions. For each word choose the definition that most closely matches the meaning of the word as it was used in the paragraphs. Write the letter next to the appropriate number on your paper. Then check your answers in a dictionary and record any words you missed in the English section of your notebook.

1. efficacious: (a) educated; (b) friendly;
                    (c) effective; (d) effortless
2. assertion: (a) desertion; (b) declaration;
                    (c) rejection; (d) aggression
3. rudimentary: (a) elementary; (b) unpolished;
                    (c) incurable; (d) bright
4. resurgence: (a) development; (b) birth; (c) rising
                    again; (d) surgical operation
5. prodigious: (a) strong; (b) very smart; (c) very
                    proud; (d) huge

6. virulent: (a) masculine; (b) cruel; (c) stingy;
                  (d) poisonous
7. anodyne: (a) energetic; (b) stimulant;
                  (c) alcohol; (d) pain reliever
8. intensive: (a) very hot; (b) meant; (c) thorough;
                  (d) well-planned
9. range: (a) scope; (b) stove; (c) wander
                  about; (d) open land
10. pathologist: (a) trailblazer; (b) disease;
                  (c) linguist; (d) scientist

■ Using Context in Research Work

The following passage contains the kind of material you might find in a book or in a magazine article about popular culture. If you were doing research for a social studies paper, you might include such an article in your bibliography.

As you did with the preceding passages, read the passage and note the underlined words. Try to determine the meaning of the words by their context in the sentences. Then jot down what you think each word means.

EXAMPLE: The durability of Superman as a symbol of American popular culture is incontestable. A native of Krypton, Superman comes to earth and makes his home in Metropolis. Always on the side of justice, he battles the perversity of countless villains. Although he has superhuman strength, Superman disguises himself as the meek and impassive Clark Kent, a newspaper reporter. No one would suspect that Kent, whose cowardice is equaled by his extreme torpor, can also operate as the dynamic Superman. Lois Lane, another reporter on the *Daily Planet*, openly admits her preference for Superman with his insatiable appetite for taking on any adversary.
      With the advent of television, it seemed that comic book heroes would cease to enthrall adventure-loving fans. Many heroes did sink into the abyss of neglect and oblivion. Superman, however, has fought his way to stardom, not only in television but in the movies. American culture is ever-changing, but the indomitable Superman lives on.

EXERCISE C: Defining Words. Use your guesses to complete the following questions. For each word choose the definition that most closely matches the meaning of the word as it was used in the paragraphs. Write the letter next to the appropriate number on your paper. Then check each answer in a dictionary and record any words you missed in the English section of your notebook.

1. dynamic: (a) engine; (b) forceful; (c) dangerous; (d) dignified
2. perversity: (a) strangeness; (b) wickedness; (c) violence; (d) overwhelming odds
3. impassive: (a) calm; (b) difficult; (c) impressive; (d) imposing
4. insatiable: (a) greedy; (b) unsatisfactory; (c) encouraging; (d) hopeless
5. oblivion: (a) kind of angle; (b) binding promise; (c) state of being forgotten; (d) geometric shape
6. incontestable: (a) answerable; (b) unquestionable; (c) competitive; (d) arguable
7. torpor: (a) antipathy; (b) vibration; (c) sluggishness; (d) stupidity
8. adversary: (a) celebration; (b) opponent; (c) acquaintance; (d) finance
9. indomitable: (a) unconquerable; (b) domineering; (c) impossible; (d) unquestionable
10. durability: (a) capability; (b) hard; (c) doubtfulness; (d) lastingness

APPLICATION: **Using Context Clues to Complete Sentences.** Choose the word from the following list that best completes each sentence. Write each word on your paper.

> anodyne   efficacious   transient
> oblivion   torpor   indomitable
> aspires   incessant   virulent
> rudimentary

1. The _____*transient*_____ nature of success leads the wise person to keep one eye on the future.
2. In any field, hard work is necessary if one _____*aspires*_____ to greatness.
3. The _____*incessant*_____ questioning finally caused the prisoner to break down.
4. Since the _____*anodyne*_____ was not long-lasting, the pain returned in an hour.
5. Plant cuttings will quickly develop a _____*rudimentary*_____ root system in water.
6. The most _____*efficacious*_____ way to diet is to forgo desserts.

7. The spider's bite was so ____*virulent*____ they feared for the victim's life.
8. Because of his ____*indomitable*____ will to live, he regained his health.
9. Her ____*torpor*____ was a result of illness, not of boredom.
10. The sensational book sold well at first but soon fell into ____*oblivion*____ .

Using Structure 16.3

Besides using the context of a word, you can sometimes use a word's structure, or parts, to find clues to its meaning. You may have noticed that many words have similar parts, such as *trans-, un-, -graph-, -ject-, -ness*, and *-tion*. These word parts are of three kinds: prefixes, roots, and suffixes. A *prefix*, such as *trans-* or *un-*, is one or more syllables that can be added at the beginning of a word or part of a word to form a new word. A *root*, such as *-graph-* or *-ject-*, is a word or the base of a word. A *suffix*, such as *-ness* or *-tion*, is one or more syllables that can be added at the end of a root to form a new word. Many prefixes, roots, and suffixes have come into English from Greek, Latin, and Old English. With an understanding of the meanings of certain prefixes, roots, and suffixes, you should be able to make reasonable guesses about the meanings of words that contain these word parts.

Use prefixes, roots, and suffixes as clues to the meanings of unfamiliar words.

Some words such as *prove, tense,* and *think* consist of roots only. Some words, such as *improve (im- + -prove)* and *intense (in- + -tense)* are made up of a prefix and a root. Other words consist of roots and suffixes: *tensely (tense- + -ly)* and *thinkable (think- + -able)*. Still other words have all three parts: *improvement, intensity,* and *unthinkable*. In the following chart, notice that while a root can often stand alone, some roots such as *-ject-* act only as a base. The meaning of each word part in the chart is given underneath the part. In the last column, you can see how the meanings of the parts are combined in the definition of each word.

EXAMPLES OF ROOTS AS BASES				
Word	**Prefix**	**Root**	**Suffix**	**Definition**
project	pro- (forward)	-ject- (to throw)		to throw forward; to send forth; to plan
reject	re- (back)	-ject- (to throw)		to refuse to take; to throw out; to deny
rejection	re- (back)	-jec- (to throw)	-tion (the act of, the state of being)	the act of refusing or throwing out; the state of being denied acceptance

■ Using Prefixes

A prefix as a word part affects the meaning of the base word or root much more strongly than a suffix does. The first two steps in increasing your stock of words are recognizing common prefixes and using them to create new words.

The following chart contains only twenty of the many prefixes that occur in English words. Yet even these few can be used to form a great number of words. Learn the meaning of each prefix and the different spellings of each prefix given in parentheses. Then try adding them to different roots or words to see how many new words you can form. (The abbreviations L. and O.E. stand for Latin and Old English, the origins of the prefixes.)

TWENTY COMMON PREFIXES		
Prefix	**Meaning**	**Examples**
ab- (a-, abs-) [L.]	away, from	abolish, avert, abstract
ad- (ac-, af-, al-, ap-, as-, at-) [L.]	to, toward	adjoin, acknowledge, affix, allure, appoint, assure, attribute
circum- [L.]	around, about, surrounding, on all sides	circumstance

com- (co-, col-, con-, cor-) [L.]	with, together	compress, cooperate, collaborate, contribute, correspond
de- [L.]	away from, off, down	decontrol, debase
dis- (di-, dif-) [L.]	away, apart, cause to be opposite of	disbelief, disconnect, divert, diffuse
ex- (e-, ec-, ef-) [L.]	forth, from, out	express, emigrate, eccentric, effluent
in- (il-, im-, ir-) [L.]	not, "un"	inhuman, illegal, impossible, irregular
in- (il-, im-, ir-) [L.]	in, into, within, on, toward	indent, illuminate, immigrate, irrigate
inter- [L.]	between	international
mis- [O.E.]	wrong	misplace
non- [L.]	not	nonsense
post- [L.]	after	postgraduate
pre- [L.]	before	prefix
pro- [L.]	forward, forth, favoring, in place of	produce, protract
re- [L.]	back, again	renew
semi- [L.]	half, partly	semicircle
sub- (suc-, suf-, sup-) [L.]	beneath, under, below	submarine, success, sufficient, suppress
trans- [L.]	across	transport
un- [O.E.]	not	unknown

The more prefixes you become familiar with, the more rapidly your vocabulary and your comprehension of new words will grow.

EXERCISE A: Using Prefixes to Build New Words. Add one of the prefixes from the chart to each of the words in the first column to form a word that matches the definition in the second column. Write each new word on your paper. Notice that you may have to use one of the prefixes in parentheses for some of the words. Use a dictionary, if necessary.

1. _____circum_____ + navigate   to sail around
2. _____de_____ + compress   to free from pressure
3. _____sub_____ + standard   not up to standard
4. _____pre_____ + mature   happening before the usual time
5. _____re_____ + submit   to submit again
6. _____dis_____ + appear   to go away
7. _____in_____ + formal   not very formal
8. _____ex_____ + change   to hand over or transfer
9. _____im_____ + moral   not moral
10. _____ac_____ + quit   to clear a person of a charge

■ Using Roots

Of all three word parts, the root is, of course, the most important in determining the meaning of a word. Roots have come into the English language from many sources. The following chart lists twenty common roots that come from Latin and Greek. Like many other roots borrowed from foreign languages, none of the roots in this chart can stand alone. The chart gives the different spellings and meanings of each root as well as examples of words containing the roots.

TWENTY COMMON ROOTS		
Root	Meaning	Examples
-cap- (-capt-, -cept-) [L.]	to take, seize	capable, captivate, accept
-ced- (-ceed-, -cess-) [L.]	to go, yield	procedure, proceed, success
-dic- (-dict-) [L.]	to say, point out in words	indicate, edict
-duc- (-duct-) [L.]	to lead	produce, conduct
-fac- (-fact-, -fec-, -fect-, -fic-) [L.]	to do, make	facsimile, manufacture, infection, defect, fiction
-graph- [Gr.]	to write	autograph
-ject- [L.]	to throw	reject
-mit- (-mis-) [L.]	to send	admit, transmission

-mov- (-mot-) [L.]	to move	movement, motion
-plic- [L.]	to fold	duplicate
-pon- (-pos-) [L.]	to put, place	postpone, depose
-puls- (-pel-) [L.]	to drive	pulsate, propel
-quir- (-ques-, -quis-) [L.]	to ask, say	inquire, question, inquisitive
-scrib- (-script-) [L.]	to write	describe, prescription
-spec- (-spect-) [L.]	to see	specimen, inspect
-ten- (-tain-, -tin-) [L.]	to hold, contain	tenure, detain, continent
-tend- (-tens-, -tent-) [L.]	to stretch	distend, extension, extent
-ven- (-vent-) [L.]	to come	convene, inventor
-vert- (-vers-) [L.]	to turn	divert, subversive
-vid- (-vis-) [L.]	to see	evident, vision

EXERCISE B: Determining the Meaning of Words Based on Roots You Know. Match each of the meanings in the second column with the correct words in the first column. In parentheses before the definitions, you will find the meaning of the word parts. Write the letter of the definition next to the appropriate number on your paper. If you are not sure of any meanings, look the word up in the dictionary.

1. predict *g*
2. transcribe *d*
3. recede *j*
4. exceed *h*
5. impulse *c*
6. transmit *a*
7. induce *i*
8. remiss *b*
9. prefect *f*
10. extend *e*

a. (across + send) to send across
b. (back + send) being in the wrong
c. (into + drive) a sudden desire
d. (across + write) to write down in a different form
e. (from + stretch) to stretch beyond
f. (before + make) a high official
g. (before + tell) foretell
h. (from + go) to be more than expected
i. (toward + lead) to persuade
j. (back + go) to fall back

■ Using Suffixes

At the beginning of this section, a suffix was defined as one or more syllables added at the end of a root to form a new word. Some word endings are used to indicate the plural of a noun or the tense of a verb. For example, to form the plural of *book*, you add the ending *-s*. To form the past tense of *laugh*, you add the ending *-ed*. Other word endings, however, when added to a base word, form totally new words. In doing so, they also change the part of speech of the words. The suffix *-ment*, for example, changes the verb *improve* to the noun *improvement*. It is this type of word ending that you will work with in the last part of this section.

The following chart shows only fifteen suffixes, along with their meanings and the parts of speech they form. However, even this short list of suffixes, combined with words you already know, will give you the ability to build a large number of words.

FIFTEEN COMMON SUFFIXES			
Suffix	Meaning	Examples	Part of Speech
-able (-ible) [L.]	capable of being; tending to	reliable, edible	adjective
-ance (-ence) [L.]	the act of; the quality or state of being	clearance, confidence	noun
-ate [L.]	making, applying, operating on	decorate, activate	verb
-ful [O.E.]	full of; characterized by; having the ability or tendency to	scornful	noun or adjective
-fy [L.]	to make; to cause to become; to cause to have	clarify	verb
-ist [Gr.]	a person who does or makes; a person skilled in; a believer in	violinist	noun
-ity [L.]	state of being; character; condition of	intensity	noun
-ize (-ise) [Gr.]	to make	idolize, improvise	verb
-less [O.E.]	without; lacking	careless, ageless	adjective

-ly [O.E.]	in a certain way; at a certain time or place	harshly, hourly	adverb or adjective
-ment [L.]	result or product of	improvement, amazement	noun
-ness [O.E.]	state of being; quality	laziness	noun
-or [L.]	a person or thing that; a quality or condition that	spectator	noun
-ous (-ious) [L.]	marked by; given to	pompous, mysterious	adjective
-tion (-ion, -sion, -ation, -ition) [L.]	the action of; the state of being	action, mission, aviation, position	noun

EXERCISE C: **Writing Words with Suffixes.** Use the underlined word in each of the following sentences plus an appropriate suffix to form a word to fill each blank correctly. Write each new word and its part of speech on your paper.

1. A person who <u>conforms</u> to expected standards of behavior is a ___*conformist*___ . *noun*
2. To be unable to <u>help</u> oneself is to be ___*helpless*___ . *adj*
3. To cause something to become <u>active</u> is to ___*activate*___ it. *verb*
4. When something is full of <u>dangers</u> it is ___*dangerous*___ . *adj*
5. The quality of being <u>generous</u> is called ___*generosity*___ . *noun*
6. To cause to become <u>legal</u> is to ___*legalize*___ . *verb*
7. The act of <u>assisting</u> another is called ___*assistance*___ . *noun*
8. A person who is characterized by <u>hope</u> is ___*hopeful*___ . *adj*
9. To give <u>glory</u> to is to ___*glorify*___ . *verb*
10. One who <u>mediates</u> an argument between persons or groups is a ___*mediator*___ . *noun*

APPLICATION: **Using Word Parts.** Choose four word parts from each of the three charts in this section. Add other word parts to make twelve complete words. Then write a short story using all twelve words. Underline each of the words.
Answers will vary. Five word samples given. Short story can be graded as composition. 1. *suc + cess + ful* 2. *ad + dic + tion* 3. *pro + ject + or* 4. *post + pone + ment* 5. *dis + ten + tion*

Chapter 17

Spelling Improvement

Spelling is an important skill to acquire. By following the suggestions and learning the basic rules explained in this chapter, you should be able to avoid many spelling problems. Your major goal in these sections should be to learn to spell words that you use again and again in your daily writing, both in and out of school.

In order to spell correctly and easily, you should have an overall strategy for spelling. The first section of the chapter will help you plan your strategy. The second section will present specific spelling rules that will make it easier for you to spell accurately.

17.1 Improving Spelling Skills

Many years ago, people who wrote in the English language were not overly concerned with spelling words uniformly. William Shakespeare, for example, was very casual about spelling. However, as time passed, spelling became more consistent. When Thomas Jefferson wrote to his daughter about her education, he included the following advice: "Take care that you never spell a word wrong. Always, before you write a word, consider how it is spelled, and if you do not remember, turn to a dictionary."

His advice still holds, for correct spelling is just as necessary today as it was 200 years ago. Spelling has become so uniform that a misspelled word stands out like the proverbial sore thumb. Careless spelling indicates either that you do not know how to spell or that you are a hurried or a careless writer. In either case, someone reading your work may be unfavorably impressed and the value of whatever you were trying to communicate may diminish.

■ Keeping Track of Problem Words

The best place to start improving your spelling is with words that are difficult *for you*. Set aside a special section of your notebook for a personal spelling list that will include words you frequently misspell in your own writing.

Make a personal spelling list of difficult words, enter it in your notebook, and keep it up to date.

Begin by collecting a reasonable sample of papers and tests that you have written over the last few months. Note spelling errors marked by your teachers and then work with a partner to identify any other misspelled words. In the special section of your notebook, make four columns across the page, as in the following sample. In the first column, headed "Misspelled Words," record each such word exactly as you wrote it on your paper or test. Knowing how you misspelled the word will help you locate and remedy your errors. Put an X through the entire column so you will not learn these spellings by mistake. In the second column, "Correct Spelling," record the correct spelling of each word as it is given in a dictionary. In the third column, "Practice Sessions," leave enough space to record your progress, following the suggestions you will find on pages 448–449. In the fourth column, "Memory Aids," leave even more space in case you decide to add the kind of hints described on pages 449–450.

	Personal Spelling List			
	Misspelled Words	*Correct Spelling*	*Practice Sessions*	*Memory Aids*
○	1. ~~artic~~	arctic	√√	*There is no art in arctic.*
	2. ~~seperate~~	separate	√	*Separate and apart both have 2 a's.*
	3. ~~alot~~	allot		*a lot (2 words) means "many"; allot (1 word) means "to apportion."*

EXERCISE A: Beginning Your Personal Spelling List. Look over all the writing you have done in the last month, including personal writing and school assignments. Following the preceding explanation and sample, record any misspelled words in a personal spelling list.

Class list of problem words could be compiled.

▣ Studying Problem Words

Some of the words on your personal spelling list may be words you seldom use and have misspelled simply through carelessness. Others may be words that you repeatedly misspell. Both kinds of problems can be attacked through the use of a systematic study plan.

Study the words in your personal spelling list using the steps in the following chart.

Once you have completed the first two columns in your personal spelling list, you can use the following steps in a series of practice sessions to master the correct spelling of the words.

LEARNING TO SPELL PROBLEM WORDS

1. *Look* at each word carefully. Observe the arrangement and pattern of the letters in the word. Consider, for example, the word *moccasin*. Notice that there are two *c*'s and only one *s* in the word. Try to *see* the word in your mind.

2. *Pronounce* the word accurately. For example, pronounce *athletic*. Notice that there are only three syllables: *ath let ic*.

3. *Write* the word on a piece of paper. As you write the word, pronounce it carefully.

4. *Check* to make sure the spelling is correct. If it is correct, enter a check in the third column of your notebook. If you have made a mistake, take note of the part of the word you misspelled. Then start over again with the first step.

5. *Review* your list of problem words at least once a week. Enter a check in the third column only when you have spelled the word correctly in the first round of a practice session. Consider a word mastered when you have three checks.

EXERCISE B: Working with Problem Words. Each of the following sentences contains a pair of words in parentheses. Choose the word that you think is spelled correctly and write it on your paper. Check each word in the dictionary. Then list the correct spellings of the words you misspelled in your notebook. Review them periodically using the Look, Pronounce, Write, Check, and Review method.

1. The (pronounciation, <u>pronunciation</u>) of some words is difficult.
2. The thunder and (lightening, <u>lightning</u>) terrified the puppy.
3. The (<u>personnel</u>, personal) office will have information about possible jobs.
4. I hate to fill out (questionairres, <u>questionnaires</u>).
5. Who is (responsable, <u>responsible</u>) for this messy room?
6. The (<u>defendant</u>, defendent) is always presumed innocent unless proven guilty.
7. Can you draw (<u>parallel</u>, paralel) lines without a ruler?
8. What kind of (milage, <u>mileage</u>) does your car get?
9. Your (<u>appearance</u>, appearence) should be very neat when you apply for a job.
10. The hotel can (<u>accommodate</u>, accomodate) 250 guests.

■ Developing Memory Aids

Some words in the English language are especially difficult to learn, often because they do not follow any set spelling rules. Many of these words can best be mastered through the use of memory aids.

Use memory aids to remember the spelling of words that you find especially difficult.

There are a number of tricks that you can use to remember the spelling of problem words. One popular way is to look for familiar words whose spelling you already know within the hard words.

EXAMPLES: bulletin Watch for the *bullet* in *bulletin*.

friend You will be my fri*end* to the *end*.

principal Our princi*pal* is like a *pal* to us.

vegetables Did you *get* the vege*t*ables from the market?

Another popular way to memorize the spelling of problem words is to associate a part of a word with the same letters in a related word. It is most effective to make up your own, but here are a few suggestions.

EXAMPLES: cellar A cell*ar* is usually d*ar*k. Both words are
spelled with *ar*.

clientele Clien*tele* means a group of customers.
Customers often order what they want on
the *tele*phone.

Once you have decided you need a memory aid to memorize a particularly difficult word, develop an aid using one
of the ideas above or some more personal clue to the word's
spelling. Then enter the memory aid in the fourth column of
your notebook.

EXERCISE C: **Working with Memory Aids.** Choose five particularly difficult words from your personal spelling list. Develop a memory aid for each and enter it in your notebook.
*Students might compare memory aids, especially for similar spelling problems. Answers
will vary. Two samples given: 1. Emma was in a* <u>dilemma</u>.   *2.* <u>Parallel</u> *has two
parallel lines in it.*

■ Reviewing Spelling Demons

Spelling demons are words that many people have problems with.

Review a list of spelling demons to find additional spelling
problems you yourself may have.

Some of the two hundred words in the following chart
are spelled according to basic rules. Others follow no rule.
Look over the list to see how many words you can spell correctly. Those you are not sure of should be added to the list
in your notebook.

200 COMMON SPELLING DEMONS			
abbreviate	condemn	foreign	privilege
absence	conscience	grammar	probably
accidentally	conscientious	guarantee	procedure
accumulate	conscious	handkerchief	proceed
achieve	contemporary	hygiene	pronunciation
acquaintance	continuous	immigrant	psychology
admittance	convenience	independence	really
advertisement	coolly	inflammable	recede
aerial	cordially	interfere	receipt
aggressive	correspondence	knowledge	recommend
aisle	counterfeit	laboratory	reference

allowance	courageous	lawyer	rehearse
all right	courtesy	library	repetition
amateur	criticism	license	restaurant
analysis	criticize	lieutenant	rhythm
analyze	curiosity	lightning	ridiculous
anecdote	curious	loneliness	scissors
anniversary	deceive	maintenance	secretary
anonymous	defendant	mathematics	separate
anxiety	deficient	meanness	sergeant
appearance	delinquent	mediocre	similar
argument	desert	mileage	sincerely
athletic	despair	millionaire	sophomore
attendance	desperate	misspell	souvenir
awkward	dessert	naturally	spaghetti
banquet	development	necessary	straight
barrel	dining	neighbor	substitute
behavior	disappear	ninety	succeed
believe	disappoint	nuisance	superintendent
benefit	disastrous	occasion	supersede
bicycle	dissatisfied	occasionally	surprise
bookkeeper	distinction	occur	suspicious
bulletin	distinguish	occurred	syllable
bureau ·	doubt	omitted	technique
business	efficient	opinion	temperament
calendar	eighth	pamphlet	temperature
capital	eligible	parallel	temporary
capitol	embarrass	paralyze	thorough
captain	emergency	particularly	tomatoes
career	envelope	permanent	tomorrow
category	environment	permissible	tragedy
cemetary	equipped	personally	truly
changeable	exaggerate	perspiration	unforgettable
chauffeur	exceed	physician	unnecessary
clothes	exercise	possess	vacuum
colonel	existence	possession	vegetable
column	explanation	prairie	villain
committee	extraordinary	precede	Wednesday
competitor	familiar	preferable	weird
concede	February	preparation	whether

EXERCISE D: Spelling Spelling Demons. Spell each of the following words by filling in the missing letters on your paper. Check your answers in the dictionary and enter any words you spell incorrectly in your notebook.

1. effic_*ien*_t
2. chang_*ea*_ble
3. permiss_*i*_ble
4. contempor_*a*_ry
5. We_*dnes*_day
6. at_*hle*_etic
7. develop_*me*_nt
8. distin_*c*_tion
9. Feb_*rua*_ry
10. allow_*a*_nce

11. counterf_*ei*_t
12. vac_*u*_um
13. correspond_*e*_nce
14. gramm_*a*_r
15. anal_*y*_ze
16. par_*a*_llel
17. el_*i*_gible
18. anx_*ie*_ty
19. rid_*i*_c_*u*_lous
20. amat_*eu*_r

APPLICATION: Spelling Problem Words Correctly in Original Sentences. Study the following words, using the steps on page 448. Then use each of the words in a sentence of your own. *Sentences will vary; samples given for first two.*

1. accumulate
2. knowledge
3. balance
4. develop
5. maintenance
6. process
7. noticeable
8. strenuous
9. presence
10. recognizable

1. He hoped to accumulate wealth in South America. 2. His knowledge of geography was meager.

17.2 Recognizing Basic Spelling Rules

Although the list of spelling demons in Section 17.1 includes a number of irregular words for which there are no set rules, it also includes a number of words that will be much easier for you to master if you become familiar with the rules listed in this section. Learning when to use *ei* and when to use *ie*, how to form plurals, and how to add prefixes and suffixes will improve your ability to spell a great number of words without having to examine each one individually.

■ *ie* and *ei* Words

Probably sometime in grade school you heard or learned the following jingle that forms the basic rule for *ie* and *ei* words.

Write *i* before *e*,
Except after *c*
Or when sounded like *a*,
As in *neighbor* and *weigh*.

This simple rule accounts for a great number of words in which the two letters *i* and *e* come together.

EXAMPLES: grieve   ceiling ⎫
                                          ⎬ after *c*   reindeer ⎫
                                                                                      ⎬ /ā/ sound
             chief   conceit ⎭   freight ⎭

As with any rule, however, there are exceptions. The spelling after a *c* with an *sh* sound is usually *ie*, as in *ancient* and *conscience*. In addition, the following common words, grouped for easy association, are exceptions to the rule.

EXCEPTIONS: either   foreign   heir   height   seize

               neither   forfeit   their

EXERCISE A: Writing *ie* and *ei* Words. Write each of the following words on your paper, filling in either *ei* or *ie* in the blanks. Check each word in a dictionary and record any words you misspelled in your personal spelling list.

1. ach _i_ _e_ ve
2. bel _i_ _e_ f
3. dec _e_ _i_ ve
4. sl _e_ _i_ gh
5. s _e_ _i_ zure

6. rec _e_ _i_ pt
7. effic _i_ _e_ nt
8. h _e_ _i_ ress
9. r _e_ _i_ gn
10. rel _i_ _e_ ve

■ Plurals

The plural form of a noun is the form that carries the meaning "more than one." Most plurals in English present no spelling problems.

The plural form of most nouns is formed by adding *-s* or *-es* to the singular.

The addition of *-s* seldom causes a problem. However, you may often have to stop and think before adding *-es*. The following chart summarizes most of the cases in which you might add *-es*.

ADDING *-es*			
Noun Ending	Rule	Examples	Exceptions
-s, -x, -z, -sh, -ch	Add *-es.*	masses, foxes, fizzes, wishes, benches	
-o preceded by a consonant	Add *-es.*	torpedoes, tomatoes	Musical terms: altos, pianos
-o preceded by a vowel	Add only *-s.*	radios, cameos	
-y preceded by a consonant	Change *y* to *i* and add *-es.*	babies, flies	
-y preceded by a vowel	Simply add *-s.*	monkeys, delays	

Nouns that end in *f* or *fe* are not so simple to classify. Some have plurals formed simply by the addition of *-s* (*chiefs, roofs*). For others, the *f* or *fe* must be changed to *v* before *-es* is added (*calves, knives*). Still others have two acceptable plural forms (*hooves, hoofs*). If you are unsure of how a plural is formed, check a dictionary. If there is any spelling change from the singular form, the plural form or forms will be given. If two plural forms are given, the one listed first is preferred.

In addition to the nouns already discussed, a few English nouns have totally irregular plural forms. Nouns such as *child, mouse, basis,* and *datum* form their plurals in ways that generally have to be memorized (*children, mice, bases, data*). A few nouns have the same form for both singular and plural, such as *sheep, trout,* and *moose.* Again, a dictionary is your safest authority if you are not sure.

NOTE ABOUT OTHER SPECIAL PLURALS: With compound nouns that are written as separate or hyphenated words, you must find the word that is being modified and make it plural.

EXAMPLES: rule of order   mother-in-law

rules of order   mothers-in-law

To form the plurals of letters, numbers, symbols, or words used as words, you must add an apostrophe and an *-s* as explained in Section 15.8.

EXERCISE B: Writing Plural Forms. Write the plural for each of the following nouns on your paper. If you are not sure of the spelling, look the word up in a dictionary. Record the correct spelling of words you had to look up in your personal spelling list.

1. volcano *es*
2. soprano *s*
3. goose *geese*
4. crisis *crises*
5. jelly *jellies*
6. alley *s*
7. sheaf *sheaves*
8. finch *es*
9. potato *es*
10. block *s*

11. belief *s*
12. brush *es*
13. ox *en*
14. class *es*
15. aquarium *s*
16. deer *deer*
17. tax *es*
18. heart *s*
19. elf *elves*
20. cry *cries*

■ Prefixes

A prefix is one or more syllables added at the beginning of a word or root. The addition of a prefix does not affect the spelling of the word or root to which it is attached.

When a prefix is added to a word, the spelling of the root word remains the same.

Following this rule will help you with the spelling of words with double letters that may look rather strange but are actually spelled correctly.

EXAMPLES: co- + ordinate = coordinate

dis- + satisfaction = dissatisfaction

Keep in mind, however, that the spelling of some of the prefixes may change before certain types of roots to make pronunciation easier. The following example shows this kind of spelling change in a prefix.

EXAMPLE: ad- + locate = allocate

EXERCISE C: Spelling Words with Prefixes. Write the new words formed by connecting the following prefixes and roots on your paper. Refer to the chart on pages 440–441 if you are not sure about a spelling change in a prefix.

1. ad- + portion *apportion*
2. de- + activate *deactivate*
3. ex- + fervescent *effervescent*
4. pre- + eminent *preeminent*
5. co- + operate *cooperate*

6. mis- + speak *misspeak*
7. ad- + fluent *affluent*
8. un- + necessary *unnecessary*
9. ad- + knowledge *acknowledge*
10. dis- + solve *dissolve*

■ Basic Rules for Suffixes

You have already studied the rules for adding word endings to form plurals. The rules for adding word endings that change a word from one part of speech to another are quite similar to those you have already seen.

Be aware of spelling changes needed in some words or roots when you are adding suffixes.

There are three basic situations in which the question of a spelling change in the root arises before the addition of a suffix: (1) when the word or root ends with *y*; (2) when the word or root ends with *e*; and (3) when the word or root ends with a single consonant after a single vowel. The chart below summarizes the rules for these changes.

SPELLING CHANGES BEFORE SUFFIXES			
Word Ending	Suffix Added	Rule/ Examples	Exceptions
consonant + *y* (rely, friendly)	most suffixes (-able, -ness)	Change *y* to *i*. (reliable, friendliness)	most suffixes beginning with *i*: rely becomes relying hobby becomes hobbyist
vowel + *y* (employ, joy)	most suffixes (-ment, -ous)	Make no change. (employment, joyous)	a few short words: day becomes daily gay becomes gaily

any word ending in *e* (desire, separate)	suffix beginning with a vowel (-able, -ed)	Drop the final *e*. (desirable, separated)	1. words ending in *ce* or *ge* with suffixes beginning in *a* or *o*: trace becomes traceable courage becomes courageous 2. words ending in *ee* or *oe*: agree becomes agreeing toe becomes toeing 3. a few special words: dye becomes dyeing be becomes being
any word ending in *e* (nice, separate)	suffix beginning with a consonant (-ness, -ly)	Make no change. (niceness, separately)	a few special words: true becomes truly awe becomes awful argue becomes argument judge becomes judgment acknowledge becomes acknowledgment
consonant + vowel + consonant in a stressed syllable (wrap', remit')	suffix beginning with a vowel (-er, -ance)	Double the final consonant. (wrap'per, remit'tance)	1. words ending in *w* or *x*: row becomes rowing mix becomes mixing 2. words in which the stress changes after the suffix is added: refer +-ing becomes referring BUT refer' + -ence becomes ref'erence

consonant + vowel + consonant in an unstressed syllable (sig'nal,ri'val)	suffix beginning with a vowel (-ing, -ed)	Make no change. (sig'naling, ri'valed)	no major exceptions

EXERCISE D: Spelling Words with Suffixes. Write the new words formed by combining each of the following words and suffixes.

1. fascinate + -ion *fascination*
2. lucky + -ly *luckily*
3. lobby + -ist *lobbyist*
4. swim + -er *swimmer*
5. cease + -less *ceaseless*
6. control + -able *controllable*
7. confer + -ence *conference*
8. manage + -able *manageable*
9. alphabet + -ic *alphabetic*
10. apply + -ance *appliance*
11. extreme + -ity *extremity*
12. occur + -ence *occurrence*
13. portray + -al *portrayal*
14. benefit + -ed *benefited*
15. fit + -ness *fitness*
16. emerge + -ence *emergence*
17. refer + -ence *reference*
18. annoy + -ance *annoyance*
19. imagine + -ary *imaginary*
20. final + ist *finalist*

■ Special Methods for Dealing with Confusing Pairs of Suffixes

Knowing when to change the spelling of a root before a suffix will make it easier for you to spell correctly a large number of words. However, some suffixes are confusing in themselves, and you must be able to choose the right one at the right time in order to spell a word correctly.

Learn to distinguish between confusing pairs of suffixes.

-ary and -ery. Although there is no hard and fast rule about which of these to choose, it should help you to know that most words end with *-ary*. Certainly if the word you need to spell is an adjective (*honorary*, *imaginary*, or *voluntary*), *-ary* is the correct choice.

Only a few words end with *-ery*. As you can see in the following chart, these are generally nouns that refer to a place. A few other nouns, such as *stationery* (note paper) and *millinery*, also end with *-ery*.

COMMON WORDS ENDING IN -*ery*	
bakery	monastery
cemetery	stationery
millinery	winery

-*cy* and -*sy*. Only a handful of English words end with -*sy*. If you learn those in the following chart, you can be reasonably safe in using -*cy* for the others. When in doubt, however, be sure to consult a dictionary.

COMMON WORDS ENDING IN -*sy*	
autopsy	epilepsy
biopsy	fantasy
courtesy	heresy
curtsy	hypocrisy
ecstasy	idiosyncrasy
embassy	pleurisy

-*ify* and -*efy*. Similar to the pairs you have seen, one of these is much more common than the other. In this case, -*efy* is rarely used except for the four words in the following chart.

COMMON WORDS ENDING IN -*efy*	
liquefy	rarefy
putrefy	stupefy

-*ance* (-*ant*) and -*ence* (-*ent*). These suffixes travel in pairs. If a noun has the *a* spelling *(elegance)*, you can be quite sure that the corresponding adjective will as well *(elegant)*. The same applies for nouns and adjectives with the *e* spelling *(adherence* and *adherent)*.

The basic problem is knowing which spelling to use after which roots. The most helpful thing to remember is that words containing a "hard" *c* or *g* sound usually end with the *a* spelling: *arrogance, litigant.* Those with a "soft" *c* or *g* sound will usually have the *e* spelling: *emergence, deficient.* There are many -*ance* and -*ence* words, however, that do not contain soft or hard *c* or *g* sounds. To learn the spelling of some of these words, study the following lists.

COMMON WORDS ENDING IN -*ance*		COMMON WORDS ENDING IN -*ence*	
abundance	importance	absence	independence
acquaintance	radiance	convenience	patience
appearance	resonance	correspondence	presence
brilliance	romance	difference	reference
defiance	tolerance	excellence	violence

EXERCISE E: Writing Words with Confusing Suffixes. Write each of the following words on your paper, supplying the correct letter in the blank.

1. bak _e_ ry
2. fanta _s_ y
3. liqu _e_ fy
4. viol _e_ nt
5. brilli _a_ nce
6. auxili _a_ ry
7. delica _c_ y
8. fort _i_ fy
9. idiosyncra _s_ y
10. millin _e_ ry
11. nurs _e_ ry
12. terr _i_ fy
13. tenden _c_ y
14. radi _a_ nt
15. agen _c_ y
16. element _a_ ry
17. correspond _e_ nce
18. biop _s_ y
19. intellig _e_ nce
20. milit _a_ ry

APPLICATION: Spelling Words in Sentences. Write ten sentences of your own using at least one plural noun and one word with a prefix and/or a suffix in each sentence. Check the spelling of all words in a dictionary.

Answers will vary; two samples given.
1. The media misrepresented the situation.
2. Impatience causes many crises.

UNIT

Study Skills

18

Basic Study Skills

Good study habits can be the key to success in school. They can make the difference between interest and boredom in class, between good grades and poor grades, and between progressing and standing still. If you have good study habits, you will know how to approach assignments and how to prepare for class. You will know how to listen attentively and how to take notes from lectures and reading material. In short, you will know how to concentrate your efforts so that you can do your best work.

No one comes by these study skills naturally. But you can acquire them through proper instruction and repeated practice. The sections in this chapter explain how you can develop and apply these skills.

18.1 Practicing Basic Study Skills

Putting time and effort into improving your study skills should result in a number of rewards. You will probably need to study less, your grades will probably improve, your self-confidence will probably grow, and your general attitude toward school may become more positive. If you are truly interested in becoming a better student, improving your study skills is worth the time and effort required.

■ Evaluating Your Study Skills

Before you begin a program to build your study skills, you should determine what skills you already have and what skills you need to develop. You may be pleasantly sur-

462

prised to learn that you have already acquired many good study habits.

Determine which study skills you need to acquire.

The following list will help you determine your strengths and weaknesses.

CHECKLIST FOR STUDY SKILLS
1. Do you always bring a pencil or pen, notebook, and appropriate books to class?
2. Do you follow a study schedule regularly?
3. Do you write down assignments for each class and check them off as you complete them?
4. Do you search for main ideas when you are listening as well as when you are reading and taking notes?
5. Do you have a system for taking notes that provides you with good material to review for tests?
6. Do you make some kind of outline and several drafts of every writing assignment?
7. Do you review regularly so that cramming for tests is not necessary?
8. Do you have a plan of attack for each test?

If you can answer a firm yes to five or more of the preceding questions, you are well on your way to developing good study habits. If you are weak on most of the questions, you should begin making plans to master the study skills you are lacking.

EXERCISE A: Listing Study Skills You Will Need. Think about the particular classes you are taking and the subjects you are studying. Then look at the checklist and the many different skills the questions cover. What five study skills will you definitely need this year? Jot them down and then circle three skills that need additional work.

Students with similar course schedules might be grouped to discuss common needs. Also, the checklist might be used to identify greatest weaknesses for the whole class.

■ Time and Work

Once you have made a decision about which study skills you need to master, you are ready to set goals and establish a timetable for reaching these goals. Whatever goals you choose, you can also benefit from making out a daily study schedule and trying to identify any potential problems in your classes so you can begin to solve them.

Setting Goals. Your main objective in acquiring good study habits is to become a better student. However, you cannot reach this overall objective without first setting a number of short-term goals. These goals and the timetable for achieving them should be recorded in writing. By putting your goals in writing you are making a commitment; you are, in fact, making a contract with yourself.

Set short-term goals for mastering study skills.

Short-term goals will prevent you from becoming discouraged by giving you something quickly attainable to work for. First, as in Exercise A, you should choose a number of goals, such as improving your listening skills or your understanding of what you read. Then, break each general goal down into short-term goals that will lead you back to your general goal. For example, if you want to improve your listening skills, you can work on listening in class for directions and assignments, listening for main ideas during lectures or discussions, and listening for major details. Once you establish the short-term goals, you should determine how much time you want to spend on each. You can then prepare a chart that has your general goal and your short-term goals, your timetable, and a column for comments on your progress. For example, to improve your ability to take notes, you might prepare a chart like the following.

SETTING SHORT-TERM GOALS		
General Goal: to take better notes in class		
Short-term Goals	Timetable	Comments
Practice writing the date and topic on all notes.	2 weeks (by Oct. 1st)	Successfully completed (except for one day when I forgot)
Practice writing all notes in ink.	2 weeks (by Oct. 1st)	Successfully completed

Take complete, understandable notes using headings and organized lists.	4 weeks (by Oct. 15th)	More practice needed; work on skill through Nov. 1st

When you have set your general and short-term goals you should concentrate on the short-term goals until each becomes a habit. When the date you have set arrives, evaluate your work to see if you have mastered the skill and thus met your goal. Once a particular skill becomes a habit, you will perform it automatically and easily.

Planning Your Time.   In addition to planning your goals and establishing a timetable, you should organize your time for each day. Because efficient management of time is essential to every student's success, you should learn to use time to your best advantage.

Schedule your studying in workable blocks of time.

Making daily and weekly schedules will enable you to fit in all your assignments and the activities you have to do and want to do. You should also plan to spend additional time working on your study skills. The following suggestions will help you make efficient use of your time.

MAKING A STUDY SCHEDULE

1. Block out study periods of no more than an hour and a half at a time.
2. Include a five or ten minute break every forty-five minutes.
3. Schedule your study blocks when you are at your best mentally.
4. Use study hall and time at school to study and to get at least some of your work done.
5. Reward yourself for carefully following your study schedule.

Handling Pressures.   As you progress through school, demands on your time and academic pressures tend to increase. Following your study schedule will help you handle some of the pressure. Knowing how much work you have to do, when it has to be done, and when you plan to do it can make a major difference. If you still feel burdened by all of the things you need to do, try to identify more clearly what is causing the problem.

Identify the source of the pressure and try to solve the problem. If you need help, ask a member of your family, your teacher, or your guidance counselor for assistance.

If you notice that you are having a problem in a class, try to solve it immediately rather than letting it continue and hoping it will go away. You might try one or all of the following suggestions.

HANDLING ACADEMIC PRESSURES

1. Ask questions when you do not understand the text or information in class.
2. Schedule time after school for special help from your teacher or a tutor.
3. Get help from a friend or relative who understands the subject.
4. Schedule more time to study for a difficult class.
5. Review notes from a difficult class on a daily basis.
6. See your guidance counselor.

EXERCISE B: **Setting Goals for Study Skills.** Select one general study skill that you want to master. Divide that general goal into short-term goals. Then make a chart for short-term goals for that study skill. Include a column for the goals, a column for the time you plan to devote to mastering each goal, and a column for comments on your progress. *Students with similar coursework might compare needs. Class time can be set aside for evaluating progress.*

EXERCISE C: **Planning the Use of Your Time.** On a large note card or on a piece of paper, block out a study schedule for yourself. Include the time you are in school and any time you can spend studying at school, time for after-school activities, time to study for each subject, and time for relaxation. *Students with similar programs might compare schedules. Attention might also be given to similar extracurricular and work schedules.*

EXERCISE D: **Identifying Pressures at School.** In one to three sentences, describe any pressures that are bothering you at school. Then choose one of the courses of action mentioned in the chart to help solve the problem. *Students could discuss these and compare successes of different solutions.*

■ Learning to Concentrate

Concentration is the ability to focus the mind on a particular subject. It is important to all study skills and related learning. You will find that there are some times when concentrating is more difficult than at other times. When you are having trouble concentrating, you can correct the situation.

Identify what is causing you to lose concentration, and change your pattern of studying or the conditions around you.

Your ability to concentrate can become weakened for a number of reasons. The following chart explains some common reasons for lack of concentration and ways to solve each problem.

IMPROVING CONCENTRATION	
Reasons for Lack of Concentration	**Ways to Solve the Problem**
1. Hunger or tiredness	Have a snack or discontinue studying until after a meal. Take a short nap.
2. Distractions	Identify the distractions (music, television, and so on) that are bothering you. Remove them from your desk or room or change your place of study.
3. Boredom	Exercise. Leave your present task and start a more pleasant one. Change to another form of study, reading instead of writing, for example.
4. Lack of organization	Make a checklist of things you have to do. To study in an organized fashion, preview the material; question, read, and take notes; and then recite what you have learned.
5. Lack of purpose	Ask yourself what you know, what you need to know, and how you are going to learn it.

6. Improper materials and setting	Gather the materials you need before beginning to study. If the setting is improper, change your place of study.

The student who studies by using different combinations of activities can concentrate more easily than the student who just reads and rereads notes and texts. By becoming an active student you can build your powers of concentration.

EXERCISE E: Checking Your Powers of Concentration. Each day for five days, rate your concentration. When you have finished studying for the night, give yourself a 5 for excellent concentration, a 4 for good, a 3 for satisfactory, a 2 for poor, or a 1 for weak concentration. Then ask yourself what helped you concentrate while you were studying and what distracted you and weakened your concentration. When you have identified the problems, apply the solutions mentioned in this section. *Students could plot a weekly graph of their concentration scores and share the lists they develop of their concentration techniques.*

APPLICATION: Evaluating Your Study Skills. After two or more weeks of working on your study skills, answer the following questions.

1. Do you have several short-term goals for mastering study skills that you are actively trying to achieve?
2. Do you plan a study schedule each week and follow it closely?
3. Do you ask questions and seek help when you do not understand assignments or material in class?
4. Do you use methods for improving your concentration?
5. Do you think that you have made progress with one or more study skills?

Students might make a conscious effort to utilize the suggestions in Section 18.1 for one week at a time and monitor their own progress during that period, using these questions.

18.2 Understanding and Organizing Information

Eighty to ninety percent of the information you learn in class one day is forgotten the next unless you make an effort to organize the information. You can organize information by taking good notes and by using the information soon afterward.

To improve your ability to record and remember information, you should first determine how you learn best. Second, you should practice and sharpen your listening skills. Then, by learning the different methods of taking notes, you can adapt your own note-taking method to the particular material you are hearing or reading. Finally, you can use formal outlining to structure the information you find in some books as well as to organize the information you present in papers and speeches of your own.

■ Different Styles of Learning

Some people understand material best when they read it. Others learn best through listening and writing down the information. If one method seems more natural to you than another, you may be able to take better advantage of your preference.

Determine how you learn best and make the most efficient use of your personal learning style.

Learning takes place through reading, writing, listening, and speaking. Most people favor the one or two ways of learning that come easiest to them. Some students learn best through a reading-writing combination, and some learn best through a speaking-listening combination. In school, you cannot use only one combination or another. However, when you study at home, you can use the combination of skills that is most appropriate for you. Examine the following chart to help you determine which styles of learning you should be using more. You should try each of the activities in the following chart to figure out which works best for you.

Learning Style	Activities
Reading	Read using a variety of speeds.
	Read summaries, outlines, and notes silently.
	Read extra material that goes along with the textbook.
Writing	Write summaries at the end of each reading section.

	Make outlines as you read and listen to lectures.
	Show the relationship between ideas through drawings and diagrams.
Listening	Listen carefully to lectures and take notes.
	Listen to library tapes.
	Make tapes of your notes and listen to the tapes.
Speaking	Summarize the end of each reading section aloud.
	Respond to end-of-chapter questions aloud.
	Study with a friend by asking each other questions.

EXERCISE A: **Determining Your Personal Learning Style.** To help evaluate the methods of learning that work best for you, answer the following questions. Then use your answers to the questions and the Learning Style and Activities chart to decide which *two* activities you are going to employ more often in your studying, particularly at home.

1. Would you rather read to get information or gather information by listening to the teacher?
2. Do you enjoy learning through the use of audio-visual materials such as filmstrips, tapes, and movies?
3. Do you do better on tests when the questions are given aloud or when you read the questions?
4. Do you understand information better when you take notes on it?
5. When you study, do you get more out of reading your notes aloud or reading them silently?
6. Do you prefer to express your ideas by writing a paper or by giving a speech?

Each student might write a personal learning-style diagnosis with ideas for making better use of preferred styles.

■ Improving Listening Comprehension

Many of the concepts and skills you are expected to learn in school will be introduced and discussed in class. How well you listen and follow your teacher's train of thought will partially determine how successfully you master the content and skills involved. You also need good listening skills to follow directions, to participate in class discussions, to do assignments, and to take tests. To listen well means to tune out distracting noises, to focus on the information being presented, and to follow the speaker's ideas.

Improve your listening comprehension by listening for clues in directions, by listening for main ideas, and by listening for important details.

Because listening, unlike hearing, is an active skill, you must train yourself to listen. Prepare your body for listening by choosing a position in which you are comfortable but alert. Prepare your mind by resolving to concentrate on what is being said. Listening also involves picking up signals from the speaker. The signals will tell you when the speaker is giving directional clues, moving to a new main idea, or stressing a particular detail.

To listen for clues in directions, you should use the following guidelines.

LISTENING FOR CLUES IN DIRECTIONS

1. Take note of signal words that indicate sequence, such as *first, second, next, then, following, before,* and so on.
2. Pick a key word from each step in the directions to remember. Link these key words together.
3. Repeat the directions after they have been given.
4. Visualize each step before performing the task.
5. Use logical thinking (What do I have to do next?) to reinforce what you are trying to remember.

When you listen for main ideas, your purpose is to understand the importance of ideas. The following guidelines can help you listen for main ideas.

LISTENING FOR MAIN IDEAS

1. Listen carefully to the beginning statements of the speaker and to the points the speaker emphasizes and repeats. These will generally be the main ideas you should keep in mind.
2. Think about the speaker's examples, facts, and details and decide if they add up to the main ideas you have in mind.
3. Try to visualize the main ideas. Restate them in your own words.

To listen for important details, follow these guidelines.

LISTENING FOR IMPORTANT DETAILS
1. As you listen, ask yourself what makes the main idea true. Keep the details that answer that question in mind.
2. Focus on words such as *for instance, for example, the following reasons, this can be explained by*, and so on.
3. Try to predict details the speaker will mention.
4. Think about the main ideas and supporting details simultaneously.
5. Try to link the main ideas and supporting details into some sort of visual pattern.

Learning to listen to directions, to recognize a speaker's main ideas, and to gather major details will help you to record information and organize it into valuable notes.

EXERCISE B: Practicing Your Listening Skills. Select one teacher in whose class you will practice specific listening skills for a week. Note how lectures begin and end, how the teacher indicates a change of topic or activity, how the teacher stresses something of importance, and how the teacher uses the chalkboard. List ways in which your knowledge of these techniques can help you in this class.
Students selecting the same class might profit from sharing their observations.

EXERCISE C: Developing Listening Comprehension. Listen to the morning public address announcements without taking notes. Rely on your listening skills and your memory alone. After the announcements, list as much factual information as you can remember. Compare your list of information with that of other students in the class. Review the guidelines for good listening habits and repeat the exercise the next day. *Students might repeat this exercise for consecutive days, making individual graphs of their progress.*

■ Methods of Taking Notes

The notes you take in class, in the library, or at home while studying can be as simple as the details of a homework assignment or as complex as the ideas in a lecture or a book about Mahatma Gandhi. In all of these situations, the purpose of taking notes is to help you concentrate on what you are hearing or reading and to record information for future use. Your notes should be neat, with dates and topics on each page. They should be clear, direct, complete, and easy for you to understand later.

Being acquainted with different methods of note-taking—modified outlines, summaries, and free-form outlines as well as formal outlines—will help you achieve the goal of taking useful notes. With a knowledge of these varied styles of taking notes, you will be able to adjust your note-taking method to the material you are hearing or reading.

Modified Outlines. An *outline* is a pattern of ideas that ranks the information according to main ideas, major details, and lesser details. In a *modified outline*, the main idea is written as a heading and is usually underlined. The major details relating to the main idea are listed under the main idea using numbers, letters, indentation, or simply dashes.

A modified outline enables you to organize information quickly. It is useful for recording information from lectures, films, discussions, and books. You may also jot down your ideas for a paper or the answer to an exam question in a modified outline.

Use a modified outline to organize information to show the relationship between main ideas and supporting ideas.

When you are using a modified outline to take notes, you should leave wide margins in case you want to add more information later or in case you want to explain a point in more detail. Remember that a modified outline is a skeleton of an idea or subject. The following chart presents some suggestions for taking notes in modified outlines.

MAKING MODIFIED OUTLINES
1. Take down important information in as few words as possible.
2. Write down each main idea as a title or heading and underline it so it stands out.
3. Group supporting information under the proper heading as you hear or read it. Indent and list each piece of supporting information using numbers, letters, or dashes.

If you heard the following portion of a lecture on Susan B. Anthony, based on an article in *Current Events* magazine, you might record information in a modified outline like the one that follows the lecture.

LECTURE:

Do you know why Susan B. Anthony's image appears on a recent coin? To honor her fight for women's right to vote, her profile was stamped on a 1979 one-dollar coin. The coin is smaller than a fifty-cent piece and is made of copper and nickel.

Susan B. Anthony was born in 1820 in Massachusetts. She inherited the love of freedom from her grandfather, who fought in the Revolutionary War. Early in life Ms. Anthony became a school teacher and a reform leader. She fought against slavery and the use of alcohol and in favor of women's rights. Her biggest fight was for women's suffrage, or the right to vote. For over thirty years, Ms. Anthony traveled throughout the country speaking out for women's rights. Finally, in 1870 Wyoming granted women the right to vote, but the other states did not follow Wyoming's lead. In 1872, when Ms. Anthony attempted to vote in a presidential election, she was fined one hundred dollars but not jailed as she had hoped to be.

In 1920 the Nineteenth Amendment, granting women the right to vote, was adopted. Unfortunately, Susan B. Anthony had died fourteen years earlier without seeing her goal achieved. For her lifelong work, many people today think she deserves to be the first American woman honored on a coin.— Adapted from *Current Events*

Notice the short phrases used in the following modified outline made from the lecture on Susan B. Anthony. Main ideas are underlined and supporting ideas are numbered.

MODIFIED OUTLINE:

Recent Coin

1. Susan B. Anthony's profile
2. 1979, $1.00 coin
3. Smaller than 50¢ piece
4. Made of copper and nickel

S.A.'s Early Background

1. Born 1820, Massachusetts
2. Grandfather fought in American Revolution
3. School teacher and reform leader

Her Causes as a Reform Leader

1. Fought against slavery
2. Fought against use of alcohol
3. Fought to gain voting rights for women

Action Taken

1. Spoke for 30 years on women's rights
2. Saw women get vote in Wyoming in 1870
3. Fined for voting in presidential election, 1872
4. Died 14 yrs. before women got the right to vote

Summaries. Another useful way to record information is to summarize.

A *summary* states the main ideas of a lecture or printed material in your own words in a few complete sentences. The length of the summary varies according to the amount of information you are summarizing. For instance, you might summarize a paragraph or a short lecture in about two sentences, but you might summarize an article or chapter in a paragraph.

Use summaries to record main ideas in your own words.

You may take notes in a modified outline and then summarize your notes, or you may take notes in a summary directly from listening or reading. Whenever you summarize, you must select the ideas that are of greatest importance, phrase these ideas in your own words, and express the ideas in complete sentences that represent fairly the information you have heard or read. The following chart offers suggestions for summarizing.

MAKING SUMMARIES
1. Listen or read for main ideas.
2. Remember these main ideas or jot them down on paper.
3. Shape these main ideas into sentences that express the point of the information you have heard or read. Always use your own words.
4. For longer summaries, you may include a few major details.

A summary developed from the modified outline on the lecture about Susan B. Anthony follows. Notice that over fifty percent of the information from the modified outline has been eliminated. In a summary, only the information that directly supports the main ideas should be included.

SUMMARY:

Susan B. Anthony is the first woman to be honored on an American coin. She was a reform leader who spent over thirty years campaigning for women's right to vote. Fourteen years after her death, the Nineteenth Amendment was passed, and her goal was achieved.

Free-Form Outlining.   Like a modified outline, a free-form outline includes main ideas, major supporting details, and sometimes minor details. If you tend to remember pictures and designs better than words and ideas, you may find free-form outlines helpful. In a free-form outline, you show the relationship between main ideas and supporting ideas through a design. The design can take any shape as long as the main ideas form the core of the pattern and related ideas branch out from the core.

Use a free-form outline to organize and remember main ideas and supporting ideas.

If you like to draw or show your ideas in diagrams, you may be able to take notes directly using free-form outlining. Or you may find that taking notes in a modified outline first and then making a free-form outline works best for you. To use free-form outlining, you should follow the guidelines given in the following chart.

MAKING FREE-FORM OUTLINES

1. Place your topic and your main ideas in the center of your design.
2. Branch off from the center with major supporting details for any or all of the major details.
3. Branch off from the major supporting details with minor supporting details.
4. Without looking at the completed design, try to visualize the pattern. This can help you fix the pattern of ideas more firmly in your mind.

If you take notes originally in free-form outlines, you may want to transfer your notes to a modified outline as part of your studying.

The following design shows notes on the lecture about Susan B. Anthony in a free-form outline. Notice the topic of the outline in the center and the main ideas in circles also in the middle of the design. Major details are added on lines branching off from each of the circles. One minor detail is shown at the upper right.

FREE-FORM OUTLINE:

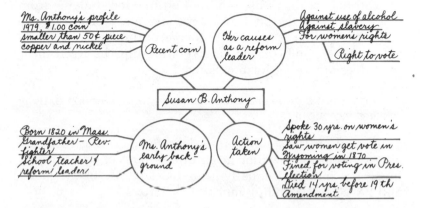

EXERCISE D: Writing a Modified Outline. Listen to a television newscast and take notes in modified outline form, using your own words. After the newscast, read your notes and fill in any information that is needed to make them clear. *Students might be assigned broadcasts so outlines can be compared. Also, students might make oral "broadcasts."*

EXERCISE E: Taking Notes in a Modified Outline from Reading Material. Choose one of the following topics and read an appropriate article in the encyclopedia. Then take notes in your own words in modified outline form. At the top of your paper, write the title of the encyclopedia, the title of the article, and the author of the encyclopedia article, if one is listed. *Answers will vary. Good outlines might be distributed.*

1. A place you would like to visit
2. A famous person from the past you wish you could meet
3. An invention you could not live without
4. The natural phenomenon (earthquake, blizzard, hurricane, and so on) you most fear
5. An unusual animal you would like for a pet
6. The career that seems the most exciting to you

EXERCISE F: Writing a Summary. Write a summary of the information you took notes on for your modified outline in Exercise E. *After writing summaries, students might exchange outlines and write summaries based on each other's notes.*

EXERCISE G: Practicing with Free-Form Outlining. Bring a magazine article on a current event or famous person to class. Read the article and then take notes on the article using a free-form outline. *One or two articles might be distributed to all students to facilitate comparison and discussion.*

■ Formal Outlines

You may want to use a formal outline for studying from well-structured textbook chapters and for preparation for your own writing or speaking. A formal outline shows more exact, complete information and relationships between ideas than does any other form of notes.

Use formal outlines to rank and arrange information exactly and thoroughly.

Formal outlines conform to definite rules. They use specific symbols and regular indentation. Items of equal importance are indented equally from the left side of the paper and have corresponding numbers or letters.

EXAMPLE: I. Main idea
    A.
    B. } Major details explaining I.
    C.
       1.
       2. } Minor details explaining C.
         a.
         b. } Lesser details explaining 2.

A formal outline should also show the order in which the information was or will be presented and the relationship between the pieces of information. The following chart explains more about the rules for formal outlining.

RULES FOR FORMAL OUTLINING
1. Statements of equal importance should be ranked equally with Roman numerals, capital letters, Arabic numerals, or lower case letters.
2. The less important a piece of information, the greater the indentation.
3. Each point should have either no subpoints or two or more subpoints. An *A* should not be presented without a *B;* a *1* should not be presented without a *2.*
4. The first word in each line should be capitalized.
5. A period should follow each number or letter.

Formal outlines can be either topic outlines or sentence outlines. In a *topic outline*, you write information in words and phrases; in a *sentence outline*, you write information in complete sentences. Thus, a topic outline is sketchier than a sentence outline and quicker to write. You should not mix topic and sentence outlines within one outline. Always use the kind of formal outline your teacher requests.

Both kinds of formal outlines show an exact ranking of information. As you write either kind of outline, you must constantly evaluate the information you are outlining and decide its level of importance. For each piece of information, ask yourself, "Is this information a main idea, a supporting idea, or a further detail of a supporting idea? What is the relationship of this fact or idea to the ones before it and the ones after it?"

Now read the following selection on phobias, based on two articles in *Read* magazine, and the topic outline of it that follows. Notice the short phrases and the relationship of ideas in the topic outline.

READING:

A phobia is an intense fear of something. Nineteen million Americans suffer from a variety of phobias ranging from fear of bees, blood, seaweed, and spiders to fear of dead flowers.

How do these fears originate? Psychologists have many explanations. Some phobias are learned fears; that is, a person learns to fear a situation because of a bad experience he or she had. For example, people with belonephobia, fear of needles, may have suffered at the hands of careless nurses or doctors who hurt them when giving an injection. People with ailurophobia, fear of cats, may have been bitten by cats in childhood.

Some psychologists explain the cause of phobias in another way. They believe that people with deep personal problems develop phobias to hide what is really bothering them. In England, for instance, there is a surprising amount of ophidiophobia, fear of snakes, yet snakes are not common in England. Psychologists conclude from this that it is not really snakes that these people fear.

Whatever the cause, when people with phobias even imagine the situation they fear, they panic. They may turn pale and their breathing may become rapid and shallow. Also, their behavior may seem odd because they will do anything to avoid confronting the situation that terrifies them. People with agoraphobia, for example, do not like to leave home because they fear open spaces, even empty streets and sidewalks. These people are forced by their phobia to withdraw from activities rather than have to go outside.

Similar effects may be seen with other less common phobias: villophobia, helminthophobia, kakorrhaphiophobia, and pantophobia. Villophobia is a fear of hairy people or animals. Helminthophobia is a fear of worms, and kakorrhaphiophobia is a fear of failure, particularly with regard to taking tests. Of all phobias, perhaps the worst is pantophobia, fear of just about everything.—Adapted from *Read*

TOPIC OUTLINE:

    I. Definition of a phobia
        A. Intense fear of something
        B. Ranges from fear of bees to fear of dead flowers
   II. Causes of phobias
        A. Learned phobias from bad experiences
           1. Belonephobia (fear of needles) caused by careless nurses or doctors
           2. Ailurophobia (fear of cats) caused by an attack by a cat
        B. Psychological phobias—only hiding deeper personal problems
  III. Effects of phobias
        A. Paleness
        B. Shallow and rapid breathing
        C. Strange behavior to avoid confronting phobia
           1. Avoiding open spaces with agoraphobia
           2. Clinging to safety of home
  IV. Less well-known phobias
        A. Villophobia—fear of hairy people or animals
        B. Helminthophobia—fear of worms
        C. Kakorrhaphiophobia—fear of failure
        D. Pantophobia—fear of everything

A sentence outline provides even more information than a topic outline. Sentence outlines can be used to take notes from textbooks, but you will probably find them most helpful when you are organizing your thoughts and information for speeches or compositions. Sentence outlines can help you make sure that you have covered your topic thoroughly and logically.

The following example shows the beginning of a sentence outline for a composition about avoiding stagefright.

SENTENCE OUTLINE:

    I. How can you face all those people out there in the auditorium when you feel so scared?
        A. Terror makes you feel and act foolish.
           1. Your hands and legs are shaking.
           2. Your throat is dry and scratchy.
           3. You are afraid your voice will crack.
           4. You are afraid you will forget everything.

    B. You can overcome these signs of nervousness, however, by following certain suggestions before and during your speech.

  II. You can lessen your nervousness by selecting a good topic for your speech.

    A. Choose a topic you will be comfortable speaking about.

    B. Know your topic well.

      1. Find information on your topic from books and people.

      2. Find human interest material that will be easy to remember and enjoyable to present.

    C. Use audio-visual devices if they are appropriate.

  III. Practice your speech extensively before you give it to a big audience.

    A. Tape record your speech and evaluate it.

    B. Give your speech to your friends and family and have someone time it.

    C. Practice by yourself in front of a mirror until you know your speech well and feel comfortable giving it.

  IV. Before and as you deliver your speech to an audience, follow these suggestions.

    A. Take a deep breath before you begin speaking.

    B. Establish and maintain eye contact with the audience.

EXERCISE H: Making a Topic Outline. Organize the following information in a formal topic outline, using Roman numerals I. for Musk deer and II. for Yak. You may have to consult an encyclopedia to make sure you have arranged the information logically and correctly. *Answers on page T-127.*

I. Musk deer	II. Yak
Himalaya Mountains	Small ox
Uses	At the shoulder—height of
Small animal	a tall man
Scent used in perfume	Milk
India	Cloth woven from hair
Height of a man's knee	Meat
Size	Asia
Habitat	Size
Gland under abdomen	Habitat
carries scent	Uses
	Tibet, near China

EXERCISE I: Using a Sentence Outline. Pretend you have to write a composition or give a speech on one of the following

topics. Choose a personal experience that would be interesting for someone else to read or hear about. Outline the experience using the sentence outline form. *Answers will vary; outlines might be checked for format and subordination of ideas. Outlines on same topics might*
1. Your first airplane flight *be compared.*
2. Your first day at camp
3. An accident you have had
4. Your scariest moment
5. A time you helped someone

APPLICATION: **Evaluating Your Ability to Gather and Record Information.** Answer the following questions about your learning style, listening habits, and note-taking methods. Then decide on a short-term goal related to note-taking that you want to work on.

1. Do you know which learning style works best for you?
2. Have you been able to follow directions given in class during the last week? If not, why not? What can you do about it?
3. Can you listen for main ideas and supporting details in lectures?
4. Have you used modified outlines to take notes during the last week?
5. Can you summarize a lecture or a chapter from your reading?
6. Can you translate information from a modified outline into a free-form outline and from a free-form outline into a modified outline?
7. Can you outline a chapter of your textbook using a formal topic outline?

For each no, students might answer the question "Why not?" or "What can you do about it?"

Chapter 19

Reading and Test-Taking Skills

Your schoolwork requires you to read many pages of material, retain the most important information, and recall specific points in tests and examinations. You may or may not be satisfied with how fast you read right now or with how well you prepare for and take tests. But most people can sharpen their reading and test-taking skills, and this chapter offers you several specific techniques for improving your performance in both of these areas.

Increasing Your Reading Speed 19.1

Every day you will encounter material you want to read and material you should read. And with each year in school, reading material increases in quantity and difficulty. Because you are expected to gather information through reading in school and on your own, how fast you read and how well you understand what you read will affect your performance in your classes.

At any particular moment, four conditions influence how fast you read and how much you understand: your purpose, the difficulty of the material, your previous knowledge of or interest in the subject, and the environment. Your speed and understanding will vary depending on whether you are reading for pleasure, gathering information, or searching for one fact you must check. Similarly, the size of the print, the level of the vocabulary, and the complexity and maturity of the ideas will probably make you read a scientific article in an encyclopedia, for example, at a slower rate than you would read an article in a newspaper. Also, if you are familiar with or interested in a subject, you will probably read material on that subject faster than you would read other material. Finally, noise or quiet, illness or health, and your own state of mind as you are reading will affect your ability to read well at a particular time.

Although these variables will always play some part in the efficiency of your general reading, you can learn to measure and develop your reading skills, as this section will explain.

■ Three Types of Reading

You can improve your reading skills through knowledge and practice. The three types of reading you need to know about and use are phrase reading (or careful reading), skimming, and scanning. Each type of reading has a different speed and a different purpose. In *phrase reading*, you should try to read as fast as you can with good understanding. Your goal should be to see words in groups. Your eyes and mind should work together to look for ideas. In *skimming*, you should triple your normal rate of reading by skipping words so that you take in just enough information to get a general idea of the material. In *scanning*, you should skip even more material than in skimming by moving your eyes rapidly over lines and pages with the single purpose of finding a specific piece of information.

Learn to choose the type of reading suitable to your purpose and the material.

As a student, you will often need to use all three types of reading. The following chart further explains the types of reading, when to use them, and what level of comprehension to expect from each. Notice that comprehension should be high for phrase reading (at least seventy percent) and that it drops to forty or fifty percent for skimming because you do not need to recall ideas thoroughly when you are skimming. Notice also that the level of comprehension for scanning is one hundred percent because you presumably find only the piece of information for which you are reading.

THREE TYPES OF READING			
Type	Definition	Use	Comprehension
Phrase Reading	Reading groups of words without eliminating words in order to understand all of the material	For studying, solving problems, and following directions	Lowest acceptable rate: 70–80%
Skimming	Skipping words in order to read rapidly and get a quick overview	For previewing, reviewing, and locating information	Lowest acceptable rate: 40–50%
Scanning	Reading in order to locate a particular piece of information	For research, reviewing, and finding information	Lowest acceptable rate: 100%

In most cases you will be using at least two out of three of the types of reading each time you read. You should practice varying your reading rate according to your purpose and the material you are reading. The following chart shows some possible ways of adjusting your reading.

VARYING YOUR READING RATE
Purpose: Reading to answer a specific question *Material:* Reference Book
1. Scan the index for the topic and page. 2. Locate the page and scan to locate the topic. 3. Skim to locate specific information on the topic. 4. Phrase read when the information is found.
Purpose: Studying for a test *Material:* Textbook
1. Skim a chapter for a preview. 2. Phrase read the entire chapter while taking notes. 3. Skim the headings, introductions, and summaries for a review.

As you become familiar with the three types of reading and their different speeds, you will learn to adjust your mind and eyes to the appropriate rate for the material you are reading.

EXERCISE A: Determining Which Type of Reading to Use. Examine each of the following purposes for reading. Decide which type or types of reading you would use for each purpose. Then briefly explain your choices.

skim— preview 1. Seeing if a book will be suitable for pleasure reading
2. Reading the questions at the end of the chapter before reading the chapter carefully *skim—preview*
3. Finding a word in a glossary of a textbook
4. Locating a particular place on a map *scan—specific information*
5. Reading and taking notes for a chapter test
6. Checking the contents of a book by using the index
7. Locating the time a bus should arrive using a bus schedule *scan—specific information*
8. Previewing a chapter *skim—preview*
9. Reading a short story for an assignment in English class
10. Finding statistics about the population in a book of facts

3. scan—specific information   5. phrase—understand all material   6. skim—preview or scan—specific information   9. phrase—understand all material   10. scan—specific information

■ Measuring Your Reading Rate and Comprehension

Your reading rate is the number of words you read per minute when you are phrase reading. Your phrase reading rate and your level of comprehension while phrase reading are the skills you should be most interested in improving. Phrase reading is the type of reading you will do about two thirds of the time. When you are assigned a novel to read for your English class or a chapter in a textbook to master for a test, you will use phrase reading.

Your phrase reading rate does change according to the difficulty of the material, your interest and knowledge, and your surroundings. Even so, a test of your reading rate can give you a good idea of your average speed. A complete test will give you a chance to measure two things: (1) how fast your eyes take in words and move down the page and (2) how well you understand what you read.

Determining Your Phrase Reading Rate. Most people would like to read faster than they do. Before you can work on increasing your rate, however, it is useful to know your current rate of phrase reading. You can measure your present phrase reading rate by reading a numbered passage, such as the one in Exercise B, or by computing your rate on an unnumbered passage on your own.

From time to time, calculate your phrase reading rate to determine how much you are improving.

You should usually calculate your reading speed using the same book each time. You might want to check your reading speed at least once a month and graph your scores. A graph will encourage you to strive for greater improvement. The following chart explains how to determine your reading speed using either a numbered or an unnumbered passage.

CALCULATING PHRASE READING RATE
For a Numbered Passage
Step 1: Have your teacher or another student time you as you read a numbered passage. If working alone, set an automatic timer for one minute.
Step 2: When the timer stops you at the end of one minute, put a dot beside the last word you read.
Step 3: Follow the dot to the end of the line and record the number. The number is your approximate phrase reading speed for one minute on this passage.
For an Unnumbered Passage
Step 1: Count the total number of words in the first three lines of the passage you are going to read.
Step 2: Divide the number by three to get the average number of words per line.
Step 3: Then count the total number of lines you read in one minute.
Step 4: Multiply this number by the average number of words per line. The result is your approximate phrase reading speed for one minute on this passage.

The following example shows the calculation of a reading rate for an unnumbered passage.

EXAMPLE: 1. There are thirty words in the first three lines of the passage.
2. Thirty divided by three equals ten words per line.
3. You read twenty-five lines during one minute.
4. Twenty-five multiplied by ten equals 250 words per minute on this passage.

Determining Your Comprehension. How fast your eyes take in the groups of words on a page is important, but how well you understand what you read must also be considered. Your reading rate and your comprehension should be closely related. A comprehension score below seventy percent will generally indicate a need to slow down the rate at which you are reading.

Calculate your comprehension of a passage by asking yourself questions about the passage and then checking your answers.

Numbered passages will most likely have corresponding questions for you to use to check your comprehension. For unnumbered passages, however, you should ask yourself the five questions listed in the following chart. Check the answers in the passage, and then score twenty points for each correct answer. You will then have a rough measurement of your level of comprehension. For instance, if you answer four or five questions correctly, your comprehension is eighty or a hundred percent. If you answer three or fewer questions correctly, you should probably slow down your phrase reading rate.

CHECKING YOUR LEVEL OF COMPREHENSION
1. What is the general topic of the passage?
2. How has this topic been developed?
3. What is the main idea of the passage?
4. What is one important supporting detail?
5. If you continued reading the passage, what questions would you be reading to answer?

EXERCISE B: Calculating Your Phrase Reading Rate. With another person in your class, prepare to read for one minute the following passage taken from Wilkie Collins' *The Woman* *in White.* While one person times, the other person should silently read the passage as fast as possible. When the minute is up, the timer should stop the reader. Use the information given in the charts on page 487 to determine your reading rate. Reverse roles so the other person can read while you time. *With a less advanced group of students, you might want to use a selection written at a somewhat lower reading level.*

The road was, for the most part, straight and level. Whenever	11
I looked back over it I saw the two spies steadily following me.	24
For the greater part of the way they kept at a safe distance	37
behind. But once or twice they quickened their pace, as if with	49
the purpose of overtaking me, then stopped, consulted together,	58
and fell back again to their former position. They had some	69
special object evidently in view, and they seemed to be hesitating	80
or differing about the best means of accomplishing it. I could not	92
guess exactly what their design might be, but I felt serious	103
doubts of reaching Knowlesbury without some mischance hap-	110
pening to me on the way. These doubts were realised.	120
I had just entered on a lonely part of the road, with a sharp	134
turn at some distance ahead, and had just concluded (calculating	144
by time) that I must be getting near to the town, when I sud-	157
denly heard the steps of the men close behind me.	167
Before I could look round, one of them (the man by whom I	180
had been followed in London) passed rapidly on my left side and	192
hustled me with his shoulder. I had been more irritated by the	204
manner in which he and his companion had dogged my steps all	216
the way from Old Welmingham than I was myself aware of, and	228
I unfortunately pushed the fellow away smartly with my open	238
hand. He instantly shouted for help. His companion, the tall man	249
in the gamekeeper's clothes, sprang to my right side, and the	260
next moment the two scoundrels held me pinioned between them	270
in the middle of the road.	276
The conviction that a trap had been laid for me, and the vexa-	289
tion of knowing that I had fallen into it, fortunately restrained	299
me from making my position still worse by an unavailing	309
struggle with two men, one of whom would, in all probability,	320
have been more than a match for me single-handed. I repressed	332
the first natural movement by which I had attempted to shake	343
them off, and looked about to see if there was any person near to	357
whom I could appeal.	361
A labourer was at work in an adjoining field who must have	373
witnessed all that had passed. I called to him to follow us to the	387
town. He shook his head with stolid obstinacy, and walked away	398
in the direction of a cottage which stood back from the high-road.	411
At the same time the men who held me between them declared	423
their intention of charging me with an assault. I was cool enough	435
and wise enough now to make no opposition. 'Drop your hold of	447
my arms,' I said, 'and I will go with you to the town.' The man	462
in the gamekeeper's dress roughly refused. But the shorter man	472
was sharp enough to look to consequences, and not to let his	484
companion commit himself by unnecessary violence. He made a	493
sign to the other, and I walked on between them with my arms	506
free.	507

We went on to the town-hall. The clerk made out a formal	520
summons, and the charge was preferred against me, with the	530
customary exaggeration and the customary perversion of the	538
truth on such occasions. The magistrate (an ill-tempered man,	548
with a sour enjoyment in the exercise of his own power) inquired	560
if any one on or near the road had witnessed the assault, and,	573
greatly to my surprise, the complainant admitted the presence of	583
the labourer in the field. I was enlightened, however, as to the	595
object of the admission by the magistrate's next words. He re-	605
manded me at once for the production of the witness, expressing,	616
at the same time, his willingness to take bail for my reappearance	628
if I could produce one responsible surety to offer it. If I had been	642
known in the town he would have liberated me on my own	654
recognisances, but as I was a total stranger it was necessary that	666
I should find responsible bail.—Wilkie Collins	671

EXERCISE C: **Calculating Your Level of Comprehension.**
Answer the following questions on your paper. Then check your answers by rereading the article. Give yourself twenty points for each correct answer.

1. What was the setting in the beginning?
2. How many people were following the narrator?
3. What was the tall man wearing?
4. From what source did the narrator look for help?
5. Where was the narrator taken when they reached town?

1. the open road   2. two   3. a gamekeeper's clothes   4. a nearby labourer
5. the town-hall

EXERCISE D: **Testing Reading Rate and Comprehension on Your Own.** Choose a story or chapter from one of your literature books. With another student, time each other's reading for one minute. Then use the method for calculating your reading rate explained on page 487. Use the questions in the chart on page 488 for determining your approximate level of comprehension. *Students might be encouraged to determine their different levels of comprehension for different subjects.*

■ Developing Your Phrase Reading Skills

An efficient reader tries to read words in groups while searching for ideas. If, however, you read every word slowly and carefully, hoping to remember everything you read, you can learn to make better use of your time and effort. Even if you are reading over 220 words per minute and are reading in phrases, you can continue to increase your eye span. Extending your eye span helps you read more quickly and enables you to grasp ideas in their entirety. A larger eye span also means that your eyes will have to make fewer stops across the line; thus, you will progress faster. You can learn to read two to seven words at a time with one eye fixation or movement.

Learn to read larger groups of words and to read for ideas in order to increase your reading speed.

With regular practice at home, you can increase your reading rate on your own. Learning to read two or three words at a time may raise your reading rate to 300 words per minute. If you can learn to read six or seven words at a time, you may raise your rate to 800 words per minute or beyond. You can double your reading rate like this by practicing only fifteen to twenty minutes a day with newspapers or paperback books. To be really successful, however, you should practice regularly for at least three or four weeks.

Dotting over Groups of Words.   A good drill to increase your eye span is dotting over groups of words. Using a newspaper and a pencil, place dots over groups of words rhythmically as you read. It does not matter exactly where you place the dots because the purpose of the dots is to keep your eyes and pencil moving along at a faster reading rate than they would normally follow. Do not change the speed of your dotting as you come to more difficult material. Continue at your established rate, dotting and focusing on the group of words below the dot. This drill should increase your reading rate as well as keep you from rereading sections before moving ahead. The following is an example of what a passage might look like after you have dotted it.

EXAMPLE: . . . . He decided on the ninth day that no help was coming. Gathering up his parachute, he began to slog his way downriver . . . .

Using a Reading Pacer Card.   The newspaper can also help you to improve your reading rate when you use it in conjunction with a reading pacer card. To make this reading pacer you will need a 3 × 5 or 5 × 7 card with a cut-out window measured to fit the line of newspaper print.

To use the pacer card, place the window over the first line of newspaper print. Then slowly move the card downward as you read each successive line. You should move the card at a constant speed and at a speed that is slightly uncomfortable for you. Never slow down or speed up as the material changes in difficulty. Whatever happens, keep moving at a constant rate.

When you begin this exercise you may be stopping two or three times per line. However, as you begin to read more rapidly, your number of focus points should become fewer. In some cases, you may be able to focus in the middle of the column and read straight down. Eventually, your eyes should not need the card at all. They should be able to drop down the page automatically, picking up group after group of words.

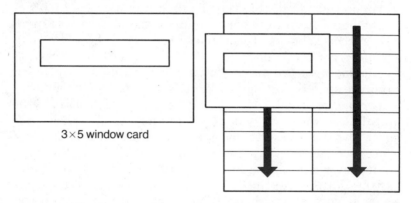

3×5 window card

Using an Alarm Clock.   A third method of increasing your reading speed at home is through the use of an alarm clock. The process explained in the following chart is simple, yet very effective for raising reading rates by 100 words per minute and more.

INCREASING READING RATE WITH AN ALARM CLOCK
1. Select a novel that is easy to read.
2. Set your alarm clock for fifteen minutes.
3. Read until the alarm goes off.
4. Count the number of pages that you read in the fifteen-minute period and record the number of pages read on a graph.
5. Continue the process nightly for at least three weeks. Try to read slightly faster each night.

EXERCISE E: Improving Your Reading Rate. Set aside fifteen minutes a night for three nights to develop your reading rate using dotting, a pacer card, or an alarm clock. If you use the alarm clock method, record the number of pages you read each night. If you want to continue increasing your reading rate, you might decide to spend fifteen minutes a night for three weeks. You might then make a graph to record your progress. After every practice session, record on the graph the number of columns or pages read. For the alarm clock method, your graph might resemble the following.

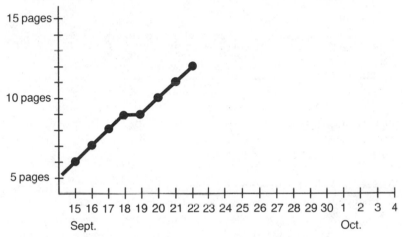

Progress—rather than absolute rate—could be emphasized for each student. Students can report progress at regular intervals.

■ Developing Your Skimming Skills

Skimming involves doubling or tripling your phrase reading rate. You can use skimming when you are doing light reading for pleasure or studying for a test. For instance, you can skim a novel or story to get an overview and then skim sections that are not vitally important to the story. Skimming a chapter you are about to read in a textbook can prepare your mind for what is to come, and skimming headings, introductions, and summaries in a chapter you have already read can remind you of the important points.

Use skimming when you need an overview of reading material.

To skim you must skip over words and phrases that are not important to your particular purpose. The following chart shows some of the words and ideas you should try to pick up when you are skimming.

INFORMATION TO LOOK FOR WHEN SKIMMING
The first sentence in each paragraph
Headings and words in italics or special print
Nouns and capitalized words
Action verbs
Dates and places
Transitions: *such as, in addition, moreover* (for examples); *however* (for contrast)
Answers to questions raised earlier in a story or chapter

When you are skimming, you should never feel guilty about skipping reading matter. Your special purpose when you are skimming does not require careful reading, and you should not waste your time.

EXERCISE F: Improving Your Skimming Skills. Skim the following paragraph, reading only the key words and phrases, which are underlined. After skimming the paragraph, try to recall in written form or in oral form the highlights of the paragraph.

Paragraph I

The whole object of the <u>stratagem</u> was now <u>disclosed</u> to me. It had been so managed as to make a remand necessary in a <u>town where I was</u> a perfect <u>stranger</u>, and where I could <u>not hope to get my liberty</u> on bail. The remand merely extended over three days, <u>until the next sitting</u> of the magistrate. But in that time, while I was in confinement, <u>Sir Percival</u> might <u>use any means</u> he pleased to embarrass my future proceedings—perhaps to <u>screen himself from detection</u> altogether—without the slightest fear of any hindrance on my part. <u>At the end</u> of the three days <u>the charge</u> would, no doubt, be <u>withdrawn</u>, and the attendance of the witness would be perfectly useless. —Wilkie Collins

Now skim read the second paragraph. Since the key words and phrases are not underlined, you will have to pick them up with your eyes alone. After skimming the passage, try to record the highlights in either written or oral form. (Use the same method you used for Paragraph I.)

Paragraph II

My indignation, I may almost say, my despair, at this mischievous check to all further progress—so base and trifling in itself, and yet so disheartening and so serious in its probable results—quite unfitted me at first to reflect on the best means of extricating myself from the dilemma in which I now stood. I had the folly to call for writing materials, and to think of privately communicating my real position to the magistrate. The hopelessness and the imprudence of this proceeding failed to strike me before I had actually written the opening lines of the letter. It was not till I had pushed the paper away—not till, I am ashamed to say, I had almost allowed the vexation of my helpless position to conquer me—that a course of action suddenly occurred to my mind, which Sir Percival had probably not anticipated, and which might set me free again in a few hours. I determined to communicate the situation in which I was placed to Mr. Dawson, of Oak Lodge. —Wilkie Collins

Students can compare number of highlights recalled. Students can then compare and discuss their records of the highlights.

■ Developing Your Scanning Skills

Like skimming, scanning involves moving your eyes two or three times faster across the page than you would for phrase reading. Scanning is useful when you are reading to answer specific questions or looking for a particular piece of information, such as a telephone number in a phone book or a city on a map. Scanning can also help you use an index or a table of contents.

Use scanning when you need to locate specific pieces of information in reading material.

To scan you should move your eyes rapidly over a page looking for the information you need. You should be able to scan and locate almost any information in a given text in ten to fifteen seconds. The best practice for scanning is through the regular use of the index in a textbook.

EXERCISE G: **Practicing with Scanning.** With your textbook in hand, think of a topic that is probably in your book. Decide which heading or category the topic would be under in the index. If no such topic appears in the index, think of another category or heading. Then scan the index to find the page number of the topic. Locate the page or pages and scan to find the topic you had in mind. Repeat this process with another textbook. *Students can work in pairs, timing each other's efforts.*

APPLICATION: **Using Your Reading Skills.** Think about how you should use the three types of reading to study the subjects you are currently taking. Remember that in doing many assignments involving reading you will probably use two types of reading. On a piece of paper, write down two specific assignments for which you will plan to use phrase reading. Write down two specific assignments for which you will use skimming and two for which you will use scanning. As you do these assignments later, practice using the three types of reading with their different purposes and speeds.

You might be given a copy of each student's plan. After they have completed their assignments, students could fill in on your copy the specific uses they made of their plans.

19.2 Taking Tests

"If only I could remember what I read. If only I could remember what the teacher told us yesterday." You may have made similar statements in the past as you read over a test that the teacher had just handed out. If you have had this experience, your memory may be keeping you from becoming a better student.

Perhaps another reason you may have found taking tests difficult is because you have trouble interpreting the questions or budgeting your time. This section explains some helpful methods for storing information you want to remember and some guidelines for preparing for and taking tests, particularly tests that require short answers.

■ Methods of Improving Your Memory

You may have wondered what is the best way to remember a list of scientific terms or the kings and queens of England or the titles of an author's books. Lists of information lend themselves to certain methods of remembering. These methods allow you to remember information by making up words and sentences and by grouping items by similarities. The use of certain formulas to aid memorization is called mnemonics (nē mon' iks). Some mnemonic methods involve the use of first letters and some involve a rhyme to help you remember. Another aid to memorization is categorizing information.

Apply various mnemonic methods and categorization to learn lists of information.

In addition to using mnemonic methods, you can improve your ability to memorize information by going over facts and lists of information repeatedly and by using the suggestions in the following chart.

GUIDELINES FOR MEMORIZING

1. Tell yourself exactly what you want to remember.
.2. Try to remember only main ideas and major details.
3. Review material to the point of overlearning.
4. Work on memorizing after you have completed your other school work.
5. Make use of help from friends or members of your family.

The mnemonic methods presented here should give you some useful study tools.

The Word or Sentence Method. One way to remember information in a list is to link the first letters of the items to form a real word or a group of real words that fall in some logical order. The first letters of the words in the list can also be used as the first letters of the words in a nonsense sentence. Some of the sentences and words that can be formed in these ways have become famous because they have been used by students for so many years. For example, piano students often learn the lines of the musical staff by memorizing the sentence <u>E</u>very <u>G</u>ood <u>B</u>oy <u>D</u>oes <u>F</u>ine. The spaces can be remembered by memorizing the word <u>FACE</u>.

To use this mnemonic method to develop words and sentences, you should first write down the information you want to remember in the order you want to learn it. Then underline the first letter of each word you want to remember. Try to make up real words or nonsense sentences using the first letters of the items. The following chart shows you how this method works.

USING THE WORD OR SENTENCE METHOD

Real Word

To remember the five Great Lakes: *H*uron, *O*ntario, *M*ichigan, *E*rie, *S*uperior
Remember: HOMES

Nonsense Sentence
To remember how to classify the animal kingdom: *Kingdom, Phylum, Class, Order, Family, Genus, Species* Remember: *King Philip Came Over From Germany Slowly.*

The Poetic Association Method. In the poetic association method, a short, simple poem can help you remember a list of information in order. First, you must memorize the following poem. Then you must link the last word in each line of the poem with the item you want to recall.

POEM: ONE IS A BUN	
One is a bun	Six is sticks
Two is a shoe	Seven is heaven
Three is a tree	Eight is a gate
Four is a door	Nine is a line
Five is a hive	Ten is a hen.

Once you have memorized the poem, you can use it to learn such information as the Articles in the Constitution by linking the subject of each article with the last word in each line of the poem.

USING THE POETIC ASSOCIATION METHOD	
Articles in the Constitution	**Link with the Poem**
1. Legislative	House of Congress wedged in a bun
2. Executive	President with only one shoe on
3. Judicial	Judge chopping down a tree with a gavel
4. Relationship of States	Two states with a door between them
5. Amendment Process	A hive being mended
6. General Provisions	Sticks lined up for a fire along with other provisions, such as food, water, and so on

Categorization. Most of the methods for memorizing emphasize remembering information in a specific order. For remembering information with no particular order, grouping or categorization works best. To help yourself remember ideas or lists of items such as vocabulary words, grouping them according to similarities will improve your ability to memorize the information.

The following chart shows two versions of the same list of words. In Column I the words are listed in no particular order. In Column II the words have been grouped or categorized. Notice how much easier it is to remember the items in Column II than in Column I.

CATEGORIZATION	
Column I	**Column II**
ice cream mittens hammer van	ice cream turkey peas doughnuts
stereo scarf skateboard turkey	mittens scarf earmuffs socks
peas chisel scooter	hammer chisel saw
speakers earmuffs socks	van skateboard scooter
doughnuts C. B. radio saw	stereo speakers C. B. radio

This same grouping method can be used for more complicated ideas and concepts.

EXERCISE A: Practicing with Mnemonic Methods. Select a list of information that you need to remember for history, English, or science. Use the words or sentences method or the poetic association method to remember the information. Write down your words, sentences, or poetic links. Test yourself the next day.

Students might be asked to report on their subjects, methods, and success.

EXERCISE B: Remembering by Categorizing. Using the following twenty words, try two ways to remember the words. First, look at the first ten words for one minute. Cover the list and recall as many words as you can. Then, group the second ten words into three or four categories. Study your categories for one minute and cover the list. Then test yourself by writing down as many words as you can remember. Compare your first list produced from memory with your second list produced after categorizing.

1. ice pick	6. tractor	11. lantern	16. light bulb
2. flashlight	7. soda	12. ink	17. restaurant
3. church	8. gas	13. cream	18. bus
4. barn	9. razor	14. go-cart	19. lotion
5. yacht	10. knife	15. candle	20. garage

Students could discuss their experiences with the two methods in terms of particular categories used, which worked best, and how many items students remembered each time.

■ Preparing for Different Kinds of Objective Tests

Doing well on tests involves more than just studying beforehand. You need to know how to take different types of tests. You also need to know how to spot word clues in questions and when and how to make a reasonable guess at an answer you do not know. If you can master these test-taking skills, your test scores will probably improve.

The two main kinds of tests are essay exams and objective tests. On essay exams, you are asked to write a short composition of a paragraph or more in which you answer a question and support your main idea with specific examples. Your answer may include a reasonable opinion backed up and supported by facts and examples. (Essay exam questions and answers are explained in more detail in Section 29.1) Objective tests, on the other hand, usually ask for short, factual answers that are clearly either right or wrong. Objective tests include such kinds of questions as multiple choice, matching, true/false, a variation of true/false in which you are asked to correct the error, and fill-in.

You can improve your performance on objective tests by following a number of suggestions.

Use your knowledge of the kinds of questions that may be asked along with certain helpful procedures to achieve higher scores on objective tests.

The format of each objective test varies; however, there are some common guidelines that apply to all objective tests.

TAKING OBJECTIVE TESTS

1. Read each question at least *twice* before deciding on an answer.
2. Give only one answer to a question unless the instructions say otherwise. Your choices usually include a single *best* answer.
3. Answer all questions on the test. If you are not certain of an answer, make an educated guess *unless you have been told not to guess.*
4. Do not change your first answer unless you have a good reason.

Besides these general suggestions for taking objective tests, you should recognize the nature of the different types of questions and the particular procedures that can make answering these questions easier.

Multiple Choice Questions.   In all your classes, you will frequently find multiple choice questions on objective tests. These questions usually include four or five possible answers. Out of the four or five answers, one or two are usually obviously incorrect, one is usually fairly close to the real answer, and the final incorrect answer is usually very close to the real answer. You must know the material well in order to distinguish between this last answer and the real answer. You should thus spend most of your time making your choice between these two answers. The following chart provides some hints for answering multiple choice questions.

ANSWERING MULTIPLE CHOICE QUESTIONS

1. Try to answer the question before looking at the possible answers. If your "instant response" is one of the possible answers, you can be almost certain that you have selected the correct answer.
2. If you are permitted to write on the test paper, eliminate obviously incorrect answers by crossing them out as you read.
3. Change the question to a statement by inserting your answer. See if the statement makes sense.

The following question from a grammar test is an example of a multiple choice question.

EXAMPLE:

> Directions: In the following sentence, which words function as *adverbs*?
>
> 1. Quite unmistakably, the small dark figure winked back.
>   a. quite, small, dark
>   b. unmistakably, back
>   c. small, winked, back
>   d. quite, unmistakably, back
>   e. quite, dark, figure, back
>
> Answer: d. quite, unmistakably, back

Matching Questions. Matching questions require that you connect items in one column with the items in a second column. Sometimes the two columns have an equal number of items, and sometimes the columns are unequal. If they are unequal, you will not know which items are meant to be left over. The following chart offers some hints for answering matching questions.

ANSWERING MATCHING QUESTIONS

1. Try to figure out the answer before looking at the answer column.
2. Work down the column matching all of the items you know first.
3. If you can write on the test paper, eliminate terms and words already used by crossing them out. Make certain that they are still visible.
4. When you come to a difficult item, attempt to recall all of the information you know concerning that item. Through this association process, a recalled fact might provide a clue to the answer.

The following matching questions are from a vocabulary test.

EXAMPLE:

> Directions: Match the words on the left with the definitions on the right by writing the letter of the definition in the blank before the word.

_____ 1. philanthropist   a. to beg; plead
_____ 2. antipathy   b. to scold
_____ 3. exasperate   c. face; appearance
_____ 4. chide   d. hatred; strong dislike
_____ 5. implore   e. someone who loves people
                         f. to make angry or irritated
                         g. muddy; cloudy

Answers: 1. e; 2. d; 3. f; 4. b; 5. a.

True/False Questions.   True/false questions usually look easy but can be very difficult. The addition or deletion of one word in these questions can make the difference between a true or false statement. Because of the importance of single words on these tests, you should follow these procedures carefully.

ANSWERING TRUE/FALSE QUESTIONS

1. If you think a statement is true, make certain the entire statement is true. A statement that is only partially true is false.
2. Pay special attention to the word *not*. It can change the meaning of the statement.
3. Pay special attention to these words: *only, no, never, all, none, always*. Often, by limiting an idea too much, they make a statement false.
4. Also, notice these words: *some, often, sometimes, usually, much, little, generally, most*. They often make a statement true.

Think about the ideas in the chart as you study the following questions.

EXAMPLE:

Directions: Identify the following statements as true or false by writing *T* or *F* in the blank before each statement.

_____ 1. You should review class notes on a regular basis.
_____ 2. A study schedule is only necessary when you have a lot of homework.
_____ 3. You should take study breaks every forty-five minutes or so.
_____ 4. You never need to write down your study goals.

Answers: 1. T; 2. F; 3. T; 4. F.

A more difficult form of the true/false question is the correct-the-error question. In this kind of question, you must first determine if a statement is true or false. If the statement is false, you will generally have to change a word, add a word, or delete a word to make the statement correct. Having to correct statements reduces your chances of simply guessing the correct answer.

Fill-In Questions. Fill-in questions, also called short answer questions, require you to supply answers in your own words. The answers can be single words, short phrases, or possibly short sentences. The only helpful clue to answering fill-in questions is to use the context to see if your answers make sense. Because there are few useful hints or guidelines for answering fill-in questions, you should study the material especially thoroughly and carefully if you know a test will include this kind of question.

EXAMPLE:

> Directions: Answer the following questions with words or phrases.
>
> 1. List *two* sound effects that Shakespeare's theater used.
>   a. _____
>   b. _____
>
> Answers: a. trumpets and horns for battles and military processions
>   b. drums for thunder

EXERCISE C: Examining Questions for Objective Tests. Using a subject you are studying in class—grammar, literature, spelling, or speech, for instance—prepare a short objective test on the material. Write five multiple choice questions, five matching questions, five true/false questions, and five fill-in questions. Exchange papers with another student and take the other student's test, writing your answers on a separate piece of paper. Exchange back and submit your own test and the other student's answers to it to your teacher. *Students may keep corrected tests as review aids. They might also make up potential test questions in preparation for any upcoming test.*

■ Taking Objective Tests

The actual taking of a test is a three-step process. First you must preview the test, then you must give your answers, and finally you must proofread your answers. You should make wise use of the test period by allowing enough time to do each of these steps.

Regulate your time by spending five to fifteen percent of your time previewing, seventy-five to eighty-five percent of your time answering the questions, and about ten percent of your time proofreading.

You should always come to a test on time with the necessary equipment, such as pens, pencils, erasers, or any books you have been told to bring. When the test has been handed out and you have been told to begin, you should begin your preview. As the suggestions in the following chart show, you should look over the test, plan your strategy, and prepare to write.

PREVIEWING A TEST
1. Put your name on each sheet of paper you will be using.
2. Skim through the entire test to get an overview of the format and type of questions that are being asked.
3. Decide on the time you plan to spend on the various sections of the test. Plan to devote the greatest amount of time to the questions that carry the most points.
4. Decide where you will begin. You do not have to start with the first question.

Once you have examined the test and decided on your approach, you are ready to follow these suggestions for answering the questions on the test.

ANSWERING THE QUESTIONS
1. Jot down the information you do not want to forget on a piece of paper. Ask the teacher for paper for this purpose at the start of the test.
2. Answer the easy questions in each section first.
3. Put a check beside difficult questions that you will want to come back to later.

Proofreading is the final step in test-taking. This step should take no more than ten percent of your total time. The following chart explains what you should look for and check as you proofread.

PROOFREADING YOUR ANSWERS
1. Check to see that you have followed directions completely.
2. Check to see that your name is on each sheet of paper used.
3. Reread test questions and answers. Do not change original answers unless you have a good reason to do so.

EXERCISE D: Practicing Your Test-Taking Skills. With another student in your class, decide on a subject for a test and the types of questions you want to include. Each of you should then make up a test of twenty objective questions. Make your questions challenging but fair. When everyone has composed a test, exchange papers with your partner and take the test. Follow the guidelines for previewing, answering, and proofreading the test. Then submit your test to your teacher. *This might be done as a group exercise, with each group making up a test together, taking another group's test, and comparing results.*

APPLICATION: Using Mnemonic Methods and Test-Taking Skills. In preparation for an upcoming tests in one of your classes, use one of the mnemonic methods in this section to study. When you receive your test, follow the three steps for taking tests. After you have turned in your test, analyze your use of memory methods and test-taking skills by answering the following questions.

1. What mnemonic method did you use to recall information? Did it help you?
2. How could you have made better use of mnemonic methods to remember the information?
3. Which questions on the test were the most difficult for you?
4. Which kind of questions should you practice making up and answering?
5. Did you spend the right amount of time previewing the test?

Students might write a brief paragraph comparing their usual methods of studying for a test with the method used in this case. Which are more successful? Why?

Chapter 20

Library and Reference Skills

Modern libraries contain many different kinds of material. Printed items such as books, pamphlets, newspapers, and journals are the most numerous. Other items, however, such as films and tape recordings, are not printed at all. Sometimes information is even computerized or put on microfilm. Regardless of its format, information is readily available and awaiting your discovery at the libraries in your area.

Becoming familiar and comfortable with your local libraries can help you move ahead rapidly, both academically and personally. For this reason you should learn about the tools of the library and practice using them so that you can develop confidence as quickly as possible. Above all, you need to recognize that most library materials, as well as the indexes that help you locate specific information in them, are arranged logically. The next two sections will help you learn to use the basic tools that are found in your library. The third section will describe the features found in most dictionaries and will help you use this valuable reference to your best advantage.

Using the Library 20.1

Whether you use the library to find a specific book or to gather information from many sources, you need to know how to use the card catalog and how to interpret location symbols in order to proceed from the catalog to the shelves. Learning how to use these guides will make your work in the library more pleasant and rewarding. But before you begin any search in the library, you should take time to plan your research. Knowing what information you should take with you will help you use your time well and increase your chances of finding exactly what you need.

■ Knowing What You Are Looking For

Although it is always helpful to check with library personnel to seek information and to make sure you are not overlooking newly acquired materials, you must help librarians before they can help you. To do so requires planning. No matter how much you have used a library, you need to come prepared with some basic information.

Begin your research by knowing basic facts about your topic.

As part of your planning, you should gather a list of names and terms related to your topic. You should also try to determine the limits of your topic, essentially in terms of time. The following suggestions should be useful in carrying out this planning stage.

Checking Your Spelling. Since the card catalogs and indexes in a library are arranged alphabetically, you must be absolutely sure of the spelling of the words that describe your topic. Incorrect spelling can defeat you before you start. For example, if you want to find information about the English writer Virginia Woolf, looking under *Wolf* or *Wolfe* would turn up either nothing or entirely wrong information.

Considering Alternative Names and Terms. Some topics may not be listed under the name you expect. If, for example, you are looking for information about ancient Iran, you may need to look under *Persia* as well. In the course of history, this geographic area has been known by both names. Similarly, if you want information about oil, you will probably have to look under *petroleum* as well. In considering alternative names, you should also try to relate small topics to the larger fields of which they are a part. For example, not all rocks and minerals are gems, but all gems are rocks or minerals. Thus, if you cannot find the specific topic *gems* in a catalog or index, you might try looking under the larger, more inclusive term *minerals*. Knowing alternative names and terms will often help you uncover just the information you need.

Limiting Your Topic to a Period of Time. When information in a reference book is arranged chronologically—that is, by date—knowing the appropriate dates of your topic will help you find the proper section or volume. In addition, assigning dates to your topic will often limit the number of sources you will need to consult. Suppose, for example, you were assigned a short oral report on the major English poets of the Romantic Period. Knowing the dates of this period (roughly 1750 to 1840) would help you limit the number of poets you research. You might study Blake, Wordsworth, Coleridge, Byron, Shelley, and Keats, but not Pope (who died in 1744) or Tennyson (who became famous in 1842).

Only when you are prepared with this sort of information can you use, or have someone help you use, the standard references effectively. Most of the information you need for planning will be found in your textbooks or can be learned from class discussion. The time spent in defining and limiting your topic will be saved many times over during your search for information.

EXERCISE A: Gathering Information Before You Visit the Library. Choose a topic for a research paper. Write the information you need to know to find the best sources in the library by answering the following questions.

1. What is the name of your topic?
2. What alternative names, if any, are there for this topic?
3. Of what larger field is it a part?
4. What are some names and terms related to this larger field?
5. Are your responses to the first four questions spelled correctly?
6. Within what span of years does your topic fall?

The class might work first on two or three common topics, with students then finding individual topics of their own.

■ Using the Card Catalog

A card catalog is to a library what an index is to a book—a convenient means of locating the information you need. The filing within the catalog is done according to common standards. To use the catalog, you must be familiar with word-by-word alphabetizing, with all types of catalog cards, and with the basic filing rules and subdivisions. In addition, you need to know how to proceed from the catalog to the shelf to locate the materials you want.

Understanding the Basic Arrangement.   There are two types of card catalogs: the *dictionary type* and the *divided type*. If your library has the dictionary type, all the cards will be filed together. In the divided type there will be separate sections for subjects and for authors and/or titles. In either type, you can expect the cards to be alphabetized word by word rather than letter by letter.

Use word-by-word alphabetizing to find information in a card catalog.

In letter-by-letter alphabetizing, the method used in dictionaries, the spaces between words are ignored. All letters are considered to be of equal importance. In word-by-word alphabetizing, however, the spacing between words is taken into consideration. The first word in a topic or title is compared with the first word in another topic or title (letter by letter within the word). If the first words are the same, then the second words are compared to determine placement, and so on.

Word-By-Word Alphabetizing	Letter-By-Letter Alphabetizing
To be young	To be young
To kill a mockingbird	Today in New York
Today in New York	Togetherness poems
Togetherness poems	To kill a mockingbird

Recognizing Different Types of Cards.   A card catalog contains three principal types of cards: *title cards, author cards*, and *subject cards*. These cards and other more specialized cards will contain all the information you need to locate the materials you want.

Use catalog cards to find information about books and other materials and to locate items on the shelves.

What you know from your planning will help determine the kind of card you will use. For example, if you already know the title of a particular book—suppose it is *A Cornish Childhood*—you would simply look it up in the catalog under the first main letter, *C*. (The words *the*, *an*, and *a* at the beginning of a title are dropped in alphabetizing.) Notice the different kinds of information a title card includes about the book.

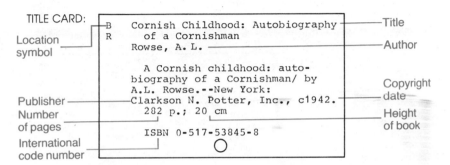

TITLE CARD:
Location symbol
Publisher
Number of pages
International code number

Title
Author
Copyright date
Height of book

Suppose instead you cannot recall the title but remember the author's name—A.L. Rowse. Looking up the author's name (last name first) would yield several author cards for this person. Under the author's name on each card would be the title of a book written or edited by him—one title per card. All the cards for one author are arranged alphabetically by title. The author card for *A Cornish Childhood* would look like this. Notice that the information about the book is the same as that found on the title card.

AUTHOR CARD:

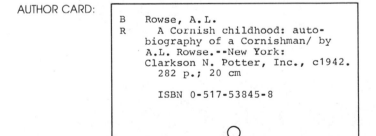

The third kind of card, a subject card, is useful when you have a topic in mind but do not know what specific titles or authors to look up. Suppose you need to begin gathering information for a report for your biology class. Looking up

Biology in the card catalog would yield many cards giving the names of authors and titles that come under that general heading. Notice in the following example that the location symbol is a number rather than letters. This kind of symbol is called a *call number*. Notice also the items at the bottom of the card that show what cards contain this information: a subject card and a title card.

SUBJECT CARD:

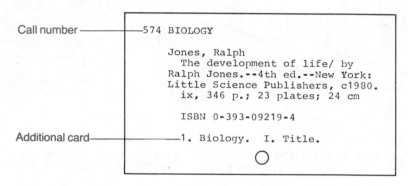

Call number ——————574 BIOLOGY

Jones, Ralph
The development of life/ by
Ralph Jones.--4th ed.--New York:
Little Science Publishers, c1980.
ix, 346 p.; 23 plates; 24 cm

ISBN 0-393-09219-4

Additional card ——————1. Biology. I. Title.

As you use subject cards to discover books you think will be helpful, you should take time to copy the essential information from the card: title, location symbol or call number, and author. You will need this information to locate the book on the shelf. Subject names (such as *Biology*) will not appear on the spine of the book, but the other information will.

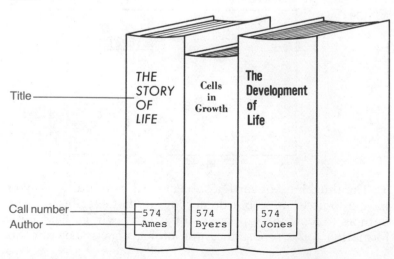

Title

THE STORY OF LIFE

Cells in Growth

The Development of Life

Call number
Author

574 Ames

574 Byers

574 Jones

Besides the three principal types of catalog cards, you should also learn to recognize two other types: *analytic cards* and *cross-reference cards*. Analytic cards indicate *parts* of books or kits. Suppose you are looking for the play *Saint Joan* by George Bernard Shaw and find the following analytic card. What it tells you is that the play you need can be found on pages 346–391 of the book *Modern English Drama* by Harry Smith.

ANALYTIC CARD:

Part title	822.08 Saint Joan, p. 346-391, in

Book editor and title	Smith, Harry, ed.
	  Modern English drama/ ed. by Harry Smith.--3rd ed.--New York: Scribner, c1971.
	    560 p.; il.; 26 cm; (Drama classics series)

Part authors and titles	Contents: Dryden, J. All for love.-- Sheridan, R. School for scandal.-- Goldsmith, O. She stoops to conquer.-- Shaw, G. Saint Joan. 1. English drama (Collections). I. Analytics. II. Title.

In using analytic cards, you must take care to distinguish the "part" author and title from the "book" author and title. The selection inside the book is what you want, but you will find it on the shelf only by looking for the title and author of the entire book. When you go to the shelf to locate the play, you must look for the book by Smith, not for the book by Shaw.

Cross-reference cards are often provided when there is a chance that the library user will look up a term different from the one the cataloguer chose to use. The cards will be marked *see* or *see also*.

A *see* card means that no information is listed under the term you have chosen. Instead, the card will direct you to another place in the catalog where the information can be found. A *see also* card may sometimes be found at the end of a series of subject cards. It will suggest additional subjects to look under. Subjects placed on *see also* cards will generally be closely related to your topic and will often prove very useful.

CROSS-REFERENCE CARDS:

OIL See Petroleum ○	PETROLEUM See also Rocks and Minerals ○

Interpreting the Information on the Cards.   As you can see from the examples already given, catalog cards contain standard kinds of information and are printed according to set formats. Some of the information is of interest primarily to librarians, but most of it is intended to help the user of the library.

Learn to recognize the standard kinds of information that can be obtained from catalog cards.

The following author card shows some of the basic kinds of information that can be learned from a catalog card.

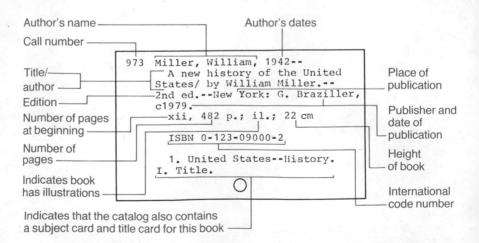

Following Special Filing Rules.   Over the years, librarians have agreed on standard ways of dealing with certain options that come up in filing catalog cards. Though there are many detailed and complicated filing rules that a cataloguer must remember, you need to concern yourself with only a few of these rules. Knowing them will help you locate certain cards that otherwise might escape your notice.

Recognize a number of special rules used for filing catalog cards.

Foremost among these rules is the one you have already learned: The cards are alphabetized word by word. Related to this is the rule that the words *a, an,* and *the* are dropped when they appear as the *first* word of a title. Thus, *A Thousand and One Nights* is found under the letter *T,* not under the letter *A.*

Another rule involves names beginning with *Mc* or *M'.* Names that begin with the sound *Mac* are mentally spelled *Mac* even when they are actually spelled *Mc* or *M'.* This filing rule makes it possible to look in just one place and to have all the names together. The following example shows the proper sequence of names in the *Mac* section of the card catalog.

EXAMPLE: MacHENRY   M'LEOD

MACHINERY   MACMILLAN

McINTYRE

A related rule states that abbreviations and numbers must also be spelled out mentally. *Dr.* is filed as if it were *Doctor; Mr.* will be under *Mister; Mrs.* will often be under *Mistress. Five Plays* would come after *50 Best Stories* because *50* is filed as if it were *Fifty.*

A final rule concerns subject cards. Large subject areas are usually subdivided, and the subdivisions are filed alphabetically under the main subject. A dash in the first line of a subject card indicates that a subdivision follows. One significant deviation from alphabetical arrangement is the chronological arrangement used when a subdivision such as *History* is *further* subdivided.

EXAMPLE: U.S.

U.S.—FOREIGN RELATIONS

U.S.—HISTORY—WAR OF 1812

U.S.—HISTORY—BLACK HAWK WAR, 1832

U.S.—HISTORY—WAR WITH MEXICO, 1845–48

> U.S.—HISTORY—CIVIL WAR, 1860–65
>
> U.S.—IMMIGRATION
>
> U.S. ARMY
>
> U.S. CONSTITUTION
>
> U.S. SUPREME COURT

Note that the last three items in the preceding example are main topics themselves, not subdivisions of *U.S.* When you are researching a small area of a large subject and do not find what you are looking for, remember to check both the place where it could be filed as a subdivision and the place where it could be filed as a main topic.

EXERCISE B: Alphabetizing Word by Word. The following items are alphabetized letter by letter, as they would appear in a dictionary. Alphabetize them word by word, as they would appear in a card catalog.

1. New Amsterdam *1*
2. Newark *7*
3. New Deal *2*
4. Newfoundland *8*
5. New France *3*
6. New Orleans *4*
7. Newport *9*
8. New South Wales *5*
9. Newton *10*
10. New York *6*

EXERCISE C: Interpreting Information on a Catalog Card. Use the following subject card to answer the questions that come after it.

```
398    BEES--POETRY

       Busch, Wilhelm, 1832-1908
         The bees: a fairy tale/ by Wilhelm
       Busch: translated by Rudolph Wiemann.
       --1st ed.-- New York: Vantage Press,
       c1974.
         72 p.; il.; 21 cm

         Translation of Schnurrdiburr.

         ISBN 0-533-01215-5

         1. Bees--Poetry. 2. Stories in
       rhyme. I. Wiemann, Rudolph. II. Title.
                      ◯
```

1. What is the complete call number? *398*
2. What is the copyright date of the book? *1974*
3. Who is the publisher of the book? *Vantage Press*

4. Who is the author of the book? *Wilhelm Busch*
5. What is the title of the book? <u>*The Bees: A Fairy Tale*</u>
6. How many pages are in the book? *72*
7. Where was the book published? *New York*
8. What is the name of the translator? *Rudolph Wiemann*
9. What was the book called in the original language? <u>*Schnurrdiburr*</u>
10. Are there any pictures in the book? *yes*

EXERCISE D: Identifying Catalog Cards. Write an author card, a title card, and a subject card using the following information.

Elizabeth Regina: The Age of Triumph, 1588–1603, by Alison Plowden, published by Times Books in New York, in 1980, with 214 pages and a height of 20 cm. The call number is 942.055, and the international number is 0-686-65925-2. The book is filed under both GREAT BRITAIN—HISTORY— ELIZABETH, 1558–1603 and ELIZABETH, QUEEN OF EN- GLAND, 1533–1603.
Cards should follow models found on preceding pages.

EXERCISE E: Using Special Filing Rules. Write each of the following pairs of card catalog entries in the correct order on your paper. (Two are correct already.) Cite the catalog filing rule that governs the order of each pair.

1. Dr. Faustus   *correct (Dr. = Doctor)*
   Doctors at work
2. 5 ways to grow   ⤴⤵ *(5 = five)*
   Fifteenth summer ⤵
3. Machinery in America ⤴⤵ *(McG = MacG)*
   McGregor's garden ⤵
4. Applesauce recipes   *correct (disregard "an")*
   An old man
5. FRANCE—HISTORY—BOURBONS, 1589–1789   ⤴⤵
   FRANCE—HISTORY—HOUSE OF VALOIS, 1328–1589 ⤴
   (within historical listing, use chronological order)

■ From Catalog to Shelf

Besides the title and author, the most important piece of information on a catalog card is the location symbol, or the more specific call number. This set of numbers, letters, or a combination of the two corresponds to a *classification system*, which determines the item's location on the shelf. To find an item, you must match the symbols and numbers on the catalog card with the symbols and numbers found on the book.

Use call numbers and other symbols given on the catalog cards to locate materials on the shelves.

A library uses one of two basic classification systems to arrange materials logically on the shelves. The traditional method is called the Dewey Decimal System. The newer method is called the Library of Congress System.

Locating Nonfiction by the Dewey Decimal System. The Dewey Decimal System divides all knowledge into ten main classes, numbered from 000 to 999. Each of the classes is divided into ten divisions and each of the divisions is divided into ten subdivisions. When necessary the subdivisions can be divided even further.

MAIN CLASS:	600–699	Technology
DIVISION:	620	Engineering
SUBDIVISION:	621	Applied Physics
FURTHER DIVISIONS:	621.1	Steam Engineering
	621.15	Engines
	621.16	Stationary Engines
	621.165	Turbine Engines

The numbers in the call number are generally followed by the first letter or letters of the author's last name. Thus, a group of books with the same number can be arranged alphabetically on the shelf according to the authors' last names. The following chart shows how three books about turbine engines—one by Jones, one by Smith, and one by Young—would be organized on the shelf.

ORDER ON SHELF				
621.1	621.165	621.165	621.165	621.2
M	J	S	Y	A

To find the book by Young on turbine engines, you would first go to the part of the library where the 600's are shelved, then find the 620's, the 621's, the 621.1's, and so on until you come to 621.165. Finally, you would use the author letters.

Locating Nonfiction by the Library of Congress System. Instead of using numbers and an author letter, the Library of Congress System uses the letters of the alphabet—

A to Z—to designate the main classes of knowledge. A combination of two letters is used to indicate divisions, and numbers are used to show subdivisions.

MAIN CLASS:	B	Philosophy
DIVISION:	BC	Logic
SUBDIVISIONS:	BC 131	Early works to 1800
	BC 135	Later works, 1801—

Books sharing the same subdivision may also be distinguished by author letters and numbers.

To find a book in a library arranged by the Library of Congress System, follow the same steps as you would in a library using the Dewey Decimal System.

Using Location Symbols to Find Fiction. Books of fiction (novels, short stories, and so on) are generally kept separate from the other books in the library. The catalog card for a work of fiction will usually have the location symbol F or Fic instead of a call number. Some libraries may include all or the first few letters of the author's last name above the location symbol. Other libraries may give no marking at all. The book you want will be in the fiction section of the library, arranged alphabetically on the shelf according to the author's last name.

ALPHABETICAL ORDER OF FICTION ON SHELF:

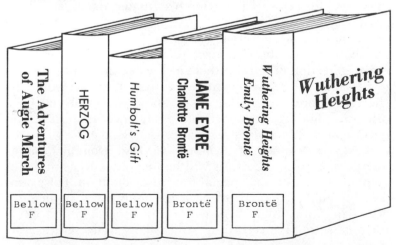

Using Location Symbols to Find Biographies.   Although they can be shelved in the history section (the 920's of the Dewey System), individual biographies are often shelved in a separate area. Marked with the location symbol B (for biography) or 92 (short for 920), biographies are arranged according to the person the book is about, not according to the author. This makes it possible to have all the material about one person grouped in the same place. Thus, *Byron: A Portrait* by Leslie A. Marchand (a biography about the English poet) would be marked with the location symbol B or 92 and either all or the first letter of the subject's last name.

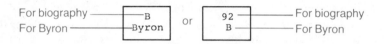

For biography ———— B   or   92 ———— For biography
For Byron ———— Byron   B ———— For Byron

Collective biographies, books that contain chapter-length biographies about a number of persons, will usually be shelved with the library's main collection. In the Dewey Decimal System they would carry the call numbers 920 through 929 rather than the location symbols B or 92.

Using Symbols and Numbers to Find Reference Materials.   Libraries may shelve reference materials in a variety of ways, although they are usually separate from the other books and almost always carry the letters R or Ref above the call number. This location symbol indicates that the item is stored in a special area and is restricted in borrowing time.

Large libraries place reference materials in a special room. School libraries often use a separate section, with books labeled R and arranged according to their usual call numbers. Some libraries place reference materials with the main collection but group them at the beginning of each section. Thus, all reference materials about music would be shelved before the regular items about music. If you have difficulty finding the particular reference materials you need, you should ask for assistance.

Using a Variety of Symbols to Find Non-Print Materials.   Non-print materials will be marked with a variety of symbols to match the special format of the item. For example, FS might be used above a call number to indicate a filmstrip. Trans might be used for a transparency and TR(C) for a cassette tape recording. Since these items will usually be kept separate, you should ask your librarian for help in finding and using these materials.

EXERCISE F: Recognizing and Sequencing Dewey Decimal and Library of Congress Call Numbers. Divide your paper into two columns and label one column Dewey Decimal System and the other Library of Congress System. Separate the following sample call numbers according to the system they represent and arrange them in proper order.

Dewey		*Library of Congress*		
320 Jones	822 Thomas	QC 3385	809 Smith	
320 Jones	*822 Thomas*	*D 767*	*ML 338*	
LB 1585	647.3 Sandone	FB 122.1	641 Eves	
641 Eves	*971 Johnson*	*FB 122.1*	*ND 623*	
647.3 Sandone	*973 Adams*	*HQ 792*	*QC 3385*	
HQ 792	QH 6525	D 767	979 Evans	
809 Smith	*979 Evans*	*LB 1585*	*QH 6525*	
973 Adams	ML 338	ND 623	971 Johnson	

EXERCISE G: Interpreting Location Symbols Used for Fiction, Biographies, and Other Special Materials. Use the card catalog to find the following items in your library. Write the location symbols, titles, and authors on your paper. *Answers will vary; cumulative lists might be made on the board.*

1. Two novels by William Faulkner
2. A biography about William Shakespeare
3. A collective biography about English poets
4. A reference book about American literature
5. A filmstrip about career opportunities

APPLICATION: Using What You Have Learned. Use the card catalog and what you have learned about the organization of a library to prepare a list of materials on any topic that appeals to you. Follow these steps. *Special attention could be paid to checking tables of contents, indexes, and multiple references to subject.*

1. Carry out the planning stage. (See Exercise A.)
2. Use the card catalog to find about ten items related to your topic. Try to find a variety of items: individual books, reference materials, and non-print items.
3. Copy the essential information from the catalog cards: title, location symbol or call number, and author.

4. Find the materials in the library and check them for suitability to your topic.
5. Revise your list if necessary. Prepare a final version for submission to your teacher. (Be sure you have identified your topic.)

20.2 Using Reference Materials

The materials in the reference section of the library fall into three basic categories: general reference books, specialized reference books, and periodicals, such as magazines and newspapers. All of them are meant to be consulted for information. Some you may want to read from cover to cover for enjoyment. The primary purpose of reference books, however, is to help people who are doing research. Thus, most reference materials cannot be checked out of the library—except, perhaps, overnight.

This section will help you become more familiar with the three kinds of reference materials you can find in most school and public libraries. It will also show you how to use them to check facts and to find the information you need for a project or report.

■ General Reference Books

When you need to check a fact or are beginning work on a topic about which you know little or nothing, you should think in terms of "first step" references. How will you get the greatest amount of help in the least amount of time? One way is to turn to general reference books, such as encyclopedias, almanacs, and atlases. (Dictionaries, the general reference book that people use most often, will be discussed separately in the next section.)

Use general reference books to check basic facts or to explore the range of a topic.

General reference books cover broad areas of knowledge and usually do not go into great detail. They will, however, provide you with basic information that can guide you as you go on to more detailed sources of information. Unless you are simply checking a fact, general references should rarely be the last stop in your research.

General Encyclopedias. General encyclopedias contain articles on a wide range of subjects. Usually published in sets of twenty or more volumes, they rely on alphabetical order and indexes to help readers find information quickly. Some encyclopedias use word-by-word alphabetizing, as in a card catalog; others use the letter-by-letter method, as in a dictionary.

A useful way to begin your search for information in an encyclopedia is to consult the index. There you will find out whether or not your topic has an entire article devoted to it. If it does, the index will direct you to the volume and page where it may be found. Some topics, on the other hand, may not be considered important enough to have entire articles devoted to them. Then, the index will tell you if your topic is covered within another article. Perhaps information about your topic can be found in parts of several articles. If so, the index will tell you exactly where to look. Notice, for example, how the index to the *Encyclopedia Americana* indicates an entire article about Queen Victoria, volume 28, page 85. Notice, too, that information about Victoria can also be found within other articles, such as within an article on Great Britain, volume 13, pages 326 and 328, within an article on Albert, Victoria's husband, and within an article on hemophilia.

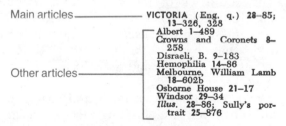

Main articles ——————— VICTORIA (Eng. q.) 28–85;
                        13–326, 328
                      ⌐ Albert 1–489
                        Crowns and Coronets 8–
                        258
                        Disraeli, B. 9–183
                        Hemophilia 14–86
Other articles ——————— Melbourne, William Lamb
                        18–602b
                        Osborne House 21–17
                        Windsor 29–34
                        Illus. 28–86; Sully's por-
                      ⌐ trait 25–876

Since information about politics, economics, science, and many other subjects is constantly changing, publishers of encyclopedias need to keep their products as up to date as possible. Most revise articles or parts of articles yearly to reflect recent developments. They may also publish yearbooks as supplements to their encyclopedias. A yearbook summarizes important events of the preceding year and describes major developments in various fields of knowledge. Most yearbooks contain an index that covers the contents not only of that particular book but also of several of the preceding yearbooks. Whenever you are researching a current or rapidly changing topic you should begin with a recent encyclopedia and then check the index of the most recent yearbook as well.

Some of the most popular general encyclopedias are *Collier's Encyclopedia, Compton's Encyclopedia,* the *Encyclopedia Americana,* the *Encyclopedia International,* the *Encyclopedia Britannica,* and *The World Book Encyclopedia.* Small one- or two-volume general encyclopedias such as the *Cadillac Modern Encyclopedia, The New Columbia Encyclopedia,* the *Columbia-Viking Desk Encyclopedia,* and *The Lincoln Library* are also available in most libraries.

Almanacs and Other Yearbooks. In addition to encyclopedia yearbooks, several other general reference books are published annually. Almanacs provide up-to-date statistics and other facts on such topics as government, history, geography, astronomy, economics, population, and sports. Relatively inexpensive, almanacs can be found in bookstores as well as in libraries. Among the most popular are *Hammond's Almanac,* the *Information Please Almanac,* the *Reader's Digest Almanac and Yearbook,* and *The World Almanac and Book of Facts.*

Other references that are revised yearly include *Facts on File,* a current events digest, and the *Statesman's Yearbook,* which provides basic information about international organizations, the countries of the world, and the individual states in the United States.

Almanacs and other yearbooks are generally arranged by topics rather than by alphabetical order. It is essential, therefore, that you use the index to locate information in these references.

Atlases and Gazetteers. Atlases and gazetteers can be very helpful when you are checking facts about geographic location. Many atlases include not only maps but also informative text. Besides showing you the borders of different countries, atlases may contain facts and charts about population distribution, seasonal temperature and rainfall, agricultural and industrial production, and natural resources.

Other atlases are historical—that is, they show the borders of nations as they were at a particular point in history. Some historical atlases also show the movement of armies or trace the migration of different groups of people. The following map, for example, shows the territory included in the Roman Empire in the second to fourth centuries. Notice the names of the regions as they were known at that time and the symbol for the frontier wall.

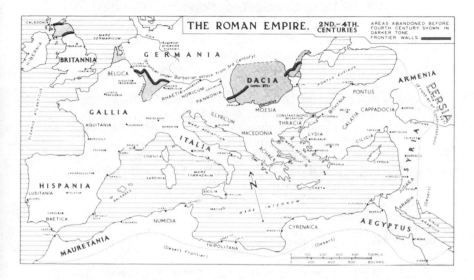

In either a modern or a historical atlas, you will need to use the index to find the information you need. It will direct you to the pages and, if necessary, to the exact location on the map grid.

Among the most popular modern atlases are the *National Geographic Atlas of the World*, the *Rand McNally Cosmopolitan World Atlas*, the *Hammond Medallion World Atlas*, and *Goode's World Atlas*. Major historical atlases are *Shepherd's Historical Atlas*, the *Atlas of American History*, the *Atlas of European History*, and the *Atlas of the Bible Lands*.

Unlike atlases, most gazetteers do not contain maps. Instead, they offer brief descriptions of places, arranged alphabetically like entries in a dictionary. In short, gazetteers are geographical dictionaries. Here is a typical entry from one. Note the kind of information it provides.

EXAMPLE: **Death Valley** \deth-\. 1 Valley in Inyo co., E California, bet. Panamint Mts. on W and Amargosa Range on E; ab. 140 m. long; Amargosa river flows into it from S; contains small pool, Badwater, lowest point in U.S., 282 ft. below sea level, less than 80 m. from Mt. Whitney (14,494 ft., highest point in U.S. outside of Alaska); has been set aside as **Death Valley National Monument:** see UNITED STATES, *National Monuments.*
2 Post office, Inyo co., E California, E of Death Valley National Monument.

Webster's Geographical Dictionary and the *Columbia-Lippincott Gazetteer* are among the most popular gazetteers.

EXERCISE A: **Using General Encyclopedias.** Use the index of a general encyclopedia or encyclopedia yearbook to locate information about the following ten items. Record the name of the encyclopedia you use, the volume and page number on which the information can be found, and the title of the article in which the information can be found.
Choices of encyclopedias will vary; note that a yearbook would be best for 5.
1. The use of cowrie shells as money
2. A description of the death of Percy Bysshe Shelley
3. The numbering system of the Maya Indians
4. Toussaint L'Ouverture's place in history
5. Recent scientific discoveries about the planet Uranus
6. The purpose of Hadrian's Wall
7. The art of the Benin people of Nigeria
8. Plants that eat insects
9. The origins of jazz
10. A description of Sarajevo

EXERCISE B: **Using Almanacs and Other Yearbooks.** Use an up-to-date almanac or yearbook (such as the *Statesman's Yearbook*) to answer the following questions. After your answers, record the names and pages of the books you use.
Specific sources will vary; factual answers given (as of 1980–81).
1. What are the chief exports of the African nation Zimbabwe? *tobacco, cotton, sugar, corn, tea*
2. How many nations were members of the United Nations last year? *149*
3. Who was Eisenhower's running mate in the U.S. presidential election of 1956? *Richard Nixon*
4. What is the most populous city in the world? *New York*
5. Who is the head of state of Canada? *Queen Elizabeth, represented by a Governor-General*

EXERCISE C: **Using Atlases and Gazetteers.** Use atlases and gazetteers to answer the following questions. After each answer, record the name and pages of the book you use.
Specific sources will vary; factual answers given.
1. Bordeaux belonged to what European territory in the 1300's? What nation encompasses this territory today?
2. What large island lies off the coast of the territory of Quintana Roo?
3. What are the two most populous cities of Puerto Rico?
4. What nations border on Lake Chad?
5. In what direction do ocean currents flow in the Pacific Ocean north of the equator? South of the equator?

1. England/France   2. Cozumel   3. San Juan and Ponce   4. Niger, Chad, Nigeria
5. clockwise/counterclockwise

■ Specialized Reference Books

After you have used general reference books to learn about the broad range of a topic, your next step will often be to find more detailed information, usually on some smaller aspect of the general topic. One way to proceed is to use the card catalog to locate appropriate materials from the main collection. Another way is to use specialized reference books.

Use specialized reference books to gather detailed information about a limited aspect of a broad topic.

You are likely to find that the reference section of your library contains specialized materials for almost every topic. Some books will be limited to a specific number of years and perhaps to a specific area, for example, a book that covers the Renaissance period (1265–1564) in Italy. Others will cover just one part of a much larger field. For example, a book entitled *A Field Guide to Wildflowers of Northeastern and North-central North America* will cover only a small part of the topic of wildflowers, which in turn is only a small part of the subject of botany. Becoming familiar with the variety of specialized reference materials at your disposal will help broaden your research abilities. In many cases, it will also save you time.

Specialized Dictionaries. Sometimes called glossaries, handbooks, or companions, specialized dictionaries provide brief entries describing the special terms, people, or events involved in the study of a specific topic. The entries are arranged alphabetically. Whether your topic is American slang, computer terminology, a foreign language, classical mythology, British literature, medicine, folklore, or mathematics—there is probably a specialized dictionary to suit your particular needs.

The information you find in these books will usually be more detailed and informative than what you could find in a regular dictionary. For example, if you were writing about a fierce storm off the coast of China and were not sure whether *hurricane* was the right word to use, a dictionary of synonyms, rather than a regular dictionary, would help you find the correct word by explaining the similarities and differences among words related to *hurricane*. In the following example, taken from *Webster's Dictionary of Synonyms*, you can see how the system works.

EXAMPLE: Asterisk indicates the entry under
⌐ which each group of words is explained

> **hurricane** 1 *wind, breeze, gale, zephyr
> 2 *whirlwind, cyclone, typhoon, tornado, waterspout, twister

whirlwind, cyclone, typhoon, hurricane, tornado, waterspout, twister share the basic notion of a rotary motion of the wind. **Whirlwind** is applied to a small windstorm which begins with an inward and upward spiral motion of the lower air and is followed by an outward and upward spiral motion until, usually, there is a progressive motion at all levels. **Cyclone**, in technical use, is applicable to a system of winds that rotate, counterclockwise in the northern hemisphere, about a center of low atmospheric pressure; such a system of winds originating in the tropics (a *tropical cyclone*) may rotate at the rate of 75 miles per hour or more, sometimes exceeding 200 miles per hour. **Typhoon** is used of a severe tropical cyclone in the region of the western Pacific ocean. A tropical cyclone in the tropical north Atlantic and tropical western Pacific, with winds rarely exceeding 150 miles an hour, occasionally moving into temperate latitudes, is called a **hurricane**. In popular use, especially in the midwestern U.S., *cyclone* may take the place of **tornado**, the usual technical term, for an extremely violent whirling wind which is accompanied by a funnel-shaped cloud and which moves with great speed in a narrow path over a stretch of territory, often causing great destruction. A **waterspout** is a tornado that occurs over water. **Twister** is a familiar term often applied to a whirlwind, tornado, or waterspout.

A related type of specialized dictionary, the thesaurus, also gives synonyms but generally does not give the detailed explanations found in a dictionary of synonyms. *Roget's International Thesaurus* and *Webster's Collegiate Thesaurus* are both popular examples.

Specialized Encyclopedias.   Many encyclopedias limit their coverage to one area of knowledge, such as religion, science, social science, medicine, sports, or the arts. Others are even more limited. For example, *The Reader's Encyclopedia of Shakespeare* covers only that playwright and information related to his works. Other well-known specialized encyclopedias you should know about are the *International Encyclopedia of Social Sciences, Cassell's Encyclopedia of World Literature,* the *Encyclopedia of World Art,* the *Encyclopedia of Oceanography,* the *Encyclopedia of Sports,* the *McGraw-Hill Encyclopedia of Science and Technology,* and the *McGraw-Hill Encyclopedia of Drama.*

Biographical Reference Books.   Biographical reference books are particularly useful when no full-length biography exists about a person. They may also be useful when you do not have the time to read an entire book. These specialized references include entries for many more persons than a general encyclopedia has room for. The coverage is also likely to be more thorough than that found in an encyclopedia.

To use biographical references efficiently, you will need to pay attention to the limitations each book sets on the dates, nationalities, or professions of the people they list. For example, the *Who's Who* series, *Current Biography*, and *Contemporary Authors* contain entries only for people who are now living or have only very recently died. On the other hand, such references as *Who Was Who in America*, the *Dictionary of American Biography*, the *Dictionary of National Biography*, *Composers 1300–1900*, and *European Authors 1000 to 1900* are devoted to people who are no longer living. They also limit their coverage to particular nationalities or professions. People who are not well known nationally or internationally can often be found in reference books emphasizing a single profession. Typical of these are *Contemporary Artists*, the *Biographical Dictionary of Film Directors*, and the *Biographical Encyclopedia of Science and Technology*.

Literary Reference Books. In addition to specialized dictionaries of literary terms and encyclopedias devoted to literature, a number of other useful references are available for almost every aspect of literature.

Collections of quotations and proverbs can be very useful when you are trying to find the source of some famous saying. Most quotation books are arranged by the subject matter of the quotations and contain an author index as well as a key-word or key-idea index. *Bartlett's Familiar Quotations* is different in that it is arranged chronologically by author rather than by subject. Standard quotation books arranged by subject include *Hoyt's New Cyclopedia of Practical Quotations, Stevenson's Home Book of Quotations,* and *Stevenson's Home Book of Proberbs, Maxims, and Familiar Phrases.* Reference materials that specialize in prose quotations are *What They Said in 19--,* a series of annual publications, and the *Dictionary of Thoughts.*

Indexes to literature can help you locate works by theme or setting. They are particularly useful whan an assignment calls for the comparison of two or more works. Among the indexes usually found in libraries are *Granger's Index to Poetry,* the *Poetry Index,* the *Short Story Index, Ottemiller's Index to Plays in Collections,* the *Index to Full Length Plays,* and the

Play Index. The *Fiction Catalog*, which lists a wide range of themes and settings, and *Historical Fiction*, which is concerned only with historical times and settings, are also very useful.

Other literary indexes can help you find book reviews printed in magazines and newspapers. Often these reviews can help you gain a greater understanding of an author's work. Both the *Book Review Digest* and the *Book Review Index* list entries by author, title, and subject. The *Book Review Digest* also gives a short summary of the contents of each book and quotes portions of the reviews. If the complete review is in a magazine or newspaper you cannot obtain, there is usually enough to work with in the *Book Review Digest* itself. The *Book Review Index* gives less information about each book, but covers more titles. It prints the location of reviews that have been listed in the *Book Review Digest*, the *Library Journal*, the *Saturday Review*, and *Choice* throughout all or most of their years of publication. No reviews are given here, only their locations.

EXERCISE D: Using Specialized Dictionaries. Find specialized dictionaries in your library that will give you information about the following items. Record the names and pages of the books you use, and be prepared to describe what you find. *Specific references will vary; factual answers and probable types of sources given. Answers to 3 and 4 appear at the bottom of the following page.*

1. Synonyms for the word *picayune* *trivial, petty, small-minded (thesaurus)*
2. A description of the musical instrument known as a sackbut *medieval forerunner of the trombone (musical dictionary)*
3. The significance of the cult of Vesta in ancient Rome
4. The causes of and treatment for rickets *sweater*
5. The meaning of the French word *chandail* *(French dictionary)*

EXERCISE E: Using Specialized Encyclopedias. Use the specialized encyclopedias in your library to find information about the following topics. Record the encyclopedia, the volume and page, and the name of the article in which the information can be found. *Specific sources will vary; probable types of sources given.*

1. The closing of the theaters in England in 1642 *encyclopedia of drama*
2. The influence of Lorenzo de Medici ("the Magnificent") as a patron of the arts *encyclopedia of art*
3. The role of satellites in modern communications
4. The making of stained glass windows *encyclopedia of art or crafts*
5. The history of the development of computers

3. encyclopedia of science
5. encyclopedia of computers or technology

EXERCISE F: Using Biographical References. Use the biographical references available in your library to find information about the following people. Record the names and pages of the books you use, and be prepared to describe what you find. *Specific sources will vary; probable types of sources given.*

1. Abolitionist Harriet Tubman *biographical dictionary (American history)*
2. Film director Alfred Hitchcock *biographical dictionary (film)*
3. Artist Georgia O'Keeffe *biographical dictionary (art)*
4. Soccer star Pelé *biographical dictionary (sports)*
5. Conductor Sarah Caldwell *biographical dictionary (music)*

EXERCISE G: Using Literary References. Use the quotation books and literary indexes in your library to find information about the following items. Record the books you use.
Specific sources will vary; factual answers and probable types of sources given.
1. Two quotations about patriotism *quotation book*
2. The title and author of the poem beginning, "April is the cruellest month" *The Waste Land by T.S. Eliot (quotation book)*
3. A work of fiction set in Cornwall, England *literary index*
4. Reviews of William Golding's *Lord of the Flies* *literary index or digest*
5. Five novels set during the American Revolution *literary index*

■ Periodicals

Periodicals are magazines and journals that are issued regularly, generally weekly, monthly, or quarterly. The term is usually applied to newspapers as well. Some periodicals, such as *Reader's Digest* and *Life*, are of general interest, while others, such as *Parnassus: Poetry in Review*, are devoted to highly specialized topics. Hundreds of different periodicals on almost every topic are published in the United States alone. Not only are periodicals a source of enjoyment, but they can also be a valuable research aid as well.

Use periodicals to supplement your research with specialized or current information.

Periodicals often contain information that cannot be found elsewhere. Moreover, they are often the only source for the most recent information on a subject. Libraries usually have a special section for these very special research tools.
3. Vesta—protector of hearth; sacred flame at shrine tended by Vestal Virgins (dictionary of mythology) 4. Cause: insufficient vitamin D; treatment: exposure to sunlight, diet rich in vitamin D (medical dictionary)

A number of different indexes make it possible for you to look up information in periodicals by subject or author. Each index analyzes a different selection of periodicals. *The Readers' Guide to Periodical Literature* is very general in its scope, while the *Art Index*, the *Education Index*, the *Humanities Index*, the *General Science Index*, the *Business and Technology Index*, and the *Social Sciences Index* are more specialized. Because all of these indexes have the same publisher, learning to use one enables you to use the others if they are available. Almost every library contains at least *The Readers' Guide to Periodical Literature*, known generally as *The Readers' Guide*.

The Readers' Guide.   This reference indexes about 180 magazines and journals, but no newspapers. It is published twice a month (except in February, July, and August when it is issued once a month). A large hardbound volume that combines all these issues appears annually.

Information in *The Readers' Guide* is arranged alphabetically by author and subject. Some subjects may have various subheadings listed under them. Notice in the following excerpt how the titles of the articles are arranged alphabetically under each heading. Notice also the abbreviations that give extra information and tell you where the article can be found.

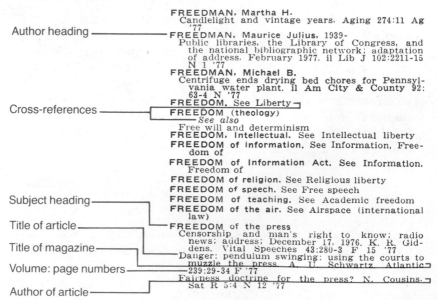

FREEDMAN, Martha H.
   Candlelight and vintage years. Aging 274:11 Ag
   '77
Author heading —————— FREEDMAN, Maurice Julius, 1939-
   Public libraries, the Library of Congress, and
   the national bibliographic network; adaptation
   of address. February 1977. il Lib J 102:2211-15
   N 1 '77
FREEDMAN, Michael B.
   Centrifuge ends drying bed chores for Pennsyl-
   vania water plant. il Am City & County 92:
   63-4 N '77
Cross-references ———— FREEDOM. See Liberty
   FREEDOM (theology)
   ——— See also
   Free will and determinism
FREEDOM, Intellectual. See Intellectual liberty
FREEDOM of information. See Information, Free-
   dom of
FREEDOM of Information Act. See Information,
   Freedom of
FREEDOM of religion. See Religious liberty
FREEDOM of speech. See Free speech
Subject heading —— FREEDOM of teaching. See Academic freedom
FREEDOM of the air. See Airspace (international
   law)
Title of article —— FREEDOM of the press
   Censorship and man's right to know; radio
   news; address; December 17, 1976. K. R. Gid-
Title of magazine —— dens. Vital Speeches 43:280-3 F 15 '77
   Danger: pendulum swinging; using the courts to
Volume: page numbers —— muzzle the press A. U. Schwartz. Atlantic
   ——— 239:29-34 F '77
   Fairness doctrine for the press? N. Cousins.
Author of article —— Sat R 5:4 N 12 '77

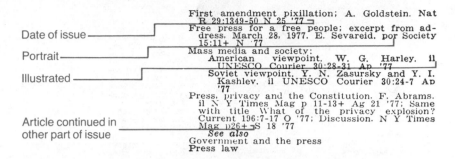

Date of issue

Portrait

Illustrated

Article continued in
other part of issue

First amendment pixillation; A. Goldstein. Nat
R 29:1349-50 N 25 '77
Free press for a free people; excerpt from ad-
dress. March 28, 1977. E. Sevareid. por Society
15:11+ N '77
Mass media and society:
American viewpoint. W. G. Harley. il
UNESCO Courier 30:28-31 Ap '77
Soviet viewpoint. Y. N. Zasursky and Y. I.
Kashlev. il UNESCO Courier 30:24-7 Ap
'77
Press, privacy and the Constitution. F. Abrams.
il N Y Times Mag p 11-13+ Ag 21 '77; Same
with title What of the privacy explosion?
Current 196:7-17 O '77; Discussion. N Y Times
Mag p26+ S 18 '77
See also
Government and the press
Press law

If you are unsure of what an abbreviation in *The Readers'
Guide* means, check at the beginning of the issue. There you
will find a section called *Key to Periodicals Indexed and Other
Symbols*, which will explain all of the abbreviations used in
the guide.

Newspapers.   Major newspapers, such as *The New York
Times*, the *Christian Science Monitor*, the *Wall Street Journal*,
and the *National Observer*, all have their own indexes. However, no general index such as *The Readers' Guide* exists for
newspapers.

Since *The New York Times* is readily available on microfilm, *The New York Times Index* is the newspaper index
found most often in libraries. It indexes articles that have
appeared in this newspaper from 1851 to the present. Not
only can you use the index to keep track of current events,
but you can also use it as a historical record. How, for example, did the nation react to the bombing of Pearl Harbor?
Checking *The New York Times Index* volume for 1941 would
tell you where to look to answer this question.

The articles in the index are arranged alphabetically by
subject. Each article is then *abstracted*—that is, summa-
rized—to help you decide whether the article contains the
information you need. Abstracts for longer articles often
provide so much information that you need not refer to the
newspaper at all. Notice, for example, the thoroughness of
the abstracts for the articles that appeared in *The New York
Times* on December 8, 1941, the day after the bombing of
Pearl Harbor. Notice, also, the frequent use of abbreviations
without periods: *Is* for island, *Gov* for Governor, *reptd* for reported, and so on. As you become more familiar with the index itself, you will also become familiar with the abbreviations that are used.

Abstract of front-page articles →

Japanese attack Hawaii; bomb Pearl Harbor, Ford Is, Wheeler Field, Honolulu munic airport, Hickam Field and U S Navy air repair base, Kaneohe; U S Fleet goes into action; Gov Poindexter declares emergency; attack described; casualties; USS Oklahoma reptd afire; Jap troops gain foothold after initial repulse, Northern Malaya; proceed toward Kota Bharu airdrome; Singapore bombed; Brit planes bomb Jap troopships off Malaya coast presumably heading for Thailand; Japanese invade Thailand; bomb Kowloon, Hong Kong; maps; Guam bombed; Hirohito issues Jap war declaration against U S and Brit; Tojo outlines war plans and policy to Cabinet; advises empire of war, radio s; blames U S; promises victory; Grew gets formal reply to Hull proposals after hostilities start; Jap Govt and Tokyo U S Embassy officials silent on Roosevelt message to Hirohito; Roosevelt conf with Cabinet and Cong leaders; conferees comment; official statement on conf; Roosevelt expected to ask Cong for war declaration; Sens comment; Roosevelt puts U S on full war basis; conf with Churchill and Hawaii Gov Poindexter by phone; full U S embargo on trade with Japan invoked; Amer lumber transport reptd sunk; freighter reptd in distress; Sen Connally comments on attack; Nomura and Kurusu give Hull Japan's reply rejecting U S proposals for multilateral nonaggression pact and ending negotiations; proposals and reply texts; Hull denounces reply; later scores Jap attack on U S; State Dept rept on conf; N Y area reaction to Jap attacks, D 8, p 1; Jap-U S relations since 1853 revd; Jap war declaration text; Sen Walsh on attack; USS Oklahoma described; Australia declares war on Japan; unconfirmed repts announce sinking of Jap aircraft carrier off Hawaii and 2 Brit cruisers, Singapore; Tokyo radio repts Guam surrounded by Jap ships; USS Gen Hugh L Scott rumored sunk; Jap choosing of Sunday for attack discussed; Wake Is rumored occupied; K K Haan, Sino-Korean People's League Wash repr, reveals he warned Sec Stimson in Oct of Jap attack plans; warning based on K Hirota s to Black Dragon Soc, D 8, 2:1-4,6-8; Honolulu harbor, Schofield Barracks, Hickam Field and Pearl Harbor illus; ← Illustrations
N Y C Mayor LaGuardia comments, D 8, 3:1; ← Date, page: column
Japan informed Brit is at war; Craigie instructed to ask for passports; Churchill summons Parliament for formal action; U S expected to assume major burden; Brit press comment; K Ohmori, acting Jap Consul Gen at Chicago, questions Japan's ability to wage long war; German communique refers to Jap-U S hostilities as clashes; scores Roosevelt; Germany believed awaiting word from Japan before acting on Jap-Axis pact; pact article on war obligations quoted; Ital comment on war; D M Nelson holds Jap attack caused by Germany; cites U S stake; Gov Gruening orders 24-hr watch, Alaska; Mrs F D Roosevelt on Jap attack, D 8, 4:1,2,4,5;

Since major newspapers contain much more than the day's news, do not overlook them as a valuable source of information on a wide range of topics.

Pamphlets.   Though not strictly periodicals, pamphlets are similar to newspapers and magazines in that they often contain very recent information. Published by government agencies, private companies, universities, and professional groups, pamphlets can be found on such topics as welfare,

Medicare, state parks, child abuse, and education. Libraries usually store pamphlets in a *vertical file*, a file cabinet with large drawers. Do not hesitate to ask the librarian whether a pamphlet exists that could help you with your topic.

EXERCISE H: Using *The Readers' Guide.* Select a topic related to what you are currently studying in school, to a hobby, to your career goals, or to any other interest you may have. Using *The Readers' Guide*, find and read three articles about your topic. Record both the names and dates of the magazines and the titles and authors of the articles. Then write a short account of what you read.
Answers will vary; a list might be compiled of the most frequently used magazines.

EXERCISE I: Using *The New York Times Index.* Use *The New York Times Index* to find an article on the topic you chose for Exercise H. Find the newspaper in the library and locate the article. Record the exact headline and the author (if given). Then list five facts from the article.
Students might make an oral report from their notes, redoing the news items.

APPLICATION: Comparing General and Specialized Reference Books. Compare the coverage of a topic in a general reference book with the coverage of the same topic in a specialized reference book. Follow these steps.

1. Choose a general reference book available in your school library.
2. Select a topic that interests you and read about it.
3. Record the name of the reference book, the topic, and the pages read.
4. Choose a specialized reference book that contains coverage of the same topic and again read about your topic.
5. Record the name of the specialized reference book and the pages read.
6. Then describe the similarities and differences in topic coverage between the two references.
7. When would the general reference be more useful? When would the specialized reference be more useful?

Answers will vary. Students working in related areas might compare notes in a class discussion. Also, the comparison of the two sources might serve as a writing topic.

Using the Dictionary 20.3

Of all general reference materials, you probably use the dictionary most often. But if you refer to it merely to check the meaning or spelling of words, you are not getting all you can out of this valuable resource. In addition to providing meanings and spellings, a dictionary can show you how to break words into syllables and pronounce them correctly; it can tell you how a word should be used in a sentence. Most dictionaries also show the histories of words; a few can even tell you what a word meant at a particular time in history. In addition, many dictionaries include essential facts about famous people, events, and places and explain the meanings of common abbreviations.

Although most of these features can be found in a typical dictionary, all dictionaries are not the same. This section will describe some of the different kinds of general dictionaries and what they contain. It will also help you learn to use them efficiently.

▪ Kinds of General Dictionaries

There are dictionaries made for almost every audience: for students to use in their studies, for adults to use at home or at work, for scholars to use in their research. There are even dictionaries with more pictures than words for preschool children just learning to read.

The kind of dictionary you use at home, in school, or in the library should be neither too easy nor too difficult for you.

Use a dictionary that suits your present academic needs.

A suitable dictionary should contain all of the words you are likely to encounter in your studies and should explain them to your satisfaction in language you can understand. Thus, a dictionary meant for children will not help you understand all of the words in a novel or science text. On the other hand, a great scholarly dictionary containing thousands of pages would be unnecessary for most of your schoolwork. Nevertheless, you should be aware of the two main kinds of general dictionaries that are available to you so that you know where to go to find the information you need. Basically, general dictionaries are either abridged or unabridged.

Unabridged Dictionaries. *Unabridged* means "not shortened." The word simply tells you that a dictionary is not the shortened version of some larger dictionary. It does *not* mean that the dictionary contains all the words of a language. Unabridged dictionaries generally contain 250,000 to 500,000 words while it is estimated that the English language contains at least 600,000 words. Assembling such great dictionaries takes many years of research and writing. Some words that might have been included are overlooked; others are intentionally excluded. Moreover, English is constantly changing. By the time an unabridged dictionary can be completed and published, thousands of new words have entered the language. Because of this flux, the editors of these dictionaries periodically publish supplements to keep their work up to date and as complete as possible.

Two well-known unabridged dictionaries found in most libraries are *Webster's Third New International Dictionary of the English Language* (published in 1966) and the *Random House Dictionary of the English Language, Unabridged Edition* (published in 1967). You should consult these books whenever you need very specific definitions and extremely detailed information about words. On most occasions, however, your regular dictionary will contain all you need to know.

Notice, in the following example, the detail and thoroughness of an unabridged dictionary's definitions.

EXAMPLE: ¹**but·tress** \'bətrəs\ *n* -ES [ME *butres, boterace,* fr. MF *bouterez,* fr. OF *boterez,* fr. *boter, bouter* to thrust — more at BUTT] **1** : a projecting structure of masonry or wood for supporting or giving stability to a wall or building (as to resist lateral pressure or strain acting at a particular point in one direction) but sometimes serving chiefly for ornament **2** : any of various things that resemble a buttress in appearance: **a** : COUNTERFORT **b** : a projecting part of a mountain or hill **c** : a horny protuberance on a horse's hoof at the heel where the wall bends inward and forward **d** : the broadened basal portion of a tree trunk or a thickened vertical part of it **3** : something that supports, strengthens, or helps to defend ⟨a ~ of the cause of peace⟩ **4** : an abutment built from a river bank to prevent logs in a drive from injuring the bank or jamming

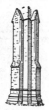

buttress 1

Another well-known unabridged dictionary is the *Oxford English Dictionary*. Its original twelve volumes took more than fifty years to write and were completed in 1928. The work was finally published in 1933 with a supplement volume. Further supplements began to appear in 1972. Probably the most ambitious dictionary ever produced, it differs from the two preceding books in that it is a *historical dictionary*; that is, it organizes a word's meanings by dates. This organization allows you to determine when a word first appeared in written English, what it meant at a particular time and how its meaning changed over the years. Each meaning is followed by dates and examples of the word in use. In the following excerpt from the *Oxford English Dictionary*'s coverage of *pandemonium*, notice how the word was first used by John Milton in 1667. Compare this with a later meaning of the word.

EXAMPLE:

Pandemonium (pæ:ndĭmōᵘ·nĭᵒ̌m). Also -dæ-mon-. [In form, mod.L. f. Gr. παν- all + δαίμων divinity, DEMON.]
1. The abode of all the demons; a place represented by Milton as the capital of Hell, containing the council-chamber of the Evil Spirits; in common use, = hell or the infernal regions.
1667 MILTON *P. L.* I. 756 A solemn Councel forthwith to be held At Pandæmonium, the high Capital Of Satan and his Peers. *Ibid.* x. 424 About the walls Of Pandæmonium, Citie and proud seate Of Lucifer. 1713 ADDISON *Guardian* No. 103 P 4 He would have a large piece of machinery represent the Pan-dæmonium [of Milton]. 1743 CHESTERF. in *Old England* No. 3 Misc. Wks. 1777 I. 116 'This .. is certainly levelled at us ', says a conscious sullen apostate patriot to his fallen brethren in the Pandæmonium. 1831 CARLYLE *Sart. Res.* II. iii, And, in this hag-ridden dream, mistake God's fair living world for a pallid, vacant Hades and extinct Pandemonium.
2. *transf.* A place regarded as resembling Pandemonium: **a.** A centre or head-quarters of vice or wickedness, a haunt of wickedness. **b.** A place or gathering of wild lawless violence, confusion, and uproar.
1779 SWINBURNE *Trav. Spain* xlii. 367 Every province .. would in turn appear a Paradise, and a Pandaemonium. 1800 COLQUHOUN *Comm. Thames* iv. 190 The various ramifications of this Pandæmonium of Iniquity. 1813 *Examiner* 17 May 317/2 The Emperor Tiberius.. wrote to the Senate from his pandæmonium at Capreæ. 1816 BYRON *Dom. Pieces* II. ii, To make a Pandemonium where she dwells, And reign the Hecate of domestic hells. 1827 LYTTON *Pelham* xlix, We found ourselves in that dreary pandaemonium,..a Gin-shop. 1876 BLACK *Madcap V.* vi. 47 She would turn the place into a pandemonium in a week. 1897 F. T. BULLEN *Cruise Cachalot* 155 Ribald songs, quarrelling, and blasphemy made a veritable pandemonium of the place.
c. Wild lawless confusion or uproar, a distracting fiendish ' row '.
1865 PARKMAN *Pioneers Fr.* I. iv. (1885) 55 When night came, it brought with it a pandemonium of dancing and whooping, drumming and feasting. 1897 *Daily News* 29 Nov. 4/5 On Saturday pandemonium again reigned in the Reichsrath.

Dictionaries for Everyday Use. Several companies publish shorter dictionaries especially suited to the needs of the general public and of students. Unless you want special information about a word or need the meaning of a rare word, you will probably find all you need to know in an abridged dictionary. Often called high-school or college dictionaries, these books are designed for everyday use at home, in the office, or in the classroom. Considerably smaller and less expensive than unabridged dictionaries, college dictionaries usually list between 150,000 and 200,000 words; high-school dictionaries list somewhat fewer.

SOME ABRIDGED DICTIONARIES FOR EVERYDAY USE	
High-School Dictionaries	**College Dictionaries**
Webster's New World Dictionary, Students Edition	Webster's New World Dictionary, Second College Edition
The Scott, Foresman Advanced Dictionary	The Random House College Dictionary
The Macmillan Dictionary	The American Heritage Dictionary

EXERCISE A: Comparing Unabridged and Abridged Dictionaries. In a library, compare an unabridged and abridged dictionary by completing the following steps. Be sure to record your findings.

Answers will vary; students should give very specific answers to 3.

1. Write the complete title of each dictionary.
2. Write the number of pages contained in each book.
3. Look up a common word in both dictionaries. How does the coverage differ? Be specific.
4. Find at least three words that are entered in the unabridged dictionary that are not entered in the other.

■ What Student Dictionaries Contain

As you read the following descriptions, keep in mind that all dictionaries are not the same. Apply what you learn here to your own dictionary.

Learn to recognize and use the various features of your own dictionary.

The place to begin learning about any dictionary is in the book's introduction.

Front Matter. A good college or high-school dictionary contains an introduction that explains how to use it efficiently. Here, in addition to a description of all the book's features, you will usually find instructions on how to look up a word, how to find words whose spelling you are unsure of, and how to interpret the pronunciation symbols. A complete pronunciation key and a list of all the abbreviations used throughout the dictionary will also be found in this part of the book.

Main Entries.   In a dictionary, each word and all the information about it are called a *main entry*. The word itself is called the *entry word*. All the entry words are listed in strict letter-by-letter alphabetical order, right to the end of the entry word.

EXAMPLE: Olaf

old

olden

Old English

old-fashioned

old fogy

oldie

An entry word may be a single word, a compound word (two or more words acting as a single word), an abbreviation, a prefix or suffix, or the name of a special event, person, or place. (Some dictionaries do not include names of persons and places. Others put them in separate alphabetical lists at the back of the book.) The following chart shows the different kinds of entry words that may be found in a dictionary.

KINDS OF ENTRY WORDS	
Single Word:	old·en
Compound Word:	Old Guard
Abbreviation:	R.S.V.P.
Prefix:	o·le·o-
Suffix:	-o·ma
Event:	American Revolution
Person:	Doug·lass
Place:	Nan·tuck·et

Preferred and Variant Spellings.   A dictionary is an authority for the spelling of words. Most English words have only one correct spelling, as shown by the entry word. Some words, however, can be spelled in more than one way. The spelling most commonly used is called the *preferred spelling*.

Less commonly used spellings are called *variant spellings*. If the form you are looking up is a variant spelling, the entry will refer you to another entry, the one that begins with the preferred spelling. Here you will also find the definition of the word.

VARIANT SPELLING: **Breu·ghel** (brü′gəl; *occas*. broi′-) *same as* BRUEGEL

PREFERRED   **Brue·gel, Brue·ghel** (brü′gəl; *occas*. broi′-), **Pie·ter** (pē′tər)
SPELLING: 1522?–69; Fl. painter

If a main entry shows two entry words, as the second example above does, the form listed first is usually more common and is, therefore, the preferred spelling. Sometimes a rather uncommon variant spelling or form may be listed only at the end of a main entry, as in the following example.

UNCOMMON VARIANTS: **bar·bell** (bär′bel′) *n.* [BAR¹ +
(DUMB)BELL] a metal bar to which
disks of varying weights are attached
at each end, used for weight-lifting
exercises: also **bar bell, bar-bell**

Syllabification.   Centered dots, spaces, or slashes in an entry word indicate where words are divided into syllables. If words are already hyphenated, hyphens will take the place of these symbols. The word *brother-in-law*, for example, has four syllables: broth·er-in-law. Most, but not all, of these divisions can be used for word breaks at the end of a line of writing. The section on hyphens (Section 15.7) gives specific rules for breaking words into syllables at the ends of lines of writing.

Pronunciation.   Pronunciations appear after most entry words, usually in parentheses or between diagonal lines. Pronunciations usually do not accompany entries that are not full words, such as abbreviations, prefixes, and suffixes. Nor are they usually found with entries that are compound words when the individual words are main entries themselves.

The dictionary indicates how to pronounce words by respelling them in a *phonetic alphabet*. This is a set of letters and special symbols. Each letter and symbol represents one sound. Since phonetic alphabets vary from one dictionary to another, it is important for you to become familiar with the one in your dictionary. A *pronunciation key* at the front or back of your dictionary lists and explains all of the pronunciation symbols used throughout the book. Study this carefully. Most dictionaries for students also provide short pronunciation keys on every other page.

Besides helping you to pronounce the sounds correctly, the dictionary shows you which syllables are stressed. The syllable that gets the most emphasis has a *primary stress*, usually shown by a heavy mark (') after the syllable. Words of more than one syllable may have a *secondary stress*, shown by a shorter, lighter mark (') after the syllable. Unstressed syllables have no stress marks. Again, symbols may vary from one dictionary to another.

When two or more pronunciations of a word are given, the preferred pronunciation is given first. Here are some entries from different dictionaries, showing their pronunciations. Notice not only the stress marks but also how additional pronunciations are indicated.

PRIMARY STRESS ONLY: **dwin·dle** (dwind′əl)

PRIMARY AND SECONDARY STRESSES: **en·gi·neer** (en′jə nir′)

MORE THAN ONE PRONUNCIATION: **ei·ther** (ē′*th*ər, ī′-)

Part-of-Speech Labels and Inflected Forms. The dictionary also tells you how a word can be used in a sentence—whether it functions as a noun, a verb, or as some other part of speech. This information is given in abbreviated form, usually after the pronunciation of a word but sometimes at the end of the entry. Entries of two or more words, such as *pony express* or *bird of paradise*, have no part-of-speech labels because they are always nouns. Some dictionaries also omit part-of-speech labels for the names of people and places since these, too, are always nouns. As you can see in the following example, some words can be more than one part of speech.

out·side (out′sīd′, out′-; *for prep. & adv., usually* out′sīd′) *n.*
1. the outer side, part, or surface; exterior [wash the windows on the *outside*] 2. outward look or appearance [a man who seems jolly on the *outside*] 3. any place or area not inside [the prisoners got little news from the *outside*] —*adj.* 1. of or on the outside; outer [the *outside* layer] 2. coming from or situated beyond given limits; from some other place, person, group, etc. [to accept no *outside* help] 3. extreme; maximum [an *outside* estimate] 4. mere; slight [an *outside* chance] —*adv.* 1. on or to the outside 2. beyond certain limits 3. outdoors [go play *outside*] —*prep.* 1. on or to the outer side of [leave it *outside* the door] 2. beyond the limits of [traveling *outside* the country] —**at the outside** at the very most —**outside of** 1. outside 2. [Colloq.] other than; except for

Part-of-speech labels

When it is necessary, the dictionary shows inflected forms after the part-of-speech label. An inflected form may be the plural form of a noun, the different forms of an adjective or adverb, or the parts of a verb.

PLURAL FORM OF NOUN: **dis cour te sy** (dis kėr/tə sē), *n., pl.* -sies.

FORMS OF ADJECTIVE: **ti·ny** (tī/nē) *adj.* -ni·er, -ni·est

PARTS OF VERB: **in·fu·ri·ate** (in fyoor/ē āt/) *v.t.,* in·fu·ri·at·ed, in·fu·ri·at-ing.

As the inflected forms in these examples indicate, the plural of *discourtesy* is *discourtesies,* the different forms of *tiny* are *tinier* and *tiniest,* and the parts of *infuriate* are *infuriated* and *infuriating.*

Etymologies.   The origin and history of a word is called its *etymology.* In dictionaries the etymology of an entry word usually appears in brackets soon after the pronunciation or part-of-speech label. In some dictionaries, the etymology comes at the end of a main entry.

The historical information in an etymology is organized in reverse chronological order. This information is written in a code made up of symbols, abbreviations, and different kinds of type. One kind of type may indicate, for example, a cross-reference to another etymology. As with pronunciation symbols, the codes for etymologies vary from one dictionary to another. It is best that you study the introduction in your particular dictionary to understand the code.

Knowing a word's etymology can often help you remember its present meaning. In the following example, see how the etymology can help you remember what *anarchy* means.

an·ar·chy (-kē) *n., pl.* -chies [< Gr. < *an-,* without + *archos,*————Etymology
leader] **1.** the complete absence of government **2.** political disorder and violence **3.** disorder or confusion in any kind of activity

The etymology indicates that *anarchy* comes from a Greek word that came from two other Greek words, *an-* meaning "without" and *archos* meaning "leader."

Definitions.   Many words in English have multiple meanings. These meanings or senses are called *definitions.* All meanings for the same part of speech are grouped together in the dictionary and numbered consecutively. Sometimes, a definition will be broken into parts to show different shades of meaning; then the different parts will be arranged by letters: *a, b, c,* and so on. One dictionary, for instance, lists forty-four definitions for the little word *set*; most of these are broken down further into as many as eight parts.

Most dictionaries help clarify the different meanings of an entry word with a phrase or sentence showing the word in use. The following entry for *render,* for example, lists eleven different definitions (one with two parts) and gives six examples of the word in use.

Definition ──────

Example of word in use ──────

Definition────── with two parts

ren·der (ren′dər) *vt.* [< OFr., ult. < L. < *re-,* back + *dare,* to give] **1.** to hand over, or submit, as for approval, consideration, payment, etc. [*render* an account of your actions; *render* a bill] **2.** to give (*up*); surrender [to *render* up a city to the enemy] **3.** to give in return [*render* good for evil] **4.** to give or pay as due [to *render* thanks] **5.** to cause to be; make [to *render* one helpless] **6.** *a*) to give (aid, etc.) *b*) to do (a service, etc.) **7.** to represent, as in a drawing; depict **8.** to recite (a poem, etc.), play (music), act (a role), etc. **9.** to translate [to *render* a Spanish song into English] **10.** to deliver (a judgment, verdict, etc.) **11.** to melt down (fat) —**ren′der·a·ble** *adj.* — **ren′der·er** *n.* —**ren′der·ing** *n.*

When you are checking a word that can have more than one meaning, read each definition carefully to find the one that matches the context of the word in the sentence you are reading or writing. You should be able to substitute the correct definition for the word in the sentence. You might, for example, have to decide which definition of *render* can be substituted for the word in the following sentence.

SENTENCE: *Rendering* e.e. cummings' poems into another language is almost impossible.

Only definition 9, "to translate," makes sense when substituted.

Usage and Field Labels.   Words and meanings that are considered acceptable in formal situations by most speakers and writers of a language are said to be standard usage. Dictionaries indicate nonstandard words and meanings with *usage labels,* such as *Slang, Informal* (or *Colloquial*), *Dialect,* and *British.* The label lets you know that a particular word or meaning may be unsuitable or not understood in certain situations.

Other words or meanings are restricted to a particular occupation, activity, or branch of knowledge. Dictionaries indicate this restricted usage with *field labels,* such as *Radio & TV, Baseball,* or *Philosophy.*

Both usage labels and field labels usually appear before the definitions to which they apply.

click (klik) *n.* [echoic] **1.** a slight, sharp sound like that of a door latch snapping into place **2.** a mechanical device, as a catch or pawl, that clicks into position **3.** *Phonet.* a sound made ⎯ Field label
by drawing the breath into the mouth and snapping the tongue
from the roof of the mouth —*vi.* **1.** to make a click **2.** [Col-⎯⎯⎯ Usage label
loq.] *a)* to be suddenly understood *b)* to work or get along together successfully *c)* to be a success —*vt.* to cause to click —**click′er** *n.*

Idioms. An *idiom* is an expression that has a meaning different from that which the individual words would literally suggest. Expressions such as "watch your step," "on the go," and "over and above" are idioms.

Idioms are usually found in alphabetical order near the end of a main entry or at the end of the definitions for a particular part of speech. The key word in the expression determines the main entry with which the idiom appears. If the idiom seems to have two or more key words, as in "watch your step," look under the noun first (*step*). If there are no nouns in the idiom, as in "over and above," look under the first key word (*over*).

The following example shows the many idioms that one dictionary lists under the entry word *rope*.

rope (rōp), *n., v.,* **roped, rop ing.** —*n.*
1 a strong, thick line or cord, made by twisting smaller cords together. 2 U.S. lasso. 3 number of things twisted or strung together: *a rope of pearls.* 4 cord or noose for hanging a person. 5 death by being hanged. 6 a sticky, stringy mass: *Molasses candy forms a rope.* 7 **give one act** freely. 8 **know the ropes or learn the ropes, a** know or learn the various ropes of a ship. **b** INFORMAL. know or learn about a business or activity. 9 **the end of one's rope,** the end of one's resources, activities, etc. —*v.t.* 1 tie, bind, or fasten with a rope. 2 enclose or mark off with a rope. 3 U.S. catch (a horse, calf, etc.) with a lasso; lasso. 4 **rope in,** INFORMAL. get or take in by tricking. [Old English *rāp*] ⎯⎯⎯ Idioms

Derived Words or Run-on Entries. Words formed by adding a common suffix, such as *-ly* or *-ness*, to an entry word are called *derived words* or *run-on entries*. The suffixes are added to change words from one part of speech to another. Derived words are found at the end of a main entry and are not defined. They simply appear with their part-of-speech labels and, sometimes, with their pronunciation. If you are not sure of the meaning of a derived word, look up the meaning of the suffix and combine that with the meaning of the entry word.

gos·sip (gäs′əp) *n.* [< Late OE. *godsibbe*, godparent: see GOD & SIB] **1.** [Obs. or Dial.] *a)* a godparent *b)* a close friend **2.** one who chatters or repeats idle talk and rumors, esp. about others' private affairs **3.** *a)* such talk or rumors *b)* chatter —*vi.* to be a gossip; indulge in idle talk or rumors about others —**gos′sip·er** *n.* —**gos′sip·y** *adj.*————————————Derived words

Synonymies. A *synonym* is a word closely related but not identical in meaning to another word. In some dictionaries you will see below the entry a block of words beginning with the abbreviation *SYN.* Here the differences in meaning among synonyms are explained. Such explanations are called *synonymies. Antonyms*, or words opposite in meaning, are sometimes found here, too.

ma·ni·a (mā′nē ə, mān′yə) *n.* [ME. < LL. < Gr. *mania*, madness < *mainesthai*, to rage < IE. base *men-, to think, be mentally excited, whence MIND] **1.** wild or violent mental disorder; specif., the manic phase of manic-depressive psychosis, characterized generally by abnormal excitability, exaggerated feelings of well-being, flight of ideas, excessive activity, etc. **2.** an excessive, persistent enthusiasm, liking, craving, or interest; obsession; craze [a *mania* for dancing] *SYN.*—**mania** in its basic sense (see definition above) describes the phase of manic-depressive psychosis that is distinguished from *depression;* **delirium** denotes a temporary state of extreme mental disturbance (marked by restlessness, incoherence, and hallucinations) that occurs during fevers, in alcoholic psychosis, etc.; **frenzy,** not used technically in psychiatry, implies extreme emotional agitation in which self-control is lost; **hysteria** is applied in psychiatry to certain psychogenic disorders characterized by excitability, anxiety, sensory and motor disturbances, and the involuntary simulation of blindness, deafness, etc. In extended use, **mania** suggests a craze for something [a *mania* for surfing], **delirium,** rapturous excitement [a *delirium* of joy], and **hysteria,** an outburst of wild, uncontrolled feeling [she laughed and cried in her *hysteria*]——————Synonymy

EXERCISE B: Alphabetizing Entry Words. Put the following words in letter-by-letter alphabetical order on your paper as you would find them in a dictionary.

1. turn *4*
2. Turkish Empire *2*
3. turpentine *7*
4. tutti-frutti *10*
5. turntable *6*
6. tutor *9*
7. turkey *1*
8. tussock moth *8*
9. turncoat *5*
10. turmeric *3*

EXERCISE C: Determining Preferred Spellings. Use your dictionary to determine whether the following words are preferred or variant spellings. If the word is considered preferred, write *preferred* on your paper; if it is a variant, write the preferred spelling.

Answers to exercises on pages 547–548 based on Webster's New World Dictionary of the American Language, Second College Edition.

1. theatre *theater*
2. gelatin preferred
3. glamorous preferred
4. ameba *amoeba*
5. hooves *hoofs*

6. heartsease preferred
7. enjambement *enjambment*
8. interrogation mark preferred
9. inclose *enclose*
10. glamor *glamour*

EXERCISE D: Understanding Pronunciations. Copy from your dictionary the preferred pronunciations for the following words. Be prepared to pronounce them aloud in class.

1. recognize *rek' - əg - nīz'*
2. usually *yōō' - zhoo - wəl - lē'*
3. literature *lit' - ər - ə - chər*
4. remembrance *ri - mem' - brəns*
5. sophomore *säf' - ə - môr'*

6. temperament *tem' - prə - mənt*
7. surprise *sər - prīz'*
8. arthritis *är - thrīt' - is*
9. February *fcb' - rə - wer' - ē*
10. history *his' - tə - rē*

EXERCISE E: Finding Part-of-Speech Labels. Use your dictionary to write the part-of-speech labels for each of the following entry words. After each label record on your paper the number of definitions listed for that part of speech.

1. hitch vi.–4; vt.–4; n.–7
2. inside n.–3; adj.–5; adv.–2; prep.–2
3. range vt.–9; vi.–6; n.–16
4. run vi.–31; vt.–25; n.–25; adj.–4
5. sea bass n.–1

EXERCISE F: Interpreting Etymologies. Find the etymologies for the following words in your dictionary. Write a sentence describing the origin and history of each on your paper.
Answers on page T-127.

1. derrick
2. radar
3. candidate
4. peninsula
5. innocuous

6. dodo
7. dandelion
8. verbose
9. mellifluous
10. sophomore

EXERCISE G: Applying Definitions to Words in Context. Look up the word *cross* in your dictionary. Decide which definition of *cross* applies in each of the following sentences. Then write the appropriate definitions on your paper.

1. Sean sat back leisurely and *crossed* his legs. *"to place across"*
2. She became *cross* when the waiter forgot to take our order. *"ill-tempered"*
   "to go from one
3. The explorer *crossed* the desert by camel. *side to the other"*
4. A shoat is not a *cross* between a sheep and a goat. *"hybrid"*
5. The *crossed* wires caused a short. *"to bring into contact"*

548   *Library and Reference Skills*

EXERCISE H: Finding Usage Labels and Field Labels. Use your dictionary to answer the following questions about usage labels and field labels.

1. What is the *Informal* or *Colloquial* meaning of *railroad?*
2. What is a *British* usage of the word *boot?*
3. What is a *pass* in the field of *Baseball?* a walk
4. What is a *period* in *Physics?* time between successive phases of a cycle
5. What does *sharp* mean in *Music?* higher in pitch by a half-step
   1. to rush or force through   2. trunk of an automobile

EXERCISE I: Finding the Meaning of Idioms. Use your dictionary to learn the meaning of each of the following idioms. Write the meanings on your paper and record the entry word under which you find each idiom.

1. shake down blackmail–shake   4. have it in for
2. under one's thumb   5. steal one's thunder
3. kick the bucket to die–bucket   2. under another's influence–thumb
4. hold a grudge against–have   5. use of another's idea without giving credit–thunder

EXERCISE J: Finding Derived Words. List the following entry words on your paper. Next to each, write the words your dictionary lists as derived words.

1. persuasive persuasively, persuasiveness   4. miscalculate miscalculation
2. mope moper, mopey, mopish, mopishly 5. giddy giddily, giddiness
3. circumnavigate circumnavigation, circumnavigator

APPLICATION: Using Your Dictionary Efficiently. Use your dictionary to answer the following questions. Write the answers on your paper and record the amount of time you spend finding each answer.
This might be used as a section test; factual answers given.
1. When did Vincent van Gogh die? 1890
2. Where is Leipzig? East Germany
3. What field labels do you find under *field?*
4. When did the Vandals sack Rome? 455 A.D.
5. What are some synonyms of *avoid?* escape, evade, elude
6. According to its etymology, what did *lady* originally mean? laf dig—bread kneader
7. What are ten idioms listed under *hand?*
8. What usage label is listed for the first meaning of *wight?* What does this label mean? Obs.—obsolete, no longer used
9. How many syllables are in the word *meteorologically?* Which syllable has a primary stress? Which has a secondary stress? eight/log/me
10. Which is the variant spelling, *litre* or *liter?* litre
3. heraldry, mathematics, physics, TV, baseball, cricket
7. first hand, at hand, second hand, by hand, force one's hand, + 41 others

UNIT

Composition

Chapter 21

The Right Words and Tone

Good writing uses neither too many nor too few words. Instead, each word serves a purpose. When you write well, your words will tend to be specific, vivid, and exact, as well as varied and appropriate. Your choice of words will reflect your awareness of the reader's knowledge, background, and perspective. In good writing, all your words should work together to create a unified tone, or impression, that is suitable for your readers.

The sections in this chapter will explain the way in which you can use the power of words to capture the meaning you want to express. They will also explain how being direct and precise can help you make your writing more effective. Finally, the last section will look at the issue of tone, the creation of a consistent impression for an audience.

21.1 Writing Concisely

In your sentences, you should choose your words carefully. If your words state your points clearly and briefly, your ideas will be easier to read and understand.

All your words should serve a constructive purpose. Although the complexity of your sentences will vary, you should look for the most direct way to express an idea. As you write and revise, you should also be careful to avoid weakening the meaning of words by saying the same thing more than once. Expressing an idea directly once is better than saying it indirectly twice. This section explains how to identify and eliminate unnecessary words to make your sentences concise.

■ Deadwood

Unnecessary words that take up space without adding meaning are called *deadwood*. Deadwood includes hedging words, made up of unnecessary qualifying expressions, and empty words that add nothing to your ideas. Deadwood can make sentences meaningless and irritate a reader who is trying to understand the ideas that are actually hidden by all the words.

Eliminate hedging words and empty words from your sentences.

A sentence with hedging words makes a statement and then waters it down by adding a qualifying word or phrase. Hedging words suggest that you do not have enough confidence in your ideas to make a strong statement about them. Sometimes you need to qualify a statement, but most often you should strive to make your sentences as direct as possible.

While hedging words dilute the meaning of a sentence, empty words contribute nothing to the ideas you want to present. Sentences with empty words may be long and sound impressive. However, when you examine them, you will realize you can express the same idea more concisely.

Hedging words and empty words are not difficult to identify. The following chart gives examples that can help you recognize both kinds of deadwood.

RECOGNIZING DEADWOOD	
Hedging Words	**Empty Words**
it seems that	it is a fact that
quite	it is also true that
somewhat	as I said before
rather	on account of the fact that
almost	despite the fact that
kind of	the reason was because
sort of	the area of
tends to	the thing is
it is my opinion that	to the extent that
in my opinion	needless to say
I think that	by way of

You can learn to eliminate deadwood from your sentences as you write and as you revise. Begin by questioning the point of your words and determining whether all of the words contribute to your ideas. Deadwood usually sounds awkward and indirect. When you find deadwood in a sentence, you should remove it. Sometimes you can simply delete the hedging words or empty words. Other times you will need to reword the sentence.

In the following examples notice that deadwood can appear anywhere in a sentence.

WITH DEADWOOD: *What I want* for my birthday, *I think,* is a typewriter *for the reason that* I *tend to* type faster than I write.

CONCISE: For my birthday, I want a typewriter because I type faster than I write.

WITH DEADWOOD: He is *of the opinion that* San Raphael's students are better players.

CONCISE: He believes that San Raphael's students are better players.

WITH DEADWOOD: She acted *sort of* like a clown when she tried to roll off the diving board.

CONCISE: She acted like a clown when she tried to roll off the diving board.

EXERCISE A: Removing Deadwood. Each of the following sentences contains deadwood. Identify the hedging words and the empty words. Then write the sentences on your paper, eliminating the deadwood.
Revisions may vary; samples given. Each problem is identified in parentheses.
EXAMPLE: I became somewhat frightened to the extent that I shook and stuttered.

I became so frightened that I shook and stuttered.

1. ~~There were~~ three ~~rather~~ sinister men﹐ standing in a doorway. *were (empty/hedging)*
2. ~~It is a fact that~~ to buy a new stereo, Sara saved half of her allowance. *(empty)*
3. ~~On account of the fact that﹐~~they can eat wooden beams and supports, termites must be exterminated. *Because (empty)*
4. ~~It seems that~~ the early pioneers came to America with ~~quite~~ high hopes of being free. *(hedging/hedging)*

5. Most computers, ~~I think,~~ can calculate and print figures ~~to the extent that they are~~ faster than any human. abili-ties to do so. *(hedging/empty/empty)*
6. The convict escaped by ~~way of~~ following a ~~somewhat~~ lonely country road. *(empty/hedging)*
7. When a ~~rather~~ large ship enters the harbor, tugboats ~~kind of~~ crowd around it. *(hedging/hedging)*
8. ~~There is~~ nothing, more disappointing to me than a friend who ~~tends to make~~ excuses for staying out of school.
9. ~~The reason~~ we stayed home ~~was~~ because the rainstorm spoiled the plans for a camp-out. *(empty/empty)*
10. ~~As I said before, the thing is~~ the coach should not allow tardiness. *(empty/empty)*

8. is/makes *(empty/hedging)*

■ Wordiness

Besides deleting hedging words and empty words, you can make your sentences more concise by looking for simpler ways to express your ideas. Often you can shorten clauses to phrases and phrases to single-word modifiers.

Reduce a wordy clause or phrase to a shorter structure or to a single word.

Adjective clauses and prepositional phrases can add important details to your writing, but they can often be replaced with structures or words that provide the same details more effectively.

Wordy Clauses. Adjective clauses add words that are not always needed to a sentence. Words such as *who is* or *which are*, the subject and verb beginning many adjective clauses, make a sentence sound drawn out. In some sentences you will want to simplify adjective clauses by omitting the subject and verb.

EXAMPLE: The young man *who was wrestling with the grocery cart* looked confused. (Omit the subject and verb of the clause to reduce the clause to a participial phrase.)

The young man *wrestling with the grocery cart* looked confused.

In the following examples, wordy adjective clauses are followed by shortened versions. Notice that adjective clauses can be reduced to participial phrases, prepositional phrases, appositive phrases, part of a compound verb or complement, or a single-word modifier.

WORDY: Explorers discovered a passage *that went through the mountains.*

CONCISE: Explorers discovered a passage *through the mountains.* (prepositional phrase)

WORDY: Brasilia, *which is the capital city of Brazil,* lies many miles inland.

CONCISE: Brasilia, *the capital city of Brazil,* lies many miles inland. (appositive)

WORDY: My grandmother, *who gave me Forever Amber,* also told me the story.

CONCISE: My grandmother *gave me Forever Amber* and told me the story. (part of a compound verb)

WORDY: The teacher *who was a coach on an Olympic team* was also a player on an Olympic team.

CONCISE: The teacher was *a coach* and a player on an Olympic team. (part of a compound complement)

WORDY: We could not lift the chest, *which was heavy.*

CONCISE: We could not lift the *heavy* chest. (single-word modifier)

Wordy Phrases. Sometimes you can replace a prepositional phrase with a single-word modifier, a noun, or a pronoun to create a shorter, clearer sentence.

WORDY: Detectives discovered that the name *of the suspect* was Smith.

CONCISE: Detectives discovered that the *suspect's* name was Smith. (reduced to an adjective)

WORDY: Aunt Bess moves *in a slow manner.*

CONCISE: Aunt Bess moves *slowly.* (reduced to an adverb)

WORDY: He sent many letters *to her* and hoped that she would visit.

CONCISE: He sent *her* many letters and hoped that she would visit. (reduced to a pronoun)

WORDY: Volunteers brought books and magazines *for the patients* to read.

CONCISE: Volunteers brought *the patients* books and magazines to read. (reduced to a noun)

EXERCISE B: Reducing Wordy Clauses and Phrases.

Each of the following sentences contains a wordy clause or phrase that is underlined. Rewrite each sentence to make it more concise.
Revisions may vary; samples given.

EXAMPLE: Vandals threw paint onto a car which was parked.

Vandals threw paint onto a parked car.

1. Many boats ~~which are~~ floating on the bay are anchored to buoys.
2. Almost half of ~~the money which was~~ the couple's income last year was paid in taxes.
3. Some of ~~the fur on our dog~~ has fallen out in clumps.
4. ~~The~~ hat ~~which was on his head~~ blew off and landed in a pool of water. *His*
5. Grandpa's favorite movie, ~~which is~~ an old silent comedy, will be shown this week on television.
6. A truck stopped and offered a ride ~~to us~~ into town. *us*
7. The puzzled expression ~~which was revealed~~ in my eyes made the stranger think that I had not heard his question.
8. The exhibit of dinosaur bones ~~in the museum~~ attracted people of all ages. *museum's*
9. Dr. Harris, ~~who~~ buys hand-carved statuettes, sells them to his friends. *and*
10. That species of flower ~~that was endangered~~ is now thriving in the wild. *endangered*

3. our dog's fur

■ Redundancy

Redundancy is the unnecessary repetition of an idea. Like deadwood and wordiness, it can weaken the expression of your ideas.

Eliminate redundant words, phrases, and clauses from your sentences.

Redundant Words.   Redundant words repeat the meaning of other words in the sentence. Adjectives that repeat the meaning of nouns and adverbs that repeat the meaning of verbs should be eliminated. The nouns and verbs should be left to do their own work in conveying meaning.

In the following examples, the adjectives repeat the definition of the nouns and should thus be eliminated.

REDUNDANT: He has studied *past* history extensively.

CONCISE: He has studied history extensively.

REDUNDANT: The Greeks celebrated their *successful* victory with food and dance.

CONCISE: The Greeks celebrated their victory with food and dance.

If an adverb repeats the definition of a verb, as in the following examples, you should delete the adverb.

REDUNDANT: They screamed *loudly* at the sight of the fake mouse.

CONCISE: They screamed at the sight of the fake mouse.

REDUNDANT: The boys advanced *forward* and shook their fists.

CONCISE: The boys advanced and shook their fists.

Redundant Phrases. Redundant prepositional phrases can clutter your sentences with ideas that have already been expressed by other words in the sentence. You should examine your sentences for these repetitious phrases and remove them.

REDUNDANT: Pat's face turned red *in color*, and he ran from the room.

CONCISE: Pat's face turned red, and he ran from the room.

REDUNDANT: She had an idea *in her mind* that would solve the problem.

CONCISE: She had an idea that would solve the problem.

Redundant Clauses. Redundant clauses can make sentences illogical or even pointless. They offer explanations that are not explanations at all, just repetitions of the ideas in the main clauses. You should delete redundant clauses either by letting the main clause stand alone or by adding a meaningful subordinate clause. The following examples show both ways to correct redundant clauses.

REDUNDANT: The television did not work because it was broken.

CONCISE: The television did not work.

CONCISE WITH TWO IDEAS: The television did not work because the channel selector was broken.

REDUNDANT: The soccer team played poorly because the team did not do well.

CONCISE: The soccer team played poorly.

CONCISE WITH TWO IDEAS: The soccer team played poorly because half of the players were sick.

REDUNDANT: The child asked unanswerable questions that no one could answer.

CONCISE: The child asked unanswerable questions.

CONCISE WITH TWO IDEAS: The child asked unanswerable questions that vexed his parents.

EXERCISE C: Avoiding Redundancy. Each of the following sentences contains a redundant word, phrase, or clause. Write each sentence on your paper, eliminating the redundancy. *Revisions may vary for some items; samples given for all.*

1. The car was so dark ~~in color~~ that it was hard to see when parked at night.
2. After sitting in silence for most of the school year, Jeff finally spoke ~~out loud~~ to the whole class.
3. We like the incumbent candidate ~~who is now in office~~.
4. When he was finally alone ~~by himself~~, Jeb took out a book and settled down to read.
5. On their way to their lockers the girls stamped ~~noisily~~ by our room.
6. He was a negligent driver ~~because he was careless~~.
7. We were assigned a biography ~~about the life~~ of Abraham Lincoln.
8. To find my keys, I retraced my steps ~~back~~ to my front door.
9. The wake from the river ~~caused a flood that overflowed~~ the town. *flooded*
10. Jennifer's report card revealed ~~an excess of~~ too many absences.

■ Other Problems with Conciseness

Two other problems with conciseness are overuse of the passive voice and the use of nouns and verbs when just a verb would do. Verbs in the passive voice require more words than verbs in the active voice do. Using a verb and noun when you could express the same idea with a single verb also creates unnecessarily wordy sentences. Learn to recognize these weaknesses in your sentences and remove them.

Eliminate unnecessary uses of the passive voice and of verb/ noun constructions in your sentences.

Passive Voice.   Verbs in the passive voice increase the number of words in a sentence. They also move the doer of the action from the beginning of the sentence to the middle or end. By lengthening and inverting a sentence, verbs in the passive voice can confuse a reader. Notice the difference between a verb in the passive voice and a verb in the active voice.

PASSIVE VOICE: The mistakes on the report cards *have been made* by the computer.

ACTIVE VOICE: The computer *has made* mistakes on the report cards.

Although occasionally you will need to use the passive voice, you should replace verbs in the passive voice with verbs in the active voice whenever you can, as in the following examples. Notice the addition of a new subject, the doer of the action, in the second example.

PASSIVE VOICE: The machine *can be used* by you to polish floors or wash carpets.

ACTIVE VOICE: You *can use* the machine to polish floors or wash carpets.

PASSIVE VOICE: The ball *was passed* to Rodriguez.

ACTIVE VOICE: Grossi *passed* the ball to Rodriguez.

Verb/Noun Constructions.   Phrases using verbs such as *have, give,* and *hold* followed by nouns sound impressive at first. On rereading, however, you will often see that the use of both a verb and a noun is heavy-handed and that the idea can be expressed more clearly with only a verb. By replacing the longer construction with a verb that carries the same meaning you can make your sentences more direct and concise. Notice the difference in sound and length in the following pairs of sentences.

WORDY: She *will give help* to you if you ask her.

CONCISE: She *will help* you if you ask her.

WORDY: The club plans to *hold discussions* on the new rules.

CONCISE: The club plans to *discuss* the new rules.

EXERCISE D: Replacing Verbs in the Passive Voice and Unnecessary Verb/Noun Constructions. Each of the following sentences contains either a verb in the passive voice or an unnecessary verb/noun construction. Write each sentence on your paper, making it more direct and concise. *The department will*
Revisions will vary; samples given.
1. Several new courses will be offered next fall. *offer several . . .*
2. Fund raising and the election of officers are included in this week's agenda. *This week's agenda includes fund raising and . . .*
3. The new counselor intends to~~provide assistance to~~ unemployed students. *assist*
4. Everyone will be required to write a library paper for Ms. Sanchez. *Ms. Sanchez will require everyone . . .*
5. The President~~delivered an address to~~ the union leaders. *addressed*
6. The nurse will~~carry out inquiries~~ about the nature of his illness. *inquire*
7. The speaker agreed to~~give answers to~~ questions from the audience. *answer*
8. Three new members have been admitted to the club.
9. A buffet dinner will be served by the staff at midnight.
10. That book~~provides a summary of~~ the Battle of Britain.
8. The club has admitted . . . 9. The staff will serve . . . 10. summarizes

APPLICATION: Writing Concise Sentences in Compositions. The following composition contains deadwood, wordy clauses and phrases, redundancy, verbs in the passive voice, and wordy verb/noun constructions. Copy the composition onto your paper, making it more concise.
Revisions will vary; samples given.

(1) ~~During the time that~~ he walked down the long, dark corridor, Ted thought he heard ~~a noise that was like~~ the sound of a window opening. (2) He~~was of the opinion~~ that ~~there was~~ someone else~~besides himself~~ in the empty building.
1. As   2. believed/was

(3) ~~There was~~ another noise ~~that~~ sounded sharply. (4) A moment later,~the sound of a window opening ~~repeated~~ again. (5) This ~~was the~~ time ~~that~~ Ted was sure of it. (6) Someone was trying to ~~gain entrance by breaking~~ into the building.
   (7) Ted had to ~~reach a decision about the idea of~~ what to do. (8) He knew that ~~there was~~ no one else ~~who~~ was in the building so ~~no one could be called to help him.~~ (9) In addition, if he made any ~~audible~~ noises that ~~the intruder could hear,~~ he might cause a confrontation ~~to happen.~~
   (10) ~~The action was chosen that Ted thought was sort of safest.~~ (11) He tiptoed as noiselessly as he could ~~walk,~~ and ~~he~~ reached ~~a door that was~~ an exit without being seen or heard. (12) Opening the door carefully, Ted stepped outside and broke into a ~~fast~~ run. (13) Within seconds, he found a telephone and dialed the ~~number for~~ police ~~emergencies.~~

3. Then   4. he heard   6. break   7. decide   8. he couldn't call for help
10. Ted chose the safest action.

21.2   Writing Precisely

Every time you write a sentence, your aim should be to make your reader understand your thought, feeling, or intention. You cannot rely on your gestures, facial expressions, pauses, or the rising and falling of your voice to communicate your meaning. Instead, you must work with words on the paper. You can learn to take advantage of the many words in the English language to make your writing more precise. First, however, you must think about words as you use them every day. Then, master a few useful principles practiced by experienced writers. These principles include the use of specific words, the creation of lively expressions, and the use of a variety of words.

■ Specific Versus General Language

Specific words have much more impact on a reader than general words do because specific words help a reader to visualize what you are describing. In the following pages, you will learn how to replace weak, general nouns and verbs with precise ones and how to replace vague adjectives with specific ones. As you will see, many of the skills are similar to those used in writing concise sentences.

Avoiding Weak Nouns.   Although sometimes a general noun will be exactly the word you want, you will usually gain accuracy by using a more specific noun.

Choose specific nouns to give the reader a clearer understanding of your ideas.

For example, if you are writing about a *coffee shop, hamburger stand,* or *steakhouse,* use one of these specific nouns rather than the general word *restaurant.* Instead of saying you watched a *television show,* you can indicate what kind of show you watched with the same number of words by saying *situation comedy, game show,* or *crime drama.* In the following sentences, notice that the specific nouns improve the clarity of the sentences.

GENERAL: Dr. West had practiced his theory at several *educational institutions.*

SPECIFIC: Dr. West had practiced his theory at several *colleges* and *universities.*

GENERAL: Most students claimed to have gained *something* from the exercise class.

SPECIFIC: Most students claimed to have gained *firm muscles* and *endurance* from the exercise class.

Avoiding Weak Verbs. Weak verbs include unnecessary linking verbs, verbs unnecessarily in the passive voice, or drab, general verbs.

Use action verbs, verbs in the active voice, and specific verbs to make your writing precise.

Some linking verbs are necessary, but others sap the action and energy from your sentences. Frequently, you can replace a linking verb and a noun with a specific action verb related in meaning to the noun.

LINKING VERB: His comment *was* an insult to my aunt.

ACTION VERB: His comment *insulted* my aunt.

LINKING VERB: Many coastal settlements *were* the victims of pirates.

ACTION VERB: Pirates *victimized* many coastal settlements.

Just as you may sometimes find linking verbs useful, you may sometimes want to use the passive voice of a verb. The passive voice focuses the reader's attention on the receiver of the action, as in this sentence: *Her collie was hit by a car.* If you do not want to highlight the receiver of the action, you will generally find the active voice more useful. Notice how the following verbs sound more definite and direct in the active voice than in the passive.

PASSIVE VOICE: A dress code *was established* by the school board.

ACTIVE VOICE: The school board *established* a dress code.

PASSIVE VOICE: An aria from *Aida was sung* by Beverly Sills.

ACTIVE VOICE: Beverly Sills *sang* an aria from *Aida.*

Like action verbs and verbs in the active voice, specific, colorful verbs give a reader sharp pictures and vivid impressions. Commonplace verbs, such as *say, speak, walk, go, cry,* and *move,* are frequently useful and appropriate. In many sentences, however, you should try to express action more precisely with verbs that go a step beyond the general action to indicate exactly how someone spoke, walked, or moved. More specific verbs will appeal to the reader's sense of sight, sound, smell, taste, or touch. Thus, *clang, buzz, rustle, creak, thump* help a reader hear in a way that the general verb *sound* does not. You can replace a general verb with a specific verb by attempting to capture the physical or mental action accurately. Notice that the specific verbs in the following sentences spark a reader's interest more than the general verbs do.

GENERAL: She *ran* from the starting line as the gun *went* off.

SPECIFIC: She *dashed* from the starting line as the gun *exploded.*

GENERAL: In the middle of the night the doorbell *rang.*

SPECIFIC: In the middle of the night the doorbell *chimed.*

GENERAL: He watched her *walk* down the hall.

SPECIFIC: He watched her *stroll* down the hall.

Avoiding Vague Adjectives.   Adjectives should sharpen or adjust the meaning of the words they modify. Some adjectives, however, are vague because they have multiple meanings. Only the writer knows the exact meaning hidden behind the general word.

Use specific adjectives and details instead of vague adjectives.

The words in the following chart are examples of adjectives that should be used with caution. You should use vague adjectives only when you intend to explain your idea further with specifics and details.

VAGUE ADJECTIVES				
interesting	typical	excellent	nice	terrible
terrific	exciting	wonderful	cute	beautiful
lovely	fantastic	great	tasty	awful

Vague adjectives prompt a reader to ask questions. If you were to write that a movie was excellent, a reader would want to know why you thought so, in what way the movie was excellent, and just what you meant by excellent. The word *excellent* can express your enthusiasm generally, but to communicate with someone else precisely you must use more specific words.

You can avoid vague adjectives by using one or more specific adjectives or by giving details that add specific meaning to what you are describing.

VAGUE: Napoleon was a *cute* puppy.

SPECIFIC: The puppy, Napoleon, was *white* with a *seal-like face* and *irregular black freckles*.

VAGUE: It was a *beautiful* day.

SPECIFIC: It was a *cloudless* day, *warm enough for swimsuits and straw hats*.

EXERCISE A: Replacing General Words with Specific Words. Each of the following sentences contains weak nouns, verbs, and adjectives that can be replaced with stronger words. Write each sentence on your paper, replacing the underlined word or words with specific words to make the sentence more precise. Remember that linking verbs can be replaced with action verbs and verbs in the passive voice with verbs in the active voice.

Revisions will vary; samples given.

EXAMPLE: My parents insisted that I pick up my things from the floor.

My parents insisted that I pick up my school books and
dirty clothes from the floor.

1. He <u>hit</u> the door with his fists over and over again. *banged*
2. <u>Members of the medical profession</u> will attend a convention at the Civic Center. *Physicians, nurses, and paramedics*
3. <u>Something</u> was bothering me, but I did not want to talk about it. *Her nagging*
4. She <u>told</u> us over and over again please not to tell Mother. *begged*
5. News magazines give us the information we need to keep abreast of <u>things</u>. *current events*
6. My little sister's singing was <u>terrible</u>. *ear-splitting*
7. We were reassured by his <u>explanations</u>.
8. The movie <u>was</u> offensive to us so we left before it ended.
9. A <u>certain look</u> on his face told us he did not understand English. *blankness*
10. The fuse <u>was lit</u> by the bandit before he ran.
11. Dr. Wilson <u>put</u> her notebook on the table with an awful thud and looked at me. *slammed*
12. Her parents gave her a <u>wonderful</u> birthday party. *tumultuous*
13. Uncle Grover was so angry at Felix that he threw an <u>object</u> across the room. *his pipe*
14. This jacket <u>is</u> a match for my new slacks. *matches*
15. The general <u>moved</u> among his guests and spoke of his trophies. *oozed*
16. Thousands of innocent people <u>were affected</u> by the invaders. *The invaders affected thousands of innocent people.*
17. We found the food <u>tasty</u>. *delicately seasoned*
18. The new student <u>was teased</u> unfairly by Meg and Allan.
19. Our team played an <u>exciting</u> basketball game last night.
20. The storm <u>was</u> a threat to shorefront properties in Maine. *threatened*

7. description of the surgery   8. offended   10. The bandit lit the fuse . . .
18. Meg and Allan teased . . .   19. a sudden-death

■ Fresh Versus Worn-out Expressions

Besides using specific words that communicate accurately, you will often want to use colorful, descriptive expressions. One problem you may encounter, however, is that many expressions that come to mind easily and that seem to describe a situation well are clichés. *Clichés* are expressions that have been used so much for so many years that they have lost their descriptive power. Once these expressions were fresh and descriptive, but now they have only vague and abstract meanings. Phrases such as *come to a standstill, walk a fine line, be an early bird, last but not least, at this point in time,* and *when the chips are down* take away from, rather than add to, the clarity of your ideas. You can strengthen your writing by eliminating these trite phrases, by using specific words instead, and by creating descriptive expressions of your own.

Avoiding Clichés. You may get by and save time by using clichés in speaking because your gestures, facial expressions, and intonation add meaning, but you cannot communicate clearly with these exhausted expressions in writing.

Replace clichés with specific words that clearly express your meaning.

In order to remove clichés from your writing, you should first become aware of some of these familiar sayings.

RECOGNIZING CLICHÉS		
slow as molasses	backbone of a jellyfish	leave much to be desired
at loose ends		
pull the rug out from under	heart of the matter	spitting image
		benefit of a doubt
in the doghouse	axe to grind	
bats in the belfry	apple of someone's eye	goes without saying
prime the pump		
hitting the nail on the head	memory of an elephant	at a loss for words
	rat race	at this stage in the game

You can remove clichés from your sentences by reexamining the idea you want to communicate and by expressing it simply and directly. Notice that the revised sentences that follow the clichés sound more precise.

CLICHÉ: His brother advised him not to *cry over spilt milk.*

REVISED: His brother advised him not to mope about losing the tennis match.

CLICHÉ: The radio club is growing *by leaps and bounds.*

REVISED: The radio club is adding new members each week.

Creating Fresh Similes and Metaphors. Another way to avoid clichés is to replace them with your own descriptive phrases. Your words will make more sense and will be more captivating if they are your own. You can add zest to your writing by creating fresh comparisons that help a reader grasp or visualize your idea. Often you may see resemblances between two basically dissimilar things. By saying one thing resembles another, you can make the first thing clearer to a reader. Comparisons that say X is *like* Y are similes; comparisons that say X *is* Y are metaphors.

Write your own similes and metaphors to sharpen your ideas and impressions.

A simile uses the words *like* or *as* to draw a direct comparison between two basically dissimilar things. To create a simile, you must make an imaginative comparison by seeing or thinking of resemblances between two things that are different in most ways. If you were to write the following sentence, you would be making an imaginative comparison between a dog and a feeble, old man: *The poodle hobbled like an old man with a cane.* However, if you were to write the following sentence instead, you would not be using a simile. You would simply be making a factual observation. No imaginative comparison between two unlike things is involved: *The poodle hobbled like an old dog.*

The following examples show how similes can create mental pictures and enhance understanding.

SIMILES: The boat skimmed into the harbor like a water bug.

Between Harriet and Mr. Pomfret there occurred one of those silences into which the first word spoken falls like the stroke of a gong.—Dorothy Sayers

Grandfather stood on the wide front porch like a captain surveying the vast unmotioned calms.—Ray Bradbury

A sudden dread here fell like a shadow across his imagination.—George Eliot (Mary Ann Evans)

Like a simile, a metaphor is a comparison between two dissimilar things. But a metaphor imaginatively identifies one thing with another by saying *X is Y* or *X was Y*. To write a metaphor, you must first imagine the likenesses between different things and then speak of one thing in terms of another. The following examples show how metaphors create images and add meaning.

METAPHORS: The bulldozer, resting in the rutted mud, was a sleeping dinosaur.

Linda Fratianne was a dancing flame in red as she whirled toward figure skating glory, only to flicker out just short of the gold.—Pete Axhelm

Sometimes you can condense or submerge a metaphor so that instead of saying X is Y, you replace X with Y. If the metaphor is effective, the reader visualizes the image and mentally fills in the comparison. Submerged metaphors are used even more often than metaphors.

SUBMERGED METAPHORS: The wave left a fringe of Venetian lace on the beach.

(The reader sees the water and salt foam as Venetian lace.)

Slowly the white wings of the boat moved against the blue cool limit of the sky.—F. Scott Fitzgerald

(The reader sees the boat as a bird; the boat's sails are wings.)

NOTE ABOUT DEAD SIMILES AND METAPHORS: When you write similes and metaphors, avoid comparisons that are familiar and overused. Such direct and implied comparisons as *easy as apple pie, irons in the fire,* and *food for thought* are actually dead similes and metaphors, a subcategory of clichés. These expressions are dead because they no longer evoke visual images. They have become abstract through overuse.

EXERCISE B: **Identifying Clichés.** Each of the following sentences contains a trite expression. Write the cliché from each sentence on your paper and then rewrite the sentence, substituting more precise language for the cliché.
Revisions will vary; samples given.
1. For me good grades are~~a matter of life or death.~~
2. She became ~~all hot and bothered~~ because I would not agree to hold the party at my house. *hostile*
3. Please ~~touch base with~~ me before the end of school tomorrow so that I can borrow your geometry book. *see*
4. My aunt puts ~~everything but the kitchen sink~~ in her homemade soup. *many exotic vegetables*
5. When he had only a pair of threes in his hand, he ~~threw in the towel~~ and decided not to play poker again. *gave up*
1. my main consideration

6. Poor Dexter has~~a spare tire~~ that he is trying to lose by exercising. *a flabby midriff*
7. The fog was~~as thick as pea soup and~~ made navigation along the coast impossible. *so thick that it*
8. Losing the class election~~took the wind out of Bob's sails~~. *humiliated Bob*
9. ~~By hook or by crook~~ Eleanor was determined to get that job. *any way she could*
10. Motorists~~flew~~ through our town ~~like blazes~~ before the 25 mph speed limit was imposed. *speeded*

EXERCISE C: Writing Your Own Similes and Metaphors. Complete each of the following similes and metaphors with a vivid, imaginative image. Identify each completed sentence as a *simile* or a *metaphor:*

Completions will vary; samples given for first two.

EXAMPLE: Sparrows sat on the fence like

Sparrows sat on the fence like clothespins on a line. simile

1. His hands and wrists stuck out of his sleeves like
2. The thruway clogged with traffic was
3. Fog enveloped the city like *simile*
4. The pet shop was as noisy as *simile*
5. Betsy cut the engine and quiet covered them like *simile*
6. The maple tree was a *metaphor*
7. The power shovel perched at the edge of the pit like *simile*
8. The needle on the sewing machine bobbing up and down was *metaphor*
9. The cluttered drugstore is *metaphor*
10. The dense ivy on the trunks and walls was *metaphor*

1. . . . new shoots on a plant/simile
2. . . . a dumping ground for ancient metal bones/metaphor

■ Varied Versus Overused Words

In addition to using specific words and original comparisons, you can make your sentences more precise by varying your choice of words. You can easily fall into using the same word or form of a word repeatedly in a sentence or in a series of sentences. Or you might find yourself using obvious modifiers, such as *green* in the phrase *green grass*. Again, increasing your awareness of the words you use will help you decide when you should repeat a word or use a familiar modifier and when you should try for varied words and new modifiers.

Avoiding Overuse of the Same Word.   You should regard every word in your sentences as an opportunity to clarify your ideas. If you use the same word or a form of it several times in a sentence just because you have not taken time to find a better word, your sentence will sound tedious and awkward. You must learn to distinguish between useful repetition and careless repetition. Sentences with useful repetition sound natural and logical to a reader. In sentences with careless repetition, on the other hand, the overused words jar and distract the reader from the idea in the sentence.

Choose your words to avoid careless overuse of words.

In the following sentences, you can see the difference between useful and careless repetition. In the first sentence, the word *played* is used logically to achieve the writer's purpose and to create a certain effect. In the second sentence, the word *picture* is overused and weakens the writing.

USEFUL REPETITION: The members of the team *played* with total concentration to show their devotion to their coach, and they *played* with all their energy to please their fans.

CARELESS REPETITION: Thomas painted a *picture* of the old barn, and in the *picture* he *pictured* the barn as mysterious and deserted.

You can avoid overuse of the same word within a sentence by proofreading aloud whenever possible. Then try to think of a word to replace the overused word. Sometimes you will have to rewrite the whole sentence. The following examples show various ways of improving sentences with overused words.

OVERUSED WORD: The construction company *housed* equipment for the building of the *houses* in a makeshift shed.

VARIED WORDS: The construction company *stored* equipment for the building of the houses in a makeshift shed.

OVERUSED WORD: We *noticed* Ricardo's bright purple shirt, which was extremely *noticeable* among the faded brown uniforms of the band.

VARIED WORDS: We easily *spotted* Ricardo's bright purple shirt among the faded brown uniforms of the band.

Avoiding Obvious Modifiers.   An obvious modifier is an adjective that has been linked so often with a noun that it has lost its meaning. Rather than sharpen your idea or description, an obvious modifier obscures it. Phrases such as *unforgettable experience, blushing bride*, and *high mountain* are also clichés in that they are familiar and trite. By examining your words carefully, you can avoid modifiers that serve no purpose in your sentences.

Replace modifiers that are obvious and unnecessary with modifiers that are more precise and vivid or with specific details.

Occasionally you will want to leave an obvious modifier in a sentence because, in that particular context, it expresses exactly what you want to say. For instance, in the following sentence, the writer intends to make the distinction between yellow bananas and green bananas; in this sentence *yellow* is not an obvious modifier.

ACCEPTABLE MODIFIER: Please buy *yellow* bananas this time because I cannot use green ones in the pie tonight.

If a modifier does sound obvious or unnecessary in a particular sentence, you can either (1) delete it and let the noun stand by itself or (2) substitute a more striking and more precise modifier, possibly by rewriting the sentence. The following sentences show different ways to make sentences more precise.

OBVIOUS MODIFIER: The *loud* siren under her window shattered her dreams.

IMPROVED: The screaming siren under her window shattered her dreams.

OBVIOUS MODIFIER: They stretched out on the park benches and gazed at the *fluffy* clouds.

IMPROVED: They stretched out on the park benches and gazed at the shapes appearing and dissolving in the clouds.

EXERCISE D: Replacing Overused Words and Obvious Modifiers. Each of the following sentences contains overused words and obvious modifiers. Rewrite each sentence on your paper, eliminating these words. Replace them with precise, vivid words or specific details.
Revisions may vary; samples given.

1. The~painter painted~ the subject's dog in the foreground of the painting. *artist included*
2. The ~yellow~ lemons and ~green~ parsley were an attractive garnish.
3. The staff at the special emergency number responds quickly ~to all emergencies~.
4. That barking dog kept me awake all night ~with its barking~.
5. A ~ringing~ bell will signal the end of the exam.
6. All ~competitors~ will ~compete~ in the final competition.
7. In ~overcoming~ a fear of heights, Sandy overcame a major obstacle to a career in sky-diving. *conquering*
8. We rode through the ~deserted~ streets of the ghost town.
9. Neither suspect recently brought in ~by the police~ had any ~police~ record with the local police.
10. The cold, ~wet~ waves turned our legs blue.

6. contestants/meet

APPLICATION: Choosing the Most Precise Language. The following short composition contains some good ideas but does not use the best words. Identify weak, general words, worn-out expressions, overused words, and obvious modifiers. Then copy the composition onto your paper, supplying specific, fresh, and varied words.
Revisions will vary; samples given.

(1) The ~dark~ moonless night gradually gave way to a dull glow. (2) A bearded man in brown ~clothes was~ motionless in the ~low~ undergrowth. (3) A rifle ~and some other things~ lay by his side. (4) Although a dull ache passed through his body, the man dared not move.

(5) Again, the burning sensation in his foot brought back memories of the last battle. (6) ~It had been so awful that it~ brought tears to his eyes. (7) ~His~ regiment ~had been attacked by the attacking guerillas~. (8) Only he had survived. (9) And the bullet in his knee kept him from flight. (10) He was ~a sitting duck~ for the enemy.

(11) The man ~sat~ himself into a sitting position. (12) Again the terrible pain ~went through~ his foot and ankle. (13) ~He was made alert by the snap of a twig~. (14) In that moment he resolved to ~push aside other thoughts and~ concentrate on survival.

2. pants and shirt lay   3. , canteen, and some biscuits   6. The horror and waste
7. Guerillas had attacked his . . .   10. an easy target   11. lifted   12. pierced
13. A snapping twig alerted him.   14. only

21.3 Maintaining an Appropriate Tone

Tone is the impression that a passage of writing makes on the reader. A writer's attitude toward the audience and the subject reflected by the words he or she uses creates the tone of a passage. This section will explain how an awareness of audience and tone can help you choose precise, appropriate words.

■ The Ingredients of Tone

Whenever you write, you are usually writing to communicate with someone. The readers to whom you are speaking in your writing are your *audience*. The topic about which you are writing is your *subject*, and your reason for writing is your *purpose*. In any piece of writing, your attitude—thoughts and feelings—toward your audience, subject, and purpose create the *tone* of the writing. The tone you adopt helps, consciously or unconsciously, to determine the words you select. At the same time, the words you choose reveal your tone to the audience.

Consider your audience, subject, and purpose to determine the tone for a piece of writing.

Before you begin to write, you should decide on a tone that will be (1) suitable to a particular audience, subject, and purpose and (2) consistent throughout each sentence and group of sentences.

Audience.   To write effectively, you must develop an awareness of your readers. Whether you are writing a postcard to a friend, a letter to a company complaining about a damaged product, a want ad for the local newspaper, an editorial for the school newspaper, or a report to be presented to your class, you should think about your audience. You can begin by trying to determine some basic information about the people who will make up your audience.

INFORMATION YOU NEED ABOUT YOUR AUDIENCE	
Age	Knowledge of subject
Educational background	Feelings about subject

Jobs or professions   Interest in subject
Geographical location   Relationship to you
Any other special characteristics (prejudices, nationality, physical limitations)

Not all of these points will be important for everything you write, and information on these points will not always be available to you. Sometimes you will have to make reasonable assumptions about your audience. No matter how much or how little you know, you should decide on an attitude toward your audience that will allow you to choose the best words to communicate with them. Notice that the writer's awareness of the audience helps to create the tone in the following selections.

The first passage, taken from *Ranger Rick's Nature Magazine*, is directed toward children in elementary school. The language is simple and direct with short sentences and a conversational tone.

Simple, conversational tone

> Have you ever noticed earthworms crawling about after a heavy rain? Once some people thought it "rained" worms!
> Now we know that earthworms live in burrows in the ground. When it rains hard, their tunnels fill with water. Then many come to the surface.— Janet Halfmann

The second passage, from a scholarly journal of literary criticism, provides ideas and interpretations for university professors and advanced college students. Notice the literary terms, the abstract words for philosophical ideas, and the complicated sentences that compare and contrast.

Serious, scholarly tone

> The two narrator-protagonists stand therefore as antitheses, Hank as empirical idealist, Huck as ideal empiricist; Hank as one who wants to order experience according to the principle of technology, Huck as one who wants to be free and easy and comfortable according to the principle of purely sensuous pleasure. —Jeffrey L. Duncan

Subject and Purpose. Also important in determining the tone you want to use is your attitude toward the subject matter and your purpose in writing. Whether you are writing about backpacking in the Rocky Mountains, about the dangers of nuclear power, about a character in a story, or about the student body's behavior at rallies, you should determine whether your attitude is objective or personal, casual or formal, indifferent or involved, humorous or serious. You should also determine your purpose in writing. For example, if your subject were backpacking your purpose could be to persuade others to backpack, to explain how to get the most out of backpacking, to inform people of the dangers involved, or simply to tell some of your experiences. Both your attitude toward the subject and your purpose in writing should be clear from the words you choose.

The Final Product: A Suitable, Consistent Tone. Once you have determined a few basic facts about your audience, considered your attitude toward your subject, and chosen your purpose, you should be able to choose your tone. The tone of a passage can be described by one or more adjectives, as shown in the following chart.

POSSIBLE TONES WRITING CAN HAVE			
serious	casual	nostalgic	solemn
light	humorous	chatty	playful
scholarly	emotional	matter-of-fact	ironic
formal	calm	familiar	condescending
impersonal	angry	conversational	somber
objective	indifferent	confidential	pretentious
informal	sentimental	aloof	coaxing

The tone of a passage is not right or wrong, but it can be either appropriate or inappropriate, consistent or inconsistent. If the tone suits the particular audience, subject, and purpose, it is appropriate. A letter to the president of a company requesting an interview in which the writer establishes a familiar, casual tone by calling the president by her first name would not be appropriate. Similarly, a composition that was objective in the beginning and became subjective and emotional in the middle would have an inconsistent tone. Notice the appropriateness and consistency in the tone of the following passages.

In the first passage, from *Soul*, a newsmagazine, the tone is light, chatty, and breezy. The short sentences, exclamation marks, and words such as *jazz lovers, odd, get a good grip on yourself* create a casual, enthusiastic tone, and show the writer's direct, familiar approach to the audience.

Casual,
direct
tone

Jazz lives! And jazz lovers live too! They live everywhere from the lower east side, to the upper west side. They are students, custodians, and stock brokers. They ride in subways, buses, Cadillacs, and jets. And if you think these combinations are odd, then get a good grip on yourself because the greatest oddity is yet to come. Many jazz lovers don't even know that's what they are!—R.A. Wilson

In contrast, the following passage from a medical magazine establishes a serious, objective, yet conversational tone, which appeals to a specially trained and concerned audience. It suggests by the use of medical terms, explanations in parentheses, and the words *you* and *ask yourself* that the writer intends to explain and teach.

Serious,
objective
tone

Your first glance at the patient may give you the feeling that a cardiac problem exists, though it takes a systematic examination to pinpoint all the clues. As you come into the room, ask yourself if the patient appears to be in distress. Note his general appearance and apparent state of health. Does he appear older (as a result of chronic heart disease) or younger (due to suppressed growth from congenital heart disease) than his chronological age?—Christine Cannon

EXERCISE A: Identifying Tone. Read the following two passages taken from books. Decide what word or words best describe the tone of each passage. Then, list the specific words in each passage that contribute to the tone. Finally, state who you think is the intended audience of each passage.
Answers will vary; samples given.

(1) Sometimes it's hard to believe that English is the official language in Sydney, Australia; so many people speak, from habit or choice, a delightful, distorted form of English called Strine. It comes out as a colorful combination of British cockney and pure Australian. Words may emerge in a rush, or be shortened beyond recognition. Thus, "How much is it?" sounds like someone named Emma Chizzit, and to "do a uey in a ute at the uni" really means making a U-turn in a utility truck at the university.—Adapted from Ethel A. Starbird
casual, light—general audience

(2) Do you know why twelve inches is called a foot? Long, long ago, a foot was the distance from a man's heel to his toe. On every man it was different. Sometimes a foot was ten inches, and sometimes more. On a very large man, a foot

might even be nineteen inches. Then <u>some wise men,</u> in the days of King Edward II of England, in the year 1324, decided that thereafter a foot would be twelve inches. —Adapted from Hester and Shane

informal, familiar—children

EXERCISE B: Examining Tone in Your Own Writing. Bring to class a short letter or composition you have written recently. Briefly describe your intended audience, your attitude toward the audience, your subject matter, and your purpose. Then describe the tone of the writing in one or two words.

Answers will vary. Students could exchange original papers to compare impressions.

■ Avoiding Words That Destroy a Consistent Tone

Once you have chosen a tone, you should strive to keep it consistent. One way to maintain a consistent tone is to avoid certain words that may destroy the tone you have chosen. Slang, or casual in-phrases, and jargon, or technical language peculiar to a special field of knowledge, will more often than not jar the tone you are trying to create.

Problems with Slang.   In most of the writing you will do, you will want to avoid slang. Slang consists of popular words and phrases used by certain age or regional groups. Most slang is short-lived; it is used frequently, to the point of overuse, by a group of people for a short time and then it passes out of the language. Only a small number of slang words become a permanent part of the English language and fewer still become acceptable in most writing. Two of the main problems of using slang in writing are (1) that slang words tend to be vague and imprecise, mainly dependent upon a speaker's intonation and expression and upon the context to make sense and (2) that slang words are often local and impermanent. If you use slang in writing, you not only risk a distortion of tone but you also risk being misunderstood by your audience.

Replace slang words with words that are suitable for your established tone.

In the following sentences, notice that the revised sentences are consistent in tone and clearer than the sentences with slang.

SLANG: Our basketball players will have to *get their act together* if they want support from the student body next year.

REVISED: Our basketball players will have to start practicing seriously if they want support from the student body next year.

SLANG: We hope that you and other members of the community will not be *hung up* on the cost of the new Fine Arts Program at Butler High. Instead, we hope that you will be *keyed up* for our performances and that you will promote them by advertising and attending them.

REVISED: We hope that you and other members of the community will not be disturbed by the cost of the new Fine Arts Program at Butler High. Instead, we hope that you will be enthusiastic about our performances and that you will promote them by advertising and attending them.

Problems with Jargon.   Jargon is specialized vocabulary consisting of technical terms from a profession or hobby. It may have its place when you are writing to an audience that shares your knowledge of a particular field. Used with the wrong audience, however, jargon can be confusing and even irritating.

Replace jargon with words that are consistent with the tone you have chosen for a specific audience.

You can maintain a consistent tone by explaining difficult terms and by rewriting sentences in simpler language.

JARGON: When the truck hit my uncle's car, he suffered injuries to his head and chest and developed an *aortic aneurysm.*

REVISED: When the truck hit my uncle's car, he suffered injuries to his head and chest and developed a sac in the weakened wall of the main artery carrying blood from his heart to the rest of his body.

JARGON: From the lodge, we watched Heidi flying down the slope, doing *wedel turns* and then relaxed *parallel christies.*

REVISED: From the lodge, we watched Heidi flying down the slope doing short, snaky turns and then relaxed, wider turns.

EXERCISE C: Identifying Slang. List ten slang expressions that you currently use when you speak. Then list five slang expressions that you consider old-fashioned but that an older person you know once used or still uses. As a class, list current and out-of-date slang expressions on the board. Write your definitions of the expressions and compare them with those of other students. *Some students might want to keep adding to these lists of current and out-of-date slang.*

EXERCISE D: Identifying Jargon. Using one of your special fields of knowledge (a sport, hobby, craft, parent's job, and so on), list five technical terms and define them so that everyone in the class can understand them. Use each term in a sentence for other experts. Then write a sentence for the average audience in which you translate the jargon into understandable words. *Students might discuss which terms can be simplified and which seem more difficult to translate.*

■ Avoiding Other Problems with Tone

To maintain a consistent tone you should also think about the effect of your words on your audience. Certain words can jolt, deceive, outrage, or insult your audience. To make sure your words convey the meaning and attitudes you wish to convey, you should think about your words. Look up words in the dictionary so that you can eliminate any words with unwanted meanings and associations. You might also find that reading your sentences aloud to others helps you to see the effect of your words. Becoming aware of the literal and suggested meanings of words and of their emotional impact will also help you choose the right words for a particular audience and tone.

Problems with Denotation and Connotation. The *denotation* of a word is its literal definition, and the *connotation* of a word is a broader area of meaning, which includes the suggested meanings and associations that word has. Often a word has general connotations, or additional meanings, that have developed over the years and that most people are aware of. A word may also have private connotations for individuals; that is, people may associate their own experiences and meanings with a word. The associations words have are either positive, negative, or neutral. For example, a denotation of the word *doctor* is "a physician or surgeon; a person licensed to practice any of the healing arts." To many people the word *doctor* might carry associations of a prestigious, successful member of society, or a hard-working professional. To a person who had had an unpleasant experience with a doctor, however, the word might have negative connotations and might be associated with pain, frightening hospital rooms, or expensive medical bills. As a writer, you will not be able to anticipate all of the private connotations of your words, but you should be aware of the general connotations. By considering the connotations of words, you can choose those words that will achieve the effect you intend.

Keep the tone of your writing consistent by choosing words with appropriate connotations.

Connotations involve shades of meaning and levels of formality. Words with unsuitable connotations can make your tone inappropriate. For a consistent tone, the connotations of your words should be appropriate in both meaning and formality.

Sometimes the connotations of a group of words differ mainly in their shades of meaning. To choose the best word for a sentence, you should consider whether the word has positive, neutral, or negative associations. Then decide which association fits the tone you are trying to create. In the following sentences, the adjectives in italics change the description from neutral to negative.

NEUTRAL CONNOTATION: The cashier was *forgetful*, sometimes adding the sales tax twice. (*Forgetful* suggests that a person has a poor memory and cannot be blamed entirely for mistakes.)

NEGATIVE CONNOTATION: The cashier was *inattentive*, sometimes adding the sales tax twice. (*Inattentive* suggests that a person has the ability to do things correctly but lacks discipline.)

STRONGER NEGATIVE CONNOTATION: The cashier was *negligent*, sometimes adding the sales tax twice. (*Negligent* suggests that a person does not try and does not care. It is the most blameworthy of the three characteristics.)

Sometimes the connotations of words differ mainly in how formal or informal they are. For example, although two words are close in meaning, one might be too dignified or too casual for a particular audience and tone. The words in italics in the following sentences show different levels of formality.

INFORMAL CONNOTATION:　The president's *chopper* skimmed over the eager crowd and landed in the parking lot amidst cheers. (*Chopper* sounds out-of-place because it is too casual.)

MORE FORMAL CONNOTATION:　The president's *helicopter* skimmed over the eager crowd and landed in the parking lot amidst cheers. (*Helicopter* is suitably formal.)

FORMAL CONNOTATION:　She asked him to *elevate* the sofa so she could dust underneath it. (*Elevate* sounds stuffy and draws attention to itself.)

MORE INFORMAL CONNOTATION:　She asked him to *lift* the sofa so she could dust underneath it. (*Lift* fits the informal tone of the rest of the sentence.)

　　With many words, you will have to consider both the precise meaning and the formality appropriate for your tone.

　　Problems with Euphemisms.　*Euphemisms* are words or phrases that are used to soften or sugarcoat a truth or fact that someone might not want to face or that might embarrass someone. Euphemisms, such as *pass away* for *die, heart condition* for *heart disease*, and *mental illness* for *insanity*, are sometimes useful to avoid hurting someone's feelings; used carelessly or frequently, however, euphemisms can give writing an insincere tone. Writers who are trying to hide their real meaning in order to manipulate the readers' response often use euphemisms dishonestly. In your writing, you should avoid even a careless manipulation of the audience.

　　Avoid an insincere tone in your writing by removing euphemisms from your sentences.

　　In the following sentences, clear and more direct words and phrases replace euphemisms and make the tone of the sentences unified.

EUPHEMISM: Three *law enforcement officers* inspected the house after the burglary and concluded that the burglar had entered through the kitchen window.

REVISED: Three detectives inspected the house after the burglary and concluded that the burglar had entered through the kitchen window.

EUPHEMISM: The foreign guests found the food well-seasoned, the service prompt, and the *comfort stations* clean.

REVISED: The foreign guests found the food well-seasoned, the service prompt, and the restrooms clean.

Problems with Emotional Language. *Emotional language* includes words with strong negative connotations and words that express strong and often unsupported opinions. Emotional language yells at the audience and sours your tone by making it offensive and insulting. Words such as *cheap, neurotic, bigoted, low class, freeloader,* and *babyish* should generally be avoided.

Replace words with strong negative connotations with reasonable words that have more neutral connotations.

Words with negative connotations can be useful but you should try to avoid unwanted negative implications and overstated opinions. Even one out-of-place, loaded word could make a reader reject your writing. In the following sentences, emotional language has been replaced with more neutral words.

EMOTIONAL LANGUAGE: Cars manufactured by that company are *rattletraps.*

REVISED: Cars manufactured by that company have a record of breaking down after a few years.

EMOTIONAL LANGUAGE: My parents will not vote for that candidate because they say he is a *pigheaded fool* who *sponges off* the community.

REVISED: My parents will not vote for that candidate because they say he is stubborn when he makes mistakes and indifferent to the needs of the community.

Problems with Self-Important Language. Another problem that can disrupt an established tone is self-important language. Self-important language works hard to sound impressive by being unnecessarily long-winded, vague, or weighty. Self-important language is showy but unclear. It may be flowery with too many adjectives and adverbs creating useless decoration. Or it may be falsely formal with vague, general nouns, long verbs ending in -*ate* or -*ize*, and heavy verb/noun constructions.

Replace self-important language with simpler, more direct words.

You should avoid self-important language by using simpler, more precise words and by rewriting your sentences when necessary. The following sentences illustrate the difference between self-important language and appropriate formality.

SELF-IMPORTANT LANGUAGE: If you *utilize* the *assorted educational opportunities* provided by the *community college system*, you can *maximize* your *learning situations*.

REVISED: If you take advantage of the classes, lectures, and free movies offered by the local community colleges, you can learn about many subjects.

SELF-IMPORTANT LANGUAGE: A *familiarity* with the subway system will *facilitate* a tourist's *movement* about the city.

REVISED: Understanding the subway system helps a tourist travel in the city.

EXERCISE E: Identifying and Correcting Problems in Tone. Each of the following short passages contains words that destroy the consistent tone. Identify the problem in each passage and rewrite the passage to create a unified tone.

Problem words are underlined and problems identified. Revisions will vary; samples given for first passage.

   (1) Older people are ~~becoming cognizant of~~ the new philosophy that says that life begins rather than ends at sixty. Many retired people are discovering new hobbies and interests as varied as jogging, oil painting, and politics. My grandfather, for example, ~~commenced his own enterprise~~ at sixty-two when he retired from a successful career as an insurance agent. He bought ~~an unprosperous~~ diner, and within five years, ~~the tiny diner metamorphosed~~ into a thriving, fashionable restaurant. *self-important language mixed with direct, simple language*

1. recognizing/started his own business/a struggling/changed the tiny diner

(2) Many people worry about the pollution in the water we drink and the air we breathe, but too few people are concerned about the effects of noise pollution on our hearing, health, and sanity. For example, think how upsetting it is to have a group of leather-jacketed dudes on motorcycles race through your quiet neighborhood, shattering the peace with their blasting engines. Or just when your children are trying to go to sleep, a car full of teeny-boppers will cruise through your community with the car radio blaring trashy music or the revving of an engine will force your hands to your ears. If you open your windows expecting to hear crickets, you will probably hear instead roaring jets. *emotional language*

(3) The small country's fight for political survival continued last month as its larger neighboring country increased its attacks. The small country's commander had to order the intelligence scouts to make a strategic relocation. Meanwhile the invading army liquidated the inhabitants of the captured villages and began a defoliation mission. Although the invading army appeared to be gaining territory and momentum, the president of the smaller country announced that his country would not resort to biological agents. *euphemisms*

APPLICATION: Improving Tone for Consistency. In the following passage, the writer has not achieved a consistent tone. First, rewrite the passage to suit the tone to a general audience. Then, rewrite the passage again, adjusting the tone for an audience of second graders. *Problem words are underlined. Revisions will vary. Students might compare their "second-grader" versions.*

(1) A leisurely voyage down the coast of Oregon makes an ideal family vacation. (2) Oregon is infested with state parks, which offer hiking, picnicking, and camping. (3) Most parks provide drinking water, comfort stations, and sometimes consultation for travelers. (4) When camping, however, travelers should avoid hippies hanging around the beaches and lakes. (5) At least, Oregon fines slobs who litter.

(6) The northernmost border of Oregon is delineated by the magnificent, majestic Columbia River, spanned by the graceful Astoria Bridge. (7) Heading south a sojourner will discover swell beaches, funky antique shops, and adequate fishing spots. (8) At Kiwanda Beach, travelers can observe anglers launching their skiffs into the breakers. (9) Travelers should also visit the Spanish Head and Surftide resorts, where no beach bums are allowed. (10) There they will find excellent recreational facilities that offer amusement for the whole family.

22

Sentence Variety and Logic

One important step toward improving your writing style is to learn how to vary your sentences. The first section in this chapter will give you practice in achieving variety in your sentences by altering lengths, complexity, beginnings, and patterns. Another way you can achieve a more advanced writing style is to learn to establish smooth, logical connections between ideas. The second section will explain how to clarify the relationships between ideas and how to make your writing flow.

22.1 Writing Varied Sentences

As a serious writer, you should be concerned not only with the words you write but also with the patterns created by the sentences you write. Part of the effectiveness of your writing will depend upon how you construct your sentences. No matter how important your ideas, if all of your sentences sound alike, your readers will quickly lose interest. If, on the other hand, you vary the lengths and structures of your sentences, you will be much more successful in capturing and holding your readers' attention. This section suggests ways to improve your sentences by using variety.

■ Developing Short Sentences

One of the most common weaknesses in style is short, choppy sentences. A series of short sentences produces a halting, awkward passage that is monotonous to read. If you find yourself writing this way, you probably have not provided your readers with enough details or explored the ways to combine your ideas into longer sentences.

Expanding Short Sentences.   There are many times when you will want to write short, direct sentences. A series of short sentences can be awkward, however, especially if the sentences are so plain and skeletal that the reader receives only a minimal amount of information. In this case, you should lengthen the sentences by including more details.

Expand short sentences by adding words and phrases that modify or rename.

Adding modifying details to your sentences not only gives a reader more thorough information but also helps to make your writing more lively. Notice that the sentences in the following chart use single-word modifiers, phrases, and appositives to add details to the subject, verb, or complement.

EXPANDING SHORT SIMPLE SENTENCES
Short Simple Sentence
The cyclist passed the van.
With Adjectives and Adverbs
The *leading* cyclist *quickly* and *unexpectedly* passed the *delivery* van.
With Prepositional Phrases
The cyclist *in the lead* passed the van *near the finish line.*
With Verbal Phrases
The cyclist, *wearing number eight,* passed the van *to avoid the vehicle's exhaust.*
With Appositives
The cyclist, *Bryon Conners, an experienced racer,* passed the van.

Joining Sentences.   Sometimes simply adding more details to a group of simple sentences will not be enough to vary the length of your sentences. You may also find that your short sentences already contain enough sharp details. Another way of creating longer sentences is to join together several shorter ones. If your sentences do contain enough details but are short and choppy, you can group your sentences into longer, smoother sentences.

Join two or more short sentences by using compound subjects or verbs, by making one or more sentences into a phrase that modifies or renames, or by forming compound, complex, or compound-complex sentences.

You can join simple sentences in many ways. Notice in the following charts how sentence structures are changed to form longer, more interesting sentences.

Some simple sentences can be joined by using a compound subject or verb.

USING COMPOUND SUBJECTS OR VERBS
Forming Compound Subjects
Michael Tores is running for class president. So is Jennifer Wise.
Michael Tores and *Jennifer Wise* are running for class president.
Forming Compound Verbs
Sandra heard the late bell. She ran to her next class.
Sandra *heard* the late bell and *ran* to her next class.

Other sentences can be joined by changing one of them into a phrase modifier or an appositive phrase.

MAKING ONE SENTENCE INTO A PHRASE
Making a Sentence a Prepositional Phrase
The husky puppy whined for attention. It was in the cramped cage in the corner.
The husky puppy *in the cramped cage in the corner* whined for attention.
Making a Sentence an Appositive Phrase
Dr. Maguire joined the staff in 1979. He is our new superintendent of schools.
Dr. Maguire, *our new superintendent of schools*, joined the staff in 1979.

Making a Sentence a Participial Phrase

She heard a police siren. She pulled to the side of the road.
Hearing a police siren, she pulled to the side of the road.

Making a Sentence an Infinitive Phrase

Here is a screwdriver. Put these shelves together.
Here is a screwdriver *to put these shelves together*.

Sometimes you can join short sentences by forming compound, complex, or compound-complex sentences. You can form these types of sentences by using coordinating or subordinating conjunctions.

CHANGING SENTENCE STRUCTURES

Making a Compound Sentence

The moon disappeared behind a cloud. A wind stirred.
The moon disappeared behind a cloud, *and* a wind stirred.

Making a Complex Sentence

Strong gusts blew leaves and branches. Drops of rain began to fall.
Strong gusts blew leaves and branches *as* drops of rain began to fall.

Making a Compound-Complex Sentence

We tried to change her mind. She insisted that we take her to the scene of the accident.
We tried to change her mind, *but* she insisted *that* we take her to the scene of the accident.

Now, take a close look at the following passage. Although all of the sentences contain enough details, they are all about the same length, and together they are awkward and monotonous to read.

Series of short sentences

(1) Denver is the capital of Colorado. (2) It sits on the Great Plains of America. (3) Denver began as a mining camp in 1858. (4) The city grew slowly. (5) However, during World War II Denver expanded rapidly. (6) Army and other federal bases were built there. (7) Many war veterans settled in Denver after the war.

When these seven short sentences are restructured using the methods presented in the charts, the passage becomes smoother and easier to read.

(1–2) With appositive (3–4) Complex sentence (6–7) Compound sentence	(1–2) Denver, the capital of Colorado, sits on the Great Plains of America. (3–4) The city, which began as a mining camp in 1858, grew slowly. (5) However, during World War II, Denver expanded rapidly. (6–7) Army and other federal bases were built, and many war veterans settled there after the war.

EXERCISE A: Adding Details to Short Sentences. The following simple sentences lack specific details. Rewrite each sentence by following the directions in parentheses.
Answers will vary; samples given.

EXAMPLE: Science boasts a staggering amount of published information. (Add an appositive phrase.)

Science, the last and probably endless frontier, boasts a staggering amount of published information.

1. Some of the local residents use the service road. (Add a prepositional phrase.) *at rush hour*
2. The house aroused people's curiosity. (Add two adjectives and an adverb.) *allegedly haunted/young*
3. Mrs. Hamilton did her best to influence the town council. (Add an appositive phrase.) *, a wealthy businesswoman,*
4. The mechanic pried the flat tire from the wheel rim. (Add a verbal phrase.) *Working deftly,*
5. My opponent easily won the game. (Add a prepositional phrase.) *With good strategy*

EXERCISE B: Changing Sentence Structure for Variety. Each of the following items contains two or more short, choppy sentences. Write each item on your paper, restructuring and joining sentences. Try to find the most effective way to group details. You can change, add, or omit words, but do not alter the ideas in any of the sentences. Note also that you do not always have to make all of the short sentences in each item into one sentence.
Revisions will vary; samples given.

EXAMPLE: A tan car sped along the highway. It attempted to turn sharply. It nearly flipped.

Speeding along the highway, a tan car attempted to turn sharply and nearly flipped.

1. ~Snow fell steadily upon the Acadian Forest. ~~It fell for seven days.~~ *For seven days,*
2. ~Jason lost his grip on the rope tow. ~~He~~ slid all the way to the bottom of the hill. *When/he*
3. Eating balanced meals ~is~ essential for good health. ~~Exercising regularly is necessary too.~~ *and exercising regularly are*
4. Thomas Jefferson ~was~ the third President of the United States. ~~He~~ helped to write the Declaration of Independence. *, /,*
5. Horses communicate with each other. ~~They snort and make~~ sounds of different pitch. *by snorting and making*
6. Reading magazines ~is a good way to stay informed. ~~They usually give several different viewpoints on a subject.~~ *that give several different viewpoints on a subject*
7. ~A walrus looks clumsy. ~~It~~ appears sluggish. ~~It~~ is quite agile when it swims. *Although a/and/, it*
8. ~~The~~ temperature rose. ~~The~~ snowbanks glistened in the sun. ~~Tiny~~ beads of water trickled down the hill.
9. ~~We were miles~ away. ~~We~~ could hear Alan. ~~He was~~ practicing his trumpet. *Miles/, we*
10. The Tower of London ~was~ built almost 900 years ago. ~~It~~ was originally a prison. Today it houses the crown jewels. *, /,*

8. As the/, the/, and tiny

■ Reducing Long Sentences

As you continue to develop your writing style, you should also try to avoid using too many long, complicated sentences in a series. Although they may be grammatically correct, such sentences can be so overloaded with details that they lack clarity. Writing some long sentences that have clearly stated ideas can strengthen a passage. But packing too much information into too few sentences will make your ideas difficult to follow. In fact, in a long, involved sentence a reader may forget the beginning before reaching the end.

If you find that you have written a series of long, overloaded sentences, you probably have too many compound and compound-complex sentences. In order to separate your ideas into shorter, more concise sentences you can (1) change rambling compound sentences into simple sentences and (2) break up long, awkward compound-complex sentences into two or more independent sentences.

Shorten lengthy, overly complicated sentences by forming some simpler, shorter sentences.

You should practice developing a balance between the number of short and long sentences and the number of plain and complicated sentences in your writing.

Read the following passage carefully. The two extremely long compound-complex sentences tangle and obscure the ideas. If you read the sentences aloud, you will hear they are not structured naturally.

Two compound-complex sentences

(1) I'll always remember my trip to White Horse Inn because there I met my best friend Karen, who was on holiday with her parents and since I was traveling with my parents, I was pleased to meet another person my age and someone who I soon discovered shared many of my interests. (2) Before long, we became constant companions, and we hiked, swam, played gin rummy when it rained, and sampled all activities offered by the Inn, and eventually we shared a common secret that we both felt awkward with groups of people our age, and that similarity especially helped to make us close friends.

Now read a revision of the same passage. The two original compound-complex sentences have been reduced to a group of shorter sentences to create a variety of lengths and structures. The variety clarifies the ideas, increases the readability, and improves the rhythm of the sentences.

(1) Complex

(1) Simple
(1) Complex

(2) Complex

(2) Compound

(2) Simple

(1) I'll always remember my trip to White Horse Inn because there I met my best friend Karen. (1) She was on holiday with her parents. (1) Since I was traveling with my parents, I was pleased to meet another person my age with many of my interests. (2) Before long, we became constant companions, hiking, swimming, playing gin rummy when it rained, and sampling the other activities offered by the Inn. (2) Eventually we shared a common secret: We both felt awkward with groups of people our age. (2) That similarity especially helped to make us close friends.

EXERCISE C: Simplifying Long Sentences. Each of the following items contains extremely long, rambling sentences. Write the items on your paper, breaking them up into shorter sentences. You can change, add, or omit words, but do not alter the major ideas in any of the sentences.

Answers will vary; samples given.

EXAMPLE: Old houses may look attractive and unusual, but buyers should not be swayed by their quaintness because old houses often require much renovation and many repairs since plumbing and electrical fixtures can be outdated and worn or roofing and siding material can be weathered and leaky, and even supporting walls and beams can be rotten or decaying.

Old houses may look attractive and unusual, but buyers should not be swayed by their quaintness. Old houses often require much renovation and many repairs. Plumbing and electrical fixtures can be outdated and worn. Roofing and siding material can be weathered and leaky, and even supporting walls and beams can be rotten or decaying.

1. Many people laughed at Adam when he first set out to find an old Spanish galleon that had sunk in 1622, ~~but~~ within a year he had converted many a disbeliever, because in that short time he had found millions of dollars of submerged treasure. . *Yet*

2. The art of wood carving was perfected so early in history that few records have been preserved, except relics, ~~such as~~ a recently excavated set of wood carver's tools, ~~which~~ prove that even before metal was used, people cut and decorated wood with tools of shell, bone, and flint.

3. I finally saw the movie, ~~and I am~~ glad that I read the book first, ~~because important~~ details that made the story understandable were left out of the movie version.

4. She clutched the letter tightly, refusing to talk about it and refusing to show it to us, ~~yet tears~~ streamed down her face and small sobs shook her body, making us afraid to take the letter from her, ~~and we~~ did want to help her, but she was unreachable.

5. In the first few hours of heavy rain, flood waters began to rise, and many people left their homes in search of higher ground, but most of these people got stuck in traffic jams and had to wait out the crisis in their stalled automobiles.

2. . For example   3. When/was/. Important   4. . Tears/. We   5. . However, most of them

■ Beginning Sentences Differently

Besides varying the length of your sentences you can achieve variety by concentrating on different beginnings.

The most common way to begin sentences is with a subject followed by a verb. You should certainly begin some of your sentences in this way. By varying the beginnings of your sentences, however, you can add life to your writing style. Even a series of simple sentences will create an interesting pattern when they do not all begin with the monotonous subject-verb pattern.

Readers tend to notice the beginnings and ends of sentences even more than they notice the middles. Therefore, placing words or structures other than the subject first can allow you to focus the reader's attention on certain ideas as well as vary the pattern of your ideas.

Vary your sentence openers by beginning not only with subjects but also with one-word modifiers, phrases, clauses, and transitional words. Occasionally consider putting a complement and verb before a subject in an inverted sentence.

The following chart gives examples of different ways to begin sentences.

VARYING SENTENCE OPENERS
Subject first: We took skiing lessons for several weeks.
Adjective first: Amused, we allowed her to finish her wildly exaggerated tale.
Adverb first: Frantically, hundreds of ants scurried in all directions.
Participial phrase first: Hearing strange noises, we crept downstairs to investigate.
Infinitive phrase first: To prepare for a short answer test, Ellen makes flash cards and quizzes herself.
Adverb clause first: Because the train was traveling so fast, it vanished in seconds.
Several adverbs first: Quickly and smoothly, the swimmers dived into the pool.
Subject with appositive first: Janet Weiss, committee chairperson, wrote more than fifty letters asking for donations.
Transition first: Nevertheless, you are still required to complete four years of English.
Inverted with phrase first: Out of the sky had come a mystery.

All of the sentences in the following passage begin with subjects followed by verbs. Read the passage aloud and listen to the rhythm of your voice. You will see that repeating the subject-verb opener in all the sentences contributes to the dull rhythm.

Sentences beginning with subjects   (1) Aunt Helen's heirs were an eager group. (2) Eight men and nine women, sitting around the giant parlor table, waited anxiously for the lawyer's arrival. (3) They exchanged enthusiastic talk of "dear, departed Helen" although most had

Writing Varied Sentences 593

never met before this evening. (4) Each pair of eyes glanced regularly toward the parlor doorway.

When the sentences are rewritten with a variety of sentence openers, their rhythm becomes more lively and some of the ideas stand out more.

(1) Subject	(1) Aunt Helen's heirs were an eager group. (2)
(2) Participial phrase	Sitting around the giant parlor table, eight men and nine women waited anxiously for the lawyer's
(3) Adverb clause	arrival. (3) Although most had never met before this evening, they exchanged enthusiastic talk of
(4) Adverb	"dear, departed Helen." (4) Regularly, each pair of eyes glanced toward the parlor doorway.

EXERCISE D: Varying Sentence Beginnings. The following sentences begin with subjects and verbs. Write each sentence on your paper, rearranging the words to make the sentence begin differently. Use as many of the different openers presented in the chart on page 592 as possible.

Revisions will vary; samples given.

EXAMPLE: I tossed and turned constantly during the night.

During the night, I tossed and turned constantly.

1. ₌Oceanographers have worked ~~endlessly~~ to study the habits of undersea animals. *Endlessly,*
2. ₌I lost my concentration ~~when the phone began to ring.~~
3. ₌The ~~confused~~ tourists stared at the timetable in the train station. *Confused,*
4. ₌Lucky contestants have won hundreds of thousands of dollars ~~on television game shows.~~ *On television game shows,*
5. ₌Burning coals and boiling lava ~~erupted from the mouth of Mount Etna.~~ *From the mouth of Mount Etna erupted*
6. ₌Clarissa, ~~running to answer the phone,~~ slipped on a magazine and twisted her ankle. *Running to answer the phone,*
7. ₌You must fulfill basic requirements ~~to be a good student and earn high grades.~~ *To be a good student and earn high grades,*
8. ₌The mountain, ~~jagged and menacing,~~ loomed above us.
9. ₌A building can be condemned ~~if it does not meet safety standards.~~ *If it does not meet safety standards,*
10. ₌My uncle, ~~however,~~ would not play golf again. *However,*

2. When the phone began to ring, 8. Jagged and menacing,

■ Using Structure for Emphasis

Besides varying the lengths, structures, and beginnings of sentences, you can experiment even further with the pattern and sound of sentences. Specifically, you can focus more closely on making and breaking patterns within sentences and within groups of sentences in order to emphasize certain ideas.

Repeating a Pattern for Emphasis.   As you become a more experienced writer, you will want to find new ways to make your writing sound interesting. You will also want to learn to emphasize your ideas by the order of words in a sentence.

Use similar sentence patterns within your sentences to underscore ideas.

The use of similar patterns within your sentences is called parallelism. *Parallelism* is the use of similar grammatical structures in a series, that is, the use of single words together, phrases together, and clauses together. The following sentences illustrate the difference between sentences with parallelism and those without.

WITH PARALLELISM: She was lazy, proud, and foolish. (parallel adjectives)

WITHOUT PARALLELISM: She was lazy, proud, and a fool. (adjective/adjective/noun)

WITH PARALLELISM: The boy ran in anger and in fear away from the accident. (parallel prepositional phrases)

WITHOUT PARALLELISM: The boy ran angrily and in fear away from the accident. (adverb/prepositional phrase)

You can use parallelism to draw attention to an idea. If an idea seems to have two or more equal parts, put the idea in a sentence using the same grammatical structures two or more times. Notice how the repeated structures in the following sentences stand out and emphasize ideas.

PARALLELISM FOR EMPHASIS: *In a dead city, in a musty warehouse, in a dilapidated laboratory*, the scientist studied his beakers and vials. (Parallel phrases emphasize the scientist's seclusion.)

While she worked with the monstrous machines in the factory, she dreamed *of running away from the city, of finding a forgotten meadow*, and *of sleeping in the quiet sunshine.* (Parallel phrases emphasize the idea of escape.)

Parallelism can also help you show contrast. Notice that the independent clauses in the following compound sentences resemble two sides of a level seesaw with a colon or semicolon in the middle. The parallelism of the clauses highlights the differences in the ideas.

PARALLELISM TO SHOW CONTRAST: The mistakes of the fool are known to the world but not to himself: The mistakes of the wise man are known to himself but not to the world.—Charles Colton

She wanted publicity and power; he wanted privacy and peace.

Breaking a Pattern for Emphasis. Another way to emphasize one or more ideas is to establish a pattern with a series of sentences and then to write a sentence with a totally different structure to break the pattern. For instance, you could write four long sentences and then write a short, forceful sentence that would have the effect of a punchline. Or you could write a series of questions and then answer the questions with a statement. Establishing and then breaking a pattern is a method frequently used in speeches, political writing, and advertising to make ideas stand out and be remembered. With such a pattern, the reader sees and hears the similarity of the sentences and then immediately notices the change to a different pattern.

Use a new structure after a series of similar structures to underscore an Idea.

If you have ideas that you want to develop in several sentences with an emphasis at the end you can express the introductory ideas in similar sentences to set up a pattern and then express the main or final idea in a sentence with a different structure. The following sentences give examples of how this repetition and variation works.

BREAKING PATTERNS: Can Robert "Bud" Gibson provide the leadership we need? Can he halt the trend of rising taxes? Can he lower the city's crime rate? *You bet he can.*

Hills of garbage, sprinkled with paper and tin, and swamps, with half-submerged machinery rusting, bordered the highway. Nearby thick smoke billowed from industrial pipes like evil vapors from a witch's cauldron. Fumes reeking of gasoline, roach and mosquito spray, burning rubber, and stewing garbage seeped through the airvents and cracks of the passing cars. *It was a wasted land.*

EXERCISE E: Emphasizing Ideas with Structure. Each of the following items uses sentence structure in some striking way to emphasize ideas. Read each item carefully. Then briefly describe the structures or pattern used and explain the idea the writer is trying to emphasize. *Basic structures or patterns given.*

Explanations may vary; sample given for first one.

EXAMPLE:　Spittle physically nauseated Dickens; slavery morally sickened him.—Jeanne and Norman MacKenzie

Two independent clauses contain the same number and kind of words in the same pattern: The parallelism emphasizes the idea of sickness.

1. Education makes a people easy to lead, but difficult to drive; easy to govern, but impossible to enslave.—Lord Brougham　*parallelism: emphasizes rewards of education*
2. The past is only the present become invisible and mute; and because it is invisible and mute, its memorized glance and its murmurs are infinitely precious. We are tomorrow's past.—Mary Webb　*pattern broken*
3. Feast, and your halls are crowded; fast, and the world goes by.—Ella Wilcox　*parallelism*
4. The country needs and, unless I mistake its temper, the country demands bold, persistent experimentation. It is common sense to take a method and try it: If it fails, admit it frankly and try another. But above all, try something.—Franklin Delano Roosevelt　*pattern broken*
5. Better by far you should forget and smile than that you should remember and be sad.—Christina Rossetti
parallelism

APPLICATION: Correcting Sentences to Add Variety. The paragraphs in the following passage have groups of short, choppy sentences, a few long, overly complicated sentences, and some monotonous sentence openers. Copy the passage onto your paper, improving it by varying the lengths, beginnings, and possibly the patterns of the sentences. You may combine, restructure, reword, or separate sentences. You may also decide to leave some of the sentences unchanged.
Revisions will vary; students could exchange papers and make further improvements.

(1) Millions of people are injured yearly in their own homes. (2) Every area of your home can possess a safety hazard. (3) No one can afford to overlook possible hazards. (4) Inspect all rooms of your house and eliminate all of the dangers you recognize.

(5) Too many home accidents happen in kitchens so you must take special care to insure safety by making sure that electric appliances are away from the sink and by preventing their cords from slipping into the water, and you should keep a fire extinguisher in the kitchen because fires can occur all too quickly. (6) They can spread rapidly.

(7) You can help prevent accidents in bathrooms. (8) Inspect for potential hazards. (9) Keep pills and medicines out of the reach of children, and label all medicines to avoid dangerous mix-ups, and place a carpet or bath rug on a slippery floor. (10) Make sure that it cannot slip. (11) Never place a telephone near the tub or sink. (12) The phone cord can become wet. (13) It can cause an electric shock.

Using Logic to Connect Ideas 22.2

As you concentrate on making your sentences varied in length and structure, you should also think about their clarity and smoothness. By using transitions—words such as *thus, on the other hand, for example,* and *finally*—you can show how one idea relates to the next. By using coordination—words such as *and* and *or*—you can group and combine equal, related parts of sentences and independent clauses to achieve clear meaning and flow. By using subordination—words such as *because* and *since*—you can group and combine related but unequal clauses to achieve smooth and logical sentences. Ordering your ideas according to certain logical plans within sentences and groups of sentences, can also improve the reader's understanding and the style of your sentences. This section will explain these four methods in more detail.

▪ Using Transitions Logically

Transitions are words and phrases that act as bridges to link your ideas from sentence to sentence and often as guideposts to indicate the direction of your thoughts. If you leave out necessary bridges and guideposts, the reader has to guess the intended relationships between ideas. If you include helpful transitions, however, you avoid confusing or frustrating the reader. Transitions enable your ideas to flow together smoothly.

Use transitions logically to clarify the relationships between ideas in different sentences.

Different transitions establish different relationships between ideas. The following chart lists some of the most commonly used transitions and shows the relationships they establish.

SOME USEFUL TRANSITIONS
To Show a Time Sequence
next   later   meanwhile   finally   before then in a few minutes   then   during   after earlier   first, second, third   at the same time
To Compare or Contrast
likewise   unlike   on the other hand   similarly however   on the contrary   in like manner conversely   nevertheless   but   yet
To Show a Cause or Effect
so   therefore   because of   thus   consequently then   as a result   on account of
To Add More Information
also   furthermore   first, second, third   and in addition   moreover   besides   too   as well
To Emphasize a Point
indeed   in other words   in fact
To Introduce Examples or Explanations
for example   in particular   for instance   that is as an illustration   namely   also

Not all pairs or groups of sentences require transitions. But those that do can be improved greatly by transitions that carry the reader along from one idea to the next or that guide the reader by indicating such things as "More information is coming up," "These two items are being compared," or "This event is a result." When you use transitions between sentences, you can put them at the beginning of the second sentence, in the middle of the second sentence, and occasionally at the end of the second sentence. Transitions are particularly effective at the beginning of the second sentence.

Notice that the following sentences without transitions are isolated and sometimes confusing. When the same sentences are rewritten to include transitions, the logical relationship between the ideas becomes clearer.

UNCONNECTED: George and Al disappeared into another room. They emerged wearing clown costumes.

WITH TRANSITION: George and Al disappeared into another room. *In a few minutes*, they emerged wearing clown costumes.

UNCONNECTED: North Americans often serve hot chocolate with whipped cream. South Americans often add cinnamon and sometimes orange rind.

WITH TRANSITION: North Americans often serve hot chocolate with whipped cream. South Americans, *on the other hand*, often add cinnamon and sometimes orange rind.

UNCONNECTED: Ken asked his friends to help clean up the vacant lot. He enlisted the help of the neighbors.

WITH TRANSITION: Ken asked his friends to help clean up the vacant lot. He enlisted the help of the neighbors *as well*.

EXERCISE A: Supplying Logical Transitions. Each of the following items contains two sentences with ideas that are not clearly connected. Write the sentences on your paper, using transitions to show the most logical relationship between the ideas. Answers will vary; samples given.

EXAMPLE: We waited endlessly for a package from home. One arrived on the day we least expected it.

We waited endlessly for a package from home. Finally, one arrived on the day we least expected it.

1. Not everyone did poorly on the exam. Janet scored over ninety percent. *For instance,* ⟨*explanation*⟩
2. My mother does not approve of dates on school nights. ˄I will not be able to go to the hockey game with you next Wednesday. *Therefore,* ⟨*cause/effect*⟩
3. The sunlight disappeared and the sky darkened. ~~Large~~ hailstones began to fall. *Then, large* ⟨*time/sequence*⟩
4. Ingrid Plotkin has been named Vice President in charge of advertising for the Bradley Corporation. ~~She~~ was a copywriter and account executive. *Previously, she* ⟨*time*⟩
5. You can plan to arrive early. ˄I will be behind schedule if you don't. *In fact,* ⟨*emphasis*⟩
6. Maryanne has built several pieces of summer furniture. ˄~~She~~ built an awning for the outdoor deck. *Also, she*
7. Nesting birds use their body heat to keep their eggs warm. ˄~~Other~~ mammals, such as kangaroos, use their bodies to incubate their young. *By contrast, other*
8. Beyond a doubt, the security guard was frightened. ˄~~He~~ shook and trembled and could not lift his arm. *Indeed, he*
9. There are many ways to save money. ˄~~You~~ can enroll in a payroll deduction plan where you work. *For example, you*
10. I will not allow you to take this test over. ˄~~You~~ may write a separate report for extra credit. *However, you*

▮ Using Coordination Logically

While transitions show the relationship between ideas in separate sentences, coordination connects ideas by placing them in the same sentence. When you want to show a relationship between ideas of equal importance, use coordination to form such things as compound subjects, verbs, complements, and sentences.

Use coordination logically to join equal and related words, phrases, and clauses within a sentence.

The following pages show (1) how to use coordination properly and (2) how to recognize and avoid problems with coordination.

Uses of Coordination. *Coordinate* means "of equal rank." By using coordination to join words, phrases, and clauses in a sentence, you can indicate to the reader that these items or ideas are related and equally important. Grouping your ideas in this way can also make your sentences clearer.

You can join ideas of equal importance using four main methods. Coordinating and correlative conjunctions can join words, phrases, and clauses. Semicolons with conjunctive adverbs (words often used as transitions) and semicolons alone can join clauses to form compound sentences. The following chart explains these methods in more detail.

METHODS OF COORDINATION		
Method	**What to Join**	**Uses**
Coordinating conjunctions: for, and, nor, but, or, yet, so	words phrases clauses	Choose a coordinating conjunction to suit the meaning you intend.
Correlative conjunctions: either . . . or neither . . . nor both . . . and not only . . . but also just as . . . so also	words phrases clauses	Choose a correlative conjunction to suit the meaning you intend.
Conjunctive adverbs: ;however, ;indeed, ;consequently, ;moreover, ;furthermore, ;otherwise, ;therefore,	independent clauses	Choose a conjunctive adverb to indicate time, contrast, result, addition, or emphasis.
Semicolon alone: ;	independent clauses	Use a semicolon alone to indicate a close relationship when no other words are needed.

As you use coordination in your sentences, make sure the ideas you are joining are equal and do belong together. Then choose a method from those presented in the chart to join the ideas. Sometimes more than one method might work. You should choose the method that best demonstrates the relationship between the equal ideas.

As you read the following examples, notice how coordination clarifies the ideas and improves the flow of the sentences.

UNCONNECTED: Don Whillans repeatedly tried to reach the summit of Mount Masherbrum. He failed.

WITH COORDINATION: Don Whillans repeatedly tried *and* failed to reach the summit of Mount Masherbrum.

UNCONNECTED: I suggest you subscribe to a morning newspaper. An evening newspaper is also acceptable.

WITH COORDINATION: I suggest you subscribe *either* to a morning *or* an evening newspaper.

UNCONNECTED: Workers at the fire department had to be promised a pay raise last month. They would have gone on strike.

WITH COORDINATION: Workers at the fire department had to be promised a pay raise last month; *otherwise,* they would have gone on strike.

UNCONNECTED: The people of Athens studied and valued the arts. Those of Sparta practiced the techniques of war.

WITH COORDINATION: The people of Athens studied and valued the arts; those of Sparta practiced the techniques of war.

Problems with Coordination.   There are three major problems with coordination that you should try to avoid in your writing: (1) excessive coordination; (2) coordination that connects unrelated ideas; and (3) vague coordination.

Excessive coordination occurs when you try to connect too many related ideas in a compound sentence. Joining too many independent clauses in one sentence results in a sentence that is tiring to read and difficult to understand. To correct excessive coordination, break up some of the ideas into separate sentences.

EXCESSIVE COORDINATION: I had planned to arrive at your party early so I could help you to get ready,

> but my car broke down, and I had to walk the last three miles, and I was wearing these uncomfortable shoes.

APPROPRIATE COORDINATION: I had planned to arrive at your party early so I could help you to get ready, but my car broke down. I had to walk the last three miles in these uncomfortable shoes.

A second common error in using coordination is trying to connect unrelated ideas. Always be sure you understand the relationship between the ideas you combine in a compound sentence. If you do find two or more unrelated ideas in a sentence, you can easily separate the ideas into different sentences. If necessary, change or add words in order to make two or more complete sentences.

UNRELATED IDEAS CONNECTED: The old Williams mansion burned down last night, and we once played in that deserted house.

UNRELATED IDEAS IN TWO SENTENCES: The old Williams mansion burned down last night. I can remember when we played in that deserted house.

A third major problem with coordination is vague coordination caused by using a conjunction that does not establish a logical connection between the ideas. To correct vague connections, simply replace the wrong conjunction with the one that will best clarify the relationship between the ideas.

VAGUE COORDINATION: The soccer field is under an inch of rain water; *for example*, the opening game will have to be postponed.

CLEAR COORDINATION: The soccer field is under an inch of rain water; *consequently*, the opening game will have to be postponed.

EXERCISE B: Adding Coordination. Each of the following pairs of sentences contains equal ideas that need coordination to clarify their relationship. Write each pair of sentences as a single sentence, forming compound subjects, verbs, complements, or compound sentences.
Revisions will vary; samples given.

EXAMPLE: Smart joggers always do warm-up exercises before beginning to run. They risk the chance of causing damage
to their muscles.

Smart joggers always do warm-up exercises before beginning to run; otherwise, they risk the chance of causing damage to their muscles.

1. To reach the senator for his comment, I telephoned his
office, ~~I called~~ his home. *both/and*
2. No one thinks of swimming in the frozen Yukon. ~~Warm~~
mineral springs make swimming possible. *, yet warm*
3. You can pay the fine to the clerk, ~~You can~~ serve thirty
days in jail. *or*
4. Hurricane damage forced many residents to make major
repairs, ~~Others~~ abandoned their property altogether.
5. Penny ~~couldn't go~~ on the retreat. ~~Tony couldn't go on~~
~~the retreat.~~ *Neither/nor Tony could go*
6. My brother forgot to screw the oil plug in, ~~The~~ new oil
passed through the car engine and spilled all over the
driveway. *; as a result, the*
7. ~~The~~ rats move out of our attic, I will move out. *Either the/, or*
8. Electric automobiles may provide more economical
transportation, ~~They~~ may significantly reduce air
pollution. *and*
9. Writers often supplement their incomes with part-time
jobs. ~~The same is true of construction workers.~~
10. The experiment found that nonsmokers who did not live
in a smoky environment had normal lung function,
~~Those~~ who were regularly exposed to smoke had a significant degree of respiratory impairment. *and that those*

4. , but others   9. Both writers and construction workers

EXERCISE C: Recognizing Problems with Coordination. Each
of the following sentences contains a problem with coordination. Rewrite the sentences on your paper, making them
logical and more readable. *Answers will vary; samples given.*

EXAMPLE: We had planned to arrive at the airport before noon;
otherwise, the trip took us longer than we had expected.

We had planned to arrive at the airport before noon;
however, the trip took us longer than we had expected.

1. My grandfather enjoys working in his garden, ~~and~~ he
spends much of his free time making furniture. *; in addition,*
2. The car is an antique Model T Ford; ~~therefore,~~ it is still
in good running condition. *however,*

3. We had planned a trip to the beach, but it rained on Saturday, ~~so~~ we stayed in the house, ~~and~~ played a long game of Monopoly, and ~~we~~ watched a movie, ~~and~~ later in the afternoon, the electricity went off. *. As a result / , / . Then,*
4. David planned to repay the loan quickly, ~~or~~ he wanted to buy a new bowling ball. *but*
5. My grandmother recently dislocated her hip, ~~and~~ she likes game shows and crossword puzzles. *; fortunately,*

■ Using Subordination Logically

Another way to connect ideas within a sentence is to use subordination. By making one clause subordinate to another, you can make that clause describe or modify another in a complex sentence. Subordination allows you to show exact relationships between ideas that are related but unequal in importance.

Use subordination logically to connect related but unequal ideas in a single sentence.

The following pages show (1) how to use subordination and (2) how to avoid problems with subordination.

Uses of Subordination. *Subordinate* means "lower in rank or importance." When you use subordination, you indicate to the reader that one idea is less important and therefore subordinate to the other idea. The subordinate idea limits, describes, or explains the main idea. By making unequal but related ideas into complex sentences, you can indicate relationships of time, contrast, comparison, result, or condition, or you can simply add information. Using complex sentences also makes your writing more interesting and varied and makes your style more sophisticated.

To form a complex sentence, you must decide which idea will be the main idea and which idea will support that idea. Sometimes the ideas you want to join are obviously unequal. Other times the choice is a matter of your preference, your writing style, and your intended meaning. For instance, in the following examples, notice which sentence in each pair becomes the main clause. Also notice which sentence becomes the dependent clause. The dependent clauses begin with words such as *while, because, as if,* and *which* and contain the supporting ideas. Whenever subordination is used effectively, it points out the logical relationships between ideas for the reader. Notice how the clarity of the following sentences is improved when they are joined by subordination.

UNCONNECTED: Carlotta was sweeping the garage. I was mowing the lawn.

WITH SUBORDINATION: *While* Carlotta was sweeping the garage, I was mowing the lawn.

UNCONNECTED: Alex always looks unkempt. He refuses to have his hair cut.

WITH SUBORDINATION: Alex always looks unkempt *because* he refuses to have his hair cut.

UNCONNECTED: The little boy walked with jerky steps and made humming noises. He was a robot.

WITH SUBORDINATION: The little boy walked with jerky steps and made humming noises *as if* he were a robot.

UNCONNECTED: The new restaurant has received much publicity lately. It has a colonial decor.

WITH SUBORDINATION: The new restaurant, *which* has a colonial decor, has received much publicity lately.

Problems with Subordination. There are three major subordination problems that you should avoid in your writing: (1) excessive subordination; (2) illogical subordination; and (3) absence of desirable subordination. Any of these problems can cloud the relationship between ideas in your sentences.

Excessive subordination occurs when too many subordinate clauses are joined in one sentence. The long, tangled, complicated sentence that results can create clutter and obscure your meaning. To correct excessive subordination, make one or more of the subordinate clauses into separate sentences.

EXCESSIVE SUBORDINATION: While trying to write a composition, Leonardo was watching a wrestling match on television, which was distracting him because he was thinking about the Regional Tournament when he would be wrestling on Saturday when he would try to do his best to please his coach.

IMPROVED SUBORDINATION: While trying to write a composition, Leonardo was watching a wrestling match on television. It was distracting him because he was thinking about the Regional Tournament on Saturday. He would be wrestling then and trying to do his best to please his coach.

Illogical subordination is another problem to avoid. As you combine two ideas to form a complex sentence, you should be careful to establish a logical relationship between the main idea and the subordinate idea. If you choose the wrong clause to subordinate, the connection between your ideas may not make sense. To correct illogical subordination, make the main idea into the main clause.

ILLOGICAL SUBORDINATION: Before you brush your teeth, go to bed.

LOGICAL SUBORDINATION: Before you go to bed, brush your teeth.

A third problem you may encounter in your writing is using coordination where subordination would be clearer and stronger. Using coordination to join certain ideas may create a weak connection between those ideas. Using subordination instead can tighten and sharpen the relationship.

WITHOUT SUBORDINATION: My grades started to drop, *and* I realized I needed to spend more time on my homework.

STRENGTHENED BY SUBORDINATION: *When* my grades started to drop, I realized I needed to spend more time on my homework.

EXERCISE D: Adding Subordination. Each of the following pairs of sentences contains ideas that would be clearer if they were joined by subordination. Write each pair on your paper, forming a complex sentence. Add or omit words as needed. Be sure relationships you establish are logical.
Revisions will vary; samples given.
EXAMPLE: The theater doors were opened. We bought our tickets.

                 We bought our tickets after the theater doors were opened.

1. The audience erupted into applause. ~~The~~ candidate reached the podium. *as the*
2. They stood tightly packed against one another. ~~There~~ was no place to sit. *because there*

3. ~~My~~ uncle had a stroke. ~~He~~ did not have the use of his left arm. *After my/, he*
4. ~~The~~ horn finally blew. ~~Our~~ basketball team walked off the court triumphant. *When the/, our*
5. The unsigned article ~~caused~~ a big debate in class. ~~It appeared in the last issue of the school newspaper.~~
6. During the war years this was a very popular recipe. ~~It~~ doesn't call for expensive milk, eggs, or butter. *because it*
7. ~~The~~ moon is full. ~~Coyotes~~ will howl. *If the/, coyotes*
8. We don't have a case. ~~We~~ can prove that the suspect was in town on the day of the crime. *unless we*
9. You can prepare supper. ~~Follow~~ the directions carefully.
10. The animal was a muskrat. ~~It~~ scurried into its den. *which*

5. , which appeared . . . newspaper, 9. if you follow

EXERCISE E: Recognizing Problems with Subordination. Each of the following sentences presents a problem with subordination. Rewrite each sentence on your paper, showing logical, precise relationships between the ideas.

Answers will vary; samples given.

EXAMPLE: Bats frighten many people; the creatures are harmless.

Although bats frighten many people, the creatures are harmless.

1. ~~She~~ was hungry and tired. ~~because~~ she decided to go home. *Because she /,*
2. Because tornadoes are powerful enough to destroy the sturdiest of buildings, many homeowners in the Middle West have built underground shelters, ~~which~~ will provide them with the necessary protection when a "twister" comes into their area, which usually happens several times a year. *. These shelters*
3. ~~Neil~~ loved the fields and woods around his new home, ~~and~~ he felt uncomfortable in the house. *Although*
4. Whenever ~~the~~ dog howled to drown the music, ~~my mother sang and played the piano.~~
5. Although I had read everything written by this author, I really had no idea what she would be like in person ~~before~~ I had the pleasure of meeting her at the airport when we were boarding the same plane, ~~which was departing~~ for New Orleans. *. Then,*

4. my mother sang and played the piano,

■ Using Logical Order

Another method of making your sentences clear and smooth involves arranging ideas within your sentences and within groups of sentences according to logical plans. When your ideas suggest an order that sets up the reader's expectations, you must follow through. For instance, if you are listing three steps in a process, you should list the steps in the order in which they naturally occur. If you are describing a view from a lookout, you should not jump back and forth from the distance to the foreground.

Among the common plans people use to organize ideas are order of importance, chronological order, spatial order, and comparison and contrast. The following pages explain ways to follow these orders (1) within individual sentences and (2) within a series of sentences.

Logical Order Within a Sentence. Related ideas within a sentence should be arranged in a logical order. When you are showing a progression from least to most important, a time sequence, or a scene from near to far, you should check the order of your ideas to make sure that they follow the pattern. If your ideas are out of order, they will appear disjointed and will distract and lose a reader.

Order your ideas logically and consistently within sentences.

As you read the following examples, notice that sentences with ideas in an illogical order force the reader to jump back and forth between unconnected ideas. Sometimes an illogical order can make ideas appear ridiculous, as in the first example. Other times the meaning may simply be clouded by the ineffective arrangement of ideas. When the sentences are rewritten with ideas in logical order, a precise, clear relationship is established.

ILLOGICAL ORDER: I dressed in my best clothes, took a shower, and left for the reception.

LOGICAL ORDER: I took a shower, dressed in my best clothes, and left for the reception.

ILLOGICAL ORDER: The tour guide showed us the dungeon deep underground, the estate around the castle, and the interior of the castle.

LOGICAL ORDER: The tour guide showed us the estate around the castle, the interior of the castle, and the dungeon deep underground.

Logical Order in a Series of Sentences. A series of sentences that contains related ideas should also be arranged in a logical sequence. If your sentences do not follow the order the reader expects, the reader will most likely become lost. The way you arrange ideas in a series of sentences determines whether your writing flows or falls apart.

Order related ideas in a series of sentences according to a logical, consistent plan.

An illogical order in a series of sentences is even more confusing to a reader than illogic within one sentence. The larger the group of ideas, the more important that you make your meaning clear. If you are explaining a process or if you are comparing and contrasting, carry through on your overall plan. The following examples show you how the clarity and even the smoothness improve when the sentences are rewritten in a logical order.

ILLOGICAL ORDER: Mix the melted butter and the brown sugar. Fold in the flour, salt, and spices. Sift the flour, salt, and spices. Add the oatmeal, nuts, and raisins to the mixture. Make sure the nuts and raisins are finely chopped.

LOGICAL ORDER: Mix the melted butter and brown sugar. Sift the flour, salt, and spices. Fold in the flour, salt, and spices. Make sure the nuts and raisins are finely chopped. Then add the oatmeal, the nuts, and the raisins to the mixture.

ILLOGICAL ORDER: Like tennis, racquetball is a game of strategy. But unlike tennis, it must be played indoors. Like tennis, racquetball requires good hand-to-eye coordination.

LOGICAL ORDER: Like tennis, racquetball is a game of strategy that requires good hand-to-eye coordination. Unlike tennis, racquetball must be played indoors.

EXERCISE F: Recognizing Logical Order. Some of the following sentences are written in logical order while others are not. If a sentence is correct, write *logical* on your paper. Rewrite the illogical sentences to follow a logical order.
Revisions will vary; samples given for 2 and 3.
1. The designated hitter choked up on the bat, watched the *logical* pitcher wind up, and then swung with all his might.
2. Write your composition about the story. Read the story. Then revise your composition.
3. The annual scholarship dinner was topped off with
2. Read the story. Write your composition about the story. Then revise your composition.

strawberry shortcake. The main course was roast beef. Shrimp cocktail was served for an appetizer.
4. The car chugged and jerked down the road. Gradually the grating and roaring of the engine increased. Then the engine screeched and died. *logical*
5. This radio station broadcasts state, national, local, and international news.
6. Both snow skiing and water skiing use muscles in the legs. In contrast to snow skiing, water skiing also strains muscles in the back. *logical*
7. We loaded the car, packed our suitcases, and left for California.
8. Intelligence sources reported that the army could not control the problem. They said total anarchy was imminent. They announced that citizens were rioting.
9. The grand prize in the drawing is a weekend in a resort hotel for a whole family. The prize for runners-up is a fifty dollar bill. The second prize is a set of golf clubs.
10. The charlatan claimed that his elixir would make dying people recover, tired people energetic, and sick people healthy.   *3. At the annual scholarship dinner, shrimp cocktail . . . appetizer. The main course was roast beef. And the dinner was topped off . . .*

APPLICATION: Writing Logically in Compositions. The following passage can be improved by adding transitions, coordination, subordination, and logical order. Rewrite the passage on your paper, creating clear, smooth, logical relationships between the ideas.
Answers will vary; this could be done at the board as an in-class exercise.

(1) Cross-country skiing offers several advantages that downhill skiing does not. (2) Downhill skiing mainly involves executing turns down wide, steep slopes. (3) Cross-country skiing can be done on the flat, on hills, or on narrow trails. (4) Downhill skiers must pay to use lifts and tows to carry them to the top of slopes. (5) Cross-country skiers can ski through parks or woods for free. (6) The boots used for cross-country skiing are flexible and comfortable. (7) They are like soccer shoes. (8) The skis are light. (9) Downhill equipment anchors the skiers' feet and ankles to the solid skis with heavy, inflexible boots.

(10) Cross-country skiing is an excellent way to enjoy exercising in the winter. (11) It is like hiking in the snow. (12) The basic stride is a gliding shuffle. (13) The stride is a combination of walking and skating. (14) Maintaining the stride uses shoulder, arm, and leg muscles and stimulates the circulation system. (15) Skiing along park trails or golf courses, skiers breathe fresh air. (16) They may see deer tracks and may hear a brook trickling beneath its layer of ice. (17) Skiers become hot from the exercise. (18) A cooling mist may blow down from the snow-covered trees.

Chapter 23

Paragraphs

One of your goals as a student should be to learn to express your ideas clearly in writing. Not only should you try to choose the most appropriate words and to write the most interesting sentences, but you should also try to express your thoughts well in logical groups of sentences called paragraphs.

Paragraphs organize ideas for the benefit of the writer and the reader. A paragraph is a group of related sentences that represent a unit of thought. It is generally marked by the indentation of the first word of the first sentence. Usually a paragraph explains and develops one main idea with specific information.

In this chapter, examples and steps will aid you in improving your own paragraphs. You will first examine models to see how other writers have presented their ideas in paragraphs. Then you will practice planning, drafting, and revising your own paragraphs. With explanations, models, steps, and exercises, the sections in this chapter will help you strengthen your thinking and writing skills.

23.1 Recognizing Clear Topic Sentences and Strong Support

Paragraphs vary in many ways, including length, organization, and purpose, but most good paragraphs have some similarities. A good paragraph is a unit of thought in which all the sentences work together to present and develop one main idea. The main idea is usually found in one sentence called the topic sentence. The other sentences contain support for the main idea in the form of examples, details, facts, reasons, or incidents. A good paragraph holds the reader's interest with specific supporting information that elaborates on, and does not shift from, the main idea. In short, a good paragraph fulfills the reader's expectations by being thorough and complete.

In this section, you will examine some of the characteristics of good paragraphs to enable you to recognize good paragraphs and to help you write your own.

■ Topic Sentences

The topic sentence in a paragraph indicates what the paragraph is about and often suggests the purpose of the paragraph—to explain, to persuade, to describe, and so on. It guides the reader in understanding the writer's thoughts.

The **topic sentence** expresses the main idea of a paragraph and limits and directs the development of that main idea.

By telling a reader what the paragraph is about, the topic sentence sets limits on the ideas and focuses the ideas in the paragraph. A reader will expect to find only certain aspects of one topic developed in the paragraph.

Many paragraphs begin with a topic sentence. Other paragraphs have topic sentences in the middle. Still other paragraphs end with topic sentences that summarize in one final statement the specific information that came before. You will also find some paragraphs by professional writers in which the main idea may be implied or may be expressed in two sentences. As you study paragraphs and as you write your own, however, you should concentrate on paragraphs with stated topic sentences.

To find the topic sentence in a paragraph, you should look for the sentence that acts as an umbrella under which all the ideas in the other sentences belong. In the following paragraph, notice that the first sentence expresses the main idea of the paragraph. By stating that Cyrus West Field "envisioned and brought about the first transatlantic cable," this topic sentence limits the paragraph to Field's role in creating the cable. The other sentences provide more specific information to explain this main idea.

TOPIC
SENTENCE

Supporting
information

Cyrus West Field envisioned and brought about the first transatlantic telegraph cable. He thought up the cable and interested others in the idea. Field also helped form the Atlantic Telegraph Company, which financed the laying of the cable, and he found talented people to work on the project. Most important, Cyrus West Field made sure that the cable was completed, even after repeated disasters had injured or discouraged others.

In the next paragraph, the first two sentences introduce the topic sentence, which is the third sentence. This sentence contains the main idea of the paragraph: creating a remarkable product each day in the newsroom. All of the sentences following this one present more specific supporting information.

Introductory
sentence

TOPIC
SENTENCE

Supporting
information

There are few places that can boast an act of creation every day. A newspaper is one of them. *Out of the daily newsroom whirl emerges a remarkable product.* In a matter of hours, thousands of words and pictures are put together in a cohesive pattern designed to inform, enlighten, and entertain the reader. To a casual observer, the men and women working in the newsroom may appear to be running about aimlessly amid the clatter of typewriters and the continually ringing telephones. Actually, the scurrying around, the occasional shouting, the general air of excitement are all part of a controlled procedure. Each editor, reporter, and copyboy has a designated job, the end result of which is the newspaper that rolls off the press on time. —M.L. Stein

The final paragraph shows how a topic sentence at the end of the paragraph can act as a summary to state the point behind all the specific supporting information.

Supporting
information

TOPIC
SENTENCE

Quarterbacks must have skill in the art of throwing a pass, and they must think quickly because football is a fast-moving, complex sport. Running backs must also be fast on their feet and quick to move away from tacklers. Linemen, on the other hand, must be good at blocking the running advances of the other team, and they must develop strength and determination. *Each position in football requires special skills.*

EXERCISE A: Identifying Topic Sentences. Each of the following paragraphs contains a topic sentence and other sen-

tences with introductory or supporting information. Write the topic sentence from each paragraph on your paper. Remember that the topic sentence can be at the beginning, in the middle, or at the end of a paragraph.
Topic sentences are underlined. In Paragraph 3, the last sentence might also be chosen.

(1) Curiously, Venetian blinds neither originated nor gained fame in Venice. A type of Venetian blind seems to have existed in Nero's Rome, and archaeologists note that Egyptian tomb walls depict a primitive prototype of blinds—an artifact made of reeds, over which slaves poured water to cool the passing air. No one is sure how or when Venetian blinds came to the Western world. Some historians believe that Marco Polo brought them to Italy early in the fourteenth century; others assert that a liberated Persian slave took them to France in order to create a livelihood for himself. Venetian traders introduced the blinds to Great Britain, which probably accounts for our name for them.—Teresa Byrne-Dodge

(2) Wall paintings of many ancient Egyptian tombs picture the deceased playing a board game called *Senet*. Other *Senet* diagrams, scratched onto the walls of ancient temples and other buildings, indicate that the game was popular among watchmen, priests, and building workers. Peasants played it in the sand, with stones or ceramic pieces. But the pharaohs played it on magnificent boards made of rare woods, ivory, and faience. Archeological evidence clearly reveals that *Senet* was played by people at all levels of ancient Egyptian society. —Adapted from an article in *Games of the World*

(3) Dr. Sidney A. Gauthreaux, Jr., a professor at Clemson University, will never forget September 28, 1977. That night he surveyed migrating birds with radar and telescope at South Carolina's Greenville-Spartanburg Airport. Dr. Gauthreaux scanned a front, or line, across the path of migration and computed the number of birds that passed through it in a six-hour period. He got a peak count of 218,700 in one hour and more than a million in the six hours. From his data, he decided it was possible that fifty million birds were flying through the area over a front extending fifty miles.—Allan C. Fisher, Jr.

(4) Approximately thirty percent of humanity lives in industrial areas, such as Europe and North America, but these people consume about sixty percent of the world's food supply. Such percentages indicate that the world faces the problem of unequal distribution of food. The majority of the world's

people, constituting about seventy percent of the population, must attempt to live on only about forty percent of the world's food. In some parts of the world, millions of people live near starvation whereas for others the food supply is adequate or even plentiful.

■ Support for Topic Sentences

While the topic sentence presents the main idea, the support in a paragraph helps the reader understand that main idea. Supporting information must explain, explore, expand, or elaborate on the idea in the topic sentence.

Support for topic sentences can be examples, details, facts, reasons, incidents, or any combination of these.

Support can be of several kinds. *Examples* are typical instances or samples of an idea, principle, or method. *Details* are small parts or particulars that make up something larger. *Facts* are happenings, conditions, or observations that can be verified. *Reasons* are explanations, justifications, or causes. *Incidents* are minor events or happenings. Each of these kinds of support is slightly different from the others, but they often overlap. Sometimes the main idea in a paragraph has only one kind of support. Frequently, however, paragraphs contain support of several kinds, called *mixed support*.

In good paragraphs the support for the topic sentence consists of enough specific information to explain, illustrate, or complete the main idea. In order to include enough support, the writer must anticipate what a reader would like to know and needs to know to understand the main idea. As you examine the paragraphs that follow, notice the kinds and amounts of support used to develop the topic sentences.

The following paragraph describes the growing popularity of computer "time-sharing." All of the sentences after the topic sentence present reasons for the popularity of the system, backed up by examples that show the many ways in which the system can be used. After reading the paragraph, you should have a good idea of just why time-sharing has become so popular.

TOPIC
SENTENCE
In recent years, a new method of using the computer called "time-sharing" has become popular. It makes the computer more convenient for many

Reasons
and
examples

people to use. Time-sharing computer systems still have all the usual pieces of equipment but, in addition, they have input/output devices called terminals which can be located in the next room, the next block, the next town, or thousands of miles away. The terminals can be connected to the central computer by ordinary telephone lines. With time-sharing, users can input their data and immediately receive the output right in their offices, at a department store check-out counter, in the warehouse, the classroom, or even in their homes. —Judith B. Edwards

In the next paragraph, which is about railroad cars, the topic sentence prepares the reader for an explanation of "a great variety of cars" to transport different kinds of goods. The support for this main idea consists of three examples—boxcars, stockcars, and refrigerator cars—each of which is explained further with facts and details.

TOPIC
SENTENCE

Examples
with
facts and
details

Railroads have a great variety of cars in which to transport different kinds of goods. Perhaps the most familiar is the boxcar, which is completely enclosed with sides and a roof. It carries products that must be protected from the weather or from theft. A stockcar is a boxcar with slatted sides, to allow air for the animals inside. Less familiar, but equally important, is the refrigerator car, a boxcar chilled by means of ice or a machine. The refrigerator car is used to preserve perishable items. These different cars are specialized to suit the many different kinds of cargo that are sent along the rails. —*The New Book of Popular Science*

A topic sentence can also be developed with an incident. The incident recounted in the following paragraph is an account of the sinking of the *Titanic*. The topic sentence at the end draws a conclusion from the incident. Notice the use of facts and details to make the incident authentic and interesting and to make the topic sentence convincing.

Incident
with
facts and
details

In April, 1912, the RMS *Titanic* left Southampton, England on her maiden voyage. Less than a week out of port, the *Titanic* was sailing through a dense evening fog when the officers on the bridge sighted an iceberg approaching on the starboard side. Veering to port, the great ship could not clear the submerged arms of the iceberg, and she sideswiped the ice below her water line. Shutting down the engines, the crew immediately closed the watertight doors between the ship's compartments and began pumping out the sea water that had flooded the forward compartments. In less than one hour, the ship had taken in enough water to submerge her bow dangerously and list to starboard. Because of the shortage of lifeboats and jackets, as well as the speed with which the ship sank, 1,517 passengers and crew—more than half of the *Titanic*'s population—perished in the frigid north Atlantic. *The sinking of the RMS Titanic was one of the worst naval disasters in modern history.*

TOPIC
SENTENCE

The final paragraph in this section is also about the sinking of the *Titanic*. It has a topic sentence similar to the one in the preceding paragraph. But unlike the preceding paragraph, which presents an incident, this paragraph simply presents reasons and facts to support the main idea. The paragraph offers three reasons—the loss of lives, the insufficient rescue operations, and poor preparations for emergencies—to explain why this was one of the worst naval disasters in modern history. Notice that facts are used to back up the reasons.

TOPIC
SENTENCE

Reasons
with
facts

One of the worst naval disasters in modern history was the sinking of the RMS Titanic in the north Atlantic on April 15, 1912. This event was disastrous because the loss of lives was staggering. Of the 2,224 persons on board, 1,517 perished. Insufficient rescue operations contributed to the disaster. One nearby ship misunderstood or overlooked the *Titanic*'s distress signals, and another ship, the *Carpathia*, was several miles' distance away. Perhaps the main reason the collision with the iceberg became a calamity was the lack of preparation for just such an emergency. The ship had lifeboat space for less than half of the ship's passengers and crew and had too few life jackets for all the people aboard.

EXERCISE B: Identifying Support for Topic Sentences. Reread the paragraphs in Exercise A and examine the support. List the supporting information given in each paragraph. Then tell what kinds of support each paragraph uses to develop the topic sentence.

The class might discuss additional kinds of support for each paragraph.

EXERCISE C: Adding Supporting Information. The following paragraph lacks enough supporting information to be complete. List three or four pieces of information you could add to develop the topic sentence. Then copy the paragraph onto your paper, adding your own supporting information to make a complete paragraph.

The class could suggest additional items and rewrite the paragraph as a group exercise.

(1) The pets people choose reflect their personalities to some extent. (2) For instance, outgoing people often have large, active dogs that jog with them, ride in the car, chase frisbees or tennis balls, and accompany them on long walks through the woods or along the beach. (3) Thoughtful, intellectual people often prefer pedigree cats that are aloof and independent.

APPLICATION: **Evaluating Paragraphs.** Read the following two paragraphs carefully and determine which one is well-written. Write the topic sentence from the well-written paragraph on your paper and list the support used. Then study the paragraph with weaknesses and try to determine how the topic sentence and the supporting information can be improved. Finally, rewrite the weak paragraph, making the necessary changes.

Paragraph 1 is weak; revisions will vary. Students may need to rewrite the topic sentence in addition to strengthening the support for paragraph.

(1) The movie *Star Wars* was released in 1977. Almost overnight it became one of the most popular films of all time. It was directed and produced by George Lucas, and starred Alec Guinness, Mark Hamill, Carrie Fisher, and Harrison Ford, with James Earl Jones as the voice of the villainous Darth Vader. The best characters, however, were Chewbaca the Wookie and the robots C3PO and R2D2.

Paragraph 2 is well-written; the topic sentence is identified. The class could list pieces of support on the board.

(2) Nothing aggravates me as much as waiting for a tardy bus. At first, I am glad to be outside on my way home, but my mood gradually sours as the minutes tick by. For the first few minutes, I breathe in the fresh air and wonder about the people passing. How far does that jogger run? Does that old man muttering to his cane live by himself? Five minutes later I realize the bus is late, put down my packages, and try to find new amusements. I watch the sun setting behind the buildings and the jets crisscrossing overhead. Glancing at my watch again, I notice that ten more minutes have passed. Is the bus trapped on the bridge in a traffic jam? Did the driver take a late coffee break? I shift back and forth on my feet, open my book, and close it again for fear the bus might drive by. I begin to think of all the things I could have done had I been home on time. By now the bus is twenty-five minutes late. I play the count-the-cars game. Maybe the bus will be

the eleventh vehicle to go through the intersection. When the thirtieth vehicle passes, I resolve to report the driver. Then from around the corner two 93 buses appear. I get on the first one, scowl at the driver, and flop down in the only empty seat, too annoyed to speak to anyone.

23.2 Recognizing Unity and Coherence

In addition to having an identifiable main idea and specific supporting information, a good paragraph has unity and coherence. It has unity because all the specific information belongs together and develops one main idea. It has coherence because the organization of the paragraph and the use of certain words throughout the paragraph help a reader understand the relationship between the ideas. A good paragraph, then, reads smoothly and logically with all its supporting ideas in harmony with each other and with the topic sentence.

In this section, you will learn more about unity and coherence and some devices for achieving them so you can work on these goals in your own paragraphs.

■ Unity

A paragraph should not stray from the main idea presented in the topic sentence. All the supporting information in the other sentences of the paragraph should concentrate on that main idea.

Sometimes, however, writers follow their spontaneous thoughts without checking them against their topic sentence. In this way they destroy the unity of their paragraphs. They either elaborate too much on one supporting idea and allow the focus of the paragraph to shift or they include information not directly related to the topic sentence. Any information outside the range of the topic sentence destroys the unity of a paragraph.

A paragraph is unified if all of its sentences illustrate and develop the topic sentence and if all the sentences are closely related.

A unified paragraph with adequate supporting information fulfills the reader's expectations because it goes into some depth on one manageable topic.

If you examine a paragraph without unity, you will see how confusing and unsatisfactory such a paragraph can be. The following paragraph begins by focusing on the color of penguins but then wanders away from the main idea.

TOPIC SENTENCE	The basic pattern of penguins, dark above and white below, has survival advantages. In the southern oceans, dense with plankton, the water is
Supporting information without unity	murky, and a penguin's dark back viewed from above as it slips through the depths is hard to see. Viewed from below, its white front all but disappears against the silvery light that filters down from the sky. *Penguins look like proud little men in tuxedos. Their flippers, which look like short, stiff arms, have prompted some scientists to argue that penguins never flew. Other scientists, however, maintain that the ancestors of penguins lost their ability to fly and developed their flippers as they adopted other methods of locomotion, such as swimming, sliding on their chests, and running.*

In contrast to the preceding paragraph, the paragraph that follows, taken in its entirety from a magazine, does have unity. It begins with a discussion of the protective coloring of penguins and sticks with this idea throughout instead of changing to a discussion of the appearance of penguins and the development of their flippers.

TOPIC SENTENCE	The basic pattern of penguins, dark above and white below, has survival advantages. In the southern oceans, dense with plankton, the water is
Supporting information with unity	murky, and a penguin's dark back viewed from above as it slips through the depths is hard to see. Viewed from below, its white underparts all but disappear against the silvery light that filters down from the sky. This natural camouflage, known as "countershading," serves the penguin well when eluding the leopard seal and the sharks. It matters little that this same bicolored pattern is blatantly conspicuous on shore; land-based predators are not usually found on the islands where penguins consort for breeding. —Roger Tory Peterson

To maintain the unity of a paragraph, you should examine your supporting information before, during, and after writing the paragraph and ask yourself what each piece of support contributes to the reader's understanding of the main idea. Any sentence that does not fit in with the sentences that come before and after it as well as with the topic sentence should be removed from the paragraph.

EXERCISE A: Identifying Paragraphs with Unity. Read each of the following paragraphs carefully. If a paragraph is unified, write *unity* on your paper. If a paragraph lacks unity, write the sentences that stray from the main idea on your paper. *Problem sentences in 1 and 3 are crossed out.*

(1) A hurricane begins as a small, seemingly insignificant tropical storm and grows into a spinning, rampaging killer. A hurricane first appears as a tropical disturbance caused by a drop in barometric pressure. Tornadoes also result partly from changes in pressure but do not always develop from tropical storms. As the drop in pressure attracts heat, wind activity builds, and the storm begins to move. As it moves, the storm then joins other warm, moisture-laden air and converts to high winds and rain. Precipitation is not usually a characteristic of tornadoes. Finally, the storm reaches hurricane intensity, spinning counter-clockwise. Few other forces in·nature are as unpredictable—and as deadly—as a hurricane.

(2) Certain advantages helped the American colonists win their war for independence. The Americans had one advantage of fighting on their own soil, whereas English troops had to travel 3,000 miles. The Americans were also more experienced wilderness fighters, having previously battled to win upstate New York and the Northwest Territory. Another advantage was the entry of France into the war. This greatly aided the American battle effort. In addition, foreign volunteers helped in the Americans' struggle. The greatest advantage for the Americans was the strength, courage, and dedication of such leaders as George Washington, General Nathanael Greene, and John Paul Jones. *unity*

(3) The plot of *Love Story* centers on two characters. Oliver Barrett IV, a boy from a wealthy New England family, is an undergraduate at Harvard University. There, he meets a girl named Jennifer Cavilleri. Though Jennifer is poor, her liveliness and wit attract Oliver, who soon falls in love with her. The story is about the problems involved in their love and

marriage. Another character, Mr. Barrett, Oliver's father, dis-approves of Oliver and Jennifer's relationship. Still another character, Mr. Cavilleri, Jennifer's father, supports their re-lationship. The story is also about religious and social differ-ences and prejudices.

■ Coherence

A paragraph has coherence if all of its supporting ideas are presented in an order that a reader can easily follow. A coherent paragraph is constructed logically, with transitions that form bridges between the supporting ideas. In a coher ent paragraph, the writer may also guide the reader by repeating main words, by using synonyms, by using clear pronouns, by using parallel structures, or by ending with a sentence that completes the thought of the paragraph.

A paragraph is coherent if all of the sentences are logically ordered and if the relationships between the ideas are clearly shown with transitions and other linking devices.

You should give thought to coherence as you plan, draft, and revise your paragraphs. The pages that follow will show you a number of different ways to organize your paragraphs and to connect your ideas.

Orders for Supporting Information. You can order supporting information in a paragraph in a number of ways. The order you choose should grow out of the topic you are developing and should help you present that topic logically. Having a definite order for the ideas in a paragraph prevents the ideas from jumping around in a way that would confuse a reader.

The following chart explains some of the most common orders used in paragraphs.

ORDERING SUPPORTING INFORMATION	
Order	**How It Works**
Order of importance	Major pieces of supporting information are arranged from least important to most important or vice versa.

Chronological (time)	Major pieces of supporting information or steps are arranged in a time sequence according to when they happened or should happen.
Spatial (space)	Major details and other supporting information are arranged by position— near to far, far to near, top to bottom, front to back, and so on.
Comparison and contrast	All of the supporting information for one item is presented and then all of the supporting information for the other is presented (AAA-BBB), or supporting information for both items is compared and contrasted point by point (AB-AB-AB).
Developmental	When none of the other orders fits, supporting information is arranged in the most logical fashion; for instance, three or more related and equally important items could be mentioned in the topic sentence and then be discussed in that order.

Sometimes a topic, such as a process or a description, will fit perfectly into one of the first four orders in the chart. Other times, a topic sentence will suggest its own *developmental* order, with three examples or three details mentioned in the topic sentence, for instance. In this case, you would just follow the order you established in the topic sentence. In still other cases, you will have to construct your own developmental order to suit a particular topic sentence.

Whatever order you choose, you must make sure that each piece of support either directly develops the topic sentence or directly expands the piece of supporting information immediately before it. Following this guideline will help you write logical paragraphs.

The paragraphs and explanations that follow show how some of the orders in the chart can be used effectively to clarify ideas in a paragraph.

Order of importance is particularly useful in paragraphs that attempt to persuade the audience as well as in many paragraphs that offer explanations and reasons. By building from least important to most important or from simplest to most complex, a writer can gradually gain the audience's understanding or agreement and then conclude forcefully. In the following paragraph, the words *heads the list, second, third,* and *most dreadful* indicate that the order of the pieces of support is from least serious to most serious.

TOPIC SENTENCE	The chief reasons for the decreases in wild animals and plants fall into understandable categories. Exploitation of the wild resources for useful products *heads the list. Second,* and increasingly rapidly, is destruction of the natural environment in which the animals and plants live. *Third* is competition from introduced species, whether livestock or pests (such as rats and plant diseases) or kinds of life from which some good was anticipated (such as starlings or mongooses). Today the *most dreadful threat* is the unselective poisoning of the environment by chemical compounds that have been added either in attempts to minimize losses from pests or merely as industrial wastes.
Support organized in order of importance	
	—Lorus and Margery Milne

Chronological order arranges supporting information in a time sequence, for example, from first to last, from the past to the present, or from the present to the future. Historical topics, procedures, and processes often follow a time order. In the following paragraph, the words *first, once, then,* and *finally* help the reader see immediately that the supporting information is organized by time.

TOPIC SENTENCE	Students who wish to become doctors must plan on many years of demanding study and strenuous work beyond high school. *First,* they must complete four years of liberal arts studies including certain pre-med courses. *Once* they have finished college, pre-med students must attend medical school, usually for an additional four years of intensive study in medicine. *Then,* following medical school, doctors must complete internship and residency requirements at a hospital or other medical facility for at least another one to two years. *Finally,* when reviewed by supervisors and other doctors, the new doctors are ready to practice their profession.
Support organized in chronological order	

Spatial order, which organizes ideas over space rather than over time, is most useful for descriptions. It gives a reader a visual understanding of the relationship of one object to another. Words such as *over, behind, in front of, beside, above, to the right of,* and so on indicate organization by space or position.

Comparison and contrast can be regarded as a purpose as well as a method of organizing ideas. For instance, your purpose or goal in writing a particular paragraph might be to compare and contrast two places you have lived. The order you would use in such a paragraph would be comparison and contrast. As an order, comparison and contrast has two main variations. You can present all of the supporting information for one item and then compare and contrast the second item with the first: AAA-BBB. Or you can present the similarities of and differences between items point by point: AB-AB-AB. Sometimes a topic can be treated equally well using either method, as the following two examples show. The first paragraph follows the AAA-BBB order. Notice that *on the other hand* indicates a shift from the first item to the second item.

TOPIC SENTENCE

Support organized in comparison-and-contrast order (AAA-BBB)

There is a definite distinction between science and engineering. The scientist is usually interested only in extending knowledge of some aspect of the natural world. Scientists want to know why things happen, but are not necessarily interested in useful applications of their discoveries. They usually do not create a product such as a steam-turbine electric generating unit. Their ideas and concepts are their products. Scientists isolate new chemical elements, explore the atom, and make discoveries in fields such as dietetics and thermodynamics. They seek answers to questions concerning space, sound, and nuclear physics. Engineers, *on the other hand*, are concerned with the intelligent application of scientific knowledge to the solution of technical problems. They want to know not only why and how things work, but how they can be made to work better and more economically. Engineers must be cost-conscious, because projects are considered practical only if each dollar invested yields a satisfactory return. Furthermore, the engineer has a definite responsibility for public safety. —Charles N. Gaylord

The same paragraph could also be written using a point-by-point method of comparison and contrast, as shown in the next paragraph. Notice the words in italics that guide the reader in understanding the similarities and differences.

TOPIC SENTENCE

There is a definite distinction between science and engineering. The scientist is usually interested mainly in extending knowledge of some as-

Support
organized
in
comparison-
and-
contrast
order
(AB-AB-AB)

pect of the natural world. Engineers, *on the other hand*, are concerned with the intelligent application of scientific knowledge to the solution of technical problems. *While* scientists want to know why things happen, they are not necessarily interested in useful applications of their discoveries. Engineers also want to know why and how things work, *but in addition*, they want to discover how things can be made to work better and more economically. Scientists usually do not create a product such as a steam-turbine electric generating unit. *Instead*, their ideas and concepts are their products. Scientists isolate new chemical elements, explore the atom, and make discoveries in fields such as dietetics and thermodynamics. They seek answers to questions concerning space, sound, and nuclear physics. Engineers, *however*, must be cost-conscious, because their projects are considered practical only if each dollar invested yields a satisfactory return. *Furthermore*, the engineer has a definite responsibility for public safety.

Many paragraphs simply proceed logically, without the framework of a rigid order. These paragraphs use developmental order in that the only requirement of the order is that the other sentences help develop the topic sentence.

As you read the following paragraph about sights and sounds in a forest, notice that each sentence follows the one that came before it logically and each adds relevant information to the topic sentence.

TOPIC
SENTENCE

Support
organized
in develop-
mental
order

The high point of our seven-park pilgrimage came at Corcovado when we stepped out of the plane into the deep, cool shade of the tropical forest. Huge trees, some more than 200 feet high and six feet in diameter, towered over a rich tangle of smaller trees and vegetation. *Here and there* we heard a sound like the patter of rain and discovered it was thousands of tiny pink and yellow blossoms floating down from tall trees. Hummingbirds hovered *above* the fallen blossoms, whose fragrance mingled with the earthy odor of the damp, decomposing leaves underfoot. *Now and then* there was loud chattering as parrots flashed by. —Robert and Patricia Cahn

Transitions. Transitions are words and phrases that connect one idea to another. They often highlight the logical order of supporting ideas and make a paragraph more than a mere list of information. To clarify the relationship between supporting ideas and to make your sentences flow smoothly, you should employ transitions. A reader can easily follow the progression of ideas in a paragraph with transitions. In the paragraphs you have just been reading, the words in italics are transitions.

Many words can function as transitions. (For more information on transitions, see Section 22.2, page 597.) The following chart presents some examples of transitions grouped according to the orders they usually clarify.

SOME WORDS THAT CAN BE TRANSITIONS			
For Order of Importance		**For Chronological Order**	
first	also	first	during
second	most . . .	next	afterwards
third	greatest	then	finally
next	least	later	moments later
one	even greater	soon	in the meantime
another	for one reason	now	at the moment
finally	moreover	after	formerly
		before	at last
For Spatial Order		**For Comparison and Contrast**	
outside	to the left	like	in addition
inside	ahead	besides	similar to
near	overhead	and	however
behind	beneath	both	on the contrary
closer	above	whereas	in contrast
around	in the distance	similarly	on the other hand
beyond		likewise	
For Developmental Order			
also	namely	as a result	along with
furthermore	moreover	consequently	next
for example	in addition	thus	in fact
for instance	other	therefore	

The following paragraph illustrates the use of transitions to clarify the ideas that the writer has organized for the reader. The paragraph explains how to start your own family history, using the transitions *then, also, once,* and *final* to explain the major steps involved.

TOPIC
SENTENCE

If you are the sort of person who enjoys a historical detective game, you can trace your own family history. Begin by getting a large looseleaf

Support
connected
by
transitions

notebook and making a chart. *Then* visit old relatives and get them to talk about their parents,
grandparents, aunts, where they came from, when
they married, maiden names, family traditions,
and so on: You can *also* try to get your hands on
old family Bibles, diaries, letters, and account
books. *Once* you have exhausted these sources,
you can try libraries with genealogical depart-
ments where you'll find such material as family
histories, town and local histories, and even collections of original documents. As a *final* resort,
you can try old wills in a local probate office,
church records, pension records, and census reports. —Adapted from Judith Chasek

Other Helpful Words. Organizing your supporting information and using transitions can help guide the reader
through your paragraph; repeating main words and using
well-chosen synonyms and pronouns can also help to connect ideas in the paragraph. By repeating certain main
words—often those important nouns and verbs in your topic
sentence—you can emphasize your ideas. Main words repeated throughout a paragraph focus the reader's attention.
A second way to unify your ideas and also add variety is to
use a synonym for a main word. However, you should not
strain to come up with synonyms simply for variety. Remember your purpose is to aid the reader and to make your
writing flow, not to confuse the reader with forced synonyms. The use of pronouns to replace main words is a third
way to make the ideas in your paragraphs hold together. If
you are careful to make your pronouns agree with their antecedents, you can lead the reader smoothly from idea to
idea and avoid monotony and unnecessary repetition.

The following paragraph on pop art uses repetition of
main words, synonyms, and a number of clear pronouns.
The words in italics form one connecting thread of ideas,
and the words in bold letters form another. Notice how
these threads contribute to the flow and clarity of the ideas.

TOPIC
SENTENCE

Support
connected
by main
words,
synonyms,
and
pronouns

For years now on the mud flats on the east side
of the San Francisco Bay, *artists* and *ordinary people* have been creating **imaginative sculptures** by
nailing together driftwood and debris. *These sculptors* build **trains** and **ballerinas**, **chickens** and **totem poles**, **whales** and **airplanes** with wood, hub-
caps, old tires, rusty cans, and whatever washes
ashore. **Some of the pieces** are skillfully done; **others** are quite crude. **Some** manage to remain
standing for a year or two; **others** last only a few

> days before succumbing to the winds or the tides or the hands of *another artist* who needs the materials for **another work**. Almost **all** are done anonymously. All for the sheer fun of it. The result is an outdoor gallery of pop art. The thousands of motorists who daily drive the nearby freeway provide the audience. —Adapted from J. Fritz Lanham

In the preceding paragraph, one thread is formed by the words *artists* and *ordinary people, these sculptors,* and *another artist.* The main thread is the idea *imaginative sculptures,* created with the following words and synonyms: *trains, ballerinas, chickens, totem poles, whales, airplanes, some of the pieces, others, some, others, another work, all.*

Parallelism and Concluding Sentences. The structure and placement of sentences can also link the ideas within paragraphs.

Parallelism is the use of similar grammatical structures in a series; single words go together, phrases go together, and clauses go together. By writing sentences with parallel clauses, you can indicate to the reader that two ideas are equal in importance. For instance, if you were writing a paragraph that had three examples, you might present the examples in three similar sentences. These similar sentences could come one after the other or could be separated by sentences containing additional details and facts.

In the following paragraph, the writer presents three facts that are "the basic ingredients" of a thunderstorm. The repetition of the subject-verb pattern and the verb *must be* identify the ingredients for the reader and link the supporting ideas in the paragraph.

TOPIC SENTENCE	The basic ingredients of an isolated air-mass thunderstorm are fairly simple. The moisture in the air must be plentiful, up to a level of 10,000 feet or higher. The surface of the ground and the air just above it must be well heated by the sun. And the atmosphere must be unstable, which means that the air at higher levels must be a great deal cooler than the air at lower levels. —Adapted from Henry Lansford
Support in parallel sentences	

A *concluding sentence* can sometimes be used to strengthen the coherence of a paragraph. A concluding sentence can summarize the supporting ideas in the paragraph, restate the topic sentence in different words, or function as a punchline by expressing a final point briefly, forcefully, and memorably. This last kind of concluding sentence is often called a *clincher*. Although a concluding sentence is not always needed, sometimes a concluding sentence can wrap up the ideas in the paragraph, making it complete.

In the following paragraph, Virginia Woolf's description of the wax statue of Queen Elizabeth in the Abbey Waxworks ends with a concluding sentence, which echoes the topic sentence and captures the mood of the paragraph.

TOPIC SENTENCE	The Queen dominates the room as she once dominated England. Leaning a little forward so that she seems to beckon you to come to her, she stands, holding her sceptre in one hand, her orb in the other. It is a drawn, anguished figure, with the pursed look of someone who goes in perpetual dread of poison or a trap; yet forever braces herself to meet the terror unflinchingly. Her eyes are wide and vigilant; her nose thin as the beak of a hawk; her lips shut tight; her eyebrows arched; only the jowl gives the fine drawn face its massiveness. The orb and the sceptre are held in the long thin hands of an artist, as if the fingers thrilled at the touch of them. She is immensely in-
Concluding sentence	tellectual, suffering, and tyrannical. *She will not allow one to look elsewhere.* —Virginia Woolf

EXERCISE B: Recognizing Orders of Supporting Information in Paragraphs. Read the following paragraphs and write on your paper which order is used in each to present the supporting information logically.

(1) The surface of a mountain may appear placid, quiet, and covered with snow. Yet beneath the surface, the weight of the snow compresses itself at the lower levels. Deep down, the weight of the snow displaces air and forms layers of ice. One layer of ice slides along another. From thousands of feet beneath the surface, a glacier "walks." *spatial*

(2) Buster Keaton produced one kind of comedy, Charlie Chaplin quite another. And Keaton's was the purer use of the form. Keaton was cool, detached, and very strictly funny, never suggesting for a moment that we need worry ourselves about what might happen to him. If a building fell on him during a cyclone, we were not to be apprehensive: When the dust cleared, he would be standing in the small space made safe for him by an open second-story window. Keaton himself

never displayed emotion. Chaplin's comedy, by comparison, was blurred. Chaplin would be in love with a girl until she snatched a bit of his food. Then he hit her. But there would be none of Keaton's detachment or objectivity in the quick slap. Chaplin would be momentarily asserting his self-interest. And yet a moment later he would sigh and share everything he had with the girl. As comedy, Chaplin's work is hopelessly impure. Yet no one has ever questioned Chaplin's superiority to Keaton. The impure comedian is greater than the pure comedian: He shows us *more*; he shows us who he is and how he got that way. —Walter Kerr *comparison and contrast*

(3) The presence of scientists is no accident, for Costa Rica is a kind of Mecca for tropical research. It has sweltering lowland rain forests along both Caribbean and southern Pacific coasts; dry, thorny forests along the northern Pacific Coast; and cool, lush cloud forests in the central mountains. As part of a narrow land bridge joining two continents, it has an exceptional variety of fauna and flora. At Corcovado, American scientist Gary Hartshorn once identified 111 different species of trees on a two-acre plot. Costa Rica has close to 800 species of birds, over 100 more than can be found in all of North America above Mexico. —Robert and Patricia Cahn *developmental*

(4) In colonial America a family's place on the social scale might vary considerably through the course of two or three generations. Several factors account for this relatively high degree of social mobility. For one, America had no titled aristocracy, no dukes and duchesses, lords and ladies, monopolizing positions of political and economic power. For another, labor was constantly in great demand, and a man willing to work hard could move up the social scale. Still more significant was the cheap land available in the unsettled interior of the country. People discontented with their life in established communities could move in search of new opportunities. —Adapted from the *Encyclopedia Americana* *order of importance*

EXERCISE C: Recognizing the Devices That Add Coherence.

Reread the paragraphs in Exercise B. Then choose two to analyze for coherence. For each paragraph make a list of (1) the transitions and (2) the repetition of main words, synonyms, and pronouns. Then write down (3) any parallel sentences and (4) the concluding sentence, if there is one.

The class might do one paragraph first as a group exercise.

EXERCISE D: Improving the Coherence of a Paragraph. In the following paragraph, the writer has not included transitions and has made no effort to make the ideas clear or to make the sentences flow. The paragraph also needs a concluding sentence. Rewrite the paragraph on your paper, adding transitions to show the relationships between the ideas. If necessary, change the words to achieve coherence with repetition of main words, synonyms, and pronouns. If you can use parallelism, do so. Then write a suitable concluding sentence for the paragraph. *Answers will vary. One method of increasing coherence would be to focus on the three possible meanings of "breaking away" presented in the paragraph.*

(1) In the movie *Breaking Away*, the title has a number of meanings. (2) The movie features a bicycle race. (3) When a rider "breaks away," takes the lead and charges ahead of the rest of the pack, the audience feels like cheering. (4) Four friends in the movie spend the year after their high school graduation drifting with little to do and no goals for their lives. (5) Dave Stoller's obsession with bicycles helps him to escape from the discontent and aimlessness of Mike, Cyril, and Moocher. (6) The setting is the university town of Bloomington, Indiana. (7) The young residents of the town, called "cutters" because the townspeople once engaged in marble cutting, resent the university students and feel inferior to them. (8) Dave leaves the "cutters" to enroll in the university.

APPLICATION: Evaluating Paragraphs for Unity and Coherence. Of the following two paragraphs, one has unity and coherence and the other does not. Identify the good paragraph and write the following information about it on your paper: (1) the order of supporting information; (2) the transitions used; (3) the repetitions of main words and any synonyms and pronouns used; and (4) any use of parallelism and the concluding sentence, if there is one. Then rewrite the weak paragraph by removing any unrelated thoughts, by improving the organization of the sentences, and by adding transitions and possibly some of the other devices for coherence. *Paragraph 1 is supported by details and examples arranged in developmental order. Transitions and other connectives are underlined. The last sentence is a concluding sentence.*

(1) Some <u>department stores</u> exhibit one attitude toward <u>shoppers: Confuse</u> and <u>conquer</u>. They cleverly <u>manipulate shoppers</u> into <u>buying</u>. With attractive displays of elegantly furnished rooms, of towels, sheets, and quilts in designer prints

and flashy colors, and of jaunty mannequins in the latest suits and sportswear, the stores overwhelm the shopper. Unintentionally the shopper flits from rack to rack like a butterfly, forgetting what he or she intended to get and finding additional things to buy. The hanging mirrors and glittering mirror walls multiply the dazzle, increasing the shopper's disorientation even more. In addition, department stores often have puzzling organizations. One item, such as blouses or shoes, may be scattered throughout the store in four or five little sections like boutiques. The shopper cannot possibly get an overview of the entire selection and then choose one item. Consequently, the shopper may wander from section to section and end up buying two blouses or two sports shirts instead of one. Or on some floors, one department may spill over into the next, again exposing the shopper to the appeal of more merchandise. Artistically stocked with everything from tie tacks to silk flowers and from swim suits to Persian rugs, some department stores have become powerful persuaders, tempting the shopper to make unnecessary purchases.

Revisions of Paragraph 2 will vary, but might focus on the benefits of running, rather than on the marathons.

(2) Minutes spent running for exercise each day can be some of the best minutes of the day. The runner is outside in the sunshine, fresh air, and soothing breeze. The ideal weather for a marathon is a clear, dry, brisk day with moderate temperatures. The runner can almost feel fat melting away and muscles building. The runner can forget the frustrations and problems of the day as he or she speeds through a park, around a reservoir, or through a neighborhood. Running is invigorating. Marathons are by definition twenty-six miles and 385 yards long. The New York City and Boston Marathons are among the most famous races in the country. Crowds gather at the finish line to greet the winners. The runner dons a tank top or T-shirt and light-weight shorts and feels comfortable and free. The runner's heart and lungs work in a fast, steady rhythm as his or her shoes tap the ground.

23.3 Planning and Drafting Your Paragraphs

Recognizing the characteristics of a good paragraph will help you know *what* you want to achieve in your own writing. However, you will also need to know *how* to practice what you have learned about good topic sentences, strong supporting information, unity, and coherence.

Although the writing process differs from person to person, certain basic steps can aid you in the planning, organizing, and drafting of your paragraphs. You can learn how to discover an idea you want to express, how to develop it, and how to write it in a paragraph that will best convey your meaning. This section will explain the steps of selecting a topic and shaping it into a topic sentence, of gathering supporting information, of organizing the supporting information, and of drafting the paragraph. When you are comfortable with these steps, you can adapt them to fit your writing needs.

■ Writing a Topic Sentence

To go from a blank piece of paper to a topic sentence and later a complete paragraph, you must be prepared to do some brainstorming and careful analysis. Most likely you have many ideas or beginnings of ideas for paragraphs that can be drawn out and expanded. In the first step of writing a paragraph, you must consider possible topics, select one, and narrow it so you can write about it in some depth in one paragraph. As you write your topic sentence, you must concentrate on presenting just one main idea about your topic, on communicating with your audience, and on achieving your purpose.

Finding a Suitable Paragraph Topic. A suitable paragraph topic is one that you can develop thoroughly in one paragraph. In order to do this, you should make sure that it is not too big and general. For instance, wind-surfing, llamas, Washington, D.C., antique cars, careers in law, twentieth-century American poets, and aircraft carriers are broad topics. On the other hand, places to wind-surf, llamas as pets, the most valuable antique car, the duties of a judge, New England poets of the sixties, and the design of the decks of aircraft carriers, although still large topics, are narrower in scope than the first group. Therefore, they could be discussed more easily within a paragraph. To write a well-supported paragraph about a topic, you should also have some interest in and knowledge of the topic. In addition, a suitable paragraph topic must fit the requirements of your particular assignment.

To find a suitable paragraph topic, brainstorm for ideas and jot down possible topics on paper. If you have already chosen a topic and it seems too large, divide it into smaller topics. When you have selected a topic, examine it to see if you can work with it in a paragraph.

Brainstorm for a topic, break down topics into smaller topics if necessary, and select a manageable paragraph topic.

If you have been asked to write a paragraph on a book you have just read, you might brainstorm for a paragraph topic in the following manner. You could not adequately describe the whole book in one paragraph, so you would have to find some part of the book to focus on. If you had read Ray Bradbury's futuristic book *Fahrenheit 451*, you might make a list of topics and smaller topics similar to the one in the following chart. Although a few of the broader topics, such as the title of the book, would make a suitable paragraph topic, you will often find it more useful to choose one of the smaller topics listed underneath a broader topic.

BRAINSTORMING FOR A PARAGRAPH TOPIC ON *FAHRENHEIT 451*	
Characters	**High Technology of the Society**

—Guy Montag
  changes in Guy
—Clarisse McClellan
  her strangeness
  her influence on Guy
—Mildred Montag
—Captain Beatty
—Professor Faber
	—mechanical gadgets in homes
	  wall-to-wall circuit television
	  thimble radios
	—the Fun Park
	—the Mechanical Hound
	—mechanical gadgets in schools

Important Episodes	**Title—*Fahrenheit 451***
—the woman dying with her books —Montag's burning his own house —Montag's escape	**Firemen's job—to burn books** **Society's philosophy of books**

After examining your list, you might decide that *the Mechanical Hound* would make a suitable paragraph topic.

Focusing on Your Main Idea, Audience, and Purpose.   To find what you want to say in your paragraph, you will have to probe your thoughts and the paragraph topic further. You should decide exactly what you want to say about the paragraph topic. Thinking about your audience will help you select and focus on a main idea. A third decision involves your purpose. Will you be explaining, persuading, describing, or entertaining? Sometimes, you will begin with a purpose and that purpose will help you find and clarify a main idea. Other times, your purpose will grow out of your main idea. When you have made these decisions, you should write your topic sentence.

Think about your audience and purpose as you write a topic sentence that presents your main idea about the paragraph topic.

A paragraph topic must be focused on one main idea in order to become a topic sentence. Often you can find a main idea about a topic if you first determine the interests, background, and knowledge of your audience. For instance, for the topic on the Mechanical Hound, you might choose to write to those students in your class who have not read the book. To determine a main idea, ask yourself a series of questions about your topic that you think your audience might like to know the answers to. You should learn to think of questions that can stimulate your own thinking as well: Why are *you* interested in the topic? What one idea about the topic would *you* like to tell others? Why is the topic important? The answers to these and other questions will give you possible main ideas for your paragraph.

If you were thinking about the Mechanical Hound, you might write this list of questions and possible main ideas.

QUESTIONS LEADING TO POSSIBLE MAIN IDEAS	
Paragraph Topic: the Mechanical Hound in *Fahrenheit 451*	
Question	**Main Idea**
Why am I interested in the topic?	The Mechanical Hound is the most frightening part of the book.
What one idea would I like to tell others?	The Mechanical Hound, though a machine, functions as a main character in the story.

Why is it important?	The Mechanical Hound stands for the society that it serves.

When you have examined different main ideas that could be developed, you should select one to write about. Make sure that the main idea you select suits your audience and your purpose. Notice that with the first main idea in the preceding chart, your purpose would most likely be to persuade. With the second main idea, your purpose would most likely be to explain. If you used the third main idea, your purpose would probably be to convince. As you choose your main idea, you should also consider which will make the most interesting paragraph for your audience, which will be the easiest to support and develop, and which will you enjoy writing about the most.

You are now ready to write your topic sentence. You should actually write at least two versions of your topic sentence. Try different wordings, maybe different lengths, as you attempt to express the main idea clearly and concisely. Your topic sentence commits you to develop thoroughly that one idea you have chosen. With it, you are setting up the audience's expectations of what will be covered in the paragraph. Therefore, experiment with your topic sentence until you express your main idea most clearly.

If you were using the third of the possible main ideas listed in the chart, you might write these versions of your topic sentence.

POSSIBLE TOPIC SENTENCES

1. In Bradbury's *Fahrenheit 451*, the Mechanical Hound stands for the society it serves.
2. In Bradbury's *Fahrenheit 451*, the Mechanical Hound is a symbol of the mechanical, destructive society that uses it.
3. In Bradbury's *Fahrenheit 451*, the Mechanical Hound symbolizes the mechanical, destructive society that it serves.
4. In *Fahrenheit 451*, Bradbury uses the Mechanical Hound as a symbol of the mechanical, destructive society that it serves.

Although you could use any of these four topic sentences, some of them are clearer than others. For example, the first topic sentence is the most open-ended of the four because it tells the reader the least about the paragraph that will follow. The other three experiment with slightly different wordings. You might choose the fourth version to be your topic sentence because it gives the most information to the reader and the clearest guidelines to you.

EXERCISE A: Choosing and Narrowing Topics for Paragraphs. From the following list of general topics, choose the five that appeal to you most and write them on your paper. Beneath each, write two smaller topics that might be suitable for a paragraph. Then circle the one smaller topic that you would most like to write about.

One topic might be broken down into smaller topics as a class exercise.

Home movies	Travel	Professional
Boats	Safety hazards	athletes
Weather	Camping	Classical music
Astronomy	Crafts	Biographies
Conservation	Deserts	
Sportsmanship	Friendship	

EXERCISE B: Preparing Topic Sentences. Use the paragraph topic that you chose in Exercise A in the following steps.

1. Write the paragraph topic on your paper.
2. Decide on your audience and briefly describe it (for example, people unfamiliar with the topic, experts, strangers, friends, and so on).
3. Find some possible main ideas about your paragraph topic by asking yourself at least three questions. Write the questions and your answers on your paper.
4. Looking at your possible main ideas, choose your purpose: to inform or explain, to persuade, to describe, or to entertain. Then choose the main idea most suitable for your audience and purpose.
5. Write three versions of your topic sentence.
6. Finally, choose the topic sentence that most clearly expresses your main idea and that has the greatest appeal to you. Circle it on your paper.

Students should follow these steps systematically; their progress at each stage might be monitored.

■ Gathering Supporting Information for a Topic Sentence

Once you have a topic sentence, your second major step is to gather the supporting information that will explain and develop your main idea. The main idea in your topic sentence, even the words you have chosen to express that idea, can help you come up with supporting information. After you have made a list of supporting information, you should evaluate it to make sure you have the best support and the right amount of support for your audience to understand your main idea.

Brainstorming for Specific Information. Throughout the planning and thinking stages you have done so far, you have probably had many ideas about support for your main idea. Your task as you gather support is to compile the ideas you already have and then find even more related supporting ideas. To do this, you should probe your main idea for supporting information that will clarify and illustrate it.

> Brainstorm for examples, details, facts, reasons, and incidents that explain and expand the main idea in your topic sentence.

Writers use a number of methods to find appropriate supporting information for their main ideas about their topics. Your goal is to produce a list of strong, relevant supporting information that will fulfill the expectations set up by your topic sentence. Two possible methods you can use to achieve this goal are (1) using questions to determine the information your audience might want to know about your main idea and (2) free-associating with your topic sentence to find related ideas.

Using the questioning method, you should put yourself in the reader's place and examine your topic sentence carefully as a reader would see it. Ask yourself: What terms in the topic sentence need to be defined or described? What part of the main idea calls for examples, facts, or reasons? Then answer the questions with information about the main idea. If you were to use the questioning method for the topic sentence on the Mechanical Hound, your list of possible questions and answers might look like the following.

QUESTIONING TO FIND SUPPORT FOR A TOPIC SENTENCE

Topic Sentence:	In *Fahrenheit 451*, Bradbury uses the Mechanical Hound as a symbol of the mechanical, destructive society that it serves.

What is the Mechanical Hound?
—made of copper and steel   —runs quickly and quietly,
—has eight legs   leaps on victims

In what way is the society mechanical?
—uses machines for
everything—recreation,
schools, transportation,
medicine, law enforcement

—homes have wall-to-wall
circuit TV
—people listen to little radios
in their ears constantly

In what way is the society destructive?
—forces everyone to be alike;
doesn't allow people to
think, ask questions, or
communicate

—gets rid of people who try
to be different
—Fun Park has such
amusements as car wrecker
and window smasher

How is the Mechanical Hound a symbol of the society's
mechanical nature?
—Mechanical Hound is one
of society's advanced,
complex machines; runs by
computers
—a robot, more powerful
than a real dog

—can be set to identify
10,000 different people at a
time by their body
chemistry
—society has complete
confidence in it

How is the Mechanical Hound a symbol of the society's
destructiveness?
—firemen enjoy watching the
Mechanical Hound kill
rats, chickens, and cats
—used to track and kill
criminals as well as people
who simply dare to be
different
—shows how inhuman and
violent society has become

—society uses the Hound to
help maintain its control
—uses metal jaws like pliers
and hollow needle to inject
poison into victims
—Hound always growls and
hisses at the main
character, Guy Montag
— Hound tracks Guy Montag
as he runs for his life

As you can see in the chart, the questioning method can
help you find many pieces of supporting information. While
you are writing down answers that occur to you, you should
put down all the different facts, examples, reasons, and details that answer the questions. Later you can sort out and
discard unimportant answers.

The second method, free-associating with your topic sentence, can also produce many possible pieces of supporting
information. To free-associate, write your topic sentence at
the top of your paper. Then read it carefully several times.
As you concentrate on your topic sentence, write down all
the ideas that occur to you. If you were to use the method of
free association with the topic sentence on the Hound, you
might jot down a list like the following.

FREE-ASSOCIATING TO FIND SUPPORT FOR A TOPIC SENTENCE

Topic Sentence: In *Fahrenheit 451,* Bradbury uses the Mechanical Hound as a symbol of the mechanical, destructive society that it serves.

—Mechanical Hound sleeps in the Fire House, tracks and kills criminals with the firemen

—Hound is a combination computer, insect, and dog

—people in the society are programmed like the Hound because they aren't allowed to think; everything is done by machines

—Hound is fast-moving, quiet; at any one time it is capable of hunting and finding one of 10,000 people

—society doesn't care about people and kills off people who try to be different

—people enjoy watching wall-to-wall circuit television, listening to radios, traveling fast in cars, motorcycles, planes

—people enjoy breaking things and sometimes casually kill each other

—Hound can only hunt and kill—uses strong poison injected through a needle it has in its metal jaws

—fear of the Hound forces the main character, Guy Montag, to burn his own house and to run for his life

—the Hound seems to sense that Guy is an enemy of the society before he really is

—the society trusts the Hound to catch and kill enemies

—society invented the Hound and brags of its powers

Like questioning, free-associating with a topic sentence can yield a long list of possible supporting information.

At this point, you may have to revise your topic sentence to fit the support you have gathered. You may change a few words for clarity and focus, shorten the topic sentence, or possibly add a few words.

Checking Supporting Information for Unity and Completeness.   With either method of finding supporting information, you will probably gather much more information than you can actually use in one paragraph. Therefore, once you have brainstormed, you should evaluate your list of information to find the examples, details, facts, reasons, and incidents that offer the strongest and clearest support for your main idea.

Check each piece of information to see if it fits in with your topic sentence. Then cross out any unrelated information and add information to fill in any gaps you may have noticed in your list.

Throughout all the steps in writing a paragraph, you can take out information you do not want to include and add new related ideas that occur to you. But you should make your main selection and evaluation of supporting information at this point. As you read each item on your list, ask yourself, "Does this piece of information help to explain or illustrate my main idea? Is this piece of information necessary to explain another piece of information?" Any item on your list that does not meet one of these requirements should be crossed out. Sometimes you will have to leave out examples or facts simply because any more would make your paragraph too long.

If you were to use the list of support from the questioning method, your deletions and additions might look like those in the following chart.

EVALUATING A LIST OF SUPPORTING INFORMATION

Topic Sentence: In *Fahrenheit 451*, Bradbury uses the Mechanical Hound as a symbol of the mechanical, destructive society that it serves.

What is the Mechanical Hound?
—made of copper and steel   —runs quickly and quietly,
—has eight legs   leaps on victims

In what way is the society mechanical?
—uses machines for   —homes have wall-to-wall
  everything—recreation,   circuit TV
  schools, transportation,   —people listen to little radios
  medicine, law enforcement   in their ears constantly

In what way is the society destructive?
—forces everyone to be alike;   —Fun Park has such
  doesn't allow people to   amusements as car wrecker
  think, ask questions, or   and window smasher
  communicate   —the society drives people to
—gets rid of people who try   kill themselves and each
  to be different   other

How is the Mechanical Hound a symbol of the society's mechanical nature?

| —Mechanical Hound is one of society's advanced, complex machines; runs by computers | —can be set to identify 10,000 different people at a time by their body chemistry |
| —a robot, more powerful than a real dog | —society has complete confidence in it |

How is the Mechanical Hound a symbol of the society's destructiveness?

—~~firemen enjoy watching the Mechanical Hound kill rats, chickens, and cats~~	—uses metal jaws like pliers and hollow needle to inject poison into victims
—used to track and kill criminals as well as people who dare to be different	—~~Hound always growls and hisses at the main character, Guy Montag~~
—shows how inhuman and violent society has become	—~~Hound tracks Guy Montag as he runs for his life~~
—society uses the Hound to help maintain its control	—the Hound can only be used to chase, find, and kill; it has no other use

Notice that seven pieces of information have been crossed out because they are only indirectly related to the main idea and that new pieces of information have been added to answer the third and fifth questions. Once you have a list of solid, strong supporting information, you will begin to see your paragraph taking shape.

EXERCISE C: Developing a Topic Sentence with Supporting Information. Use the topic sentence that you prepared in Exercise B in the following planning steps. *After completing this exercise, students might exchange papers to elicit further information.*

1. Write your topic sentence on your paper.
2. Use either the questioning method or the free-associating method to find supporting information for your main idea. If you use the questioning method, be sure to show all your work by writing the questions as well as the answers. After brainstorming, using either of these methods, you should have a list of supporting information. Revise your topic sentence if necessary to fit your supporting information.
3. Check your list of support for unity and thoroughness. Does each piece of information develop your main idea or help to explain an important piece of supporting information? Using another color pen, cross out the pieces

of information that do not directly contribute to your main idea. Add other pieces of information you may have overlooked that will help to develop your main idea.

■ Organizing Your Paragraph

In addition to choosing the supporting information that your paragraph will contain, you should organize your supporting material logically. Before you actually write your paragraph in complete sentences, you should arrange the supporting information. Choosing a logical order for the paragraph will aid you as you write and will help you communicate your main idea clearly to a reader. Once you have decided whether the paragraph should follow order of importance, chronological order, spatial order, comparison-and-contrast order, or developmental order, you should prepare a modified outline to guide you as you write.

Organize your supporting information logically and prepare an outline.

Both your topic sentence and your list of supporting information should offer clues to finding a logical order. Study your main idea and your list of support to see if a time order, space order, comparison-and-contrast order, or order of importance is implied. If none of these fit, you should organize your supporting information by developmental order. Then select the pieces of support that will be major points, and select other pieces that will back up and develop those major points. Look for the arrangement of ideas that will be clearest and easiest for a reader to follow. You may decide first to number your ideas on your rough list of support or you may make a modified or topic outline directly from your list.

If you were organizing the supporting information that begins on page 643, you might decide that developmental order would most logically fit the main idea and supporting information. After reexamining the topic sentence, you might decide to organize the paragraph around two major supporting ideas: the Hound as a symbol of the technology of the society and the Hound as a symbol of the destructiveness of the society. You would then list all the other information logically under each of these points. You might also jot down a possible concluding sentence. Your outline might then resemble the following.

Topic Sentence: In *Fahrenheit 451*, Bradbury uses the Mechanical Hound as a symbol of the mechanical, destructive society that it serves.

Hound—one of society's many complex machines
—Society dependent upon machines for everything—recreation, daily living, education, transportation, and law enforcement
—Hound—computerized robot more efficient than a real dog
—Can be programmed to identify over 10,000 different people by their body chemistry
—Made of copper and steel with eight legs and rubber padded paws for running quietly and quickly and leaping
—Complete confidence placed in computerized bloodhound by society
Hound—symbol of society's destructiveness
—People who try to be different arrested and executed—people driven to kill themselves and each other
—Hound—society's instrument of control
—Used in tracking and poisoning people labeled enemies of society
—Used only to hunt and kill
—Equipped with metal jaws like pliers— hollow needle to inject poison into victims

Concluding Sentence: As the deadly weapon of its society, the Hound reveals how technologically advanced but how violent that society is.

EXERCISE D: Arranging Support in a Logical Order. Use the supporting information that you gathered in Exercise C in the following steps. *Outlines could be checked for logic and organization.*

1. Examine your list of supporting information to see which order fits your topic the best and which most clearly develops your main idea for your audience. Then choose an order (order of importance, chronological order, spatial order, comparison-and-contrast order, or developmental order) and write your choice on your paper.

2. Put your supporting information in an outline according to the order you have chosen. Write your complete topic sentence and your complete concluding sentence, if you can think of an appropriate one, at the beginning and end of your outline.

■ Drafting Your Paragraph

Once you have an outline, you should be able to draft the paragraph rapidly. With your outline before you, begin writing your paragraph by putting your ideas in complete sentences. As you move from thought to thought and sentence to sentence, use transitions and other linking devices to make the relationships between your ideas logical and clear to a reader.

> As you draft your paragraph, connect the ideas in your outline using transitions, repetitions of main words, synonyms, pronouns, and, possibly, parallelism and a concluding sentence.

As you read over your outline, you should be able to tell where you will need transitions and what words you should emphasize to guide the reader. For instance, in the paragraph about the Mechanical Hound, you will definitely need a transition as you begin the second major point; the word *also* might be chosen to connect the ideas in the first part of the paragraph with the ideas in the second part. A word such as *both* could then function as a transition in the concluding sentence to wrap up the ideas in the paragraph. In addition, repeating such main words as *Hound, symbol of, mechanical,* and *destructive* would add coherence to the paragraph. You might also want to use synonyms for these main words, such as *technological, computerized, represents, stands for, symbolic,* and *reveals.* Besides linking words, you might want to use similar sentence lengths and structures (parallelism) for similar and equal ideas.

If you were to write a draft from the preceding outline, your paragraph would probably resemble the following. Notice the important transitions *also* and *both,* the synonyms for Hound—*robot, computerized bloodhound, instrument,* and *weapon*—and the pronouns *it* and *its.* Also, notice that some of the ideas in the outline have been worded slightly differently in the complete draft.

TOPIC
SENTENCE

Complete
supporting
information
in develop-
mental
order

In *Fahrenheit 451,* Bradbury uses the Mechanical Hound as a symbol of the mechanical, destructive society that it serves. The Mechanical
Hound is one of the complex machines invented
by the society, and as such it symbolizes that society for the reader. Bradbury describes a society
totally dependent upon machines for having fun,
for traveling, for daily living, and for learning; the
Mechanical Hound is the machine used for enforc-
ing the laws. It is a robot that is more powerful
and efficient than a real dog. Its copper and steel
body has eight legs with rubber-padded paws capable of leaping and running quickly and quietly.
The Hound can be programmed to identify over
10,000 different people by their body chemistries.
The society has complete confidence in its computerized bloodhound. The Mechanical Hound
also reveals the society's destructiveness. Bradbury presents a society that drives people to kill
themselves and their neighbors and that executes
anyone who tries to be different from the majority. As an instrument of the society's control, the
Hound is used in tracking and poisoning people
who are labeled enemies of society. Its only purpose is to hunt and kill. With its metal jaws like
pliers and its one tooth, a hollow needle, it injects
deadly poison into its victims. As a lethal weapon
of the society, the Mechanical Hound stands for

Concluding
sentence

both that society's technological advancement and
its violence.

As you draft your paragraph from an outline, some new
ideas may occur to you. Include these new ideas in your paragraph only if they help to communicate your main idea or
help to explain another piece of information. When you have
a complete first draft of your paragraph, you should read it
both silently and aloud, and examine it for sense and flow.
You will notice that the more you have planned, the more
easily you will be able to write your paragraph.

EXERCISE E: Writing the Paragraph. Before you begin to
write your paragraph from your outline in Exercise D, list
some of the transitions and some of the main words with
synonyms that you will want to use in the paragraph. Then,
with your outline in front of you, draft your paragraph. Put
all the ideas in the outline in complete sentences. Try to include transitions as you move from thought to thought and
sentence to sentence. When you have completed your first
draft, proofread it. Underline the transitions and add others

if you need them. Label your topic sentence and your concluding sentence, if you have one. *Student paragraphs might be
discussed in class, and authors could explain their progress, step by step.*
APPLICATION: Preparing and Writing Paragraphs. Choose
one of the following topics or think of one of your own and
follow the instructions. Show your work at each stage. *Students work
might be monitored at various points. Final products could be discussed by class as a whole.*

Modern music	Our solar system	Car engines
Gardening	South America	School spirit
Part-time jobs	Photography	Favorite movies
Hobbies	Scuba diving or	Unforgettable
Team sports	sky diving	books
Archeology	Unusual	
	occupations	

1. Narrow the topic to one suitable for a paragraph topic.
2. Choose your audience and think about your purpose.
3. Ask yourself questions to find a main idea about your
   paragraph topic and write a topic sentence.
4. If you have used the questioning method before, use the
   free-association method (or vice versa) to brainstorm for
   supporting examples, details, facts, reasons, or incidents. Revise your topic sentence, if necessary, to fit
   your supporting information.
5. Study your list of support and eliminate unrelated information. Add information to give complete support.
6. Choose an order for the supporting information in your
   paragraph and outline the paragraph.
7. Then draft the paragraph from the outline. Concentrate
   on connecting your ideas logically with transitions,
   main words, synonyms, and pronouns.
8. Exchange paragraphs with someone in your class and
   write down two strengths and two weaknesses of the
   other student's paragraph.
9. Then reread your own paragraph and the person's comments. Make any necessary changes for clarity and
   smoothness.
10. Rewrite your paragraph.

Revising and Rewriting Paragraphs

23.4

Once you have completed your first draft, you have accomplished a big task. However, your writing should not
stop here. Now you should reexamine your paragraph to

make sure that all the parts work together to communicate your ideas. This final step is called revision.

To revise does not simply mean to recopy your first draft. Revising involves reading and examining your writing from your audience's perspective; it includes reconsidering your purpose, your presentation of ideas, and your choice of words; it means recognizing and eliminating weaknesses. When you revise a paragraph that you have planned and written, you will often discover ways to make it even more clear and interesting for your audience. If you brainstormed and evaluated as you planned and wrote your paragraph, you have actually been revising mentally and on paper all along. But when you have a complete draft, you can look at the whole and the parts from a fresh perspective.

You should use the following questions as a tool for revising. Whenever you complete a first draft, ask yourself these questions about your paragraph. The questions will help you analyze your paragraph objectively as a reader might and will uncover weaknesses that you can improve.

CHECKLIST FOR REVISING

1. Does the topic sentence clearly focus and express the main idea of the paragraph?
2. Does the paragraph contain enough examples, details, facts, reasons, or incidents to develop the topic sentence?
3. Is all of the supporting information appropriate? Is any of the supporting information weak, vague, or repetitive?
4. Does the paragraph stick to the main idea?
5. Is the supporting information presented in the most logical order?
6. Have you used transitions, repetitions of main words, synonyms, and pronouns to enable the audience to follow your ideas?
7. Is a concluding sentence needed to wrap up the ideas of the paragraph?
8. Does the paragraph as a whole achieve your purpose? Will the audience find the paragraph interesting?
9. Have you improved all choppy, awkward, or confusing passages?
10. Have you corrected all mistakes in grammar, punctuation, and spelling?

This section will give you practice in using the checklist and will explain further how to strengthen and correct your writing as you revise.

■ Revising Your Topic Sentences

You must make sure that your topic sentence does not set up false expectations in the reader. A topic sentence that does not fit in with the paragraph will cause a reader trouble in understanding your main idea.

Overly General Topic Sentences. If the topic sentence uses words that are too general or too vague, the reader will expect the paragraph to cover more than it actually does. A vague or overly general topic sentence is a confusing signal to the reader.

Revise an inexact, vague, or overly general topic sentence by sharpening the focus to fit the supporting information in the paragraph.

In the following paragraph, the broad topic sentence at the end does not accurately sum up the preceding details.

Overly general topic sentence

Lines now etched his forehead and circled his eyes. He had developed an uncontrollable quiver about the hands, and his eyelids seemed to blink more rapidly than normal. When he walked, his strides were short and unsure, and his shoulders had acquired a droop. As each month of worry, unsolved problems, and new conflicts passed, his body resisted more feebly. *Many people in his position have suffered similarly.*

If you can make a topic sentence more precise, rewrite it. Make sure that it presents your main idea in a way that focuses the content of the paragraph. The writer could improve the preceding paragraph by rewriting the topic sentence to give a clear general statement of the man's appearance and possibly also the reason for his appearance: *His short term as President had aged him immensely.*

Overly Narrow Topic Sentences. You should also check a topic sentence to make sure it does not mislead a reader because the idea it presents is too narrow. Ask yourself if the topic sentence really does state the main idea that all the other sentences in the paragraph explore.

Revise a topic sentence that is too limited and specific by rewriting it to state the main idea of the entire paragraph.

In the following paragraph, the overly narrow topic sentence prepares the reader for only one of several supporting ideas in the paragraph; in other words, it does not state the main idea of the paragraph at all. Thus, the reader may have difficulty comprehending the ideas in the paragraph.

Overly nar-   *Dr. Harris invented some unusual machines to*
row topic   *treat physical problems.* Elderly asthmatics and
sentence   those afflicted with other diseases common to ag-
                ing sought the doctor and paid handsomely for his
                services. Harris had designed elaborate "muscle
                machines" complete with levers and weights as
                well as gadgets with which he clamped, rubbed,
                pulled, and pressed ancient legs, arms, necks, and
                thighs. The long-hidden secret of Dr. Harris's suc-
                cess, however, was the age of his patients. He
                never accepted a patient younger than seventy. Al-
                though he worked overtime making a fortune
                from his over-extended practice, a prospective pa-
                tient could expect an opening before long because
                his patients rarely lived long. Death was Dr. Har-
                ris's miracle "cure."

In addition to his unusual machines, the supporting information in the preceding paragraph mentions Dr. Harris's concentration on elderly patients, his reputation for miraculous cures, and the truth behind his questionable fame. None of these other ideas is suggested by the topic sentence. The writer can improve this paragraph by rewriting the topic sentence so that it will capture the main idea behind all the information. A better topic sentence for this paragraph would be: *The legendary Dr. Harris fooled the world for years with his unusual machines and their miracle "cures."*

EXERCISE A: Identifying and Revising Weak Topic Sentences. Identify the topic sentences in the following paragraphs as *too general, too narrow,* or *appropriate.* Then on your paper revise each weak topic sentence to suit its paragraph.
Revisions will vary; sample given for first one.

(1) <u>Shakespeare's plays are noted for happy endings</u>. Among his comedies, *Measure for Measure* and *The Tempest* are mostly serious, dramatic pieces, but they end satisfactorily

for the principal characters. Other comedies, such as *The Taming of the Shrew* and *A Midsummer-Night's Dream*, are boisterously funny and, again, end happily. But among Shakespeare's many tragedies, happy endings are not on the program. At the ends of plays such as *Hamlet*, *Macbeth*, and *Othello*, the principal characters die tragically or suffer terrible emotional pain. *too narrow: Shakespeare's plays might be classified as comic or tragic according to their endings.*

(2) <u>Insomnia is one of many health problems experienced by Americans.</u> One cause, some claim, is poor eating habits. Drinking coffee or tea late at night may result in wakefulness. Overeating, particularly on a regular basis, can result in a continual state of indigestion, robbing the overeater of normal sleep patterns and routines. Most experts, however, believe that nervous conditions—worry and deeper forms of anxiety—are the chief villains. And although doctors will often explore an insomniac's eating habits, treatment for insomnia usually depends on curing or easing nervous conditions. *too general*

(3) The Colosseum of ancient Rome stood imposingly at the center of the great city. An enormous circular amphitheater, it was more than six hundred feet in diameter. And more than four stories high, it seated at least fifty thousand spectators in long, semicircular tiers. The condition of the structure today, however, will disappoint the sightseer who does not expect the ravages of centuries. The Colosseum now stands partly, or largely, in ruins. The central tiers have long since fallen, and the vast arena and subterranean passages are buried. The grand outer walls, including two layers of proud arches, have partially crumbled. <u>Yet by inspecting the ruins and using imagination, the visitor can still piece together the splendor</u> that once was Rome. *appropriate*

(4) <u>Every year many people visit Greenfield Village near Detroit.</u> The Village was created by Henry Ford and contains a motley group of special exhibits. One building jumbles together thousands of watches from the medieval period to the present. The Wright brothers' bicycle repair shop, bodily transported from its original site, is next door. Thomas Edison's workshop is perhaps even more striking. In homage to Edison, Ford had the workshop transported from its original location in Menlo Park, New Jersey. Ford had workers sift through all the dirt around the Menlo Park site for relics of Edison's genius. Consequently, bits of paper, pieces of trash,

and fossilized lumps of chewing gum have all been placed on display in Greenfield Village for posterity to wonder at.

too general

■ Revising Supporting Information in Your Paragraphs

Besides reexamining your topic sentence, you should look again at the extent and quality of your supporting information.

Inadequate Support.   Most paragraphs should contain at least three pieces of supporting information, and some require much more. When you revise your paragraphs, you may discover that you did not include enough specific information or that you accidentally left out information as you drafted your paragraph. As you revise, you can make a weak, undeveloped paragraph into a strong, complete one by adding the specific information a reader needs or would like to know about your main idea.

Revise weak paragraphs by including additional examples, details, facts, reasons, and incidents to fulfill the reader's expectations.

If your topic sentence leads the reader to think that your paragraph will explain how to cut a coconut or will offer reasons in favor of a new school policy, and your paragraph only begins to do these things, a reader will be disappointed. As you revise, make sure that you have covered your main idea thoroughly.

The following paragraph illustrates the problem of inadequate support. The topic sentence suggests that many examples will follow, but the writer has mentioned only a few.

Paragraph with scanty supporting information

Washington, D.C., can occupy a visitor for days with trips to museums, monuments, and important government buildings. A visitor can study the replicas of Colonial American homes and the displays that document the history of our government in the National Museum of History and Technology. The National Museum of Natural History houses some of the world's largest diamonds, rubies, sapphires, and emeralds as well as meteorites, mummies, dinosaur skeletons, reptiles, birds, and mammals.

By giving more thought to the paragraph, the writer could revise it to include enough examples to fulfill the promise of the topic sentence.

Paragraph with thorough supporting information	Washington, D.C., can occupy a visitor for days with trips to museums, monuments, and important government buildings. A visitor can study replicas of Colonial American homes and displays that document the history of our government in the National Museum of History and Technology. The National Museum of Natural History houses some of the world's largest diamonds, sapphires, rubies, and emeralds as well as meteorites, mummies, dinosaur skeletons, reptiles, birds, and mammals. Yet another museum, the National Air and Space Museum, chronicles the history of flight from balloons and Lindbergh's *Spirit of St. Louis* to today's rockets and missiles. Gleaming in the sunshine by day and glowing white at night, the Lincoln and Jefferson memorials and the Washington Monument offer the visitor impressive views of the city. After seeing these massive architectural tributes to some of the country's leaders, a visitor could spend hours touring the Senate Chamber and the House Chamber in the nation's Capitol, seeing the Supreme Court, and stepping inside the Library of Congress. And once a visitor has seen these places, hundreds of other attractions and sites—Georgetown, Arlington National Cemetery, the National Cathedral, art galleries, the zoo, and nearby Mount Vernon—await exploration.

Inappropriate Support. As you read your paragraphs with a critical, objective eye, you should also determine if you have provided the kind of supporting information that you need to fulfill your purpose, whether it be to inform, persuade, or describe. Check to make sure you have not simply said the same thing several times, made hasty generalizations, or offered unconvincing opinions. Even if a paragraph has a good topic sentence, a writer will fail to communicate the main idea if the support is repetitious, general, or full of opinions.

Revise a weak paragraph by replacing repetitions, generalizations, and opinions with strong, specific examples, details, facts, reasons, and incidents.

Each of these weaknesses has a negative effect on an audience. Repetition can lead a reader around in circles and become irritating. Generalizations do not adequately explain or illustrate the topic sentence. Also they are often unfair. A topic sentence may contain an opinion to be supported, but the support itself should consist not of opinions but rather of facts, reasons, and examples.

The following paragraph contains repetitious sentences, generalized statements, and unsupported opinions. Notice that the paragraph is vague and unconvincing.

Repetitions, generalized statements, and unsupported opinions

Recently a number of near accidents involving taxis on Pelham Road have caused concern among residents. Taxis collecting and discharging commuters and travelers at the train station are entirely to blame. Taxis should not be allowed in the town. All the taxi drivers exceed the speed limit and drive recklessly. Every day residents see taxis jumping the traffic lights, careening around corners, and barely missing children on bicycles and elderly residents with their shopping carts. The taxis are completely at fault for these near collisions. Taxis are a menace to life and limb.

The paragraph mainly repeats several opinions and generalizations. A reader concludes that the writer feels strongly about the subject but has provided little evidence and has given little logical thought to the problem. The writer could improve the paragraph by concentrating on specific, accurate evidence and logical reasons. When specific support replaces the repetitions, generalizations, and opinions, the paragraph gains strength and credibility.

Specific supporting information

Recently a number of near accidents involving taxis on Pelham Road have caused concern among residents. Taxis collecting and discharging commuters and travelers at the train station have been involved in most of the close calls. Four residents have filed complaints with the town police reporting that taxis have exceeded the speed limit. Last month our neighbor observed a taxi jumping the light and careening around a corner, barely missing two children on bicycles and an elderly woman with a shopping cart. Last week another taxi sideswiped a parked car on Pelham Road. As a result of these dangerous incidents, the town police and officials have promised to investigate the driving practices and safety records of local taxi drivers.

EXERCISE B: Identifying and Revising Problems with Supporting Information. Some of the following paragraphs lack ade-

quate support, and others have inappropriate support. Read the paragraphs carefully and briefly describe the problem in each paragraph. Then rewrite one paragraph on your paper, adding the best specific support you can.
Revisions will vary; problems identified.

(1) By the end of the nineteenth century, immigrants from Europe had good reasons to come to America. They saw America as a land of opportunity, where steady work was available and where farming land could be purchased cheaply. Immigrants looked to America for acceptance and equality.
inadequate support

(2) People who smoke have neither respect for their own bodies nor concern for the health and comfort of those around them. People are foolish to continue this dreadful habit despite the warnings of the Surgeon General. Smoking is not a healthy habit, and it is unclean besides. Smoking is an irritating habit that infringes on the rights of others.
inappropriate support—opinion

(3) Many television commercials insult the audience in a variety of ways. Some commercials for detergent, for example, make the people in them appear stupid. Other commercials make idle boasts about the superiority of one product over another. Viewers can sense that the comparison is unfair and that the results are fabricated. *inadequate support*

(4) The first landing on the moon was an exciting historic event. What a thrill it was to see people actually walking on the moon. Nothing people have ever done, or ever will do, can rival the accomplishment of the first landing on the moon. It was a truly earth-shaking occurrence. Everyone was proud to witness this epoch-making event.
inappropriate support—opinion

■ Revising for Unity

Another weakness that can be corrected during revision is lack of unity. Sometimes a piece of information that at first seemed to be related to your topic sentence and the other sentences appears, on second reading, to stray from your main idea. You may have become sidetracked by one of your supporting ideas, or you may have included a new idea without checking it against your topic sentence. You can improve paragraphs that lack unity by removing the sentences and ideas that do not belong. You may then have to rewrite some of the other sentences in your paragraph to make your words read smoothly.

Restore unity to a paragraph by eliminating unrelated or insignificant ideas and rewriting sentences, if necessary.

The following paragraph is about Canada's size. However, in the middle of the paragraph, the writer gives examples of Canada's industries. The unrelated sentences are disruptive and confusing to a reader.

Paragraph
with
unrelated
ideas

Canada's geographical dimensions are impressive. Canada covers the continent of North America from the Atlantic to the Pacific. *It is a growing nation producing nuclear power as well as other industrial commodities. And it is a nation of fishermen. Canadians export tons of cod and lobsters annually.* Canada's northern boundary stretches toward the North Pole and includes the frozen Arctic region. On its southern boundary, it borders the entire United States from the state of Washington to the state of Maine, a distance of 4,000 miles. As a result, Canada covers an area of 3.8 million square miles, second in size only to the Soviet Union.

In this case, the writer can improve the paragraph by simply removing the unrelated ideas and thus shortening the paragraph. If you reread the paragraph leaving out the unrelated sentences, you will notice how much clearer the paragraph is.

EXERCISE C: Identifying and Correcting Problems with Unity. Each of the following paragraphs lacks unity. Read the paragraphs carefully. Then write them on your paper, removing unnecessary and unrelated information and making any other small changes for smoothness. *Problems identified*

(1) Three kinds of soups are my all-time favorites. One of these is vegetable soup, especially the kind containing peas, carrots, and lentils. Even more, I like cream soups, such as

cream of spinach and cream of tomato. In fact, I like any-thing in cream: strawberries, bananas, and some other fruits. My favorite soups, however, are chowders. These taste espe-cially good with seafood dinners. Lobster tails, flounder, and scrod will appeal to me any time of the year.

Underlined sentences destroy unity.

(2) Twenty years ago roller-skating was almost the exclusive activity of children after school and on Sunday afternoons. But recently the sport has been taken up by a much wider age group. Skating has become both a method of transportation that is faster than walking and an opportunity for a new form of dancing, which brings discos out onto the sidewalks. Disco music is a phenomenon of the 1970's much the same as rock music was a creation of the 1960's. People used to sit around and simply listen to rock music, but people dance to disco music. Rock music fans look unfavorably on disco in the same way that the waltzers found rock and roll offensive.

Paragraph turns to different focus (disco) at first underlined sentence.

■ Revising for Coherence

The coherence of your paragraphs requires special atten-tion during the revising stage. During the drafting stage, you are mainly trying to express your ideas in complete sen-tences and to follow your outline. When you write your par-agraph for the first time, you may not be able to supply all the necessary connections or you may wander away from a logical order. The revising stage enables you to examine your writing for logical order, clear relationships between ideas, and the flow of your ideas and words.

Improve the coherence of paragraphs by checking to make sure your ideas are in a consistent, logical order, by adding helpful transitions, and by clarifying the repetitions of main words, synonyms, and pronouns.

As you revise for coherence, you can correct weaknesses and polish and refine your ideas for clarity and style.

Illogical Order.   One major problem often found in first drafts is the failure to follow the order set up or implied in the topic sentence. For example, if your topic sentence im-plied that your paragraph would recount the highlights of a basketball game from the beginning to the end, the reader would expect you to proceed from the beginning of the game to the final play. If instead you jump around from the first five minutes, to overtime, and back, the reader will be bewildered. As you revise, you can restore the ideas in a paragraph to the order that the topic sentence leads the reader to expect, whether it be order of importance, chronological order, spatial order, comparison-and-contrast order, or a particular developmental order.

In the following description of a room, the topic sentence leads the reader to expect the details to follow spatial order. Instead the discussion jumps around from one side of the room to the other and from the floor to the ceiling to the floor in a way that disorients the reader.

Paragraph
with
details in
illogical
order

We didn't know where to begin hunting for the baseball glove in that compost heap of a room. Bowls of crusty cereal, cans of soft drinks, and candy wrappers surrounded the bed. Two wrinkled helium balloons huddled in the upper right corner. To our right, a bike rack and an old ten-speed with flat tires covered the wall. The clutter also hung like stalactites from the ceiling. From the light in the center of the room, an I Love NY T-shirt, a scarf, and a belt dangled. Underneath the bicycle was a bookshelf holding a tattered stack of *Mad* comic books. From the bottom shelf, Tarzan and Hardy Boys books had toppled like dominoes onto the floor. On the next wall, the bed's sheets and blankets were barely visible under the albums, gym clothes, muddy jeans, and stacks of socks. An overflowing closet occupied the next wall. The floor, carpeted by ripped maps, a month's worth of sports pages, clipped articles, school books, and dirty bath towels and shirts, allowed no movement from the door to the closet. To the left of the closet, more shelves were littered with a transistor radio, bowling trophies, erasers, bubble gum, chess pieces, and a plastic tarantula. A heap of cleats, thongs, ragged sneakers, a baseball bat, a hockey stick, and an electric train set spilled out of the closet toward the bed.

When the paragraph is rewritten so that the details proceed from right to left and top to bottom, the reader can see the relationship of objects in the room more clearly. When the details follow spatial order, the reader's eye moves with the writer's eye around the room, across the ceiling, and across the floor.

Paragraph
with
consistent,
logical
order for
details

We didn't know where to begin hunting for the baseball glove in that compost heap of a room. To our right, a bicycle rack and an old ten-speed with flat tires covered the wall. Underneath the bicycle was a bookshelf holding a tattered stack of *Mad* comic books. From the bottom shelf Tarzan and Hardy Boys books had toppled like dominoes onto the floor. On the next wall was the bed with its sheets and blankets barely visible under the albums, gym clothes, muddy jeans, and stacks of socks. Bowls of crusty cereal, cans of soft drinks, and candy wrappers surrounded the bed. An overflowing closet occupied the next wall. A heap of cleats, thongs, ragged sneakers, a baseball bat, a hockey stick, and an electric train set spilled out toward the bed. On the left wall, more shelves were littered with a transistor radio, bowling trophies, erasers, bubble gum, chess pieces, and a plastic tarantula. The clutter also hung like stalactites from the ceiling. From the light in the center of the room an I Love NY T-shirt, a scarf, and a belt dangled. Two wrinkled helium balloons huddled in the upper right corner. The floor, carpeted by ripped maps, a month's worth of sports pages, clipped articles, school books, and dirty bath towels and shirts, allowed no movement from the door to the closet.

Insufficient Transitions. In many paragraphs, the order of ideas may be logical but the coherence can be improved with transitions. Transitions can make your important pieces of supporting information stand out for the reader. They can also make examples clearly recognizable and can improve the meaning as well as the flow of ideas.

The following paragraph has a clear topic sentence and appropriate supporting information. When you read the paragraph, however, you will notice that it is a little choppy. Also, the relationship of the ideas could be clearer.

Paragraph
without
transitions

Students interested in geology must understand the term "mineral." Minerals are chemical elements or compounds of different chemicals. These solid substances can be identified by their physical and chemical properties. A characteristic of many minerals is color. Jadeite is often bright green, although it sometimes appears brown or yellow. Spodumene appears pink or opaque. Minerals can be identified by their relative hardness. Some minerals can be scratched with a fingernail. Others can only be scratched by a harder substance, such as a knife. Many minerals, particularly crystals, can be split and examined for shape. When the mineral obsidian is fractured, it splits in a clearly circular pattern.

When just a few transitions are added to identify examples and connect ideas, the paragraph gains smoothness and sharpness.

Paragraph
with
transitions

Students interested in geology must understand the term "mineral." Minerals are chemical elements or compounds of different chemicals. These solid substances can be identified by their physical and chemical properties. *The most noticeable characteristic* of many minerals is color. Jadeite, *for example*, is often bright green, although it sometimes appears brown or yellow. *Another mineral*, spodumene, appears pink or opaque. Minerals can *also* be identified by their relative hardness. Some minerals, *for instance*, can be scratched with a fingernail. Others can only be scratched by a harder substance, such as a knife. *And* many minerals, particularly crystals, can be split and examined for shape. When the mineral obsidian is fractured, it splits in a clearly circular pattern.

Other Inconsistent Connections.   Repeating certain main words and using synonyms and pronouns for those words can help you connect the ideas in a paragraph. On the other hand, overusing synonyms and pronouns or using them carelessly can confuse a reader with too many terms and shifts in point of view. As you revise, you should determine if you have used main words clearly and if you have employed useful synonyms and consistent pronouns.

In the following paragraph, the writer uses too many synonyms for the main words. Also, the writer switches pronouns by using *you, one,* and *he or she.* Consequently, instead of connecting and clarifying ideas, the writer complicates straightforward ideas.

Paragraph
with
confusing
synonyms
and
pronouns

The first time on water skis can be a strain on nerves and muscles. The beginner usually wades out waist deep in the water and tries to put on the awkward, buoyant skis. Then the *nervous skier* crouches with the tips of the skis sticking out of the water. Soon the people in the boat throw the *skier* the towline. *You* tell the driver to "Hit it," and the boat leaps ahead, the line tightens, and *one* is yanked out of the water. If the *novice* does not weight both skis equally and pull against the tug of the boat, *he or she* will fall over. After getting up on skis, the *newtimer* must face the boat's bumpy, frothy wake by skiing in it or outside it. The choppy little waves can upset the *tyro's* balance. When *your* muscles have fought the steady pull for awhile, someone in the boat usually motions to *you* asking *you* for instructions to slow down, speed up, or head for the shore. To stop, *one* lets go of the towline and skis off toward the shore, gradually sinking into the water. If the *skier* has succeeded in staying on top of the water for long, *your* shoulders, arms, back, and thighs will probably feel sore and stiff the next day.

When the writer revises and limits the synonyms for skier to *beginner* and *new skier* and the pronouns to *he or she*, the paragraph becomes easier to understand and more pleasant to read.

Paragraph with consistent main words, synonyms, and pronouns

The first time on water skis can be a strain on nerves and muscles. The beginner usually wades out waist deep in the water and tries to put on the awkward, buoyant skis. Then the nervous skier crouches with the tips of the skis sticking out of the water. Soon the people in the boat throw the skier the towline. The skier tells the driver to "Hit it," and the boat leaps ahead, the line tightens, and the skier is yanked out of the water. If the beginner does not weight both skis equally and pull against the tug of the boat, he or she will fall over. After getting up on skis, the skier must face the boat's bumpy, frothy wake by skiing in it or outside it. The choppy little waves can upset the skier's balance. When the beginner's muscles have fought the steady pull for awhile, someone in the boat usually motions to the skier asking him or her for instructions to slow down, speed up, or head for shore. To stop, the skier lets go of the towline and skis off toward shore, gradually sinking into the water. If the beginner has succeeded in staying on top of the water for long, his or her shoulders, arms, back, and thighs will probably feel sore and stiff the next day.

EXERCISE D: Identifying and Correcting Problems with Coherence. The following three paragraphs have problems with either illogical order, insufficient transitions, or inconsistent connections. Read each paragraph carefully, and briefly describe the problem you find in each. Then rewrite each paragraph on your paper, reorganizing the supporting

information, adding helpful transitions, or correcting confusing synonyms and pronouns. Read your rewritten paragraphs aloud to yourself to listen for smoothness and clarity.
Problems are identified; revisions will vary. Sample given for first one.

(1) First-time visitors to the Grand Canyon are often surprised at the sheer length of this amazing gorge. ~~We expect~~ this natural wonder to be deep, but photographs never ~~prepare you for~~ the miles of twists and turns along the crevasse's upper rim. No single vantage point allows one to see most of this national treasure. ~~Instead, it seems that you must board~~ an airplane ~~and climb~~ thousands of feet in the air ~~in order to get~~ an accurate idea of the shape and dimensions of this awesome sight. *Pronouns need to be consistent.*
One expects/capture/Perhaps only/view/can give one

(2) Until the mid-1960's scientists thought that no animals were capable of mastering a language. A chimpanzee named Washoe communicates in a form of "speech." Allen and Beatrice Gardner conducted an experiment at the University of Nevada. A female monkey was trained from infancy to use a number of gestures in AMESLAN, the sign language of the deaf. Washoe learned the symbols for such words as baby, water, bird, and drink. Using a word in a new context demonstrates true understanding of a language. The process of comprehending concepts is a big step. Washoe began independently to combine gestures to make such new words as "candy-drink," which means watermelon. "Water-birds" mean ducks. Actual sentences were made. The Gardners found evidence that humans are not alone in their ability to translate reality into a system of symbols.
Needs transitions.

(3) A new driver in a standard shift car may think that tollbooths were invented for an octopus: Eight arms or legs *might* be enough to perform the many simultaneous actions required. While the car immediately ahead goes through the tollbooth, the new driver must find a quarter in a pocket or wallet. Downshifting, the driver must choose a toll gate and head for it, all the while watching for other cars which may try to scoot in ahead. The driver must steer the car to no more than an arm's length from the metal mesh basket. As the tollbooth comes in sight, the driver must brake gently and cruise to a crawl. Then with the left arm, the driver must toss the quarter into the basket. The driver may then accelerate away from the tollbooth, shift, and roll up the window. If the coin drops in the basket or rebounds off the side, a green sign flashes "Thank you," and the driver may pass through. If the coin misses the basket, a buzzer sounds alert-

ing an attendant who appears to retrieve the lost coin. Then finally the embarrassed new driver may accelerate, shift, roll up the window, and try to hide his or her shame by disappearing amidst the stream of cars.
Needs better organization.

APPLICATION 1: Revising Your Own Writing. For this exercise, reconsider a paragraph you have recently written. First, use the checklist for revising on page 650 to identify the weaknesses. Read your paragraph silently and aloud and examine it closely. Then, revise it by making any necessary improvements. Finally, rewrite your paragraph and submit both your original and revised versions to your teacher.

APPLICATION 2: Revising Someone Else's Writing. On a topic of your choice, write a paragraph using the planning and drafting steps you have learned. Then exchange papers with another student. Evaluate that paragraph using the checklist and the methods you have learned in this section. Make proofreading corrections on the original paper. On another piece of paper suggest any necessary changes in topic sentence, supporting information, organization, and connections. Return the paper to the writer. Then rewrite your own paragraph in final, revised form by following the suggestions of the evaluator, when you think they are beneficial. If you do not follow a suggestion, write a brief note explaining why. Submit all copies of your paragraph to your teacher.

Application 1: *Students might exchange papers and compare the other students' originals and revisions, pointing out two or three clear improvements in the second versions.*

Application 2: *Authors and critics might then present their work in teams to the rest of the class, which could offer its own critique.*

Chapter 24

Kinds of Paragraphs

In this chapter you will study four kinds of paragraphs that represent four different kinds of writing: (1) *expository paragraphs*, which set forth information, explain, or instruct; (2) *persuasive paragraphs*, which attempt to convince others to agree or act; (3) *descriptive paragraphs*, which paint pictures or recreate experiences for the reader; and (4) *narrative paragraphs*, which relate experiences or sequences of events for the reader.

In each of these kinds of paragraphs, the writer's particular purpose influences every part of the paragraph—the topic, approach, and choice of language. Each kind of writing attempts to fulfill its special purpose by having a particular effect on the audience. Studying these kinds of paragraphs separately will help you focus on purpose and audience and develop skill with different kinds of writing. Later, on your own, you can learn to combine some of the features of expository, persuasive, descriptive, and narrative writing as professional writers often do.

24.1 Expository Paragraphs

Expository writing sets forth information with the purpose of explaining it to the reader. Some common examples of expository writing are reports for classes, answers on exam questions, instructions to a neighbor on caring for a dog or plant, and an account of a person's job experience on an application.

Because much of all writing is expository, you have probably already written many expository paragraphs. Perhaps, however, you have not fully realized what kind of writing you were doing. This section will sharpen your understanding and help you write even better expository paragraphs by pointing out the main features of an expository paragraph (and of all expository writing). Writing this specific kind of paragraph will also help you apply your knowledge of paragraph writing in general.

■ The Main Features of Expository Paragraphs

Expository writing should have the qualities of all good writing, but it should also have several distinguishing features. In expository writing, the writer must concentrate on explaining an idea, thing, or process to the reader. The writer's goal is to make sure that the reader will understand the explanation. Although the tone of an expository paragraph may be serious or humorous, formal or casual, the tone must always be informative or instructional as well.

An Explanatory Purpose.　In an expository paragraph, the writer must explain a main idea. Both the topic sentence and the supporting information should reflect and serve this explanatory purpose.

The purpose of an expository paragraph is to explain an idea, event, object, or process by setting forth information.

The topic sentence in an expository paragraph is a factual statement that clarifies for the reader exactly what is to be explained in the paragraph. It should not express an opinion that would call for a defense. Notice the difference between the following two types of statements.

STATEMENT OF FACT:　A tsunami, or tidal wave, is one of the most dangerous natural disasters.

STATEMENT OF OPINION:　A tsunami, or tidal wave, is the most dangerous natural disaster.

STATEMENT OF FACT:　Some astronomers think the strange star called SS-433 has a black hole inside.

STATEMENT OF OPINION:　The strange star called SS-433 has a black hole inside.

The supporting information in an expository paragraph should provide explanation for the factual statement presented in the topic sentence. The specific information in the paragraph should answer a reader's questions about the topic sentence with examples, details, facts, and possibly reasons and incidents. Most of all, supporting information should be complete and logically arranged to serve the explanatory purpose.

In the following paragraph, the topic sentence makes a factual statement about the Aztecs' calendars: *The Aztecs used two calendars simultaneously.* The supporting information provides facts and details that thoroughly explain two questions that a reader might ask about the topic sentence: What were the two calendars? How were they used together?

TOPIC SENTENCE (Factual statement)	The Aztecs used two calendars simultaneously. The first was a calendar of 365 days, based on the apparent movement of the sun around the earth. This was the calendar which determined the seasons and the times for planting and harvesting, and it is known to have been more accurate than the solar calendar used in 16th-century Europe.
Explanatory facts and details	The second calendar, used only for religious and ritual purposes, was based on a 260-day cycle. Each day of the year was thus fixed in terms of two independent calendar cycles and, since the solar and ritual years were of different lengths, it was 52 years before any particular combination could come round again. According to their beliefs these 52-year periods had great significance, for at the end of one of them they thought the universe was due to be destroyed by earthquakes. —Adapted from *The Last Two Million Years*

An Informative Tone.   A second major feature of an expository paragraph is its informative tone. The writer's effort to teach the reader and to help the reader reach a new level of understanding contributes to the informative tone. The writer tries to present ideas and information in the clearest, most direct and unbiased manner.

Create an informative tone by defining terms and using precise explanations and by having an instructional attitude toward the reader.

To enable the reader to understand, the writer must choose the most accurate words—words that the reader is most likely to comprehend. The writer should consider the reader's background and knowledge of the topic so that the explanation can be delivered at a suitable level of difficulty.

For example, if you are explaining how to clean a horse's hoofs you will give a simple and more basic explanation to readers who have never been around horses than you will to readers who are frequent riders.

In the following paragraph, from a skiing manual, notice the informative tone used to present the detailed but simple and precise explanation. Notice that the writer is "instructing" the reader.

TOPIC SENTENCE (Factual statement) Explanation with instructions and details	To do the snowplow, simply push out the tails of your skis, keeping the tips together. This should be done with a gentle brushing motion. Avoid jerkiness, keep your knees well flexed and hold your body erect. Except for angling the skis inward, the snowplow stance is essentially the same as for straight running. The skis will ride slightly on their inside edges, the knees being closer together than the feet, and this, combined with the V angle of the skis, produces the plow effect. Be careful not to overdo the edging by pressing the knees together as this will lock you into a cramped position. To increase the braking power, simply push the tails out farther and flex more in the knees and ankles. —*The Skier's Handbook*

EXERCISE A: Identifying an Expository Paragraph. Read the following two paragraphs carefully. Then identify which one has an expository purpose. Give two reasons why you think the writer's purpose is to explain. Then tell what you think the writer's purpose is in the other paragraph and explain why you think so. *Specific reasons may vary; samples given.*

(1) The lunar surface is similar to earth's in basic form and composition although different in minor details. The moon has irregular surfaces like the earth's. Both have tall mountains and some jagged peaks. The lunar surface, however, is more rigid, or firm. Rocks on the moon do not sink beneath the surface, as earth rocks can. Lunar and earth rocks are composed of the same minerals and elements. Both contain minerals such as pyroxene, ilmenite, and olivine, and both contain elements such as titanium and nitrogen. But while the same minerals and elements are found in both places, they exist in very different amounts. An element such as titanium is much more abundant on the moon, whereas oxygen is very scarce. In addition, enormous amounts of glass exist on the moon. *expository: informative tone, factual support*

(2) Consider spending your vacation with us, the Explorer Line, on a seven-day, fourteen-day, or eighty-day cruise. We can take you to all those places you have always wanted to visit: the Caribbean, the Mexican Riviera, South America, the Pacific Islands, the Far East, and Africa. With us, you will cross the oceans and seas Columbus and Magellan once traveled but in comfort undreamed of by those explorers. You will have your own clean, spacious stateroom with a view. In a comfortable dining room, you will enjoy delicious meals, prompt, attentive service, and evenings of music and dancing. As we sail, you can sunbathe, swim in one of the three pools, or play tennis, ping pong, and shuffle board. At each port of call, you can sightsee, shop, and often golf, swim, and hike. On your next vacation, let us do the navigating so you can have the adventures.

persuasive: appeals directed to reader, attempt to "sell" cruise

EXERCISE B: Identifying Problems in an Expository Paragraph. Read the following paragraph, assuming it was written for people who know little about pianos and harpsichords. Find three terms or statements in the explanation that the writer fails to explain to the general reader. Then write three questions that you wish the writer had answered about these terms or points. *Problem terms underlined; questions will vary.*

(1) Surprisingly enough, playing a harpsichord requires an entirely different technique from playing a piano. (2) For one thing, the harpsichord player must employ a quicker finger action, almost a plucking motion, whereas a pianist will apply weight through the fingers to depress keys. (3) This is partly because key movements on a harpsichord are stiffer than on a piano. (4) In addition, a harpsichord does not have dampers, as does a piano. (5) So the harpsichord player will not use a pedal to hold notes and chords, as a pianist will.

■ Writing an Expository Paragraph

When writing an expository paragraph, you will follow the planning, brainstorming, organizing, drafting, and revising steps for writing any good paragraph. Throughout these steps, however, you should concentrate on fulfilling your explanatory purpose and on achieving an informative tone.

As you prepare an expository paragraph, focus on explaining your main idea and on helping the audience to understand it.

You should begin by letting your purpose guide you in finding a suitable topic, main idea, and supporting information. You should choose a topic you know well, either from your reading or from experience. You should also select an aspect of the topic that can be treated in a factual, explanatory manner; focus on facts and ideas, not on opinions. For instance, if you wanted to write about the Abominable Snowman, your topic sentence should focus on theories about the Abominable Snowman rather than your opinion that the Abominable Snowman does exist. To explain your idea, you may use specific information from books, particularly reference books. As long as you indicate the sources of your facts and examples, such supporting information can strengthen and clarify your explanation.

As you draft and revise your paragraph, strive to be a good instructor by putting yourself in your reader's place. Because you may have experienced the frustration of trying to follow a recipe or instructions that had an ingredient or step missing, you will want to avoid putting your reader in this position. You probably also know how annoying a fuzzy or incomplete explanation can be. Try to avoid technical terms beyond the reader's knowledge or define such terms clearly. Do not assume that the reader knows the topic as well as you do. Be thorough in your explanation. As you begin to revise your paragraph, you should consult a checklist for revision, such as the one in Section 23.4. You may also find the following suggestions useful for checking the clarity and completeness of your expository paragraph.

SUGGESTIONS FOR EVALUATING EXPOSITORY PARAGRAPHS

1. Read your paragraph to someone unfamiliar with the topic. Ask that person to tell you what your paragraph has explained.
2. Have someone else read your paragraph and list any questions your paragraph should answer but does not.
3. If your paragraph explains a process, try to do the steps or have someone else try using your explanation. See if you have omitted any important steps or details.

EXERCISE C: Planning and Organizing an Expository Paragraph. Choose one of the following topics, narrow the topic, and think about your explanatory purpose and your audience as you write a topic sentence. Then, gather supporting information through reading and brainstorming or simply through brainstorming. Finally, outline your paragraph using the most appropriate logical order.

Topic sentences and outlines might be checked.

A landmark or historical site	How an instrument produces sound
How icebergs form	Junior high school and high school
Rugby and American football	Styles of dancing
Unusual pets	A school sport
Space travel	A detective story

EXERCISE D: Drafting and Revising an Expository Paragraph. Use the outline you prepared in Exercise C to draft your paragraph, striving for smoothness, clarity, and completeness. Use the checklist in Section 23.4 on page 650 to revise your paragraph. Also, use one of the suggestions in the chart on page 671. Then make any necessary changes in your paragraph and recopy it.

Students could exchange papers, or paragraphs could be discussed by entire class.

APPLICATION: Writing and Analyzing Expository Paragraphs. Choose one of the following processes or think of one of your own to explain in an expository paragraph. Follow the steps for narrowing the topic, writing a topic sentence, brainstorming for support, organizing support, and drafting your paragraph. Then exchange papers with someone else in the class and try to follow the process explained in the paragraph. Make notes to the writer of any instructions and details that are unclear or incomplete. Then return the paragraph to the writer, revise your own, and recopy it. *Paragraphs that treat the same process might be compared in class.*

How to tie a shoe	How to get from school to your house
How to unlock a combination lock	How to play Hangman
How to change a typewriter ribbon	How to shoot a basket
	How to make an omelet
How to start a car	How to wash dishes
	How to do a dance step

24.2   Persuasive Paragraphs

Persuasive writing attempts to influence others, to convince others, or to move others to take action. It is found in editorials, reviews of movies and books, and advertisements.

Any time you are asked to take a stand on an issue or to offer your own interpretation of something you have read, you are using persuasive writing. Like expository writing, persuasive writing is one of the basic kinds of writing. Because you will often read and have occasion to use persuasive writing, you can profit from a study of its main features. This section will also explain how to adapt your general paragraph writing skills to writing persuasive paragraphs.

■ The Main Features of Persuasive Paragraphs

Persuasive writing should resemble other forms of good writing, but it should also have some specific features. The writer of a persuasive paragraph must concentrate on defending an opinion or course of action. The writer's goal is to convince the reader to agree with an opinion or at least to consider the writer's viewpoint. The tone can be casual or serious, but it should always include a logical, persuasive appeal.

A Persuasive Purpose. The persuasive purpose should be apparent in the topic sentence and in the supporting information. The topic sentence should state the writer's opinion or proposal for action clearly and directly. And the supporting information should give the reader reasons why he or she should think or do as the writer advocates.

The purpose of a persuasive paragraph is to persuade a reader to agree with an opinion or to take action by offering convincing evidence.

The topic sentence in a persuasive paragraph should be a statement of opinion. To be a suitable opinion, it should be controversial; that is, it should be a statement with which some people disagree, not a factual statement.

CONTROVERSIAL STATEMENT: Tests for new drivers should be longer and more difficult.

FACTUAL STATEMENT: Most tests for a driver's license involve a written test and a driving test.

The opinion should also be significant, of interest to others, rather than trivial or highly personal.

SIGNIFICANT OPINION: Bull mastiffs make reliable, companionable
                          watchdogs for families.

INSIGNIFICANT OPINION: I like bull mastiffs.

In addition, the opinion for a persuasive paragraph
should be supportable with reasons, facts, and examples
rather than an opinion that you cannot reasonably defend.

SUPPORTABLE OPINION: Classical musicians must have more tech-
                          nical skill than rock musicians.

UNSUPPORTABLE OPINION: Michelangelo would like the paintings of
                          Picasso.

The support in a persuasive paragraph should consist of
specific information that interests the reader and makes the
reader see the reasonableness and importance of the writer's
opinion. Like support in an expository paragraph, support
in a persuasive paragraph will often include information
that explains. But it should also attempt to influence the
reader or change the reader's mind. To serve this persuasive
purpose the writer must provide complete support in a logical order.

In the following paragraph, the writer begins with an
opinion: *Any individual interested in physical activity should
consider jogging.* The supporting information defends that
opinion by offering four reasons with details: (1) Jogging is
beneficial to health; (2) it is inexpensive; (3) it is enjoyable
and fulfilling; and (4) it is an independent sport. These reasons tell the reader why the writer's opinion is reasonable
and worthwhile.

TOPIC SENTENCE (Statement of opinion) Reasons	Any individual interested in physical activity should consider jogging. According to a recent study sponsored by the President's Council of Physical Fitness, the sport is beneficial to a person's general health and wellbeing. It tones muscles and improves physical endurance. And running is inexpensive since little equipment is necessary. Although perhaps not the most exciting of sports, jogging can be quite enjoyable. It is fulfilling to watch your pace and endurance increase with practice. Joggers can move as fast and as far as they choose, when they like, and thus can blame no one but themselves for failure. Similarly, if you take up jogging and succeed at it, the victory belongs to you and you alone.

A Reasonable, Persuasive Tone.　Good persuasive writing also has a persuasive tone. The writer's effort to convince the reader of the opinion in the topic sentence with strong, interesting evidence contributes to the persuasive tone. The writer's choice of language also helps to create a persuasive tone. The words in a persuasive paragraph should appeal to a reader's interest, reason, and understanding.

Create a reasonable, persuasive tone by using language that is forceful but fair, as well as specific and clear.

Using fair, unemotional language will help to create a persuasive tone. When writing persuasive paragraphs, you should avoid becoming emotional. Misusing words with strong negative or positive connotations, including unsupported opinions, or using emotionally loaded words will distort the tone. Emotional language offends rather than persuades. Few people are persuaded by insults, unfair accusations, or name-calling. Words such as *redneck, numbskull, prude, brain, hog, crook,* and *idiot* destroy a persuasive tone. (For more information on emotional language see Section 21.3.)

In order to be persuasive, you must often interest and inform. Specific concrete language can help to create a persuasive tone, while adding interest and information. A reader is more likely to respond to your reasons if you say a product will save twenty dollars a month than if you are vague and say the product has economic benefits. You should also take into account the reader's background and knowledge of the topic. If you explain difficult technical words and ideas so that the reader can understand them, the reader will be more apt to follow and agree with you.

The tone of the following paragraph, adapted from a book by Vance Packard, is forceful and insistent. The writer even uses the words "urgent and immediate problem." Notice that the information offered as support and the language of the paragraph appeal to the reader's reason and understanding. Also, notice that the writer has used words that are accurate and fair, such as *heavy users*, has given specific, familiar examples of water needs, such as *dishwashers* and *lawn sprinklers*, and has explained such terms as *water tables* and *mining of the water*.

TOPIC
SENTENCE
(Statement of
· opinion)

Persuasive
tone with
reasonable,
specific
language

The task of maintaining an adequate water supply for a violently expanding population accustomed to heavy use of water presents an urgent and immediate problem. The water needs of the average American citizen have doubled in this century, partly because of the demand for showers, flush toilets, air conditioners, dishwashers, lawn sprinklers, and swimming pools. The really heavy users of water, *however*, are industry and farmers. It ordinarily takes 60,000 gallons of water to make a ton of paper or steel. Farmers use quantities of water for irrigation. Because of the increase in use, water tables are falling. In some communities water is being withdrawn twenty times as fast as it is being replaced. And in some areas of North Dakota and Long Island, underground water levels have fallen so low that further "mining" of the water is curbed by regulation.
—Adapted from Vance Packard

EXERCISE A: **Identifying a Persuasive Paragraph.** Read the following two paragraphs carefully. Identify which one has a persuasive purpose, and describe two characteristics of the paragraph that indicate its persuasive purpose. Then identify the purpose of the other paragraph and tell why you think that is its purpose.

(1) The ancient Egyptians sought eternal life above all else. If they could but placate the hundreds of deities who regulated every event; if they could save prized possessions for perpetual use; if they could preserve their bodies as permanent shelters for their souls; then, surely, they would live forever, free from illness and harm, continuing the colorful existence they enjoyed along the fertile banks of the Nile. —Alice J. Hall
expository: to inform readers about Egyptian custom

(2) The concerned citizens in this school district urge that the members of the school board correct unsafe conditions on the elementary school playground. The blacktop area needs to be repaved. Loose chunks of cement and large surface crevices can easily snag a child's foot as he or she walks or runs through these areas. Also hazardous are the sidewalks and drainage ditches near the school's rear entrance. Slabs of the walkways have been upturned by heavy rains, and mud slides across these passageways occur during every rainstorm. The stairway leading to the lower playing field is even more dangerous. Children use this route all day long, running to and from recess and other activities. Many wooden steps are

cracked and several wooden supports are splintered and shaky. If the steps or supports should collapse, serious injuries could result. Let's think ahead and prevent these playground tragedies.

persuasive: statement of opinion, attempt to convince audience ("let's")

EXERCISE B: Improving Tone in a Persuasive Paragraph. In the following paragraph, the writer fails to be persuasive. Read the paragraph carefully. Then list examples of emotionally loaded words, vague, general words, and unexplained terms. Look up the unexplained terms in the dictionary. Then rewrite the paragraph to create a reasonable, persuasive tone. You can add or rearrange supporting information to make the paragraph more persuasive.

Revisions will vary; problem words underlined and classified.

(1) All students should be required to take a speech course in high school. (2) Most students cannot get up in front of the class without making total fools of themselves. (3) They tend to be mumbling, rambling idiots. (4) A speech course could correct these problems, however, by teaching students to project their voices and to think out and practice their speeches. (5) A speech class would also help them with enunciation and effective eye contact. (6) All jocks, super brains, and conceited student officers could use public speaking in their classes and later in job and college interviews and in their careers. (7) Students could benefit from learning how to give informative speeches, sales talks, dramatic interpretations, and impromptu and extemporaneous speeches. (8) Finally, a speech course could give mousy students confidence and could help loudmouths have something meaningful to say.

1. OK   2. vague/loaded   3. loaded   4. unexplained   5. unexplained/ unexplained   6. loaded/loaded/loaded   7. unexplained   8. loaded/loaded/ vague

▪ Writing a Persuasive Paragraph

As you write a persuasive paragraph, you should plan, brainstorm, organize, draft, and revise, always concentrating on your persuasive purpose and tone. Directing your paragraph toward readers who disagree will help you be persuasive. Your goal should be to change the opinion of the reader who disagrees with you or does not care about the issue. To reach this goal, you must consider the opposing viewpoint at all times.

As you prepare a persuasive paragraph, focus on convincing an unsympathetic or apathetic reader to agree with your opinion or to take action.

Concentrating on your persuasive purpose will help you to find an appropriate controversial topic and to develop a strong, clear opinion on that topic. You should choose a topic that you believe in and know something about, and one that you think others should care about too. You should state your opinion about the topic in a sentence that will become your topic sentence. Then test the validity of your topic sentence by thinking of an opinion opposite to yours. If you cannot come up with an opposite or different opinion, you have probably written a statement of fact. Make sure your topic sentence is a direct, supportable statement of opinion.

As you gather supporting information, consider the opposing opinion but focus on defending your opinion. You should find convincing facts, examples, and reasons. Evidence from reference books or from experts can make your defense more believable. Remember that the more controversial the opinion, the more persuasive you must be. You should particularly avoid support that consists simply of weak, general opinions.

One method of gathering support to defend a controversial opinion is to list the evidence for and against your opinion. Listing the arguments against your opinion can help you think of stronger evidence to support your opinion. It can also help you fill in the gaps in your defense. The following chart shows an example of building a defense.

BUILDING YOUR DEFENSE		
Topic Sentence: Residents of apartments should not be allowed to have cats or dogs.		
Evidence For	Evidence Against	Additional Evidence For
—Cats and dogs are noisy— meowing, howling, barking —Cats and dogs can bring odors and fleas	—Cats and dogs give joy to their owners —Dogs, especially, can provide protection —Owners can train pets to	—Not all residents enjoy people's pets in close quarters —No room for everyone to have pets so allowing anyone is unfair

—Cats and dogs damage rugs, floors, woodwork, drapes —Cats and dogs have no place to exercise or take care of their needs	be quiet and obedient and housebroken	—Many people spoil their pets

Besides helping you strengthen your defense, considering evidence of the opposing side can also help you plan the persuasive approach you will take in your paragraph. As you outline your paragraph, you may decide to admit that the other side does have a good point. This practice is called *conceding a point.* Conceding a point can show the reader how reasonable and knowledgeable you are. It reveals that you have thought about the other side's viewpoint and that you are fairminded. For example, in the paragraph on jogging, the writer concedes that jogging may not be an exciting sport but then emphasizes jogging's positive points. In your outline, you can plan to mention an opposing argument or even concede a point and then counter with strong evidence in your favor.

As you organize your support, remember that you want to hold the reader's attention and win at least the reader's consideration of your opinion. You can arrange supporting information in many ways, but you may find order of importance particularly useful. Building from your least important reason to your strongest and most important reason can help you maintain the reader's interest and end forcefully. A concluding sentence that contains a summary, warning, personal appeal, or call to action can also strengthen a persuasive paragraph.

While drafting and revising your paragraph, thinking about winning the reader's agreement can help you make a final check for persuasiveness. You should use a checklist such as the one in Section 23.4. Also, consider the following suggestions as a means of testing the effect of your paragraph on a reader and of improving the persuasiveness of your paragraph.

SUGGESTIONS FOR EVALUATING A PERSUASIVE PARAGRAPH

1. Have someone who *disagrees* with your opinion read your paragraph. Ask that person if your paragraph is reasonable and convincing.
2. Have someone who *agrees* with your opinion read your paragraph. Ask that person what other reasons or evidence would strengthen your defense.

EXERCISE C: Planning, Brainstorming, and Organizing a Persuasive Paragraph. Choose one of the following topics, state your specific opinion about it, and write a clear, supportable topic sentence. Then write an opinion opposite to yours. Brainstorm for strong supporting evidence, and list at least two points that someone who disagrees with you might make. Finally, outline your paragraph using order of importance or another order.
Topic sentences and outlines might be checked before actual writing begins.

The best place for a vacation	A book everyone should read
The highest quality television show	The most economical car
The animal that makes the best pet	The most fulfilling career
The most important subject in school	The most effective diet
The most talented (athlete, singer, dancer)	The most exciting spectator sport

EXERCISE D: Drafting and Revising a Persuasive Paragraph. Use the outline you prepared in Exercise C to draft your paragraph, giving special attention to fair, reasonable, understandable language and complete, logical support. Then use the checklist in Section 23.4 on page 650. Finally, follow one of the suggestions in the chart above. Make any necessary improvements in your paragraph and recopy it.
Students could exchange papers before doing revisions.

APPLICATION: Writing and Analyzing Persuasive Paragraphs. Choose one of the following topics or use one of your own, and develop a statement of opinion. Follow the steps for writing a persuasive paragraph. Also, make a chart like the one on page 678 for building your defense. Write your topic sentence at the top of your paper. Then divide your paper into three columns: one column for evidence *for* your opinion, one for evidence *against*, and one for additional evidence *for* your opinion. Try to strengthen your evidence by considering both sides. Plan to concede one point to the opposing side somewhere in your paragraph. Organize your evidence using order of importance or another logical order. As you draft your paragraph, remember to use fair, specific, understandable language. As you revise, follow one of the suggestions in the chart on page 680. Then make any necessary changes in your paragraph and recopy it.

A needed change at your school

The driving age for young people and elderly people

Stricter laws against pollution (noise, factories, garbage)

The need to pass competency tests before graduating from high school

Smoking in public places

The need for more national parks

Neighborhood organizations to prevent crime

Increasing the national budget for space exploration

Littering

Nuclear energy

Students could exchange papers and try to add to other students' pro or con arguments. Building a defense around an interesting topic could be a good class exercise to prepare for this assignment.

Descriptive and Narrative Paragraphs 24.3

Descriptive writing paints pictures with words or recreates a scene or experience for the reader. Description enlivens magazine articles, interviews, and reviews, and helps to make characters and places seem real in works of fiction as well. In your own writing, description can add vividness to your letters, stories, and compositions.

Narrative writing, like descriptive writing, is particularly lively and imaginative. It draws the reader into a series of events—either real or imaginary—by relating them in chronological order, from a particular point of view, and in vivid and interesting language. Your own letters and compositions, even your daily conversations, are likely to be filled with brief narratives.

This section will explain the features of both descriptive and narrative paragraphs. It will also give you practice in exercising your imagination to write these special kinds of paragraphs.

■ The Main Features of Descriptive Paragraphs

Descriptive writing makes special demands on the writer who must try to appeal to the reader's senses and imagination. The writer's goal is to make the reader see, hear, smell, or experience what is described. In addition, the writer often attempts to convey a dominant impression or mood, perhaps a gloomy, peaceful, solemn, or joyful mood. To achieve these multiple goals, the writer must use descriptive language: sensory impressions and figures of speech.

A Descriptive Purpose.   In a descriptive paragraph, the descriptive purpose affects the choice of topic, the topic sentence, and the support. All the parts of the paragraph should work together to paint a picture or to recreate an experience for the reader.

The purpose of a descriptive paragraph is to describe a particular person, place, object, or experience by presenting specific details.

The topic of a descriptive paragraph should be a particular person, place, object, or experience: a specific street musician, a specific beach in Maine, a specific cat in the neighborhood, a specific broken umbrella, or a specific stormy night. The topic you describe can bring to mind all other objects or places like it, but the paragraph should not give general ideas about a general category of things.

A descriptive paragraph should also be unified by a dominant impression or mood, which is usually stated in the topic sentence. Some descriptive paragraphs, often those within longer stories, may leave the dominant impression unstated. However, many descriptive paragraphs do use a topic sentence to focus the reader's attention on a single, overall impression of someone or something. A topic sentence at the beginning of the paragraph can set the scene, give the reader a preview, and often arouse the reader's curiosity. A topic sentence in the middle can focus the reader's attention on the most important impression to be drawn. A topic sentence at the end of the paragraph can indicate to the reader that all the specific description in the paragraph adds up to that one dominant impression or mood.

The support in a descriptive paragraph should make the person, place, object, or experience real to the reader. It should include sensory impressions—sights, sounds, smells, textures, feelings—that the writer has experienced or imagined. Most of all, support in a descriptive paragraph should consist of specific details that give the reader a complete impression of someone or something.

Strong description consists of many specific details whereas weak description consists of general remarks with few details. Weak description is brief and sketchy. It presents the writer's judgment by summarizing, and it often includes vague adjectives such as *terrible, beautiful,* and *big.* Strong description, on the other hand, involves the reader to a greater degree. It places the reader right in the scene by offering specific details about such things as color, size, texture, shape, condition, and movement. To capture specific details, a writer can use colorful action verbs, specific nouns, and vivid, exact adjectives. Notice the difference in the amount and quality of the details in the following two descriptions.

WEAK DESCRIPTION: The woman was small and somewhat fat, with dark eyes, messy hair bound with vines and jewels, a dirty robe, and big feet.

STRONG DESCRIPTION: Facing him was a short and rather plump little woman with a round, lumpy face and a pair of very sharp black eyes. Her hair hung like a clump of discolored marsh weeds, bound with vines and ornamented with bejeweled pins that seemed about to lose themselves in the helpless tangle. She wore a dark, shapeless ungirt robe covered with patches and stains. Her feet were bare and exceptionally large. —Lloyd Alexander

In addition to using complete, specific details, the writer should organize the details so that the reader can visualize them easily or experience them realistically. Often a description can be organized in spatial or chronological order. For instance, if the writer is describing a room as he or she looks around that room, the specific details should follow that spatial order, from wall to wall, or ceiling to floor. You may have noticed in the preceding description of the enchantress that the writer began with the total impression and then moved from her face to her feet. If the writer is describing such things as laundry flapping on the line, a passing train, or the changing colors of the sky as the sun sets, specific details could follow chronological order to give the reader a moment by moment description. No matter what order is used, specific details should always be arranged logically with transitions to guide the reader.

The following paragraph develops the dominant impression of wonder at the perfection of an object. Notice the specific details of the trees, fruit, birds, and animals. Also notice that the presentation of these details follows spatial order. (The transitions are in italics.)

TOPIC SENTENCE (Dominant impression)	The visitor gazed in wonder at the king's invention: a mechanized miniature forest perfect in every detail. Encased in a carved box, approximately two feet square, the little forest shone deep green in the sunlight. Dense sugar pines, elms, and walnut, apple, and pear trees clustered *around the inner walls of the box.* The little trees had real, scratchy bark and bristled with leaves and needles. Some of the branches held tiny pine cones, walnuts, apples, and pears. *Toward the inner part of the forest*, the trees thinned. *On the ground*, amidst the scrubby brush, twigs, and fallen leaves, tiny animals romped. A squirrel dug among the leaves for nuts, and a deer grazed. A rabbit sniffed the wind not far from a bushy red fox hiding behind a log. When the king turned a switch, the fox lunged and the rabbit hopped into the thicker trees.
Specific details in spatial order	

Descriptive Language. Besides focusing on a dominant impression and developing it with specific details, a writer can fulfill the descriptive purpose by using descriptive language. Descriptive language, with its sensory impressions and figures of speech, appeals to the reader's senses, imagination, and emotions. It helps to create pictures, to recreate experiences, and to establish a mood.

Sensory impressions and figures of speech help to make a dominant impression or mood real to the reader.

Sensory impressions are a kind of specific detail. They are impressions gained through the sense of sight, smell, hearing, touch, taste, or feeling. The writer can convey these impressions to the reader by using sharp, precise verbs and vivid nouns and adjectives. Sensory impressions can enable the reader to experience with the senses and imagination. The following chart gives examples of sensory impressions, many of them written by professional writers. Notice that the sensory impressions for sounds actually use words that imitate the sounds.

SENSORY IMPRESSIONS		
Sights	**Sounds**	**Smells**
The shadows of the trees were long and twisted. —Madeleine L'Engle	A woodpecker went into a wild ratatattat. —Madeleine L'Engle	the smell of starch in her crisp, white apron —Catherine Marshall
eyes lined with tiny red veins	a sudden hiss of arrows —Lloyd Alexander	The night air was scented with burning pine chips and resin. —Sid Fleischman
Tastes	**Feelings (touch)**	**Sensations**
the gluey licorice of cough syrup	the cool, rounded smoothness of marble polished by many feet	Her legs and arms were tingling faintly, as though they had been asleep. —Madeleine L'Engle
hot chili, peppery and spicy	a soft, fluffy apple blossom	the breeze tickling her forehead with wisps of hair

Figures of speech can also appeal to a reader's imagination and understanding. Figures of speech are imaginative comparisons formed by seeing similarities between essentially unlike things. By describing one thing as like another, the writer helps the reader see the thing described in a fresh, vivid way. Some examples of figures of speech are similes, metaphors, and personifications. (For more explanation of similes and metaphors, see Section 21.2.) The following chart explains these figures of speech and gives several examples of each.

FIGURES OF SPEECH

Figure of Speech	Example
simile: a comparison of two unlike things introduced by *like* or *as*	The furnace purred like a great, sleepy animal. —Madeleine L'Engle He was swift and light on his feet as a ball bouncing away ahead of me. —Sid Fleishchman
metaphor: a comparison of two unlike things by complete identification (X is Y); the comparison may be implied, not written out, in a *submerged metaphor*	the lake of melted butter in the steaming mound of hominy grits —Catherine Marshall The sky had begun to unravel in scarlet threads. —Lloyd Alexander
personification: giving objects or ideas human characteristics; describing objects or ideas as if they were human	Unmasked now, the ship went swaggering before the wind as if with a knife clasped between her teeth. —Sid Fleischman There was a faint gust of wind and the leaves shivered in it. —Madeleine L'Engle

NOTE ABOUT PERSONIFICATION: Personification should not be overused because too much personification can make description seem artificial and forced.

EXERCISE A: **Identifying the Descriptive Features.** Read the following paragraph. State the dominant impression that the writer describes. Then list at least five specific details and identify any other features that contribute to the descriptiveness of the paragraph.
Details and descriptive language are underlined.

(1) Then the sun was <u>sinking</u> and <u>every prismatic color</u> was <u>reflecting</u> back from this <u>ice-encased world</u>. (2) The valley had become like <u>Ali Baba's Treasure Cave</u> that I had read about as a child. (3) I found my <u>eyes and throat aching</u> with the <u>beauty</u> that <u>blazed</u> outside the train windows. (4) <u>Jewels</u> seemed to <u>glitter</u> from every bush, <u>every withered blade</u> of grass, every twig: <u>sapphires and turquoise, emeralds and amethysts, rubies, crystals, diamonds.</u> —Catherine Marshall

impression of wonder at landscape

EXERCISE B: **Identifying Sensory Impressions and Figures of Speech.** Identify each of the following items as a sensory impression or a figure of speech. If the item is a sensory impression, also write which sense it appeals to (for example, *sensory impression: sound*). If the item is a figure of speech, also write what kind it is (for example, *figure of speech: personification*).

1. From the bulwarks her crew peered down at me like vultures. —Sid Fleischman *figure: simile*
2. jangling of her alarm clock —Madeleine L'Engle *sensory: sound*
3. There was even a cold slice of moon rising in the sky to help me. —Sid Fleischman *figure: metaphor*
4. the greasy smoothness of hot vinyl car seats *sensory: touch*
5. The petals were pink and white confetti on the lawn.
6. the earthy scent of molding leaves *sensory: smell*
7. Rain danced on the decks... —Sid Fleischman
8. The captain's face flushed red as a sunset. —Sid Fleischman *figure: simile*
9. A ceaseless thrumming and groaning trembled in the air. —Lloyd Alexander *sensory: sound*
10. The sun was feeble, wrapped in gray clouds. —Lloyd Alexander *figure: personification*

5. figure: metaphor   7. figure: personification

EXERCISE C: **Using Sensory Impressions.** For each of the following items, write a sensory impression that appeals to the sense in parentheses. *Answers will vary; samples given for first two.*

EXAMPLE: A dandelion (touch)—the soft, whispering feel of the downy petals

A parade (sound) *blaring trumpets*   An old apple (taste)
A restaurant (smell) *pungent onions* A baby's hair (touch)
A bridge (sight)   A rainstorm (sensation)
A train (sound)   A parking garage (smell)
A Ferris wheel (sensation)   Corn on the cob (taste)

EXERCISE D: **Using Figures of Speech.** Follow the instructions and write similes, metaphors, and examples of personification. *Answers will vary; samples given for first two.*

1. After observing an animal, write a simile.
2. After observing a child, write a metaphor.
3. After observing a machine in motion, write an example of personification.
4. After observing a person in motion, write a simile.
5. After observing traffic, write a metaphor.

1. a chick fuzzy as a dandelion head   2. a little island of a boy

■ Writing a Descriptive Paragraph

Throughout the planning, brainstorming, organizing, drafting, and revising of a descriptive paragraph, you should assume that the reader is not familiar with the subject you are describing. Consequently, you must concentrate on your descriptive purpose and descriptive language to appeal to the reader's senses, imagination, and understanding.

As you prepare a descriptive paragraph, focus on enabling a reader unfamiliar with what you are describing to see or know your topic.

You should choose a subject that has affected you strongly or one that stands out in your mind. Sometimes some preliminary observation or thinking will be necessary for you to arrive at a single, overall impression or mood. Once you have reached a dominant impression or mood, you should state it clearly in a topic sentence.

You can gather support for a descriptive paragraph in a number of ways: through direct observation, through memory, or through imaginative thinking. With all three ways, however, you should look for features that identify and distinguish your subject. Ask yourself, "What would a person unfamiliar with this subject need to know to recognize it and understand it from my description alone?" List your observations carefully as specific details, sensory impressions, and even figures of speech, if any occur to you. Try to take a mental photograph and reproduce it with your words.

In order to make someone or something seem real, interesting, and memorable to the reader, you must gather exact, specific information. The following chart suggests some kinds of details you should gather.

DETAILS AND IMPRESSIONS TO GATHER	
Topic of Description	What to Describe
A person	size, shape, mannerisms, facial expressions, features, gestures, voice, walk, clothing, mood
An object	size, shape, texture, function (use), color, condition, location, any motion, noise, speed, smells, tastes

A place or an experience	dimensions, weather or season, time of day, number of people, activity of people, atmosphere, surroundings, sounds, smells, sensations

As you select and organize your details, you should concentrate on making them clear to the reader. Whether you order details from near to far, far to near, top to bottom, inside to outside (in spatial order), by time, or by any other order, keep the relationship of one detail to another clear for the reader.

In the drafting and revising steps, you can polish your description. As you write, try to use strong action verbs, specific nouns, and exact, vivid adjectives. Use specific details that include the reader. Think of any figures of speech that could make your description more exact, vivid, and imaginative. As you revise, you should use a checklist such as the one in Section 23.4. Also consider the suggestions in the following chart.

SUGGESTIONS FOR EVALUATING A DESCRIPTIVE PARAGRAPH

1. Ask someone *unfamiliar* with what you are describing to read your paragraph and react by saying what the description made him or her see, feel, sense, and so on.
2. Ask someone *familiar* with what you are describing to read your paragraph for accuracy and completeness of details.
3. Put your paragraph aside for a short time and then reread it. Look for too little or too much detail, or details that are too fuzzy.
4. If possible, return to observe your person, place, or object again. Check the accuracy, vividness, and completeness of your description against the original.

EXERCISE E: Planning, Organizing, Drafting, and Revising. Choose one of the following general items and focus on a specific person, place, object, or experience that fits into this category. Observe the topic of your description closely or use your memory or imagination. Determine a dominant impression or mood, and write a topic sentence that expresses it. Then jot down details and sensory impressions, and organize your support in an outline. Using the outline, draft the paragraph, keeping in mind your reader and making use of vivid, specific words. Also try to include at least one figure of speech. Finally, revise your paragraph, first using the checklist in Section 23.4, and then using one of the suggestions in the chart on page 689. Finally, recopy your paragraph. *The class might work through the first few steps with a common topic to generate images and colorful language.*

A certain beach	A piece of	A frightening
A room in a	machinery	person
building people	A new car	A person you'll
say is haunted	A pet	never forget
A hospital at	A favorite piece	A teacher you
night	of clothing	remember
Your hideout as	A favorite	from your
a child	childhood toy	childhood

■ The Main Features of Narrative Paragraphs

Narrative writing has a great deal in common with descriptive writing: It involves readers very powerfully by appealing to their imaginations, senses, and emotions. Like descriptive writing, it often conveys a particular mood and draws upon the vivid language of sensory impressions. But narrative writing is distinguished by the fact that it always tells a story: It relates a series of events from a particular point of view in chronological order, using the graphic language of description and action.

A Narrative Purpose.   When you write a narrative paragraph, you set out to tell a story—real or imagined—for any one of a variety of reasons. You may want simply to entertain your readers, you may want to share an experience you have had, or you may want to pass along a lesson that an experience has taught you. Whatever your reasons for telling a story, your writing will be governed by its basic narrative purpose. Your paragraph will connect a series of related events into a single chain, holding them together by means of a single point of view and a chronological organization.

> The purpose of a narrative paragraph is to relate a series of events, real or imaginary, from a single point of view, in chronological order.

The topic of a narrative paragraph is an experience—a series of events with a beginning, middle, and end—which can be related in a single paragraph. The experience might be real or fictional, but the topic of a narrative paragraph must be a series of events that the author can report in clear, specific, and interesting terms.

The topic sentence of a narrative paragraph makes the writer's narrative purpose clear. It usually comes at the beginning of the paragraph telling the reader to expect a story of some kind, setting the scene, and providing necessary background information. If the narrative is meant to illustrate some lesson or truth, the topic sentence, which will generally explain the meaning of the experience may, sometimes be found instead at the end of the paragraph.

In most cases, the topic sentence will also establish the *point of view* from which the narrative will be presented. In telling a story, a writer is free to choose from among several different points of view, or *narrators*, explained in the following chart. The important thing to keep in mind is that once a particular point of view is selected, it must be maintained consistently throughout a narrative.

DIFFERENT POINTS OF VIEW	
Narrator or Point of View	**Definition**
First person	The narrator, using the word "I," tells the story and participates in the action; the narrator gives the reader details as he or she sees them. The "I" may be either you yourself or a character you have created.
Third person, objective	The narrator, who is not in the story, tells the story as it happens to the characters through the use of "she" or "he"; the narrator makes only factual observations, no subjective comments.
Third person, partially omniscient	The narrator, who is not in the story, tells the story as it happens to the characters through the use of "she" or "he." The narrator can see into at least one character's mind and can tell what that character's thoughts and feelings are.
Third person, totally omniscient	The narrator, who is not in the story, tells the story as it happens to the characters through the use of "she" or "he." The narrator can see into the minds of several or all of the characters and can tell what the characters' thoughts and feelings are.

The point of view chosen for a story helps determine the kind of supporting information used to develop the story. The supporting information in any narrative will consist of the major events involved in the experience being related. These events can be both physical and mental and can include both actions and thoughts. But obviously they will vary according to the point of view that the author chooses. An experience revealed through the eyes (and thoughts and feelings) of a first-person participant would be quite different from one related by a third-person objective observer, who can report only physical appearances and actions.

The supporting information in a narrative paragraph is usually arranged in straight chronological order, proceeding step by step from beginning to end. Occasionally, however, a writer may vary this order by establishing the endpoint, or result of the experience, and then narrating the events that led up to it.

The Language of Narration.   Because narrative writing reproduces action and experience, the language of narration should be *graphic*, capturing the dynamic and vivid quality of real experience.

Use graphic language to transmit the feel of a real experience in writing narrative paragraphs.

The language of narration should be as dynamic as possible, drawing the reader along through a series of changing thoughts, feelings, and actions. Narration uses descriptive language as well; the word choices of narrative writers should be specific, lively, and full of sensory impressions. But, unlike descriptive writing, narrative writing must *move*; it must recreate the flow of real experience through time. In particular, writers of narration should choose precise and active verbs to capture this sense of movement; for example, *lumbered* creates a much sharper picture than *walked*, because it conveys much more of the quality of the action related.

The sentences as well as the words of narrative paragraphs should work together to carry the reader through the action. Good narrative writing makes particularly good use of transitions and other connecting words to make the sentences flow into one another. Sentence structure itself also has a great impact on the pace and flow of a narrative passage, pulling the reader along from word to word and phrase to phrase.

Note how the following story by Jean Kerr uses first-person narration, clever and exact word choices, and many linking words to give the reader a moment-by-moment sense of her comic misadventures as May Queen. The transitions and other connecting words are in italics.

TOPIC
SENTENCE
(Sets the
scene and
establishes
first-person
narrator)

Developed
with active
verbs and
specific, lively
language

A silence fell as I picked up the wreath and walked slowly up to the statue. It was *then* that I realized, and with a stab to the heart, why I had been chosen May Queen. I had been chosen because I was the tallest girl in the school. *It was equally clear*, as I peered at the massive stone figure looming four or five feet above me, that, tall as I was, I wasn't tall enough. Was it possible, I wondered, that we would all have to stand here until I grew another six inches! *Then* I remembered Mother Claire's oft-repeated adage, "Desperate diseases require desperate remedies." I took the wreath firmly in my two hands, grasping it like a basketball, and hurled it up onto the head of the statue. *For a brief moment* it looked as though I had succeeded, for the wreath seemed to be resting firmly on the prongs of the stone crown. *But then*, slowly and majestically, it slid down until it settled rakishly over one large stone eye. The effect was decidedly disreputable, and there was a hiss of horror from the nuns as well as a gasp from the girls that quickly degenerated into muffled laughter. The *first* to be affected were the flautists, who, in an effort to suppress their giggles, had blown spit into their flutes and rendered them useless. The singers, without a flute to guide them, fell silent. The little girl who had borne the wreath burst into tears and a first grade flower girl was heard to inquire loudly, "Is it over?" — Jean Kerr

EXERCISE F: Identifying Narrative Features. Read the following narrative paragraph and identify the point of view used in the paragraph. Then, identify the kinds of support used in the paragraph as physical or mental activity. Next, list at least five examples of transitions and other connecting words used in the paragraph. Finally, list at least five examples of vivid, graphic nouns, verbs, and modifiers.

See explanation below.

(1) A short distance away a young eagle dragged a partially eaten salmon carcass out of the water. (2) Gripping the nearly frozen fish awkwardly, the bird tore off pieces of meat with a force that threw it back several feet in the snow each time. (3) Composing itself, the bird cautiously eyed the other eagles, then lifted its head up and finished the meat. (4) A magpie and gull landed on the dead fish and began eating. (5) As the eagle waddled back for more food, the two stepped gingerly aside, stopping just two feet away. (6) Again the eagle fell back with a huge piece, and again the two smaller birds returned to the carcass. (7) This dance for dinner was repeated until the eagle was so gorged that despite labored beats of its four-foot wings, it couldn't take off. —Vic Banks

Point of view is third-person objective; support is physical. Examples of transitions and connecting words are shaded; examples of vivid language are underlined.

■ Writing a Narrative Paragraph

In planning, brainstorming, organizing, drafting, and revising a narrative paragraph, you should concentrate on telling your reader a story. Capture the reader's attention in the beginning, hold his or her interest throughout, and satisfy his or her expectations by the end. Every element of your narrative—your choice of a topic, of a narrator, of supporting information, and of language—should appeal to your reader's curiosity and imagination.

In preparing a narrative paragraph, focus on making the experience you narrate come to life for your reader by choosing a topic, narrator, support, and language that stimulate your reader's interest and imagination.

Whether you relate something that happened to you, something that happened to someone else, or something completely imaginary, you should write about an experience that you can envision fully, one that you can relate with authority, in detail.

After you have a basic story in mind, you must select a point of view and create a narrator for yourself. Decide which of the several narrative points of view listed in the chart on page 691 is most suitable for your topic. A first-person narrator might work well for a story about a personal experience, but even in this instance, you might give yourself more freedom if you talked about yourself in the third person. In any case, choose your point of view carefully, and maintain it consistently throughout your paragraph.

At this point, you can draft your topic sentence, either one that sets the scene while arousing interest or one that focuses on some general truth or principle. Then you should decide which aspects of the experience—which events and details—should be included in your support. Remember that your choice of a narrator will determine the kind of support that you can use. For example, a first-person narrator cannot read another character's mind and probably cannot even be expected to be aware of *all* the physical activity around him or her. Once you have chosen your pieces of supporting information, make sure that you arrange them in chronological order and that the relationship of one item to the next is clear.

When you actually write your paragraph, concentrate on making the connections between the events in your story clear to your reader. In your opening sentences, try to set the scene and attract the reader's curiosity and interest. As you proceed, try to satisfy the expectations you have aroused, without leaving any loose ends.

Keep your language as specific as possible, using strong verbs, precise nouns, and lively adjectives. Remember that you want your reader to see and feel the experience as it happens: Strong sensory impressions will help to place your reader at the scene of the action and will catch him or her up in your story. Link your sentences with transitions and other connecting devices to make sure that the narrative flows smoothly from beginning to end. As you revise, you should use a checklist such as the one in Section 23.4. The suggestions in the following chart may also be useful.

SUGGESTIONS FOR EVALUATING A NARRATIVE PARAGRAPH

1. Ask someone unfamiliar with the experience you are relating to read your paragraph and tell you what he or she saw, felt, or thought as the narrative unfolded. Ask also if your reader has noticed any skips or breaks in the narrative and whether or not the reader thinks the ending brought the story to a satisfying close.

2. Reread your story yourself, trying to approach it as if you were an outsider coming across the paragraph in a magazine or book. Ask yourself if your story arouses your interest, if it makes sense, and if it comes to a satisfactory resolution.

3. Look closely at the language of your story: How graphic is the language? Can it be made more lively, more real, more specific? Do your sentences seem connected to one another?

EXERCISE G: Planning, Organizing, Drafting, and Revising.
Choose one of the following general experiences or develop a topic of your own and build a narrative paragraph around it. Think through the experience, decide on the point of view that you want to use, write a topic sentence, and list the major events, actions, and thoughts that your narrator will relate, making sure that the events follow a chronological order. Then draft your narrative, keeping in mind your reader's need to follow the actions you relate and using graphic language that vividly communicates the experience as it unfolds. As a final step, revise your paragraph, using the checklist in Section 23.4 as well as one of the suggestions in the chart on page 695.
Particular attention might be paid to chronological order and use of transitions.
A familiar legend, myth, or fairy tale from a fresh perspective
An interview, test, audition, or other challenging experience
A day without food or a day of silence
The longest moment of someone's life
A funny or painful lesson

APPLICATION: Writing Descriptive and Narrative Paragraphs. Follow the instructions to write one descriptive and one narrative paragraph on the same topic.

1. Write a descriptive paragraph about a place that you can actually observe—a specific bus station, restaurant, classroom, theater, or park, for example. Describe the place as fully as you can, giving a precise and detailed account of the look, sound, atmosphere, and so on of your subject. What people and what objects are in this place? What do they look like? What are they doing? Make your reader feel as if he or she is in the middle of your scene. Use as many sensory impressions as you can, choosing your language carefully. Then revise your paragraph, using the checklist in Section 23.4 and one of the suggestions in the chart on page 689.
2. Use the scene that you described in your descriptive paragraph as the setting for a narrative paragraph. You may use a real-life incident that took place in that setting or you may invent one of your own. Set the scene, assuming that your reader has *not* read your descriptive paragraph, and narrate the experience that takes place there, choosing an appropriate point of view and using language that draws your reader along through the experience as it progresses. Then revise your paragraph using the checklist and one of the suggestions in the chart on page 695.

Particular attention might be paid to use of detail in the description and to point of view and the connections between actions in the narrative.

Chapter 25

Essays

Once you are familiar with analyzing and writing paragraphs, you are ready to study essays. An *essay* is a group of paragraphs that focus on one main point, which is presented in a thesis statement. Each paragraph develops some part or aspect of that main point. An essay has a title, an introduction, a body, and a conclusion.

In this chapter you will examine the structure and content of essays in more detail. In the first section, you will learn more about the function of each part of an essay and the features that contribute to a good essay. In the second section, you will learn some practical steps to follow in writing essays. When you can write essays, you will be prepared to handle many of the writing assignments and situations you will meet in and out of school.

Characteristics of Good Essays 25.1

All the principles of good writing that you have learned apply to essays: awareness of audience, clarity of purpose, completeness, smoothness, conciseness, and exactness. An essay is a longer composition written to communicate a main point to a particular audience for a specific purpose. It is a shaped and structured piece of writing with a series of well-connected paragraphs.

Your understanding of the structure of a paragraph will help you comprehend the similar structure of an essay. The following diagram points out the resemblances between the parts of a paragraph and the parts of an essay. Notice that the topic sentence of a paragraph corresponds to the introduction and thesis statement, or main point, of an essay.

The supporting information in the body of a paragraph corresponds to the supporting information in the body paragraphs of an essay. And the concluding sentence in a paragraph functions similarly to the conclusion in an essay.

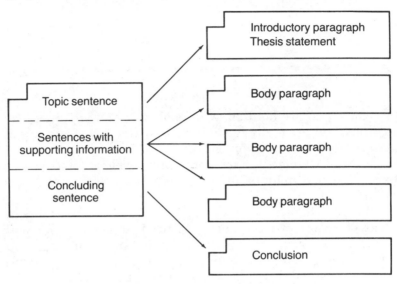

An essay differs from a paragraph mainly in its length, amount of detail, and complexity. Because an essay consists of a number of paragraphs, usually four or more, it allows you to go into more depth on a topic or to explain a bigger topic than you would in a single paragraph. An essay must also sustain a reader's interest longer than a paragraph and must include more supporting ideas.

■ Main Features of an Essay

An essay is more than just a group of paragraphs on one topic, however. To cover a main point on a topic thoroughly, to hold a reader's interest, and to enable a reader to follow the development of a main point, the parts of an essay usually follow a basic pattern. The title usually indicates the topic of the essay and gives the reader a clue to the writer's main point. The introductory paragraph usually begins by presenting general background or attention-getting material on a topic. The paragraph then zeroes in on a main point about the topic in one sentence, called a *thesis statement*.

Each paragraph in the body of the essay develops and explains the thesis statement by adding information and leading a reader to a greater understanding of the main point. Finally, a concluding paragraph reminds the reader of the thesis statement and pulls together all the ideas in the essay. The following diagram illustrates this pattern.

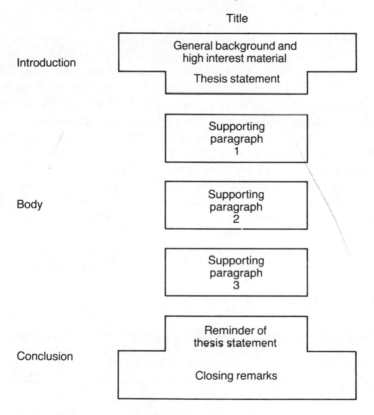

The following pages explain in greater detail each of the parts and features of an essay.

The Thesis Statement. The thesis statement is usually not the first sentence of an essay, but it is the single most important part. It is the core or controlling idea of the entire essay. The thesis statement contains the idea you must support and develop in the essay; it is the point you are making. All of the other information you include in the essay and the arrangement of those ideas will depend on your particular thesis statement. For the reader, too, the thesis statement indicates the direction and focus of the essay; it tells the reader exactly what the essay will be about. Just as the topic sentence of a paragraph creates expectations in the reader which the paragraph must fulfill, so also the thesis statement of an essay functions as a commitment to the reader.

The thesis statement should express the main point of an essay in a sentence that is both direct and clear.

Although a thesis statement must always narrow and focus the topic of the essay to one main point, the thesis statement will vary according to the topic, the audience, and the writer's purpose. Some thesis statements will contain stated subtopics. These subtopics will then help you order the essay by indicating parts of the main point that you must explain. Some thesis statements will present an opinion that must be supported and defended in the essay. Others will present a theory or factual statement that must be explained in the essay. For every essay, the thesis statement should always be written with a particular audience and purpose in mind, and it should be appropriate for that audience and purpose.

The following chart gives sample thesis statements. Notice that some have stated subtopics while one does not and that the writer's purpose is usually clear.

SAMPLE THESIS STATEMENTS		
Thesis Statement	**Stated Subtopics**	**Purpose**
Citizens in our community should vote money for a paramedic service.	None	to persuade
Doctors and scientists think diabetes may be caused by viruses, a body's abnormal immune response, and overeating.	(1) Viruses (2) A body's abnormal immune response (3) Overeating	to explain

Hitting a golf ball involves choosing a club, assuming the correct position, and swinging properly.	(1) Choosing a club (2) Assuming the correct position (3) Swinging properly	to explain a process

The most effective location for the thesis statement is toward the end of the introduction. When it is the last sentence in the introductory paragraph, it stands out in the reader's mind and serves as a guide for the reader throughout the body of the essay.

The Title. The title is the first part of the essay that a reader notices. It should function as a preview of the thesis statement and an advertisement for the essay.

A title should attract the reader's attention and hint at the topic, the main point, and the tone of the essay.

A well-written, appropriate title will make the reader want to read the essay. It will be remembered during and after the reading of the essay. A title should provide clues to the topic of the essay and the writer's focus on that topic. Usually a title should be original, short, and direct. To arouse a reader's curiosity and to prepare the reader for the thesis statement of an essay, the title can be clever or catchy, but it should never be cute or misleading. For example, a humorous title should prepare a reader for a humorous essay.

The following chart gives some sample topics and titles. Notice that the titles give some indication of the writer's idea about the topic and of the essay's tone in addition to encouraging the reader to read on.

SAMPLE TOPICS WITH TITLES	
Topic	**Title**
Untruths about wolves	The Most Slandered Animal: The Wolf
The development of early airplanes	Airborne At Last
Walking as better exercise than jogging	Walk, Don't Run

The Introduction.   The introduction is the first major part of the essay. It is usually the first paragraph, although it can be longer than one paragraph. Its purposes are (1) to clarify the topic of the essay in a way that will spark the reader's interest, (2) to establish the tone of the essay, and (3) to zero in on the thesis statement. The introduction should make a reader want to continue reading the essay.

The introduction should present the topic, engage the reader's interest, and pave the way for the thesis statement.

Your introduction should be particularly well thought out and carefully written. An introduction will usually begin with general remarks about a topic that serve to identify the topic for the reader. Sometimes an introduction contains necessary background information or raises questions that will be answered in the essay. This first paragraph of an essay should make a reader want to learn more about the topic by stirring up interest and, sometimes, by arousing curiosity. The words and flavor of the introduction will also set the tone for the entire essay by creating certain expectations in the reader. From the introduction, the reader will expect the tone of the essay to be, for example, scholarly, casual, objective, formal, or familiar.

By identifying the topic, by appealing to the reader's interest, and by setting the tone, the introduction is also serving its most important function: zeroing in on the thesis statement. Like a funnel narrowing to its smallest end, the introduction should begin with general remarks and end with the focused thesis statement. In this key position at the end of the introduction, the thesis statement signals the reader that this idea is the main point that the rest of the essay will develop.

An introduction can begin with a thought-provoking question, an incident, startling facts, an historical account, or concise, lively statements about the topic. Notice some of these methods used in the following introduction. Also notice that the introduction paves the way for the thesis statement, which is the last sentence.

Background information	Why do people dress up in masks and costumes on Halloween and imagine ghosts and goblins behind gravestones and dark trees? Halloween gets its name from "All Hallows' Eve," the night before All Saints' Day. Actually, in establish-

Thesis
statement

ing All Saints' Day, the Catholic Church adopted an older celebration. The customs and beliefs behind the ghosts and ghouls go back much further in history. *Halloween appears to trace its origin to two ancient festivals: the Celtic festival of the New Year and the Roman tribute to the dead.*

The Body of an Essay. The body of an essay consists of two or more paragraphs in the middle of the essay. The body contains the supporting information for the thesis statement. The number of paragraphs and the amount of information in each paragraph will vary according to the thesis statement. However, to be complete and well developed, the body must have enough support to explain the thesis statement with facts and examples or to defend it with facts, examples, and reasons.

The body paragraphs of an essay should include specific supporting information for the thesis statement: examples, details, facts, reasons, or incidents.

The paragraphs in the body of an essay develop the subtopics, either stated or unstated, of the thesis statement. For example, if a thesis statement includes three subtopics, then the body should develop each of these subtopics. A writer could choose to devote one or more paragraphs to each subtopic. If a thesis statement does not present subtopics, then the writer must think of two or more subtopics of the main point. Each of these implied subtopics can then be treated in one or more paragraphs. The topic sentences of the body paragraphs often restate the subtopics, which become the main ideas of the paragraphs.

The Conclusion. The conclusion completes the essay by summarizing the ideas. It is usually one final short paragraph. The conclusion should include a reminder of the thesis statement. It should also suggest to the reader that the main point has been covered thoroughly, that the essay has achieved its purpose.

The conclusion should remind the reader of the thesis statement and should end smoothly and convincingly.

Usually the conclusion begins specifically with a different version of the thesis statement and then ends generally, with closing remarks on the topic. In a long essay, the conclusion may be used to summarize the ideas presented in the essay, although it should not simply repeat in a tedious fashion the information from the body. Nor should it bring in a group of new ideas not closely related to the thesis statement or not developed in the body of the essay. The conclusion is neither a rehash nor the beginning of a new essay. Instead, it is the place to mention a final, short incident directly related to the main point, to show the reader the relevance of the topic to his or her life, to make sharp observations on the main point, or simply to end strongly and concisely. The final sentence in a conclusion may be a forceful, witty, or memorable statement, called a *clincher*.

Notice that the following conclusion begins specifically with a reminder of the thesis statement. The paragraph moves from the past to the present, ending with a statement about modern day activities. Notice that this conclusion returns to the starting point of the introduction on page 702.

Reminder of thesis statement

The ancient Celts, dancing in animal masks and skins, and the ancient Romans, honoring their dead, have influenced the way Halloween is celebrated today. Over the past 2,000 years these ancient festivals joined with those of other cultures and gradually became our Halloween. Today, people shrieking in a deserted house and haunting the streets in the likenesses of ghosts and other creatures are following traditions that have ancient roots.

Student Essay Showing the Main Features of an Essay. The following six-paragraph essay by a student shows the features and structure of the basic essay. As you read the following essay, notice that it is aimed at the general reader, that the purpose is to explain a process, and that the tone is casual and instructional. The comments in the margins identify the main features of the essay.

Wrap That Parcel Right

Introduction

Thesis statement with four subtopics

Have you ever received a package with the box mangled and the contents damaged? Or have you mailed one that never arrived? Damage and disappearance can happen when packages are not properly wrapped and labeled. To give items a better chance of reaching their destinations in good shape, follow this easy process: Secure outside containers, protect the inside with padding, close and seal the parcel properly, and label it correctly.

First
body
paragraph
(Develops
first
subtopic)

Always begin with strong, secure outside containers. The United States Postal Service allows self-supporting paperboard boxes or padded draft paper bags for most clothing and noncrushable items up to ten pounds. The United Parcel Service recommends that a corrugated carton be used. Although you will probably have to pay for a box of this type at a department store, they are yours for the asking at any supermarket. When choosing a carton, check the bottom for the pounds-per-square-inch figure. The higher the number, the sturdier the carton. Also check to see that the flaps are intact and that the box is in no way broken.

Second
body
paragraph
(Develops
second
subtopic)

Secondly, provide protection inside the carton with padding. A parcel that gets dropped from a high platform or hit by some object can suffer heavy damage. To make the package shockproof, put several inches of cushioning on the bottom, along the sides, and on the top. Crumpled grocery bags, newspapers, foamed plastic shells, and air-pocket padding are all good choices. When mailing more than one item in the same carton, wrap each separately, and then package all the items with padding around. Never package fragile and heavy items in the same carton.

Third
body
paragraph
(Develops
third
subtopic)

Another step involves closing and sealing the parcel properly. Use sealing tape, not string or twine, because string can become tangled in the postal sorting machines. Nylon and glass reinforced tape are best. You must use water to activate the gummed surface and apply the tape immediately. Close the flaps, tape them together securely, and then band the box with two tapes around the length and two around the girth. You may want to tape the midsection for added strength. The Postal Service frowns on outer wrapping paper. If you use it, it should at least be the weight of a standard grocery bag.

Fourth
body
paragraph
(Develops
fourth
subtopic)

As the final step, you should label the package properly. Remove all other labels from the parcel you have prepared. In the lower right-hand side of the box, print with indelible ink the name and address of the recipient, including the zip code. In the upper left-hand corner, mark "From:" with your complete name and address. If you use a gummed label, type or print your name and address clearly, and make sure it is attached securely.

Conclusion
(Reminder of
thesis
statement)

Following these easy steps will help you and the post office work together to insure that your package reaches its destination safely. You can save yourself the frustration of sending someone a package that looks as if it has been in a tug-of-war or has been stepped on by an elephant. And your friend will not be angry at you for supposedly forgetting his birthday. —James Dattilo

EXERCISE A: Identifying the Features of an Essay. Read the following essay carefully. Then answer the questions that follow the essay. You may have to reexamine the essay to answer the questions.

Those Mystifying Allergies

For some people the little green tassels dropping from the trees and the fluffy pink, white, and yellow blossoms announce the arrival of allergy season. For others a big, furry dog or a soft feather pillow brings on the sneezes or itchy eyes. Still others are in trouble if they accidentally eat honey, chocolate, or water chestnuts. Although millions of Americans have allergies, no one knows definitely how allergies develop or why some people have them and others do not. Doctors have made some progress in diagnosis. Yet allergies remain a mystery that is only partially solvable and only partially treatable.

Doctors do understand that allergies are abnormal reactions of the body to ordinarily harmless substances. Why these abnormal reactions occur, however, is unknown. Despite this common root cause, the symptoms of allergies vary greatly. Most allergic people only suffer for a week or two each year. For example, as the ragweed or grass pollen blows in the wind, these people become rapid-fire sneezers or develop red eyes, stuffy heads, or runny noses, but in a few weeks they return to normal. Slightly more serious allergic reactions can occur throughout the year, either during several seasons or whenever a person comes in contact with certain foods, materials, or drugs. Varied substances such as penicillin, soap, flowers, duck meat, wool, cigarette smoke, and sunshine may cause symptoms ranging from severe asthma to hives to serious sinus congestion. And a small percentage of allergy victims suffer near-crippling migraine headaches and even nausea that can leave them bedridden.

Given these diverse allergic reactions, doctors, not surprisingly, are only moderately successful in diagnosing the specific causes of allergies. Some allergies are easy to figure out. A person whose tongue swells after eating strawberries is clearly allergic to strawberries. Other times, diagnosis proves more complicated, such as when symptoms do not appear immediately after contact. Some food allergies, for example, are characterized by delayed reactions. Pollen and ordinary house dust are other common causes of allergic reactions, but identifying the exact cause from among the grasses, trees, and flowers and their seeds and pollen and from among fibers, lint, mold, food particles, and pet hair can be difficult. Treatments for these numerous and confusing allergic reactions vary in effectiveness. Most treatments, though, can boast only temporary success. For many allergies the best treatment is to stay away from the apparent cause by avoiding certain animals, foods, and drugs. But what about such substances as cigarette smoke, pollen, and dust, which are in the air and consequently unavoidable? Partial treatment for allergies to these substances may involve staying away from all fields and gardens, sleeping in an air-conditioned room, and not having indoor pets. Over-the-counter and prescription decongestants, antihistamines, and other medicines can provide some relief. In even more severe cases, the person can undergo allergy tests in a hospital. During one such test, a grid is drawn on the person's back, and a small pronged instrument is used to scratch each square of skin and inject a different substance under the skin. If a swelling like a mosquito bite and itching occur in a square, the person is allergic to that substance. The doctor can then prepare allergy shots to be given over many months in order to increase the person's tolerance to that substance.

Despite relief from planned avoidance, from medicine, and from shots, the cause and treatment of some allergies puzzle doctors, and the cures still elude them. Some people outgrow allergies while others develop them. Each year victims wheeze with asthma, itch with rashes, and suffer from nosebleeds. Even worse, about fifty people die every year from violent allergic reactions to bee and other insect stings. Undoubtedly, allergies remain a mysterious menace.

Answers may vary unless specified.

1. What is the title of the essay? Is it a good title for the essay? Why or why not? *"Those Mystifying Allergies"*
2. How long is the introduction? *one paragraph*
3. What is the thesis statement? Does it have stated subtopics? *Paragraph 1, Sentence 6 / yes: two*
4. How does the writer try to spark the reader's interest in the introduction?
5. From the introduction and the thesis statement, what would you say is the intended purpose of the essay? What audience did the writer have in mind? What tone does the writer establish?
6. How many body paragraphs does the essay have? *three*
7. What subtopics of the thesis statement does the writer develop in the body of the essay? What are the topic sentences in the body paragraphs?

5. to inform / general audience / objective, instructive
7. partially understood / partially treatable / Sentence 1 in each

8. What are three pieces of specific supporting information in each body paragraph?
9. How long is the conclusion? What sentence in the conclusion reminds the reader of the thesis statement?
10. Is the conclusion effective? Why or why not?

9. one paragraph / Sentence 1

■ Unity and Coherence in an Essay

Unity and coherence are characteristics of good paragraphs (as explained in Section 23.2). They are also characteristics of good essays. In fact, the longer the composition, the more important unity and coherence are to sustain the reader's interest and aid the reader's understanding. Unity and coherence should appear in an essay on two levels: within each paragraph and within the essay as a whole. (For more information on unity and coherence in paragraphs see Section 23.2.) The following sections will explain some ways to achieve unity and coherence in the essay as a whole.

Overall Unity.   In a unified essay, the reader senses that all the information in the paragraphs and all the paragraphs themselves belong in this piece of writing. The introduction and thesis statement, the body, and the conclusion stick to one main point and, together, cover that main point completely.

An essay is unified if each paragraph has unity and if all the paragraphs develop and relate to the thesis statement.

A clear, concise thesis statement can contribute greatly to the unity of an essay. By clearly focusing on only one main point to be developed, the thesis statement helps the writer weed out vague or unrelated supporting information.

Carefully thought out subtopics can also contribute to overall unity. Subtopics, either stated or implied, should be natural, significant steps, parts, or categories of the main point. For example, the following thesis statement could have a number of related subtopics: *A person dwelling in an average city apartment must accept certain difficult living conditions.* Some subtopics that represent "certain difficult living conditions" might be the noise of neighbors and traffic, limited parking space, old appliances and plumbing, and little storage space. If you make sure that there is a close relationship between every subtopic and the thesis statement and between all the subtopics, your essay will have unity. The introduction and conclusion can function as another aid to overall unity. The introduction should set the tone of the essay, the body should follow through with the tone, and the conclusion should end with that tone. In other words, if an essay begins with a casual, conversational tone, that tone should be maintained from beginning to end. Besides emphasizing the consistent tone, the introduction and conclusion should highlight the essay's consistency of ideas. The introduction directs the reader's attention to the main point, and the conclusion redirects the reader's attention to it. Furthermore, sometimes the conclusion can echo ideas or words mentioned in the introduction.

Overall Coherence. Besides exploring only one main point in depth, a good essay should read smoothly and should carry the reader along from idea to idea. The reader should be able to grasp the underlying order of the ideas within each paragraph and within the essay as a whole. If the order of ideas is logical and consistent and if appropriate connections are used, the essay will hold together. A coherent essay resembles a coherent paragraph, but on a larger scale.

An essay has coherence if the ideas within each paragraph and within the whole essay are logically ordered and smoothly connected.

Like a paragraph, an essay should have a logical, consistent overall order. The subtopics in the body of the essay should be arranged according to one of many possible orders, such as order of importance, chronological order, spatial order, comparison-and-contrast order, or developmental order. (For a detailed explanation of orders and coherence see Section 23.2.) The order of stated subtopics in the thesis statement dictates their order of development in the body of the essay. For instance, if a thesis statement presents subtopics X, Y, and Z, in that order, then the body of the essay should develop subtopic X first, then Y, and finally Z. The logical order appropriate for subtopics will depend on the topic, the thesis statement, and the supporting information. The following chart suggests orders that would be suitable for certain subtopics.

POSSIBLE ORDERS FOR SUBTOPICS ON CERTAIN TOPICS	
Subtopics	**Possible Order**
Four reasons to vote for a new community center Some causes of chemical fires	Order of Importance
Stages of my first experience in mountain climbing Steps in building the Golden Gate Bridge	Chronological Order
Four important sights along the Mississippi The design of the Wright brothers' famous airplane	Spatial Order
Three differences between gasohol and gasoline Lake fishing and stream fishing	Comparison-and-Contrast Order
The best way to insulate a home Four kinds of skiers I have observed	Developmental Order

Each paragraph in the body of an essay should either present a new subtopic or expand upon the subtopic immediately before it. And, in addition to following the larger overall order, each paragraph should contain information that is logically arranged.

Like a coherent paragraph, a coherent essay links ideas for ease in reading and understanding with transitions, repetitions of main words, synonyms, and pronouns. Transitions often come in the first and last sentences of body paragraphs to indicate the movement to a new subtopic. Transitions can also be used in these sentences to tell the reader that a paragraph is elaborating on the preceding subtopic. Repetitions of main words, synonyms, and pronouns can further connect ideas from paragraph to paragraph. Main words and synonyms, particularly, can keep the thesis statement and important ideas in the essay in the forefront of the reader's mind. The following diagram illustrates the way all the parts and the paragraphs in an essay can be connected.

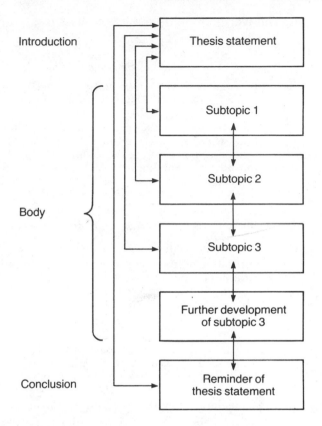

Introduction — Thesis statement

Body — Subtopic 1

Subtopic 2

Subtopic 3

Further development of subtopic 3

Conclusion — Reminder of thesis statement

Student Essay Showing Unity and Coherence. The following student essay analyzes a character in a novel. Notice that the essay sticks to the thesis statement and that the subtopics are a natural part of the thesis statement. The writer also unifies the essay by returning in the conclusion to Scarlett and Melanie's relationship, which was mentioned in the introduction and the body. The conclusion ends with a clincher that redelivers the writer's main point: Melanie was a strong person.

The writer also creates coherence in the essay by using a logical order and some important linking devices. The subtopics follow a developmental order both in the thesis statement and in the body of the essay. The three subtopics—loyalty, naiveté, and simplicity—are main words that the writer repeats throughout the essay. These words and a few other main words are circled. Notice that they connect each paragraph to the thesis statement and often to the preceding paragraph. The words in bold type function as transitions to connect the paragraphs.

Title	*Melanie: The Silent Pillar*
Introduction	*Gone with the Wind* is not just Scarlett O'Hara's story; it is also the story of another remarkable woman, Melanie Wilkes. The author describes Melanie as having "the face of a sheltered child who had never known anything but simplicity and kindness, truth and love, a child who had never looked upon harshness or evil, and would not recognize them if she saw them" (page 155). *Strangely enough, the qualities that weakened Melanie in Scarlett's eyes—loyalty, naiveté, and simplicity—actually proved to make Melanie a strong person.*
Thesis statement: subtopics— (1) loyalty (2) naiveté (3) simplicity	
Subtopic 1A: loyalty to a way of life	Melanie Wilkes was a truly loyal person. Many times during the reconstruction of the South, life would have been easier for Melanie if she had chosen to join the Yankees. Yet she remained loyal to the only way of life she really knew or understood. Because of this loyalty her friends, family, and even strangers "clung to her skirts" (page 1000). She was an oasis in a desert of people who were suspended between a way of life which was no more and a new way of life, which was utterly confusing.
Subtopic 1B: loyalty to loved ones	Melanie was **also** loyal to her loved ones, especially to Scarlett O'Hara. Although Scarlett intensely disliked Melanie, Scarlett could not even make Melanie disloyal to her. Melanie once said, "Now, dear, I love you and you know I love you, and nothing you could do would make me change" (page 863). Scarlett did not even attempt to disguise her dislike for Melanie, just as Rhett Butler (another recipient of Melanie's loyal love) did not try to disguise his dealings with the "Watling woman" and the scalawags. But Melanie defended them both vehemently and protectively as a mother would her children. Her loyalty to these two in particular occasionally put her in situations where she had to fight "Yankees, fire, hunger, poverty, public opinion, and even her beloved blood kin" (page 1000). Though the public might ridicule her, she remained loyal. It takes a strong person openly to defend people and causes which others openly shun.
	To many, Melanie's loyalty to certain people seemed unwarranted, and yet if they had seen the

Subtopic 2A: naiveté with a focus on good	world through Melanie's naive eyes, they would have understood her. Her naiveté led her to overlook the ugly qualities and to concentrate on the redeeming qualities in a person. She saw the good before the bad, and when she finally did see the bad, she chose not to accept it. Because of this vision of people, "that cames incerely and spontaneously from a generous heart, everyone flocked about her, for who can resist the charm of one who discovers in others admirable qualities undreamed of even by himself?" (page 156).
Subtopic 2B: naiveté and reliability	Those that flocked to Melanie did so for **other reasons as well.** Her naiveté made her reliable. She lacked the desire to put up a façade. Because of her naiveté she had a serene innocence, not like that of a child, but rather like that of a placid soul, untouched by irrational prejudice. And just as her naiveté kept her from seeing the bad qualities in others it also kept her from realizing the strong characteristics in herself. Her naiveté strengthened her by preventing her from discovering that so many people depended on her.
Subtopic 3: simplicity	The bad qualities in others that Melanie could not overlook by her naiveté could be condoned by her simplicity. Her emotions were not complex. Melanie did not allow new, unpleasant facts to complicate her feelings about people. For example, at one point in the novel, Melanie found out that Scarlett had entertained scalawags. Even though the thought was horrid to Melanie, she said to Scarlett, "Darling, what you do, you always do for a good reason. Everybody thinks differently and everybody's got a right to their own opinion" (page 863). Melanie's simplicity also made her refuse to listen to talk of Rhett Butler's bad qualities. And another example is Melanie's relationship with her husband, Ashley Wilkes. She knew all along that he was a dreamer, that he wasn't practical, but she loved him anyway. Being able to accept others as they were strengthened Melanie more than anything else. Her simplicity enabled her to realize that a person cannot expect to make changes in other people.
Reminder of thesis statement	Loyal, naive, simple Melanie was the underlying strength of so many people. Even Scarlett finally had to admit that Melanie was the one upon whom "she had relied unknowingly for so many years" (page 1000). She eventually realized that

Melanie had been her "sword and her shield, her comfort and her strength" (page 997). Melanie may not have tackled the job of building a new world, but she was the essential link which kept others in touch as they daringly forged ahead. People like Melanie are the maintainers of sanity,

Clincher   the stabilizing influences. Only at her death did her friends fully appreciate the "terrible strength of the weak, the gentle, the tender-hearted" (page 1001). —Tracy Martin

EXERCISE B: Recognizing Unity and Coherence in an Essay. Reread the essay entitled "Those Mystifying Allergies" and examine it for unity and coherence. Then answer the following questions.

Answers may vary unless specified.

1. What is the single, clear point the writer makes in the thesis statement? *Allergies are mysterious.*
2. What is the relationship between the subtopics and the thesis statement? What is the relationship between each subtopic and the other subtopics?
3. How does the conclusion echo the introduction? How does it maintain a consistent tone with the introduction and body?
4. How would you rate the overall unity of this essay?
5. In what order has the writer arranged the subtopics?
6. Why is this order of subtopics appropriate?
7. What small-scale order does each body paragraph follow? *order of importance*
8. What words or phrases function as transitions in the essay?
9. What repetitions of main words and synonyms connect the ideas in the essay?
10. Choose one paragraph in the essay to examine for coherence. What transitions, repetitions of main words, synonyms, and pronouns does the paragraph have?

5. developmental

APPLICATION: Examining an Essay for Main Features, Unity, and Coherence. Find an essay or article of about five hundred words in a book or magazine. Read your essay or article carefully, looking for similarities and differences between it and the basic essay features and structure you have just studied. Then answer the following questions about your essay or article.

Answers may vary; students might work in teams.

1. What is the title? Does the title fit the essay?
2. What is the main point or thesis statement? Where is it located in the piece of writing?

3. Does the essay have an introduction, body, and conclusion?
4. How does the introduction attempt to interest the reader?
5. What are the subtopics developed in the body of the essay?
6. What supporting information is given under each subtopic?
7. In what order has the writer arranged the subtopics?
8. Does the conclusion mention the thesis statement? Does it refer to the introduction in any other way? Does it have a clincher?
9. What transitions connect the ideas in the essay?
10. What repetitions of main words, synonyms, and pronouns make the essay coherent?

Steps in Writing an Essay 25.2

Writing an essay involves thinking, shaping and developing your ideas, and making many decisions. In this section, you will learn how to simplify the writing process to create an essay that will represent your best work.

■ Writing a Thesis Statement

As the first step in writing an essay, you must be prepared to do some thinking, discovering, and examining to find an essay topic. Spending time choosing your essay topic and planning your thesis statement will make the rest of the writing go more smoothly and quickly.

Finding a Suitable Essay Topic.   A suitable essay topic is one that you, with your interests and knowledge, can develop thoroughly in approximately four to five paragraphs. Remember that the larger the topic, the less depth your essay will have; conversely, the smaller the topic, the more depth you can go into. Choosing a narrow topic can also help you find specific supporting information.

General topics will usually become more manageable if they are reduced to smaller, narrower essay topics. For instance, general topics such as homing pigeons, sailing, modern ballet, pianos, and boxing can be narrowed to these more manageable essay topics: care of homing pigeons, the best sailing conditions, one famous modern choreographer, materials used in constructing pianos, and a boxer's training. Even these topics can be refined and narrowed further. At the same time, beware of topics that are more suitable for a single paragraph than for an essay. A suitable essay topic, then, is neither too broad nor too specific. It should interest you, draw upon your knowledge, and fit your particular assignment.

To find a suitable essay topic, you should make a list of possible topics you could write about. Then you should examine those topics, select one that particularly interests you, and narrow it if you think it is too big for an essay.

Brainstorm for topics, break down topics into smaller topics if necessary, and select a manageable essay topic.

If you have been asked to write an essay on a topic of your own choice, you might search for an essay topic in the following manner. The thinking stage is a time of discovery and exploration. Let your mind work freely and then jot down possible topics on paper. Think about books and articles you have read, about your special skills and interests, and about issues that concern you. Jot down all of the ideas that occur to you. If a topic interests you but seems too general, break it down into smaller topics. Using this brainstorming method, you might make a list of topics similar to the following. Notice that a few of the topics—the tests a seeing-eye dog must pass, tips on moving, and a few others—would make suitable essay topics, whereas others need to be broken down further.

BRAINSTORMING FOR AN ESSAY TOPIC

Dorothy Sayer's mystery *Strong Poison*
—the character of Lord Peter Wimsey
—the character of Katherine Climpson

The tests a seeing-eye dog must pass

Insurance rates for young drivers

Tips on moving without a moving van

The Hawaiian Islands
—how they were formed
—Hawaiian kings and queens
—characteristics of the Hawaiian language
—modern industries
—Hawaiian volcanoes

Golf
—basic equipment
—different swings and grips
—the beginner's view of golf
—the first golf course in St. Andrews, Scotland
—the rewards of golf
—famous golf tournaments

The training of a circus clown

Playing a guitar
—playing an electric guitar
—playing flamenco guitar
—teaching yourself to play

Physical education as a high school requirement

After examining your list, you might decide that *the beginner's view of golf* would make a suitable essay topic.

Focusing on Your Main Point, Audience, and Purpose. To arrive at a main point or thesis statement for your essay, you should carefully examine your essay topic and your thoughts about it. Ask yourself questions and use your answers to find a main point that you can make interesting, believable, and understandable in an essay. Ask yourself, "What do I want to say about this essay topic? Who are my readers, my audience? What do I want to tell them? What is my purpose and what effect do I want the essay to have on the readers?" Often, your purpose will grow out of your main point and your consideration of audience. Other times, you will begin with your purpose, to persuade, for example, and that purpose will help you determine and shape a main point. Once you have made decisions about your main point, audience, and purpose, you are ready to write a thesis statement.

Think about your audience and purpose as you write a thesis statement that clearly presents your main point about your essay topic.

An essay topic must be shaped and refined to one main point to become a thesis statement. You can do this shaping and focusing by thinking about your interest in the essay topic and often by considering your audience's interests, background, and knowledge. For the topic *the beginner's view of golf*, for example, you might decide that your audience will be made up mainly of nonplayers who are thinking of taking up golf. Now you can begin your focusing of the essay topic by asking yourself questions such as those in the following chart. By answering these questions, you can discover possible main points for your essay.

QUESTIONS LEADING TO POSSIBLE MAIN POINTS	
Essay Topic: the beginner's view of golf	
Question	Main Point
How can I define the beginner's view of golf?	Golf is an easy game to lose and a difficult game to win.
What one idea would I like to tell others about it?	Golf will tease and frustrate the new golfer in a number of ways.
What is the most important idea the audience should know about it?	Only people with patience and determination should take up golf.
What are some things that beginners have to learn?	To learn golf, beginners must learn to concentrate on their stance, grip, and swing, all at once.

Once you have a number of main points, you should choose the one you will write about. Consider each main point in light of your audience and purpose. Each of the main points in the chart speaks to nonplayers, the chosen audience. The first three main points express opinions and could be used in essays that would try to persuade the audience to understand and agree. The fourth main point would suit an explanatory purpose. Besides clarifying and matching a main point and purpose, you should select the main point that interests you the most and that prompts you to think about specific supporting information.

When you have an interesting main point that suits your audience and purpose, you are ready to write a thesis statement. You should begin by experimenting with different ways to express your main point in a sentence. Each of these versions of your thesis statement will further refine and focus your main point. Some wordings of your main point may even help you discover a slightly different angle. And although you may revise your thesis statement after you have planned your whole essay, you should try to write and select a complete version of your thesis statement at this stage. The following chart gives sample thesis statements you might write if you chose the second of the possible main points listed in the preceding chart.

POSSIBLE THESIS STATEMENTS
1. Golf will tease and frustrate the new golfer in a number of ways.
2. For new players, golf can be extremely frustrating.
3. Golf will challenge but frustrate new players in a number of ways.
4. The three main frustrations of the beginning golfer are the hazards of the course, other players, and inconsistent shots.
5. For new players, golf can be extremely frustrating, a constant conflict between the way they try to play and the way they do play.
6. For beginners, golf is a fascinating frustration because fun and success are often just out of reach.

When you have at least three possible thesis statements, you should select the one you will use in your essay. Notice that the six versions of the thesis statement in the chart each give a slightly different emphasis and focus to the main point. Notice also that the first three thesis statements are less specific and give less information than do the last three. The fourth thesis statement includes stated subtopics while the others do not. After reading each of your thesis statements carefully, you might decide to use the sixth version because you like the twist that the word "fascinating" gives to the main point.

EXERCISE A: Selecting and Refining Topics for Essays. From the following list of general topics, choose one that you could write about. Write it on your paper and then examine the topic and break it down into smaller topics suitable for an essay. When you have listed at least three smaller topics, circle the one you are most interested in and are prepared to write about.

Answers will vary; students might handle this assignment in teams to facilitate discussion.

Your town or city	Part-time jobs	Architecture
Advantages and disadvantages of a small (or large) family	Bowling	After school sports
	Making movies	Your favorite National Park
	Painting	
	Reading mysteries	

EXERCISE B: Preparing a Thesis Statement. Use the essay topic you chose in Exercise A and follow these instructions.

Audience, questions, and thesis statement could be checked for appropriateness.

1. Write the essay topic on your paper.
2. Decide on your audience and briefly describe it.
3. As you think about communicating with your audience about your essay topic, write at least three questions to yourself on your paper. Then write the answers to make a list of possible main points.
4. Examine your list of main points and decide which purpose each fits. Decide the purpose you will have in this essay. Then choose the main point you will develop and make sure it suits your audience as well as your purpose.
5. Write at least three versions of your thesis statement.
6. Finally, circle the thesis statement that seems to you to be the most interesting and most workable.

■ Gathering Support for a Thesis Statement

Once you have your thesis statement, you can begin gathering the supporting information that will become the body of your essay. This step should involve probing, questioning, and discovering.

As you prepared your thesis statement, you probably began to think of specific information that you would include in your essay. Now, when you brainstorm for supporting information, you should try to recall all those ideas and think of even more related information. Your thesis statement, through its focus and its words, should guide you to supporting information that will explain and develop your main point.

Brainstorm for examples, details, facts, reasons, and incidents that expand and support your thesis statement.

The goal of the brainstorming stage is to produce a long list of supporting information from which you can choose the strongest, clearest pieces of support for the body of your essay. To reach this goal, professional writers use a number of methods. Among them are the formulation of questions that they think their readers would ask and the use of free association based on the thesis statement. (For more information about questioning and free association, see Section

23.3.) To use the questioning method, you should write your thesis statement at the top of your paper. Then put yourself in the reader's place and ask yourself questions about the thesis statement. Ask yourself, "What words in the thesis statement should be defined? What do I mean by this idea? Why is this idea true?" You should then answer these questions with specific information. Write down all the ideas, facts, and examples that come to mind. In general, you should follow this principle: Think and write now, sort and evaluate later.

If you were to use the questioning method for the thesis statement on golf, you might write a list of questions and answers like the following.

QUESTIONING TO FIND SUPPORT FOR A THESIS STATEMENT

Thesis Statement: **For beginners, golf is a fascinating frustration because fun and success are often just out of reach.**

Why is golf fascinating? (Why do people want to play?)

—the golf course is a world of lawns, hills, greenness, lakes, ponds, trees

—players are outdoors for hours in the sun getting tan

—players can take up golf at almost any age

—people of all ages can play golf

—a person gets away from everyday concerns on a golf course

—courses are often scenic— overlooking oceans, lakes, in mountains, hills

—a person can get the amount of exercise he or she wants—walking or riding in a golf cart

—a person can play against himself or herself or against others

—golf challenges a player to be accurate, precise, to keep on trying to improve

—a person can hope to do better on each hole, each game

—a person gets away from crowds of people

—the joy when the player really connects with the ball

—the joy when drives, fairway shots, and putts go well

—the joy when a player gets a low score near par (considered the best reasonable score for that hole)

—the chance to meet friendly golfers

—the chance to play a relaxing, leisurely game

Why is golf frustrating? (Why are fun and success out of reach for beginners?)

—new players hit some good shots and some bad ones

—courses are too long for beginners

—on some holes players have a strong start and a bad finish
—on other holes players have a bad start and a strong finish—can't do all things well
—new players get angry at themselves
—there are many ways to make bad shots
  —miss completely
  —top the ball
  —hit behind the ball
  —slice
  —hook
—courses require accuracy and control that beginners don't have
—often other players try to give beginners advice
  —new players lose confidence, become upset, flustered
—other players want to play faster—get irritated with new players hunting for their golf balls or making many short shots
  —new players try to hurry and play worse
—bad shots often lose the ball

—bad shots are embarrassing
—tall grass and shrubbery at the sides of course swallow up golf balls
—trees on sides of course obstruct players' shots and hide or cause balls to bounce
—players lose balls in water hazards—lakes, ponds, creeks, nearby ocean
  —difficult for beginner to avoid water hazards— must hit just the right direction and just the right distance
—backyards border golf courses—players can't hunt for their golf balls in people's yards
—other players could be fun to watch and meet
—other players criticize and make fun of new players
  —new players get embarrassed and discouraged
—other players on other holes lose their golf balls, take the new players' by mistake
—beginners are not sure of grip and stance—varies from swing to swing

EXERCISE C: Brainstorming for Supporting Information. Use the thesis statement you wrote in Exercise B and follow these instructions.

After initial brainstorming, students might exchange papers for additional suggestions.

1. Write your thesis statement at the top of a sheet of paper.
2. On the left side of the paper, write two or more questions about your thesis statement that you think your audience would be likely to ask.
3. On the right side of your paper, answer each question with as much supporting information as you can think of. List all of the examples, details, facts, reasons, and incidents that come to mind. Do not think about sorting the information at this time; just write.

■ Organizing Your Essay for Unity and Coherence

Once you have a long list of supporting information, you will have the raw materials for your essay. Now you must find a way to organize the information so that it will clearly and thoroughly develop the thesis statement.

Deciding on Subtopics. To organize the supporting information you have gathered, you must think of two or more subtopics of your thesis statement. If you have stated these subtopics in your thesis statement, you may have already grouped your supporting information by the subtopics. But if your thesis statement does not provide subtopics, you must examine your list of support to determine natural subtopics of your main point. Then you should arrange these subtopics by determining which will come first, second, third, and so on in the body of your essay.

Examine your list of supporting information, choose appropriate subtopics, and then order your subtopics logically.

Begin looking for subtopics by rereading your thesis statement and your list of supporting information. Do any natural categories, steps, or divisions emerge from your list of support? Ask yourself, "Does the list of support break easily into two or more groups of information? What steps, parts, or categories would organize this information clearly for the reader and develop the thesis statement thoroughly?" Jot down or circle two or more subtopics on your list of support. Then check to see if they are appropriate subtopics by examining each in relationship to your thesis statement and by examining the relationship of all the subtopics to each other. If your subtopics fit with the thesis statement and with each other, you have suitable subtopics.

For the list of supporting information based on the golfing thesis statement, you might observe that much of the information seems to fall naturally into three groups. These three groups are three frustrations: frustration caused by inconsistency, frustration caused by the golf course, and frustration caused by other players. These three categories could then become your subtopics.

To order your subtopics for the body of the essay, you should decide what is the most effective way to arrange them. If your subtopics are locations, you will probably choose spatial order. Other types of subtopics could be arranged in order of importance, in chronological order, in comparison-and-contrast order, or in developmental order. To check the logic of using these orders, ask yourself, "Is one subtopic more important than the others? Does a natural, logical order emerge?"

Thinking about the three subtopics for the golfing thesis statement, you might decide that they actually follow an order of importance, from least frustrating to most frustrating. Then, using order of importance, you could arrange the subtopics so that frustration caused by the course would be first, frustration caused by other players would be second, and frustration caused by the players' own inconsistency would be third.

Checking Support for Unity and Completeness.   Once you have decided how to arrange the subtopics in your essay, you can reexamine your list of supporting information to see if you have enough and the right kinds of information to support each subtopic.

Adjust and group your supporting information to fit with your subtopics and thesis statement.

Although each writer will handle this checking, grouping, and revising step differently, the goal remains the same: a rough plan for the body of your essay with complete, unified supporting information grouped under the subtopics. You may choose to group, cross out, and add information right on your original list of support. Another alternative is to list your subtopics on a clean sheet of paper and, under each, list information that will develop the subtopic. As you group your supporting information on the paper by subtopic, you should eliminate those pieces of support that are repetitious or unnecessary. You should also jot down any helpful ideas that you may have overlooked and that you now need to round out your subtopics. At this point, you may also need to revise your thesis statement so that it will fit your subtopics and chosen supporting information.

For the essay on golfing, you might jot down the three subtopics—frustration caused by the course, frustration caused by other players, and frustration caused by playing inconsistently—as headings. Then you could select and list the pieces of support from your original list under the appropriate subtopics. Looking at the original list of supporting information on pages 721 and 722, you might also decide that most of the answers to the first question and a few of those to the second will not fit or are unnecessary in the body of the essay.

Outlining Your Essay. Writing an outline that shows the decisions you have made about subtopics and supporting information can speed up the drafting of the essay. You can use a modified outline or a formal topic outline. In your outline, you should include your thesis statement, your subtopics, and your supporting information logically ordered under each subtopic. You can choose to make the information under each subtopic into one or more paragraphs. You may also include concluding sentences at the end of any one of the subtopics or at the end of the body.

Write a modified or topic outline for the body of your essay that shows the logical order of your subtopics and the logical order of supporting information under each subtopic.

For the essay on golfing, you might write a topic outline like the following. Notice that the subtopics follow order of importance and that the information under the first subtopic follows developmental order, the information under the second and third subtopics follows order of importance.

Thesis Statement: For beginners, golf is a fascinating frustration because fun and success are often just out of reach.

I.   The new player's first frustration: the course itself
   A.   Long, winding, hilly course
      1.   Need for accuracy and control beginners lack
      2.   Beginners take many strokes to reach green
   B.   Rough on the sides of course
      1.   Tall grasses and shrubbery hide golf balls
      2.   New players often lose one or more balls a game
   C.   Trees on sides of fairways
      1.   Golf balls disappear in and under trees
      2.   Golf balls bounce off trees and disappear
   D.   Water hazards
      1.   Players lose balls—hit right distance but wrong direction
      2.   Players lose balls—hit right direction but wrong distance

II. Second frustration: other players
   A. Need to team up with other players
      1. Experienced golfers try to give advice—fluster new golfers
      2. Experienced or other golfers criticize new golfers—discourage and annoy new golfers
   B. Relaxing, uncrowded course becomes crowded when players behind want to go faster
      1. Players behind interrupt the new golfers' game
      2. Cause new players to hurry and play more poorly
III. Greatest frustration: unfulfilled expectations of doing well caused by new golfers' inconsistency
   A. New players lack control and aim so make many mistakes
      1. Swing and miss
      2. Top the ball
      3. Hit behind the ball
      4. Slice
      5. Hook
   B. New players' anger at alternating good shots and bad shots
      1. Anger at self for ruining a good score with bad putts
      2. Anger at self for not beginning as well as they ended
   C. Concluding idea for subtopic: Whatever the problem, new players feel embarrassed when, after one good shot, they hit a terrible shot.

EXERCISE D: Arranging Supporting Information in the Body of Your Essay. Use your list of supporting information from Exercise C to organize and develop the body of your essay. Follow these instructions. *Special attention could be paid to fullness and logical development in this planning stage.*

1. Examine your thesis statement and your list of supporting information to determine appropriate subtopics. List two or more subtopics that grow naturally out of your thesis statement and support. Make sure your subtopics are related to the thesis statement and to each other.
2. Arrange your subtopics in a logical order that fits the thesis statement and the subtopics.
3. Examine the supporting information that will develop each subtopic. List the support you plan to use under each subtopic and weed out the examples, details, facts, and reasons that are unnecessary or unrelated. Include only the related pieces of support. Add any pieces of support that are needed for a thorough treatment of your subtopics.

4. Reexamine your thesis statement. If it should be revised to fit the subtopics and list of support, make any necessary changes in the wording or length.

EXERCISE E: Outlining Your Essay. Prepare an outline for the body of the essay you have been developing in the previous exercises by following these instructions.
Outlines should be checked for logic and ample support for each subtopic.
1. Decide tentatively how many paragraphs you will have in the body of your essay; in other words, decide how many subtopics you will have and whether you will devote more than one paragraph to each subtopic.
2. Decide what order you will use to arrange the supporting information under each subtopic.
3. Finally, prepare a modified or topic outline that shows your thesis statement, your subtopics in logical order, and the supporting information under each subtopic in logical order.

■ Drafting Your Essay

As you draft your essay, you should concentrate on putting all the parts together into a unified, coherent whole.

Before you draft your essay, sketch or draft an introduction and possibly plan a title and conclusion. Then draft the complete essay, focusing on connecting ideas smoothly with transitions and repetitions of main words, synonyms, and pronouns.

To plan and draft an introduction, jot down ideas, general remarks, background information, colorful examples, or incidents. You may find that your original list of supporting information contains some ideas not used in the outline of the body. If not, you may have to brainstorm for other ideas that will serve to clarify the topic, capture the reader's interest, set the tone, and lead into your thesis statement. You may have to write several versions of your introduction until you have one that successfully performs all these functions. Always avoid boring beginnings such as "I am going to tell you about . . . " and introductions that are cute or misleading.

Although a title can be added as late as the revising step, and a conclusion can be written at the end of your draft, you may want to jot down possible titles and plan a conclusion at this point. Try to think of a short, direct title that attracts attention, maybe even arouses the reader's curiosity, and provides a clue to the main point of the essay. A title, like the introduction, should suit the tone and content of the essay. For the conclusion, you should plan a reminder of the thesis statement, which should convey the main point of the essay in different words. Think of ideas that will neither repeat your essay nor launch a new essay but instead give the reader a sense of completion and mental satisfaction. If an appropriate clincher comes to mind, jot it down too.

Now, equipped with an introduction that ends in your thesis statement, an outline of the body of your essay, a possible title, and possible ideas for the conclusion, you are ready to draft your essay. As you draft your essay, try to make the underlying order of ideas within each paragraph and within the essay as a whole clear to the reader. You can achieve this clarity and smoothness by using transitions within paragraphs and between paragraphs to indicate a new subtopic or further development of the preceding subtopic. Also, try to repeat the main words in your thesis statement and in your subtopics and to use synonyms for these main words. Main words and synonyms can focus the reader's attention on the thesis statement and important ideas in the essay. You may also find consistent pronouns, parallel structures, and concluding sentences—at the end of subtopics—useful for guiding the reader through your ideas.

The thinking and planning you have done earlier will make the drafting of your essay a smooth, satisfying step. You can simplify your task further by writing legibly and by leaving large margins and spaces between the lines for revisions. If new ideas or changes in your outline occur to you as you write—and they probably will—check them against your thesis statement and subtopics, and include them in your draft if they fit.

EXERCISE F: Planning an Introduction, Title, and Conclusion. With your outline and your original list of supporting information before you, jot down ideas for an introduction, making use of any suitable ideas in your list of support that you are not using in the body of the essay. Think of ideas that would make the reader want to read more. Jot down three possible titles for your essay. Then draft a reminder of your thesis statement in one sentence and list three other ideas you could use in your conclusion.
Students might discuss ways of tying together introductions and conclusions.

EXERCISE G: Completing a First Draft. Use your introduction and outline to draft your essay. As you write the draft in complete sentences, use transitions, repeat main words, and use synonyms for main words to connect and clarify ideas. *Students might check transitions and other connectives by underlining them.*

■ Revising Your Essay

The revising step allows you to correct, improve, and polish your essay. It is a last opportunity to add good ideas, try for greater clarity, and make your essay your best effort. As you revise, you should try to view your essay objectively, as a reader would read it.

Revise your essay by proofreading for sense and flow, by using a checklist for revision, by adding, removing, or sharpening ideas, and finally by correcting problems of word choice, grammar, usage, mechanics, and spelling.

You should proofread your essay several times. Read it silently and aloud immediately after you finish writing. Later read it aloud to yourself again or read it to someone else. Listen for long, confusing sentences, short, choppy sentences, and illogical connections. Try putting your essay aside for awhile and coming back to it with an open mind. Then use a checklist similar to the following to make final changes and corrections in structure, content, grammar, punctuation, and spelling.

CHECKLIST FOR REVISION

1. Does the title attract attention, suit the essay, and give clues to the main point of the essay?
2. Does the introduction capture the reader's interest, provide any necessary background information, establish the tone, and lead smoothly into the thesis statement?
3. Does the thesis statement present a clearly focused main point of the essay?
4. Does each body paragraph develop a subtopic of the thesis statement or part of a subtopic with enough specific examples, details, facts, reasons, and incidents? (See p u 14-17)
5. Are the subtopics natural outgrowths of the thesis statement? Are they arranged in the most logical order?
6. Does each paragraph in the body of the essay have a clear topic sentence?

7. Does the supporting information in each body paragraph follow a logical order clarified by transitions?

8. Have you guided the reader from paragraph to paragraph with appropriate transitions and repetitions of main words, synonyms, and pronouns?

9. Does the conclusion include a reminder of the thesis statement, echo the introduction, and bring the essay to a satisfactory completion?

10. Have you tried to make the thesis statement, its development in the body, and the entire essay catch and hold the reader's interest?

11. Have you used clear, varied sentences that sharpen your ideas and read smoothly?

12. Have you chosen the most precise and concise words and used correct grammar, punctuation, and spelling?

After you have marked your first draft with any necessary changes and corrections, and perhaps rewritten sections of your essay, you are ready to recopy it in final, neat form.

If you were to draft and revise the essay on golfing, it might resemble the following finished essay. The marginal notes point out the essay's structure. The words in italics are transitions. Also notice the repetition of the main words and synonyms: *frustration, aggravation, problems, new golfers, new players,* and *beginners.*

Title

The Most Frustrating Game

Introduction

Tan, trimly muscular, Nancy Lopez and Lee Trevino walk on the golf course, address the ball with confidence, swing with powerful control, and watch the ball drop neatly on the green near the hole. Their appearance and actions have summed up the glamor, challenge, and rewards of golf. No doubt golf does have much to offer. Players can leave the strains of everyday life behind as they enter a world of grassy slopes and rugged cliffs, sparkling ponds, manicured greens, and swaying trees. Players can walk for exercise or ride in golf carts for comfort. Players can smile with satisfaction as they beat their last week's score by ten strokes. *Furthermore,* golf is a sport players can take up at almost any age and play long into their retirement years. For beginning golfers, *however,* the problems and aggravations equal the benefits and rewards. Golf will tax new golfers' patience

Thesis
statement

and test their determination. For beginners, golf is a fascinating frustration because fun and success are often just out of reach.

Subtopic 1
First
frustration:
the course

The *first* frustration new players must contend with is the scenic, appealing course itself. Every feature that contributes to the peaceful charm makes the course more impossible for beginners. The area, called the hole, between the teeing ground, where players begin to play each hole, and the putting green, where players end each hole by putting the ball into a small hole, can be as long as 550 yards. On many holes, golfers will not be able to see the putting green from the teeing ground because the course is so long, or because it bends, drops down a cliff, or climbs a hill. To hit from the teeing ground to the putting green in the fewest possible strokes requires accuracy and control that most players lack. While professionals might take two strokes, beginners might need as many as seven to reach the green. The unmowed or scrubby territory on the sides of the course, called the rough, can *also* pose definite problems for beginners. The tall grass and shrubbery seem to swallow golf balls, and new players can plan to lose one or more golf balls a game. Trees in the rough and between the holes can obstruct beginners' shots, causing the ball to lodge in some dense thicket or ricochet out of sight. The refreshing ponds, creeks, and lakes bordering holes, called water hazards, are guaranteed to frustrate beginning golfers. A shot can go the right distance but curve and land in the pond to sink in the mud, where only the ducks or fish could find it. *And* a ball hit in the right direction, but hit too soft or too hard, can have exactly the same miserable fate.

Transitional
sentence

Subtopic 2
Second
frustration:
other golfers

Most new players accept the hazards of the course as a challenge and reconcile themselves to losing some golf balls. Few new golfers, *however*, realize that other friendly golfers and seemingly uncrowded conditions can easily become frustrations. Usually golfers must play in groups of three or four. *Thus*, two new golfers could be teamed up with one or more other players, usually strangers, who are likely to be better golfers. When these experienced players see any new players struggling, they often begin giving advice: "Where did you learn that grip? You're going to hurt your wrist if you hold the club like that. Do it this way." Or "Uh, uh, uh, you moved your head again. You've got to watch the ball." This analysis of their mistakes easily unhinges new golfers. Since golf is largely a game of attitude and concentration, the more flustered new golfers become, the worse they play. *Besides* the Friendly Advisors, the Wise-Guy

Commentators can annoy and discourage new players: "Well, you'll never find that ball. It's a goner for sure. In the creek." *Perhaps the most frustrating players* are those speedy threesomes who turn an uncrowded course and a relaxing game into just the opposite when they play behind beginners. No sooner do new golfers begin to look for one lost ball or have one bad short shot, than the impatient players behind yell, "Can we play through?" *Then* the new players have to step aside and wait while the golfers behind play the hole and go on ahead. *Meanwhile* the new golfers have lost time and become even slower. *Soon* other players behind want to play through too. *Now* feeling guilty about taking more time, the new players rush their strokes, lose more balls, and play progressively worse.

Subtopic 3
Third and greatest frustration: inconsistency

But of all the frustrations encountered by new golfers, inconsistency will tease and frustrate them the most, giving them that "if only . . . " feeling. New players lack the control and aim needed to hit the ball the right distance in the right direction every time. In golf, there are many ways to make mistakes, and new players usually find them all. Drawing back from the ball can cause new players to swing and miss. Poor form can cause players to top the ball, making it hop or roll only a short distance. Or players can swing awkwardly and gouge the ground, sending a huge piece of dirt flying instead of the ball. If players do swing into the ball, it can arc off to the right in a slice or curve away to the left in a hook, out of bounds either way. Hitting bad shots like these can make new players feel ineffective, unskilled, and foolish. Hitting some good shots and some bad shots, *however*, can be *even more frustrating*. When new players hit a long, straight drive and then hit three poor shots and take four putts to sink the ball, they become furious with themselves for throwing away the chance for a good score. On the other hand, a poor beginning with a strong finish on a hole can lead new players to ask themselves, "Now why couldn't I do that before?" And nothing is quite as embarrassing and aggravating as, after one good hole, teeing off in front of other players, only to watch the ball bound off the tee and land five yards away in a hedge.

Reminder of thesis statement

One golfer confided to his friend, "Golf's got to be the most frustrating game in the world. Those good times and good shots every now and then won't let me give up, but golf makes me so mad sometimes." Many new golfers would probably agree. Those cartoons of golfers with broken clubs attacking their golf carts or their partners must have captured some truth. But just when new golfers have vowed to forget golf and stick to tennis, they swing and hear a solid "thwack," as the ball soars 200 yards onto the green. Suddenly the fascination of the game returns. And the sun, relaxing breeze, lush grass, and trees seem very appealing. After all, the new players think, I have thirty years to learn this sport. Again, golf demonstrates its true nature; it is not just a frustra-

Clincher   tion, but a lure and a challenge as well: a fascinating frustration.

EXERCISE H: Examining and Revising Your Essay. Proofread the essay you drafted in Exercise G by reading it aloud to yourself and then to someone else. Then, use the checklist for revision on page 729 to locate and correct any weaknesses in your essay. Make your additions, corrections, and improvements on your draft, and then recopy your essay in final form.

APPLICATION: Evaluating, Writing, and Revising Essays. Before you begin to write your next essay, read an essay published as a short article in a magazine. Evaluate the essay's thesis statement, supporting information, and overall unity and coherence. Then write down three or four observations about this essay. List one good point or feature that you would like to include in the next essay you write. Then follow the steps you have learned in this section and prepare an essay on a topic of your choice. Begin by brainstorming for five or more topics you could write about and jotting them down on a piece of paper. Narrow any topics that are general to smaller, more manageable topics. Choose the topic for your essay from among these possibilities. Then find a main point, write versions of your thesis statement, choose a thesis statement, brainstorm for support, decide on subtopics, organize your support by subtopics, outline, and draft your essay. Finally, revise your essay by reading it aloud to another person and using the checklist on page 729. Correct, polish, and recopy your essay in final form.

Chapter 26

Kinds of Essays

Once you know how to write a standard essay, you can learn to write essays with a particular purpose. Expository essays, persuasive essays, and personal experience essays each serve a different function and are meant to have a specific effect on the reader. In writing these essays, you will learn to focus on achieving a different goal for each: (1) The *expository essay* attempts to explain an idea, process, or event with factual information; (2) the *persuasive essay* attempts to convince a reader with reasonable arguments and evidence; (3) the *personal experience essay* attempts to recreate an experience for a reader with vivid description of events. The sections that follow give useful pointers on writing these three kinds of essays.

26.1 Expository Essays

An expository essay provides facts and ideas to inform and instruct the reader. It can be used to share information in a variety of different situations: in writing a scholarly article, in writing a how-to manual, or even in writing an answer to an examination question. This section will explain the features and help you plan and write this kind of essay.

■ The Distinctive Features of Expository Essays

Writing an expository essay is an opportunity for you to explain what you know about a concept, event, or process to someone who probably has not done the reading you have done or had the experiences you have had.

An Explanatory Purpose. The expository essay should explain a factual main point to the reader. All the material in the essay, from the beginning of the introduction to the end of the conclusion, should work together to achieve this purpose.

The purpose of an expository essay is to explain a concept, event, or process by presenting information.

Like any other essay, the expository essay begins with an introduction that establishes the essay's topic, purpose, and tone and presents a thesis statement. The thesis statement should be a statement of fact that you intend to explain and elaborate on in the body of the essay. It should not offer an opinion suitable for an argument or one that requires a defense. Notice the difference between a statement of fact appropriate for an expository essay and a statement of opinion. The statement of fact can be checked in a public record whereas the opinion is a judgment, open to disagreement and debate.

STATEMENT OF FACT: Most American Presidents retire from public office when they leave the White House.

STATEMENT OF OPINION: Most American Presidents make no significant contributions after they leave the White House.

The following chart gives other examples of thesis statements for expository essays. Notice that all present factual main points that can be developed with objective information. The first thesis statement includes stated subtopics.

SAMPLE THESIS STATEMENTS FOR EXPOSITORY ESSAYS	
Thesis Statements	**Stated Subtopics**
While *The Magic Three of Solatia* by Jane Yolen and *Greenwitch* by Susan Cooper both incorporate myth and	(1) Length (2) Intended readers (3) Use of myths and fairy tales

fairy tale, they differ in their length, in their intended readers, and in their use of myths and fairy tales.	
You can learn to take excellent photographs of your tropical fish with a closeup lens.	None stated
Benjamin Disraeli played an important role in British government and politics in the mid-nineteenth century.	None stated

The body of an expository essay should develop the main point with a complete explanation. In the body, you should include enough examples, details, and facts to fulfill the reader's expectations and to cover the main point thoroughly. You may find supporting information through your reading and by consulting reference books and knowledgeable people.

An Informative Tone.   An expository essay should also be informative in its tone. This tone should flow easily and naturally from your aim to lead the reader to new knowledge and to communicate your information in a direct, matter-of-fact manner.

Create an informative tone by defining terms, by using precise language, by being objective, and by focusing on instructing the reader.

To create an informative tone, you should present your information in an unbiased, explanatory way that is appropriate to both your topic and your readers. You should take into account the background and knowledge of the audience and write your explanations at an appropriate level. For instance, if you were teaching inexperienced people how to set up a tent, you would have to explain each step slowly and in simple language. When writing an expository essay, you should define all difficult or specialized terms, use examples to illustrate ideas, and explain all concepts thoroughly.

EXERCISE A: Evaluating an Expository Essay. Read the following expository essay that makes observations on the changes in television shows from the 1950's to the 1970's. Then answer the questions that follow the essay.

Ozzie Goes to the Office

Throughout the three decades of commercial television in the United States, the situation comedy—or "sitcom"—has remained one of the most popular and successful forms of television entertainment. Certain basic aspects of the sitcom have persisted unchanged since the early 1950's. Sitcoms have always been geared to entertaining a mass audience for half-hour chunks of time during the prime viewing period between 7:30 p.m. and 10:00 p.m. Also, they have always involved a small core of regular characters who are very different from one another and who behave in a consistent and predictable manner. But television critics have noted that the main setting of the sitcom has shifted over the last few decades from the family in the home to the office family. Although the location and the members of the families in many situation comedies have changed, several elements of the family structure have been preserved in the new setting.

The "real" family situation comedies of the 1950's focused almost entirely upon the home and relations among parents and children. *Ozzie and Harriet, The Donna Reed Show, Father Knows Best,* and *Leave it to Beaver*—to name a few—took place almost without exception in a single-family house located in a small town or suburb. The family usually consisted of a mother, father, and two or three children of varying ages. The mother was usually a housewife. The father was always employed outside the home, but his job, if discussed at all, rarely entered the family drama. (One exception, *Make Room for Daddy*, with Danny Thomas, involved a father with a colorful show business career.) Because the setting was confined to the home, the personal and professional difficulties of the adult characters received very little attention. As a result, these series tended to center on the problems and accomplishments of the children. The parents acted chiefly as counselors and benevolent authorities, guiding the children through the process of growing up.

In the 1970's, however, a number of situation comedies moved out of the home into the workplace with a new core of characters, called the "office family." The "office family" series are populated almost entirely by adults thrown together because of their occupations. While the "real family" situation comedies were set in small towns and suburbs, the office family sitcoms take place principally in large cities: *The Mary Tyler Moore Show* in Minneapolis, *The Bob Newhart Show* in Chicago, *WKRP in Cincinnati* in Cincinnati. The absence of children in the office usually carries over into the personal lives of the characters as well. Nearly all of them are childless, and a large percentage are single. The office family series focuses, therefore, entirely upon the problems of adults— on their professional, personal, and romantic triumphs and tribulations. Still, some of the old family relationships remain. Members of the office family get to know each other well from working closely together. Like the real family, the office family has a clear structure of authority. The bosses in the office family even have some of the wisdom and authority that the home family granted to parents. Sometimes members of the office family take on the role of children. Occasionally, these adults act "childishly" as other members of the family offer more mature, "parental" counsel.

Thus, despite differences in setting and characters, the "real family" comedies of the 1950's and the "office family" comedies of the 1970's share some parallel features and relationships. In a sense, the "office family" carries the structure of the "real family" into a new setting. One might even say that the Ozzies and Harriets of the old family sitcoms have not entirely departed from America's living rooms. They have simply left their kitchens and backyards for office cubicles and coffee machines.

Answers may vary unless specified.

1. What does the title add to the essay? Can you think up alternative titles?
2. How does the introduction prepare the reader for the rest of the essay?
3. What is the thesis statement? *Paragraph 1, Sentence 6*
4. What are two pieces of supporting information given in the body paragraphs?
5. What order does the body of the essay follow? Can you suggest another possible order for the supporting information? *chronological*
6. What terms does the writer explain? Do any of these terms require more explanation than the writer has given? Are other terms confusing?
7. What transitions link ideas between paragraphs?
8. How is the concluding paragraph related to the thesis statement? What words and ideas link the introduction and the conclusion?
9. What does the last sentence add to the essay? Write a final sentence of your own to substitute for it. What have you added or taken away from the essay?
10. To what extent does the essay fulfill its explanatory purpose? To what extent does the essay maintain an informative tone?

6. sitcom and prime time

■ Writing Expository Essays

When writing expository essays, you should follow the usual planning, brainstorming, organizing, drafting, and revising steps. You should also focus on your explanatory purpose and informative tone throughout the steps.

As you prepare an expository essay, concentrate on explaining your main point to a particular audience.

Your explanatory purpose should help you choose a topic and plan and develop an expository essay. First, be sure to select a topic that lends itself to an explanatory purpose. You should know your topic well so that you can comfortably explain it to someone else. You should find a main point about your topic that can be illustrated and developed objectively and factually.

In the brainstorming step, ask yourself questions your audience would expect your essay to answer, and gather as many relevant pieces of supporting information as you can. Consult books and reference works if you need more facts and other support, but be sure to mention these sources of information in your essay or at the end of it. A logical organization for your particular information can also help you make your ideas comprehensible to the reader.

While you draft, you should think about writing clear, thorough explanations. First, rough out an introduction that will spark the reader's interest in your topic, give background information, establish the objective tone, and lead into the thesis statement. Think of lively ideas and a fitting reminder of your thesis statement for your conclusion, and jot down possible titles for your essay. Maintain the informative tone throughout the drafting by pretending you are speaking to your audience, explaining your main point in language the audience can understand. Connect your ideas smoothly with transitions and repetitions of main words and synonyms so the reader can follow your explanation.

When you have completed your first draft, revise your essay for clarity. Use a checklist for revision such as the one in Section 25.2. In proofreading an expository essay, you should also pay special attention to any jargon, any vague or confusing ideas, and any incomplete explanations. To identify and eliminate these weaknesses, you may find the following suggestions helpful.

SUGGESTIONS FOR REVISING AN EXPOSITORY ESSAY

1. Check the clarity of your explanation by having someone not familiar with your topic read and summarize the information you present.
2. Check for clarity by having someone unfamiliar with your topic read your essay and write down any questions that your essay does not answer but should and any terms that are confusing.
3. Ask a reader to identify any places where the tone is not objective and informative.
4. If your essay explains a process, ask someone to follow the steps as you have presented them.

EXERCISE B: Planning and Organizing an Expository Essay. Choose one of the following topics or use one of your own for an expository essay. Narrow it and find a main point. Write a thesis statement and brainstorm for supporting information. Then select subtopics and organize your supporting information logically to develop your thesis statement as effectively as possible. Finally, prepare an outline of the body of your essay. *Students' progress through these stages might be monitored.*

Hairstyles popular among teenagers in the 1940's and today
Planning a garden (or tool shed, playroom, display cabinet)
The design changes in this year's new automobiles
Preparing for a final exam
The causes of the Great Depression
The steps involved in repairing a watch (radio, television, or other appliance)
The accomplishments of a famous person (for example, Henry Ford, Thomas Edison, Marie Curie, Carrie Nation)
Designing a stage set
The earliest forms of written communication
Planning fire escape routes from your home

EXERCISE C: Drafting and Revising an Expository Essay. Use the thesis statement and outline of the body of your essay from Exercise B to sketch an introduction, think of ideas for your title and conclusion, and draft your complete essay. Then use the checklist for revision in Section 25.2 to evaluate your essay. Also, use one of the suggestions in the chart above. Then revise your essay and recopy it. *Students could also exchange essays for further suggestions before revising.*

APPLICATION: **Analyzing and Writing Expository Essays.** Find a piece of published writing that you think illustrates the features of good expository writing. Bring your selection to class, identify it by name and writer, and list three features found in the essay that you would like your next expository essay to include. Then choose a topic and write an expository essay that demonstrates all you have learned about expository writing. Work with another person on revising your essay for clarity and thoroughness. Finally, recopy your essay and submit it and your comments on your expository selection to your teacher.

Students who read other students' papers might list two or three things they learned from reading them.

Persuasive Essays 26.2

A persuasive essay defends an opinion or takes a stand on an issue in order to convince others. It may seek to change people's minds or it may attempt to move them to action or prevent them from acting. Knowing how to write persuasive essays can be useful to you in school, in future jobs, and in your personal writing. This section will point out the essential features of persuasive essays and will help you incorporate them into your own writing.

■ The Distinctive Features of Persuasive Essays

In a persuasive essay, you must convince the audience to accept or at least think about your opinion, interpretation, or recommended course of action. You must win the reader's attention and consideration. The tone of persuasive essays will vary according to the urgency and importance of the topic and the strength of your own convictions. However, whether the tone is humorous or serious, formal or informal, it should always be reasonable and persuasive.

A Persuasive Purpose. Your purpose to convince the audience should be evident throughout the essay and should govern every choice you make. You should make your opinion or position clear to the reader in the thesis statement and develop it with compelling supporting information in the body.

The purpose of a persuasive essay is to convince the reader to accept an opinion or take some action presented in the thesis statement by offering strong evidence in support of that opinion or action.

The introduction and thesis statement should establish the persuasive purpose. The introduction of a persuasive essay should begin persuading by catching the interest of the audience. It should lead comfortably and gradually toward the thesis statement without antagonizing the reader who may disagree. Your thesis statement should express your position clearly and forcefully but rationally and calmly as well, so that the reader will continue to weigh your supporting evidence with an open mind.

In addition, the main point should be a controversial statement. That is, it must be an opinion, open to disagreement, not a fact. Notice the difference between the following controversial thesis statement and the factual one.

CONTROVERSIAL THESIS STATEMENT: Smoking should be banned from all public places.

FACTUAL THESIS STATEMENT: The Surgeon General's Report links cigarette smoking to the causes of lung cancer and other respiratory ailments.

The opinion in your thesis statement must also be significant and defensible. It should seem worthwhile and not trivial to the reader, and you must be able to support your stand with convincing evidence. The following chart provides further examples of significant, defensible thesis statements that are suitable for persuasive essays. Notice that the thesis statements take opposing positions on two issues. Also notice that the last two of thesis statements include stated subtopics.

SAMPLE THESIS STATEMENTS FOR PERSUASIVE ESSAYS	
Thesis Statements	**Stated Subtopics**
The rights of farm and other domesticated animals deserve more attention in the United States.	None stated

Farm and other domesticated animals exist purely to serve human needs.	None stated
In *Romeo and Juliet*, the young couple's impatience and Romeo's hot temper bring about their tragic end.	(1) Young couple's impatience (2) Romeo's hot temper
In *Romeo and Juliet*, both families' foolish feuding and the Capulets' insensitivity to Juliet bring about the young couple's tragic end.	(1) Both families' foolish feuding (2) The Capulets' insensitivity to Juliet

To carry through your persuasive purpose, your support-ing information should defend your thesis statement. It should include numerous facts, examples, and reasons that will appeal to your reader's reason and understanding. In many cases, you will want to organize your support by order of importance so that you can lead your reader slowly up to your final and most convincing argument.

A Reasonable, Persuasive Tone.   The entire essay should have a reasonable, persuasive tone. The wording of the the-sis statement and the choice and arrangement of the support should contribute to the persuasiveness of the tone. Your choice of language can help convince the reader that you are a reasonable person whose opinions are worth thinking about.

Create a reasonable, persuasive tone by using language that is forceful but fair, as well as specific and clear.

You should assume from the start that your readers dis-agree with you and must be won over to your viewpoint. Ef-fective persuasive writing pays attention to the opposition. It is written with the opposition in mind. It may state the opposing position and it may even admit that the opposition has one or more good arguments.

Your own opinions should be presented forcefully, but not in a way that automatically offends those who disagree with you. Name-calling, words with inappropriate shades of meaning, and other emotional language can destroy a reasonable tone and alienate readers. Because persuading involves informing, too, specific and clear language will help your readers follow your arguments.

EXERCISE A: Analyzing a Persuasive Essay. Read the following essay on air travel, and answer the questions that follow it.

Why Fly?

Not everyone flies. In fact, some people go to a good deal of trouble to avoid taking airplanes altogether. This attitude may be difficult to understand, particularly for veteran air travelers, who appreciate the benefits of airplane travel and could not accomplish half of what they do if they did not fly. Confirmed nonfliers, however, mention problems of air travel, and those most hostile to flying cite the dates and locations of airplane disasters. Yet in spite of complaints and some travelers' deep-seated fears of flying, air transport continues to offer a combination of convenience, speed, and safety unmatched by any other means of transportation.

Opponents of flying point out that air travel can be inconvenient. They maintain, for example, that passengers on closely connecting flights may have to wait several hours at their destinations before their luggage appears. Actually, though, airlines provide conveniences unparalleled anywhere else in the travel industry. Luggage is almost never lost or mishandled, and if it should be delayed, the airlines always arrange to deliver the luggage to the passenger. Statistics vary among airlines, but most confirm that only one passenger in ten thousand will suffer a loss or delay with baggage. Unlike train and bus stations, most airports also have set aside long-term parking areas where passengers can safely leave their cars for extended periods of time. In addition, most have rapid transfer systems, such as buses and carts, which conduct passengers and their luggage from the parking areas to the terminal. The airlines also relieve their customers of the burden of hauling their luggage, with curbside check-in service.

Some people may say that flights are often delayed or cancelled, but such problems are really infrequent and do not lessen the overall speed of air travel. Even with an occasional few hours delay, travel time by air is well ahead of travel by car, bus, or train. No one can deny that airplanes cut to a fraction the traveling time between two points. And for great distances, anything but air transport is inconceivable. Imagine spending three and one-half days of a short vacation or of a work week sitting on a bus between Washington, D.C. and

San Francisco, when an airplane could have flown you from coast to coast in about five hours.

Despite the speed and convenience of air travel, however, many people are troubled by an overwhelming fear of flying, based quite understandably on the attention given to airplane crashes. But these events are truly rare, almost freakish, occurrences. In fact, it is their rarity that makes them newsworthy. The chances of being involved in an airplane accident are miniscule for any air traveler. Those who ride in automobiles are one hundred times more likely to suffer injury than air passengers, and yet people quite routinely ride in and drive automobiles every day. Most people do not realize that airplanes actually enjoy the best safety record of all the modes of travel, given the huge numbers of people they carry and the millions of miles they cover every year.

Clearly, flying makes traveling easier, faster, and safer than other methods of transportation. While those who shun airplanes constitute only a small percentage of travelers, they might be fewer still if they examined the facts and statistics. And if these people could conquer their fears enough to give flying a chance, they might make some pleasant discoveries. With veteran travelers, they might come to enjoy the automatic ramps that whiz passengers from one end of a terminal to another, the thrill of takeoffs, and the view of clean clouds, rainbow sunsets, and the earth curving thousands of feet below. These people would then know why they fly.

Answers may vary unless specified.

1. Do you consider the title of this essay appropriate or inappropriate?
2. How does the introduction prepare the reader for a persuasive essay? *introduces controversial issue; expresses opinion*
3. At what point did you first realize what the writer's position was? *Paragraph 1, Sentence 5*
4. What is the thesis statement? What, if any, are the subtopics? *Paragraph 1, Sentence 5 / convenience, speed, safety*
5. What are the major arguments offered in support of the thesis statement? What supporting information is provided for each of these arguments?
6. Where does the writer mention opposing arguments? Which points, if any, are actually conceded?
7. What additional arguments for or against the controversial main point can you think of?
8. What is the arrangement of subtopics in the body? Would another order be possible and effective?
9. What transitions and repetitions of main words and synonyms do you find in the essay?
10. What are some examples of the writer's reasonable, persuasive tone? Where is the tone not reasonable or persuasive?

6. *opposing arguments mentioned in all but last paragraph*

8. *order of importance*

■ Writing Persuasive Essays

All of the familiar steps that you follow in writing an essay—planning, brainstorming, organizing, drafting, and revising—should be directed in a persuasive essay toward achieving your persuasive purpose and tone. Imagine that your audience disagrees with you or simply does not care. Keeping the opposition in mind will help you sharpen your own reasoning and be more convincing.

During each of step of writing a persuasive essay, concentrate on persuading an unsympathetic or uninterested reader to think about and accept your viewpoint.

In choosing your topic, select a topic that you know well and consider important for others to care about. Shape your topic to a main point by asking yourself questions and finding an opinion you can state in a single clear and forceful sentence. Make sure that your thesis statement is indeed an opinion and not a fact by drafting a sentence that presents an opposing position. Be sure that the controversial main point you choose and your wording of it are defensible with factual evidence and reasonable arguments.

When gathering supporting information, you should concentrate on presenting your position reasonably, forcefully, and convincingly. Ask yourself questions as you brainstorm for examples, details, facts, and reasons that will appeal to a reader's understanding and reason. You may want to consult and include information from outside sources, such as reference books and experts in the field, to bolster your position. Your support should always be specific and complete.

As you brainstorm for and organize the support for your thesis statement, you can plan to be casually persuasive or strongly persuasive. But in developing any persuasive essay, you should anticipate the arguments of readers who disagree with you. Your support should answer these opposing arguments. After thinking about the other side, you may choose simply to list the strongest, most persuasive arguments for your side. However, if your main point is especially controversial, you will need to be particularly persuasive. Two very effective ways of planning such an essay are (1) to begin by listing opposing arguments and then think of your own arguments in response or (2) to list first the evidence on your side, then the evidence against your side, and finally to use the con arguments to help you think of additional pro evidence. Building your defense using either of these methods will help you see where you need to strengthen your support. The following chart shows how you can build your defense by taking account of the evidence on both sides.

BUILDING STRONG ARGUMENTS FOR THE BODY OF A PERSUASIVE ESSAY		
Thesis Statement: Smoking should be banned from all public places.		
Evidence For	Evidence Against	Further Evidence For
—smoking represents a proven health hazard to which nonsmokers should not be exposed —many people have allergic reactions to nearby cigarette smoke —smoking adds to the dirt and litter of public places —people should not be encouraged to take up smoking by the example of others	—such a ban would restrict personal liberty over a matter of taste and opinion —a ban on smoking would be impossible to enforce —if litter is a problem, why not restrict eating, drinking and reading newspapers as well?	—the state has the right to restrict liberty in the general interest, and voters could reject a ban if the majority opposed it —even if only partially successful, the ban would improve the situation for nonsmokers —creating of litter is just one more strike against smoking, not the major problem

If you are writing a forceful, highly controversial essay, you may find it very helpful to include in the body of your essay a few of the con arguments you have thought about. Mentioning the arguments of the other side can actually add to the persuasiveness of your essay. It enables you to answer objections to your opinion which might come up in your reader's mind. Also, you might find that conceding a point to the other side will tell the reader that you have really thought the issue through from all sides and, consequently, that your opinion is reasonable and knowledgeable. You might even consider organizing your essay around answering the strongest arguments against your own position. If you are going to mention or concede opposing arguments, you should use a con-pro, con-pro pattern. Present the opposing arguments early in the essay or early in the subtopic sections, and then give all the evidence on your side. Always leave the reader with the evidence in favor of your opinion.

Whether you plan to mention only your arguments or the opposition's arguments as well, you will probably find order of importance most useful in arranging your supporting information. Order of importance places your strongest argument last where it will clinch your defense and stay in the reader's mind.

When drafting your essay, bear in mind the effect you want to have on the reader. As you write your introduction, try to capture the reader's attention and lead up to your thesis statement gradually. You should express your main point clearly and strongly yet encourage the reader to keep an open mind. Try to maintain a consistent, reasonable tone in your draft of the whole essay. You might imagine that you are speaking to or debating with the reader, and that you have to make your reader *want* to listen to you and, ultimately, agree with what you say. You should write a striking, fitting title and a conclusion that restates the controversial main point in different words. The conclusion can also wrap up the essay by ending with a warning, a call to action, a statement relating the issue to the reader's life, or an echo of the title.

As you revise your essay, use a checklist similar to the one in Section 25.2. You might also use the following suggestions to make your essay more persuasive.

SUGGESTIONS FOR EVALUATING A PERSUASIVE ESSAY

1. Have someone with a neutral viewpoint read your essay. Ask that person to evaluate how interesting and convincing your essay is. Then make any necessary improvements in your essay.

2. Have someone who disagrees with you read your essay. Ask that person to comment on the strength, development, and order of your arguments. Make any necessary improvements to strengthen your essay.

EXERCISE B: Planning and Organizing a Persuasive Essay.
Choose one of the following topics for a persuasive essay.
Determine your stand on it, sharpen your main point, and
write a thesis statement. Brainstorm for supporting information by thinking about opposing arguments as well as
listing your own evidence and arguments. If your opinion is
highly controversial, use a chart for building your defense.
Choose and order your subtopics and your supporting information under your subtopics. Then outline your essay showing any opposing arguments you plan to mention or concede.
Students could exchange papers to generate additional arguments.

The need for
improvements in the
school cafeteria (or
classrooms or gym)

The necessity for people to
vote (in school elections
or national elections)

The quality of television
commercials

The usefulness of the
Electoral College

The quality of movie
sequels as compared to
the original films

The value of athletic
scholarships

The contributions of
activist students in the
1960's

The need for gasoline
rationing

The most talented popular
musician

The inventor (politician,
artist, and so on) who
has made the biggest
contribution to society

EXERCISE C: Drafting and Revising a Persuasive Essay. Prepare to write the essay you outlined in Exercise B by drafting an introduction suitable for your persuasive purpose and
by jotting down ideas for your title and conclusion. Then
draft your essay, trying to be persuasive, reasonable, and
clear throughout. Finally, use the checklist for revision in
Section 25.2 and one of the suggestions in the chart on page
748 to revise your essay. Recopy your essay in complete, re-
fined form. *Essays taking different positions on the same question could be presented
to the whole class for discussion.*

APPLICATION: Writing and Evaluating Persuasive Essays. With
your classmates, list on paper or on the board five to ten
controversial statements (for example, *The two-party system
is dead* or *Curfews are a violation of individual freedoms*).
Choose to write for or against one of these issues. Then follow the writing steps you have learned, including making a
chart to build your defense. Exchange the first draft of your
essay with another student who took the opposing stand on
the issue. Suggest how the other student's essay might be
strengthened. Then revise your own essay, taking the other

student's comments into account. Recopy your essay and submit it to your teacher.

Again, opposing papers might be presented in a kind of debate to the whole class.

26.3 Personal Experience Essays

A personal experience essay recounts some experience that you have had, something scary, funny, or embarrassing, something that taught you a lesson, something you will never forget, something that happened to you recently or long ago. It attempts to make your experience real, to involve the reader, to help the reader visualize what you are describing and experience the situation vicariously. It is a flexible kind of essay that combines expository, persuasive, descriptive, and narrative writing and adapts the essay structure to its needs.

Narrative writing tells a story by relating a series of events. In personal experience essays, narrative writing can be used to tell your real experiences.

■ The Distinctive Features of a Personal Experience Essay

A personal experience essay is an account of something that happened to you and that you feel is worth telling others about. Your purpose may be primarily to inform or to entertain your reader. But whatever reaction you intend the audience to have, you will be telling a true story in such a way that the reader will understand. You should also focus on communicating the *feeling* of the experience to your reader by choosing words that paint pictures, capture sensory impressions, and convey the action.

A Narrative Purpose.   The introduction, body, and conclusion of a personal experience essay should combine to make an experience come alive for the reader. The essay should relate a series of events that really happened, presenting them in the order in which they occurred.

The purpose of a personal experience essay is to recreate a significant, true experience by presenting a sequence of events in a natural, clear order.

The narrative purpose influences the choice of topic and the shaping of the thesis statement and the introduction. The topic of your personal experience essay should be an experience that made a strong impression on you. It should also be one that can be made interesting to others. Like any other essay, the personal experience essay should have a thesis statement that presents the main point of the essay. But the main point of this type of essay can vary a great deal, depending on the story that you plan to tell. It might be a factual idea, as in expository writing, or an opinion you developed through the experience, as in persuasive writing. It might be a dominant impression, as in descriptive writing. For example, in a story about a trip to a haunted house, the main point might be the idea that there is really no such thing as a "haunted" house. Or the main point might be how frightening or funny the experience was. Or you might choose to show how gullible you were ten years ago (or last week). Still another choice might be a main point that presents the dominant impression of depressing decay or sadness. The following examples show some possible thesis statements for personal experience essays.

POSSIBLE THESIS STATEMENTS: It is true that the top of a mountain is a dangerous place to be in the late afternoon.

Accepting a blind date can be a big mistake.

As the hours passed in the sea cave, the ocean became an enemy seeking our lives.

The introduction to thesis statements such as these should lead up to the main point by setting an appropriate mood and scene and capturing your reader's interest.

The body of the essay should also concentrate on the narrative purpose. It should develop the experience by presenting a series of events with many specific, concrete details. Usually, the events should follow chronological order, but you might at some point want to jump forward or back in time. For instance, in your introduction, you might want to *foreshadow* (look forward to) the outcome of the experience you are about to describe. In your concluding paragraph, you might want to look back over what happened. You might also, somewhere in your essay, use a *flashback* to some past event or previous point in your story to clarify what you are saying.

The conclusion of a personal experience essay should be memorable, with some interesting twist or reflection on your experience. The more colorful your ending, the more it will contribute to the reader's enjoyment and remembrance of your experience.

Language of Description and Action. The tone of the personal experience essay may vary from light to solemn, depending on the topic, but the language should be as concrete and vivid as possible. This type of essay should be written in the first person because it tells about something that happened to you. That is, when you refer to yourself throughout your essay, you should use the pronouns "I," "me," "my," "myself," and "mine."

> The personal experience essay should be written in the first person. It should also use many specific details, sensory impressions, and occasionally figures of speech to recreate the experience for the reader.

The language of a personal experience essay should be lively and specific. It should include sensory impressions—sights, sounds, smells, tastes, feelings, and sensations—and imaginative comparisons such as similes and metaphors. Action verbs are also particularly important in narrating events. These verbs should be precise and graphic, clearly conveying the action that you are describing to your reader. (See Section 24.3 for more explanation of sensory impressions and figures of speech and Section 21.2 for information on precise language.)

EXERCISE A: Analyzing a Personal Experience Essay. Read the following essay about the painful experience of a piano recital. Then answer the questions that follow it.

Piano Painissimo

Just knowing that I must perform in a piano recital was enough to make my hands and feet clammy for weeks in advance. I actually play the piano very well. But that is not the point. The day of my first big recital turned me into a pitiful creature, who could not call her mind or her body her own.

The day of the recital began poorly. When I woke up, I felt as if my stomach and heart were trying to escape. I wanted to call my teacher to say that I was sick, but that would have been silly. Instead, I breathed deeply over my cereal and told myself: "Relax. There is nothing to worry about. It will all be over in a few hours." But my body refused to listen.

After breakfast, I ran to the piano and tried to practice my piece, the *Second Hungarian Rhapsody* by Franz Liszt. Soon I discovered that my fingers had joined my insides in plotting against me and would not play the piece correctly. They stumbled into each other, got stuck between the keys, and refused to bend. I bit them and slapped them to show them who was the boss. I told myself that if I just played the piece through one time perfectly, everything would be all right, but my efforts were futile.

Somehow I lived through the hours until I sat captive at the recital in the school auditorium. My teacher stood before the seated assemblage and announced that before the recital actually began, all the performers would rise separately to introduce themselves. I squeaked out my name and age. (My voice had joined the rest of my body's conspiracy.) This formality completed, we all turned with tremendous concentration to follow our printed programs, and one by one the performers took their seat at the piano.

The solemnity of the surroundings made my rising panic take a strange turn. I emitted a low chuckle and tried to disguise it as a cough, but I could not seem to cough properly. A few students turned to look at me, and I shifted awkwardly in my seat. Everyone else seemed so controlled, so incredibly self-possessed. I put my clenched fist to my mouth to try to muffle my laughs, but as my shoulders shook, the entire row in front of me turned as if their heads were on a spit to look at me reproachfully. The performer before me finished his piece, somewhat distracted by my choked outburst, and I rose to take his place. Suddenly, a deathly calm descended over me. I know that this is the way I would face a firing squad, with a blank stare that some people might mistake for courage. I sat at the piano and started to play.

As I began the piece, I felt like a player piano or an airplane on automatic pilot. I had no idea what I was doing. I was not consciously directing my body to do anything. In fact, I didn't even remember the piece that my fingers were playing and probably could not give my own name. Much amazed, I stared at the keyboard and my flying fingers, which were expertly picking out the notes of the *Second Hungarian Rhapsody*, the piece which they had refused to play only hours before. Soon my fingers had gotten past the slow, heavy part at the beginning and had hit their stride in the perkier section in the middle. I wondered idly what they would do when they came to the maniac movement at the end, but I did not worry. They seemed to know what they were doing.

When the piece was finished, I rose to bow. My legs wobbled, I was drenched with perspiration, and I knew that my eyes and cheeks were blazing as if I had a fever. But the ordeal was past and I had come through it alive. I could take possession of my life and body once again. Giddy with relief, I even felt a tiny and quite insane pang of regret that it was all over. I wondered if I would ever play in a recital again.

Answers may vary unless specified.

1. What impression does the title give you of the essay?
2. What three things does the introduction tell you?
3. What is the thesis statement? *Paragraph 1, Sentence 4*
4. What details or events in the essay can you remember without rereading it?
5. What is the sequence of events that make up the writer's experience in the essay? What words and ideas serve as transitions to take the reader from one event to the next? *events of recital day*
6. Before you got to the paragraph that actually described how the writer performed in the recital, how did you expect her to perform? Were you surprised by what actually happened? Why or why not?
7. What examples of sensory impressions (sight, sound, taste, smell, feeling, and sensation) can you find in the essay? Which sense(s) does the writer refer to most often? Which passages make you see and feel the writer's experience most strongly?
8. What especially vivid verbs are used in the essay?
9. What figures of speech are used in the essay?
10. What reactions do you think the writer wanted you to have?

1. humorous   2. plays well, nervous, sense of humor

■ Writing a Personal Experience Essay

As you plan, develop, and revise a personal experience essay, you should concentrate on helping the reader to identify with your experience.

During each writing step, focus on making the reader see things through your eyes and experience them with you.

In the planning stage, be sure to select an experience that you can recreate in a vivid, interesting way for your reader. In trying to choose your topic, you might think of three or four experiences that you could write about. Then give yourself about five minutes to jot down whatever ideas each experience calls to mind for you. The experience for which you think of the most responses is probably your richest topic.

To prepare a thesis statement for a personal experience essay, you can use the usual method of asking yourself questions to find a main point. You can also try to organize your various jottings about the topic into a pattern. Ask yourself, "Does one type of feeling seem to stand out or be repeated among my ideas about the experience? What one point connects my various reactions?" You should then express this point in a clear thesis statement.

As you brainstorm for and organize supporting information, you should ask yourself questions with your audience in mind. You should think through your experience, step by step and detail by detail. You might, for instance, imagine that you are telling the experience to a friend. Give the time and setting, and set the mood. You should jot down a description of the people involved, how they reacted, what you did, and how you felt. Think about the information the reader needs to know to follow the events and how you intend the reader to react to what you are describing. What particular details are most worthy of attention? You should organize the events in a smooth, natural order, which will usually be chronological.

When you begin to draft your essay, you should write a lively introduction that draws your reader into your story and leads up to the thesis statement. At this stage, you might jot down a few ideas for your title and conclusion as well. As you draft your essay, choose specific nouns and exact action verbs. You should also include sensory impressions and any fitting figures of speech that come to mind.

When you revise your essay, use the checklist in Section 25.2. The suggestions in the following chart can also help.

SUGGESTIONS FOR EVALUATING PERSONAL EXPERIENCE ESSAYS

1. Have someone who is not familiar with your experience read your essay once. Then have this person tell you which details and events seemed most vivid and memorable. Examine your writing in those passages, and then see if you can make the rest of the essay as vivid.

2. Have someone read your essay and identify any parts of the essay that seem confusing and in need of further explanation.

EXERCISE B: Planning and Organizing a Personal Experience Essay. Choose one of the following experiences or recall one of your own. Think about the main point that you would like to make about the experience and write a thesis statement that expresses it. Then think about the details and events that you want to include. Follow the suggestions in the section as you brainstorm for and organize support. Finally, outline the body of your essay. *Class discussion could generate descriptive details and examples of descriptive language.*

A memorable game (baseball, tennis, Monopoly, checkers, and so on) that you won or lost

An embarrassing moment

Learning something you did not know about another person

Your most terrifying experience

Something from your childhood that you miss now

A mistake that taught you something

Your attempt to learn something new (for example, a driving lesson or a dancing or swimming class)

The best present you ever received (or the worst one)

Being lost

EXERCISE C: Drafting and Revising a Personal Experience Essay. Use the thesis statement and outline you developed in Exercise B to draft your personal experience essay complete with a title. Focus on using language of description and action. Then use the checklist for revision in Section 25.2 and the suggestions offered in this section to revise your essay. Finally, recopy it in final form. *Students might exchange papers and identify particularly striking details and uses of descriptive language.*

APPLICATION: Analyzing and Writing a Personal Experience Essay. Read two personal experience essays published in magazines such as the *Reader's Digest*. For each selection, comment on (1) how interesting and significant the writer's choice of experience is; (2) how engaging the introduction is; (3) whether the specific details and events are well chosen and clearly presented; (4) how well the writer uses descriptive language and conveys action; and (5) whether the conclusion is suitable and striking. Then follow the steps to write another personal experience essay that shows how much you have learned about this kind of writing from the section and from examining other people's accounts of personal experiences.

A list of interesting introductions, conclusions, descriptive details, and phrases could be compiled by each student for class discussion. Students might be encouraged to continue adding to this list whenever they read.

Chapter 27

Library Papers

In school and later on in your work, you will often need to prepare reports based on research about particular topics: historical subjects, famous people, foreign countries, financial conditions, and so on. In most cases, you will find the information you need in a library. You will digest the information you find, integrate what you have learned with what you already know, and express this new understanding in a report or library paper.

The first section of this chapter focuses on the special characteristics and structure of the library paper. The second will guide you in preparing and writing one.

Characteristics of the Library Paper 27.1

The library paper, like an essay, must be focused on and logically organized around a particular point: the thesis statement. Unlike many essays, however, a library paper must *always* be based upon information that is gathered through *research*. A library paper may begin with your own ideas about a particular topic, but it must be developed through outside sources that provide new information.

This section will explain how and when you should cite the sources for the information that you use in your paper. Then it will show you how this information can be incorporated into the basic structure of the paper.

■ Sources of Information in the Library Paper

The library paper is by definition the product of research. You will generally begin with a number of ideas about a topic that interests you and then explore that topic further by consulting a variety of sources in the library. You will need to check the card catalog, *The Readers' Guide to Periodical Literature,* and the vertical file for potential references to your subject. Then you will have to follow up your leads by reading books, newspapers, magazines, and such specialized reference works as encyclopedias, almanacs, atlases, and biographical dictionaries. (For a detailed guide to the use of the library, see Chapter 20.)

Remember above all that the library paper depends for its success upon two elements: your own thoughts and the outside information you acquire in the course of your research. You should gather enough information to become somewhat of an "expert" on a particular aspect of your subject. As a result, your own ideas will carry more weight because you will be able to back them up with reliable sources throughout your paper. Without your individual perspective, however, the information you gather and present will simply be a jumbled mass of facts and quotations. Therefore, you must use your sources well to support and lend authority to what you yourself want to say.

How to Cite Sources of Information.   Since the library paper is based upon your research on a topic, you will need to identify the sources of your information. The citation of outside sources will increase the authority of your ideas by persuading your readers that you do have special knowledge of your subject. Such citations will also give your sources the credit that is due to them and will direct your readers to the appropriate materials, if what you say stimulates them to explore the subject further.

You can cite your sources of information in a number of ways. A widely accepted form of citation is the *footnote,* which directs the reader by means of a number or some other symbol to another place in the paper where the source is given (usually at the bottom of the page on which the reference occurs or at the very end of the paper). You may also use a less formal type of citation, in which you identify your source immediately after the borrowed fact, quotation, or idea. Either form is acceptable, but is it important that you be consistent throughout your paper and use the same method of citation for all of the sources in your paper.

A library paper should give credit to its sources of information either in footnotes or within the text of the paper. One method of citation should be consistently used throughout the paper.

If you are using the footnote method of citing your sources, you should place a small number above the line just after the quotation, idea, or fact that you are taking from your source. You should then place the same number at the bottom of the page or at the end of the paper and write the following information for different types of citations. For *books*, you should include the name of the author, the title of the book, the place of publication, the publisher, the date of publication, and the page from which your reference is drawn. For *articles*, you should include the author's name, the title of the article, the magazine or journal in which it appears, the date of the periodical, and the page of your reference. Citations are numbered consecutively.

The following passage about the painter Pablo Picasso footnotes two sources, a magazine and a book.

Use of footnotes

Pablo Picasso, one of the greatest artists of the twentieth century, was also one of the most productive painters of all time. In his ninety-one years, he created over six thousand paintings, and when he died, his estate was valued at $1.1 billion.[1] Picasso's great and varied output had a tremendous influence over the artists of his time, and the abstract movement in twentieth-century painting owes its origin largely to the work of Picasso.[2]

---

[1] Pete Hamill, "Picasso the Man," New York, May 12, 1980, p. 35.
[2] H.W. Janson, History of Art (Englewood Cliffs, N.J.: Prentice-Hall, 1962), p. 521.

If you are using the less formal method for citing your sources, you can omit some of the details. For books, you simply insert the name of the author, the title of the book, and the page number in parentheses immediately after the borrowed information. For articles, however, you will need to insert all of the information found in the footnote. If the person who wrote the passage about Picasso had chosen this form of citation, the passage would look like this.

Use of informal citations

Pablo Picasso, one of the greatest artists of the twentieth century, was also one of the most productive painters of all time. In his ninety-one years, he created over six thousand paintings, and when he died, his estate was valued at $1.1 billion (Pete Hamill, "Picasso the Man," New York, May 12, 1980, p. 35). Picasso's great and varied output had a tremendous influence over the artists of his time, and the abstract movement in twentieth-century painting owes its origin largely to the work of Picasso (H.W. Janson, History of Art, p. 521).

Most of the sources that you will cite in your library papers will be either books or articles, and the bulk of your citations will probably follow the patterns of the preceding citations. But occasionally you may need to cite other sources as well: encyclopedia articles, edited collections, translated books, and so on. The following chart shows you an acceptable method of citing a number of different kinds of sources. Forms are given only for footnotes. As you can see in the preceding examples, you can omit the publishing information in informal citations of books.

FORMS FOR THE CITATION OF SOURCES	
Kind of Source	**Footnote**
Book	¹H. Stuart Hughes, Contemporary Europe: A History, 2nd ed. (Englewood Cliffs, N.J.: Prentice-Hall, 1966), p. 167.
Book (with two authors)	¹Jean Lipman and Alice Winchester, The Flowering of American Folk Art (New York: Viking, 1974), p. 86.
Magazine article (signed)	¹Frank Trippett, "The Human Need to Break Records," Time, June 16, 1980, p. 88.
Magazine article (unsigned)	¹"Upset Win for an Unknown Colt," Time, June 16, 1980, p. 44.
Encyclopedia article (signed)	¹The Encyclopedia Americana, 1980 ed., "Embroidery," by Donald King and Monique King.
Collected or selected works of a single author (edited)	¹William Shakespeare, The Complete Plays and Poems of William Shakespeare, ed. by William Allan Neilson and Charles Jarvis Hill (Cambridge, Mass.: Riverside Press, 1942), p. 7.
Translated work	¹Fyodor Dostoyevsky, The Idiot, trans. by Constance Garnett (New

	York: Dell Publishing Co., 1959), p. 210.
Work in several volumes (edited)	¹Elting E. Morison, ed., <u>The Letters of Theodore Roosevelt</u>, vol. 3 (Cambridge, Mass.: Harvard University Press, 1951), p. 425.
Newspaper article (signed)	¹Jennifer Dunning, "The Rise of a Young Ballerina," <u>The New York Times</u>, June 13, 1980, p. C13.
Newspaper article (unsigned)	¹"Draft Registration Approved in Senate; July Sign-Up Likely," <u>The New York Times</u>, June 13, 1980, p. A1.

When to Cite Outside Sources. Besides knowing *how* to acknowledge your sources of information, you need to know *when* to indicate that you have incorporated outside information into your paper. If you do not cite the use of outside sources, you will be guilty of *plagiarism*, the act of presenting someone else's work as your own.

A library paper should identify any source from which words, ideas, or little-known facts have been taken.

Since a number of the ideas in your library paper will be your own, or will represent your own thoughts about the information that you have found, you will not need to footnote every single statement in your paper. But three kinds of information always require citation.

First, whenever you repeat a source's exact words, the statement must be placed in quotation marks and the source must be acknowledged. This is true no matter how short the quote and no matter whether it was written or spoken.

Second, whenever you summarize or reword the ideas in a single source, you must acknowledge the source of the ideas. If you read an article that describes the evolution of the automobile engine, or one that presents the argument that the loom was really the earliest form of the computer, you will need to identify your source in order to use the ideas.

Third, whenever you refer to an individual fact or idea that is not widely known, you will need an acknowledgment. You would *not* need to provide a source for the date of the bombing of Pearl Harbor, but you *would* need to footnote more specialized information about the bombing—how many battleships were sunk, how much damage was actually done to the naval base, how many casualties there were, and so on. Similarly, you would *not* need to credit the widely held idea that the Industrial Revolution represented a significant development in world history. But you *would* need to cite a source for the more original and less commonly held idea that the Industrial Revolution concluded with the invention of the computer.

Imagine that in doing research on television technology, you came upon the following passage about videodiscs in *New York* magazine.

Passage from a magazine   But now, after nearly a decade and a billion dollars' worth of worldwide development, the videodisc is here. The disc offers the same pleasures of ownership and control as the videocassette . . . but it is cheaper, of markedly sharper quality, and performs functions that turn your TV set into a very different instrument. . . . Simply and crudely, a videodisc is a record that plays images. Anything you see and hear in a movie theater or on TV can be captured on a disc. —Michael Schrage

The following passage from a library paper shows the incorrect use of this research material. Both the words and ideas of the magazine article have been used without acknowledgment. The italicized words and phrases are lifted directly from the article. The article's information about videodisc research and the advantages of the videodisc have also been borrowed without credit.

Unacceptable library paper with plagiarism   *After nearly a billion dollars' worth of research over the last decade, the videodisc is now here.* The videodisc, like the videocassette, *offers* television viewers *the pleasures of ownership and control.* But the disc is less expensive than the cassette: its images are *markedly sharper,* and *it can perform functions that turn* the television set *into a very different instrument.* Basically, *the videodisc is a record that plays images.* Special effects that can be shown *in a movie theater or on television can be captured on a disc.*

In contrast, the following passage is also based on the *New York* article, but it combines this information with the writer's own ideas, expresses it in the writer's own language, and gives credit where credit is due.

Acceptable library paper with source cited   Thanks to the development of the videocassette and videodisc, it is now possible for television viewers to collect their favorite movies and television programs, just as they own their own books and record albums. Videocassettes and videodiscs are comparable to audiocassettes and records, but they both store images as well as sounds. The videodisc is the more advanced of the two new products because it not only provides better images than the videocassette but is also less expensive than its predecessor.[1]

---

[1]Michael Schrage, "Good-bye 'Dallas,' Hello, Videodiscs," New York, November 17, 1980, p. 38.

Writing a Bibliography. In doing the research necessary to write a library paper, you will probably consult a number of different sources. You may end up citing most or all of these sources in the body of your paper whenever you borrow a quotation, idea, or specialized fact from them. But there may be other sources among your readings that supplied you with general background information, but which you do not refer to at any particular point in your paper. All of the sources that you consult in your research—both those cited in the body of the paper and those that are not specifically cited—must be presented at the end of the paper in a list, which is called a *bibliography*.

Every library paper must include a bibliography listing all of the sources consulted in the preparation and writing of the paper.

The bibliography shows the extent of the research that you have done. Like the citations, it also directs the interested reader of your paper to the appropriate sources of information about your topic.

The bibliography is usually a separate page at the very end of the library paper. Each entry in the bibliography gives complete information about every book, magazine, encyclopedia, or newspaper that you have consulted in your research. In your bibliography, you should list the author's name, last name first, followed by all of the information found in a formal footnote. The one exception is for page numbers. You do not need to list the page numbers of books in bibliographic entries since you are simply identifying the work as a source that you consulted. You should, however, give the pages on which an article in a periodical can be found. The entries in your bibliography should be listed in alphabetical order, by the author's last name, or by the title of the article or book if the author is not given.

The following chart includes the basic forms for the bibliographic entries of a number of different types of sources.

FORMS FOR BIBLIOGRAPHIES	
Kind of Source	**Bibliographic Entry**
Book	Hughes, H. Stuart. Contemporary Europe: A History, 2nd ed. Englewood Cliffs, N.J.: Prentice-Hall, 1966.
Book (with two authors)	Lipman, Jean and Winchester, Alice. The Flowering of American Folk Art. New York: Viking Press, 1974.
Magazine article (signed)	Trippett, Frank. "The Human Need to Break Records." Time, June 16, 1980, p. 88.
Magazine article (unsigned)	"Upset Win for an Unknown Colt." Time, June 16, 1980, p. 44.
Encyclopedia article (signed)	The Encyclopedia Americana, 1980 ed. "Embroidery," by Donald King and Monique King.
Collected or selected works of a single author (edited)	Shakespeare, William. The Complete Plays and Poems of William Shakespeare. Edited by William Allan Neilson and Charles Jarvis Hill. Cambridge, Mass.: Riverside Press, 1942.
Translated work	Dostoyevsky, Fyodor. The Idiot. Translated by Constance Garnett. New York: Dell Publishing Co., 1959.
Work in several volumes (edited)	Morison, Elting E., ed. The Letters of Theodore Roosevelt, vol. 3. Cambridge, Mass.: Harvard University Press, 1951.
Newspaper article (signed)	Dunning, Jennifer. "The Rise of a Young Ballerina." The New York Times, June 13, 1980, p. C13.
Newspaper article (unsigned)	"Draft Registration Approved in Senate; July Sign-Up Likely." The New York Times, June 13, 1980, p. A1.

EXERCISE A: Practicing the Citation of Sources. Look in the library for sources on *one* of the following topics. Use the card catalog, *The Readers' Guide to Periodical Literature,* and any other means you can to find sources on your topic. Choose at least *five* sources, including at least one book and one magazine article. Write down the information for each source that would be included in a footnote or citation within the text of the paper. If you cannot find at least five sources on your topic, choose another one. *Students could also be presented with incorrect or incomplete citations and asked to identify the errors in each.*

Solar power	Medieval armor and
A famous movie star	weapons
Scuba diving	A tourist attraction
The San Francisco	Extrasensory perception
earthquake	(ESP)
Modern American painters	Dinosaurs
	The space shuttle

EXERCISE B: Writing Bibliographic Entries. Take the sources that you found for your topic in Exercise A and write entries for them as they would appear in a bibliography. List them together, in the order that they would follow in a complete bibliography. *Students might benefit from discussion of specific differences between footnote and bibliographic citations.*

■ Structure of the Library Paper

The library paper is organized like an essay. It also includes references to sources of information and a bibliography of sources consulted.

A library paper should have a title, an introduction with a thesis statement, a body, a conclusion, the citation of sources throughout, and a bibliography.

Your *title* and your *introduction* should prepare your reader for the information that you will present. Your introduction should also offer a thesis statement, the main point of your paper. This statement will keep your paper focused on a topic that you can cover reasonably. Even more important, this statement represents your chance to present the purpose of your paper. As in an essay, you should try to write an opening paragraph that will interest your reader and indicate why your main point is worth making, why the information you are going to communicate is worth communicating.

The *body* of your paper will develop your thesis statement. You will present the information you gathered in your research and arrange it in a logical sequence that supports and elaborates upon the point you made in your introduction.

Your *conclusion* should tie together your thesis statement and the evidence presented in the body of your paper. It should do this in a way that is clearly related to the rest of the paper without being repetitive. You should think of it as the place where you can put the "finishing touch" on your arguments or ideas.

A library paper must also include the systematic and consistent citation of sources throughout and a bibliography at the end listing all of the sources you have consulted. The purpose of the citations and the bibliography is to set forth the extent of the research behind the paper, to give credit for all the facts, ideas, and statements taken from outside sources, and to lend authority to the information and arguments presented in the paper.

The following paper incorporates all of these special features. Notice how the footnotes are given in full for the first citation of a work but later abbreviated.

The Boy Genius

The Austrian composer Wolfgang Amadeus Mozart achieved great fame during his short but brilliant life two centuries ago. He composed an amazing number of highly original, imaginative works and contributed many new ideas to the classical music of his time. But Mozart is especially remembered as a boy wonder, a child prodigy who showed an incredible aptitude for understanding and composing music at a very early age. For example, Mozart wrote his first symphony—a complex musical composition consisting of a number of separate sections or movements—at the age of nine.[1] This ability to create complex music was truly a rare gift, and the young Mozart was fortunate to be encouraged from infancy to develop his talents. As a result, he spent much of his childhood in the glare of public attention, and his early years were both difficult and stimulating.

Born in January of 1756 in Salzburg, Austria, Wolfgang Amadeus Mozart was the last child of Anna Maria and Leopold Mozart, a musician. As an infant in a musical household, young Wolfgang showed a profound interest in music. When he was only four years old, he began to listen to his sister's music lessons. He was soon able to copy her music, having learned notation partly from his father and partly on his own. At the age of five, he composed his first original piece of music, a piano concerto.[2] Moved by his son's accomplishment,

Leopold decided that this child was sent from God, and that it was his special duty to train the boy.[3]

Leopold Mozart believed that his son's talents as a composer as well as his skills as a pianist should receive recognition. Embarking with his son and daughter on a tour of Europe, Leopold first presented his children in concert in Vienna, Austria, where they received overwhelming ovations and became an instant success. They were invited to perform at the homes of wealthy Austrian aristocrats and they even played for the Emperor and Empress. Soon the children became the "darlings of Vienna" and were showered with gifts.[4]

One of Mozart's most remarkable youthful achievements took place in Rome during Holy Week, when he heard a choir sing Allegri's *Miserere*. This was a sacred piece of church music which singers were not allowed to copy under the threat of excommunication. After hearing it only once, Wolfgang wrote down the entire work from memory—note by precise note. Scholars have compared Mozart's version with the original and have found it flawless.[5]

Leopold Mozart continued to present his brilliant son to the public, developing but also exploiting his talent. For example, he advertised his son's concert in Frankfurt in 1763 like a barker at a carnival: "He will play a concerto for the violin, and will accompany symphonies on the harpsichord, the manual or keyboard being covered with a cloth, with as much facility as if he could see the keys; he will instantly name all the notes played at a distance, whether singly or in chords on the harpsichord or any other instrument, bell, glass, or clock. He will finally improvise as long as may be desired, and in any key, on the harpsichord and organ."[6] These exhibitions earned young Mozart considerable accolades and some important appointments as a church and court musician. It was not until Mozart was in his early twenties that he escaped the domination of his father and sought important and lucrative appointments, which, unfortunately, never came to him.

Mozart lived only thirty-six years but produced highly original works that often departed from the traditional music of his time. While his career was characterized by frequent disappointments and financial problems—he failed to receive coveted court appointments and he made several powerful enemies in the Church—his life was distinguished by an outstanding talent. Mozart's experiences as a child prodigy led to a highly productive mature career and helped to establish him as a legend in his own brief lifetime.

---

[1]Alfred Einstein, Mozart—His Character, His Work, trans. by Arthur Mendel and Nathan Broden (New York: Oxford University Press, 1945), p. 215.

[2]Charlotte Haldane, Mozart (London: Oxford University Press, 1960), p. 7.

[3]Erich Valentin, Mozart—A Pictoral Biography (New York: The Viking Press, 1959), p. 153.

[4]J.E. Talbot, Mozart (London: Duckworth, 1934), p. 25.

[5]Talbot, Mozart, pp. 60–61.

[6]Milton Cross and David Ewen, New Encyclopedia of the Great Composers and Their Music (Garden City, N.Y.: Doubleday and Company, Inc., 1963), pp. 641–42.

BIBLIOGRAPHY

Cross, Milton and Ewen, David. New Encyclopedia of the Great Composers and Their Music. Garden City, N.Y.: Doubleday and Company, Inc., 1953.

Davenport, Marcia. Mozart. New York: Charles Scribner's Sons, 1956.

Einstein, Alfred. Mozart—His Character, His Work. Translated by Arthur Mendel and Nathan Broden. New York: Oxford University Press, 1945.

The Encyclopedia Britannica, 14th ed. "Mozart, Wolfgang Amadeus."

Haldane, Charlotte. Mozart. London: Oxford University Press, 1960.

Kolb, Annette. Mozart. Westport, Conn.: Greenwood Press, 1975.

Talbot, J.E. Mozart. London: Duckworth, 1934.

Valentin, Erich. Mozart—A Pictoral Biography. New York: The Viking Press, 1959.

NOTE ABOUT OTHER FEATURES: In most cases, your library paper should also have a special, separate title page, which includes the title of your paper, your name, the date, the class for which the paper was written, and any other information that your teacher might require. You might also be asked to provide a separate formal outline of your paper.

EXERCISE C: Recognizing the Structure of the Library Paper. Answer the following questions about the library paper on Mozart. *Answers for some items may vary within reason.*

1. makes reader want to know why   2. background on Mozart   3. underlined

1. How does the title capture the reader's interest?
2. What does the reader learn in the paper's introduction?
3. What is the thesis statement of the library paper?
4. How has the writer organized the supporting information in the body of the paper? *chronologically*
5. How does the conclusion refer to the thesis statement?
   5. in final sentence

APPLICATION: Analyzing a Library Paper. Answer the following questions about the use of sources in the library paper on Mozart.

1. Which of the two systems for citing sources has been followed in the paper? *formal footnotes listed at end of paper*
2. How many different sources does the writer cite in the body of the paper? *5*
3. What kind of citations are being given in each case: quotations, ideas, or specialized facts?
4. How many different *types* of sources are consulted: books, magazines, and so on? *books, encyclopedias*
5. What additional sources might have been consulted? *Answers will vary.*

3. quotations—1/ideas—0/facts—5

Steps in Writing a Library Paper 27.2

Your library paper will be both better and easier to do if you approach the assignment as a series of research and writing steps. This section describes ways to plan your research, locate information, and organize, draft and revise your paper.

■ Finding an Appropriate Topic

You should select the topic for your library paper with great care, taking into account the assignment, your own interests, and the amount and kinds of information you are likely to find.

Choosing and Narrowing a Topic. To make sure you have a workable topic, you should spend a fair amount of time in choosing and narrowing your topic. Your topic should be something that interests you, that you know at least a little bit about, and that you would like to explore further. It should also meet a few more specific criteria.

Select a topic that is interesting, that can be supported with research, and that can be reasonably handled in a library paper.

You might give yourself three or four general areas of interest to choose from, and then visit the library to see the amount and kind of research material available on each topic. After checking the card catalog and *The Readers' Guide to Periodical Literature*, you may find that one of your topics simply does not lead you to enough sources. The information on another topic may be so abundant that you would not know where to begin. You can thus avoid these topics and select one that is more manageable.

Your review of the sources can also help you decide on a specific topic that can be handled in a short paper. Suppose, for example, that you have chosen the general topic of science fiction movies. This subject is too broad to be covered in a few pages. Even before you begin your research, you will have to narrow it to something more specific. Your survey of the material available on your topic will help you to focus it, since the library's card catalog and *The Readers' Guide to Periodical Literature* will suggest a number of specific topics within your general area of interest.

The general topic of science fiction movies could lead you to a number of smaller, more manageable topics, some of which are shown in the following chart.

NARROWING A GENERAL TOPIC	
General Topic	**More Specific Topic**
Science fiction movies	Heroes in science fiction movies
	Monsters in science fiction movies
	Space travel in science fiction movies
	Special effects in science fiction movies
	Themes in science fiction movies

Note that this is only a preliminary narrowing. You may need to limit your topic even further, once you have begun to collect information.

Making Your Initial Bibliography Cards.   Even at this early stage of preparation for the library paper, you should begin to keep track of the sources you consult. Once you have decided on a topic, you should begin making bibliography cards.

Record all information necessary for citations and bibliographic entries for every source you consult.

On each card, you should list the library location symbol, or call number, and the appropriate data about the author, title, and publication of the work. The following chart offers several guidelines for preparing bibliography cards.

PREPARING BIBLIOGRAPHY CARDS

1. Use one card or one sheet of paper for each source.
2. At the top of each card you prepare for a book, record the author, title, city of publication, name of the publisher, and date of publication. For magazine articles, note the author, article title, magazine, publication date, and page numbers.
3. Include the location symbol or call number since you may need to consult the book or periodical later on.
4. Note any mention of illustrations, maps, charts, or tables that you may want to use.

The number of sources that you will need will depend on your topic and your teacher's requirements. You should definitely plan to use at least five sources. Since all sources may not be useful, it may be helpful to have a few more than you need listed on your bibliography cards.

EXERCISE A: Choosing and Narrowing Your Topic. Choose one of the following topics or use one of your own. Consult the card catalog and *The Readers' Guide to Periodical Literature* in the library to see how much material is available on the topic. Then break the topic down into five more specific topics, and choose one that you would like to research and write about. Find five sources on your narrowed topic, including as many different *kinds* of sources as possible (books, magazines, newspaper articles, encyclopedia items, and so on). Then make bibliography cards with the necessary information for each source.

Dolphins	The discovery of oil
Earthquakes	Presidential campaigns
Changes in clothing styles	American generals
The Ice Age	Space stations
Stonehenge	Volcanoes

Feel free to add to list of topics. Cards might be checked for format. Students could also be encouraged to set up a schedule for the completion of their papers.

■ Researching the Library Paper

You should begin your actual research by developing several key questions about your topic and a preliminary thesis statement.

Planning Your Research. Make up about five questions that you would like to pursue in your research and then state your thesis statement in preliminary form.

Always direct your research with several key questions and a rough statement of your thesis statement.

If your topic were *special effects in science fiction movies*, you might ask yourself questions such as those in the following chart.

SAMPLE QUESTIONS TO DIRECT RESEARCH
1. Just what are "special effects" in movies and how are they different from the rest of the movie?
2. Are special effects in science fiction movies different from those in other movies? If so, how?
3. How have special effects in science fiction movies changed over the years?
4. Who are the principal creators of special effects in science fiction movies?
5. How do they actually *do* particular special effects in science fiction movies (for example, space ships moving through space)?

These questions will help you to formulate a one sentence main point for your paper, which will serve as a very rough version of your thesis statement. You will sharpen this statement as you do your research. You may even have to alter it considerably, depending on the information that you find. But you will need this preliminary focus to pull your thoughts together and guide you through the quantities of information that you are likely to scan in doing your research. For the topic *special effects in science fiction movies*, you might begin with the following rough thesis statement.

PRELIMINARY THESIS STATEMENT: Advances in technology have made science fiction special effects highly sophisticated.

Taking Notes on Your Sources.   At this point, you will have already done a fair amount of thinking about your topic and acquainted yourself with a number of sources of information about it. With your questions and preliminary thesis statement to guide you, you should scan these sources, read the relevant sections, and take notes to answer your questions and develop your main point. Keep these notes as neat and organized as possible.

Take accurate notes, recording page numbers and direct quotations exactly, to answer your key questions and develop your thesis statement.

Scan every source listed in your bibliography cards, taking note of the pages likely to contain information relevant to your topic. Set aside the sources that do not directly pertain to your topic as you have defined it, although you may want to include these materials in your bibliography. Then begin to take notes on each of your sources.

The following chart offers a number of suggestions for orderly note-taking.

TAKING NOTES

1. Take notes from each individual source on a separate card.
2. In the upper left-hand corner of each card, record the information necessary for citing the source in the paper (the author's name, title of the work, city of publication, year of publication, and so on).
3. In the top right-hand corner of each note card, set up a subject heading to indicate what the card covers. You are likely to have several cards for each source, each card referring to a particular subject within your topic. Later you can sort the cards by subject.
4. Remember to include the page numbers for each fact, idea, or quotation you note.

Your note-taking will proceed more quickly and efficiently if you begin with the source that covers your subject most clearly and thoroughly. It will give you a good grasp of the available information early on, and it will help you avoid duplicating your efforts in other sources. For each source, record only that information that you have not recorded elsewhere, and remember to confine yourself to the topic as you have defined it in your preliminary thesis statement. Always skim your material first, and then take notes as you reread.

For some sources, you will want to record quotations that are particularly appropriate. These quotations should be clearly marked and listed separately from the other notes on the card. Outlining or summarizing can be used for other types of information you find in your sources, depending on the nature and quantity of the information involved. No matter how you take your notes, you *must* include the page numbers for every item of information you record. The following sample note cards demonstrate different methods of note-taking.

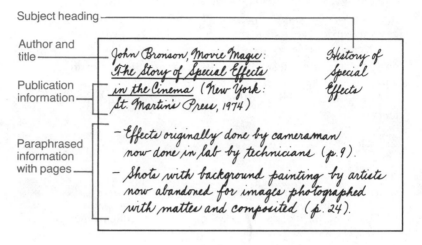

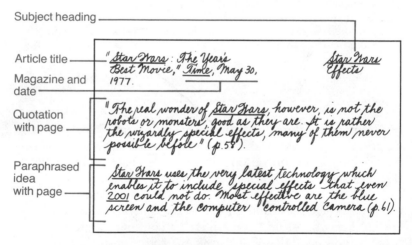

As you take notes, try to decide if the information you are gathering is answering all the key questions that you raised about your topic. If you find gaps in your research, try to fill them in with additional sources. Once you are satisfied, you can start to plan the writing of your paper.

EXERCISE B: Taking Notes for the Library Paper. Use the topic you selected and narrowed down in Exercise A, and follow these instructions. *Student progress could be monitored to identify problems. Special attention should be paid to the thesis statement.*

1. List five key questions you will want to answer in your research.
2. Compose a rough draft of your thesis statement.
3. Scan the sources you listed in Exercise A for those that contain the information most relevant to your thesis statement and questions.
4. Read these sources carefully and take notes. Include several direct quotations in your notes. Remember to record the appropriate information (author, title, page number, subject heading) on each card.

■ Planning and Writing the Library Paper

In writing your library paper, you will sharpen your thesis statement, select and organize supporting information from your research, plan your introduction, and draft a paper from your note cards and an outline.

Writing a Precise Thesis Statement.   The information you gather in answer to your key questions will prepare you to write a more precise thesis statement.

Write a clear thesis statement that takes account of both your audience and purpose.

Your thesis statement should cover all of the information that you plan to use and should tell your audience what you want them to learn from your paper. Take into account the level of understanding, experience, and knowledge of your audience in your thesis statement. For the paper on special effects in science fiction movies, a revised thesis statement might resemble the following.

REVISED THESIS STATEMENT: Special effects in present-day science fiction movies such as *Star Wars* are highly advanced over their predecessors because of space-age technological development.

Preparing an Outline.   Keeping in mind your thesis statement and the supporting information that your research has supplied, you can plan your paper so that it presents your knowledge of your topic clearly and logically.

Organize your information in an outline that is based on your thesis statement, your notes, and your ideas for linking them together into a coherent whole.

Begin ordering your ideas and your research information by performing the steps in the following chart.

ORGANIZING A LIBRARY PAPER
1. Determine the subtopics you want to develop in order to explain your thesis statement. 2. Group the note cards containing information on each of these subtopics together. 3. Decide on an order for presenting your supporting information in the body of your paper. Try to find the order that will serve your thesis statement and subtopics most effectively. Support can be organized by order of importance, in chronological order, in spatial order, or in developmental order.

You should then write an outline that reflects the order that you have chosen for your library paper. (For more information on outlines, see Section 18.2.

The following topic outline for the paper on special effects in science fiction movies will give you an idea of the kind of outline you should prepare for your own library paper.

Thesis Statement: The special effects in present-day science fiction movies such as Star Wars are highly advanced over their predecessors as a result of space-age technology.

Subtopic 1   I. The definition and history of special effects in movies
                   A. Definition
                   B. History of early effects
                       1. Introduction by Melies
                       2. Use of effects to supply elements of background
                           a. Use of mattes in camera; effects done by cameraman
                           b. Use of large glass mattes
Subtopic 2   II. Changes in 1933 King Kong
Subtopic 3   III. 1933 King Kong compared to present
Subtopic 4   IV. Present-day special effects
                   A. Improved photography
                   B. Computers
                   C. Blue screen
Subtopic 5   V. Result seen in Star Wars

When you have completed your outline, examine it to decide if you need to add anything or change the order in which any of the ideas are presented. If you prepare your outline carefully and critically, you will find that it will be easier to write your paper and that your paper will be much more logical.

Writing the First Draft. At this point, you should be ready to write your paper, expanding the points in your outline into sentences and paragraphs. You may wish to start by drafting a few ideas for your introduction and conclusion, so that you will have the main points of your paper firmly in mind as you proceed. Then draft your entire paper.

Use your outline, notes, and ideas to write a first draft of your paper.

After collecting your thoughts about what you want your introduction and conclusion to include, begin your first draft by writing an introduction that leads up to your thesis statement. Follow your outline and the grouping of your note cards in presenting your supporting information. Remember to cite the sources for every quotation, borrowed idea, and fact that you include in your paper. Be consistent in your method of citing these sources. You should also make certain that every paragraph that you write has a clear topic sentence and that your ideas are linked by transitions within and between paragraphs. Your conclusion should remind your audience of your thesis statement, should refer to the important points in the paper, and should bring the paper to a definite and satisfying end.

EXERCISE C: Organizing and Writing a Library Paper. Use the information you gathered from at least five sources in Exercises A and B to develop a precise thesis statement. Then follow the steps outlined in this section for organizing your information and preparing an outline. Jot down ideas for your introduction and conclusion, and then begin the first draft of your paper, writing your introduction first. Cite your sources for every borrowed statement, idea, or fact, using a consistent method.

Outlines should be checked for logic and completeness before students begin to draft their papers. Special attention should be paid to documentation of source material.

■ Preparing the Final Paper

The final steps in the writing of the library paper involve revising, preparing a final neat copy, proofreading, and adding a title page and bibliography.

Revising the Paper.   In revising your paper, read it with a critical eye, noting any gaps in logic, weak spots, and confusing statements, as well as any errors in grammar, usage, mechanics, and spelling.

Check your first draft for weaknesses in both form and content.

You should evaluate your first draft using questions such as those in the following checklist.

CHECKLIST FOR REVISION
1. Does the introduction include ideas that will help interest the reader? Does it provide necessary background information? Does it include a thesis statement?
2. Is the thesis statement clearly presented?
3. Is the thesis statement intelligently developed in the body of the paper by means of subtopics?
4. Does each paragraph contain a topic sentence?
5. Do the ideas flow logically within each paragraph and from paragraph to paragraph? Are transitions used to link ideas within and between paragraphs?
6. Does the conclusion refer to the thesis statement and summarize the content of the paper without being repetitious?
7. Are all sources used in the paper given credit throughout the body of the paper?
8. Does the writing follow the rules of grammar, usage, mechanics, and spelling?

Rewriting and Preparing the Final Copy.   After you have revised your paper to your satisfaction, you should recopy it or type it.

Prepare a clean copy of your paper.

The final version of the library paper on special effects in science fiction movies follows in its revised and retyped form. The marginal notes highlight the citations and the organization of the paper.

Title   *Advances in Special Effects in Science Fiction Movies*

Introduction   Anyone who has seen the film <u>Star Wars</u> has left the theatre dazzled with such special effects as duelling swords made out of light, chess pieces that appear to be tiny animals wiggling on a board, and intergalactic dogfights that end in the massive destruction of a huge, dark, armored war satellite. These, like hundreds of other powerful and often witty special effects in <u>Star Wars</u>, are fascinating because they seem impossible to do in real life, and yet the movie manages to make the viewer believe in them. They seem to go beyond the limitations of "trick photography" and clever sleight-of-hand. And, in fact, they do. The special effects seen in contemporary science fiction movies are greatly advanced beyond their predecessors because of space-age technological development. These special effects are the creations of highly imaginative and skilled technicians who have refined techniques used for years and combined these with new technology to produce a reality never before seen on the movie screen.[1]

Although we normally think of special effects in connection with science fiction and space exploration movies, a special effect can be anything that is not directly and straightforwardly photographed in a film. Special effects—or "FX" as they are called in movie terminology—are as old as movies themselves. At the turn of the century, George Melies, a French magician turned filmmaker, pioneered in special effects in movies, using a combination of animation, projection, and double exposure to produce images of space flight in <u>A Trip to the Moon</u>.[2] These practices became the standard tools that special effects technicians used to create, for example, the illusion of a mountain looming behind the action. At first these special effects were done by the film editors, who would combine two different elements by blotting out a portion of one frame with a small glass slide or "matte." The missing element could then be added on the unexposed portion of the film. Later on, these effects were created by artists, who would paint the required images on huge glass mattes. These could then be placed in front of the action being photographed without interfering with it as long as the real and painted scenes were photographed at just the right angle.[3]

In the 1920's, as movies became more popular and elaborate, convincing <u>moving</u> effects (as opposed to stationary background images) were developed with the more sophisticated use of mattes, scale models, and composite photography. These advances culminated in 1933 with the tremendously popular movie, <u>King Kong</u>. <u>King Kong</u>, which is considered to have been the <u>Star Wars</u> of

Margin notes:

Thesis statement

Citation of borrowed idea

Subtopic 1

Citation of borrowed facts

Citation of borrowed fact

Subtopic 2

Citation of
paraphrased
source

Subtopic 3

Subtopic 4

Borrowed fact
Borrowed fact

Borrowed fact

Subtopic 5

its day, included numerous scenes combining animated miniatures and models of monsters in what, at that time, seemed to be frighteningly convincing effects.[4]

When we look at King Kong today, however, the images seem crude and unconvincing in comparison with the movies that are now being released. We notice the somewhat jerky movement of the monster models in King Kong. Although we may not be conscious of it, we can sense the difference between the separately photographed elements that are combined in one scene (for example, the heroine's body wriggling in Kong's huge paw). What we take for granted today are the refinements that the years have added to the technology of special effects, which allow today's movie-makers to make the fantastic completely plausible to our eyes.

These advances have occurred in a number of areas. Photography has itself improved, as lenses have been refined and cameras have been developed that can travel in a number of different directions.[5] Attention to detail in the creation of mattes and models has been heightened, as movies with special effects face increasingly sophisticated audiences who have been exposed to many believable effects in films. Transistors and other miniaturized elements of space-age technology have made it possible to create models that really can move, guided by remote control.[6] But probably the most valuable contributions to special effects technology have been the blue screen and the development of a computer program that can guide the camera.[7]

While special effects used to be created with the camera alone, today they are created in the laboratory where a special optical printer blends several different shots together into a single frame. Such composites, up until the time of Star Wars, still called for a tremendous amount of laborious measuring on the part of the people behind the cameras. They would have to be sure that they had photographed each separate element in the scene from the proper angle and distance so that the pieces would fit together convincingly. In the filming of Star Wars, however, director George Lucas used a camera guided by a computer that would automatically reset the camera in the proper position. Several of the shots in the film involved as many as eighteen separately photographed elements to be assembled in a composite. Throughout the filming, the computer-controlled camera was able to make as many identical shots as were needed. The use of the computer-guided camera made it possible for Star Wars to include some 420 special effects shots. (2001: A Space Odyssey had included only about thirty-five, just ten years before and at a relatively much greater cost.)[8]

The other major advance, the blue screen, was not new in Star Wars. But combined with the computer technology used in that film, the blue screen enabled the makers of the movie to create unprecedented varieties of moving effects, particularly of spacecraft in motion. The blue screen makes it possible for objects in motion to be photographed and then believably combined with other elements, such as actors and backgrounds. The blue screen acts as a large matte that blots out areas of the shot, which can then be exposed in another shot, as an object moves across the field of vision. Thus, the space ships in Star Wars could move through a ground of stars and planets without looking superimposed over them.[9]

We now take the spectacular effects that new technology has made possible in movies for granted and expect to be convincingly shown beings and worlds we have never seen. In a way, the sophistication of present-day audiences has taken away some of the wonder that people used to feel when anything out of the ordinary occurred on screen. But such sophistication is unavoidable, given the images we are exposed to on the screen. And audiences are still not too sophisticated to become excited by an effect that helps them believe that they are entering into worlds where they have never been and, probably, never will be in "real" life.

Margin labels:

Paraphrased idea

Paraphrased idea

Conclusion

---

[1]Richard Schickel, "Far Beyond Reality," The New York Times Magazine, May 18, 1980, p. 40.

[2]Schickel, "Far Beyond Reality," p. 40.

[3]John Brosnan, Movie Magic: The Story of Special Effects in the Cinema (New York: St. Martin's Press, 1974), p. 9.

[4]Brosnan, Movie Magic, p. 23.

[5]Jack Kroll, "Fun in Space," Newsweek, May 30, 1977, p. 61.

[6]Robert Kerwin, "Star Wars," The New York Post, May 28, 1977, p. 31.

[7]Schickel, "Far Beyond Reality," p. 52.

[8]John Brosnan, Future Tense (New York: St. Martin's Press, 1978), p. 268.

[9]Schickel, "Far Beyond Reality," p. 52.

Preparing a Title Page.   In most classes, you will be expected to place your title on a separate title page.

Prepare a title page that resembles the following sample.

You should begin by centering the title of your paper in the middle of the title page and placing your name immediately below it. At the bottom of the page, you should write the title of the course for which you are preparing the paper and the date on which you are handing in the paper.

```
              Advances in Special Effects
              in Science Fiction Movies

                          by

                  Christine Hansen




                      English 10
                  February 1, 1981
```

NOTE ABOUT FORM: Because there are many different forms used for title pages, in some classes your teacher may assign a somewhat different form.

Writing a Bibliography.   After writing your paper and preparing your finished copy, you should list the sources you consulted as you recorded them on your bibliography cards.

For the bibliography, make an alphabetical listing of all the sources you consulted in the preparation of your paper.

You should place your bibliographical entries on a separate page at the end of your paper, listing every source that you cited in the paper as well as any other sources that you consulted during your research.

The bibliography for the paper on special effects in science fiction movies follows. Notice that the sources are arranged alphabetically according to the last name of the author or by title when the name of the author is not given. Notice, also, that the name of the author is not repeated when two books by the same author are consulted. Instead, a blank underscore is used.

BIBLIOGRAPHY

Brosnan, John. Future Tense. New York: St. Martin's Press, 1978.
_____ . Movie Magic: The Story of Special Effects in the Cinema. New York: St. Martin's Press, 1974.
Kerwin, Robert. "Star Wars." The New York Post, May 28, 1977, p. 31.
Kroll, Jack. "Fun in Space." Newsweek, May 30, 1977, pp. 60–63.
Schickel, Richard. "Far Beyond Reality." The New York Times Magazine, May 18, 1980, pp. 40–62.
Sobchak, Vivian C. The Limits of Infinity: The American Science Fiction Film. Cranbury, N.J.: A.S. Barnes and Co., 1979.
"Star Wars: The Year's Best Movie." Time, May 30, 1977, pp. 53–62.

EXERCISE D: Writing the Final Paper. Proofread and revise your paper following the checklist on page 778. Then recopy your paper and add a title page and bibliography.
Students might also be asked to note the major improvements made.

APPLICATION: Evaluating and Preparing a Complete Library Paper. Exchange library papers with another student in the class. Read the other person's paper and answer the following questions. *Class discussion could be organized around the presentation of several sets of papers and evaluations.*

1. How many sources has the writer cited?
2. How many sources has the writer consulted? What kinds of sources have been used?
3. What is the thesis statement of the paper?
4. What are the subtopics used to develop it?
5. How could the thesis statement be improved to present the paper's main point more clearly?
6. How could the topic sentence in each paragraph be made clearer?
7. Which undocumented facts and ideas seem to need documentation?
8. Which sources, if any, are cited incorrectly?
9. Are all of the sources listed correctly in the bibliography?

Return the paper to its writer with your answers to Questions 5–9. Look at the comments written about your own paper and revise it accordingly. Submit your first paper, your revised paper, and your fellow student's comments to your teacher.

28

Letters

Letters serve a number of different needs. Most people write hundreds of letters in their lifetime—for school, for business, and for formal and informal social reasons. As a means of transmitting personal information, letters compete with telephone calls. As a means of conducting business, letters are often even more crucial than the telephone. Unlike calls, letters act as concrete records of dates, meetings, applications, orders, and other important business information.

In this chapter you will study the structure and style of both personal and business letters. You will also examine models of letters and practice writing your own.

28.1 Personal Letters

In your personal life, many occasions will prompt you to write letters. Writing good letters involves both form and ideas. Your reader will expect to find a certain structural and stylistic arrangement in your letter as well as a number of ideas worth reading. In this section, you will look first at form and then at suggestions for making your ideas as clear and interesting as possible.

■ The Structure and Style of Personal Letters

When you prepare a personal letter, you must know what to place in the heading, how to arrange the other parts of the letter, and how to conclude the letter. You must also choose a style for the letter, most likely the indented style or the semiblock style. And you must prepare an envelope correctly to ensure the letter's arrival at its destination.

Following the Basic Structure. Most personal letters contain five basic parts, which follow an expected order.

Arrange the five basic parts of a personal letter—the heading, the salutation, the body, the closing, and the signature—in the expected order.

The *heading* should be placed in the upper right-hand portion of your letter. It should consist of your street address, town or city, state, and zip code. (You should also include the name of your country if you are sending the letter to another country.) This information serves a very important purpose. It ensures that the person who receives the letter can easily write back. In the last line of your heading, you should also add the date.

The *salutation*, or greeting, should be placed below the heading at the left of the letter. In most personal letters, the salutation begins somewhat formally with "Dear" followed by the name of the person who will receive the letter. A comma then follows the salutation.

FORMAL: Dear Aunt Millie, Dear Mrs. Donovan,

Dear Dr. Larkin, Dear Ms. Rivera,

To greet close friends and family members, however, you might use less formal salutations.

INFORMAL: Hi Jim, Greetings Tom and Pat,

My good Friend, Hello Pal,

The *body* of a personal letter should begin two or three lines below the salutation. This section can include as many paragraphs as you need to communicate ideas, feelings, and other personal information.

The *closing* should be written in the lower right-hand portion of the letter, about two or three spaces beneath the body. You should capitalize the first word of your closing, but not the following words. Then place a comma at the end. Your closing word or phrase should suit the tone of your letter.

FORMAL: Sincerely yours, Very truly yours,

INFORMAL: Regards, Love,

Your *signature* should be placed directly beneath the closing word or phrase. If you do not know the person to whom you are writing very well or if there is a large age difference between the two of you, you should sign your full name. Otherwise, you should use your first name or a nickname. Write your signature in ink, even if you have typed the rest of the letter.

If your letter is an invitation, you may also want to add an *R.S.V.P.* This abbreviation tells the person who receives the invitation to respond, stating whether he or she will accept or decline the invitation. (The abbreviation stands for the French words *répondez s'il vous plait* which means "Respond please.") An R.S.V.P. is usually placed in the lower left-hand corner of the invitation.

Choosing a Style.   While the five basic parts of a personal letter must appear in designated places on the paper, the style that you use for arranging the lines is a matter of choice.

Use either an indented style or a semiblock style for arranging the lines of a personal letter.

The *indented* style calls for indented lines in the heading and in the closing and signature. In the *semiblock* style, on the other hand, the heading, closing, and signature all begin at the same point.

Indented Style		Semiblock Style
	Heading	
	Salutation	
	Body	
	Closing	
	Signature	

Mailing the Letter. Once you have completed your letter, there are still a few additional formal matters that you should attend to.

Fold your letter correctly and prepare an envelope.

The way in which you fold your letter depends on the size of your stationery and your envelope. You may only need to fold the paper in half. A larger piece of paper, however, must be folded into thirds before it will fit into an envelope. To do this, simply fold the lower third of the letter upward to cover the center third. Then fold these two thirds over the upper third of the letter. This can be done in two steps, as shown in the following diagram.

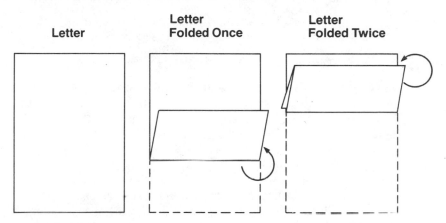

| Letter | Letter Folded Once | Letter Folded Twice |

When you write your envelope you must remember to use the same style, indented or semiblock, that you used to write the letter. Your envelope should look like one of the following models.

Indented Style   **Semiblock Style**

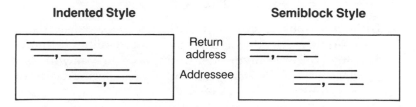

The following guidelines may be useful in carrying out this last step of letter writing.

WRITING YOUR ENVELOPE

1. Prepare the envelope in the same manner that you wrote the letter: typed or handwritten.
2. Place your name and address, including zip code, in the upper left-hand corner.
3. Do not use titles such as Mr., Miss, or Ms. in your own name.
4. Place the name and address of the person who is to receive the letter in the center of the envelope. Include all necessary mailing information: apartment number, route number, and zip code.
5. Avoid any abbreviations in addresses that will not be immediately clear to everyone who reads the envelope.
6. Use the proper punctuation in addresses.
7. On small envelopes, write your own name and address on the back instead of in the upper left-hand corner. (With a very small envelope, you may need to check with your post office to see if it is large enough to mail. The post office will not deliver envelopes that are too small.)

EXERCISE A: **Practicing with Structure and Style.** Prepare two skeleton letters, with lines instead of words in the body. For one letter, use the indented style. For the other, use the semiblock. Fill in the five parts of each letter by using your own address for the heading and someone else's name for the salutation. Include all five parts of a personal letter.
Answers should follow the formats on page 786.

EXERCISE B: **Mailing Personal Letters.** Prepare envelopes for the skeleton letters in Exercise A. Use the other person's address as well as your own. Make sure that each envelope matches the style of its letter. Then fold each letter properly and slip it into its envelope. *Answers should follow the formats on page 787.*

■ Writing Personal Letters

Different types of letters suit different personal needs. A long letter to a friend, for example, would differ in many ways from a letter of invitation. In this section, you will consider ideas for writing general and more specific types of personal letters.

Writing a Friendly Letter. A friendly letter, like many more formal pieces of writing, should contain an interesting opening, a body of interesting information, and a suitable conclusion. While your friendly letters are not likely to be as unified as an essay, many of the skills used in writing good paragraphs and essays can be applied to a friendly letter.

Include well organized statements of personal information, recent happenings, and other ideas of interest when you write friendly letters to friends, family, and acquaintances.

Above all, your friendly letters should be interesting to the people who receive them. The following suggestions should help you gather ideas and express them well.

SUGGESTIONS FOR YOUR FRIENDLY LETTERS
1. Think about any questions the person may have asked in his or her last letter. Be sure to answer these questions, briefly or at length.
2. Think about previous contacts with the person, through letters, visits, or phone calls. Consider mentioning any thoughts you have had about these occasions.
3. Provide facts and details about people, places, or events that the person will understand and find interesting.
4. Be careful not to concentrate solely on your own experiences. Share information about yourself, but mention the recipient's interests as well and ask questions that he or she will enjoy responding to.
5. Proofread your letter for mechanical errors and for clarity of ideas. Will the person understand the ideas you are presenting? Is more information needed?
6. Rewrite the letter, if necessary, to make any corrections or additions.

Writing Invitations and Letters of Acceptance and Regret. Although most of your personal letters are likely to be friendly letters, you can also write letters to plan events with friends. Similarly, you may receive written invitations from friends that require written responses.

Invitations and letters of acceptance and regret tend to be shorter and slightly more formal than friendly letters. They are among the many forms of personal letters generally referred to as social notes.

Use short and very direct social notes to extend invitations to social events and to respond to such invitations.

Like a friendly letter, a letter of invitation includes a heading, salutation, body, closing, and signature. In addition, there are a number of other specific details that must be included if you hope to get the response you desire. The steps in the following chart give you the essentials.

WRITING A LETTER OF INVITATION

1. Give specific details about the time, date, and place of the occasion as well as what kind of event it will be.
2. Mention what to wear and bring, if necessary.
3. Give the people you are inviting time to respond.
4. Include an R.S.V.P.

Whenever you receive a written invitation, you should reply promptly with a *letter of acceptance* or a *letter of regret* unless a phone number is given with the R.S.V.P. Again you must include a heading, salutation, body, closing, and signature as well as certain special details.

WRITING A LETTER OF ACCEPTANCE OR REGRET

1. If you accept, repeat the date, time, and place to avoid any misunderstanding.
2. If you must refuse, offer a reason for being unable to attend.
3. Always express your appreciation for the invitation.

Notice that the following letters of invitation and acceptance contain the basic parts of all personal letters as well as the special details needed in each specific letter.

1030 Franklin St.
Delmar, Iowa 52037
November 12, 1980

Dear Bill,

I am planning a surprise birthday party for my sister Eileen. Knowing that you and my sister have been friends for several years, I sincerely hope that you can attend.

The party will begin at 4:00 p.m. on Sunday, November 30. It will be held at our house and will include an informal dinner.

I certainly hope that you can attend.

Sincerely,
Eleanor Donovan

R.S.V.P.

220 Pierce St.
Delmar, Iowa 52037
November 14, 1980

Dear Eleanor,

I will be pleased to attend your party for Eileen. I am glad that you thought of me, and I will look forward to the occasion.

I plan to arrive at your house promptly at 4:00 p.m. on the 30th, with a very special present for Eileen.

Sincerely,
Bill Derby

Writing Other Kinds of Social Notes. Social notes are written to perform a single special function. Besides offering and responding to invitations, they can be used to send thanks for a present or hospitality. They can also be used to relay your feelings about special events in another person's life.

Use short, direct social notes to express appreciation, to say congratulations, or to send condolences.

Whenever you receive a gift, you should always reply as promptly as possible, mentioning the gift by name. If you are thanking someone for acting as your host, you should again be prompt and specific. Promptness is also important when you send a letter of congratulations or condolence. The most important thing in these last two types of notes, however, is a sincere tone, either of joy or sorrow.

Notice that the thank-you note in the following example contains the five basic parts of any personal letter, while mentioning a specific gift and other related details. The tone of the letter is friendly, gracious, and certainly thankful.

> 820½ North Uhl Street
> Allentown, Pennsylvania 18103
> December 30, 1980
>
> Dear Uncle Albert,
>
> On December 23, a package addressed to me arrived at our door. Because Mom and Dad would not let me open it until Christmas morning, I could barely contain my curiosity. I shook the package gently, marveled at its size, and did my best to guess what it could be.
>
> When finally I opened it (and it was the first gift that I attacked), I became the proud owner of a Space Shooter Pinball Machine, much to my delight. You could not have chosen a present that I'd have loved more. You remembered my fascination with pinball!
>
> Thank you again and again and again. I think of you immediately, every time I begin another "round" on the machine.
>
> Love,
> Tommy

EXERCISE C: Getting Ideas for a Friendly Letter. Choose someone to whom you might write a friendly letter. This person can be real or imaginary. Then jot down ideas that you might want to include in a letter to this person, using the suggestions in the chart on page 789. Finally, draw up an organized list of these ideas and, next to each idea, tell why you think it would be interesting to the person whom you have chosen.

Some students might enjoy writing a friendly letter to a famous person, as well.

EXERCISE D: Writing Invitations and Letters of Acceptance or Regret. Think of a real or imaginary social event that you could plan and organize. Then write a letter of invitation to someone whom you would like to attend. Exchange your letter of invitation with someone else in your class. Read his or her letter and write a letter of acceptance or regret.

Students could also check the format and mechanics of their partners' letters.

EXERCISE E: Writing Other Kinds of Social Notes. Write a note or letter responding to a gift or hospitality, or to an event in someone else's life. Use one of the following suggestions. *Students could exchange papers and write responses to these letters.*

1. A thank-you note for a birthday gift that you received
2. An apology for an accident that you caused
3. A thank-you note following a weekend at a friend's ski lodge
4. A note to a friend at a private school who has won an award
5. A note to a distant cousin who has broken his or her leg

APPLICATION: Writing Your Own Personal Letters. Choose a type of personal letter that you can actually send to someone: a friendly letter or a letter of invitation, acceptance, regret, gratitude, congratulations, or condolence. When you complete the letter, prepare an envelope. Fold the letter properly and place it in the envelope.

Envelopes could be checked for format.

28.2 Business Letters

A business letter is the most frequently written type of correspondence. It may request or share information, order merchandise, or serve any of a number of other purposes that a person or a business may have.

■ The Structure and Style of a Business letter

The structure and style of business letters are similar but not identical to those of personal letters. There are also a number of special rules of form to be followed when writing a business letter.

Following the Basic Structure. Usually written on plain white paper that measures 8½ × 11 inches (21.6 × 27.9 cm), a business letter contains a minimum of six parts, all of which must follow an expected order.

Arrange the six basic parts of a business letter—the heading, the inside address, the salutation, the body, the closing, and the signature—in the expected order.

The heading of a business letter presents your complete address as well as the date on which you wrote the letter. You should place the heading at least one inch (2.54 cm) below the top of the paper.

The inside address states the name and address of the person or business to whom you are writing. You should place it two to four spaces beneath the heading.

EXAMPLES: Ajax Rug Cleaning, Inc.
140 Main Street
New Rochelle, New York   10801

Dr. Bertram Baker
Director of Admissions
Atlas Community College
St. Paul, Minnesota   56556

The salutation, placed two spaces beneath the inside address, greets the person to whom you are writing the letter. For business letters, a proper salutation should be very formal. It should also be followed by a colon.

EXAMPLES: Dear Sir: Gentlemen:

Dear Sir or Madam: Dear Mrs. Appleby:

The body of a business letter should include all of the information that you wish to convey. Any requests, orders, or other ideas must be presented clearly and efficiently. The body can be any length, but short and direct statements are generally appreciated by busy men and women.

The closing follows two or three spaces beneath the body. As in the friendly letter, a closing begins with a capital letter and ends with a comma. In business letters, closings are usually more formal than in friendly letters.

EXAMPLES: Respectfully,   Sincerely,

Very truly yours,

The signature appears in full beneath the closing. In writing your signature, you should include your first and last name as well as a middle initial, if this is how you sign your name formally. If you have typed the rest of the letter, you should then type your full name beneath your signature. Women sometimes indicate how they prefer to be addressed (Miss, Mrs., Ms.) by placing the abbreviation in parentheses before the typed name.

Choosing a Style.   The six basic parts of a business letter can be arranged and written in at least three different ways.

Use either a block style, modified block style, or semiblock style for arranging the lines of a business letter.

In the *block style*, all parts of the letter begin on the left side of the paper. Notice in the model on page 795 that no lines are indented, not even the first line of a paragraph. Space is left between paragraphs, however, to show where one ends and the next begins. Block style is a very common choice among business men and women.

In the *modified block style*, the heading is placed in the upper right-hand portion of the letter, and the closing and signature are placed in the lower right-hand portion of the letter. The other parts of the letter—the inside address, the salutation, and the body paragraphs—begin on the left. Again, each paragraph begins on the left and a space is left between paragraphs.

In the *semiblock style*, the parts of the letter follow the same arrangement as in modified block. The first line of each paragraph, however, is indented, as shown on page 796.

The second page of a business letter, if one is necessary, should follow the same style as the first. For purposes of identification, you should begin the second page with a short heading listing the name of the recipient, the page number, and the date.

Block Style

Heading	
Inside address	
Salutation	
Body	
Closing Signature Name	

Modified Block Style

Heading	
Inside address	
Salutation	
Body	
Closing Signature Name	

Semiblock Style

Heading	————
	————, —— ——
	————, ——
Inside address	————
	————
	————, —— ——
Salutation	————:
Body	
Closing	————,
Signature	
Name	————

Following the Special Rules of Business Letters. Just as business letters are more formal than personal letters, they also follow a stricter form.

Recognize and follow a number of special rules when preparing business letters.

The following rules should help you prepare business letters that will be well received in the business world.

SPECIAL RULES FOR BUSINESS LETTERS

1. Write on unlined, 8½ × 11-inch (21.6 × 27.9 cm) white paper with matching envelope.
2. Type your business letter, if possible.
3. Double-space between paragraphs and between other parts of the letter.
4. Leave margins of at least one inch (2.54 cm) on all sides of your paper.

Mailing the Letter. Keep a copy of your letter for your records and prepare to send the original.

Fold your letter correctly and prepare an envelope following the standard business style.

The envelope you use for a business letter should be the standard-sized white envelope that matches your stationery. To place the letter in the envelope, fold it into thirds.

To complete the envelope, begin by placing your name and address in the upper left-hand corner. In the center, place the name and address of your recipient. This information should match the inside address on the letter. Notice in the following example that the envelope style will be the same, regardless of the style in the letter.

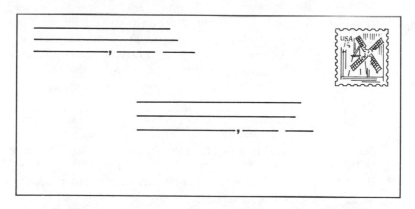

EXERCISE A: Practicing with Structure and Style. Use three pieces of paper to set up three skeleton business letters, with lines instead of words in the body. Write one in block style, one in modified block style, and one in semiblock style. Use your own name and address, as well as the following inside address: Complaint Department, Minimart Department Store, 500 S.W. Fifth Avenue, Cooper City, Florida 33328.

Answers should follow the formats on pages 795 and 796.

EXERCISE B: Addressing an Envelope for a Business Letter. Choose one of the skeleton letters that you wrote in Exercise A. Fold it properly and then prepare envelope.

Answers should follow the format above.

■ Writing Business Letters

Because different needs and situations require that you write different types of business letters, you should become familiar with a number of the most common types of these letters.

Writing Request and Order Letters.   In school and later in your career, you may often need to request information from a business or a government agency. Perhaps you will need facts for a report about South America or details about a new investment program. It is also likely that you will at some time order merchandise by mail. Sometimes order blanks will be available, but sometimes only a letter will do. Well-written request and order letters will help you obtain exactly what you want.

Use clear and direct business letters to request information or to order merchandise.

Request and order letters must contain the basic parts of any business letter: a heading, inside address, salutation, body, closing, and signature. But the body of such a letter should also contain a number of special details. The steps in the following chart should help you cover all of the essentials.

WRITING REQUEST AND ORDER LETTERS

1. State your specific request, for information or merchandise, in the first or second sentence.
2. If you require information, give a reason for the request.
3. Make all requests or orders brief and to the point, specifying precisely the items required.
4. If payment is essential, state the total amount of your order and mention the method of payment you are using, such as check, money order, or C.O.D.
5. Offer any other details that will clarify your needs and help the recipient respond.

Notice that the model of an order on page 799 contains all the essential parts of a business letter. It also covers all necessary details briefly in an orderly fashion.

Writing Letters of Complaint, Application, and Opinion. Other situations—a mistake in an order you have placed, your need to find a new job, or your feelings about a television program—might lead you to write other kinds of business letters.

Use clear and direct business letters to make a complaint or seek an adjustment, to make an application, or to express an opinion.

```
                              1160 Beaufort Drive
                              Stockton, Arkansas 72031
                              March 15, 1980

Supply Department
Crosby's Department Store
1200 Highway 101
Riverside, California 92501

Dear Sir:

    Please send me the following items, which were
listed in your 1980 Supply Catalog:

        1. Canton 3-setting Blow Dryer
           Order number:  006            $11.95

        2. Python Styling Brushes
           Order number:  107               9.90
                                         _____
                              Total      $21.85

    Enclosed you will find a money order for $21.85.
I understand that postage and insurance costs are
included in the sales price.

                         Sincerely,

                         Jane Hathaway
                         Jane Hathaway
```

A *letter of complaint* is often the speediest way to achieve a solution to a business problem. If you are writing to report a badly filled order or faulty goods, be sure to include enough specific details to allow the problem to be identified quickly. Always include any order number you may have and, if possible, a copy of any relevant documents.

When you seek employment, you may find it very useful to send *letters of application*. Begin by identifying the position you are applying for. Then summarize the main points of your résumé, if you are including one, or briefly itemize your experience. You may also want to specify your schooling, age, and other details about your past work experience.

If it seems appropriate, include the names of people who know you well and for whom you have worked previously. Finally, include your address and phone number.

If you want to express your views to the editor of a newspaper or the head of a television station, you may find that a *letter of opinion* works best. State your view clearly and politely and offer support for your position.

A model of a letter of complaint follows. Notice that the specific problem is stated in the second sentence after introductory background remarks. The writer also includes information that should help the business respond to the customer's satisfaction.

```
                              1812 Ferndale Avenue
                              Westlake, Ohio 44155
                              May 20, 1980


   Mr. Leo Benjamin, Manager
   Benjamin Jewelers
   3380 Erie Avenue
   Cincinnati, Ohio 45208

   Dear Mr. Benjamin:

        I enclose my Armitex digital watch, which I
   purchased last month at your store. As you will
   notice, links in the wristband have broken apart.
   Since this problem arose after only two weeks of
   normal wear, I expect that you will repair the
   band at no further cost to me.

        Please return the repaired item as promptly
   as possible. Thank you for your help.

                              Sincerely,

                              Betty Bower

                              (Mrs.) Betty Bower
```

EXERCISE C: Writing a Request or Order Letter. Write a letter requesting information or ordering merchandise using one of the following suggestions.
Students could exchange and check each other's letters.
   1. Write to an automobile company for details about a new car.
   2. Write to an embassy or tourist service for travel information about a foreign country.
   3. Write to a store in another city to order some item that you cannot find locally.
   4. Write to a major department store chain to order an item you found in their catalog.

EXERCISE D: Writing a Letter of Complaint, Application, or Opinion. Write a letter of complaint, application, or opinion using one of the following suggestions.
Letters might be distributed for a class discussion on their effectiveness.
   1. Write to a store complaining about broken merchandise or an item that you ordered but have failed to receive. (Address your letter to the company's complaint department.)
   2. Write to a business, government agency, or some other place (park service, hotel, restaurant) where you might find a summer job.
   3. Write to a television station to criticize or praise a show that you recently watched. (Address your letter to the General Manager of the station.)
   4. Write to your local newspaper to express your views on some public issue, such as trash removal or bus service. (Address your letter to the editor of the paper.)

APPLICATION: Writing Your Own Business Letter. Choose a type of business letter that you can actually send: an order letter, a request letter, or a letter of complaint, application, or opinion. When you complete the letter, prepare an envelope. Fold the letter properly and place it in the envelope.
Envelopes could be checked for format.

Chapter 29

Essay Examinations

Essay examinations are likely to be a part of your school life and professional life for many years to come. In cases where a question requires an answer longer than a sentence, you must plan and organize a written response. But with a knowledge of paragraphs and essays, you already have many of the skills needed.

29.1 Preparing Answers to Essay Exam Questions

In this section, you will practice writing both paragraph-length and essay-length answers to questions on essay exams. You will also look at time considerations and ways of interpreting exam questions. And, as you will see, such planning and interpreting will aid you greatly in writing your final answer.

■ Planning Your Timing

Timing is essential in writing good answers to essay exam questions. If your classroom does not have a clock, or if the clock is hard for you to see, make sure you bring a watch or other timepiece with you on examination days. Then use the clock or watch to plan the time you can spend on each question.

Plan your time carefully before you begin an essay exam and check your timing occasionally to make sure you are roughly on schedule.

As suggested in Section 19.2, spend a few minutes at the beginning of any test previewing the instructions and the questions. This makes just as much sense for an essay exam as it does for a multiple choice test. It will give you a chance to begin thinking about all the questions you need to answer and to judge which ones will take the most time. During this quick preview you should plan your timing for the entire test.

If you have about an hour to answer three equally difficult essay questions, you will obviously want to spend about twenty minutes on each question. During each twenty-minute period you will want to spend about five to ten minutes interpreting the question, gathering information to answer it, and making a rough outline of your ideas. The actual writing should take about ten minutes, but be sure to save a little time for proofreading.

If you follow such a schedule you may not be able to make each of your answers perfect. But you will seldom be penalized for failing to answer all of the questions.

EXERCISE A: Planning Ahead. Explain how you would divide your time in each of the following situations. Do not forget to add a few minutes of preview time at the beginning. Note that in many of the questions, no single answer is correct but a general plan is desirable.
Answers will vary; samples given.
1. Fifty minutes for three equally difficult essay questions
2. Forty-five minutes for a ten-item true/false test and two essay questions. *5 minutes for true/false portion; 20 minutes for each essay*
3. Forty-five minutes for a ten-item true/false test and a single essay question. *5–10 minutes for true/false portion; 35–40 minutes for essay*
4. One hour for a twenty-item multiple choice test and two essay questions
5. Thirty minutes to plan, write, and proofread a single essay exam
1. 15–17 minutes for each   4. 10–15 minutes for multiple choice portion; 20–25 minutes for each essay   5. planning: 5–10 minutes; writing 15–20 minutes; proofreading 5 minutes

■ Interpreting the Question

Before you begin to respond to a question, you must have a clear idea of what the person who wrote the question expects.

Look for word clues and other indications in the question that show what kind of information you should supply.

The best written answer will not be adequate if it does not cover all points required by the question. For this reason, you must read and reread the question. You must recognize the extent to which you must supply information, and you must recognize the types of information needed.

Finding Word Clues in Questions. Many questions will include words that tell you the type of information needed. Examine each question and look for words that point to the types of supporting information you will need. The word *compare*, for example, tells you to show how one person, place, or thing resembles another. The following chart can help you identify many of these words.

LOOKING FOR CLUES IN THE QUESTION		
Kind of Question	**Words That Offer Clues**	**What You Should Do**
Compare	*compare, similarities, resemblances, likenesses*	Look for and stress comparisons.
Contrast	*contrast, differ, differences*	Look for and stress differences.
Definition	*define, explain*	Tell what something means or is. Give examples.
Description	*describe*	Give the main features with specific examples.
Diagram	*diagram, draw, chart*	Give a drawing or chart in your answer. Label and explain it.
Discussion	*discuss, explain*	Make a general statement that shows you understand the main idea of the question. Support it with examples, facts, and details.
Explanation	*explain, why, what, how*	Give information that answers how, what, why. Support the idea with facts and examples.
Illustration	*illustrate, show*	Give concrete examples and explain them. Show the truth or significance of the general idea in the question.

Identifying the Required Task. Aside from the word clues listed in the preceding chart, a question may offer other clues and directions that will lead you to an answer. Often, essay exam questions will ask you to perform a specific task. The question might, for example, ask you to give your opinion about something that you have studied or to imagine some unlikely event.

The following chart can help you identify the specific task you need to carry out in certain common types of questions.

LOOKING FOR SPECIFIC TASKS

1. *Defending Your Opinion.* If a question asks for your opinion on a subject, you must take a stand and develop your stand with examples, reasons, and other information at your disposal.

   Example: What, in your opinion, were the principal contributions of Louis XIV to France?

2. *Answering an If . . . Then Question.* If a question asks you what would happen *if*, you must use your knowledge of the subject to present a logical answer. You must state your answer clearly and offer facts, examples, and reasons to support your position.

   Example: If you were stranded on an island for a long period of time and could not find fruits or berries to eat, how would your physical condition be affected?

3. *Analyzing Someone Else's Words.* If a question asks you to consider a statement, quotation, or opinion and tell why you think it was expressed in that way, you must offer both your own opinion and examples from the other person's life or work to support that opinion.

   Example: Why did the author say that the hero was "a man of little worth"?

EXERCISE B: Interpreting Essay Exam Questions. Read each of the following test questions carefully, looking for word clues or tasks in each question. Then identify the type of question being asked, using the charts on pages 804 and 805 if necessary. Finally, without actually answering the question, prepare to tell what kind of information you would need to write an answer. *Clue words are shaded.*

1. How do archaeologists determine the age of a particular artifact? *explanation: support with facts, examples, procedures*

2. Why was the Magna Carta an important civil document for medieval England? *explanation: provide reasons, facts, examples*
3. Show how two different animals have different "nesting" practices. *contrast: cite and stress differences*
4. What do you think was the emperor's reason for killing the flier in "The Flying Machine"?
5. According to the author of *Flowers for Algernon*, was Charlie happier with an I.Q. of 60 or with an I.Q. of 160 + ? Include examples from the book in your answer.

4. opinion: state opinion, support with reasons

5. another's opinion: state opinion and support with facts, examples, quotations

■ Outlining Your Answer

After you have interpreted the exam question, you must plan your support and arrange it in a logical order.

Write down all the ideas and information that occur to you, and then organize them in a modified outline.

Because you have only a limited amount of time to write your answer, you will often have to think and write quickly. Skimping on the planning process to save time, however, can be dangerous. The quality of your answer will depend greatly on good support and clear organization.

Thinking and Recalling Information. On scratch paper or your test, list as many details, facts, and examples as you can. Write only those that will answer the question precisely and directly. If you were answering a question about the ways in which travel in outer space affects the human body, you should recognize that your answer must contain examples, at the very least. You must explain and describe *what* happens to the human body in outer space. List all examples that come to your mind. Recall your studies and reading on the subject. Allow a little time to just sit and think, but begin your list as quickly as you can.

Writing the Outline. When your list is complete, you should write a modified outline. Begin by writing a sentence that states the main idea of your answer. This can be the topic sentence of a paragraph answer. Or if your answer will be as long as an essay, you can use this sentence as the thesis statement.

Then choose a logical order for your support and arrange your support beneath the main idea. Be on the lookout for insignificant or unnecessary support, and eliminate any as you write the outline.

The two outlines that follow could be used to answer the question about the effects of space travel on the human body. The first outline is for a paragraph-length answer. The second outline is for an essay-length answer.

SAMPLE OUTLINES

Paragraph

Topic Sentence: The traveler in space will suffer a loss of fluid, periods of "lightheadedness," and occasional blackouts.

—Weightlessness causes kidneys to speed up, producing loss of fluids

—Without gravity, more blood reaches the upper body, causing the head to be "flooded"

—Confinement, lack of exercise, and perhaps stress cause some problems with equilibrium, producing occasional blackout

Concluding Idea: Happily, scientists find that effects of outer space are not serious.

Essay

Thesis Statement: By studying the effects of space travel on astronauts, scientists have discovered that the traveler in space will suffer a loss of fluid, periods of "lightheadedness," and occasional blackouts.

—Loss of fluids
 –Weightlessness
 –Kidneys work faster
—Lightheadedness
 –Lack of gravity causes more blood to reach upper body
 –Head becomes "flooded"

—Blackouts
 –Pressures of confinement, lack of exercise, stress
 –Equilibrium is affected

Concluding Ideas:
—Scientists find that effects are not serious

—Effects can be combated easily

EXERCISE C: Outlining an Answer. Use one of the questions from Exercise A or another from your class work. List all facts, examples, details, and other forms of support that you need to answer the question. Then write a modified outline for a paragraph or essay answer.

Students working on the same question or subject area could exchange papers and evaluate their partners' answers.

■ Writing and Proofreading Your Answer

Always leave enough time to write your answer, proofread it quickly, and make any final corrections.

Use your outline as a guide to writing the answer. Then proof-read your answer to make sure it is complete and free of mechanical errors.

As you write, you should stick to the basic plan of your outline. Flesh out your outline with related examples and facts that you recall from your reading and study of the topic. If new ideas occur to you while you are following your outline, check them against your main idea. Include these ideas if they explain or defend your main idea.

If your mind temporarily goes blank and you lose your momentum while you are writing, reread your main idea, your outline, and what you have written so far. These ideas will put your mind in action again.

You can both help your thoughts flow freely and make your answer understandable by using transitions. Use transitions between paragraphs and between major supporting ideas.

The following essay is an answer to the question about space travel. Notice that the main point of the answer is presented in the introductory paragraph. Three body paragraphs then develop the subtopics of the answer. Finally, a brief conclusion ends the essay with a restatement of the main point and related optimistic findings.

Essay answer
to exam
question

Before human beings were actually sent into space, scientists feared that weightlessness and other factors in outer space would undermine an astronaut's ability to function. But by studying the effects of space travel on American and Soviet astronauts, scientists have discovered that the human body suffers only minimal discomforts: loss of fluid, periods of "lightheadedness," and occasional blackouts.

Every astronaut loses fluid in outer space. Because weightlessness allows blood to circulate more readily through the upper body, the kidneys work faster. As a result, the kidneys process and eliminate fluids at an increased rate. The astronaut loses fluids, as well as weight, more rapidly than if he or she were on earth.

In addition to more blood circulating in the mid-body region, blood will flow more freely to the head during weightlessness. Most astronauts feel lightheaded, as a result, especially during the early stages of a mission in space.

Even worse, some astronauts have experienced blackouts, either during a mission or when returning to earth. Scientists believe that confinement, lack of exercise, and perhaps stress during the mission cause problems with equilibrium and, hence, cause blackouts.

Happily, scientists find that effects of outer space on travelers are not serious. These effects can be combated. Exercise routines in particular will help astronauts combat fatigue and light-headedness. And special fluid diets can keep fluid losses to a minimum.

Before turning in your answer, remember to proofread it carefully. Check to make sure your answer is complete and contains no mechanical errors. You should also make sure that all of your ideas are expressed clearly and precisely.

The following checklist shows the kind of questions you should ask yourself.

QUESTIONS TO ASK WHILE PROOFREADING

1. Does at least one sentence present the main answer to the question?
2. Does the answer stick to the topic?
3. Is there enough supporting information?
4. Is the answer organized logically?
5. Do transitions connect the ideas?
6. Are there any spelling or other mechanical errors?
7. Are all of the words, including any corrections, readable?
8. Does the answer end clearly and persuasively?

EXERCISE D: **Writing and Proofreading the Answer.** Following the outline that you prepared in Exercise C, write your paragraph-length or essay-length answer. When you are done, use the checklist above to proofread your answer. Then make any corrections and revisions that you think will improve the piece. *This answer could be graded as if it were part of a real test. Attention should be paid to well-focused topic sentences, logical progression, and specific support.*

APPLICATION: **Planning, Writing, and Revising an Answer to an Exam Question.** Choose three questions that you have recently received on tests or as homework in any of your classes. Each question should be suitable for a paragraph or essay answer. Then complete the following steps.

Students could be given a time limit to simulate conditions of a test.

1. Choose the question that you prefer to answer.
2. Decide how much time it should take to prepare your answer. If you wrote a paragraph-length answer in Exercise

D, you should now plan to write an essay-length answer, and vice versa.

3. Interpret the question. Gain a clear idea of the types of information that you must offer.
4. Write a sentence that presents the main idea needed to answer the question.
5. List supporting information and then outline your answer.
6. From the outline, write your answer.
7. Proofread and revise the answer.

Manuscript Preparation

The most important part of any writing you do is, of course, the ideas that it contains. The composition unit offers many suggestions for developing, organizing, and expressing your ideas in clear and interesting language. However, when you hand in a paper there are also certain technical things that you should provide. The following pages give suggestions for basic manuscript preparation, for dealing with mechanical and other technical aspects of writing, for giving credit to your sources, and for understanding and using correction symbols.

Basic Preparation

Whether handwritten or typed, your manuscript should follow certain basic rules. The following chart shows the suggested procedures for each style.

PREPARING A MANUSCRIPT	
Handwritten	**Typed**
1. Use white 8½ × 11 inch (21.5 × 28 cm) lined paper, but never pages ripped from a spiral binder.	1. Use white 8½ × 11 inch (21.5 × 28 cm) paper.
2. Use black or blue ink only.	2. Use a clear black ribbon.
3. Leave a margin of 1 inch (2.54 cm) on the right, using the paper's own rules as your margin on other sides.	3. Leave a margin of at least 1 inch (2.54 cm) on all sides.
4. Indent each paragraph.	4. Double-space all lines and indent each paragraph.
5. Use only one side of each paper.	5. Use only one side of each paper.
6. Recopy if necessary to make your final copy neat.	6. Retype if necessary to make your final copy neat.

You must also identify your manuscript, following either an elaborate or simple style. For long and important papers, such as library papers, you will probably want an elaborate style. Set up a title page as shown on page 812. The next page and all the other pages should carry only your name and the page number, beginning with page one.

With Title Page

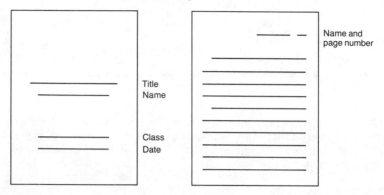

For shorter papers, use the simple style. Basic identification appears on the first page, while the second page carries your name and the page number, beginning with page two.

Without Title Page

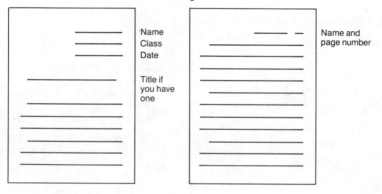

Dealing with Mechanics

The following chart offers basic guidelines for using punctuation marks and other mechanical items that seem to cause most manuscript problems.

CHECKING MECHANICS		
Item	**Basic Guidelines**	**Further Reference**
Capitalization	Use common sense in capitalizing proper nouns, proper adjectives, and first words.	Section 14.1, pages 308–328

Abbreviation	Avoid most abbreviations in formal writing. Feel free, however, to use abbreviations such as Mr. and Mrs., a.m. and p.m., and well-known abbreviations for organizations such as NATO and VISTA.	Section 14.2, pages 328–344
Commas	Take care not to overuse commas. Also check to make sure you are not dividing compound verbs with commas.	Section 15.2, pages 353–368
Hyphens	Check compound words in the dictionary. Hyphenate at the end of the line only when absolutely necessary and only at a syllable break.	Section 15.7, pages 403–411
Apostrophes	Avoid using apostrophes incorrectly in personal pronouns such as *its* and *theirs*.	Section 15.8, pages 411–420

Handling Other Technical Matters

Other technical matters should also be checked to make your paper more readable and more persuasive.

CHECKING OTHER ITEMS		
Item	**Basic Guidelines**	**Further Reference**
Spelling	Keep a dictionary at your side and check it whenever you are in doubt.	Section 17.2, pages 452–460
Usage	Take special care to make sure your subjects and verbs agree.	Section 11.1, pages 244–258, for subject-verb agreement; Section 13.2, pages 284–301, for a list of sixty common usage problems
Sentence Faults	Check for fragments, run-ons, and problems with modifiers.	Chapter 8, pages 163–181
Numbers	Spell out most numbers that can be written in one or two words and all numbers at the beginning of a sentence. Use numerals, however, for lengthy numbers, for dates, and for addresses.	Section 14.2, pages 337–341

Giving Credit to Sources

Whenever you are quoting the words or using the ideas of another writer, make sure you have given credit to that person. The chart in Section 27.1 on pages 760–761 shows the different forms for these kinds of citations.

Using Correction Symbols

You may find the following symbols very useful when you are proofreading your own manuscript. Your teacher may also choose to use these or similar marks when grading your papers.

USING CORRECTION SYMBOLS		
Symbol	**Meaning**	**Example**
ℓ	delete	The colors is red.
⌒	close up	The color is re d.
∧	insert	The color ∧ red.
#	add space	The coloris red.
∿	transpose	The colro is red.
¶	new paragraph	¶ The color is red.
no ¶	no paragraph	no ¶ The color is red.
cap	capitalize	the color is red.
lc	use small letter	The Color is red.
sp	spelling	The colar is red.
us	usage	The colors is red.
frag	fragment	The red color and the blue.
Ro	run-on	The color is red the house is blue.
mod	problem modifier	Newly painted, I saw the house.
awk	awkward	The color is, I think, kind of red.

Index

Bold numbers show pages on which basic definitions and rules can be found.

Acknowledgments

The authors and editors have made every effort to trace the ownership of all copyrighted selections found in this book and to make full acknowledgment of their use. The dictionary of record for this book is *Webster's New World Dictionary*, Second College Edition, copyright © 1980 by Simon & Schuster, Inc. The basis for the selection of vocabulary words appropriate for this grade level is *The Living Word Vocabulary: The Words We Know* by Edgar Dale and Joseph O'Rourke, copyright © 1976.

Citations follow, arranged by unit and page for easy reference.

Study Skills: Pages 474 *Current Events* magazine, "Susan B. Anthony: Freedom Fighter" (January 31, 1979), p. 12. Special permission granted by *Current Events*, published by Xerox Education Publications © 1977, Xerox Corp. **479–480** *Read* magazine, adapted from "A Handful of Weird Fears" and "Fighting Fears and Phobias" (October 19, 1977), pp. 5–7. Special permission granted by *Read* Magazine, published by Xerox Education Publications © 1977, Xerox Corp. **489–490** Wilkie Collins, *Woman in White* (New York: Penguin, 1975). **523** *The Encyclopedia Americana*. Reprinted with permission of *The Encyclopedia Americana*, copyright 1980, The Americana Corporation. **525** (map) *An Outline Atlas of World History*, by R. R. Sellman (New York: St. Martin's Press, Inc.), p. 19. **525** (second item) By permission. From *Webster's New Geographical Dictionary* © 1980 by G. & C. Merriam Co., Publishers of the Merriam-Webster Dictionaries. **528** By permission. From *Webster's New Dictionary of Synonyms* © 1978 by G. & C. Merriam Co., Publishers of the Merriam-Webster Dictionaries. **532–533** *Readers' Guide to Periodical Literature* Copyright © 1977, 1978 by The H. W. Wilson Company. Material reproduced by permission of the publishers. **534** From *The New York Times Index* © 1941 by the New York Times Company. Reprinted by permission. **537** By permission. From *Webster's Third New International Dictionary* © 1976 by G. & C. Merriam Co., Publishers of the Merriam-Webster Dictionaries. **538** From the *Oxford English Dictionary* (Oxford, England: Oxford University Press, 1979). **541** (first, second, third items), **542** (second, third, fourth items), **543** (second, fourth items), **544, 545** (first item), **546** (first item) With permission. From *Webster's New World Dictionary*, Students Edition. Copyright © 1981 by Simon & Schuster, Inc. **542** (first item), **543** (third item) From the *Macmillan School Dictionary*. Copyright © 1981 Macmillan Publishing Co., Inc. **543** (first item), **545** (second item) From THORNDIKE-BARNHART ADVANCED DICTIONARY by E. L. Thorndike and Clarence L. Barnhart. Copyright © 1973 by Scott, Foresman, and Company. Reprinted by permission. **546** (second item) With permission. From *Webster's New World Dictionary*, Second College Edition. Copyright © 1980 by Simon & Schuster, Inc.

Composition: Pages 573 Janet Halfmann, "Burrowing with Earthworms," *Ranger Rick's Nature Magazine* (March 1977), National Wildlife Federation. **573** Jeffrey L. Duncan, "The Empirical and the Ideal in Mark Twain," Reprinted by permission of the Modern Language Association of America from *PLMA* (March 1980). **575** R. A. Wilson, "Jazz," *Soul* (March 1980), p. 8. **575** Christine Cannon, "Hands-on Guide to Palpation and Ausculation," *RN* (March 1980), p. 24. **575** Adapted from Ethel A. Starbird, "Sydney: Big, Breezy, and a Bloomin' Good Show," *National Geographic* Magazine (February 1979), p. 215. **575–576** Hester and Shane. By permission of LAIDLAW BROTHERS, A Division of Doubleday & Company, Inc. Adapted from Hester and Shane, *Magic and Laughter*, 1962. **614** M. L. Stein, *The Newswriter's Handbook* (New York: Cornerstone Library Publications, 1971). **615** Teresa Byrne-Dodge, "Venerable Venetians," *Americana*, Vol. 8, No. 1 (March/April 1980), p. 72. Copyright

Americana Magazine, Inc. **615** Adapted from an article in *Games of the World,* Federic V. Grunfeld, ed. (New York: Holt, Rinehart & Winston). **615** Allan C. Fisher, Jr., "Mysteries of Bird Migration," *National Geographic* Magazine (August 1979), p. 165. **616–617** Judith B. Edwards et al, *Elements of Computer Careers* (Englewood Cliffs, NJ: Prentice-Hall, Inc., 1977), p. 51. **617** *The New Book of Popular Science,* 1981. Published by Grolier, Incorporated, Danbury, CT. **621** Roger Tory Peterson, "An Appreciation of His Favorites from 'The King,'" *Smithsonian* (October 1979), pp. 57–59. **625** Drs. Lorus J. and Margery Milne, "Will the Environment Defeat Mankind?" *The Saturday Evening Post* (September 1979), p. 103. **626** Charles N. Gaylord, "Modern Engineering," *The New Book of Popular Science,* 1981. Published by Grolier, Incorporated, Danbury, CT. **627, 632** Robert and Patricia Cahn, "Treasure of Parks for a Little Country That Really Tries," *Smithsonian* (September 1979), p. 66. **628–629** Adapted from Judith Chasek, "How to Plant Your Own Family Tree," *Americana,* Vol. 1, No. 1 (March 1973), p. 9. Copyright Americana Magazine, Inc. **629–630** Adapted from J. Fritz Lanham, "The Result Is Mad When Urban Wastes Become Public Art," *Smithsonian* (January 1980), p. 86. **630** Adapted from Henry Lansford, "The Frightening Mystery of the Electric Storm," *Smithsonian* (August 1979), p. 78. **631** Virginia Woolf, "Waxworks at the Abbey, "GRANITE AND RAINBOW" by Virginia Woolf, Harcourt Brace Jovanovich, Inc. **631–632** Walter Kerr, *Tragedy and Comedy.* Copyright © 1967 by Walter Kerr. Reprinted by permission of SIMON & SCHUSTER, a Division of Gulf & Western Corporation. **632** Adapted from *The Encyclopedia Americana.* Reprinted with permission of *The Encyclopedia Americana,* copyright 1980, The Americana Corporation. **668** Adapted from *The Last Two Million Years,* The Reader's Digest Association, 1979, p. 196. **669** Excerpt from p. 14 in THE SKIER'S HANDBOOK by the Editors of *Ski Magazine.* Copyright ©1965 by Universal Publishing & Distributing Corp. Reprinted by permission of Harper & Row, Publishers, Inc. **676** Adapted from Vance Packard, *The Waste Makers* (New York: David McKay Company, Inc., 1960). **676** Alice J. Hall, "Dazzling Legacy of an Ancient Quest," *National Geographic* Magazine (March 1977), p. 293. **683** Lloyd Alexander, *The Black Cauldron* (New York: Dell Publishing Co.), p. 120. **686** Catherine Marshall, *Christy.* By permission of McGraw-Hill, New York. **693** Jean Kerr. Excerpt from "When I was Queen of the May" from THE SNAKE HAS ALL THE LINES, copyright ©1959 by Jean Kerr. Reprinted by permission of Doubleday & Company, Inc. **694** Vic Banks, "Bald Eagles Flock in Cottonwoods on Alaskan River," *Smithsonian* (December 1979), p. 55. **762** Michael Schrage, "Good-bye 'Dallas,' Hello, Videodiscs," *New York Magazine* (November 17, 1980), p. 38.

Key of Major Concepts

Grammar

Usage

Mechanics